D1598150

The Threat On The Horizon

Also by Loch K. Johnson

INTELLIGENCE, 4 vols. (New York, 2011), editor

NATIONAL SECURITY INTELLIGENCE (Cambridge, UK, 2011).

THE OXFORD HANDBOOK OF NATIONAL SECURITY
INTELLIGENCE (New York, 2010), editor.

INTELLIGENCE AND NATIONAL SECURITY: THE SECRET WORLD
OF SPIES; AN ANTHOLOGY. 3d. ed. (New York, 2010), edited with
James J. Wirtz.

STRATEGIC INTELLIGENCE, 5 vols. (Westport, CT, 2007), editor.

HANDBOOK OF INTELLIGENCE STUDIES (London, 2007), editor.

SEVEN SINS OF AMERICAN FOREIGN POLICY (New York, 2007).

WHO'S WATCHING THE SPIES? ESTABLISHING INTELLIGENCE
SERVICE ACCOUNTABILITY (Washington, DC, 2005), edited with Hans
Born and Ian Leigh.

AMERICAN FOREIGN POLICY: HISTORY, POLITICS, AND POLICY
(New York, 2005), with John Endicott and Daniel S. Papp.

FATEFUL DECISIONS: INSIDE THE NATIONAL SECURITY COUNCIL
(New York, 2004), edited with Karl F. Inderfurth.

BOMBS, BUGS, DRUGS, AND THUGS: INTELLIGENCE AND
AMERICA'S QUEST FOR SECURITY (New York, 2000), German edition:
BOMBEN, WANZEN UND INTRIGEN: AMERIKAS GEHEIMDIENSTE
(Düsseldorf, 2002).

SECRET AGENCIES: U.S. INTELLIGENCE IN A HOSTILE WORLD (New
Haven, CT, 1996).

AMERICA AS A WORLD POWER: FOREIGN POLICY IN A
CONSTITUTIONAL FRAMEWORK (New York, 1995).

RUNOFF ELECTIONS IN THE UNITED STATES (Chapel Hill, NC, 1992),
with Charles S. Bullock III.

AMERICA'S SECRET POWER: THE CIA IN A DEMOCRATIC SOCIETY
(New York, 1989).

DECISIONS OF THE HIGHEST ORDER: PERSPECTIVES ON THE
NATIONAL SECURITY COUNCIL (Pacific Grove, CA, 1988), edited with
Karl F. Inderfurth.

THROUGH THE STRAITS OF ARMAGEDDON: ARMS CONTROL
ISSUES AND PROSPECTS (Athens, GA, 1987), edited with Paul F. Diehl.

A SEASON OF INQUIRY: THE SENATE INTELLIGENCE
INVESTIGATION (Lexington, KY, 1985).

THE MAKING OF INTERNATIONAL AGREEMENTS: CONGRESS
CONFRONTS THE EXECUTIVE (New York, 1984).

The Threat On The Horizon

LOCH K. JOHNSON

An Inside Account of

America's Search for Security

after the Cold War

JAN 19 2012

Montante Family Library
D'Youville College

OXFORD
UNIVERSITY PRESS

2011

OXFORD
UNIVERSITY PRESS

Oxford University Press, Inc., publishes works that further
Oxford University's objective of excellence
in research, scholarship, and education.

Oxford   New York
Auckland   Cape Town   Dar es Salaam   Hong Kong   Karachi
Kuala Lumpur   Madrid   Melbourne   Mexico City   Nairobi
New Delhi   Shanghai   Taipei   Toronto

With offices in
Argentina   Austria   Brazil   Chile   Czech Republic   France   Greece
Guatemala   Hungary   Italy   Japan   Poland   Portugal   Singapore
South Korea   Switzerland   Thailand   Turkey   Ukraine   Vietnam

Copyright (c) 2011 by Oxford University Press, Inc.

Published by Oxford University Press, Inc.
198 Madison Avenue, New York, New York 10016

www.oup.com

Oxford is a registered trademark of Oxford University Press

All rights reserved. No part of this publication may be reproduced,
stored in a retrieval system, or transmitted, in any form or by any means,
electronic, mechanical, photocopying, recording, or otherwise,
without the prior permission of Oxford University Press.

Library of Congress Cataloging-in-Publication Data

Johnson, Loch K., 1942-
The threat on the horizon : an inside account of America's search for security
after the Cold War / Loch K. Johnson.
p.   cm.
Includes bibliographical references and index.
ISBN-13: 978-0-19-973717-8 (hardcover : alk. paper)
ISBN-10: 0-19-973717-7
1. Intelligence service—United States.   2. National security—United States.
I. Title.
JK468.I6J67 2010
355'.033073—dc22   2010016333

9 8 7 6 5 4 3 2 1

Printed in the United States of America
on acid-free paper

JK
468
.I6
J67
2011

To Les Aspin,
who led the way,
and to
Leena and Kristin,
who inspire

"All we are trying to do, I suppose, is to tell it true."
—Hollis Summers
American novelist

CONTENTS

Entering the Shrouded World of Intelligence

I FIRST BECAME INTERESTED IN the subject of intelligence in 1975. That year I read in the newspaper that Senator Frank Church (D-ID) had been asked by the Senate majority leader, Mike Mansfield (D-MT), to chair an investigative panel that would look into charges of domestic spying by the Central Intelligence Agency (CIA). With a research trip to Washington already planned for the following week, I decided to use the occasion to drop by the Capitol and offer my good wishes to Senator Church, for whom I had worked as an American Political Science Association congressional fellow five years earlier.

We sat in his Russell Senate Office Building suite, which was dominated by an oil portrait of his childhood hero, Senator William Borah (R), another Idaho and former chair of the august Senate Foreign Relations Committee. Unlike Church, an internationalist, Borah had been a leading isolationist. As Senator Church told me about his new assignment, I became more and more intrigued. At the end of the visit, I ventured to ask if he needed any help with the investigation. He picked up the telephone and told the staff director of the new committee to sign me up and begin a background security clearance, a procedure required for all staff members participating in what was to become one of the most sensitive inquiries in the history of the Senate. The panel's focus, Church explained to me, would be the question of whether the CIA had spied on American citizens, in violation of its 1947 legislative charter. My job, he continued, would be to prepare him for committee meetings and hearings, write speeches for him, take part in the committee's research and investigative work, and help write the final report.

I reminded him that I knew virtually nothing about the CIA, or any other intelligence agency, beyond what I read in the newspapers. "I don't either," he replied with a smile, "but we'll learn together. The important thing is I know you and I can trust you." Despite these reassurances, I knew that my learning curve would be far steeper than his. Senator Church had served as a U.S. Army intelligence officer during World War II (earning a Bronze Star for meritorious service). Moreover, as a member of the Foreign Relations Committee for many years, he had received countless briefings on CIA activities and had chaired a subcommittee that examined its operations in Latin America. I would be starting from scratch.

I returned home to Ohio, where I was on the political science faculty at Ohio University in Athens, and discussed with my wife the events that had transpired in Washington. A fellow political junkie, she was thrilled at the possibility of returning to the nation's capital. The academic term was coming to an end, and soon we were packing our bags. We had lived in DC before, in 1969–70, when I was a congressional fellow, fresh out of graduate school with a PhD and ready to conquer the world. Each spring, the fellowship program selected a handful of individuals from academe (the numbers varied slightly from year to year), along with a small group of journalists and bureaucrats. The luck recipients could choose any member of Congress they wished to work for as an assistant during the fellowship year, or they could divide their time between two lawmakers, one in the House and one in the Senate. The only hitch was that the member of Congress had to agree to accept the fellow as a staff member. As a longtime admirer of Senator Church, an articulate opponent of the Vietnam War, I had listed him as my top choice. I was happy to learn that he was willing to take me onto his staff for the fellowship year. During this time with Senator Church, I worked mainly on the Cooper-Church Amendment and other proposals designed to prevent the expansion of the Vietnam War into Cambodia and Laos.

When I returned to academe, I kept in touch with the Senator, and, as the time drew near for his reelection bid for a fourth term in the Senate in 1974, I requested a leave of absence from the university, traveled to Idaho, and helped out in the campaign. Early on I came across a broken-down double-decker bus that had been transported some time ago from London to Boise, Idaho. Still bright red, the bus had come to rest in a junkyard adjacent to a potato field west of the city. At little cost, I had it towed into town and repaired the engine. I covered the sides of the bus with "Vote for Church" signs trimmed in red, white, and blue bunting. A friend and I drove it around Boise for a few hours each day, over a span of several weeks—an eye-catching mobile billboard. Idaho was becoming increasingly Republican, and the outcome of the election was in doubt until the final ballots were counted. Church won, but narrowly. Six years later, in 1980, he would be less fortunate, suffering defeat not long after assuming the chairmanship of the Foreign Relations Committee—his lifetime ambition.

I looked forward to being Senator Church's assistant again in 1975. He was a man of strong intellect, quick wit, high integrity, and an easygoing demeanor, and he was dedicated to the reform of America's foreign policy, which was the focus of my own academic research. Miraculously, during his student days at Stanford University he had recovered from testicular cancer. His chances for survival seemed slim at the time, but at the suggestion of a physician he submitted himself to painful daily doses of an experimental X-ray treatment. The radiation worked, and, following a period of recuperation, he managed to complete his coursework, win the university's coveted debating award (the Joffre medal), and graduate high in his class from its prestigious law school in 1950. With no more signs of cancer, Church returned to Idaho, passed the bar, and started a law practice. Always interested in party politics, he ran for a state legislative seat in 1952 on the Democratic ticket but was soundly drubbed, coming in fifth in a field of eight—a twelve-thousand-vote defeat.

In 1956, Church tried again, this time aiming higher: the United States Senate. Although it seemed an unrealistic goal at the time, he threw his hat into the ring, running against a long-serving incumbent. He campaigned without rest, and a sparkling oratory and sound grasp of the issues propelled him to a surprise 46,315-vote victory. It was an amazing recovery from his first stumbling attempt at electoral politics just four years earlier. At age thirty-two, Frank Church set out for Washington, DC, as the fourth-youngest person ever elected to the United States Senate. For sixteen months in 1975 and 1976, the Church Committee (as his Senate investigative panel came to be called) examined various allegations of intelligence abuse and recommended a long list of reforms.[1] Foremost among them was the creation of permanent intelligence oversight committees in both the Senate and the House. Lawmakers established these two panels in 1976 and 1977, respectively, and they are known formally as the Senate Select Committee on Intelligence and the House Permanent Select Committee on Intelligence. Less formally, the panels are referred to simply as the Senate and the House Intelligence Committees or, more commonly, by their acronyms: SSCI (with the unfortunate pronunciation of "sissy") and HPSCI ("hipsee").

Following my stint on the Church Committee, I joined Senator Church's brief run for the presidency in 1976 as his "issues director." It was a spirited but unsuccessful bid. The campaign began on a high note when Church defeated his main rival for the Democratic party nomination, Governor Jimmy Carter of Georgia, in the Nebraska primary (May 1976). It was the first head-to-head contest between the two candidates. Carter was far ahead in the delegate count, and our victory caused a media stir. Church went on to win as well in Idaho, Oregon, and Rhode Island, but he had entered the race far too late and with limited resources. In contrast, Governor Carter had been planning his race for the presidency over the previous four years and rolled forward with a well-organized national organization to capture a majority of the delegate votes. Those of us in the Church camp held out hope that at least Governor Carter might select our champion as a running mate, based on the Senator's strong showing against him in the Midwest and his extensive knowledge of foreign affairs. Instead, the future President picked another good man, Senator Walter F. Mondale of Minnesota, who had been a stellar member of the Church Committee. In the fall, the Carter/Mondale ticket proved to be a winner.

Not long after the 1976 presidential election, I accepted a position on the newly formed staff of the House Intelligence Committee, which had just set up shop in a low-ceilinged, bunker-like suite of offices nestled next to the Capitol Rotunda. I would be HPSCI's first staff director for its Subcommittee on Intelligence Oversight, led by Les Aspin (D-WI), a relative newcomer to Congress, elected in 1970 and, like Frank Church, a rare Phi Beta Kappa intellectual on Capitol Hill.

After three years, I left the House of Representatives and returned to the leafy glades of academe. I wanted to further pursue my writing and teaching activities in the field of political science. This time I moved to the South, joining the faculty at the University of Georgia, a public institution of higher learning a beautiful magnolia-shaded campus in another Athens. It seemed determined to improve its national standing—and would do so dramatically over the next three decades. In 2007, for example, it was the only state university in the nation to have two students win Rhodes scholarships. In light of my experiences on the Church Committee and with the House Intelligence Committee, the study of the CIA and America's other secret agencies became one of my research and teaching priorities.

Washington Revisited

It was thus with considerable interest that I read in the newspaper in 1994 that President Bill Clinton had appointed Les Aspin to lead an inquiry into the current state of U.S. intelligence. On one of my periodic research trips to Washington, I went by to see Aspin in his House office. Much as I had asked

Frank Church two decades earlier if I could help with his investigation, I asked Aspin if he needed help with the probe. He expressed an interest in my assistance and promised to telephone me soon. Thus began a lengthy dialogue between us, chiefly by telephone and fax, about all aspects of the envisioned study, and later in the year, when a special commission was created for this review, he asked me to join the effort as his "special assistant." Here was a chance for me to get actively involved with real-life intelligence again—an opportunity to see how the secret agencies were operating after the Cold War, compared to my earlier experience on the Church Committee in the middle of that superpower conflict. I would also be able to observe from the inside how a blue-ribbon commission functioned. Beyond these scholarly interests, I hoped to play some small role in helping the intelligence agencies chart a new course through the uncharted waters of the post–Cold War world.

This time I had to pack my bags for Washington alone. Now I had a daughter, aged sixteen, in high school, and she had little interest, understandably, in being uprooted from her good teachers and friends. She and my wife would remain in Georgia, with plans to join me in the nation's capital during the summer months. In the meantime, I would commute between Georgia and Washington each week. The plan was to board an airplane every Friday evening at National Airport across the Potomac River from Washington and fly to Charlotte, North Carolina. Then, on a small commuter plane, I would continue on to Athens. I would reverse the sequence on Monday mornings. I had a pretty good idea the commute would be taxing, both on me physically and on family relations.

Of course, hardship is a relative matter. In the early days of World War II, the British government called my father away from his wife in Te Kuiti, New Zealand, near Auckland, and sent him to Canada to learn how to pilot a twin-engine Vickers Wellington bomber. His next stop was England where he and his crew (part of the 75 NZ Squadron) flew sorties over Europe against the Nazis, in concert with the Royal Air Force (RAF). He would never return to New Zealand. Two days before Christmas in 1941, and shortly before my birth, he perished at the age of twenty-eight during a crash landing in a dense fog at Bernards Heath, north of Cambridge, England, on his return from a combat mission against the port city of Brest, France, where the Germans had sheltered the war cruisers *Scharnhorst*, *Gneisenau* and *Prinz Eugen*. A battle commendation read: "Although the raids in which the New Zealand Squadron operated did not inflict decisive damage on the enemy ships, their confinement to port during the year was a major contribution to the Battle of the Atlantic."[2]

Later in the war, my mother met an American soldier in Auckland who had been sent to the Pacific theater to fight against the Japanese. When the conflict finally ended in 1945, he married her and brought the two of us (I was four years old) from the antipodes to the United States, no doubt to the shock of his mom, dad, and multiple siblings in tiny Spanish Fork, Utah. He was soon called up again to fight in another war, this time on the Korean peninsula in 1950–53. He remained in the military and, during two subsequent tours of duty in Europe during the Cold War, spent many a long winter month as an artillery officer bivouacked beneath brown canvas tents at Graffenvier in the freezing northern reaches of Germany, where he trained to defend the Fulda Gap against a possible Soviet invasion of Western Europe.

My time away from home in Washington working for Les Aspin would be nothing compared to these sacrifices. Nonetheless, I would not recommend to anyone the kind of weekly commuting arrangement I undertook, nor would I do it again. The long hours and turmoil of service on a national commission were eased, though, by a gratifying sense that I was in a position to assist the United States, even if modestly, by providing research support to Aspin and other commission members as they weighed how the intelligence agencies should be oriented against ambient dangers that had arisen in the wake of the Cold War. I felt a joy in this opportunity to serve my adopted homeland that an immigrant often feels with special poignancy.

Compensation for the grueling year spanning from March 1995 to March 1996 came in another form as well: here was an extraordinary opportunity to learn more about intelligence, as well as the workings of a high-level commission, and to do so in the company of bright, knowledgeable, and dedicated coworkers. This book is a citizen's report on what I found during this journey into the dark regions of America's government. In these pages, I examine the shifts and starts of the commission's inquiry—such enterprises never move forward in leaps and bounds—and I try to impart a sense of how a prominent government panel on national security carries out its duties. In addition, I use the story of the commission to explore broader questions about the strengths and weaknesses of America's intelligence agencies on the eve of the terrorist attacks of 9/11 and other challenges that would soon confront the United States at the dawn of a new century.

Reorienting the Nation's Intelligence Agencies After the Cold War

The Cold War, fought chiefly between the intelligence services of the Soviet Union and the United States,[3] ended in 1991 with the dissolution of Moscow's vast empire. A decade later, in 2001, terrorists from the organization known as Al Qaeda ("The Base" in Arabic) struck New York City and the Pentagon in the worst surprise attacks against the homeland ever experienced by the United States. In the interval between the end of the Cold War and the onset of the Age of Al Qaeda, President Bill Clinton and the Congress formed a special commission to consider the future of U.S. intelligence. Officially designated the Commission on the Roles and Capabilities of the United States Intelligence Community, the panel bore the less formal name of "the Aspin-Brown Commission," after its two consecutive chairmen, Les Aspin and Harold Brown. Both men had served as secretary of defense, Aspin for Bill Clinton and Brown for Jimmy Carter.

The purpose of the Commission was to determine how best to adapt the nation's secret services to the new and very different world that had emerged in the aftermath of the superpower struggle. Between 1946 and 2009, the intelligence community was the object of forty government studies.[4] Paring this list down to the most significant probes, the Aspin-Brown Commission takes its place alongside the first Hoover Commission of 1948; the Dulles Commission, also in 1948; the second Hoover Commission of 1953; the Schlesinger Committee of 1971; the Murphy Commission of 1972–75; the Rockefeller Commission and the congressional inquiries (the Church and Pike Committees) of 1975–76; the Inouye-Hamilton congressional investigation into the Iran-*contra* scandal of 1987; the Gore Commission of 1993; and the investigations of the Kean Commission in 2003 and the Silbermann-Robb Commission in 2005 that examined the intelligence failures related, respectively, to the terrorist attacks of 9/11 and the faulty Iraqi weapons estimate in 2002 that contributed to the outbreak of the Second Persian Gulf War.[5] Of these various panels, the Church Committee and the Aspin-Brown Commission have been by far the most extensive inquiries into the activities of America's secret agencies.[6]

A study of the Aspin-Brown Commission is important for a number of reasons. The work of the Commission sheds light on the state of intelligence in the United States in the years immediately following the close of the Cold War. The commission's work also provides insights into why the nation's intelligence agencies proved to be unable to provide specific warnings about the 9/11 terrorist strikes against the U.S. homeland, and why these agencies produced inaccurate estimates of the likelihood of Iraq having unconventional weapons. A close look at the commission is useful, too, for improving our understanding about America's use of panels of inquiry to resolve policy disputes. Despite the frequent creation of blue-ribbon commissions, the scholarly literature on their activities and their influence remains thin—and especially so in the realm of national security, where commission doors have been shut tight against scholars and journalists. An occasional study has been published about security probes;[7] but this is the only book-length, behind-the-scenes dissection of a major commission that looked exclusively and deeply into the operations of America's intelligence agencies.

My intention has been to crack open a security commission for a close look inside at how they operate. I aspire to show how the work of the Aspin-Brown Commission unfolded, as participants at the time saw it and lived it. I want to illustrate how a commission goes about identifying weaknesses in government agencies, and how it communicates its findings and recommendations to those in positions of authority. I am less interested in hypotheses and statistical analyses than I am in trying to breathe life into an important period of American political and intelligence history. My hope is that, as we learn more about commission experiences, we can make better use of these panels in the future.

Peering into the Hidden Recesses of Government

This book focuses on a number of vital questions about how a security commission functions. It explores as well the question of how the U.S. intelligence community attempted to shift its focus from the U.S.-Soviet superpower standoff to a far more complicated global setting with many newly independent powers—a dramatic change from a "bipolar" to a "multipolar" world, as political scientists put it. I wanted to examine what happens behind the closed doors of a commission. What are a commission's internal dynamics? What outside institutions and individuals aid or hinder its work? With respect to America's intelligence agencies, my objective was to explore how well the CIA and its companion spy organizations managed the transition from the Cold War to a new world of terrorists, rogue nations, civil wars, and failed states. What weaknesses within America's intelligence agencies contributed to the errors of warning and judgment that would plague the United States in the years leading up to the 9/11 terrorist attacks and the faulty assessment of Iraqi armaments?

Questions of methodology are important for every researcher. The social sciences offer a wide array of tools for studying government activities, from the use of historical archives and advanced econometric analysis to conducting interviews and making personal observations. I have relied on a thorough sifting of government documents and media reports related to the Aspin-Brown

Commission; on interviews with participants involved in the inquiry; and, above all, on my own eyewitness impressions of its proceedings—what social scientists refer to as "participant observation."[8] In employing the methodology of participant observation, I follow in the footsteps of many researchers who have demonstrated the value of this approach.[9] In the preface to *The Gathering Storm*, the first volume of a history of World War II, Winston S. Churchill wrote that he intended to emulate "the method of Defoe's *Memoirs of a Cavalier*, in which the author hangs the chronicle and discussion of great military and political events upon the thread of the personal experiences of an individual."[10] I am under no illusion that I can match, or even approach, the great literary and reporting skills of Sir Winston, but I do admire his and Defoe's approach and adopt it in this work as I explore how individuals shaped the outcome of the Commission's work.

The archival research consisted of an examination of all key public documentation on America's intelligence agencies from 1991–2010: unclassified government archives, books and journal articles by scholars, memoirs from practitioners, and congressional hearings. The interviews were with members and staff on the Aspin-Brown Commission, along with most of the nation's intelligence chiefs in recent years and a wide selection of lower-ranking intelligence officers, other government officials, and fellow intelligence scholars. These interview sessions have ranged from informal discussions with participants during the course of the Aspin-Brown inquiry (1995–96) to more formal, tape-recorded sessions with intelligence directors in the years before and after the commission issued its report. As for the methodology of participant observation, I attended and closely observed (as the only academic present) every one of the Commission's formal meetings and most of its key staff sessions. In addition, when possible, I have incorporated empirical measures into the research, including a unique analysis of participation patterns by Commission members.

My presentation is straightforward and free of esoteric methodologies. This story of the Aspin-Brown Commission proceeds chronologically, but it is interspersed with what I hope are useful insights into the practice of intelligence by the United States before, during, and after the commission's work. My day-to-day exposure to the commission's proceedings provided an opportunity to trace its evolution and discuss with members and staff its management and policy choices. Being so close to the action inevitably raises questions about objectivity. As a social scientist, I have undergone formal training in the methods of participant observation and other techniques of detached scholarly analysis. I have done my best to honor these professional principles and to provide an unbiased account. The reader will be the ultimate judge of whether I have succeeded.

As I wrote this book, a quote from a short story by the great American author John Updike came loose from its moorings in my memory. Describing a sense of frustration I suppose every writer feels, Updike lamented that "from the dew of the few flakes that melt on our faces we cannot reconstruct the snowstorm."[11] I noted this observation in a study of the Church Committee, my first attempt to chronicle the inner workings of American government.[12] Again, it strikes me as an apt description of how difficult it is—indeed, impossible—to convey the full texture of a significant political event. In what follows, I offer only a few snowflakes.

ACKNOWLEDGMENTS

R ARE IS THE BOOK THAT comes to birth solely because of its author. This volume, too, has had many helping hands along the way. First of all, I am grateful to Les Aspin for encouraging me to write a history of the commission. I thank my wife, Leena, as well, and my daughter, Kristin, for putting up with all the time I spent away from home during the commission's tenure. With deep feelings of affection and devotion, I dedicate this book to Les and to my family. My companion, political and intellectual soul mate, and editor for over forty years, Leena also lent her keen eye to reading several drafts of the work. Her unyielding support in a thousand other ways cannot be adequately acknowledged in words.

I want to express my appreciation, as well, to the members and staff of the Aspin-Brown Commission for their conversations and interviews with me about the panel's activities and intelligence challenges facing the United States. Statements attributed to individuals in the following pages are based on my handwritten notes of their remarks, which I have taken great care to record accurately. I am further indebted to more than a hundred intelligence officers who responded to my questions about the events examined in the book. The opportunity during the 1990s to exchange thoughts about intelligence in interviews with every director of central intelligence (DCI) from 1966 to 1996—Richard Helms, James R. Schlesinger, William E. Colby, George H. W. Bush (by letter exchanges), Admiral Stansfield Turner, William J. Casey, William H. Webster, Robert M. Gates, R. James Woolsey, John Deutch, and George J. Tenet—also helped me understand better the perspectives on intelligence from the pinnacle of the espionage establishment. I offer my heartfelt thanks to each of these spy chiefs.

Indispensable, too, has been the chance to rub shoulders at conferences with the world's top intelligence scholars, from whom I have learned a great deal and whose influence on my own research is reflected in the reference notes at the end of this book. I thank, too, the journals *Intelligence and National Security* (published in London and for which I am the senior editor), *Washington Monthly*, *Presidential Studies Quarterly*, *Yale Journal of International Affairs*, *Studies in Intelligence*, *American Intelligence Journal*, *Nonproliferation Review Comparative Strategy*, and *SAIS Review of International Affairs* for allowing me to draw on my articles about intelligence oversight and intelligence analysis in parts of this book. In addition, I have had many stimulating conversations over the years with reporters on the intelligence beat for the *New York Times*, National Public Radio, and other leading media organizations; their influence can be seen, too, in my reference notes. Journalists seldom read scholarly work on intelligence, it seems, but we academics greatly value their insights and their skill in exposing government incompetence and scandal. There is no more important check on intelligence abuses in American society than the media, however imperfect.

When writing a book, thousands of facts need to be checked, footnotes traced, the spelling of names authenticated, interviews transcribed, and library books acquired and returned. These tasks were cheerfully assumed by my graduate research assistants, Kelley Johnson, Larry Lamanna, and Marie Milward, and an undergraduate assistant, Alexander B. Johnson. The help from these students went beyond routine chores, though, as we discussed together time and time again the leading issues in the study of intelligence. In this project they were more like professional colleagues than student assistants, and I thank them profusely. I have appreciated, too, the insights of Lt. Col. James B. Borders of the U.S. Air Force, a PhD candidate in intelligence studies at the University of Georgia.

In order to work on the commission, I needed to renew my top-secret security clearance from the days of the Church Committee. A clearance requires an extensive background check, as well as the signing of a "secrecy oath" in which one vows not to disclose classified information to any unauthorized person. In 1995, the oath committed the signatory to submit subsequent writings about the commission to the CIA's Publication Review Board (PRB). This is a disconcerting obligation for an author living in a democracy, because it smacks of government censorship. Yet the procedure does make sense. I certainly did not want to reveal, intentionally or inadvertently, any classified information, and it is useful to have a group of experts review one's work with this in mind. I would have preferred to submit my writings to a more independent review board located somewhere outside the government. Officials in Washington should create such a board In its absence, the intelligence community requires some kind of accountability concerning its sensitive information and has created the PRB.

I have been through the PRB process twice. The first time was for a book I wrote on the Church Committee in 1985. My second experience occurred a few years ago when I submitted an article to the PRB about the Aspin-Brown Commission. In both cases, its members concurred with my belief that the works contained no classified information. This book draws on that earlier article, using the same method of participant observation, augmented by interviews and new research I have conducted since my days on the Commission staff. I take this opportunity to thank the PRB for its prompt and courteous reading of the original study, and for its endorsement of the principle that a work of this kind on intelligence can be written without disclosing classified information. As with that article, there are no national secrets in these pages; this is a book about how a commission functions, not the details of the sensitive policies scrutinized by its members.

In addition, I would like to thank the professor who most influenced me in graduate school: Dr. Francis M. "Hank" Carney. His passion was the study of real politics, not the arid theoretical abstractions that have predominated in so many scholarly journals in the field of political science. I would also like to express my appreciation to Thomas P. Lauth, dean of the School of Public and International Affairs at the University of Georgia. In 2008, Dean Lauth provided me with a vital research leave to complete this project, along with encouragement and support. He is a true friend, though one without mercy on the golf course.

I want to acknowledge, too, the marvelous support I received from Oxford University Press, starting with Niko Pfund, always a reliable source of enthusiasm and encouragement. David McBride and Alexandra Dauler kept the project moving forward.

Finally, my heartfelt thanks go to Kristin and Jamil Swati for their wonderful hospitality on Long Island during the final stages of this project. I'll never forget the exhilarating runs to Sammy's Beach, the shared meals, and the spirited discussions about world affairs.

LKJ
Gardiners Bay
East Hampton

N̲O ONE LIKES TO READ government acronyms or abbreviations, not even those in the government. The most famous director of central intelligence, Allen W. Dulles (1953–61), once complained in a memo to an underling (Richard Helms, who would become director in 1966): "If you want me to learn 20 or more pseudonyms such as KUBARK, ODACID, ODYOKE, etc., I will willingly do so, but I have about reached the end of my patience on reading telegrams where pseudonyms abound and the content becomes unintelligible" (January 14, 1958, unclassified, and provided to me by a retired intelligence officer in 2009). Yet every profession has its own set as a means for easier communication. It would be peculiar to write a book about intelligence without reference to the profession's abbreviations, since they are a part of everyday life in the world of espionage. I have tried to keep their usage to a minimum; but occasionally they arise in these pages, and when they do, this glossary provides a ready guide for the reader.

ABA	American Bar Association
ABM	antiballistic missile
ADCI/A&P	assistant director of central intelligence/analysis and production
ADCI/C	assistant director of central intelligence/collection
AFIO	Association of Former Intelligence Officers
AG	attorney general
A-12	a U.S. spy plane
AWAC	airborne warning and control system (U.S. spy plane)
BDA	battle damage assessment

BMD	ballistic missile defense
BW	biological weapons
CA	covert action
CAS	Covert Action Staff
CB	chemical-biological
CBW	chemical-biological warfare
CE	counterespionage
C4I	command, control, computer, communications, and intelligence
CFR	Council on Foreign Relations
CHAOS	cryptonym (code name) of a CIA domestic spying operation
CI	counterintelligence
CIA	Central Intelligence Agency (the "Agency")
CIC	Counterintelligence Center
CIG	Central Intelligence Group
CINC	commander-in-chief (regional military commander)
CIO	Central Imagery Office
CMS	Community Management Staff
CNC	Crime and Narcotics Center (DCI)
CNO	Chief of Naval Operations
COINTELPRO	FBI Counterintelligence Program
comint	communications intelligence
CORONA	codename for the first U.S. spy-satellite system
C/O	case officer (CIA)
COed	"case-officered"
COS	chief of station, the top CIA officer in the field
CSIS	Canadian Security and Intelligence Service
CTC	Counterterrorism Center (CIA)
CW	chemical weapons
DA	directorate of administration
DAS	deputy assistant secretary
DBA	dominant battlefield awareness
DCIA or D/CIA	director of the Central Intelligence Agency
DCI	director of central intelligence
DDA	deputy director for administration
DDCI	deputy director of central intelligence
DDCIA	deputy director for the Central Intelligence Agency
DDIC	deputy director for the intelligence community

DDI	deputy director for intelligence
DDO	deputy director for operations
DDS&T	deputy director for science and technology
DEA	Drug Enforcement Administration
DEC	DCI's Environmental Center
DHS	Department of Homeland Security
DI	Directorate of Intelligence (CIA)
DIA	Defense Intelligence Agency
DIAC	Defense Intelligence Agency Center
DIA/Humint	Defense Humint Service
DMA	Defense Mapping Agency
DO	Directorate of Operations (CIA), also known as the Clandestine Services
DoD	Department of Defense
DoE	Department of Energy
DoS	Department of State
DoT	Department of Transportation
DMI	Director of Military Intelligence (proposed)
DNI	Director of National Intelligence
DS&T	Directorate for Science and Technology (CIA)
elint	electronic intelligence
EO	executive order
EOP	executive office of the president
EPA	Environmental Protection Agency
FAS	Federation of American Scientists
FBI	Federal Bureau of Investigation
FISA	Foreign Intelligence Surveillance Act
FY	Fiscal Year
GATT	General Agreement on Trade and Tariffs
GEO	Geosynchronous Orbit
GOP	Grand Old Party (the Republican Party)
GPO	Government Printing Office
GRU	Soviet Military Intelligence
HEO	highly elliptical orbit
HPSCI	House Permanent Select Committee on Intelligence
HUD	Housing and Urban Development (Department of)
humint	human intelligence (espionage assets)
IC	intelligence community
ICBM	intercontinental ballistic missile

ICS	Intelligence Community Staff
IC-21	*Intelligence Community in the 21st Century* (hearings and report title in the U.S. House of Representatives)
IG	inspector general
IM	intelligence memorandum
ints	intelligence collection methods (as in "sigint")
imint	imagery intelligence (photography)
INR	Bureau of Intelligence and Research (Department of State)
IOB	Intelligence Oversight Board (also known as PIOB)
IRTPA	Intelligence Reform and Terrorism Prevention Act (2004)
IT	information technology
I&W	indications and warning
JCS	Joint Chiefs of Staff
JIC	Joint Intelligence Committee (U.K.)JMIP joint military intelligence program
JMIP	joint military intelligence program
JROC	Joint Reconnaissance Operations Center
JSTARS	Joint Surveillance Target Attack Radar Systems
JTTF	Joint Terrorism Task Force
KGB	Soviet Secret Police and Foreign Intelligence: Committee for State Security
KH	Keyhole (satellite)
KJ	Key Judgment (NIE executive summary)
KP	"kitchen police" (U.S. Army slang for mess-hall duty)
LEO	low earth orbit
MAGIC	Allied code-breaking operations against the Japanese in World War II
masint	measurement and signatures intelligence
MI	military intelligence
MIA	missing in action
MIP	Military Intelligence Program
MIRV	multiple, independently targeted, reentry vehicle
MI5	British Security Service
MI6	Secret Intelligence Service (SIS—United Kingdom)
MIT	Massachusetts Institute of Technology
MP	member of Parliament (United Kingdom)
MRBM	medium-range ballistic missiles
MRC	major regional conflict
MX	Missile Experimental (a U.S. ICBM)
NAC	National Assessment Center (proposed)

NAFTA	North American Free Trade Agreement
NAO	National Applications Office (Department of Homeland Security)
NASA	National Aeronautics and Space Administration
NATO	North Atlantic Treaty Organization
NCPC	National Counterproliferation Center (for the DNI)
NCS	National Clandestine Service
NCTC	National Counterterrorism Center (for the DNI)
NEOB	New Executive Office Building
NFAC	National Foreign Assessment Center
NFIP	National Foreign Intelligence Program (now NIP)
NGA	National Geospatial-Intelligence Agency
NGO	nongovernmental organization
NIA	National Imagery Agency (proposed)
NIC	National Intelligence Council
NID	*National Intelligence Daily*; also (when not italicized), national intelligence director (a variation of DNI)
NIE	National Intelligence Estimate
NIPF	National Intelligence Priorities Framework
NIO	national intelligence officer
NIMA	National Imagery and Mapping Agency
NIP	National Intelligence Program
NIPF	National Intelligence Priorities Framework
NOC	nonofficial cover
NPC	Nonproliferation Center
NPIC	National Photographic Interpretation Center
NRO	National Reconnaissance Office
NSA	National Security Agency
NSC	National Security Council
NCTC	National Counterterrorism Center
NTM	National Technical Means
NZ	New Zealand
OBE	overtaken by events
OC	official cover
ODNI	Office of the Director of National Intelligence
OEOB	Old Executive Office Building
OMB	Office of Management and Budget
ONE	Office of National Estimates
OPC	Office of Policy Coordination (CIA)
OPEC	Organization of Petroleum Exporting Countries

osint	open-source intelligence
OSS	Office of Strategic Services
PAC	political action committee
PBCFIA	President's Board of Consultants on Foreign Intelligence Activities
PDB	*President's Daily Brief*
PDD	Presidential Decision Directive
PFIAB	President's Foreign Intelligence Advisory Board (since 2008, PIAB)
phoint	photographic intelligence
PIAB	President's Intelligence Advisory Board
PIOB	President's Intelligence Oversight Board
PM ops	paramilitary operations
PNG	*persona non grata*
POW	prisoner of war
PRB	Publication Review Board (CIA)
PRC	People's Republic of China
radint	radar intelligence
RAF	Royal Air Force
RANDa	Washington and California think tank
R&D	research and development
RMA	revolution in military affairs
RPG	rocket-propelled grenade
SAIS	Paul H. Nitze School of Advanced International Studies (Johns Hopkins University)
SAM	surface-to-air missile
SecDef	secretary of defense
SHAMROCK	cryptonym for a specific NSA domestic spying operation that involved electronic eavesdropping, revealed in 1975 by Senate investigators
sigint	signals intelligence
SDO	support to diplomatic operations
SLBM	submarine-launched ballistic missile
SMO	support to military operations
SNIE	Special National Intelligence Estimate
SOCOM	Special Operations Command
SOG	Special Operations Group (CIA)
SOVA	Office of Soviet Analysis (CIA)
SR-21	Strategic Reconnaissance aircraft (a U.S. spy plane)
SSCI	Senate Select Committee on Intelligence

SVR	Russian Foreign Intelligence Service (post–Cold War)
TCA	Technical Collection Agency (proposed)
techint	technical intelligence
telint	telemetry intelligence
TIARA	tactical intelligence and related activities
TOR	terms of reference (for NIE drafting)
UAV	unmanned aerial vehicle (drone)
UAW	United Auto Workers
ULTRA	British and, later, US-UK interceptions of German communications during the Second World War
UK	United Kingdom
U-2	a US spy plane
UN	United Nations
USAF	United States Air Force
USC	United States Code (a statutory identification system)
USIB	United States Intelligence Board
USSR	Union of Soviet Socialist Republics
USTR	United States Trade Representative
VENONA	the codename for sigint intercepts used to detect Soviet espionage in the United States from 1943 to 1957 (disclosed by the NSA in 1995)
VX	a deadly nerve agent used in chemical weapons
WIPACC	Weapons Intelligence, Proliferation, and Arms Control Center
WMDs	weapons of mass destruction

TABLES

APPENDIXES

ABOUT THE AUTHOR

L OCH KINGSFORD JOHNSON HOLDS THE Regents Professorship of Public
and International Affairs at the University of Georgia. He is author or
editor of over two hundred articles and twenty-seven books on America's
foreign policy, national security, and elections, including *The Oxford Handbook
of National Security Intelligence* (editor, 2010). He has served as special assistant
to Chairman Frank Church of the Senate Select Committee on Intelligence
(1975–76), as the first staff director of the House Subcommittee on
Intelligence Oversight (1977–79), and as special assistant to Chairman Les
Aspin on the Aspin-Brown Commission on Intelligence (1995–96). He has
won the Certificate of Distinction from the National Intelligence Study
Center, the Studies in Intelligence Award from the Center for the Study of
Intelligence, the V.O. Key Prize from the Southern Political Science
Association, and an American Political Science Association Congressional
Fellowship. He has been a visiting fellow at Oxford University, a distin-
guished visiting scholar at Yale University, and a Phi Beta Kappa visiting
scholar. Professor Johnson served as secretary of the American Political
Science Association and as president of the International Studies Association,
South. He is the senior editor of the international journal *Intelligence and
National Security*, published in London. Born in Auckland, New Zealand,
Professor Johnson took his PhD in political science at the University of
California, Riverside. He and his wife live in Athens, Georgia.

The Threat On The Horizon

PART I | The Beginning

CHAPTER I | # Uneasy Birth
Disaster in Somalia

A CONFLUENCE OF EVENTS related to intelligence led to the creation in 1994 of what was initially known as the Aspin Commission. Within the executive branch, the impetus behind the establishment of the Commission was a military encounter in Somalia the previous October, one that turned sour.[1] Under orders from President George H. W. Bush, American troops (some twenty-five thousand) went to Somalia in August of 1992 to buttress a failing UN-sponsored humanitarian relief operation. The primary goal of the Bush administration was to airlift food to starving people living on the Horn of Africa. The president had been moved by the horrifying televised images of babies and children perishing in Somalia, their bodies shriveled, flies crawling across eyes that could no longer blink. Twenty countries supported the American troops by contributing an additional thirteen thousand soldiers.

Somalia was a dangerous place for foreign troops to enter, plagued by violence between local warlords who vied against one another for power in a nation that was on the verge of collapse. The most prominent warlord, General Mohamed Farrah Aideed (sometimes spelled Aidid), was locked in a pitched battle against a rival, Ali Mahdi Mohamed, for control over the capital city, Mogadishu—"Dish," in local Somalian slang. Tens of thousands died in the showdown. On top of the violence, a persistent drought brought famine to the nation. The result of these twin catastrophes was a full-blown humanitarian crisis.

By the end of 1992, and shortly before Les Aspin entered the new Clinton administration as secretary of defense ("secdef" in Pentagonese), the United

States decided to provide not only food but security to the people of Somalia, who continued to be buffeted by factional violence among opposing clans. This escalation of U.S. policy objectives worried several members of Congress, as well as the Pentagon brass; absent a clear rationale as to why Somalia was important to America's security interests, the placement of troops in the crossfire of warring African clans seemed to some observers a sure prescription for trouble. The concerns proved warranted. In June of 1993, Somali warlords gunned down twenty-three Pakistani peacekeepers sent to the region by the United Nations.

In response to these and other killings, the incoming Clinton administration expanded the U.S. mission in the Horn of Africa to include the disarming of the warring Somali clans, the political reconciliation in the country between rival factions, and the capture of the most vexing of the warlords, General Aideed, who was deemed responsible for the theft of large quantities of food supplies from the United States and other foreign donors. For critics, this escalation of America's objectives looked more like a high-risk gamble on nation building than a traditional UN relief operation. "In the case of Somalia, the winds have blown us from a narrow well-defined humanitarian mission to taking sides in a prolonged hunt for a Somalia warlord," worried Senator John McCain (R-AZ, who would become the GOP presidential nominee in 2008). "We have moved from a relief effort to peace enforcement to taking sides, and we now seem to be on the edge of moving toward nation building."[2] Several other lawmakers, however, called for a stepped-up U.S. presence in the region to curb the senseless killing.

At the same time that its objectives were expanding, the Clinton administration decided to reduce the number of U.S. troops in Somalia to four thousand—only half of whom were combat-ready forces. Moreover, the administration banned from this battlefield AC-130 aircraft armed with 40mm cannons. The goal was to lower America's profile in Somalia, a reaction to criticism from a number of Washington lawmakers as well as from some other nations about the use of military force on the Horn—an argument that struck Aspin with particular resonance. He believed at the time that there was too "much emphasis, almost exclusively, on the military force track and not enough on the political track."[3] Beyond his own personal belief in the inappropriateness of American troops in Somalia, he was responding to what he thought were signals from the White House that the president now wanted to lower America's profile in the region, not raise it.[4]

The outcome of these policy decisions by the Clinton administration was to stretch thin the capacity of the U.S. military forces to defend themselves in Somalia. The chairman of the Joint Chiefs of Staff, General Colin Powell, urged Aspin to honor the request of the local American commander for additional tanks and heavy-armored vehicles to protect his troops. Aspin rejected the request, later explaining that he had misunderstood the commander's intentions. Aspin feared that the commander was attempting to expand the humanitarian assistance beyond the bounds of prudence.

The lack of adequate military equipment for the American troops in Somalia soon spurred a major dispute in Washington, as the sophisticated firepower and determined will to fight displayed by Aideed's lieutenants and their ragtag Somali fighters took U.S. forces by surprise. No pushover, Aideed had been trained by the French military and had formerly served as a general in the Somali armed services. Shrewdly, he and his men avoided using satellite phones vulnerable to signals-intelligence ("sigint") interceptors aimed at the Horn by the National Security Agency (NSA)—the largest U.S. intelligence organization.[5] Instead, Aideed and his soldiers resorted to old-fashioned walkie-talkies and a mobile radio transmitter—both beneath the power grid of the sophisticated interception systems fielded by the NSA and the CIA.[6] The Aideed forces also possessed many more rocket-propelled grenades (RPGs) than anticipated, which they used with precision and unexpected effectiveness.

During a struggle over control of the capital city (the Battle of Mogadishu on October 3–4, 1993), the Somali fighters managed to shoot down three American Black Hawk helicopters. When Army Ranger and Delta Force reinforcements came to rescue the stranded crew members, the resulting combat—the longest sustained firefight involving U.S. troops since the Vietnam War—led to the deaths of eighteen American soldiers and the wounding of seventy-five more in an intense firefight in the city. Television footage recorded by international media at the scene relayed back to the United States and around the world images of Somalis dragging the naked body of a murdered Black Hawk crew member, Sergeant Randy Shughart, through the dirt alleyways of Mogadishu.[7] Prompted by these sickening images, lawmakers immediately called for Aspin's resignation and introduced language in an appropriations bill to halt funding for further U.S. military operations in Somalia, unless President Clinton explicitly requested additional monies and Congress approved the request.[8] The administration bowed to these pressures from Capitol Hill and quickly withdrew American troops from the Horn of Africa.

The president had already grown lukewarm toward his defense secretary, with whom he had developed little personal rapport. A controversy over the role of homosexuals in the military had led to early strains between the two men at the beginning of the Clinton administration. Aspin attempted to find a middle road between those who sought to ease restrictions on gays in uniform and those who wanted them ousted from the military altogether. Eventually, the administration settled on a "don't ask, don't tell" policy; but not before Aspin had managed to anger all sides, politically harming himself and the president as well. Aspin had also opposed the president's dispatch of U.S. troops to Haiti in 1993, as well as his decision to airdrop humanitarian aid into Bosnia that same year. Further, the secretary of defense feuded with the Office of Management and Budget over how much the Defense budget should be trimmed in the aftermath of the Cold War. Aspin understood that cuts were inevitable as the superpower conflict faded into history, but he rejected the deep reductions sought by budget analysts at OMB. Faced with the prospect of cutting into domestic programs to meet Aspin's request for funding increases in the Defense Department's budget, President Clinton leaned in the direction that had gotten him elected in the first place: a focus on economic conditions at home—jobs, health care, and education, not new weaponry for the admirals and generals.

To begin with, neither President Clinton nor Secretary Aspin had many allies in the Pentagon. "Not since Carter has a President been so disliked by the military," a Joint Chiefs staff officer told *Time* magazine early in the administration.[9] Inside the corridors of the Pentagon, the commander in chief was known as "the Draft Dodger," because of his successful efforts as a student to seek deferments from military service in Vietnam. The new defense secretary had at least served in the Army; however, Aspin came to the DoD job with a reputation as a poor manager. His mind was, as *New York Times* journalist Johnny Apple once put it gently, "more ruminative than executive."[10] He had never run anything larger than the eighty-person staff of the House Armed Services Committee.

Undeterred by the flap over the rights of uniformed gays, Aspin attempted to expand the participation of women in combat roles and to accelerate their advancement in the armed forces—not a position likely to win the hearts and minds of the older generation of four-stars running the services.[11] And while he was prepared to fight the White House and OMB over their desire to radically downsize the Pentagon, Aspin showed signs that he would be willing to accept a more modest $60-billion cut in military spending. This "caving in" to the White House was guaranteed to stimulate a negative response from entrenched DoD bureaucrats, whose chief motivation is turf and budget protection (like most every other government entity, although DoD has the lobbying power on Capitol Hill to resist change better than most government departments and agencies).

A Savage Peace

In 1993 the tragedy in Somalia came across as yet another intelligence failure, arriving in the wake of a terrorist detonation of explosives at the base of the World Trade Center in February of that year that luckily failed in its objective to topple the Twin Towers. Other events around the globe also took the United States by surprise during the early 1990s and raised further questions about the capacity of the nation's intelligence agencies to understand the dynamics of world affairs in the new era. In August 1990 Iraq invaded and occupied Kuwait, threatening the security of Saudi Arabia—a primary producer of oil for Western consumers. If the Saudi kingdom fell into the hands of the Iraqi dictator Saddam Hussein, he would be in a position to influence worldwide oil production and prices. In a hundred-hour war in 1990–91, the United States drove the Iraqi Army out of Kuwait and sent it fleeing home to its Baghdad stronghold.[12]

Moreover, during the early 1990s, over half a million people died in Bosnia, victims of ethnic conflict between Muslims and Serbs.[13] In Haiti, a coup staged in 1992 drove the democratically elected president Jean-Bertrand Aristide from office. The ensuing violence that swept across the poverty-stricken, AIDS-ridden island nation created a massive exodus of refugees, most of whom boarded rickety boats and headed for the Florida coast. If only to stem this tidal wave of refugees into the United States, the Clinton administration deemed it necessary to intervene militarily in Haiti. It ousted the coup plotters and restored Aristide to power, at least temporarily.[14] In each of these cases, the intelligence provided to the president and other officials was at best uneven.

Most shocking of all, in mid-1994 some 800,000 to 1,000,000 people perished in an unanticipated civil war in Rwanda, initiated by the Hutu tribes against the minority Tutsis.[15] The United States and other Western nations stood on the sidelines watching the massacre as it unfolded over three months, first surprised by the scope of the violence and then unwilling to risk the lives of their own troops to stop the bloodshed—especially after the anguishing outcome of America's recent intervention in Somalia.

At the end of the Cold War, President George H. W. Bush had expressed hope for a "new world order."[16] Instead, the world seemed an even angrier place. Since 1981, the Committee to Protect Journalists (an independent group that defends the rights of media personnel) has kept track of how many reporters are killed each year around the world in circumstances related to their work. The most lethal year between 1981 and 2008 was 1994, when sixty-six journalists died in the line of duty.[17] The end of the Cold War appeared to bring with it less of a new world order than a time of "savage peace."[18]

America's intelligence agencies reeled from the mounting criticism that they had failed to prepare leaders in Washington for the violence that erupted in Rwanda, Bosnia, Kuwait, Haiti, and Somalia. These were not the only crises to descend upon U.S. intelligence in the years that followed the end of the Cold War. The CIA, known as "the Agency" by insiders, found itself buffeted by a series of embarrassing news stories that tarnished its reputation. The highest-ranking spy job overseas for an American intelligence officer is the "chief of station," or COS. The individual who holds this position within a U.S. embassy serves as the senior intelligence adviser to the American ambassador. Between 1991 and 1994, at least seven CIA station chiefs had been removed from office. Their offenses included such activities as the theft of a religious icon from a church in Cyprus and the waving of a pistol in threatening manner against fellow intelligence officers in the U.S. embassy in Peru.[19]

In a new, uncertain world, the CIA seemed to have lost its way.

In yet another embarrassment, at the Agency's headquarters in Langley, Virginia, several hundred female intelligence officers brought a class-action sex-discrimination suit against the Directorate of Operations (DO)—the component of the CIA that runs agents abroad and carries out covert action. (It is now called the National Clandestine Service, with the same duties, and is still located within the Agency.) The suit accused intelligence managers of failing to promote women as fairly as men.

In addition, pressures mounted in Washington to reduce the budgets of the CIA and its companion agencies (reported to be $28 billion per annum in 1994),[20] just as the Defense Department budget was undergoing its own steep funding declines. Now that the Cold War was over, politicians squeezed the national security apparatus in search of a "peace dividend"—money that could be spent on roads and bridges, health care, and education, instead of fighter aircraft, bombers, surveillance satellites, and reconnaissance spy planes. President Clinton and Vice President Al Gore charged the staff of the National Security Council (NSC) to review how the missions of the intelligence agencies might be redefined and money saved, in light of the Soviet collapse. Brent Scowcroft, the highly regarded former national security advisor in both the Ford and first Bush administrations, added fuel to the fire by declaring that the intelligence agencies were "way overblown."[21] The vice president, too, believed they were "bloated."[22] It appeared as though funding for the government's secret agencies faced the possibility of substantial cuts.

As if any more shocks to the intelligence agencies were needed, the CIA also experienced the earthquake of a major counterintelligence failure within its own headquarters. One of the Agency's high-ranking officers in the Operations Directorate, Aldrich Hazen Ames, turned out to be a traitor. Agents with the Federal Bureau of Investigation (FBI, or "the Bureau") arrested him on February 21, 1994. Ames had worked for Soviet foreign intelligence (the KGB) during the final stages of the Cold War and, subsequently, for Russian intelligence (essentially the same old KGB, renamed the SVR). His treachery had led to Moscow's execution of at least ten CIA agents inside Russia. "They killed them, click, click, click, one after another," recalled a former senior CIA official. "We were out of business in Moscow. There was an orgy of bloodshed, and we didn't know why."[23] In a "damage assessment," the CIA calculated further that Ames had compromised upwards of nine hundred Agency operations against the Soviet Union and later Russia.[24]

In light of the Ames case and the snafus in Somalia, some members of Congress wondered aloud about the reliability of America's espionage services, and even whether they were necessary now that the superpower confrontation was over. In 1991, a widely respected senator, Daniel Patrick Moynihan (D-NY), called for the abolition of the CIA.[25] Inside the intelligence agencies, it was clear that "the public has concluded something bad and incompetent has occurred," a top official recalled in reference to the Ames disaster. "Now the administration has taken this and are [sic] saying, 'Let's put it all on the table.'"[26]

Aldrich Ames and all the other troubles not withstanding, for key officials within the Clinton administration the intelligence failure in Somalia had been the last straw. It was time to do something about the nation's spies. In 1975, the Senate created the Church Committee to investigate charges of law breaking by the CIA; now, in 1994, the charge was one of incompetence across the spectrum of the intelligence services. Vice President Gore, National Security Advisor Anthony Lake, and Defense Secretary Aspin wanted answers to why the search for the troublesome Somali warlord Aideed had ended in a debacle for the U.S. military in the labyrinthine streets of Dish. Members of Congress, quick to blame the Clinton administration for the humiliating defeat, sought answers, too.

As criticism concerning the misfortune in Somalia mounted, President Clinton responded by forcing his secretary of defense to take the hit for the administration. After eleven tumultuous months in office at the Pentagon, Aspin was through. At a December 15, 1993, press conference, the president referred to "personal reasons" for the secretary's sudden resignation.[27] Many observers assumed Clinton was referring to Aspin's well-known health problems. When I had worked with Aspin in the House of Representatives almost twenty years earlier, we played tennis once a week. Neither one of us were Wimbledon material, but we did approach the game with enthusiasm. He was reasonably fit and displayed a boyish devotion to the sport. He was also a competent sailor who loved to ply the waters of the Chesapeake Bay. In the early 1990s, however, he began to experience shortness of breath and occasional dizziness, symptoms diagnosed by his physician as a serious congenital heart ailment known as hypertrophic obstructive cardiomyopathy: Aspin's heart muscle had thickened over the years, interfering with its ability to pump blood efficiently throughout his body.

Earlier that year, in February of 1993, just a few weeks after he became secretary of defense at age fifty-four, Aspin's bouts of coughing and loss of breath became worrisome enough for him to be hospitalized twice within three weeks. On the second visit to the intensive care unit, his physician decided to implant a pacemaker the size of a silver dollar beneath his left collar bone, not to regulate the heartbeat but to reduce the force of each contraction of the heart. The ninety-minute surgery at Georgetown University Medical Center went well, but now he was on a strict regime of heart medication and under doctor's orders to rest as much as possible.[28] He slowed down a step or two, but not much. He remained essentially an unreconstructed workaholic and avid tennis player. This same blinkered devotion to his work had ended his only marriage, and probably explained why he never married again. National security was his most cherished companion.

So, yes, he had some health concerns, but that was not the "personal reason" that accounted for his resignation. The truth was that the president would have fired him had he not resigned.[29]

Angry, mortified, Aspin packed his personal belongings into boxes spread around room 3E880, the secretary's spacious suite in the Pentagon, and departed from the prestigious cabinet position. In a brief statement released by his office to the media on December 16th, he said simply: "I have been working continually for over twenty years to help build a strong American military. It's time for me to take a break and to undertake a new kind of work, so I have asked the president to relieve me of this duty as secretary of defense as of Jan. 20."

To soften the blow, President Clinton noted in the press conference at which he announced Aspin's resignation that "after he takes the break he's requested, I very much hope he will consider other assignments for this Administration." In April of 1994, Clinton appointed him chairman of the President's Foreign Intelligence Advisory Broad or PFIAB (pronounced "piff-ee-ab"), a group of civilian advisers to the White House on intelligence matters established during the Eisenhower administration.[30]

The president was reportedly "largely indifferent to bureaucratic reform" and had "only a passing interest" in the nation's intelligence agencies.[31] As a result, Aspin turned to Gore and Lake for permission to use his new position as PFIAB chairman to conduct a probe into the intelligence deficiencies that had contributed to the Somali tragedy. The idea of some sort of intelligence inquiry, perhaps a commission, had been floating around Washington since the end of the Cold War. In 1992, a Carnegie Endowment task force recommended a serious study into how the intelligence agencies ought to be reoriented toward the new geopolitical reality that followed the disintegration of the USSR.[32] The task force suggested that the White House sponsor the study and assign mainly outside experts and a few PFIAB members to the job. Upset by the Somali debacle, Aspin dusted off this idea and was now shopping it to Gore and Lake in the White House. While still serving as secretary of defense, Aspin had led a "bottom-up review" of the Defense Department's roles and missions—a sweeping examination of what needed to be done to prepare the military services for the challenges of a new world. A steering group led by John M. Deutch, the under secretary of defense for acquisition and technology at the Pentagon, spearheaded the review on Aspin's behalf, although with uncommonly active participation by the secretary himself. Such defense reviews were the air he breathed. Now Aspin wanted to peer into the even darker world of intelligence.

In June 1994 the media reported on the prospect of a presidential commission that would address intelligence reform, with Aspin at the helm in his capacity as PFIAB's chair. A friend of mine in Washington telephoned me with the news, knowing of my interest in intelligence and recalling that I had once worked for Aspin. I was pleased to see that my old boss would have a chance to redeem himself after taking the rap for the administration's train wreck in Somalia.

Preparing for an Intelligence Inquiry

Upon receiving permission from the president to lead a PFIAB review of intelligence (thanks to Gore and Lake), Aspin, in his typical fashion, immediately began to reach out to experts on the subject who he had come to know over the years. Here was a chance to make a comeback in Washington—a rare second act in the higher reaches of American politics—and he wanted to make sure the inquiry was a success. This meant extensive preparation: thinking about what subjects to probe, hiring knowledgeable experts to augment PFIAB's own small staff, and finding out what it would take to improve the capacity of the intelligence agencies to deal with the new perils of outlaw regimes, failing states, and terrorists.

In 1977, Aspin had selected me to serve as staff director when he began his inaugural chairmanship of the Subcommittee on Intelligence Oversight, a part of the House Permanent Select Committee on Intelligence (HPSCI) established that year in reaction to the Church Committee's discovery of domestic intelligence abuses. The aspiration was to provide better legislative supervision over the nation's secret agencies. The Senate had set up a similar oversight or review panel the year before. Working with Aspin on HPSCI had been intellectually challenging and enjoyable. He had a lively mind, a puckish sense of humor, and a determination to improve America's security. He could also be quirky. Sometimes he and his girlfriend at the time, a journalist of rising prominence, would hide out in the secure HPSCI quarters, situated near the Capitol Dome and guarded by police. They would coo in a corner office like a couple of teenagers.

Less than a month after I went to work for him that year, he showed up on a snowy evening at my home in northwest Washington. I opened the door to his grinning face and noticed that he was carrying a large brown bag in his arm. "Here," he said thrusting it in my direction. "What's this?" I asked.

His answer was a whistle that summoned from the open door of his car an enormous fluffy white sheepdog. The frolicking beast, named "Junket," bounded across the lawn and through the front door of the house, racing toward the kitchen at the end of the hallway. I looked inside the brown bag. It was filled with cans of dog food. I was beginning to get the idea.

"I'll be back in a week, okay?" Aspin said, still smiling, with a twinkle in his eyes. Then he was gone, like a ghost at cockcrow.

This could have been a disaster. For all Aspin knew, my wife or I might have been allergic to dogs. We already had two cats, who definitely suffered from that affliction. Junket turned out, though, not just to be rambunctious, but an irrepressible, affectionate, slobbering, beloved houseguest who liked to wrestle with me on the floor and play hide-and-seek with my wife. He instantly became a member of the family. Even the cats accepted him. When the week was up, we were reluctant to see Junket go. I soon learned that he was practically an appendage to Aspin. He came to the House of Representatives with the congressman each day, and, when not greeting constituents with zeal and slobber, he slept under his master's desk.

At the time Aspin was preparing himself and PFIAB to take on the task of a "bottom-up" intelligence review in 1994, I was a political science professor at the University of Georgia and on the list of intelligence experts he contacted. Soon we were exchanging a flurry of faxes and telephone calls about the new assignment he had taken on (e-mails were still uncommon at the time). His fax machine and telephone lines hummed throughout the summer as he engaged in dialogues with scores of individuals inside the Beltway, along with a few people outside that dense zone of policy wonks. In a letter typical of those he was receiving from experts at the time, a retired general wished him luck in this "daunting endeavor" and offered his services as staff director for the anticipated commission.

As I mentioned in the preface to this book, I had visited Aspin early in the summer of 1994 and volunteered for a role on the new commission. In July, he telephoned me in Georgia and asked me to come to Washington to discuss what an intelligence commission might try to achieve. My classes were over for the year, so I flew to National Airport the next day. We met in the PFIAB suite of offices, located in the Old Executive Office Building. The OEOB, in Washington-speak (now renamed the Eisenhower Building), is a vast, ornate gray granite edifice that has stood next door to the West Wing of the White House since 1888. The thick drapery and polished mahogany tables gave the suite more the feel of a high-class law firm than a government agency. Next door, the director of central intelligence (DCI), the head of both the CIA and the dozen other agencies that comprised the "intelligence community" in 1994, also had a suite of offices.[33] These digs served as a supplement to the DCI's lofty aerie on the seventh floor of CIA Headquarters at Langley, although the intelligence chiefs rarely used the OEOB space.

My prior service in Washington had been in the Senate and in the House, with occasional consulting stints at the State Department and the NSC. Capitol Hill was a plebeian setting for the most part, outside of a few luxurious offices reserved for senior lawmakers near the Capitol Dome. The Office of the Presidency, of which the OEOB was a part, presented a markedly different world, I thought to myself as Aspin and I settled into oversized leather chairs for a conversation. In contrast to the bedlam of crowded staff office space on the Hill, here was tranquility, opulence, and a heady sense of proximity to the center of power in Washington. At his request, I gave Aspin an account of what I thought the commission should try to accomplish. My core message was: here is an opportunity to conduct the first comprehensive reappraisal of the nation's secret agencies since the end of the Cold War, and it would be a mistake to limit the inquiry to intelligence shortcomings in Somalia. Clearly, he had been hearing the same theme from many other people, and he agreed. As our meeting wound down, he asked me to put my thoughts down on paper when I returned to Georgia and to send them to him as soon as possible.

When I returned home, I sent Aspin a lengthy fax that laid out the "first-order questions" (a favorite Aspin phrase) that the PFIAB commission would have to tackle in its inquiry. Among them:

- What are the new, and the enduring, threats to the United States in the wake of the Cold War?
- What new opportunities are now available for the advancement of U.S. global interests?
- How might America be expected to use covert action to protect its interests in this changed world?

Before a thoughtful redirection of the intelligence agencies could take place, America's political and intelligence leaders would presumably have to arrive at an understanding of the forces at work in the world since the Soviet implosion. This new strategic environment called for fresh thinking about a grand global strategy for the United States in the twenty-first century. A new strategy would, in turn, provide guidance to America's worldwide intelligence collection activities. Central to the determination of intelligence priorities in this far different world would be the drafting of a formal "threat assessment." What nations, factions, and individuals should be the targets of U.S. collection operations and other intelligence activities as a new century approached? Without question, North Korea and Libya would continue to pose a challenge to the United States; and an increasingly muscular China demanded ongoing attention. Although no longer the prime threat that it was during the Cold War, Russia, too, would have to be closely watched; its leaders in Moscow still possessed the capacity to destroy the United States in a half-hour hail of nuclear-tipped missiles streaking across the Arctic ice cap toward New York City, Chicago, Los Angeles, and other A-list targets from coast to coast. That was enough to make Washington pay close attention to the Kremlin, even if the tensions between the two major powers had lessened significantly.

The commission would have to try to "imagine the future," I wrote to Aspin. We both knew how difficult that would be, since none of us owned a crystal ball. My mind, and my memos to Aspin, quickly filled with questions that PFIAB investigators would need to consider. For example, how could the United States continue to collect signals and communications intelligence (especially telephone conversations) against adversaries who were acquiring sophisticated means of encoding their messages? In my long list of key questions, I was insufficiently prescient to raise a red flag about the threat of terrorism to the American homeland. I should have thought more about that possibility, given the attempt by terrorists just a year earlier to bring down the World Trade Center. Instead, my thoughts were focused on traditional dangers posed by the schemes and arsenals of foreign nations.

Aspin's ardor for any project he undertook was infectious, and I was now spending a good part of each day wondering how his work could have a lasting, positive effect on the nation's security. The most important goals would be to improve the ability of the United States to gather information from around the world, and to make sure that the quality of insights drawn from this information—intelligence analysis—was high. A thorough examination of the secret agencies would also have to look at the controversial subjects of covert action (CA) and counterintelligence (CI).

Covert action, the hidden intervention by the CIA into the affairs of other countries or factions, was always cause for concern. This aggressive use of the Agency by presidents is nothing less than an attempt to change the course of world events in a direction favorable to the United States—"giving history a push," in the words of a senior Agency operative.[34] Here was the CIA's department of "dirty tricks," including assassination plots, secret wars, and coups against foreign governments—even when their leaders had been democratically elected (as was the case with Chile in the early 1970s).[35] Sometimes covert action had proven useful, as when the CIA supported pro-democracy forces after World War II in Greece and Turkey, in France and Germany, and throughout Latin America and Asia.[36] More recently, in the 1980s, covert action had helped drive the Soviet army out of Afghanistan (though not without long-term negative consequences, chief among them the rise of the Taliban in that nation and its support for Al Qaeda). Further, it had supported Eastern European dissidents in the years leading up to the dismantling of the Berlin Wall in 1989 and the crumbling of Soviet hegemony over that part of the world soon afterward.[37]

Spending on this aggressive form of secret foreign policy had declined to less than 1 percent of the overall annual intelligence budget by September 1993.[38] The PFIAB commission, I thought, would have to determine whether the United States should use covert action more aggressively against the world's remaining tyrants, or maintain this low rate of funding.

Further, counterintelligence—the protection of America's secrets from hostile intelligence agencies—could hardly be dismissed as a trivial matter. One word was enough to show why the commission would have to confront this subject: Ames. Here was treason at the highest levels of the CIA, a circumstance that for some officials in Washington—especially in Congress—far overshadowed whatever errors may have been made by the intelligence services in Somalia or other distant lands.

I hoped, too, that Les Aspin would use this opportunity to review the effectiveness of intelligence oversight—that is, how well supervisors in the executive, legislative, and judicial branches of government were establishing effective safeguards against the misuse of secret operations at home and abroad.[39] The darkest stain on the reputation of America's intelligence agencies had come in 1974, when the journalist Seymour Hersh alleged in a series of *New York Times* articles that the CIA had engaged in illegal spying against Vietnam War dissenters—an operation known by the codename CHAOS. Subsequent investigations by Congress and the White House in 1975 revealed that this domestic spy operation was only the tip of the iceberg; most of the intelligence agencies, not just the CIA, had been involved in illegal activities carried out within the borders of the United States. The targets were chiefly anti–Vietnam War protesters and civil rights activists.

In response to these disturbing revelations, Congress and the White House created in 1976 the Senate Select Committee on Intelligence (SSCI) and an Intelligence Oversight Board (IOB) in the Executive Office of the President, and HPSCI a year later. I had the sense, however, that the achievements of these panels had fallen far short of expectations. Certainly they had done little to tighten counterintelligence against a cunning mole like Ames, or to improve collection and analysis, which should have warned U.S. soldiers about the dangers of urban guerilla warfare in Mogadishu. These panels hadn't even managed to prevent the Iran-*contra* affair in the 1980s, in which the Reagan administration secretly bypassed the Congress and conducted its own covert actions in Central America through private funding. With their hands on the nation's purse strings, lawmakers had good leverage for ensuring that the secret agencies operated as effectively as possible and within the bounds of the rule of law, but nevertheless they often failed in their oversight responsibilities.[40]

The new commission also presented the opportunity to study the appropriate level of resources the nation should devote to intelligence. The core security question for the United States, and every other nation, has always been: how much security is enough? In the case of intelligence, how much money should be dedicated to the collection of information from around the world with piloted U-2 aircraft; remote-controlled drones (unmanned aerial vehicles, or UAVs); surveillance satellites (many the size of a Greyhound bus and costing a billion dollars just to launch into space, not to mention the costs of building and managing them); eavesdropping devices, large and small; human agents; and the rapid sifting of "open sources," such as newspapers and magazines published in Moscow or Kigali?

Further, the commission could benefit from weighing the merits of institutional reform. It might consider the value of establishing, at long last, an effective director of central intelligence, turning this titular command post into a position that had real budget and appointment powers over all of the secret agencies—a genuine leader of national intelligence, not just the paper tiger the role had been since the CIA was created in 1947. Ever since those early days of the Cold War, the nation's spymaster has had little authority to make the intelligence agencies work together, sharing information and planning operations as if they were on the same team instead of rival bureaucracies. In 1994, the thirteen staves of the intelligence community were in desperate need of a hoop that could bind them together.

The number of possible topics to investigate began to pile up inside Aspin's in-box, as faxes and memos from his various contacts descended on the PFIAB offices like a tropical downpour. Among the many suggestions of things to consider: how well were the CIA and the other agencies cooperating with friendly foreign intelligence services against common targets, such as international drug dealers and terrorists? This relationship, known as "foreign liaison" or "burden sharing," is vital; the world is simply too immense for the United States to watch alone. In addition, how well was the United States progressing on the technological side of intelligence, particularly when it came to developing new machines that could improve upon the performance of the current fleet of spy aircraft and satellites?

At Aspin's request, I provided him with a roster of individuals who I thought would serve as good researchers and staff assistants. I divided the list into full-time staff, paid consultants, and unpaid advisers. I reminded him that I would be interested in joining the staff as his aide, if I could secure a leave of absence from the University of Georgia. Finally, I suggested a timetable for the inquiry:

- September and October 1994: organizing the staff and brainstorming with all the experts we could find, inside and outside the government;
- November 1994 through February 1995: a period of "discovery," for sketching out by way of formal interviews and hearings the most useful findings and recommendations;
- March through July 1995: drafting the final report;
- August through September 1995: working on final revisions;
- October 1995: presenting the report to the president and the public.

It was an optimistic schedule that unexpected circumstances—some beyond anyone's ability to predict—would sidetrack.

Early Opposition

The idea of an intelligence commission headed by the upstart Les Aspin did not sit well in some parts of Capitol Hill, where he had served in the House of Representatives for twenty-one years as a Democrat, representing the blue-collar neighborhoods of Milwaukee, Wisconsin. Elected to Congress in 1970, he was a member of a reform-minded class of lawmakers sent to Washington in the midst of the failing war in Vietnam; they were an incoming group of skeptics intent on restoring the war powers to Congress—an impulse that would gain popularity on the Hill as the executive branch cratered in the midst of the Watergate scandal. Aspin's earlier experiences as a systems analyst in the Defense Department had turned him against the Vietnam War, and when he arrived back in Washington as a thirty-two-year-old rookie law-maker, he brought with him dovish views and something of an anti-military attitude, despite his service as an army officer.

In 1975 he lobbied successfully for an appointment to a controversial House panel, the Pike Committee, assembled to investigate the charges that the CIA had engaged in domestic spying.[41] While serving on this committee, Aspin evolved into an unabashed critic of the Agency. Then, in 1977, Democratic House leaders selected him for membership in the newly created House Permanent Select Committee on Intelligence. While a member of HPSCI, Aspin furthered his reputation as a workaholic, putting in fourteen-hour days and six-and-a-half-day weeks. Keeping up this level of intensity over the next decade, he climbed the seniority ladder in the House to one of the top perches on an even higher-profile panel: the venerable Armed Services Committee, which he led from 1985 to 1993.

Practically from the beginning of his service in Congress, he had clashed with the crusty and hawkish old chairman of the Armed Services Committee, Edward Hebert (D-LA). In 1975, Aspin had been instrumental in ousting Hebert, who was replaced by the somewhat younger and more responsive Mel Price (D-IL). Ten years later, Aspin led another internal committee revolt, this time against Price, by then an octogenarian. The rebellious lawmaker from Wisconsin managed, with the help of votes from younger colleagues, to skip from the seventh rung on the seniority ladder of the Committee to its chair-manship, alienating in the process the conservative-leaning seniors over whom he had leapfrogged. He soon became known as "Dr. No" in the Pentagon because he opposed so many Defense Department initiatives.

In the 1980s, though, he shifted more toward the center of the political spectrum on security issues, estranging himself from his former allies, the young liberal faction that had helped him gain the Armed Services chairman-

ship. In 1987, he lost control of the Committee for two weeks after its liberal faction finally rose up against his ongoing support of President Reagan's MX missile proposal and covert aid for Nicaraguan rebels (the *contras*). Holding their noses, the young turks joined forces with anti-Aspin conservative Democrats in a brief coup.[42] Aspin soon won back the support of the liberals, though, by tacking again to the left. For the rest of his career in the House, he seemed torn between the center and the left. Privately, he urged his liberal friends to help him shed the dovish image of the Democratic Party, in the same way that he had begun to shed his own dovish image.

During the Reagan years, Aspin traveled far from his previous role as a House maverick and dependable critic of the Pentagon and the CIA. In addition to the administration's MX missile program and its aid to the *contras*, he supported President Reagan's record peace-time military buildup. He also broke ranks with the formidable senator Sam Nunn (D-GA) and other defense experts in the Democratic Party by supporting the plan of the first Bush administration to use armed force to drive the Iraqi military out of Kuwait in 1991. He accurately predicted that the war would entail few U.S. casualties. Aspin had not exactly become Dr. Yes—he remained skeptical about the need for a "Star Wars" strategic missile defense system, for instance—but he was no longer the knee-jerk, anti-DoD, liberal firebrand of his first decade in Congress.

Despite his more moderate political stance, Aspin as the new head of PFIAB was still distrusted by the security hawks in Congress in 1994, who remembered his criticism of the CIA when he was a member of the Pike Committee and HPSCI. Moreover, the loss of U.S. troops in Somalia during his tenure as secretary of defense made him doubly suspect to conservative Republican and Democratic lawmakers alike. Besides, conservatives had a far different agenda when it came to intelligence than he did. The force driving Aspin was a lingering resentment over the poor information the CIA had provided to him in 1993 about the dangerous circumstances in Somalia. The lack of solid intelligence on the military capabilities of local warlords had led to the calamity that cost him his job as SecDef and lowered his standing among defense intellectuals and the progressive wing of the Democratic Party. This harm to his reputation was doubly painful for a man who had become a fixture in the federal government, someone who lived and breathed Washington politics and frequented the most exclusive Georgetown salons. He was determined to find out why the quality of intelligence had been so poor in Somalia—not to mention Haiti, Bosnia, and Rwanda—and what it would take to improve the performance of the CIA and its companion agencies.

The reform of America's intelligence capabilities was a cerebral subject, tailor-made for the brainy Les Aspin, sometimes referred to in Washington as "The Secretary of Analysis"—not a compliment among those who resented his gimlet-eyed scrutiny of defense budgets and programs.[43] Born on July 21, 1938, in Milwaukee, the son of a father from Yorkshire, England (Les Aspin, Sr., an accountant, who died young of heart disease), and a mother of German heritage (Marie Orth, a legal secretary), he had been a standout in the reputable public schools of Milwaukee. At Yale University he was a member of the secret Society of Book and Snake, and in 1960 he graduated *summa cum laude* with a degree in history. After graduation his interest in politics led him to take a staff position on Capitol Hill with Senator William Proxmire (D-WI), where he was able to observe a master politician at work. Then he moved on to the White House as a staff assistant to Walter Heller, chairman of President Kennedy's Council of Economic Advisers. Intent on continuing his formal education, Aspin next traveled to England. He had fallen short in his bid for a Rhodes scholarship while at Yale but, undeterred, he decided to study at Oxford University anyway, where he earned a master's degree in 1962 while pursuing studies that combined economics, politics, and philosophy.

In 1964 he returned to the United States to complete a PhD in economics at MIT, further honing his skills in policy analysis. During this time, he also managed Senator Proxmire's successful bid for reelection, concentrating on the policy issues of the campaign, rather than on the organizational details.

From 1966 to 1968, Aspin served as a captain in the U.S. Army, assigned to the Pentagon staff as a systems analyst under Secretary of Defense Robert S. McNamara, who would become known as the chief architect of the Vietnam War. During this time, he traveled to Indochina and observed the ill-fated war in person. When he returned to Wisconsin after his military service, Aspin taught economics as an assistant professor at Marquette University, immersed himself in local Milwaukee politics, and worked on Lyndon B. Johnson's short-lived reelection bid for the presidency in 1968. The president withdrew from the campaign after failing to perform as well as he and the media thought an incumbent chief executive should have in the New Hampshire primary. After Johnson's departure from the presidential race, Aspin made an unsuccessful try for the Democratic nomination for Wisconsin state treasurer. He returned to full-time teaching at Marquette and, unfazed by his initial political defeat, he jumped into the political ring again in 1970. Remarkably for a young candidate, this time he won a seat in Congress by defeating a Republican incumbent in Wisconsin's First District. Opposition to the war in Vietnam was the centerpiece of his campaign platform.[44]

He would be reelected eleven more consecutive times. In 1992, while still in Congress, he served as Clinton's adviser on defense and national security issues during the presidential campaign. Then, when Clinton won the presidency, Aspin left the House of Representatives to become secretary of defense.

Drawing on his analytic training at Yale, Oxford, and MIT, and as a systems analyst in the Pentagon, Aspin was sometimes ridiculed by congressional colleagues for attempting to "look at all five sides of a triangle."[45] Others, however, viewed this trait as a great strength. "He could awe a listener by ruminating aloud, masterfully examining arcane issues with a kind of brilliant dispassion," recalled one reporter.[46] In sharp contrast to Aspin's abiding interest in the quality of U.S. intelligence, most conservatives in Congress had only a passing interest in the CIA's analytic products, and the question of how well the secret agencies were evaluating the meaning of foreign events and conditions. They were more concerned with how to protect America's secrets from the likes of another Aldrich Ames. If the CIA and the other intelligence agencies were going to be the subject of a major investigation, those on the political right reasoned that counterintelligence should be the focus.

As the general counsel on the Senate Select Committee on Intelligence (SSCI) at the time, L. Britt Snider, recalls, the "principal motivation" on Capitol Hill for an inquiry into intelligence activities was the Ames spy case.[47] A liberal-leaning senator, though, had his own distinct views on the subject. Senator Daniel Patrick Moynihan's skepticism about the need for even having a CIA was growing; he thought the Senate ought to investigate the possibility of abolishing the Agency altogether and redistributing its component parts among the Departments of Defense and State.

So the Senate had a number of members who were less than enthusiastic about a comprehensive PFIAB probe into intelligence activities. The conservatives believed their own institution would be more likely to conduct a review that focused on the proper subject: Ames and the nation's counterintelligence weaknesses. And members of the Moynihan faction believed they could lead an inquiry that would be much tougher on the CIA than one conducted by the increasingly conservative Les Aspin.

Aspin was uncertain of where one key senator stood on the subject of a PFIAB commission: the formidable Republican from Virginia, John W. Warner, ranking minority member and vice chairman of SSCI, as well as a powerhouse on the Armed Services Committee. Warner, whose stern, chiseled, high-cheekboned profile seemed ready-made for Mount Rushmore, had become one of the leading voices in the Senate on matters of national security. When he spoke on this topic, officials and journalists in Washington listened.

In February 1994, soon after Aspin resigned as SecDef, Warner wrote a letter to President Clinton asking him to establish a task force that would investigate the Ames treachery. He also wanted the task force to reassure the public that, despite the horrendous counterintelligence failure that the Ames case represented, the CIA still remained a vital part of America's security. Weeks passed without a reply from the White House. The president's intelligence chief at the time, R. James Woolsey, was wary of efforts on Capitol Hill to reduce intelligence spending and wanted to avoid an inquiry, whether led by Congress, PFIAB, or anyone else. He asked the White House to delay its response to Senator Warner while he looked further into the political dynamics within the intelligence community and on Capitol Hill. The DCI quickly discovered that most intelligence officers were strongly opposed to any kind of congressionally mandated task force or commission.[48] Eventually, Clinton wrote back to the senator, saying that he saw no need for a special task force; the President's Foreign Advisory Intelligence Board, guided by its chairman, Les Aspin, could examine the Ames case at the same time as it looked into intelligence failures associated with Somalia.

The SSCI counsel, L. Britt Snider, remembers that Senator Warner was "annoyed" by this letter from the president; after all, the Virginian was simply trying to be supportive of the administration's interest in improving intelligence. In response to this perceived slight, Warner asked Snider to draft legislation that would establish an intelligence commission, but one based on a Senate initiative introduced by Senator Warner. He opposed a purely presidentially appointed panel. The statutory language would make it clear that members of Congress—not just Clinton and Aspin—would have a hand in selecting the commissioners and determining the scope of the inquiry.[49]

It was widely believed in Washington that Senator Warner had been displeased with Aspin's appointment as secretary of defense in the first place, not to mention his role in the Somalia debacle. In September 1995, Warner would coauthor the introduction to a report issued by the Senate Armed Services Committee on Somalia that claimed Aspin had rejected sending tanks and armored vehicles to the Horn of Africa for fear of creating a worldwide political backlash that would undermine the administration's support for a UN peacekeeping mission in the region. Warner maintained that Aspin had "misread the mood in Congress." Further, lawmakers were troubled by Aspin's failure to consult with them before escalating U.S. policy from humanitarian relief to nation building. They also opposed the administration's plan to capture Aideed. Warner recalled, however, that this did not mean the Congress wanted the secretary of defense to deny "U.S. forces in Somalia the equipment requested by their military commander on the scene."

In Warner's opinion, the administration's policy in Somalia had been "shifting, uncoordinated, unclear, inconsistent," and "the level of review" by civilians "fell short."[50]

Word filtered back to Aspin that Senator Warner opposed a PFIAB commission and, instead, would sponsor legislation to create a congressionally appointed intelligence commission. In a telephone conversation with me on March 22, 1994, Aspin expressed hope that the Virginian was not dead set on this course of action, and that he still might be persuaded to let PFIAB carry out an intelligence review on its own. As the summer of 1994 began, Aspin decided to find out where Senator Warner stood. He flagged down a taxi on M Street in Georgetown and traveled cross town to the Dirksen Senate Office Building, named after Everett Dirksen of Illinois, the colorful and popular Republican minority leader in the Senate during the 1950s. Aspin strode down the hallways, crowded with tourists carrying umbrellas that dripped from a recent thunderstorm, to Senator Warner's office on the long west corridor of the building. He was determined to convert the Virginian, if at all possible, into an supporter of a PFIAB intelligence study, free of Senate and House interference.

Aspin greeted Warner with a broad grin and his standard Milwaukee salutation: "Hey, whadda ya know?" This stab at charm, delivered in a distinct Great Lakes accent, often worked miracles, at least on the campaign trail in Milwaukee (even though Aspin, a surprisingly reserved person for a politician, was uncomfortable asking people for money or even votes). Yet Aspin's best attempt at cordiality seemed to be having no effect on Senator Warner's granite bearing.

Admittedly, the PFIAB Chairman was inept at small talk, the schmoozing that most politicians engage in as easily as breathing. When I traveled with Aspin in 1978 to inspect CIA operations in Europe, I found myself at embassy receptions in various capitals participating in light conversation with our hosts (spies, diplomats, and their spouses), while he had corralled the nearest weapons expert in the room into a lengthy discussion of the latest arcane developments in arms-control verification, missile throw weight, and first-strike vulnerabilities, ignoring the Agency's chief of station altogether. Unlike many of his legislative colleagues on trips abroad, he had no interest in alcohol or women; a shy teetotaler, Aspin wanted to spend his time on the details of warhead yields and deterrence strategies. At parties in the States, he had a reputation for overlooking his hapless date while joined in animated debate with the nearest available defense-policy wonk.

Undeterred by Senator Warner's stony reception to his pitch for a stand-alone PFIAB inquiry, Aspin went straight to the point: his colleagues on the board were well prepared to do the job, and it would be a nonpartisan, balanced inquiry. Moreover, he would make sure that the Ames counterintelligence disaster, not just events in Somalia, was thoroughly investigated.[51]

Bracing for a rejection from Warner, to be offered, no doubt, with the senator's usual blend of courtliness and square-jawed firmness, Aspin brought his pitch to a close and waited for a response. To his astonishment, Warner was suddenly all smiles and encouragement. He wanted to work with Aspin to put together a good commission. The senator said that he viewed a PFIAB study as an opportunity to buoy up the CIA, where morale had dipped dramatically with the revelation of Ames's treason—"lower than Death Valley," according to a *New York Times* report.[52] Then, just as quickly as they had materialized, the smiles vanished from Warner's face and he insisted that any new commission should be based on a legislative mandate and should have strong congressional representation among the panel's members.

Since the 1980s, Democratic lawmakers had become increasingly interested in having a role in the appointment of members to commissions, in response to President Reagan's vigorous use of blue-ribbon panels that were overwhelmingly composed of Republicans.[53] Now, with a Democrat in the White House, Warner wanted to carve out a role for the GOP in making appointments to whatever intelligence panel Bill Clinton might establish. Warner told Aspin that he had floated the idea of a combined legislative-PFIAB inquiry with a number of colleagues in the Senate, and they approved of this approach, rather than having the board—or, for that matter, the Congress—go it alone. It was plain to Aspin that he would have to work with Warner; the PFIAB chairman would not be able to have his own handpicked panel of inquiry.

Most of the CIA's employees lived and voted in Warner's Virginia constituency. The senator explained to Aspin that he was concerned about a movement among some of his more liberal colleagues to establish a separate Senate inquiry into intelligence. He distrusted the motives of certain members of Congress behind this movement, notably Senator Moynihan. The New York lawmaker had already circulated a draft bill in favor of the outright abolition of the CIA, on the grounds that the Agency had demonstrated its incompetence by overestimating the strength of the Soviet economy and—the clincher—by failing to predict the collapse of the Soviet empire.[54]

The preemption of a potentially more damaging investigation is a common motivation for the establishment of blue-ribbon panels.[55] In this instance, Warner hoped to prevent a Moynihan-led Senate inquiry that would display little sympathy for the CIA. Aspin may have desired a strictly fact-finding PFIAB commission, focused largely on Somalia; but Warner wanted a panel that would protect the CIA by keeping its sharpest critics in Congress at bay and, at the same time, that would mollify public concerns about the Ames counterintelligence setback.

Still other lawmakers wondered whether the CIA had adequately mapped out its new responsibilities since the fall of the Soviet Union. Was the intelligence community focused on a bipolar world that no longer existed? Why had it failed to understand more about conditions in Iraq, Somalia, Haiti, Bosnia, and Rwanda? These senators appeared ready to support a responsible inquiry comprised, as Warner desired, of lawmakers and members of PFIAB, but only if a joint executive-legislative probe looked broadly into the question of intelligence performance—not just Ames and Somalia. James Woolsey, Clinton's first DCI, had been unable to articulate a vision, at least to the satisfaction of key congressional leaders, about the role of the intelligence agencies in the uncertain era that followed the Soviet demise. "Warner's Commission proposal is the only way to get [the CIA] back on track, because Woolsey hasn't put it there," declared the influential senator Dennis DeConcini (D-AZ), the SSCI chairman, who went on to call for Woolsey's resignation.[56] DeConcini and Woolsey had rubbed each other the wrong way because of their differing views on intelligence priorities. The SSCI chair wanted to improve human intelligence—spies on the ground; Woolsey, in contrast, sought a new generation of expensive surveillance satellites—mechanical eyes in space. In pursuit of his spy satellites, the DCI attempted to sidestep DeConcini and SSCI altogether by aligning himself with the two congressional Armed Services Committees. (Woosley had served as general counsel for the Senate Armed Services Committee earlier in his career.) This subterfuge sent DeConcini into a fury.[57] Woolsey attributes the friction with DeConcini to the DCI's unwillingness to accept the deep intelligence-budget cuts (especially for satellites) advocated by the SSCI chair in his search for a post-Cold War peace dividend. DeConcini "fought us on everything," Woolsey claims. In response, the Senator says that he supported increased funding for more human agents, but remained skeptical about the DCI's projected spending levels for spy machines.[58]

The relationship was also not helped by a threat from Woolsey to have DeConcini investigated for leaking information, a charge the SSCI chairman denied.[59] Charges flew between the two men like bullets. DeConcini accused Woolsey of "total obstructionism" with respect to the Congress.[60] Criticism of Woolsey ran deep on Capitol Hill, far beyond the tensions that had arisen between him and Chairman DeConcini. Some viewed the DCI's cocksure personality as arrogance, bred at Oxford University (where he was a Rhodes

Scholar) and at Yale Law School. Les Aspin was distrustful of Woolsey, too. "He's a fucking egomaniac," he remarked to me over the telephone one day, in a rare use of profanity. "He has a trial attorney's mentality. He wants to win every battle. Instead, he loses the war."[61]

Woolsey further alienated key lawmakers in both chambers by failing to dispense harsh penalties against eleven CIA officers who had served as Aldrich Ames's supervisors during his decade of treason. The agency inspector general had recommended strong punishments for these individuals, ranging from reprimands to outright dismissals; the DCI, perhaps leery of the Agency's powerful Operations Directorate and its retaliatory capabilities, had elected to issue only reprimands.[62]

As for Aspin's hope for an intelligence inquiry led by PFIAB alone, some members of Congress felt strongly that the former secretary of defense had been discredited by his fatal missteps in Somalia; a panel established by Congress was likely to provide a more objective appraisal of what had gone

FIGURE I.I Herblock on R. James Woolsey's Reprimands at the CIA in 1994
Source: Herblock Cartoon, *Washington Post*, October 13, 1994 Copyright by the Herb Block Foundation and used with permission.

wrong on the Horn of Africa in 1993. So ran the arguments for a congressionally authorized inquiry along the lines proposed by Warner, one that would bring lawmakers into the process as full members of the commission. An experienced former lawmaker himself, Aspin knew how to count votes, and he calculated that this view had gained enough proponents on the Hill to win; Warner would probably be able to pass legislation that mandated a joint executive-congressional probe into intelligence. SSCI counsel Snider remembers that the Warner initiative "was clearly going to be enacted as part of the intelligence authorization bill that year, whether Aspin agreed with it or not."[63]

Warner was not a natural ally—that much Aspin understood; but Aspin was also well aware of the old truism that politics makes for strange bedfellows. Circumstances in the Senate were uniting Aspin and Warner in opposition to an independent Senate inquiry into intelligence, perhaps led by the anti-CIA Moynihan faction. Warner was especially worried about the emergence of an unusual coalition of conservatives angry at the CIA over Ames and liberals fed up with the Agency's analytic failures. This outcome, Warner reasoned, could lead to a disastrous intelligence probe that might jeopardize the very existence of the CIA, or at least produce deep cuts in the intelligence budget. Congress already had sent intelligence spending sliding downward. In 1994, for example, the spy-budget bill proposed by HPSCI chairman Dan Glickman (D-KS) sought a 2.1 percent cut to the president's requested amount, and the Senate's version was also below the White House recommendation.[64] A joint executive-legislative investigation along the lines envisioned by Senator Warner might be a way of heading off those senators and representatives intent on attacking the CIA.

So Aspin and Warner joined forces, and even DCI Woolsey came to see the advantage of Warner's approach over something worse from Daniel Patrick Moynihan and his allies.[65] Warner hoped, further, that he could keep the president from selecting his appointees strictly from the Aspin-led PFIAB pool of recruits.[66] All but one of Clinton's choices (Paul Wolfowitz) ended up coming from the board, however, just as Les Aspin had hoped. Yet Aspin was now stuck with a group of lawmakers who would also be part of the commission's membership. He began to worry about who these interlopers might be.

Early Shaping of the Commission's Agenda

As the sun beat down relentlessly in Georgia during the waning days of summer in 1994, I sat at my computer, silently praising whoever had invented air-conditioning and drafting memos to Aspin on how he might best organize the PFIAB inquiry. I also sent him additional thoughts on what topics needed to be covered. Based on my experiences as Senator Frank Church's "designee" (special assistant) on his investigative committee in 1975, I recommended the use of task forces with responsibilities for important subjects: on military intelligence, on foreign intelligence outside of the military domain, on domestic intelligence; on command and control (the management of intelligence, from the president down), and one that would try to anticipate intelligence needs in the year 2020. I also laid out a full array of intelligence topics that the commission ought to review, stretching far beyond Ames and Somalia.

On August 19, 1994, Aspin telephoned and asked me to write a "statement of objectives" for the commission. "Think about what the panel's specific goals should be," he said, "and see if you can get this on one page." In between beginning fall lectures and a burgeoning agenda of faculty committee meetings on campus, I distilled the commission's responsibilities into what I thought were the key issues:

- Targeting: Toward what targets, both old and new, should the intelligence agencies orient their finite resources for collection, analysis, covert action, and counterintelligence?
- Organization: Was it useful—and possible—to develop a more integrated intelligence community, with clearer and stronger management authority in the hands of the DCI?
- Costs: Could reductions be made in intelligence expenditures without jeopardizing national security, or did the dangers of the new era require even greater spending on espionage and related activities?
- Dissemination of intelligence: Could communications links between policy makers and intelligence analysts be improved and closer bonds of trust nurtured?
- Liaison: Could U.S. intelligence sharing with other nations be strengthened, to the mutual benefit of all? How about with international organizations, like the UN?
- Accountability: Could legislative and White House supervision of the intelligence agencies be improved, as a check against possible abuse of secret power?

Whether or not these memos and faxes were having any influence, I had no idea. I knew that Aspin was consulting with many other people as well. Seeking information from a wide array of sources was one of his strengths. I supposed, too, that he was hearing diverse opinions, since I understood there were almost as many proposals for intelligence reform in Washington and in academic circles as there were individuals thinking about the subject.

Throughout the summer of 1994, rumors floated around Washington about the prospects for a PFIAB inquiry. I received telephone calls from friends in Washington each week, warning me that the CIA had taken over the investigation by arranging to have its people staff the commission. An independent study was no longer possible, they concluded. In July, I was happy to escape this gossip with a backpacking trip into the rugged terrain of Zion National Park in southwest Utah. An encounter with a lively rattlesnake proved an excellent way to forget all about intelligence reform, at least for a while.

When I returned home in August, Aspin called again, this time seeking more ideas about who might staff the commission. I recommended against relying on the current PFIAB staff, which was too small and too closely tied to the intelligence community. I thought the commission needed a group of investigators who came mainly from outside the secret agencies. I was well aware that Aspin would need to have some insiders, too, who could help him understand current problems within the spy bureaucracies; but he had to be cautious about hiring active-duty intelligence officers who might join the effort chiefly to defend their own agency.

Among the list of potential staff recruits, I listed several people who had written insightfully on intelligence topics in leading scholarly publications, experts like Richard K. Betts and Robert Jervis of Columbia University, along with Mark M. Lowenthal and Gregory F. Treverton, who at the time were affiliated with Washington think tanks. I thought of the SSCI counsel, L. Britt Snider, whom I had known when we had served together on the Church Committee staff. I admired his thoughtfulness and political acumen, and I noted to Aspin that he would be a solid addition to the staff. I mentioned, as well, other former Church Committee staffers who lived in the Washington area.

A Joint Executive-Legislative Commission

The formula Warner and Aspin had settled on to prevent a separate Senate inquiry—a combined presidential-congressional commission—was essentially Warner's prescription, with an added element that he would just as soon have done without: as PFIAB chair, Aspin would head the effort. The legislative language proposed by Warner would allow President Clinton to choose nine members of the commission "from private life," and the leaders of Congress would choose eight (four "from private life" and four incumbent lawmakers). This was at least better than the other way around, Aspin reckoned with a sense of resignation.

In an echo of sentiments that Warner had expressed to Aspin in their meeting on the Hill, SSCI counsel Snider told a Georgetown University symposium in September of 1994 that the purpose of the joint commission would be to "rebuild the political consensus" in support of the intelligence mission.[67] Warner and Snider, both on SSCI, appeared to think alike about what the central objective of the proposed intelligence inquiry should be: the prevention of a decline in public support for intelligence. This goal had its merits; the nation, after all, does need a strong intelligence shield. It seemed to me, though, that the main purpose of a commission should be to arrive at a sensible reorientation of the intelligence agencies toward a vastly more complicated world than the Cold War setting had been. It was obvious already, though, that Warner would have powerful allies who would back his core objective of defending and touting the activities of the secret agencies. Led by Minority Whip (and later Speaker) Newt Gingrich, a Republican from Georgia, House GOP lawmakers similarly viewed the commission as a venue for bolstering intelligence operations and blocking cuts in the spy budget.[68]

On the other side of this budget debate, however, stood the imposing figure of former senator Warren Bruce Rudman (R-NH). He was vice chairman of PFIAB and, in this capacity, was the presumptive vice chairman of the proposed intelligence commission. In addition, he was a leader of the Concord Coalition, a highly visible private organization dedicated to lowering the national debt. Presumably, he could be expected to wield a sharp scalpel in trimming the intelligence budget, now that the Soviet nemesis had vanished. With Warner already sounding the clarion call in defense of intelligence and Gingrich cheering him on in the background with calls for expanding the nation's espionage activities, and with Rudman—a champion of debt reduction—well positioned to fight for cutbacks in spy spending, it didn't take a fortune teller to envision the possible eruption of a political free-for-all inside the commission.

Aspin was disappointed not to have his own PFIAB probe into intelligence, free and clear of the potentially significant complications that might accompany the presence of several lawmakers on the commission roster— including some from the opposition party. Nonetheless, he was personally pleased that both the executive and legislative branches had moved toward the idea of a broader look at intelligence, in the same direction his own thinking had evolved over the summer. A spate of exhaustive Defense Department and congressional studies of the Somalia disaster had satisfied

Aspin's interest in that subject, especially since his judgment during the events had been questioned by these inquiries. Enough about Somalia; he now had his eyes on a more extensive "bottom-up" review of intelligence, in keeping with the well-received similar exercise for the Defense Department that he had ordered during his brief tenure as SecDef.

Although Senator Warner and Counsel Snider had adopted rebuilding the CIA and repairing its damaged morale as the commission's primary missions, at least Snider acknowledged at the Georgetown symposium that the creation of a joint commission had the effect of putting "everything on the table, including the very existence of the [intelligence] agencies." He stressed that some lawmakers had "great discomfort" about too much money being spent on intelligence and wanted a careful review of espionage funding.[69] Even Warner had begun to express some support for a broader inquiry, the price he had to pay to garner enough votes for passage of his proposal in the Senate for a combined executive-legislative panel. Despite his rhetoric in favor of a wide-open approach by the commission, I wondered to what extent Warner would maneuver to limit its work as much as possible to his primary interest: boosting the CIA's sagging image.[70]

The annual intelligence authorization bill came to the Senate floor in August of 1994. At Warner's behest, the SSCI leadership presented an amendment to establish a bipartisan "Commission on the Roles and Capabilities of the U.S. Intelligence Community." During the floor debate, senators emphasized the need for the development of a consensus on the future of the intelligence agencies.[71] In drafting the statutory language for the commission on SSCI's behalf, Britt Snider listed a dozen topics that he thought the proposed panel should investigate, including such matters as intelligence collection and analysis, the spy budget, and counterintelligence. He circulated the list to key senators who had cosponsored the legislation. In addition to Warner, the chief sponsors were Senators DeConcini, Bob Graham (D-FL), and Bob Kerrey (D-NE). Each added a topic or two to the list, bringing the total number of subjects for study by the commission to nineteen. An example was: "To what extent, if any, should the budget for United States Intelligence activities be publicly disclosed?" (See Appendix A for a full listing.)[72]

Warner's proposed language for an executive-legislative commission, as prepared for him by Snider, passed the Senate on August 12, 1994, by a unanimous vote of 99 to 0.[73] As Warner recalls:

When I drafted the legislation creating this Commission, the Intelligence Community was "under siege" from certain members of Congress and others in the wake of the Aldrich Ames spy case and the revelations surrounding the NRO Headquarters controversy [the National Reconnaissance Office, in charge of surveillance satellites, had been accused of fiscal mismanagement[74]]. Members of Congress were advocating "slash and burn" of the intelligence budget. One even proposed the abolition of the CIA, preferring to merge its functions into other government agencies. It was clear that a "cooling off" period was essential. Time was needed to ensure that our vital intelligence capabilities were not sacrificed as an overreaction to the problems— though very serious—of the day.[75]

On September 22, House and Senate conferees reached agreement on the final bill and stated in the accompanying report that it was their intent "to produce a credible, independent, and objective review of the intelligence community."[76] Snider recalls: "There was a small effort in conference to organize the nineteen topics more logically and make them more coherent, but, frankly, they did not receive a great deal of attention."[77]

As anticipated, the commission would consist of seventeen members: nine selected by the president (this number included chairman Aspin) and eight by the Congress. This membership array would give Aspin only a one-vote PFIAB margin over the congressionally appointed delegation. He would have to contend, as well, with a sizable group of Republicans, because the bill allowed President Clinton to appoint only five Democrats among his nine appointees. The bill further stipulated that all but three of the commission staff members would have to be private citizens, a rule meant to limit the influence of active-duty intelligence bureaucrats who might otherwise have filled all of the staff positions, potentially co-opting the proceedings. As it turned out, most of the "private citizens" selected for the staff were former intelligence officers.

The president signed the bill (Public Law 103–359) on October 14, and the Aspin Commission was now a reality.[78] The legislation set a March 1, 1996, deadline for the panel's final report, providing several months more than Aspin and I had anticipated—a welcome cushion in case things got bogged down, as they always seemed to in enterprises of this size and scope.

Opinions about the legislation varied. "I have warned for the last several years that if the intelligence community did not move boldly and publicly to change, that change would be forced upon it," observed Robert M. Gates, former DCI under President George H. W. Bush (and who would later serve as secretary of defense in both the second Bush administration and the Obama administration). "That has now happened with the creation of the Commission."[79] DeConcini predicted that the joint panel could be of tremendous help, "if it doesn't get co-opted by the intelligence community."[80] His counterpart in the House, HPSCI Chairman Larry Combest (R-TX), had the opposite concern. "Partisans" might "hijack" the commission, he feared, "to validate their efforts to dismantle the intelligence community."[81] Exactly who he had in mind was unclear; perhaps he worried that Senator Moynihan would manage to find a place on the panel's final list of members.

Thus the commission was born, not in the quiet sanctuary of PFIAB's plush quarters in the OEOB but on the political battlefield of Capitol Hill. In the spectrum of commission types from strongly presidential to non-presidential, this panel would be viewed as a "moderately presidential" blue-ribbon group, thanks to the slight PFIAB majority.[82] I wondered who would hold sway over its course: Les Aspin or John Warner? The two men were poles apart in their views about national security and just about everything else, one an urban blue-collar Wisconsin liberal with centrist leanings on security issues, the other a rural patrician Virginian who leaned toward the right on military matters.

———

The fall semester at the university was rapidly approaching, and Aspin still had not worked out his staffing arrangements for the commission. I faxed him in August, saying that I was looking forward to hearing from him about my role "as soon as the fog rises." When classes began in mid-August, it was clear that I would be unable to work full time on the commission staff in Washington, as I had hoped; I was committed to a schedule of fall teaching. At the very least, though, I could probably arrange a leave of absence for the spring semester and, if necessary, into the next academic year.

The banality of daily existence as a professor had thwarted my lofty dreams of helping out with a major restructuring of America's secret agencies. My thoughts alternated between the arcane intricacies of intelligence reform in Washington and such pressing matters at home as serving on the homecoming committee, participating in University Council meetings, leading a workshop on teaching for new graduate students, proofreading my daughter's school essays, and spotting the first gray hairs in my eyebrows. Each time the telephone rang, I was sure it was Aspin with a job offer. Weeks went by. A sense of rejection set in.

At one point during these weeks of uncertainty, someone must have introduced strange chemicals into the Athens water supply, because I began to delude myself into thinking that perhaps I could serve as a commissioner, not just as the chairman's assistant. This would allow me to breeze into commission meetings periodically, offer my profound wisdom, and then breeze out again, reentering the stream of teaching, research, and committee duties at the

University of Georgia. In a moment of madness, I had overlooked the fact that to become a commission member one had to be well connected, either to President Clinton (being a high-rolling fund-raiser would have helped) or to those members of Congress who were making appointments to the panel. I was neither. The madness not yet dissipated, I asked Aspin about the possibility when he telephoned one afternoon in September. He paused, then gave a sympathetic, brotherly laugh. "You're dreaming," he said. He was right, and I came rapidly back to earth. He consoled me that the real work of the commission would be done by the staff anyway, not the commissioners; yet he had still not worked out his staffing plans.

In another phone call in September, Aspin and I discussed my current teaching obligations, and he asked me to join the staff as his special assistant in January when the semester was over. At last, the fog was lifting. In another call later in the year, he informed me that SSCI counsel Britt Snider would serve as the commission's staff director. I felt a twinge of envy: Snider would be able to devote full time to the effort immediately, while I was in Athens attending tedious faculty meetings, writing academic articles that few people would read, and—the saving grace—teaching classes. But that was the way things had worked out, and I knew that Snider was well qualified for the assignment, especially given his ties to Senator Warner and others on the Hill. Aspin would need good connections in Congress if he expected to pass intelligence reform legislation at the end of the Commission's work.

A graduate of Davidson College in North Carolina and the University of Virginia's School of Law, Snider had spent nearly ten years as general counsel for the Senate Select Committee on Intelligence and, before that, had served for another decade as assistant deputy under secretary of defense for counterintelligence and security. He knew the subject of intelligence inside and out, and, moreover, was close to many of the vital players in the bureaucracy and on the Hill. It was a solid choice.

CHAPTER 2

Starting Up
The Commission's Membership

T HE CONGRESS WAS QUICK to name its commission members: two incumbent senators, two incumbent representatives, and four private citizens. The presidential side of the selection process got off to a slower start. The legislation that established the panel prevented the president from naming more than five commission members from the same political party, and no more than four could have previous intelligence experience. The intention was to ensure a bipartisan inquiry that would bring together the perspectives of the executive and legislative branches, as well as the private sector. It took more than two months of jockeying before President Clinton finally managed, in December 1994, to present the names of the eight appointees who would join the already announced Commission Chairman, Les Aspin. In an unsigned editorial the next month, the *New York Times* warned that unless it sped things up, the new Aspin Commission would soon be "road kill," run over by the House Permanent Select Committee on Intelligence.[1] Undaunted by the razzle-dazzle surrounding the creation of the national commission on intelligence, HPSCI was gearing up, under Chairman Larry Combest's leadership, to conduct a probe of its own, starting with a set of hearings designated "IC21" (short for the "Intelligence Community in the 21st Century"). As Combest explained it: "We have a responsibility to undertake our own assessment of the intelligence community's strengths, weaknesses and future role, whether or not a separate Commission exists.... The issue is too important to relegate Congress to a consultative role."[2] Aspin and Warner had managed to head off a separate Senate probe, but evidently not one in the House.

The Presidential Appointees

In establishing blue-ribbon panels, presidents usually have a preferred outcome and carefully pick commission members who will advance the White House agenda.[3] Not so for the Clinton White House and the Aspin Commission, simply because the president had very little interest in the subject of intelligence. When Clinton announced his commission appointees, he noted that the panel's work was "an effort to which I attach the highest personal priority."[4] It was an exercise in hyperbole that few knowledgeable observers actually believed, given the president's limited attention to foreign and security affairs.[5]

Eight PFIAB members—all but one of the president's appointees—made it onto the seventeen-person commission; but Aspin's original hope for a panel chosen exclusively by the White House, based on his recommendations, was dashed by the presence of eight "outsiders" picked by the Congress.[6] I was surprised to see listed on the presidential side of the commission's member list three former managers from a single intelligence organization: the National Security Agency, home of the nation's code breakers and signals interceptors. This had the markings of a major lobbying coup for the NSA.

As I studied the list of commission members (see Figure 2.1), I felt a sense of dismay. How was Aspin going to guide such a large and eclectic group of people? The 1941 Commission to Investigate the Japanese Attack of December 7, 1941 (the Roberts Commission), had only five members; the 1975 Commission on CIA Activities Within the United States (the Rockefeller Commission), eight; the 1986 President's Special Review Board (the Tower Commission) that looked into the Iran-*contra* scandal, three.[7] My experience as an aide to the chairman of the Church Committee in 1975 had taught me that the eleven members on that panel had been hard enough to lead; now Aspin would have to deal with a half-dozen additional individuals who would serve on his commission.

Moreover, the members of the Church Committee had been all senators, several of whom were good friends and political allies. In contrast, the Aspin Commission was a grab bag of politicians, intelligence bureaucrats, political fund-raisers, and miscellaneous souls with the right connections to either the Clinton White House or congressional VIPs (the *sine qua non* for selection). Also, some of the appointees had little, if any, experience with the subject the commission had been formed to study: the U.S. intelligence agencies. Others may have had too much experience in a sense, notably the former leaders of the NSA, whose impartiality would be in doubt—although they would clearly bring important technical expertise to the table.

Presidential Appointees	Congressional Appointees
Les Aspin, Chair	Tony Coelho
(D, Wisconsin, politician)	(D, California, politician)
Warren B. Rudman, Vice Chair	David H. Dewhusrt
(R, New Hampshire, politician)	(R, Texas, businessman)
Lew Allen, Jr.	Norman D. Dicks
(NSA intelligence professional)	(D, Washington, politician)
Zoë Baird	J. James Exon
(D, Connecticut, businesswoman)	(D, Nebraska, politician)
Ann Z. Caracristi	Wyche Fowler
(NSA intelligence professional)	(D, Georgia, politician)
Stephen Friedman	Porter J. Goss
(R, New York, businessman)	(R, Florida, politician)
Anthony S. Harrington	Robert E. Pursley
(D, Maryland, businessman)	(Air Force military professional)
Robert J. Hermann	John Warner
(NSA intelligence professional)	(R, Virginia, politician)
Paul D. Wolfowitz	
(R, defense and foreign affairs expert)	

FIGURE 2.1 Members of the Original Aspin Commission, 1994

Aspin had his work cut out for him in bringing this team together, a task made all the more difficult by his meager management skills. He was a thinker and, as his many terms in the House indicated, an effective political campaigner, but he was widely regarded as one of the most disorganized individuals ever named to the cabinet. And, ironically, he had been called upon, as secretary of defense, to take charge of a sprawling, possibly unmanageable bureaucracy that, more than any other department in the government, needed a topflight administrator. It surprised few who knew him that Aspin spent his short time at the Pentagon immersed in debates about force structure and arms control, not messy day-to-day management issues. I doubted that his approach would be much different at the helm of the new commission.

I thought of the first time I had gone to Aspin's modest townhouse in Georgetown, when I worked for him on the Hill in the 1970s. He had asked me to drop by on a Saturday morning to brief him before a trip to Mexico he was about to take. Greeting me cheerfully at the door, Aspin ushered me into a disheveled bachelor's pad. His hair had begun to thin and showed hints of gray. He was tall, but stoop-shouldered, and his rumpled clothes had long ago forgotten what it was like to experience the press of an iron.

"Coffee?" he asked. That was exactly what I needed, and I accepted the offer. Instead of entering the townhouse's small kitchen, however, Aspin disappeared out the front door, leaving it ajar as I stood in the foyer. He returned ten minutes later, out of breath, with a Styrofoam cup of coffee he had purchased at a café on M Street, several blocks away in the heart of Georgetown. Apparently, he was insufficiently organized even to make a cup of coffee at home or, more likely, he'd simply rather talk policy with visitors or read a book than fuss in the kitchen.

Given his minimal interest in the subject of intelligence, President Clinton accepted most of Aspin's recommendations regarding who the White House should appoint to the commission from among the members of PFIAB. The president insisted, though, on moving a few campaign allies whom he had already appointed to the board to the front of the line for commission membership.

As anticipated by the media, Warren B. Rudman, the current PFIAB vice chairman and former GOP senator from New Hampshire (1980–92), would serve as the panel's vice chairman. He had earned a bachelor's degree from Syracuse University and a law degree from the Boston College Law School. Early in his career, Rudman was elected attorney general for New Hampshire. He and Aspin had gotten along well together in their PFIAB leadership positions, and I presumed Rudman would be a reliable partner for him, despite their different political parties.

Stocky and imposing, Rudman had served as a combat platoon leader and rifle-company commander in the U.S. Army during the Korean War. He exuded a decisive air that would complement Aspin's milder temperament and tendency to engage in endless debate.[8] Fittingly, Rudman was known in the Senate as "Sledgehammer," although the moniker was applied with affection by most of his colleagues and he had been a popular figure in Congress's upper chamber.[9] Rudman was also well known for his independence. During the Iran-*contra* affair in the mid-1980s, most Republicans rallied behind President Ronald Reagan. Rudman, though, was appalled by the scandal. He publicly assailed Lt. Col. Oliver L. North, a leading conspirator in the illegal covert actions, as well as other administration officials on the NSC staff who, as Rudman put it, "wrap themselves in the flag and go around spitting on the Constitution."[10] I viewed the New Hampshire senator as one of the heroes of the congressional Iran-*contra* hearings, and I imagined that he would bring a tough, no-nonsense attitude to the commission's proceedings.

Rudman had also served as chair of the Senate Ethics Committee, a position granted by the Senate's leadership only to individuals considered above moral reproach. Further, he had been a member of the prestigious and powerful Senate Appropriations Committee. I found attractive, too, his work since retirement from the Senate as the founding co-chairman of the Concord Coalition, a national interest group dedicated to the reduction of government spending. His concern for fiscal responsibility was long-standing. While still in the Senate, he cosponsored the celebrated Gramm-Rudman-Hollings deficit reduction legislation, designed to impose discipline and accountability on government spending. If anyone was likely to bring a sharp scrutiny to the intelligence budget, surely it would be Warren Rudman. Since retiring from the Senate, he had returned to his law practice in DC with the international firm of Paul, Weiss, Rifkind, Wharton, and Garrison.

Noticing two politicians at the commission helm, Aspin and Rudman, I scanned the list of presidential appointees to see what other political figures were among the members. I wondered what kind of partisan mix Aspin would have to handle. There were no other former or sitting members of Congress in the group among the president's appointees; but some of those chosen by Clinton were political activists, while the remaining members were former intelligence bureaucrats. The political activists included Zoë E. Baird, Stephen J. Friedman, Anthony S. Harrington, and Paul D. Wolfowitz.

Just a year earlier, Zoë Baird had been the president's nominee for attorney general. Had she been confirmed by the Senate, she would have become the first woman to serve as the nation's chief law-enforcement officer. During the confirmation hearings, though, she found herself quickly embroiled in controversy over failing to pay employment taxes for two illegal aliens, a couple from Peru, whom she had employed for almost two years as a chauffeur and a nanny. This put her in violation off the Immigration Reform and Control Act of 1988. Baird also failed to verify the citizenship status of her workers before they were hired, another provision of the law. In light of these revelations, senators, journalists, and the public questioned the propriety of appointing Baird to head the department responsible for enforcement of immigration laws. Her two visits to the chairman of the Senate Judiciary Committee, Joseph Biden (D-DE), ended with her in tears after he warned her of the strong objections to her candidacy.[11] Soon the opprobrium "Nannygate" blazed in newspaper headlines around the country. The opposition to her candidacy mounted and she was forced to withdraw her name.

On February 1, 1993, Baird appeared on the cover of *Time* magazine, although hardly in the manner she may have once hoped; the caption for the lead story read "Clinton's First Blunder." In a letter to Baird, the president consoled her with words that echoed those he had used when Les Aspin resigned from the office of SecDef: "I hope that you will be available for other assignments for your country in my Administration."[12] Shortly afterward, he appointed her to membership on PFIAB. Since duties on PFIAB are a part-time responsibility (the board usually meets only two to three days a month), Baird remained in her job as senior vice president and general counsel of Aetna, a leading insurance company based in Hartford, Connecticut. Previously in her career, she had worked as head of the legal department at General Electric, as a partner in the Washington, DC, law firm of O'Melveny & Myers, and as associate counsel to President Jimmy Carter. She held a law degree from the University of California at Berkeley and was married to Paul Gewirtz, a constitutional law professor at the Yale University Law School (the alma mater of both Bill and Hillary Clinton). In the television news coverage of her failed bid for the office of attorney general, she came across as smart, attractive, and energetic. She was, at forty-two, the youngest member appointed to the Aspin Commission.

Stephen J. Friedman was a more obscure figure in Washington, although certainly not in the financial circles of New York City. He had climbed to the top of the (at least then) highly regarded investment banking firm Goldman Sachs, where he was director from 1992 to 1994, and was its leading expert on corporate takeovers. Between leaving Goldman Sachs and joining the Aspin Commission, he held the position of senior principal at Marsh & McLennan, an investment and insurance company. Along with Warren Rudman, Friedman was a leader in the Concord Coalition and the national movement to cut back on federal budget deficits. Born in Brooklyn, he graduated from Cornell University and Columbia Law School. Friedman was clearly a financial whiz and was no doubt in serious contention for the title of the richest person appointed to the commission (along with a number of other millionaires). He was one of the three Republicans named by the president to the panel, along with Rudman and Wolfowitz. While Friedman was often described in newspaper accounts as a "mainstream Republican," he occasionally sprinkled some of his wealth in the direction of Democratic candidates for high office whom he liked, including Bill Clinton. Though diminutive in stature, the wiry Friedman had been a standout wrestler in college, winning the Eastern Intercollegiate 157-pound championship in 1959. His induction into the Cornell Athletic Hall of Fame was a badge of honor guaranteed to accelerate advancement in the macho world of Wall Street financiers.

Rumor had it that in an impromptu wrestling match at a Goldman Sachs corporate retreat, he had quickly—and repeatedly—pinned a much larger colleague, Henry Paulson, a tall, broad-shouldered former Dartmouth wrestling and football star who was later secretary of the treasury in the second Bush administration and who, at the time, had been unaware of Friedman's wrestling achievements in college.[13] At Cornell, Friedman's substantial financial donations supported the construction of the Friedman Strength and Conditioning Center and the Friedman Wrestling Center.

Still more obscure in the public eye was Anthony S. "Tony" Harrington, a native of Taylorsville, North Carolina, and a partner in the large DC law firm of Hogan and Hartson. I knew he was chair of the White House Intelligence Oversight Board (IOB), a three-person panel established by President Gerald R. Ford in 1976 to provide the chief executive with improved internal accountability with respect to intelligence activities. In the newspapers, I learned further that he was a founder and director of Ovation, an arts television network, as well as the founder and director of Telecom USA—the fourth largest U.S. long-distance telephone company before its merger with MCI Communications (sold for over $1 billion). During his time with Telecom USA, I figured he must have learned a fair amount about sigint ties between the NSA and private American telephone companies, including the history of the discovery by the Church Committee in 1975 that the NSA and leading telecommunications companies had conspired throughout much of the Cold War to eavesdrop on U.S. citizens. Because of this finding, Congress had passed the Foreign Intelligence Surveillance Act (FISA) in 1978, requiring a warrant from a special court for national-security wiretaps and related surveillance practices.[14]

Harrington's Democratic Party credentials were strong. He had served as chief counsel to the Democratic National Committee and as general counsel to the victorious Clinton-Gore campaign in 1992. He had dipped into academe for a brief stint as assistant dean at the Duke University School of Law, where he had earned his law degree following undergraduate studies as a prestigious Morehead Scholar at the University of North Carolina in Chapel Hill.

With Baird, Friedman, and Harrington—all businesspeople—the commission was beginning to look more like a gathering of the chamber of commerce than an inquiry into strategic intelligence. The next commissioner, though, was cut from different cloth. Perhaps of all these political activists, Paul D. Wolfowitz was the biggest surprise among the president's appointees, if only because he had developed strong ties over the years to the Republican Party (even though he had worked in the Pentagon during the

Carter years and was a registered Democrat until the end of the 1970s). He has been described as "steely, staunchly conservative."[15] Wolfowitz was also the only non-PFIAB member among the president's appointees. Born in Brooklyn, the son of a renowned mathematician who had emigrated from Warsaw to New York in 1920, Wolfowitz majored in math at Cornell University. For graduate studies, he switched to his deeper passion: international relations, a subfield of political science, in which he earned a PhD at the University of Chicago while studying under the famous military strategist Albert Wohlstetter. A veteran of both the Reagan and the first Bush administrations, Wolfowitz had served with President Reagan as Director of Policy Planning in the Department of State, as assistant secretary of state for East Asian and Pacific affairs, and as ambassador to Indonesia. His performance as ambassador to Indonesia was widely praised.[16] In the administration of George H. W. Bush, he had been the under secretary of defense for policy. Under the next Bush administration—that of George W. Bush—he would rise even higher in the DoD bureaucracy, to become deputy secretary of defense. In this position, he was much berated for the fitful progress of the war in Iraq. Afterward, he became a controversial and short-lived head of the World Bank.[17]

Wolfowitz was the closest thing to a scholar among the commission members, to the extent that busy college administrators can engage in scholarship while juggling their managerial responsibilities. In 1994, he had become dean and professor of international relations at the Paul H. Nitze School of Advanced International Studies (SAIS), a Washington campus of the Johns Hopkins University in Maryland. Earlier, he had taught political science at Yale University. Before his tour of duty as dean at SAIS, Wolfowitz published widely on questions of international development, including articles on water desalination in the Middle East (his doctoral-dissertation topic) and on the effectiveness of agricultural subsidies to poor nations. Over the course of his career he learned Arabic and five other languages. His cerebral credentials were unassailable, and he evolved into something of an intellectual high priest for Washington's neoconservatives. He was a reliable foreign-policy hawk, even if he sometimes displayed liberal tendencies on social issues. Certainly his decades of service in the government and his close study of international affairs made him, like Aspin, a preeminent policy analyst on the commission—perhaps the reason why President Clinton, Washington's policy wonk in chief, had been attracted to him as an appointee.

Of the president's appointed commission members, that left the three intelligence bureaucrats: Lew Allen, Ann Caracristi, and Robert Hermann, all with skeletal public resumes—hardly surprising, given their careers within the hidden side of government. According to news accounts, Gen. Lew Allen Jr. was born in Miami, Florida, went to high school in Texas, and graduated from the U.S. Military Academy. He later earned a PhD in physics at the University of Illinois (writing a dissertation on high-energy photonuclear reactions). In the Air Force, he learned how to fly B-29s and B-36s, and became expert as well in nuclear weaponry. From 1962 to 1965, he worked in the Pentagon's Space Technology Office, where he gained expertise in satellite surveillance. One of his projects involved a study of the effects of radiation on the photographic film used in the early CORONA-class of spy satellites. (His boss at the time was Harold Brown, then the Defense Department's director of defense research, who would later become SecDef for President Carter. The degrees of separation are few among security specialists in Washington.) At the Pentagon, Allen headed up procurement, launch, and on-orbit operations for all of America's satellite-based espionage platforms. He would clearly be one of the commission's key internal experts on questions related to space-based spying. He also served briefly as deputy to the DCI in 1973, then from 1973 to 1977 as director of the NSA, where he concentrated on the improvement of electronic intelligence collection. He also devoted considerable time to ensuring that the agency operated according to sound ethical guidelines, and he was the first NSA director to discuss some of the ultra-secret agency's work in public hearings on Capitol Hill.[18] In 1977, he headed up the Air Force Systems Command and earned a fourth star. The next year President Carter appointed him chief of staff of the Air Force.

Since his retirement from the Air Force in 1982, Allen had served as vice president of the California Institute of Technology (another connection to Harold Brown, who had been Cal Tech's president) and director of its Jet Propulsion Laboratory. In 1990, he led an investigation into the defective mirror on the Hubble Space Telescope and then retired for a second time in 1991. Allen was from the intellectual side of the military, a brainy technocrat rather than a warrior in the mode of, say, generals George Patton or James Doolittle. He had progressed through the ranks of the Air Force with a slide rule and a calculator, without ever having an assignment outside the United States. In 1994 he was in his second term of service on PFIAB, having been initially appointed by President George H. W. Bush.

Ann Z. Caracristi was an unknown to me, beyond the fact that she had been an officer and manager in the NSA for forty years, reaching the position of deputy director in 1980—the only female to achieve this distinction and an enormous accomplishment in a secret world dominated by males. She graduated with a BA from Russell Sage College in Troy, New York, and began her career in intelligence as a cryptanalyst with the Army Signal Intelligence Service in 1942, sorting through Japanese military messages intercepted by the United States. She quickly advanced to a supervisory position over crypt-analysis (the art and science of code breaking and message interpretation), and she helped introduce the use of computers for the collection and analysis of signals intelligence. After the war she came to the NSA, and, in 1975, Caracristi became the first woman in that agency promoted to GS-18, the highest of three "supergrades" in the U.S. civil service. Among other distinc-tions, she went on to win the Defense Department's Distinguished Civilian Service Award, its highest civilian honor. Evidently at home in a man's world, Caracristi no doubt could handle being surrounded by mostly male colleagues on the commission (Baird was the only other woman). At seventy-three, Caracristi was tied with Senator Warner as the panel's most senior member.

I didn't know much about Dr. Robert J. Hermann either, but his creden-tials immediately introduced him as another person who could help the commission in the domains of electronic and space-based espionage. His BS, MA, and PhD from Iowa State University were all in the field of electrical engineering. From 1979 to 1981, he simultaneously led the National Reconnaissance Office and served as assistant secretary of the Air Force for research, development, and logistics. Previously, he had worked for two decades at the NSA. Moreover, his government experience included a spell as principal deputy assistant secretary of defense for communications, command, control, and intelligence (1977–79) and as special assistant to NATO's supreme allied commander in Europe (1975–77). At the time of his appoint-ment to the commission in 1994, Hermann had retired from government and was senior vice president for science and technology at the United Technologies Corporation.

The presidential selection process had yielded two former politicians (Aspin and Rudman), three businesspeople who were also political activists (Baird, Friedman, and Harrington), a foreign- and defense-policy expert and political activist (Wolfowitz, although Aspin fits into this category too), and three former intelligence managers (Allen, Caracristi, and Hermann). Three were Democrats (Aspin, Baird, and Harrington)—two fewer than he was allowed to name; three were Republicans (Friedman, Rudman, and Wolfowitz), and three were intelligence bureaucrats with unknown partisan affiliations, if any (Allen, Caracristi, and Hermann). The group's credentials in their respective fields were first-rate. The businesspeople, though, seemed to have limited intelligence experience; and I was concerned that the former NSA managers might end up being more interested in the protection of their old agency than an objective examination of whatever shortcomings it might have. Nonetheless, each of these nine individuals was a person of substantial achievement, and I had to revise my cynical view that landing a seat on a national commission was simply a matter of having political connections. Granted, it did take that; but it also seemed to require an unassailable curriculum vitae—at least in the case of the presidential appointees to the Aspin Commission. I wondered if Congress's choices would match the quality of the president's major-league lineup.

The Congressional Appointees

While Aspin and Warner were negotiating in 1994 over what kind of commission should examine the intelligence agencies, the American voters triggered a political tsunami at the polls. Contrary to the predictions of leading political scientists around the country, the Democrats lost control of both houses of Congress. Clinton's new intelligence commission may have had a majority of Democrats on board, but Democrats were no longer the majority on Capitol Hill. The first session of the 104th Congress would begin with 230 Republicans in the House, 204 Democrats, and one independent; the Senate would have 53 Republicans and 47 Democrats. Since GOP lawmakers were less likely to support intelligence reform,[19] Aspin's job of selling this product on the Hill—the end game of the commission's work—had just become substantially more difficult.

This political sea change, ending forty years of Democratic rule in the House of Representatives, had no effect on Congress's appointments to the commission, however, because the new legislative leadership would not take over until January of 1995. The Senate and House leaders of 1994 would select the commissioners. The appointment procedure turned out to be a quicker process on the Hill than in the White House, even though the process in Congress was much more complicated and rancorous. The authority for choosing went to a quartet of legislative leaders: House Speaker Thomas S. Foley (D-WA), House Minority Leader Robert H. Michel (R-IL), Senate Majority Leader George J. Mitchell (D-ME), and Senate Minority Leader Bob Dole (R-KS). Each would have two picks: one sitting member of Congress and one person from outside (not necessarily a former lawmaker). The incumbent congressional appointees turned out to be Rep. Norman D. Dicks (D-WA), Senator J. James Exon (D-NE); Rep. Porter J. Goss (R-FL); and Senator John Warner (R-VA).

Among these officeholders, Senator Warner was practically a given, since he had sponsored the legislation to create the joint commission in the first place. Minority Leader Dole made sure he was on the final list. Just as he had been in the events leading up to its creation, Warner would most likely be a force to be reckoned with on the panel itself. Aspin had already made significant compromises with the senator in their odd alliance to block a separate Senate probe. Above all, Aspin had relinquished several positions on what was originally meant to be an all-PFIAB venture; now Warner and several other non-PFIAB members would participate in the proceedings. What else would Aspin have to yield to the tough-minded Virginian along the way?

Warner had the hardened looks of an old warrior, and he had been a young warrior, serving in both World War II (as a petty officer in the navy) and the Korean War (as a Marine Corps officer). In between and after these wars, he finished his higher education at Washington and Lee University and at the University of Virginia School of Law. He subsequently practiced law in Washington, DC, was appointed an assistant U.S. attorney, and later served in the Department of the Navy as under secretary of the Navy and as secretary of the Navy (1969–74). In 1978, when the leading Republican candidate died in a plane crash, he belatedly entered the Virginia GOP primary for the U.S. Senate and went on to win the seat in the general election. He would serve as a senator for the next three decades. At the time of his appointment to the commission in 1994, he was second in seniority on the Armed Services Committee, behind the aged Strom Thurmond (R-SC), as well as vice chair of the Senate Select Committee on Intelligence.

Warner had some of the flamboyance of a Hollywood leading man as he shuttled in black tie or business suit between a posh home in Georgetown and a farm in Virginia horse country. He first married the banking heiress Catherine Mellon, then dated media celebrity Barbara Walters, and was married again (briefly) to one of America's most glamorous movie stars, Elizabeth Taylor, whose Hollywood pizzazz brought some dazzle to his inaugural Senate campaign.

Though a reliable conservative Republican on many issues, Warner could exhibit a maverick streak. He angered his party in 1987 by opposing Supreme Court nominee Robert Bork, and again in 1994 by helping to defeat a bid by Oliver L. North (of Iran-*contra* infamy) to oust Virginia's Democratic senator Charles S. Robb. Some Republicans went so far as to label Warner a "liberal," but that was a stretch by any objective measure. More accurately, he was part of a vanishing breed of American politician: a bona fide centrist.[20] For that reason, he and Aspin could perhaps manage to work together on the commission, given that Aspin had moved much closer to the middle of the political spectrum since I had first worked for him two decades earlier.

The other Republican incumbent selected from Congress, Porter J. Goss, a native of Waterbury, Connecticut, was a House member with Yale University credentials (he studied classics as an undergraduate, and had been a member of the same secret society as Aspin—Book and Snake). He then served in Army intelligence and went on to the CIA. As an Agency man from 1962 to 1972, he worked in the DO, assigned to recruit espionage assets in Latin America and Europe. While a case officer, he contracted a debilitating bacteriological infection that sent him to the hospital for several months at the age of thirty-one. He emerged gaunt and pale, with a weakened heart, kidneys, and lungs. Rather than take a desk job at Langley, he chose early retirement. With the cushion of his own considerable family wealth (his father had run a metal company) and his wife's even greater family fortune, the Connecticut Yankee and his wife moved south with four children, two dogs, a cat, and two turtles in tow, settling in Florida on Sanibel Island, off the Gulf Coast.[21]

Along with two other former Agency officers on the island, he started a small company, the Island Boat Rental (a shoebox served as the cash register). The trio next founded a newspaper, the *Island Reporter*. Riled by the mushrooming commercial development on Sanibel, he and his friends at the paper soon found themselves swept up in local politics. The "Sanibel Spooks," as they were nicknamed, led an effort to incorporate the island; then they set up a city council in Lee County. Evidently, in the Operations Directorate one picked up all kinds of useful skills. The CIA had taken over the island—or so critics claimed at the time. Despite this criticism, the new council members appointed Goss as mayor, and he held the job for eight years. He was then appointed a county commissioner for five more years. In 1988, he won a seat in the U.S. House—one of only a few former intelligence officers to campaign successfully for Congress.

At the time of his appointment to the Aspin Commission, Goss was a member of HPSCI with a conservative GOP voting record and a winsome way that had attracted the favorable attention of his party's leaders in the House. He was no friend of Bill Clinton, having lashed out at him in 1994 for his policies toward Haiti. "We need a negotiated solution," he declared, in a speech, "not send Marines to enforce a solution."[22] The serrated edge of Goss's foreign policy pronouncements made me wonder whether the Aspin Commission would become yet another battlefield in Washington for the shrill partisan rhetoric that had increasingly dominated relations between Democrats and Republicans since the end of the Cold War.

A colleague of Goss's on HPSCI, Norman Dicks came from the opposite end of the country and the political spectrum. He was a Washington State liberal Democrat. Educated at the University of Washington as an undergraduate and as a law student, Dicks joined the staff of Warren G. Magnuson (a longtime U.S. senator from the state) right out of law school. His political skills honed through eight years of apprenticeship with Magnuson, Dicks took a shot at a congressional career of his own in 1976, winning a seat in the U.S. House on his first try. He had been reelected ever since, aided by a rare first-term appointment to the influential House Appropriations Committee.

In his media photographs, Dicks looked like a brawler, an impression heightened by piercing eyes and a firm jaw. His aggressive temperament had won him a position as a starting linebacker on the University of Washington football team, where the joke was that on every play he was five yards offside. His experience on HPSCI made him a good choice for the commission, but exactly how objective he would be when it came to technical intelligence matters was uncertain. The huge defense contractor Boeing was in his district, and the corporation had entered into the business of surveillance-satellite manufacturing with an eye on the bounty of federal funding for intelligence. President Eisenhower had warned of the "military-industrial complex" in his famous farewell address of 1959; that complex now had another hyphenated partner: "-intelligence." As Adm. William O. Studeman then acting DCI, had once observed: "Intelligence has become a very big business in the United States."[23] I could envision Rudman and Friedman wielding the budget axe and Dicks fending them off with his muscular girth. On social issues, Dicks lined up with the liberal Democrats; but on defense issues, he had a voting record that frequently fell right of center.

Senator James Exon, another Democrat, was the fourth congressional incumbent. On a multiple choice test, most Americans would probably have circled "Exon" as a gasoline brand, not a member of the world's most exclusive club, the U.S. Senate. Yet, obscure as he may have been to me, he had enjoyed a long and distinguished career in politics representing the state of Nebraska. Born and raised in South Dakota by a family of Democratic political activists, Exon attended the University of Omaha for three years, then entered World War II as a soldier stationed in the Pacific theater. After the war, he founded and directed a prosperous office-equipment firm. On the side, he participated in volunteer activities for the Nebraska Democratic Party, beginning at the precinct level and working his way up to party chairman. From this high partisan perch, Exon ran for governor in 1971 and won, going on to serve a record eight years in that position. In 1978, he tried his luck in a U.S. Senate race and won again, being reelected in 1984 and 1990.[24]

Exon was a member of the Armed Services Committee and the Budget Committee, where he was known as a fiscal conservative. Lawmakers are "wild-eyed spenders," he once declared.[25] With at least three commissioners—Rudman, Friedman, and now Exon—with a reputation for cutting government budgets, the intelligence community may have begun to feel a little nervous about the Aspin Commission. During the congressional debate on the MX missile in 1983, Exon had demonstrated an ability to savage a commission's findings, laying into the plans for the basing of the missile proposed by members of the Scowcroft Commission (and backed at the time by Representative Les Aspin).[26] What Exon's views were on intelligence, though, was hard to say; he had virtually no public record on the subject. His World War II service had been with the U.S. Army Signal Corps, so perhaps he still had an interest in sigint. Maybe that was why he had lobbied Majority Leader Mitchell for an appointment to the commission. Even with Exon's strong Democratic credentials, one thing was clear: Aspin would not be able to count on him for automatic support. The Nebraskan had a reputation for siding with Republicans on security and budget issues.

That left the four congressionally appointed members from outside the Congress. On this list were Tony Coelho, David H. Dewhurst, Lt. Gen. Robert E. Pursley, and Wyche Fowler—respectively, a former member of the House, a businessman and state political activist, a military man, and another former lawmaker.

Tony Coelho, a native of California, had become a fairly well-known national figure, though not for reasons he would have liked. He grew up on a dairy farm near Modesto, California, and, upon completion of his undergraduate studies in political science at Loyola University in Los Angeles in 1964 (where he was elected student-body president), he planned to enter a Jesuit seminary. During a routine physical examination, however, his physician discovered he had epilepsy. Since canon law bans epileptics from the priesthood, he had to abandon those plans. He turned to his other main interest, politics, and joined the staff of Rep. B. F. "Bernie" Sisk of California's Fifteenth District, in the Central Valley. He worked for Sisk from 1965 to 1978. When Sisk retired, he gave Coelho his blessings to run as his successor. Coelho won the election with 60 percent of the vote and was reelected five times. An ebullient individual, he rose through the Democratic leadership hierarchy in the House of Representatives during the 1980s to the third rung from the top, majority whip. Among his accomplishments as a lawmaker was passage of the landmark Americans with Disabilities Act.

All this was the good news. The bad news was that in 1989 Coelho was forced to resign as majority whip when he was accused of personal financial improprieties, namely, that he had accepted a sweetheart loan from a troubled savings and loan company, then failed to disclose to the Justice Department his purchase of a $100,000 junk bond with the loan. Although the Justice

Department decided not to bring charges against Coelho, his reputation had been dealt a blow, and within a month he left the House, a step ahead of a House Ethics Committee investigation. With his close ties to the Democratic establishment, he landed on his feet. His gregarious, winning personality, as well as his bulging Rolodex, helped Coelho secure a position in New York City as an investment banker. He got down to the business of making serious money.

Newspaper reports over the years described Coelho as partisan, aggressive, harsh, intelligent, fun loving, fascinating, and mischievous; no one, however, had ever accused him of knowing much about the subject of intelligence. While still in the House, he had chaired the Democratic Congressional Campaign Committee, setting fund-raising records; now in the private sector, he continued to use these skills, endearing himself to leading national Democrats, most recently the Clinton-Gore reelection campaign in 1994. Assignment to the Aspin Commission was a reward for his stellar fund-raising accomplishments, along with his services as a vocal and witty Republican-basher for the Bill Clinton political juggernaut.

David H. Dewhurst III was a native of Texas with a BA degree from the University of Arizona, where he played on the basketball team. He was a black hole in my knowledge of commission appointees. The media didn't seem to know much either. From the scraps of information I could find, I learned that he was a GOP political activist in his home state. He had made a fortune as a businessman and given large chunks of it to the Texas Republican Party. From 1990 to 1994, he served as the party's finance chairman. However obscure he might have been nationally, he had a leg up on the Democratic political activist Coelho when it came to understanding intelligence issues. Like Goss, he had served in the CIA's Operations Directorate, with assignments in Latin America, from 1971 to 1973. Before that, he had been an officer in the U.S. Air Force and an aide in the Department of State. When Dewhurst left the CIA, he tried his hand at ranching, breeding Black Angus cattle, riding cutting horses in national competition, and following other cowboy pursuits. His fortune came through his Houston-based company, Falcon Seaboard, which specialized in petroleum, electricity, and investments. The commission had a genuine Texas cowboy and oil tycoon among its members.

While these two outsider appointments made by Congress had obvious partisan backgrounds, Robert E. Pursley was a military man. A retired air-force lieutenant general, he hailed from Indiana, graduated from the U.S. Military Academy, and had picked up a Harvard University MBA while on leave from military service. During the Korean War, he flew fifty combat missions as a B-26 pilot. He ascended through the ranks of the Air Force to become the commander of U.S. forces in Japan and commander of the Fifth Air Force. As is common with most successful generals, he had made some useful political contacts in Washington along the way, especially while assigned to the Pentagon where he had worked for three SecDefs. His primary political connection was to Secretary of Defense Melvin R. Laird, the former Wisconsin Republican dynamo in the House of Representatives who once chaired the Armed Services Committee. Now in the private sector as president of the Logistics Management Institute (a "beltway bandit" consulting firm), Pursley had kept up his ties with Laird, who continued to have influence with the GOP leadership on the Hill. When Pursley expressed an interest in serving on the commission, Laird made it happen.

Last but not least was Wyche Fowler Jr., from my own state of Georgia and the only appointee other than Aspin whom I knew personally. I had worked with Fowler on HPSCI in its initial years of 1977–78. He was a member of that committee at the same time I was staff director of its Subcommittee on Intelligence Oversight. Wyche served in the House for ten years, until he was elected to the U.S. Senate in 1986. In both chambers he had been an active participant on the Intelligence Committees, and he understood the subject as well as any lawmaker. He was known for his advocacy of strict legislative accountability for covert action, especially paramilitary operations, and for his promotion of international democracy and human rights.[27]

A seventh-generation Georgian, Fowler was born in Atlanta. As a boy he could pick a country guitar and sing every major Presbyterian hymn by heart through the fourth stanza. His vocal abilities won him a statewide talent contest as a country singer on the television program "Stars of Tomorrow." The singer Brenda Lee joined him on the winner's podium before she went on to musical stardom. The two were so popular that they were often asked to perform "The Old Rugged Cross" together, with the eleven-year-old Fowler taking the high notes. In high school, he played basketball and won two cross-country state championships. Fowler earned a BA in English from North Carolina's Davidson College in 1962. Serving in the military from 1962 to 1964, he was stationed at the Pentagon as an Army intelligence officer. During off-hours he did volunteer work for a freshman lawmaker in Congress, Charles Weltner, a liberal Democrat from Atlanta's Fifth District. After his tour of duty in the military, Fowler signed on full-time with Weltner and soon became his chief of staff. When Weltner decided to forgo a third term rather than run on the same ticket as the right-wing gubernatorial candidate Lester Maddox, Fowler returned to Atlanta to study law at Emory University, earning a JD in 1969.

During his first year of law school, Fowler approached Atlanta's mayor, Ivan Allen Jr., offering to act as the mayor's ombudsman in the evening hours. In that way, Fowler argued, the mayor's office could help the people of Atlanta handle problems like broken street lights even when city offices were officially closed. Allen let the energetic young law student try his hand at the idea, and Fowler kept at it throughout law school. In 1968 and 1969, the media frequently referred to him as the "night mayor of City Hall." Riding on this reputation, Fowler ran for city council in 1970 under the banner "Night Mayor Runs for Alderman." At age twenty-nine, and still in law school, he won by defeating a thirty-year incumbent. Four years later, council members chose him over the well-known African American activist Hosea Williams to serve as city council president, a position he held until his election in 1977 to the U.S. House of Representatives. During his time on the city council, he also practiced law in Atlanta.

In Fowler's first bid for the Fifth District congressional seat in 1972, he lost by a wide margin to popular civil-rights leader Andrew Young; but when Young left Congress to join the Carter administration, Fowler ran again and won. He became the only white member of Congress to be reelected four times by a constituency that had become, through redistricting, majority black (65 percent). He even defeated the legendary civil rights activist John Lewis, who eventually represented the Fifth District after Fowler gave up the seat to run for the U.S. Senate. In the House, the congenial Fowler managed to win a position on the Ways and Means Committee after only one term in office, sidestepping the leadership's slate of candidates and going directly to all the members of the Democratic caucus for votes. In addition to HPSCI and Ways and Means, he served on the Foreign Affairs Committee.

As a member of HPSCI, he drafted a law that would eventually become known as the Boland Amendment, after the panel's chair, Edward P. Boland (D-MA). This law, actually seven different amendments that were increasingly restrictive and enacted over several months, prohibited CIA paramilitary operations in Nicaragua. The efforts by the Reagan administration to circumvent the Boland statute by conducting illegal covert actions in Nicaragua would precipitate the Iran-*contra* scandal of 1986–87.

In 1986, Fowler defeated incumbent Republican senator Mack Mattingly, by the slim margin of 51 percent. No Atlantan had ever won a seat in the U.S. Senate. Fowler succeeded despite long odds—he trailed by twenty-four points in the polls just three weeks before election day—pulling off a victory at the last minute by dint of his humorous and folksy stories, personal magnetism, and exhaustive campaigning. He traveled to each of Georgia's 159 counties, and held two hundred town meetings. During his first days in the

Senate, Fowler promised to support Maine's Senator Mitchell in a three-way race for the majority leadership position, and he seconded Mitchell's nomination. The Maine senator became majority leader and repaid Fowler's gamble by awarding him a coveted seat on the Appropriations Committee. Mitchell also created a special leadership position for Fowler—assistant floor leader—that catapulted the rookie into the upper reaches of the party hierarchy. This close association between Fowler and Mitchell, both avid baseball fans, would land Fowler a spot on the Aspin Commission in 1994.

The remarkable upward trajectory of Fowler's career suddenly moved downward in his bid for reelection to the Senate in 1992.[28] He seemed to lack the enthusiasm he had displayed in 1986, and some observers found his campaign unfocused—a pudding without a theme, in Churchill's phrase. Voters were unaware of his many accomplishments during his first term, and they were unclear about his goals for a second term. His votes against the war in the Persian Gulf in 1990 and for a tax increase hurt him with white male voters; and his support for the controversial Clarence Thomas, a Georgian, as a nominee to the U.S. Supreme Court in 1991, led to disaffection among white, pro-choice women, who opposed Thomas's anti-abortion stance. The substantial federal money Fowler had brought to Georgia and the work he had done in the Senate on such issues as health care, education, jobs, intelligence reform, the environment, alternative energies, and historical preservation seemed to matter little in the absence of his own personal zeal to carry on in the Senate.

Overconfidence also seems to have played a role in Fowler's loss. He underestimated his Republican challenger, Paul Coverdell (a former Peace Corps director), who he had previously defeated when Coverdell tried to unseat him in a race for the Fifth District congressional seat. This time Coverdell proved to be a formidable opponent: determined, tireless, and clever in debate—even if he didn't know, as Fowler pointed out in one debate, the pitching lineup for the Atlanta Braves. Fowler also seemed preoccupied with the health of his old friend and mentor, former congressman Charles Weltner, who died in August of 1992. Before Weltner's passing, Fowler interrupted his campaigning to take his ailing former mentor on a trip to Turkey and Iraq, where they explored religious and archaeological sites together. During August, Fowler visited Weltner in the hospital each morning, much to the dismay of his campaign staff. On election day, Fowler found himself forced into a runoff with Coverdell by a mere seventeen thousand votes (just 0.6 percent short of the majority necessary to avoid a runoff). In this second election, Coverdell edged to victory with less than 51 percent of the vote.

I was pleased that Fowler was on the commission. I knew from observing him on HPSCI that he would bring wit to the proceedings, as well as a strong sense of ethical principles for intelligence operations (a contradictory relationship for some, but not for Fowler, who believed in limits and full accountability even in the shadowy world of spies, at least within a democratic society). Fowler could be mercurial, however, as his lackluster campaign for reelection to the Senate had revealed. He appeared easily distracted, and I wondered how engaged he would be in the commission's work.

So that was the lineup. The average ages of the presidential and congressional appointees were about the same: 58 and 59, respectively (see Table 2.1). Of those with an identifiable party affiliation (that is, all but the intelligence and military officers), seven were Democrats and six were Republicans (although some of the Democrats, like Dicks and Exon, had rightward leanings on national security issues). Geographically, the president's appointees were overwhelmingly northeastern, while Congress's chosen men—no women were in this group—were predominantly southern.

Lawyers were in a minority among the total membership, but they were a sizable minority: seven out of the seventeen, or 41 percent. For me, the potential benefit of having so many nonlawyers on the commission was that we might achieve a broader review of intelligence issues, rather than getting bogged down by narrow legal points (which is not to deny that they can be important at times). The voting indexes for the commissioners who had once served in Congress revealed that Rudman, Warner, and Goss were markedly conservative; Aspin, Coelho, and Fowler were on the more liberal side; and Dicks and Exon were somewhere in between (see Table 2.1). These voting measures suggested potentially serious ideological fault lines among the commissioners.

The most significant dimension, perhaps, was the level of intelligence expertise on the commission. Here the presidential appointees brought more to the table, with an average rating near the "high experience" range (based on my judgments), compared to the "moderate" average for the congressional appointees. This skewing of expertise toward the executive-branch appointees—notwithstanding three "low experience" commissioners on this side—was attributable mainly to the president's appointment of the three former NSA managers. Those with the greatest knowledge about intelligence might well be able to frame the debate as commissioners pondered how to reorient the secret agencies in the aftermath of the Cold War.

The commission was a group of seventeen talented individuals with an astonishingly broad set of backgrounds, interests, and abilities, a far more diverse gathering than the Church Committee had been, although neither

TABLE 2.1 A Profile of the Aspin Commission Membership in December, 1994

Member	Age	Origin	Party ID *	Lawyer	Voting**	Intelligence Expertise
Presidential Appointees						
Aspin	56	Midwest	D	No	75	high
Rudman	64	Northeast	R	Yes	25	high
Allen	69	West	–	No	—	very high
Baird	42	Northeast	D	Yes	—	low
Caracristi	73	Northeast	–	No	—	very high
Friedman	57	Northeast	R	Yes	—	low
Harrington	51	South	D	Yes	—	low
Hermann	59	Midwest	–	No	—	very high
Wolfowitz	51	Northeast	R	No	—	high
Ave:	58					
Congressional Appointees						
Coelho	52	West	D	No	90	low
Dewhurst	49	South	R	No	—	moderate
Dicks	54	West	D	Yes	65	high
Exon	73	Midwest	D	No	65	moderate
Fowler	54	South	D	Yes	75	high
Goss	56	South	R	No	10	high
Pursley	67	Midwest	–	No	—	moderate
Warner	67	South	R	Yes	20	high
Ave:	59					

* The blank entries indicate that the bureaucrats on the Commission had no publicly known party affiliation.

** The numbers are voting profiles compiled by the interest group ADA (Americans for Democratic Action), in which a 100 score means a perfect liberal on the issues (by its lights) and 0 a perfect conservative. The ADA scores for Dicks, Goss, Exon, and Warner are for 1994 and are drawn from Philip D. Duncan and Christine C. Lawrence, *Politics in America: the 105th Congress* (Washington, D.C., 1997); and the scores for Fowler, Rudman, Coelho, and Aspin are for 1988 and are drawn from Michael Barone and Grant Ujifusu, *The Almanac of American Politics, 1990* (Washington, D.C.: National Journal Press, 1989). Blanks in the column indicate that a commissioner was never a member of Congress and, therefore, had no ADA index.

panel displayed much ethnic diversity. Coelho could claim Portuguese heritage, but, for the most part, the commissioners were white, middle-aged men—Washington's favorite species, judging by the demographics of the Congress, the Supreme Court, and most of the directors inside the bureaucracy. (No black or Hispanic headed any of the intelligence agencies in 1994, nor today; and only one woman led an intelligence agency that year, Toby T. Gati of INR: there is only one today.) The Aspin Commission members were, as a group, rich businesspeople; political fund-raisers; policy wonks; former high-ranking intelligence officers, military men, and technocrats; and former or incumbent politicians with sharp partisan teeth. The cliché about herding cats came to mind as I studied the membership roster—although given the strong egos involved, it would be more like herding Bengal tigers. Aspin may have had it easy during his bumpy days in the Pentagon compared to the challenge of holding this assemblage together.

The Commission Staff

Throughout December, while the president sauntered along with the selection of his commission members, Aspin sifted through hundreds of applications for staff positions: K Street attorneys, think-tank analysts, retired intelligence officers, generals and admirals, beltway bandits of various stripes, students of all ages and levels of education, legislative staff aides, and university professors. In the final compilation, he selected seventeen staff members. Ten (six of whom were retired) had served in the intelligence agencies; five had worked on intelligence issues as Capitol Hill aides; one came from the president's Office of Management and Budget; I was the only one from academe (although I had previous Hill experience). The CIA had the largest representation, contributing six staff members. A contingent of three people from the NSA included two of the most senior staffers, one of whom had worked at the sigint organization for thirty-three years. It looked like the sigint agency had scored a coup at the staff level, too.

The former intelligence officers on the staff would bring to the proceedings expertise on a wide range of subjects, including technical issues (did we need a few big or many small spy satellites?), the challenges of collection (more machines or more agents?) and analysis (how can we do this better?), covert action (should we do this at all?), and budget needs (how much money is enough?). Peculiarly, given the prominence of the Ames case as an impetus for the creation of the commission, no one on the staff was a specialist in counterintelligence, nor did anyone know much about Somalia.

Remarkably for a commission staff, only five of the seventeen were lawyers. Often in Washington, the ratio is the reverse. Three of the attorneys made up for this small representation, though, by commanding the top staff positions: the director (L. Britt Snider, the former SSCI counsel and a Democrat), deputy director (John H. Moseman, a Republican and a former aide to Senator Frank H. Murkowski, R–AK), and general counsel (John B. Bellinger III, another Republican and a former aide to William H. Webster, the only DCI to have also served as FBI director). This legal troika would run the show at the staff level.

On the Church Committee, the staff had often split along the lines of lawyers and nonlawyers. As the committee's chief counsel, Frederick A. O. Schwarz Jr., once said to me about one of his staff assistants: "He has the kind of discipline I need. Lawyers do things in a certain way."[29] He was right. As I had observed during my years on Capitol Hill, attorneys have their own manner of thinking and ways of doing things. Their great strength is in organizing materials and events chronologically, then searching through documents to determine what the hard facts are in a case—obviously an important skill for any inquiry. Broader philosophical, historical, and moral issues, for which the historian and the social scientist have a heightened sensitivity, are sometimes pushed aside as the attorney—magnifying glass in hand—searches for cracks and crevices in the evidentiary trail. The differing methodologies and interests of the two groups can lead to tension and sometimes even estrangement.[30] There was nothing inevitable about this division, though, and I had seen both groups work together amiably on some projects taken up by the Church Committee (most notably, the probe into CIA assassination plots abroad); but unfortunately there was a tendency for the two groups to go their separate ways, even though commissions and committees benefit from a balanced integration of both perspectives.

My job on the staff was to work with Aspin to prepare him for meetings and hearings, to work with him on special projects, to help with the commission's research and writing, and to keep a history of the proceedings. He had telephoned me in Georgia on January 4, 1995, and asked playfully: "Where are you? Why aren't you serving your country?" These were welcome words, since I was beginning to wonder if he had forgotten about his earlier invitation for me to join the fray. I explained that I had to fulfill some obligations at the university, but that I could report for duty at the end of the month. We discussed a few projects he wanted me to work on, including research into the topic of "economic intelligence." The next day he added another subject to the list of research tasks he wanted me to address: an appraisal of the CIA's successes and failures in its analytic predictions about the Soviet Union during the Cold War. A few days later he called with yet another topic: "environmental intelligence." How good was the CIA at anticipating global strife as a result of environmental conditions, such as water shortages in nations in the Middle East? I was tempted to have my telephone disconnected before the list grew impossibly long.

During January 1995, as their security clearances were being checked by the FBI, the staff began to trickle into the commission's quarters in the modern New Executive Office Building (NEOB) on 17th Street, around the corner from the White House and well guarded by the Secret Service. As PFIAB's chairman, Aspin already had a spacious suite of offices in the Old Executive Office Building (OEOB), adjacent to the West Wing of the White House. In these early weeks, the staff leaders—most frequently, the legal triumvirate—shuttled between the two buildings for planning sessions with Aspin. The chairman spent much of his time making telephone calls around Washington and the country, consulting on intelligence topics with his wide network of contacts in the government, think tanks, and academe. The questions poured out of the commission chairman: What topics should we focus on? In what sequence? Who should we call as witnesses? Should we hold public hearings?

Aspin issued a steady flow of press releases to keep the media up to date on the commission's activities. (During his time on Capitol Hill, he had been ridiculed by some for being a media hound, determined to write a press release every day, and to hold hearings during holidays when a slow news period might encourage reporters to cover his committee work.) As January 1995 faded into February, he made himself available for media interviews and lectures to organizations interested in intelligence issues, beginning with an American Bar Association breakfast in January. Aspin summarized for the crowd of attorneys the commission's mandate—well beyond a narrow focus on Ames and Somalia. The panel, he said, was expected to address the question: "What happens to the intelligence community now that the Cold War is over and the Soviet empire has broken up?" The most important issue facing the commission was: "What is the intelligence community for?" He vowed to examine closely America's intelligence "targets, organizations, costs."[31]

As always with commissions, this one was constantly buffeted by external events. In December 1994, Jim Woolsey resigned from his DCI post, grumbling about a lack of access to President Clinton. Deteriorating relations with Congress doubtless added to his sense of frustration, as did a classified CIA inspector-general report critical of his failure to fire those who had been Ames's supervisors during his period of treachery. Thus, as the commission began its work, the intelligence community was without a director. The Clinton administration finally settled on Air Force General Michael P. C. Carns to replace Woolsey, but the candidate soon withdrew his name from Senate consideration under a cloud of innuendo about ethics. The next prospect, John M. Deutch, a former chemistry professor and provost at MIT, and at the time deputy secretary of defense, publicly balked at leaving his job at the Pentagon.

Whether or not the intelligence community had a leader in place, we were about to launch our inquiry. The initial gathering of the commissioners was scheduled for the first week of February in 1995.

<table>
<tr><td>CHAPTER 3</td><td>Seeking Answers
The Commission Convenes</td></tr>
</table>

O N FEBRUARY 3, 1995, OVER THREE MONTHS after its creation, the commission convened for its first session, held in suite 3201 of the New Executive Office Building at 725 17th Street. Beneath a cerulean blue sky, unusual for February in Washington, I made my way on foot from an apartment near Georgetown to the NEOB. Athens, Georgia, is a quiet, even bucolic place; in Washington, the streets were noisy and jammed with buses and cars. A grizzled middle-aged man was begging by the roadside, and a raggedly dressed old woman lay curled up in a sleeping bag on top of a subway grating, enveloped in dank clouds of steam from underground. The sirens of police cars and fire trucks filled the air throughout the day, punctuated by the incessant honking of taxicabs. On Pennsylvania Avenue, the sweet aroma of weed came from inside a bus-stop shelter where an emaciated man sprawled on a bench, sucking on the stub of a joint and watching with mild amusement as briefcase-toting bureaucrats raced by. Near the NEOB, a woman with several missing front teeth approached me and said, "I need a lawyer, man, I need a lawyer. You a lawyer?" I told her that I was not. She was certainly in the right town, though; a local newspaper had just reported that some thirty-three thousand attorneys labored in DC's legal vineyards.

Two of the commission members, Vice Chairman Rudman and Senator Exon, were absent when I arrived at the conference room on the third floor. The other commissioners talked amiably among themselves with an air of anticipation about the challenges before them. Some sipped coffee or snacked on donuts. Staff members chatted with them or leafed through the morning newspapers. A fly dozed on the ceiling.

After studying the commissioners' résumés and seeing some of them on the news, I now had a chance to meet them in person. The intelligence technocrats gathered in a corner of the conference room. General Allen, tall and bald, a red handkerchief peaking nattily from a breast pocket, was expounding on some technical issue to two sympathetic listeners: the trim and wise-looking Ann Caracristi, who wore an emerald hummingbird broach at her throat, and, next to her, a chunky, tanned, and smiling Bob Hermann. Like General Allen, Caracristi and Hermann had served together on PFIAB for years already, through the era of James Woolsey's tenure as DCI (1993–95). They had also worked with Allen at the National Security Agency on technical issues related to signals intelligence collection. This trio had a combined knowledge of sigint and satellite surveillance that would have been hard to match anywhere in the world. Allen and Hermann were in a festive mood; and Caracristi, though more reserved, was clearly pleased to be a part of the NSA class reunion.

Zoë Baird stood in another corner of the room. Dark-haired, pretty, and animated, she swapped stories with Harrington and Friedman—legal birds of a feather. Harrington, short and bespectacled, looking like a pharmacist who had somehow slipped into the NEOB, beamed back at Baird with the self-assurance of someone who had just broken the bank at Monte Carlo. I expected Friedman to be a fiercer specimen, given the tales of his wrestling prowess, but he was short, curly-haired, slight of build, and quiet. He had shed his sports coat, revealing a blue-striped shirt with rolled-up sleeves. A red-checkered handkerchief dangled from his back pocket, and he wore an elaborate chronograph watch. He looked more Jackson Hole than Wall Street. One had the sense that all three of these commissioners often used the word "summer" as a verb.

Wolfowitz, more than Friedman, qualified as Manhattan chic, wearing an expensive pin-striped suit, a Ralph Lauren tie, and gold cufflinks that flashed in the room's fluorescent lighting. He peered at the crowd over half-lens eyeglasses. I took the opportunity to introduce myself, observing that he and I were the only academics on the commission. "I'm not an academic," he replied, with a high-wattage, sardonic grin. "I'm an operator."

The congressional appointees gathered at the back of the room, with the exception of Pursley. Standing ramrod straight, the white-haired general with a West Point class ring had walked over to chat with the NSA contingent; in Allen, he had spotted Another Air Force general and West Point grad. Aside from Pursley, the presidential appointees and the congressional appointees stood apart and were beginning to look like two rival fraternities that had crashed the same party.

Even in a room full of politicians, Coelho's schmoozing skills stood out. A master of bonhomie, he worked the group of fellow lawmakers, both former and current, as if the commission's inaugural meeting were a fund-raising event. "Let's talk politics soon, over lunch," he said to Dicks, who seemed restless, ready to jump the line of scrimmage. Dicks's former linebacker muscles had grown soft, giving him the appearance more of a prosperous banker than an athlete; but his square jaw and hawk eyes suggested a powerful resolve.

Fowler and Goss were trading jokes. Fowler was relating how he and a friend had recently driven down to Atlanta from the north Georgia mountains. They passed through a county called Fayette and disagreed on how it was supposed to be pronounced, with an emphasis on the first or the second syllable—"Fáy-et" or "Fay-et"? Fowler had pulled into a fast-food restaurant to settle the wager. He asked the girl at the drive-through window how to pronounce the name of the place. To make sure these strangers would get it right, she replied slowly: "Bur-ger-King." Goss grinned.

Fowler had a high forehead, graying eyebrows, and a head full of wavy, graying hair. He had stripped off his suit jacket, revealing the slender carriage that had carried him to cross-country running championships in his school days. Goss reminded me of a riverboat gambler: suntanned, self-assured, and slightly bemused—someone accustomed to winning. His Brooks Brothers garb may have been frayed at the edges, but he owned a summer home on Fisher Island, a 575-acre gentleman's farm in Orange County, Virginia, and a sleek yacht moored at Sanibel Island.[1]

At six foot six, David Dewhurst was a towering presence in the room. His jet-black hair, combed straight back, framed a still youthful and handsome face. An expensively tailored business suit, starched shirt, and well-polished cowboy boots combined to create a Hollywood image of a Texas rancher with more than a few oil wells on the lower forty. I supposed that he had a ten-gallon hat in a Mercedes somewhere, or maybe in a big red pickup truck in the parking lot beneath the NEOB building. He didn't fit in with the rest of the commissioners, a gunman from out of town in a saloon filled with inside-the-beltway policy wonks.

Much of the informal conversation revolved around two topics. The first was the political tidal wave that had struck Washington, sweeping aside the Democrats on Capitol Hill and leaving the GOP in charge of lawmaking and oversight. The second was the ongoing search for a DCI to replace James Woolsey.

Overnight, congressional Democrats had been tossed from their high thrones into the dungeon of minority status. The House was now led by what

Congressional Quarterly called "a revolutionary leadership," with the strident Newt Gingrich of Georgia as Speaker.[2] It had been four decades since the GOP had last run the House, and they hadn't commanded the Senate since 1986. In the NEOB conference room, the Republican commissioners betrayed a note of gaiety in their voices, perhaps savoring their party's sudden ascendance. Leading up to this startling turn of events, Gingrich's anti-Democratic rhetoric had been inflammatory and relentless. A graduate of the Lee Atwater school of negative campaigning (Atwater was a GOP strategist from South Carolina who advocated dirt-road attack politics), Gingrich was a master at exaggerated rhetoric aimed at his rivals. Now he had an ideal platform—the Speakership—to carry on his crusade against the "Democrat party." An outbreak of partisan civil war on Capitol Hill seemed likely. I just hoped it would not spill over into the work of the commission.

As for Woolsey's replacement, the Clinton administration had reportedly struck out in its efforts to recruit either Deputy Secretary of Defense John Deutch or the former chair of the Joint Chiefs of Staff, Adm. William J. Crowe. Another choice, Deputy Attorney General Jamie Gorelick, was rejected by SSCI chair Senator Arlen Specter (R-PA). In turn, Specter's own candidate, Maurice R. "Hank" Greenberg, chairman of American International Group, had attracted little support from the White House.

In some ways Deutch would have been an ideal choice. He had served on PFIAB and knew a good deal about technical intelligence. Further, he was an expert on military hardware, including surveillance platforms (the satellites and reconnaissance aircraft used by the United States for spying). To top things off, he had been a close friend of Les Aspin's since their graduate-school days together at MIT; and he had much closer ties to President Clinton than Woolsey, since he had attended many NSC meetings with the president over the past two years in his capacity as deputy secretary of defense. Still, Deutch refused to budge. "I was enjoying my position in the Pentagon," he recalls, "enjoying it very much. I thought that we had a good team. We were working on some problems, working well. So I had no desire to change."[3]

Deutch felt, too, that the DCI job looked like one big headache. "The director doesn't really control many resources," he said, reflecting back. "The secretary of defense controls the resources." He continued: "The [intelligence] director has an ambiguous relationship to the other intelligence community agencies. The CIA is a troubled and confused agency. Jim Woolsey, who was my predecessor and a person I respect greatly, had terrible problems as director, and I didn't see why I was going to do any better. For all those reasons, I was very content to stay where I was."

The president's next choice, retired general Michael P. C. Carns, a former jet fighter pilot, was eventually rejected as a result of media reports about ethical improprieties during his military career, primarily bringing a Philippine domestic to the United States to work for his family, in violation of immigration laws (a variation of the problem that had ended Zoë Baird's bid for the attorney generalship). No one knew who would be called upon next to serve as DCI, or what the implications of this vacancy were for the work of the Aspin Commission. The administration was reportedly "at an impasse."[4]

I glanced over at Chairman Aspin, who was standing where Senator Warner had corralled him next to a photocopying machine. The Virginian was intently explaining something *soto voce*. Looking disheveled and a little overweight, as usual, Aspin peered at Warner through thick, round brown-rimmed glasses, nodded his head several times, then took a seat at the head of the long oval table in the room. He called the meeting to order, and the commissioners seated themselves, with the staff taking places in chairs behind them. Aspin cheerfully welcomed everyone and began the session with a brief history of the commission's origins. He skated over his protracted negotiations with Senator Warner in the lead-up to its creation. Saying nothing about Somalia, he mentioned the Ames case and rumors of financial misman-agement at the NRO. "We're going to have to make some tough decisions about what to leave out [of the commission's report]," he said. "Otherwise, we are going to get swamped." He wanted the commission to work together as a group, rather than divide into subcommittees or task forces, "partly because so many of the pieces of this puzzle are mutually interdependent." Less long-winded than most politicians, he soon stopped and opened the floor for comments.

Representative Dicks needed no urging. "We need to downsize and restructure the intelligence community," he declared. He referred to the Goldwater-Nichols Act, which in 1985 had helped to re-organize and unify the military services. He cited it as a prototype to remedy the institutional fragmentation that plagued the government's secret agencies.[5] His HPSCI colleague, Porter Goss, jumped in next, warning that some people on the Hill wanted to slash the intelligence budget; it would be up to the commission to demonstrate the foolishness of that idea.

Staking out his position in favor of the status quo early on, Warner joined Goss in expressing concern that some lawmakers were intent on a "major raid" against the spy budget. "That would be unwise," he cautioned. He referred to intelligence as a "force multiplier," indicating that in a time of funding reductions in the Department of Defense, good intelligence would permit the military "to do more, smartly, and with a smaller number of troops." In time of war, for example, intelligence could direct the Pentagon's shrinking arsenal of "smart bombs" more precisely and efficiently to their intended targets.

In response to a question from Coelho about the result of the commission's labors, Aspin predicted that its findings could be translated into new executive orders and budget directives, as well as possible legislation. Fowler observed, delicately, that some members of the commission might not understand the entire intelligence system. He urged the chairman to set up a series of briefings for the less seasoned panel members.

As the commissioners discussed their objectives and likely witnesses to appear before the panel, Anthony Lake, the national security adviser, arrived at the conference room. Aspin had invited him to come by if the press of business in the West Wing that day permitted. Thin, pale skinned, and bright eyed, Lake looked like a professor who had been spending too much time in the library. He presented a list of topics he said ought to be central to the commission's work. At the top of the list were two questions: Did we have the right structure for the intelligence community? And: Were we keeping up with technological advances?

The national security advisor mentioned, as well, the importance of improving human intelligence (humint), along with the need for more efficient spending on intelligence and a strengthening of counterintelligence. He informed the commissioners that President Clinton would soon name a new DCI to replace the departed Woolsey, and that Clinton would issue a presidential decision directive (PDD)—number 35, entitled "Intelligence Priorities"—laying out a hierarchy of global information requirements for his administration. PDD-35 was the culmination of two years' worth of NSC staff work, guided by George Tenet, the senior intelligence officer on the Council's staff. It would underscore the administration's foremost intelligence priority, Lake said, namely: support to military operations "wherever U.S. forces are deployed."

Lake added that the incoming DCI would most likely also have some thoughts about plans for intelligence reform, rather than remaining (in Lake's phrase) "brain dead" until the commission completed its work in March of 1996. "We believe the new DCI must move forward in changing the community and can't wait for the commission to report," he said. This sounded to me like a prescription for conflict between commissioners and the new intelligence chief, whoever he or she might be. I looked over at Aspin, who stared down at his notepad, expressionless, doodling on a yellow pad of paper as the national security advisor made these pronouncements.

When Lake departed, the discussion turned to the question of which people the commission should interview about the challenges confronting the secret agencies. A raft of suggestions for "witnesses" came forward from the commissioners, including the usual suspects in Washington: current and former national security elites, such as the two-time national security advisor Brent Scowcroft. "We should also hear from people who think the agencies are doing well as is," General Pursley argued in another nod toward the status quo.

The meeting seemed to be winding down, and Warner, speaking in his signature grave manner with Moses-like authority, looked down the length of the table at Aspin and said: "You must be the leader. First, we should focus on getting everyone up to speed. Second, you should draft some of your ideas and put them on the table for the rest of the commissioners to respond." Aspin agreed, and, wrapping up the session, he reminded commissioners and staff that no one—absolutely no one—should talk to the press, other than the chairman or the vice chairman. It was the same rule we had adopted on the Church Committee in 1975; otherwise, investigative panels fly apart, with leaks to the media right and left, followed by internal dissension.

Planning

Aspin's main concern in these early weeks was figuring out how the commission's work should be organized. For help, he turned to friends at the RAND (short for "Research and Development") Corporation, a think tank with headquarters in Santa Monica and a division in Washington, DC. It engaged chiefly in research projects for the Department of Defense, but was always on the outlook for consulting fees elsewhere. The intelligence inquiry offered a perfect opportunity for a symbiotic relationship between RAND and the commission. RAND saw the commission as a fresh source of government funding, its lifeblood, and Aspin believed that RAND's brainpower could help him structure the work of the commission. He asked the RAND division in DC to set up a series of strategy sessions; the search was on for an analytic framework to guide our work through the next year. "What should the intelligence community be doing now that the Cold War is over?"—this was the cardinal question that Aspin posed in a January memo to RAND experts, echoing a speech he had given at an American Bar Association breakfast earlier that month.

Analysts at RAND have their own particular algorithms. They are fond of exercises that start with a clean piece of paper, looking at a problem anew as if it had just been pulled out of the earth, unwashed, unpeeled, and uncooked. "How would we do this better if we could start over?" is a favorite question posed by RAND analysts. This approach can be useful for stimulating fresh thinking about possible reforms; but, as former DCI Robert M. Gates (1991–93) observed, "You don't start with a clean piece of paper. You can't. There is too much experience and too much that's gone past."[6] The former acting DCI Adm. William O. Studeman further noted: "If they [members of the commission] came up with a clean sheet of paper . . . there would have been hell to execute it, given what have been the lack of money and the resistance of the IC [intelligence community] cultures."[7]

———

"There's good news and bad news," Aspin said when he and a couple of his aides met with the RAND staff in early February of 1995 at the think tank's offices in downtown Washington. (The organization has since moved to Virginia.) The good news was that reform was likely to happen because so many people had an interest in it, as demonstrated by HPSCI's "IC21" project and the lively concern for the subject within the White House—if not in the Oval Office, at least with Vice President Gore and security advisor Lake. The bad news was that all of these parties might go off in different directions, fragmenting the reform efforts.

Some people have personal trainers or psychoanalysts; Aspin relied on RAND for logic therapy. Adopting the tone of an advanced graduate seminar on intelligence (interspersed with such quintessential RAND jargon as "tilting the matrix" and "by orders of magnitude"), the commission chairman and his senior staff exchanged views throughout the morning with the think-tank specialists on how the commission should proceed. For RAND, it was imperative that the panel establish a "baseline"—a firm understanding of how the intelligence agencies currently do their work. Then commissioners could appraise what changes were necessary, matching the baseline against a wide range of reform proposals.

Aspin agreed, and added: "We've got to establish intelligence targeting priorities." This was a "first order issue," in his view, along with organizational reform and prudent intelligence spending. "What is the target list?" he asked. "If we don't get this right, the CIA will be bitten in the ass by all kinds of people in the media who claim the Agency has had an intelligence failure on this or that." He paused, then conceded in a raised voice and with a sense of exasperation: "*I don't know what the fuck the priorities are!*" His candor brought laughter in the room. The chairman continued: "You can't just go to the policy makers and ask them. Hell, they don't know either."

He recalled his experience as SecDef and the unexpected "pop up," as he put it, of the African nation Rwanda as an intelligence target in 1994. "When I became secretary of defense, I served several months without ever giving Rwanda a thought. Then, for several weeks, that's all I thought about. After that, it fell abruptly off the screen and I never again thought about Rwanda."[8] The African nation had become the "flavor of the month" for policy makers, and, in turn, intelligence officers scrambled to meet the information needs of Secretary Aspin and others about the why exactly Rwanda was in turmoil. Similarly, two decades earlier, in 1963, how many policy makers in Washington had anticipated that within a year Vietnam would become one of the most important intelligence priorities for the United States, and would remain so for a decade? Very few, if any.

In response to Aspin's questions, the RAND experts argued that the CIA didn't have to know about everything, but did need to have the capacity to mobilize information in a hurry, with access to the fax and telephone numbers of the nation's top experts. The Agency needed to have agile resources able to respond to new flavors of the month. In short, it needed Rolodex intelligence. Furthermore, the RAND experts stressed, it would be useful for the commission to define the universe of subjects for which the intelligence community was responsible, instead of relying on the vague "threat assessment" or "targeting list" currently used. Aspin mentioned that he had just discussed the subject of intelligence tasking with Bob Gates. The former DCI had recommended the use of an occasional "requirements review"—essentially, periodic discussions between senior policy makers and intelligence managers that would update what targets were of highest priority.

Of concern, too, was another first-order issue: how to organize the intelligence agencies. Of the thirteen major American intelligence entities that existed in 1994 (today there are sixteen), eight were housed within the organizational framework of the Department of Defense, four in civilian policy departments, and one—the CIA—stood alone as an independent agency. As the Herblock cartoon in Figure 3.1 depicts, the intelligence community had evolved in fits and starts, with agencies added on from time to time, and with no attempt at rational integration of the new organizations. Their jerry-built construction seemed in desperate need of reform.

The military intelligence agencies included the NSA, with its sigint mission; the Central Imagery Office (CIO), dedicated to the gathering of photographic or "imagery" intelligence from cameras mounted on spy satellites and lower-altitude reconnaissance aircraft; the National Reconnaissance Office, which supervises the construction, launching, and maintenance of the nation's spy satellites; the Defense Intelligence Agency (DIA), involved in writing assessments about military-related subjects; and the intelligence units of the

"WHAT WE NEED IS AN ARCHITECT"

FIGURE 3.1 Herblock on the U.S. Intelligence Community in 1994
Source: Herblock Cartoon, *Washington Post,* December 30, 1994.
Copyright by the Herb Block Foundation and used with permission.

respective branches of the armed forces, each preoccupied with collecting and analyzing tactical intelligence from theaters overseas where U.S. personnel serve in uniform. Together, the NSA, CIO, NRO, DIA, and the four service intelligence units accounted for some 85 percent of the total annual U.S. intelligence budget—about $28 billion per year at the end of the Cold War—and employed around 85 percent of the nation's espionage personnel.[9] (See Figure 3.2 for an organizational blueprint of the intelligence community in 1994.)

On the civilian side, in 1994 the four major intelligence agencies included the FBI, located in the Justice Department and assigned with both a counterintelligence and a counterterrorism mission (along with its law enforcement responsibilities); the Treasury Department Office of Intelligence Support, which concentrates on a variety of global financial topics, such as tracing the flow of petrodollars and the hidden funds of terrorist organizations; the State Department's Bureau of Intelligence and Research (INR), the smallest of the secret agencies, but one of the most highly regarded, in part because of its talented corps of foreign service officers; and the Energy

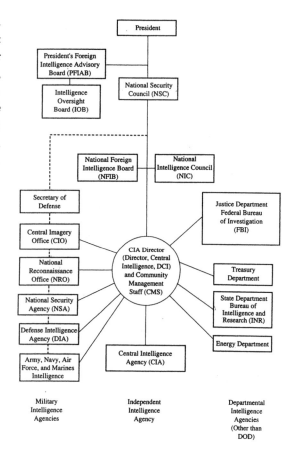

FIGURE 3.2 The U.S. Intelligence Community at the End of the Cold War Source: Loch K. Johnson, *Secret Agencies: U.S. Intelligence in a Hostile World* (New Haven: CT: Yale University Press, 1996), p. 10.

Department's Office of Intelligence and Counterintelligence, which tracks the worldwide movement of nuclear materials (such as uranium, plutonium, heavy water, and nuclear-reactor parts) and maintains security at the nation's weapons laboratories.

One other agency, the CIA, is also civilian in character, but is located outside the framework of the policy-oriented cabinet. During the Cold War, the Agency held a special cachet as the only espionage organization formally established by the National Security Act of 1947. More important still, it became the place where the Director of Central Intelligence, or DCI—the titular leader of all the intelligence agencies—hung his hat (no woman has held that position), in a suite of offices on the seventh floor of the Agency's Old Headquarters Building in Langley, part of McLean, Virginia.[10]

As the names imply, the *Central* Intelligence Agency and the Director of *Central* Intelligence were meant to be the heart of the intelligence establishment, playing the role of coordinators for the community's activities and the collators of its "all-source" (all-agency) reports, in an otherwise highly fragmented mélange of spy organizations.[11] R. James Woolsey, who held the position of DCI during the early years of the Clinton administration, has described the role of America's intelligence chief: "You're kind of chairman and CEO of the CIA," he said, "and you're kind of chairman of the board of the intelligence community."[12] He emphasized, though, that the director does not have the authority to give "rudder orders" to the heads of the various intelligence agencies. (Woolsey served for a time as under secretary of the Navy). Rather, he went on, "it's more subtle"—a matter of personal relationships, conversations, and gentle persuasion.

The CIA's organizational framework, as it stood in 1994, is presented in Figure 3.3. Adm. Stansfield Turner, who served as DCI during the Carter years (1977–81), once referred to the four directorates within the Agency—at the time: Operations, Administration, Science and Technology, and Intelligence—as "separate baronies." He was underscoring the point that the CIA has several different cultures within its walls that are not always in harmony with one another, or with the Agency's leadership cadre on the seventh floor.[13]

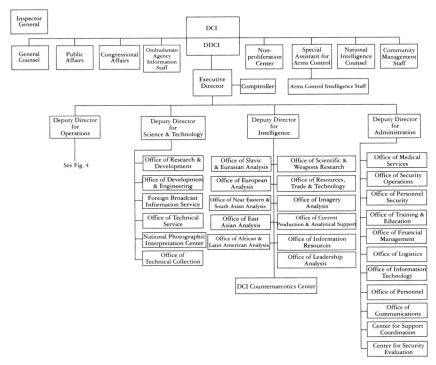

FIGURE 3.3 The Central Intelligence Agency at the End of the Cold War
Source: Adapted from Loch K. Johnson, *Secret Agencies: U.S. Intelligence in a Hostile World* (New Haven, CT: Yale University Press, 1996), pp. 8–9.

Aspin brought up this particular problem at the meeting with the RAND experts: How do we overcome the challenge of the "gorillas in the stove-pipes"? This was another bit of professional jargon that referred to the habit of individual intelligence agencies acting as if they were in isolated "stove-pipes," under the leadership of their own strong program managers—the "gorillas," such as the directors of NSA or NRO—beyond the control of the DCI. I was seated next to Aspin, and I watched him jot down on his notepad: "Do we need a Director of National Intelligence?"

Inevitably, the subject of money came up. The $28 billion for the intelligence agencies was divided among the National Intelligence Program (NIP, where the most well known of the secret agencies are located), the Joint Military Intelligence Program (JMIP, a few military units that respond to national intelligence needs, as opposed to the needs of a particular military service), and Tactical Intelligence and Related Activities (TIARA, the intelligence programs of the four military services).[14] Was it possible for the United States to reap a "peace dividend" by taking a meat cleaver to the Cold War defense and intelligence budgets, using the savings to pay for pressing domestic programs such as education reform and health care? During the session with RAND, Aspin tipped his hand about his own preferred approach to the intelligence budget—the last of the first-order topics on his personal list. He wanted to "squeeze the water out" by consolidating the number of surveillance satellites on the drawing board, and by reducing duplication in the activities of the secret agencies. The chairman also thought that improved liaison relations with the intelligence services of friendly foreign nations would help America develop a better understanding of ongoing world affairs. The globe was too large for America's espionage agencies to cover alone; improved "burden sharing" would have to be part of the answer. This, too, could reduce intelligence costs for the United States.

In Aspin's view, the overarching question about the budget was: had the old world (the Cold War) been more expensive or less expensive than the new world? In the old world, the United States had just one main target: the USSR, and it was easy to locate. Now we had a multitude of lesser targets, including terrorist groups that were as elusive as ghosts and dangerous as vipers. It has become a commonplace among intelligence officers to note that the old enemy was easy to find but hard to kill, while the new enemy is hard to find but easy to kill. As DCI Woolsey observed soon after the end of the Cold War, the United States had slain the Soviet dragon, but "we live now in a jungle filled with a bewildering variety of poisonous snakes."[15] However much prelapsarians might have longed for a new and peaceful era after the demise of the Soviet Union, realists properly anticipated a future still dark and filled with danger. Did we need a huge intelligence apparatus to track all of these new threats; or, as one senior intelligence officer had argued to me some years back, should we have a spy capability more along the lines of the British model As he put it: "Small, efficient, a few good—very good—spies, small budget, some military gear"?[16]

Aspin had in mind a set of second and third-order issues, as well. Collection, analysis, processing, and dissemination were his foremost second-order topics—the elements of the intelligence cycle, a concept used by intelligence officers to describe the pathway of information from the time of its collection in the field through its dissemination to decision makers. The overarching purpose was to provide the president and other top officials with a decision advantage enhanced by reliable, timely information[17] (see Figure 3.4.). Stated simply, the main purpose of intelligence is to provide information to the president and other policy officials that may help illuminate their decision options—"eliminating or reducing uncertainty for government decision-makers," as a leading intelligence professional has defined the goal.[18] The assumption is that good—that is, accurate, comprehensive, and timely—information will allow the president and other officials to make more effective choices. "A sensible nation will seek to be as well informed as possible about its opponents, potential or otherwise," a seasoned British intelligence expert once observed, adding: "and, for that matter, its friends."[19] Of course, policy makers receive information from a variety of sources, not just the nation's secret agencies; intelligence is but

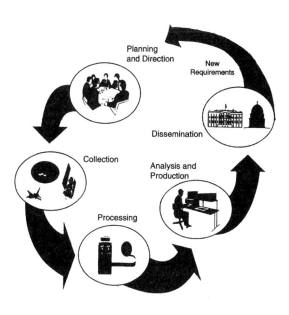

FIGURE 3.4 The Intelligence Cycle Source: Adapted from *Factbook on Intelligence* (Washington, DC: Office of Public Affairs, Central Intelligence Agency, 1993), p. 14

Planning and Direction

New Requirements

Dissemination

Collection

Analysis and Production

Processing

one, current, albeit sometimes a vital one, in the "river of information" that flows through Washington, DC.[20]

Although it is easy enough to state the purpose of intelligence, the challenge of actually gathering, assessing, and delivering useful information to policy makers is an intricate business, with many opportunities for error. One objective of this book is to provide a sense of what the investigators into the 9/11 attacks never really explained sufficiently to the public: the many pitfalls in the conduct of intelligence that make some degree of failure inevitable.[21] Despite the inherent impossibility of perfect intelligence, it is nonetheless feasible to reduce the frequency and severity of mistakes; therefore, another objective throughout this work is to explore the subject of intelligence reform to see how the performance of America's intelligence agencies can be improved. Despite its oversimplification of a complex process, the idea of the intelligence cycle offers a useful analytic construct for understanding how the secret agencies gather, interpret, and disseminate information—often called "collection and analysis," for short, and considered the most important obligation of the intelligence community.

Looming large in Aspin's mind as he traded ideas with the RAND specialists was the question of how to strengthen relationships between the producers of intelligence (the secret agencies) and the consumers (the decision makers). All too often, those in policy positions claim not to know a single intelligence analyst personally, and therefore they never seek information from analysts about world affairs; on the other side, intelligence officers often never bother to find out what decision makers want to know and instead simply send them whatever information they think might be useful—maybe a research topic of personal interest. The CIA analyst might be working on the question of excessive vodka consumption among males in Outer Mongolia, whereas the decision maker's in-box is filled with problems related to Iraq, Iran, North Korea, and Burundi. Somehow this gap in priorities has to be bridged if the intelligence agencies are going to be of any practical use to those in high office.[22]

The third-order topics on Aspin's list included covert action, counterintelligence, liaison with foreign intelligence services, the recruitment of the brightest young Americans into the intelligence services, and accountability. One of the subjects that I thought was of greatest importance—accountability—had come in last among the third-order topics by my own boss's reckoning! My recent talks with Aspin on the topic of intelligence accountability had been depressing. Once he had been a champion of rigorous intelligence oversight; now he wondered aloud whether lawmakers had become micromanagers, stifling the initiative of the secret agencies. It sounded like some of the polemics I had been reading by right-wingers who believed in an unfettered presidency, with Congress serving (at best) as a cheerleader on the sidelines.[23] It wasn't the risk of micromanagement that concerned me the most, but rather the question of why lawmakers had largely failed to provide effective supervision over the intelligence agencies—as if Operation CHAOS and COINTELPRO, improper domestic espionage activities investigated by the Church Committee in 1975, had never happened.

Counterintelligence didn't rank much higher on Aspin's list of priorities, despite Ames. He relegated this subject as well to the third order of commission priorities. Covert action struck me as another odd third-order choice, since it had gotten the CIA and the United States into so much trouble over the years—at the Bay of Pigs, for example, to name the most obvious "covert" disaster that didn't stay covert very long. I knew Wyche Fowler would be far less blasé about the subjects of accountability and covert action, and I imagined other commissioners would have a list of their own top priorities—counterintelligence, for one—that could be quite different from the chairman's.

The "seminar" ended with Aspin issuing a clear directive to RAND: build a baseline for the commissioners. I knew, and he knew, that the commission's staff would be working on this assignment, too, but it wouldn't hurt to see what RAND came up with. Aspin was a firm believer in "competitive analysis": having a number of people working on the same problem separately, then comparing notes and adopting the strongest parts of each interpretation. It was an approach to governance favored by President Franklin D. Roosevelt, and is referred to by political scientists as "competitive administration."

———

The deep thinkers at RAND were not the only sources of advice pouring into the commission. In January and February of 1995, we averaged about six hundred telephone calls a day from individuals (frequently job seekers), each offering guidance on how the commissioners should proceed. A similar downpour of mail fell on our offices, some from distinguished retired generals and admirals with helpful suggestions, others from citizens worried about their civil liberties, and a few from cranks and outright nutcases. Think tanks and beltway bandits turned up on the NEOB doorstep in search of government contracts, armed with fancy, four-color briefing books on how they would organize the panel's work. Especially impressive was a set of documents and briefing overheads presented to the commission by Dr. Paula Scalingi, director of the Decision and Information Sciences Division at the Argonne National Laboratory, near Chicago. Many of the ideas offered by

Dr. Scalingi and others were sound; but none of these thoughtful policy entrepreneurs enjoyed the close ties with Les Aspin that the RAND Corporation had developed over the years. Aspin turned to RAND's analysts as the chief outside consultants to the commission.

Credible study groups interested in intelligence reform sprang up, as well, during late 1994 and the early months of 1995, including forums at Georgetown University in Washington, DC, and at the Council of Foreign Relations in New York City. The Georgetown group provided the commission, and any other interested party, with an impressive early checklist of recommended reforms, high among them the consolidation of the nation's military intelligence agencies.[24]

By the end of February, the commission staff had drafted a tentative "scope paper." It was designed to plot out the boundaries of the inquiry; working in harness with the RAND consultants, we had developed the "baseline" document that Aspin sought. The framework consisted of four guiding questions, presented in logical progression:

1. What are the intelligence needs of the United States in the post–Cold War world?
2. What are the intelligence capabilities necessary for collecting, analyzing, and disseminating such information?
3. To what extent do existing intelligence capabilities correspond to those needed to satisfy future requirements for global information?
4. To the extent that existing capabilities fall short, what changes— organizational, managerial, programmatic, or budgetary—should be made?

Finding answers to these questions became the commission staff's abiding concern, which in turn led them to prepare (in telephone consultations with commissioners) long lists of specialists inside and outside the government who could help guide us. Further, the staff initiated requests that went to each of the intelligence agencies, asking them to provide documents that explained their individual baseline activities and budgets. During this period, RAND forwarded to us the first of many project memoranda designed to assist the commission in its planning. According to the memo, the central question the commission should keep coming back to as it worked through its agenda was *"how to make intelligence both more useful to customers, and more used by them."*[25]

The RAND consultants also came quickly to the crux of the organizational dilemma facing the DCI: "The current intelligence system is organized and dominated by the owners of collection systems," the memo went on,

"—that is, by the suppliers."[26] Here were the gorillas in the stovepipes who had undermined the centralized coordination of intelligence that President Truman initially sought when he endorsed the creation of a *Central* Intelligence Agency in 1947.[27] It was a dilemma that had continued to haunt the nation's DCIs over the years—and now haunted the Aspin Commission. Surely we had to do something about structural reform of the community; as things stood, information was simply not being shared well among the thirteen agencies. The sharing of information struck us as the first step toward a more integrated intelligence community (the same conclusion the 9/11 Commission would reach almost a decade later in 2004[28]).

A friend of mine from high school days at a U.S. military base in West Germany, Lt. Gen. James R. Clapper Jr. had climbed to a high intelligence perch in Washington, serving as director of the Defense Intelligence Agency at the time of the Aspin Commission inquiry. (In 2010, he would become director of national intelligence.) He corroborated my argument on the need for organizational change. "Structural reform is necessary," he said to me over the telephone in January, "and the intelligence community is incapable of reforming itself."[29]

––––––

On March 1, 1995, the staff held its first formal meeting, with Aspin presiding—the only commissioner present. The chairman wore a nicely cut dark-gray suit in need of ironing, a new blue shirt, and an expensive Italian tie. His hair was thin and gray, as it had been for years, and his face clean shaven. With gray-flecked eyes that sparkled with intelligence, he examined the staff through his large-framed glasses. In light of his heart problems, I wondered how he was holding up under the strain of starting up a commission. He seemed to be in a good mood, but looked tired and wan. He began the meeting by "reviewing the bidding," as he phrased it—that is, explaining the origins and purposes of the hybrid executive-legislative panel.

"At first, PFIAB alone was going to do this," the chairman noted, "but Warner needed a combined PFIAB-congressional panel to head off [Senator Daniel Patrick] Moynihan and keep the CIA's budget intact." He reprised the good news/bad news remarks he had made at RAND. "Changes are likely to happen," he said, going on to emphasize that the commission would not just be presenting its recommendations, but trying to implement them through executive orders and legislation. His comments, which had devolved into a pep talk, lasted only a few minutes and ended with the upbeat prediction that "we are going to learn a great deal as individuals, and do some good things."

Drinking coffee from a cup with a CIA logo, staff director L. Britt Snider announced that questions of oversight—holding the secret agencies accountable and within the rule of law—were off the table. That challenge would be left to others (presumable SSCI and HPSCI) to work out, while the commission concentrated on how to improve intelligence gathering, analysis, and dissemination (the intelligence cycle). A wave of disappointment washed over me. The Church Committee had demonstrated in 1975 that accountability was vital to maintaining the integrity of the intelligence agencies. To ignore this dimension was like trying to improve the performance of a police department without examining how to keep cops from abusing their authority.

I presumed that Snider and Aspin had decided not to take on oversight because this would mean criticizing lawmakers for being negligent in these responsibilities—the very people we would have to rely on to help carry out whatever reform proposals the commission settled upon. I could see the politics of this well enough, but that was an insufficient reason for abandoning one of the most vital pieces of intelligence reform.[30] In 2004, the Kean Commission on 9/11 would come to a similar finding. It acknowledged that intelligence oversight on the Hill had become "dysfunctional," yet it did nothing to investigate why, or what could be done about this lapse—and failed to hold even a single hearing on the subject.[31]

Snider underscored the point that we were not going to be advocates. Rather, the commission's job would be to "look at the big picture" and to be "honest brokers." Our task was to determine "what the problems are." That seemed right, except for one thing: surely we were going to have to come up with some solutions, too, and didn't that mean advocacy? The euphoric first formal staff meeting and associated pep talk was not the time for raising such vexing questions, it appeared; still, we obviously had some more thinking to do about our goals. Turning to the anticipated schedule, Snider observed that throughout most of 1995 the commission would go through a "discovery phase," which would include a series of interviews, briefings, and formal hearings with experts. One of our assignments was to make a formal roster of experts and practitioners whom the commissioners and staff ought to interview about intelligence issues. To write a solid report, we first had to educate ourselves further.

Thus began a series of staff meetings, usually once a week, occasionally with Aspin presiding, but more often Snider. Now and then, RAND experts would sit in, and occasionally, and awkwardly, a PFIAB member not among the president's official appointees (usually Maurice Sonnenberg) would drop in to offer views on intelligence reform. In the absence of commissioners, the staff meetings often became a free-for-all featuring exhilarating no-holds-barred debates about important intelligence topics. We were free to run with the hare or hunt with the hounds.

"The NSA is like a huge vacuum cleaner," complained a staffer at one of the meetings. "It collects way too much information."

"Which is to say 'NSA sucks,'" suggested another with a smirk, before the former NSA officers on the staff came to their agency's defense.

During one of our early gatherings, the staff director invoked Warner's chief objective for the commission: Moynihan's call for the abolition of the CIA had to be rebuffed. "Our goal is to *sell* intelligence," Snider proclaimed. "We have to establish a political consensus in the country favoring intelligence."

Snider was not always in agreement with Senator Warner. For one thing, Warner was a Republican, and Snider had a long history of working for Democrats. Yet the staff director had begun to behave like a Warner surrogate as he echoed the theme the Virginia senator had espoused to Aspin and other commissioners. The theme was not without merit: we had an obligation to reassure the American people about the value of the intelligence agencies—what President George H. W. Bush (himself a former DCI) frequently referred to as the nation's "first line of defense." But that was only half of the equation. The other half, I thought, should consist of a candid appraisal of flaws in the intelligence system, and how they might be corrected. I hoped that as we moved along we could achieve a proper balance between the need to sell and the need to reform.[32]

———

By the end of April, the staff had conducted sixty-six interviews, mostly with intelligence officers, but also with a wide range of policy makers, academics, and Hill staffers. Businesspeople were on our list, as well, reflecting the interest in economic intelligence that had become fashionable in Washington, fueled by concern over the 1994 financial crisis in Mexico that threatened to damage our own economy. Plus, "commercial activity" was on our list of mandated topics to study. On the staff, we were beginning to see the outlines of some major shortcomings in the state of intelligence. For starters, the budget process in this secret domain was a morass with little overall account-ability. The DCI had minimal authority to coordinate spending among the thirteen secret agencies. "Strange" was how Snider described the spy budget process at our second staff meeting in March.

Further, it was obvious that since the end of the Cold War, the intel-ligence community was staggering under the weight of many requests for information about many targets. "We shouldn't have to track Norwegian whaling activities—or the Burundian navy," one exasperated intelligence officer said to us, only half joking. Vice President Gore was interested in using surveillance satellites to monitor the migration of whales; and Burundi is a landlocked African nation with only a few boats on Lake Tanganyika. We got the point. When I mentioned this to Aspin, he replied: "We need a good 'no shit' set of targets. This may require new collection systems, and we need to figure out what kinds of new systems we may need."

Early on, the staff recommended to the chairman an organizational strategy adopted by the Church Committee in 1975 and one that I had suggested to him when the idea of a commission first emerged. Instead of trying to involve all the staff and commissioners in every phase of the work before us, we could divide ourselves into task forces. Although at the first meeting of the commission, he had discouraged this approach in favor of commission unity, he now began to see the merit of some division of labor, and eleven task forces soon took shape on the following topics:

1. Needs and Priorities: the targeting task force, meant to address the question of what threats the nation faced.
2. Macro-Organizational Issues: the possibility of strengthening the authority of the DCI.
3. Military Intelligence Restructuring: Should there be a director of military intelligence?
4. Analysis and Production: improving the quality of intelligence reporting to policy makers.
5. Programmatic Change in the Imagery Area: Did we have the right mix of "imint" (imagery intelligence) platforms?
6. Programmatic Change in Sigint: Did we have the right mix of signals intelligence collection systems?
7. New Ways of Doing Business: Did we need new technologies and more outsourcing to the private sector?
8. The Budget Process: all the spending issues.
9. International: the question of liaison with foreign intelligence services, as well as the matter of whether the United States should assist the UN with its intelligence needs—a highly charged political issue for some lawmakers.
10. Personnel Policies: Should there be a downsizing of the intelligence work force?
11. "Cats and Dogs": whatever else we needed to think about.

The "cats and dogs" task force would serve as a catchall category that would include such matters as counterintelligence and covert action—the chairman's third-order priorities—and, I hoped, at least some attention to accountability.

Snider and his legal team of two other attorneys began to organize the task forces, talking individually with commissioners about their own particular interests. We soon discovered that the commissioners did not wish to be put into separate boxes; they wanted the freedom to engage in all of the work as the commission moved forward, just as Aspin had originally envisioned. We reached a compromise: we would have task forces to help organize the work, but commissioners could join as many—or as few—as they wanted.

In the meantime, as these organizational details were being worked out, I immersed myself in writing research papers for Aspin, beginning with an appraisal of how well the CIA had performed in forecasting the end of the Cold War, followed up by a broader examination of the Agency's analytic successes and failures against the Soviet target. These were not easy assignments. In search of answers, I spent much of my time going through CIA documents and interviewing top-level analysts around the intelligence community. I found out that, contrary to Senator Moynihan's allegations, the CIA had done a reasonably good job of tracking the decline of the Soviet economy during the 1980s, as well as the concomitant rise in political instability inside Russia and its satellite nations in European Europe.[33] These analytic conclusions reached by the CIA's Soviet experts—the Office of Soviet Analysis (SOVA) in the Directorate of Intelligence—were largely rebuffed by the first Bush administration, and even by the DCI, Robert M. Gates, a Soviet specialist. The administration and Gates remained convinced that Soviet President Mikhail Gorbachev was part of the Old Guard, merely intent on lulling the United States into believing that genuine reform might occur in the USSR.

True, the CIA's SOVA analysts never pinpointed the exact day that the Soviet Union would disintegrate, but they did warn that its economy was in a state of acute distress, and that genuine reform was likely—again, an estimate the first Bush Administration and DCI Gates initially dismissed. By the beginning of 1991, SOVA analysts were forecasting serious political upheaval in the USSR that could even lead to a coup. "The current political system in the Soviet Union is doomed," warned analysts in May of 1991. Still, the administration refused to believe that deep change was coming. On August 18, 1991, Soviet military officers led a *putsch* against President Mikhail Gorbachev; it failed, but the attempt sealed the fate of the old Soviet regime. The SOVA experts had not predicted this precise event, but they had alerted the White House to the deteriorating conditions in the Soviet empire and the likelihood of major social unrest. No one in the world, even inside the Kremlin, had precisely predicted the stunning events that actually occurred, leading to the end of the Soviet empire.

As for the CIA's analytic record throughout the Cold War, I documented for Aspin a substantial list of successes and failures. The Agency had properly anticipated, for example, the Soviet launching of Sputnik in 1957, the Sino-Soviet chasm in 1962, and the creation of a Soviet antiballistic missile (ABM) system in 1968. In addition to these successes, I reminded Aspin that CIA analysts had been unable to forecast the Soviet placement of nuclear-tipped missiles in Cuba in 1962, its invasion of Hungary in 1956 and Czechoslovakia in 1968, or the rapid expansion of its ICBM force in the 1960s.[34] Further, the intelligence community seemed to oscillate between underestimating, then overestimating, the production levels of Soviet weapons.

While poring over this data, Aspin and I discerned a rising accuracy in U.S. intelligence reports about the numbers and capabilities of Soviet weaponry as our collection "platforms" (satellites and reconnaissance aircraft) became more sophisticated during the 1970s and 1980s. What didn't change much was our inability to fathom, with any precision, the *intentions* of our adversaries in Moscow. (Recently, a former acting director of central intelligence, John McLaughlin, would note that we knew the Soviets's capabilities but not their intentions, whereas today we know the terrorists' intentions but not their capabilities.[35]) Machines were of little help in this regard. A good recent example is the difficulty of figuring out what makes the eccentric leader of North Korea, Kim Jong Il, tick. That would require a CIA asset (a local agent recruited by the Agency) close to him, ideally a board-certified psychiatrist with access to the Great Leader.

Over take-out lunches in Aspin's PFIAB office, we discussed the papers I prepared after each was finished. Sometimes we would head for the McDonald's around the corner on 17th Street and engage in one of Aspin's favorite pastimes: eating hamburgers and fries while debating how to improve America's security (all at an abstract level, of course, mindful that classified information was not to be discussed in restaurants). It was amusing to watch a former secretary of defense dining out at McDonald's. Most Washington VIPs at Aspin's level sat in posh French restaurants around town, feigning attention to lobbyists who were going to pick up the sizable bill when the last drop of Beaujolais was poured. But he was, after all, a blue-collar guy from Milwaukee and had few pretensions—a large part of his charm. I was personally glad we weren't going to expensive restaurants, because Aspin never seemed to have any money with him. McDonald's I could afford, at least now and then.

As the weeks passed, he asked me for additional papers, including one on intelligence related to the Cuban missile crisis. This dangerous 1962 incident resulted in a mixed record of success for the CIA.[36] On the one hand, its U-2 flights provided vital information about the presence of Soviet missile bases on the island. Photographs from sophisticated cameras on U-2s alerted

President John F. Kennedy to the potential danger, and it also gave him hard, empirical evidence that the missiles would not be operational (ready for firing) for two weeks—a blessed fortnight to think through a range of options open to the United States. The president finally settled on a blockade rather than an outright invasion of the island.

Yet, on the other hand, CIA analysts had informed the White House in 1961 that the Soviet Union would never try such a risky venture. Moreover, despite its U-2 successes, the Agency never discovered at the time what we now know: that the Soviets had over two hundred tactical nuclear warheads on the ground in Cuba ready for firing, or that Soviet bombers on the island carried nuclear weapons in their bomb bays. It became clear only after the Cold War (when Moscow gave U.S. officials limited access to Soviet files from that era) that a U.S. invasion, the favored option during the preliminary days of the crisis, "would have been an *absolute disaster* for the world."[37] The tactical warheads would probably have been used against a U.S. invasion force, quite possibly triggering a cataclysmic ICBM nuclear exchange between the superpowers.

My next assignments were on economic intelligence, the threat of global terrorism, and environmental intelligence (for example, what were the national security implications, if any, of global warming, vanishing rain forests, or contamination of the North Sea through the dumping by Russia of radioactive waste?). Aspin wanted a tabbed notebook for each of these subjects, with a synopsis of the key issues, my recommendations, and an annotated bibliography. I was burning the midnight oil on these projects while the rest of the staff was busy researching other first-, second-, and third-order subjects that the commission would have to address.

The staff also requested a series of specific documents from the intelligence agencies to help us understand their current activities. We were soon inundated by responses to these requests, and we had to set up a library in our NEOB offices to give the staff and commissioners easy access to the materials. With the help of the CIA's Office of Security and the Secret Service, we created a secure storage vault for all of the sensitive documents and interviews. We were constantly concerned about maintaining security; nothing would discredit the commission faster than leaked documents or idle talk in public places about our work (as opposed to abstract debates about global strategy of the kind Aspin and I engaged in at McDonald's). We were especially worried that commissioners might take documents out of our secure space to study at home. "Give members huge dayglow notebooks that they will never carry out of here," joked one staffer. Aspin sent a memo to the staff and commissioners reminding them about security precautions and the prohibition against talking to the media or removing documents from our secure third-floor suite of offices.

One of the most aggravating circumstances during March, the commission's first month, was the slowness with which the FBI seemed to be conducting its background checks on commissioners and staff, a required step before they could have access to top-secret documents and briefings. My own clearance was fairly simple and quick, since I had gone through an exhaustive background check in 1975 and the record only needed to be brought up to date. Most of the staff were in similar circumstances. Some of the commissioners, though (Baird, for one), had never been previously cleared for access to highly classified information, and getting clearance could be a time-consuming process—fifteen to eighteen months in some earlier cases.[38] Aspin sent a letter to the Office of Management and Budget, which oversees the clearance process, urging an accelerated FBI effort on behalf of the commission so as not to stymie our progress. We were ever mindful that we only had a year to complete our work.

At least progress had been made on one important front: the administration had finally talked John Deutch into standing for confirmation as the new DCI. This would give us a focal point for our dialogues with the intelligence community—and a very good one, too, in the sense that Deutch and Aspin had known each other for years and were close friends. We had made progress, as well, in polishing up our "scope paper": the staff's effort to lay out for commissioners the boundaries of the inquiry. The paper presented an almost comprehensive catalogue of the topics we needed to study and present in our final report—essentially an elaboration of the first-, second-, and third-order topics that Aspin, RAND, and the commission staff had been tossing around in informal discussions since January.

I say "almost comprehensive" because the subject of intelligence accountability was now missing altogether. In a memo to Aspin, I reviewed the scope paper and wrote:

> Above all, WE NEED A SECTION ON ACCOUNTABILITY. We cannot, it seems to me, conduct the most thorough review of the intelligence agencies ever and leave out an explicit examination of whether improvements can be made in this area. Think back to Operation CHAOS and COINTELPRO [improper domestic intelligence activities], to the Huston Plan [a master domestic spy plan authorized by President Nixon in 1970], to the assassination plots, to the Iran-*contra* affair, to the Ames case—perhaps all of these could have been avoided with closer accountability. How is the new CIA Inspector General

position working out? The Foreign Intelligence Surveillance Court? Does the Intelligence Oversight Board need to be revived [the IOB had been downgraded during the Reagan administration]? Can PFIAB be strengthened? Are the reporting provisions to Congress adequate? This subject should not be the centerpiece of the review, of course; BUT IT SHOULD NOT BE LEFT OUT   and an implicit nod is not good enough.

The scope paper was important for several reasons. First, it provided the commissioners with a roadmap for our inquiry; and, second, the legislation that created the commission stipulated that by May of 1995 we had to provide the congressional intelligence committees with a document outlining our topics for investigation. Aspin had suggested a third reason at one of our staff meetings: by disseminating the scope paper throughout the intelligence community and in selected academic circles, we could solicit and respond to constructive criticism, as well as smoke out critics. By finding out where our weaknesses were, so we could address them before we dove too deeply into the writing of the final report. Motivated by these incentives, the staff devoted much of its energy into the preparation of this document during February and early March. Then, based on comments by commissioners, the paper went into a second drafting period throughout the rest of March. Soon it would be ready for wider distribution.

Important, too, at least in the chairman's view, was a commission "outreach program." Aspin wanted to make sure that the work of the commissioners was understood by the media and the public. As his media assistant, Kim M. Simpson, explained, the purpose was "to educate both the public and policy makers about the appropriate future, roles, mission and organization of the intelligence community, as determined by the Commission."[39] Aspin's refined media consciousness was at work; he understood the significance of good press for advancing a political agenda in Washington. As a new member of Congress in 1971, he had labored assiduously to develop ties with the media. Even earlier, as a Hill staffer, he had learned from his mentor, Senator William Proxmire of Wisconsin, the value of issuing multiple press releases; one or two might even get one's name in the newspapers—important for reelection purposes. Like Proxmire, he initially focused on wasteful spending by the Pentagon: overly expensive uniforms for officers, questionable poison-gas experiments, cost overruns for shipbuilding. A *New York Times* reporter once chided him for this practice, and Aspin conceded: "You're a junior member of a committee, and you don't have the leverage of a subcommittee or committee chairman, so what do you do?"[40]

The chairman's outreach program would involve "town hall" meetings at the major intelligence agencies; mailings to members of Congress about our work; roundtable discussions in DC, New York City, and other locations around the country (a session on intelligence reform was already scheduled for March 16 at Georgetown University), supplemented by face-to-face meetings between Aspin and senior lawmakers. The chairman was a seasoned pro when it came to commissions and Congress. While still a lawmaker, Aspin helped steer the Scowcroft Commission's report on the MX missile through the House in 1983; and as a member of the Pike Committee, he had dealt with the Rockefeller Commission on intelligence in 1975.[41] He understood the importance of keeping members of Congress informed if one wanted their cooperation, and he knew that public relations skills could matter as much as investigative tenacity when it came to the success of a commission.

The groups targeted for outreach by Aspin (with help from Rudman) would include:

- private sector organizations interested in intelligence (such as the Association of Former Intelligence Offices, AFIO, and the Business Executives for National Security)[42]
- individuals who were "players" (former secretary of state Henry Kissinger, for one)
- the U.S. House and Senate
- PFIAB members not on the commission
- key government officials in the executive branch
- reform groups (such as the American Bar Association, an intelligence studies group at Harvard University and another at Georgetown University, and the Council on Foreign Relations)
- the media

The chairman had created an exhausting schedule for himself. I could not help but worry about how he was going to lead the commission while traveling all over the place, especially given his less than perfect health.

The Briefings Begin

On March 16, the commission convened in the NEOB staff offices for a series of briefings by intelligence officers whom we had invited to address the nuts and bolts of the spy trade. The education of commissioners and staff—those who needed it, at any rate—was about to begin. The staff had distributed pitchers of water, paper cups, and candies wrapped in red-and-white cellophane along the conference-room table. In front of each commissioner was a name card and a white briefing book stamped SECRET, with a world map on the cover and multicolored tabs marking sections relevant to the day's briefing. With the exception of Goss and Dewhurst, all the commissioners were present. Dewhurst arrived late, striding into the room like a young Clint Eastwood with a healthy, reddish glow on his face, as if he'd just come from a spa for cowboys.

His suit uncharacteristically pressed for the occasion, Aspin greeted everyone affably, and then, being a listener and thinker more than a talker, he turned the meeting over to Vice Chairman Warren Rudman. Broad-shouldered and barrel-chested, with a booming, authoritative voice, Rudman took charge with enthusiasm. He said that the commission would begin by looking at some "threshold questions." The scene was distinctly hierarchical, with the staff sitting silently in the back rows and Rudman, one of the most well-known Washington fixtures in the room, holding forth in the front. After his welcome and a review of the commission's importance, he asked Britt Snider if he had any comments.

Snider stood up behind a shabby wooden dais that looked like a relic from the days of the Founding Fathers. He briefly addressed the commissioners, noting at one point: "If anyone tries to give you something to influence you, let us know."

"What if it's something really nice?" asked Rudman, grinning mischievously.

"Then you have to share it," said Tony Harrington with a wink and a smile. The commissioners were in a jocular mood on their first real workday.

Senator James Exon, attending his first commission meeting, guffawed at this touch of humor in such a serious setting. He was a big man with wide, squared shoulders and a deep baritone voice. He wore a hearing aid, and a red ballpoint pen protruded from his shirt pocket. I could imagine him baling hay in Nebraska or coaching high school linebackers in Omaha, but I knew he had actually made a fortune as a savvy businessman.

One trait that most of the commissioners shared became clear right away: they liked to travel. The conversation turned immediately to places where they should go to learn more about intelligence practices in other nations: Europe, Asia, Canada, Australia, Israel. "Wherever, don't fly with the military; fly commercially," advised Rudman. "Those military planes are like toothpaste tubes. No windows. You fly for hours and never know where you are."

Stephen Friedman had removed his coat and rolled up his shirt sleeves. At our first commission gathering, I had addressed him as Mr. Friedman. "Call me Steve," he replied. "Mr. Friedman is playing tennis in Florida," a reference to his father. The former investment banker caught Aspin's eye and asked if "we'll have enough time to bring everything together."

"I think we will," Aspin said. "There are about six…eight…ten really critical questions we have to address. We need to talk these out."

"Right," Bob Hermann added, chewing gum as if this were the junior high cafeteria. "Let's lay out the key issues." With a suspicion that the "ten issues" Aspin had in mind might not find a ready consensus, and that other issues were bound to emerge, he smiled wryly and said: "This doesn't mean there won't be some upstate counties voting differently."

"I hope we can prevent this from simply being a budgetary process for the agencies," said Wyche Fowler.

"Look, this is not a consensus-building situation," Coelho interjected. "We need to be led, Les. We can argue with you and oppose you, but we need to be led."

"Okay, let's do this the way we used to do things in Congress," Aspin responded, his eyelids wrinkling as he squinted in Coelho's direction. "We'll have some discussion, set the parameters; then I'll put together a 'chairman's mark' that brings things together. We can then have amendments, changes, modifications, whatever."

Rudman cleared his throat and, looking over at Exon, a former Senate colleague, asked if the Nebraskan had considered whether NRO's satellites could have a role in U.S. agriculture. Out of Rudman's view, a few staffers' eyes rolled. "You do grow corn out there in Nebraska, don't ya, Jim?" the vice chairman asked.

"Yeah, and football players," Exon replied with a chuckle. Nebraska had recently become a dominant force in college football and would win the national championship later that year.

"See, Warren, that's what I have in mind," said Coelho. "That's leadership!"

Exon's face grew sober. "We have as much or more waste in intelligence than we do in the Pentagon," he said, speaking authoritatively as a longtime member of the Senate Armed Services Committee. "There are too many agencies, and too much duplication." A faculty colloquium at Georgetown University had just released a report that listed a number of intelligence-reform proposals, including the suggestion that "consolidation [within the intelligence community] should begin in the Department of Defense, where duplication in organization and process is the most extensive and obvious."[43]

Baird squeezed in a comment: "We need a threat assessment."

"Right," Fowler agreed. "What information does a modern state require to defend itself, both at home and abroad? This is the key question. Les and I were on HPSCI for eight years. We don't want to fall into the 'bonsai approach,' where we trim the pretty bonsai tree but never get around to asking the fundamental questions." He paused, looked around the room, and concluded with a slight Southern twang: "The bonsai trap awaits."

"I'd rather ask the big questions, even if we fail," Rudman agreed.

"The public wants something done," added Coelho.

"Yes, we need change," said Dewhurst, the commission's resident oil tycoon. "Now I won't say 'I'm a simple cowboy from Texas...'"

"Yeah, sure," grinned Coelho.

"...but this is scary. We're close to Chapter 11 when it comes to recruiting good intelligence officers." Dewhurst continued: "I've been away from intelligence for twenty years, but I'm trying to look at this like a businessman and a private citizen. Let's be two inches wide and a mile deep, rather than the other way around. We owe this to the folks in intelligence, who risk their lives every day."

Rudman brought the meeting back to its central purpose. "Les, what can you tell us about the scope paper?"

"We have to understand the new intelligence technology, for one thing," Aspin replied. "Hell, they don't get that in the Senate."

"Just a little dig there, in case you didn't get it," Rudman added. Members and former members of the House and the Senate didn't mind scoring points against the opposing chamber now and then, even in retirement.

Coelho piled on: "We read our reports in the House."

Going step by step through the scope paper, Aspin was now in his element. He talked about how intelligence requirements could pop up suddenly, like a jack-in-the-box. He used the example of Rwanda.

"Targets should not just be countries, like Iran," Coelho stressed, "but cultures, too, like Islamic extremism."

"Yes, you're right," Aspin acknowledged, with nodding approval in Coelho's direction. Part of being a chairman meant building rapport with the commissioners.

"We need to educate the American people on the dangers we face," Coelho added.

"There is no consensus on national strategy, and we're not going to have one fall on our doorstep," Wolfowitz said. "We are in a period of uncertainty; we need flexibility and multiple capabilities."

Friedman weighed in quietly, "We have to look at organizational cultures within the intelligence community, not just costs and how the boxes are aligned on a government chart."

This was beginning to sound too much like a graduate seminar for Tony Coelho, the irrepressible activist. "Are we going to do an academic study or *change things?*" he blurted out. "Who do we have to capture, so they will support what we are trying to do? This is how it's done in politics. We have to reach out, build alliances."

"We are," Aspin assured him, informing the commissioners about his outreach program.

Time ran out for further discussion. A team of intelligence briefers had arrived, scheduled to give the commissioners an overview of the nation's intelligence activities. The first up was Admiral William O. Studeman, acting director of central intelligence, a thin, scholarly looking fellow who said that his remarks would be just "a motorcycle ride through the art gallery." Switching metaphors, he spoke of intelligence as a "river of information" that ran deep and wide. He pointed out that the community produced "thousands of intelligence reports every day." The main purpose of the espionage agencies, he said, was to penetrate targets to find out about secret plans that might threaten the United States. Further, the agencies had to defend the nation against hostile secret services, the counterintelligence mission. They also had to serve the customer's needs. He emphasized that the Department of Defense was the most demanding—even "snarling"—consumer of intelligence.

Admiral Studeman referred to the president's new intelligence document, PDD-35, issued on March 2, 1995. It laid out a "threat matrix"—an array of threats facing the United States, organized by tiers: O, for targets during a time of crisis; 1A, for especially dangerous countries and factions; 1B, for "functional" topics that needed security attention, such as weapons proliferation or drug trafficking; and tiers 2, 3, or 4, for target of decreasing urgency, but which still could not be ignored. As Studeman read from his notes, his head down, I could see the eyes of commissioners beginning to wander. The Acting DCI, a pleasant and well-meaning individual, was violating the cardinal rule of oral presentations: maintain eye contact with the audience.

When the admiral finished, Exon—apparently taken by Rudman's earlier suggestion that the NRO might be beneficial to the economy of Nebraska—asked if satellites could be used for weather reporting, which could assist his state's agricultural community. The staffers' eyes rolled again. Studeman politely sidestepped that suggestion, knowing full well that the use of surveillance satellites over the territorial United States would cause a political uproar on Capitol Hill—domestic spying!—not to mention on the editorial pages of the nation's leading newspapers. While spy satellites had been deployed at home during special emergencies, such as floods or hurricanes (with explicit permission from the White House and Congress), if this became routine practice, it would—quite properly—draw protests from civil libertarians across the country.[44]

A few minutes later, Exon slipped a handwritten note to Aspin and Rudman, informing them that he had to get back to the Senate. "Votes!" read the note. "Remember? Republicans still causing T-R-O-U-B-L-E!" Rudman, a Republican, gave Exon a comical grimace as the Nebraskan departed from the room.

Later that same day, the three-term senator from Nebraska announced that he intended to retire at the end of the current session of Congress. "The old fire horse within me wanted to answer the bell for another race," he said, but he had decided that twenty-five years in statewide office was enough— "some kind of record," he noted, "especially for a Democrat in Nebraska."[45] I wondered how this decision would affect his commitment to the commission's work. That morning, though, he was certainly engaged. Before his departure, he had looked down the table to Aspin and asked about the problem of duplication in the intelligence community: "This is open ended right? We can look at these things?"

The chairman nodded. "Yes, we can do anything we want."

After Exon departed the room, Coelho said to Admiral Studeman: "What if we placed the entire intelligence budget under the control of the DCI?" Such a move would take the intelligence purse strings away from the secretary of defense and the various agency managers (the gorillas in the stovepipes) and hand them over to the nation's intelligence chief on the seventh floor at the CIA. *Washington Post* reporter Walter Pincus had once succinctly summed up this topic: "The Pentagon exercises almost total control over its intelligence agencies, despite the DCI's supposed authority."[46]

"Major heart attacks at the DoD!" said Aspin immediately, before Studeman could respond. Ripples of laughter radiated across the conference room. The chairman was right. The biggest gorilla of all, the SecDef, would rise up against such an attempt to strip away his control over military intelligence spending—the lion's share of the total annual intelligence budget.[47]

The admiral smiled at Aspin, recognizing the tension between the DCI and the SecDef. Coelho's question was a vital one, and his standing shot up among staffers for getting to the heart of the matter this time. A central reason why the intelligence community was fragmented and lacked a tradition of sharing information was the absence of a strong DCI, a community-wide leader with full authority over budgets and personnel for all of the intelligence agencies. As former representative (and later co-chair of the 9/11 Commission) Lee H. Hamilton (D-IN) would tell a congressional panel investigating the 9/11 attacks, "I can't think of another enterprise in America, public or private, that is so decentralized and has such little direct authority at the top."[48] In acknowledgment of this fact, DCI Robert M. Gates once said to a secretary of defense: "You rule with authority; I 'rule' only with persuasion."[49]

Since the creation of the modern American intelligence establishment in 1947, the DCI had remained a weak figure, with an office at the CIA, but with little formal control over the other intelligence agencies.[50] The DCI had been provided with an "intelligence community staff" (ICS), and later (under Gates) a "community management staff" (CMS) to extend his reach over each of the secret agencies; but these management appendages proved to have limited effectiveness. DCI William Webster (1987–91), for example, always referred to his ICS as if they were some distant entity, rather than a group that worked directly for him. The commission's Q-and-A session with Studeman inevitably turned to spending. I expected Rudman or Friedman to ask where the fat was in the intelligence community, but instead it was Fowler who posed the question to the admiral: "Where would you go to make some real cuts in the intelligence budget?" Studeman squirmed in his chair and asked for more time to consider that subject. Fowler gave him a dyspeptic stare.

————

When the briefings resumed the next morning, St. Patrick's Day, the first speaker was an experienced intelligence manager. He noted that the ties between intelligence officers and policy makers were often strained, and sometimes nonexistent. "If we were a business, we'd be out of business," he admitted. "Our customer relations are terrible." All too often, analysts were writing papers that no one in the policy departments cared about, because they failed to address the hot issues that dominated in-boxes around town. "We end up writing for ourselves," the manager said. "We have become a self-licking ice cream cone." The CIA was now forty-seven and evidently undergoing a mid-life crisis.

Fowler tried his budget question again: where do we cut? The answer this time was that the commission could downsize the budget, say, by as much as $12 billion a year; but it would have to cut an entire agency. "And you better pray for world peace," the manager added with a grim and lingering glance at the Georgian.

The briefings, which lasted all day, covered the nation's primary espionage activities and pointed to a raft of new challenges the intelligence community had to face. For example, fewer international telephone calls were traveling from one transmitter to another through the air; the new means of communications was via underground and undersea fiber-optic cables—"glass pipes." Snatching communications out of the air between transmitters was a snap for the NSA; fiber-optic cables, though, had to be physically located, which meant digging into the ground or into a seabed to find them. Then a special clamp had to be applied to the glass pipe—all risky activities inside sovereign nations abroad or even at sea, with foreign ships often nearby. It was one thing for the FBI to tap the wire of a land-line telephone belonging to a suspected criminal in, say, Chicago, but quite another matter for the NSA to find a buried communications cable, then place a listening clamp on it, deep inside another country. Some commissioners had questions about the need for downsizing personnel in some of the larger intelligence agencies. The current low morale at the spy agencies was another favorite topic. A few commissioners also wanted more details about targeting, as well as more information about the technical aspects of satellites. "How do you move a satellite from one battlefield to another?" inquired a commissioner.

Several of the commissioners urged one of the briefers to say more about the problem of integrating the intelligence agencies, a goal referred to in the Pentagon as "jointness." The briefer responded by noting that the community was more like a guild, with everyone in the same business, competing against one another. He told a story about a car wreck. One driver was an army man, the other a Navy man. No one was hurt. "In the spirit of jointness, have a swig of Jack Daniels," the Navy fellow said, reaching into his satchel for a bottle. His offer was readily accepted. The Army guy gulped down the whiskey and handed the bottle back. "Here, now it's your turn." The navy man replied, "Naw, I think I'll wait until the police arrive." So much for jointness. At least, though, the story brought a much needed round of laughter that dissipated the somber air that had filled the conference room.

Perhaps the cleverest remark of the day came from DIA director James R. Clapper, Jr. "Downsizing, right-sizing, fine," he said, "but let's avoid capsizing." Clapper took the opportunity to comment as well on the seemingly endless list of targeting requirements ("tasking") that had been laid on the intelligence agencies by policy makers since the end of the Cold War. "I'll welcome the day when someone tells us what we can quit doing, but it doesn't happen," he lamented. "Tasking is addictive."

As the answers came back to commissioners, often in a dull monotone in the case of some of the less skillful briefers, they began to drift out of the room one by one. By 2:00 PM, only half remained. Throughout the briefings, Aspin and Rudman (wearing suits of the same color and style—Rudman's nicely pressed) sat next to each other, whispering about the presentations and joking quietly now and then. It was good to see such a cordial relationship between the panel's two leaders, so different in basic political philosophy and temperament. The briefing sessions, though, were getting bogged down; the staff had attempted to cram too much information into too short a period. Aspin provided the liveliest moment in the final hour when he accidentally knocked over a pitcher as he reached for a candy. Water and ice cubes spilled in the direction of Friedman's lap. With an athlete's quick reflexes, the finance guru whipped out a red handkerchief from his back pocket and made an effective cloth dam against the flood.

The hearings droned on until the final guest arrived, Louis "Judge" Freeh, the director of the FBI. He was known around Washington as a tough, competent former prosecutor with a Phi Beta Kappa key in his vest pocket and a no-nonsense attitude. Despite his short stature and youthful looks, he commanded attention with his steely demeanor. Freeh told the commissioners that his biggest intelligence problem was the "interface" between the Bureau and the CIA. The two agencies were notably poor at the "handoff problem," he advised, that is, transferring responsibility for the surveillance of a dangerous suspect—a terrorist, criminal, drug dealer, or foreign intelligence agent—from the CIA to the FBI as the person entered the United States from abroad. This admission is strikingly fateful in retrospect, now that we know how poorly the two agencies handed off surveillance responsibilities with respect to the 9/11 terrorists who entered this country in 2001.[51]

The FBI and the CIA had been at odds for decades. Bureau director J. Edgar Hoover looked on CIA officers as rich Ivy Leaguers (which they often were in the 1950s and 1960s, less so today); they were, in his opinion, rank amateurs who regarded intelligence as a hobby. In turn, CIA officers viewed Hoover as an uncouth street cop who had no understanding of international affairs. During the 1960s, Hoover refused even to talk to DCI Richard Helms because of a CIA/FBI disagreement over the *bona fides* of a Soviet defector—one of many counterintelligence disputes that would plague the relationship between the agencies over the years. During the Cold War, for instance, the agencies disagreed sharply on the trustworthiness of Soviet defectors Ivan Isidorovich Nosenko and Anatoliy Mikhailovoch Golitsin.[52]

The two organizations had a different approach to their jobs. The FBI, dominated by law-enforcement officials ("cops"), sought indictments against criminals; the CIA, home of America's spy handlers ("spooks"), preferred to watch suspects from afar to learn more about their contacts and their *modus operandi*. As the journalist Tim Weiner aptly put it, "A cop confronted with an evildoer wants to string him up. A spook wants to string him along."[53] Moreover, intelligence managers at the CIA worried that their assets (sources) might be exposed during the FBI's criminal investigations and trials.[54] As a result of the distrust, a wall had grown up between the two agencies, fortified by executive orders and laws designed to keep law enforcement and espionage apart from one another in order to ensure that rigorous standards for criminal investigations were not diluted by less stringent standards for intelligence surveillance.

Freeh ended his remarks, as well as the commission's inaugural education session (Intel 101), with this core message: "The FBI needs more money to make the country less penetrable." Some of the commissioners were well-known budget trimmers; yet, in these briefings, one intelligence official after another had requested additional funding. The prospect of conflict within the commission over the "mother's milk of politics"[55]—money—loomed on the horizon.

Our initial briefings had made it clear to the commissioners that the nation faced multiple intelligence problems. Less apparent—hiding, elusive as spies—were the answers.

PART II | Seeking Answers

CHAPTER 4

A New Intelligence Chief

I N MARCH, THE PRESIDENT MANAGED to persuade John Mark Deutch to accept nomination as DCI, apparently with the hint that he might later be favorably considered as a candidate for secretary of defense, reputedly his ultimate career ambition. Deutch was well regarded on the Hill and unlikely to have any problems with the confirmation proceedings. One of the Aspin Commission members, Rep. Porter Goss, observed that he would bring "so much horsepower" to the job.[1] Deutch certainly had stellar public-service credentials, having been chief of acquisitions at the Pentagon and, at the time, the deputy defense secretary responsible for the day-to-day operations of the Defense Department (the second highest position). He had also made his mark on Congress by skillfully negotiating a peace between the NRO and SSCI lawmakers over the satellite organization's shocking cost overruns, racked up during the construction of its new headquarters near Dulles Airport, overruns that were concealed from Capitol Hill and the public.[2]

A former chemistry professor and provost at MIT (where he had the nickname "shoot-ready-aim" for his brashness),[3] the fifty-six-year-old Deutch fit the bill as a smart defense intellectual in the style of Les Aspin and Harold Brown. Some lawmakers worried, though, that such a high-profile public official might find it difficult to step back and assume the role of a policy-neutral intelligence director. "The CIA is for analysis, not advocacy," cautioned the respected senator Richard G. Lugar (R-IN).[4]

Deutch added to these misgivings by requesting, according to rumors, that the president give him membership in the cabinet. An earlier DCI, William J. Casey, of the Reagan administration, had also made this demand and used the leverage of cabinet status to weigh in on political debates in the

White House—an activism that many lawmakers (and scholars) found inappropriate for an intelligence director.[5] Jon Kyl (R-AZ), who held a seat on SSCI, strongly objected to a cabinet position for Deutch. "Once he becomes a cabinet officer, he is making policy," the senator opined. "A CIA director must be above suspicion in the advice that he is giving."[6]

In retrospect, Deutch recalls this debate as "somewhat of a comedy."[7] The White House chief of staff, Leon Panetta (who would become director of the CIA in the Obama administration), had been delighted that Deutch finally agreed to take on the DCI job; an inability to fill the position was becoming an embarrassment for the Clinton administration. Capitalizing on Panetta's good mood, Deutch turned to him after accepting the post and said, as an afterthought, "Oh, and by the way, I want to be a member of the cabinet." The response from Panetta, who was relieved to have the DCI job search behind him, was an offhanded "fine." Deutch made the request because, as he remembers, he wanted "to signal to the people in the intelligence community, but especially to the CIA, that this director had the president's confidence—the single most important asset the DCI has." He probably had in mind as well the difficulties that his successor, Jim Woolsey, met with in trying—and failing—to have regular contact with President Clinton.

Just before Deutch accepted the DCI position, the president had named the head of the Small Business Administration to the cabinet. "If someone in that position could serve on the cabinet, so should the director of central intelligence," Deutch said to me in 1998, adding: "Besides, I didn't see it as being any great substantive matter because the cabinet is not that important."

He found the argument that the DCI might be drawn improperly into policy discussions as a cabinet member off the mark. "If the intelligence director is going to get involved in policy, he's going to get involved in policy," Deutch said, adding a phrase likely to have made Sherman Kent, the renowned dean of CIA analysts, spin in his grave (early in the Agency's history, Kent had advocated the erection of a high wall between intelligence and policy).[8] "I was the sort of person who was going to get involved in policy," Deutch went on, "so it didn't matter whether or not I was in the cabinet."

Former DCI Stansfield Turner also rejects the philosophy of a watertight barrier between policy makers and intelligence officers. Although the DCI should not volunteer policy views (such as DCI John A. McCone frequently offered in the early 1960s), it was the admiral's view that

> surely, when the president of the United States says to the DCI, "What is your opinion of what I should do?" I'm not going to be a wallflower and say: "Mr. President, I'm not allowed to do that for you."

Realistically, I can't be at a policy meeting without having an opinion; but you try to stay neutral, and if you're asked to drop that cloak of neutrality, you do—and as soon as you're finished, you go back.[9]

A State Department official has acknowledged that "officers in INR often even write policy papers."[10]

More in the Kentian tradition was DCI Richard Helms (1966–73). "There is a disagreement between people like John McCone and me, or William Casey and me," he once observed. "My view was that the DCI should be the man who called things the way he saw them, the purpose of this being to give the president one man in his administration who was not trying to formulate a policy, carry out a policy, or defend a policy." Helms continued:

> In other words, this was the man who attempted to keep the game honest. When you sit around the table and the secretary of state is propounding this and defending that, and the secretary of defense is defending this and propounding that, the president has the right to hear somebody who says, "Now, listen, this isn't my understanding of the facts" or "That isn't the way it worked." . . . I just don't think that in this large town, with all the people who are in the government, that it's too expensive to have one man who worries about the facts.
>
> That's what the DCI is supposed to do in foreign affairs.[11]

A chairman of the National Intelligence Council (NIC), the premier panel of intelligence analysts in the government, seconded this view, using a comparison unlikely to endear him to policy makers. "We're like chaplains in a whorehouse," he suggested. "We have to go inside, but we don't have to participate."[12] The dilemma can be simply stated: for purposes of objectivity, intelligence officers require a certain distance from policy makers. Yet unless there is a degree of closeness between the two, intelligence officers will never gain access to the high councils of government to provide information in the first place.[13]

———

As Deutch prepared for his Senate confirmation hearings (nothing new to him, as he had been confirmed twice before for DoD positions), the commission staff moved forward with still another draft of the scope paper. The plan was to complete this statement of our objectives by March 21, then give it to Aspin and RAND for a further close reading before wider distribution. It was important to make sure this roadmap was right. The staff was also busy planning a retreat for the commission, which would take place at a CIA training facility in rural Virginia. This would give commissioners a chance to get to know each other better in a relaxed atmosphere. The staff would invite some additional intelligence briefers, but this time the Q and A would be more laid-back. On the "outreach" front, Aspin's scheduling and media aide, Kim Simpson, had lined up various events for the chairman, including a visit to Harvard University, "town meetings" with the CIA and NSA, and sessions with SSCI and HPSCI members on the scope paper.

Aspin and I continued our two-person "intelligence seminar" as the weather in Washington began to turn warm. In his PFIAB offices, he said to me: "What if everything were organized in the intelligence community by function, instead of the usual agencies?" This would mean lumping together all sigint entities into one government building; all imint (now called geoint, short for geospatial-intelligence) in another; humint (human intelligence) in a third, osint (open-source intelligence—information available in the public domain, without spying) in a fourth; masint (measurement and signatures intelligence—telltale emissions that could be captured, such as chemical residues in laboratories where sarin nerve gas had been manufactured) in a fifth; along with separate buildings for analysis, covert action, and counterintelligence. My next assignment was to think radically about restructuring the intelligence community along functional lines—a RAND-like "clean paper" exercise. Aspin also wanted me to generate an outline of unclassified "talking points" for his use in the outreach meetings with various groups. In the meantime, we met periodically to talk about the research I was already pursuing on economic intelligence and environmental intelligence.

The question of America's economic competitiveness in the global marketplace had served as a centerpiece in Bill Clinton's 1992 presidential campaign. After his election, the president's now-famous campaign mantra—"It's the economy, stupid"—continued to resound in Washington. As a natural extension of this focus on the economy, officials and pundits began to wonder if maybe the CIA should do more to assist America's global competitiveness by ramping up espionage activities against U.S. corporate trade rivals. A champion of this point of view was former DCI Adm. Stansfield Turner. "We would have no compunction about stealing military secrets to help [America] manufacture better weapons," he argued. "If economic strength should now be recognized as a vital component of national security, parallel with military power, why should America be concerned about stealing and employing economic secrets?"[14]

However logical this perspective may have sounded, I soon discovered many reasons to doubt the wisdom of an economic espionage mission against foreign companies. In the first place, American corporations didn't seem to want the CIA's help in spying against competitors. They already had such capabilities (a topic corporate CEOs refuse to discuss on the record), in part because they had hired platoons of former CIA and FBI officers over the years to engage in industrial espionage on their behalf. Moreover, what exactly was an "American company" these days? In contemporary society, corporations were multinational conglomerates; sharing intelligence with them might well mean providing secret information to board members from a wide variety of nations—a counterintelligence taboo.

Further, as another DCI, Robert M. Gates, pointed out, officers in the CIA's Operations Directorate had signed on to protect the United States against foreign enemies, not to help out General Motors. "Some years ago," Gates recalled, "one of our clandestine service officers overseas said to me: 'You know, I'm prepared to give my life for my country but not for a company.' That case officer was absolutely right."[15] Another former DCI, R. James Woolsey, weighed in on Gates's side.[16] I remembered discussing this topic several years earlier with former DCI William E. Colby (1973–76). He, too, was unimpressed by this mission and dismissed it, saying: "You don't need to use satellites to count Toyotas."[17]

Yet beyond spying for American companies (if any purely American corporations still existed), there were some aspects of economic espionage that did appear to have merit. For instance, if foreign competitors were bribing officials in other lands and thereby obtaining business contracts in an unfair manner, wouldn't the United States benefit from blowing the whistle on the cheaters? Woolsey explained how this might work:

> We collect intelligence on those efforts to bribe foreign companies and foreign governments into, for example, awarding an airport contract to a European firm rather than an American firm.... And when we find out about those, and we do a fair amount of the time, we go not to the American corporation that's competing, but the Secretary of State, and he sends an American ambassador to see a president or a king, and the ambassador says, "Mr. President or Your Majesty, your minister in charge of construction is on the take, and you have a lot going on with the United States, and we don't really take kindly to your operating that way".... Frequently, but not always, the contract is rebid and the American firm gets a share of it.... Sometimes the whole thing is done right, sometimes not.[18]

This could be a positive outcome for the United States; so the mission of economic intelligence, I had begun to realize, could not be rejected out of hand. Moreover, the FBI had a valuable role in the economic domain: its counterintelligence officers were expected to block espionage inside the

United States, either against our government or against companies residing within our borders. So, industrial espionage by the CIA targeted against foreign companies on behalf of GM: no; but spying against foreign corrupt business practices, and the use of FBI counterintelligence agents to protect our own economic strategies as a nation and the secrets of individual business enterprises inside the United States: yes.[19] And finding out about the international economic negotiating positions of other countries (as opposed to companies): yes.

Less widely discussed was the subject of environmental intelligence. Indeed, I soon found out that this "greening of intelligence" was ridiculed by many professional intelligence officers—the gathering of environmental data was a "rather squishy" mission, complained an officer in the Operations Directorate to me on one of my many trips to the CIA in the spring of 1995. Solidly built, and with three days of stubble on his face, he looked like he would much rather be scaling the walls of an enemy stronghold at midnight with a dagger between his teeth than clandestinely procuring water samples from the Aral Sea. "What are we supposed to do," he asked with a twisted smile, "creep around the mountains of Patagonia counting the number of blind rabbits?" (According to some ecologists, retinal damage in rabbits could indicate the degree of harm being done by the hole in the ozone over Argentina.) I thought the DO officer had a point; nonetheless, I persevered and came across convincing arguments in favor of at least some attention to environmental intelligence.

Environmental conflicts could lead to war between nations, and the United States certainly needed to know about that possibility. Relations between Indian and Pakistan sometimes flare with respect to water that flows from mountain glaciers into Pakistan's agricultural heartland and which India threatens to divert with a dam; African nations compete for access to water from the Nile; Chinese dam projects in the Himalayas worry Indians; Israel and Jordan bicker over Jordan River water rights. "One state's behavior can radically change the amount of resources available to other states," ecologists have observed. "Drift net fisheries of one country may devastate a fishing ground used by all—and in the realm of management of the atmosphere there is no problem that does not cross national frontiers: acid rain, greenhouse gases, and ozone depletion are salient."[20] Further, the CIA had a rich archive of satellite photographs taken of the earth's surface since the early 1960s. These pictures were meant to reveal such things as Soviet missile sites and Chinese nuclear facilities, but, as a byproduct, they had also captured over the years the condition of rain forests, coral reefs, and lakes around the world—information of great interest to ecologists. In addition, scientists in the intelligence agencies had engaged in studies of cloud-size variability (affecting satellite performance); snowfall, glaciers, and permafrost; climate change; and measurements of sea-ice thickness (important for submarine operations). Intelligence mapmakers had charted geological erosion; traced wetlands, the growth of vegetation, and the spread of deserts; and monitored industrial air pollution, population growth, urbanization, and industrialization. These topics were of obvious relevance to the rest of us, not just to spies and security officials.

If one were to accept a broad definition of national security (rarely the case in Washington, where the term usually applies strictly to military and economic matters), one could more readily appreciate how changes in the environment could affect the well-being of Americans. I was becoming more and more intrigued by the possibility that this overlooked domain of intelligence might be of greater significance than conventional wisdom held, and not only in terms of national security. If environmental data collected by the intelligence agencies were shared with American ecologists, much good will could be generated between the U.S. scientific community and the secret agencies. Maybe the CIA, with its rich archival portraits of the planet, could help basic science and, in turn, scientists could assist the CIA in the interpretation of its satellite data for more strategic geopolitical purposes.

A program at the CIA known as MEDEA (pronounced "ma-day-a", a reference to the sorceress of Colchis in Greek mythology who helped Jason of the Argonauts steal the Golden Fleece) had already brought some scientists and spooks together for this purpose. The program was stalled, however, because of the problem of security clearances for academic researchers who did not want to sign secrecy oaths that might obstruct their future publication opportunities. Skepticism about how useful the CIA's ecological data really was presented a further stumbling block. The two parties had decided to continue cooperating, though at a low level of activity and funding, as they worked out the knots in the relationship. At any rate, I was fascinated by this new (for me at least) area of research, and I was impressed with the work being done on environmental issues and a host of other scientific topics at the CIA's Directorate of Science and Technology—"DS&T," as the Directorate's suite of offices and labs in the Langley Headquarters Building is called less formally.[21]

———

As spring arrived in Washington in 1995, bringing cloudless blue skies, four RAND consultants walked from their offices downtown to the NEOB. Our conference room was no longer just bare walls, table, chairs, and a dilapidated dais; we now had a few green plants. Moreover, the colorful crests of all the intelligence agencies adorned the walls and brought some warmth to the otherwise sterile government offices. The bold blue-and-green shield that served as the logo of the Energy Department's Office of Intelligence, and the NRO's emblem of a satellite circling the earth, stood out for their vivid designs.

Chairman Aspin and the staff greeted the RAND analysts, and we began a candid critique of the scope paper. The chief RAND spokesman came right to the point. "The paper is comprehensive in substance, but deficient in structure," he stated, and suggested that the document needed clearer segues between its component parts. "You should start with a section on the 'national interests,'" he recommended, "then move to the information needs related to each of these interests." Aspin's eyes brightened. Now this was how to start a day! Soon he was talking with the RAND people about the budget as a "dependent variable," just like in the good old days of his graduate seminars in economics at MIT.

The chairman homed in on the question of targeting. "The problem here is, the list goes on and on," Aspin said. "How do you decide what to target [for intelligence collection]? What are the priorities? And at what cost?" RAND's vague answers to these questions left Aspin annoyed. "Maybe we should have policy makers take a vote on what to target," he finally suggested sarcastically.

"Well, you should dismiss targets that are third rate," RAND tried again.

"Okay, okay, I got it, I got, I got it—you already said that," Aspin admonished, slumping over the conference table with his hand on his forehead. His mood had turned foul, which was unusual for him.

RAND tried another tack related to FBI espionage priorities.

"Don't be an asshole," the chairman responded to this new line of thought.

"It's hard, it comes so naturally," said the senior RAND spokesman, grinning in an attempt to disarm Aspin. It didn't work.

"Don't pursue that [FBI] argument," the chairman persisted. "It's a waste of time." The session was going poorly, and staffers' eyes were beginning to stare at the floor or the ceiling—anywhere but in Aspin's direction. Suddenly the chairman laughed at our discomfort, and the tension in the room dissipated like air rushing out of a balloon. Aspin's inherent good nature and his old-boy ties with the RAND analysts had trumped our ineptness in defining how America should determine its threat matrix. The exchange of ideas, however tense, had reminded us of one thing, though: it was difficult to reach agreement on solutions to even the most basic intelligence problems, even among like minds.

Another venturesome RAND analyst decided to try his luck: "We need to concentrate on what key *questions* policy makers want answered, not what targets we should choose. This will give us a sense of intelligence priorities. For example, what nations are proliferating weapons of mass destruction? And what can we do about it?"

"Right," said Aspin, sitting up in his chair as his energy returned, "and don't forget the political side of this: we have to sell the public on intelligence." The chairman had morphed into Senator John Warner for a moment. He continued, "I agree: the question is not Iran or Iraq, but how to collect against rogue states. How much we have to spend on intelligence will depend on how sophisticated these countries are in hiding their activities."

"Woolsey's approach was simple enough," interjected Britt Snider, the staff director. "Just spend more money on satellites."

"Right, but we need to be more explicit and rational about our spending priorities," Aspin replied.

"We need a study of how we've made intelligence resource decisions in the past," urged one of the RAND analysts experienced in milking the government for more funding—but, in this case, he was correct.

Aspin redirected the discussion toward a detailed examination of the scope paper's organization. I was happy to see that a paragraph had been added on the need to examine the "adequacy of oversight arrangements in the post–Cold War era." Maybe that topic would survive after all. As we went through the document, section by section, new debates sprang up. "Do we require a stand-alone NRO?" a staffer asked, for instance. "Maybe we could fold it into the Department of Defense."

"Or NSA," suggested another staffer from guess-which-agency.

"Let's remember what we need most of all," said a staff aide with years of experience on the Hill. "Just like Taco Bell, we need intelligence that is fast, hot, and at a reasonable price." This brought smiles around the room.

As additional staffers grew emboldened, the discussion expanded. "The trouble is, the barons are too strong," said one. He was referring to the program managers running each of the spy agencies. The gorillas in the stovepipes had once again entered into our deliberations.

Yawning, Aspin added slyly: "The community is designed to make sure that no one understands how it works." He rose from his chair and announced that he had to go, but he noted in parting that we had to decide which of three options we wanted to pursue: sweeping changes in the intelligence community, a few changes, or simply some fine-tuning. With this, he left the room, and the meeting came to an end. For the staff, it was back to the drawing boards on the scope paper.

The staff was also moving into a phase of intensive interviewing. Over the next few months, we intended to sit down with some 150 intelligence experts and practitioners to learn as much as possible about prevailing views on intelligence reform. The list of potential interviewees included former president George H.W. Bush (the only president to have served as America's intelligence chief), along with a host of national security advisors, DCIs, intelligence officers, military brass, diplomats, budget analysts at OMB, SSCI and HPSCI staff members, lawmakers, people in industry who dealt with intelligence (such as satellite manufacturers), the leaders of former defense or security commissions, and academics who studied intelligence and national security.

As March wound down, we had our plates full, especially as the commission's document requests were beginning to harvest reams of paper, which flowed from the intelligence agencies to our staff quarters in the NEOB, everything from budget justifications to organizational charts and statements of purpose. Aspin warned the staff again on the last day of March: no contact with the media; no speeches; no discussions with intelligence agency personnel about the internal work of the commission. Except for the chairman's outreach program, we would remain low-key and out of the limelight, if possible.

––––

The staff circulated the latest version of the scope paper to commission members in early April. After hearing back from them, we planned to send a final revision to top congressional leaders, along with lawmakers on SSCI and HPSCI. Some in the intelligence community were already complaining about various aspects of our approach. For example, the CIA balked at having RAND consultants—"outsiders"—attend commission briefings in the NEOB, and some agency directors insisted that they should be allowed to have "note takers" present whenever an intelligence officer from one of their agencies was interviewed by the commission. We were willing to compromise on the question of RAND's presence at all the briefings, but we were not going to allow "note takers," who would have a chilling effect on candid interview responses. Snider jokingly threatened to write each of the "gorillas," warning that those agencies that insisted on a note taker were the most bureaucratic and should have their budgets cut.

On April 6 and 7, our briefings designed to educate commissioners and staff about ongoing intelligence activities and challenges resumed. The first "witness" was, the deputy director for operations (DDO), who served as the chief for the Directorate of Operations (DO), the component of the CIA responsible for running spies abroad, carrying out covert actions, and supporting counterintelligence activities overseas.[22] The DO (now known as the National Clandestine Service or NCS) is arm of the Agency that extends overseas, housed for the most part in U.S. embassies around the world. The directorate's structure at the end of the Cold War is illustrated in Figure 4.1.

The DO's overseas personnel are known as "case officers" or (in a recent change of nomenclature) "operations officers," and they are led by a chief of station (COS) within each embassy. The job of the case officer is to recruit foreigners to engage in espionage against their own country. As DCI R. James Woolsey once stated in a speech: "What we [the intelligence community] really exist for is stealing secrets," a task partially accomplished through the recruitment of local spies.[23] For this recruitment effort, case officers need to be gregarious individuals: charming, persuasive, and daring; perhaps the popular

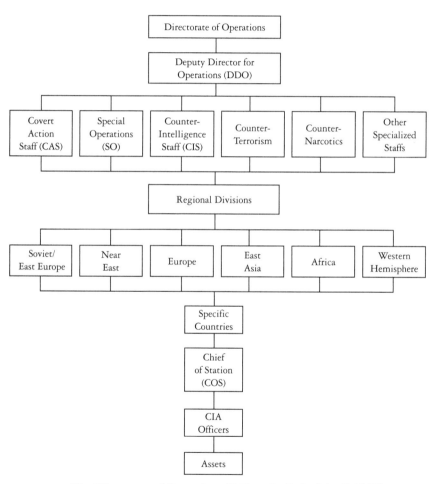

FIGURE 4.1 The Directorate of Operations (DO) at the End of the Cold War
Source: Loch K. Johnson, *America's Secret Power: The CIA in a Democratic Society* (New York: Oxford University Press, 1989), p. 46.

types likely to have been presidents of their college fraternities or sororities. To fall under their spell and become an espionage asset secretly employed by the United States is, in CIA lingo, to be "case officered" or "COed."

The DDO who appeared before the commission on April 6 looked like an ordinary enough fellow, in his fifties, with a thick head of brown wavy hair. He had an Ivy League degree and wore a well-tailored suit of clothes. He could just as easily have been a successful bond trader, except that his work had been in Bangkok, Taipei, Rangoon, Hong Kong, Singapore, Addis Ababa, and Beijing, rather than Wall Street. His career at this point was in a downward trajectory. He had already been censured by Woolsey for inadequate supervision of Aldrich Ames, and he was most likely going to be moved out of the top DO position by John Deutch, the DCI designate.

The DDO walked the commission through his directorate's responsibilities, beginning with insights into the difficulty of recruiting spies overseas, especially since all too often case officers in the Agency rarely knew the languages, cultures, and history of foreign countries as well they should. He turned next to the controversial subject of covert action, and the commissioners pricked up their ears. During the Cold War, covert actions had included such activities as propaganda operations (say, planting newspaper articles abroad with the help of a "media asset," or secretly leafleting against a cause anathema to American interests); political activities (behind-the-scenes election campaigns against adversaries, money and advertising for friends); attempts to disrupt the economies of adversaries (counterfeiting foreign currencies, blowing up power plants, mining harbors); and paramilitary initiatives (supplying weapons to friends overseas, advising surrogates in secret wars against common adversaries, engaging in assassination plots).[24]

Although covert action was out of favor with some administrations, others have spent enormous sums of money on this approach to American foreign policy, sometimes known as the "Third Option" between reliance on diplomacy and the use of military force. A prominent example was its bold use by the Reagan administration in Nicaragua and Afghanistan. Indeed, the 1980s was the Golden Age of covert action—the historical high point of America's spending on secret interventions abroad.[25]

Covert action can be tricky in several senses. Frequently, the outcome of the events it sets in motion is difficult to predict. In 1953, this approach (chiefly through the use of covert propaganda) permitted the United States and the United Kingdom to depose the incumbent leader of Iran, Mohammad Mosaddeq, and reinstall as emperor (Shah) Mohammad Reza Pahlavi, who was more friendly toward the West's primary interest in the region: access to cheap oil. The very next year, the CIA was able—also mainly through the use of propaganda operations—to frighten the president of Guatemala, Jacobo Arbenz Guzmán, out of office after he threatened to nationalize the United Fruit Company, a banana export business owned by Americans.[26] It all seemed so easy. An irritant on the world stage? Send in the CIA—far less noisy than the marines, and perhaps more effective. Similar efforts to overthrow Fidel Castro in 1961, however, demonstrated that trying to change the world through paramilitary operations (PM ops) was not simple but simpleminded; covert action as a panacea for America's foreign policy woes crashed on the beaches at the Bay of Pigs.[27]

The two major Reagan administration covert actions, in Nicaragua and in Afghanistan, further underscored the unpredictability of this approach. In the early 1980s, Congress closed down CIA paramilitary operations against the quasi-Marxist regime in Nicaragua, believing they were unnecessary. This set of decision by lawmakers—the Boland Amendments, supported mainly by Democrats—drove the Reagan administration underground. The administration decided to pursue paramilitary methods against the Nicaraguan regime by other means, despite the legal bans, creating a super-secret organization outside the intelligence community, known as "The Enterprise." The result was the Iran-*contra* scandal.[28] Against the Soviets in Afghanistan, though, properly authorized PM ops proved remarkably successful, in large part as a result of Stinger missiles supplied to the anti-Soviet Mujahideen forces in Afghanistan by the CIA. These weapons gave the Afghan fighters the capacity to shoot down Soviet military aircraft and contributed to Moscow's second thoughts about continuing the war.[29] Unfortunately, many of these fighters would later become members or supporters of Al Qaeda.

Surmising the long-range consequences of covert action is a challenge. In the case of the Guatemalan coup of 1954, for example, the United Fruit Company was no doubt pleased at the outcome; but the impoverished citizens of that nation have lived under repressive regimes ever since; in the words of the journalist Anthony Lewis, "The coup began a long national descent into savagery."[30] Similarly, the twenty-six years of repressive rule by the Shah in Iran led to a revolt in 1979 that resulted in a fundamentalist religious regime. This same regime allowed Iran students to take Americans hostage in their own embassy in Tehran in 1979, and the United States remains at odds with the government of Iran.

The rise of Al Qaeda in Afghanistan underscores the unpredictability of CIA covert actions. The celebrated ousting of the Soviets from Afghanistan during the 1980s had a downside. The Soviet defeat set the stage for the rise of the fundamentalist Taliban regime in Afghanistan, which in turn provided a safe haven for Al Qaeda during the time when its leaders backed the 9/11 terrorist attacks against the United States. Moreover, the Stinger missiles (shoulder-held rockets that could bring down not just Soviet jet fighters and bombers but, in the hands of terrorists, commercial aircraft as well) were never returned to the CIA. They remained in the hands of future Qaeda terrorists, Taliban extremists, and Iranians who purchased them on the open market from Mujahideen warriors after the Soviets fled Afghanistan. "You get all steamed up backing a rebel group for reasons that are yours and not theirs," President John F. Kennedy's national security advisor, McGeorge Bundy, once said to me, adding: "Your reasons run out of steam and theirs do not."[31]

One form of PM ops—the assassination plot—has had a residual negative effect on the reputation of the United States. Although these plots never succeeded, the CIA's efforts to "terminate with extreme prejudice" foreign heads of state (Fidel Castro of Cuba and Patrice Lumumba of the Republic of the Congo, among others) eventually became known to the world. It seemed as though this country had become a global Godfather, in the harsh Mafia sense of that word.[32] This was hardly the image most Americans desired, or the smartest approach in a Cold War contest that hinged on the ability of the West to win the allegiance of other nations.[33]

Of course, one person's agony over the long-term negative effects of covert action may be offset by another person's joy over its short-term benefits. Looking back on the Iranian coup, for instance, DCI William E. Colby stressed that "the assistance to the Shah to return in 1953 was an extremely good move which gave Iran twenty-five years of progress before he was overthrown. Twenty-five years is no small thing."[34] And, Colby might have added, neither is a quarter-century of low gas prices for Americans.

Another DCI, Stansfield Turner, points to the CIA's covert propaganda program aimed at communist regimes during the Cold War as an effective operation. "Certainly one thinks that the book programs [smuggling through the Iron Curtain books and other reading materials that were critical of communism in general and the Soviet regime in particular], the broadcast programs (most notably, Radio Free Europe), the information programs do good," he said to me. "When you get facts into a country where the truth is not a common commodity, you're doing some good."[35]

Clearly, covert action had proponents as well as opponents.

The DDO told the commission that, since the end of the Cold War, these kinds of operations were directed not so much against foreign governments as against terrorism, illegal drug trafficking, and the proliferation of

WMDs. Much of what used to be done through CIA covert actions was now carried out openly, by way of funding for U.S. aid agencies, nongovernmental organizations (NGOs), and government-funded groups like the National Endowment for Democracy; nevertheless, I suspected that the Agency still had an oar deep in these covert waters in 1995. Indeed, a week after the DDO briefing, newspapers reported on alleged CIA covert actions in both Iraq and Iran.[36] One feature of the DO, though, remained consistent during and after the Cold War: "We deal with thugs," said the DDO, "not church elders."

The DDO's biggest complaint about the current state of intelligence was the "lack of clarity" from consumers in Washington when it came to collection tasking: what were their priorities? "This is what's broken," he stressed. He emphasized, too, that the DO needed more cover abroad—credentials that appeared genuine and could help disguise the espionage activities of Agency case officers. The trouble was that few groups—journalists, academics, missionaries, development aid workers, businesses—wanted spies using their organizations or trades as cover, for fear it would jeopardize their own safety.

While Aspin, Dewhurst, Fowler, and Pursley dug into the nuts and bolts of the DO's current operations, Steve Friedman dug around in a travel bag next to his chair, finally pulled out a bagel, and began chewing on it. The DDO said that he liked the concept of "co-location"—a new experiment at the CIA of having DO operatives and DI analysts working side by side, so that the ground-truth case officers fresh from overseas assignments and the "intellectuals" fresh from the library or the Internet could share information more effectively about foreign intelligence targets. The idea was to blend spy-based findings with library and Internet research on a country or topic. Still, he said with a sigh, if certain analysts wanted an "air gap" between themselves and "us grubby DO types," so be it.[37] The whole idea, though, he continued, was to create "teams of people, not stovepipes—CIA analysts, the FBI, NSA, imint personnel all working together."

"Yeah, like the rest of the world," Friedman interrupted. The company he had come from, Goldman Sachs, took pride in its reputation for organizational teamwork.

"But it would take a clear legislative mandate to force the FBI to share information," the DDO added glumly. Or an act of God, I thought to myself.

Shifting direction, he lamented how the Operations Directorate was stretched thin. There were too many demands from policy makers flooding the DO's in-boxes, without any sense of priorities. "We don't have time to think about what we're doing," he concluded. It was the same point that General Clapper had made to us in an earlier briefing, and it reminded me of when I had once asked former DCI William Colby if the United States was trying to gather too much information from around the world. "Not for a big nation," he replied. "If I were Israel, I'd spend my time on the neighboring Arab armies and I wouldn't give a damn about what happened in China. We are a big power and we've got to worry about all of the world."[38]

The director of the NSA arrived next to brief the commission—a vice admiral named J.M. "Mike" McConnell, covered in ribbons and chevrons, with three stars glittering on his shoulders.[39] Here was the first of the big shot collectors, the man who ran the largest intelligence agency in the United States—and in the world. "If you're not in collection, you're not in the game," was an oft-heard quote attributed to him. Soft spoken and slight in frame, the South Carolinian had the physical attributes of a preacher, not a warrior. He was known for his ability to distill complex ideas into simple, under-standable explanations.[40] McConnell spoke of how the millions of telephone calls in the world each day made the NSA's job of intercepting messages exceedingly difficult, particularly with the movement of global communications companies toward "pipe lights"—the underground and undersea fiber-optic cables that were replacing through-the-air messaging from above-ground transmitters. "There has been an explosion of communications," he said wearily.

"I have an explanation," Fowler offered with a mischievous grin. "There are now more woman ambassadors, and they're on the phone more."

There was a chorus of boos in response from female staffers, joined by Commissioner Zoë Baird.

"You're in big trouble now, Wyche!" warned Aspin. "Big trouble!"

Fowler beamed, then deftly switched gears by telling McConnell that he objected to widespread NSA wiretapping in the first place.

"You remind me of that Henry Stimson guy," Warren Rudman replied to Fowler, as the admiral stared at the Georgian in disbelief. "The secretary of state who said, 'Gentleman do not read each other's mail.'[41] That didn't work, Wyche."

Next, an NRO representative dazzled the commission with four-color slides that showed pictures of elaborate surveillance satellites orbiting in space. By now, Friedman was on his second bagel, as the discussion in the room grew more technical by the minute: LEO (low earth orbit), HEO (highly elliptical orbit), GEO (geosynchronous orbit), digit exploitation, electrical-optical, long-dwell, pop-up radars. Except for the techies—Allen, Caracristi, and Hermann—the commissioners were finding it difficult even to formulate a good question. We may have had plenty of high-tech satellites, but I noticed that the wall clock in the conference room had been stuck at a quarter to six for the past two days.

A briefer on osint appeared after the NRO presentation, bringing commissioners back to earth. They could easily understand the idea of open-source intelligence, and they had a host of questions about the relationship between information in the public domain and the "secret nuggets" of clandestinely collected—stolen—information. After the end of the Cold War, the United States could now gain much insight into the rest of the world from public sources. With respect to Russia, for example, the CIA formerly had to spy to find out anything about that nation; now Moscow had some ten thousand magazines that Americans could buy at street-side newsstands. In Q and A, Rudman asked if documents in foreign languages could be translated quickly into English by machine. The answer was: not in our lifetime.

Throughout these sessions on collection, one conclusion stood out clearly: in the information gathered by America's spy machines and human agents, there was always more noise (the chaff) than signal (the wheat—the vital information affecting America's security). Trying to locate the important signals amid all the noise was part of the "processing" phase of the intelligence cycle. Intelligence pours into the U.S. secret agencies "like a fire hose held to the mouth," to quote a saying made popular by a former director of the National Security Agency, Adm. Noel Gayler, who was exasperated by all the information rushing into his agency from sigint satellites, giant listening antennae, and thousands of small eavesdropping devices planted by CIA and NSA teams overseas.[42] This glut of incoming information creates a daunting IT challenge with which the United States continues to grapple.

After the morning briefings, the commissioners had a working lunch, eating sandwiches the staff had ordered from a nearby deli while they pondered what they had learned. Wolfowitz asked Aspin for the floor. "We need to keep in mind that we might have to face a major hostile country—say, China or Russia—not just some third-rate nations," he said. "We can't afford to cut too much into our collection capabilities." He went on: "Also, I haven't heard anything about counterintelligence yet. That needs attention, too."

Aspin asked him: "What would you do differently? How would you buy differently? How would you organize?"

While Wolfowitz paused to consider these questions, Bob Hermann jumped into the discussion: "You don't have to name the risk, but you need to build the capability and the assets you need. Plus, better foreign liaison."

"Yes," Wolfowitz agreed, "and we need more R & D. We shouldn't dismantle our intelligence agencies recklessly. To what extent can we mothball certain capabilities? And by all means let's improve our foreign liaison—maybe even build some relationships with the Russian intelligence agencies."

"I don't know about that," Dewhurst said, who suddenly stopped doodling on a notepad and looked over at Wolfowitz with a skeptical expression. "The Russians still seem to threaten us." The commission's cowboy was right in a sense. It was widely discussed in U.S. counterintelligence circles that Russian espionage activities against the United States had, if anything, picked up since the end of the Cold War. Wolfowitz was aware of this, but he was thinking about the possibility of working with Moscow against common enemies—"terrorists, drug dealers, international criminal organizations," as he put it. (The fact that the Kremlin continued to spy on the United States would become obvious to all through media reports in 2010, when the FBI arrested a ring of eleven Russian agents operating in the United States; in a deal reminiscent of the Cold War, these agents were quickly traded back to Moscow in exchange for the release to the United States of four CIA assets languishing in Russian prisons.)

"What bothers me most in what I have heard so far," reflected Friedman, "is the discordant relationship between the FBI and the CIA, most recently over access to the Stasi [East German intelligence] files." When the Berlin Wall fell in 1989, leading to the reunification of Germany, the CIA sought to mine this valuable source of information on terrorists supported by East Germany. The FBI had similar interests, but ran into a CIA roadblock. Some thought the Agency was simply trying to keep the Bureau away from discovering that every one of the Agency's East German assets had been turned back against the United States—a rather embarrassing aspect of DO humint recruitment during the Cold War. This "doubling" of the Agency's agents had happened in Cuba as well, and both the Stasi and the Cuban double agents had fed disinformation to the CIA (and, therefore, to American policy officials) throughout the Cold War.[43]

The Agency, though, had a different explanation for blocking FBI access to the Stasi files: its own access had come courtesy not of the German government, but of a secret source who would be jeopardized if the "witting circle" of those in the know grew wider. The Bureau, however, was not easily dissuaded. After raising Cain at Langley and on Capitol Hill (a skill it had elevated to a fine art over the decades), the FBI got its hands on at least some of the East German intelligence files.

At Wolfowitz's mention of international crime, Baird began to stir in her chair. "International crime is something I know about," she said, when

Friedman had finished his observation about FBI-CIA discord. "We have to get these agencies working together on this and many other issues. Cooperation is vital."

Hermann thought that the attention to targeting issues was misplaced. "We need to define our strategy first, then work out the threats or targets. Decide on a course of action for the United States." While sensible, this plan required the development of an American grand strategy for world affairs in the post–Cold War era. That task was probably beyond the mandate, and perhaps the capabilities, of the commission; this was a geopolitical matter that the White House, the NSC, the State Department, and Congress should have been grappling with, although there was no sign they were. The government is usually too busy making day-to-day decisions to engage in much long-range thinking. The containment doctrine had served the nation well as a grand strategy against the Soviet Union, but now what? That was Hermann's concern, and it was warranted: how could you select targets and allocate spending for intelligence collection unless you had a good idea of what you were trying to accomplish in the world?

I remembered a conversation I had with George Tenet about this subject in 1994, just as the commission was taking shape. At the time, he was the top intelligence staffer on the NSC (and would later become DCI). "The burden is on policy makers to determine how the intelligence community should react to the new world we live in," he said. "They must decide on the roles, the missions, and the priorities for the CIA. The intelligence community can't be expected to make those decisions on its own."[44] For that reason, he was pleased that an intelligence inquiry—what would become the Aspin Commission—was in the works. It could decide on the new missions and priorities. "Take a dramatic look," as Tenet put it. "What are the nation's priorities?" was the first question to ask, in his view, followed by "How does the intelligence mission fit into these priorities?" For him, the central issue was this: "Does the intelligence-collection apparatus designed against, and focused on, the Soviet military target really meet the needs of the world that we now face?" The answer was obviously no; change was needed, just as the National Security Act of 1947—still the nation's chief statutory guidance for its defense and security policies—could stand revision to reflect the world we live in today. But exactly what a new grand strategy, and a new National Security Act, should embody was hardly self-evident. Defining this strategy was the commission's main job, Tenet thought, and so, apparently, did Bob Hermann.

The formulation of a fresh grand strategy for the United States was a tall order, and the commissioners sidestepped that challenge. Instead, they focused on matters that seemed more immediately answerable. The questions flowed around the table—some basic and some highly technical, depending on the experiences of the commissioner:

> What do we know about the industrial base for intelligence hardware?
> Do we have the right specifications for satellites?
> Do we have enough humint in the right places?[45]
> How can we determine the intelligence requirements of each policy department?
> What mix of collection systems do we need?
> Can we identify a realistic budgeting process for the intelligence community?
> And the ever-present, overarching question: how much intelligence is enough?

As always, the questions came more readily than the answers.

———

In April, an intelligence flap broke out in Washington that underscored my concerns about intelligence accountability. The cause was a pair of murders in Guatemala that put acting DCI William Studeman in the hot seat. A CIA asset in the Central American nation, a colonel in the military named Julio Roberto Alpirez, had been implicated in the 1990 killing of an American innkeeper, Michael DeVine, as well as the death of Efraín Bámaca Velásquez, a Guatemalan guerrilla fighter who had been married to a vocal and articulate American attorney who was now successfully drawing attention to the case. By law (the Intelligence Oversight Act of 1980),[46] the DCI is expected to report to both oversight committees in Congress—SSCI and HPSCI—on any intelligence failure or suspected impropriety. Discovering that a suspected murderer was on the Agency payroll qualified as a reportable event; yet for three years the CIA kept the Congress in the dark. Senator William S. Cohen (R-ME), an SSCI member and one of the leading Iran-*contra* investigators during 1986 and 1987, told Studeman flatly: "The oversight committees have been misled and . . . may have been lied to."[47]

The case raised troubling questions, too, about whether lawmakers could be trusted to keep sensitive intelligence intact. Rep. Robert G. Torricelli (D-NJ), a member of HPSCI, had taken it upon himself to identify—in a press conference—the name of the CIA asset in Guatemala (Alpirez), even though at the time this was classified information. Evidently, Torricelli had done so in moral outrage at the colonel's alleged criminal activity, although some claimed that the congressman was just a publicity hound intent on raising his profile in the media before entering a race for a Senate seat in New Jersey (which, in fact, he won the next year, though his political career in the Senate was later cut short by a corruption scandal). The *New York Times* concluded that Torricelli sometimes came across as a "bumptious grandstander."[48]

As much as I thought the CIA had seriously erred in hiring this military thug in Guatemala and in failing to report on the murders, Torricelli had no right to reveal Alpirez's name or the identity of any other CIA asset. Instead, the congressman could have expressed his concerns privately in any number of places: to the CIA's inspector general, the Justice Department, the congressional leadership, the Intelligence Oversight Board, even to the president. Instead, he went to the media—a terrible breach of trust that cast a shadow over the reliability of all SSCI and HPSCI members. Could they be counted on to keep the nation's secrets? I knew firsthand that they could, and I also knew that Torricelli was the single significant exception to the rule since the Senate and House Intelligence Committees were established in the mid-1970s. The two committees had been virtually leak-proof over the years, but—thanks to Torricelli—the perception would remain that Congress had misused its privileged access to sensitive information.

In SSCI hearings on Capitol Hill, Admiral Studeman admitted that the CIA had failed to inform the intelligence committees about the criminal actions of its asset in Guatemala. The acting DCI said this outcome was a result of a bureaucratic slipup, noting lamely that "someone in the CIA was thinking about it, but it never connected. . . . It slipped under the carpet."

This admission prompted SSCI member Richard C. Shelby (R-AL) to remark: "That's a big carpet over there at Langley, isn't it? To hold all the things that have slipped under it. It'd have to be a large carpet."

"They [SSCI and HPSCI] should have been informed," the admiral repeated, probably wishing he were on an aircraft carrier, somewhere far away at sea. "And we do have lists that describe the kinds of information and categories of data that we are to convey to this and the other committee [HSPCI]."

"I guess whoever is carrying out that list didn't come to work that day," Shelby concluded dryly.

The hearing ended with a statement of profound concern from Senator Cohen. "In the past, we used to have a mentality that if you asked the wrong question of the Agency you never got the right answer," he said. "If you asked the right question, you got only half the right answer."[49] That had been my experience, too, on occasion, when I had taken depositions from leading intelligence officials while on the Church Committee staff in 1975. For example, I had a devil of a time trying to pry information out of former DCI Richard Helms about why he signed a presidentially initiated—and clearly improper—master spy plan (the "Huston Plan") in 1970 that ordered the CIA, the FBI, the NSA, and the DIA to engage in domestic espionage.[50]

Several years earlier, former DCI Colby maintained that "Congress is informed [about intelligence] to the degree that Congress wants to be informed."[51] There was an element of truth to that point of view; if lawmakers were lazy, they would never gain access to the information they needed to understand the operations of the secret agencies. Yet even when members of SSCI or HPSCI were industrious, there was no guarantee they would be told about all operations. During the Iran-*contra* scandal, CIA officers lied to members about the Agency's involvement in questionable covert actions against Nicaragua. When called on the carpet later, one high-ranking Agency official argued that his sworn testimony to lawmakers had been "technically correct, [if] specifically evasive."[52] That kind of gobbledygook made oversight nearly impossible. At the time of the hearing on Guatemala in April of 1995, Cohen feared that the old mentality of evasion was still alive and well.[53]

This was not the last time we would hear about the Alpirez case. The White House ordered an inquiry into the matter by the Intelligence Oversight Board, and two of its three members (Caracristi and Harrington, the IOB Chair) were on the Aspin Commission.[54] I hoped all the commissioners would view the Alpirez matter as a warning that accountability should not be treated as an afterthought to our work, relegated to the "cats and dogs" grab bag of miscellaneous issues—or forgotten altogether.

———

In Washington, the scent of pink cherry blossoms filled the morning air on April 19, 1995. Spring was in full bloom, and, as always at this time of year, the world seemed filled with new possibilities. In fact, though, it would prove to be one of the most tragic days in American history. As I walked from my apartment toward the NEOB for a commission staff meeting, thirteen hundred miles away in Oklahoma City a Ryder rental truck sat parked in front of the Alfred P. Murrah Federal Building. In its storage space, a homemade bomb made up of fifty-five-gallon drums suddenly erupted in a powerful blast, fueled by a mixture of ammonium nitrate and nitromethane.

The date marked the second anniversary of the fatal assault by the FBI on the Branch Davidian sect near Waco, Texas, that resulted in the deaths of seventy-six people. The Oklahoma City explosion, triggered by an alienated young military veteran, Timothy McVeigh, seething with antigovernment rage, was a domestic terrorist event of a magnitude never before seen in the United States—the worst terrorist attack in the nation since a bomb exploded in front of the Morgan bank on Wall Street on September 16, 1920, killing thirty-eight men and women.[55] In a letter written shortly before the bombing of the Oklahoma City federal building, McVeigh said that he had shifted from being an "intellectual" in the antigovernment movement to being an "animal" determined to shed blood in honor of his cause.[56] The bombing left 168 people dead, including nineteen children, and injured more than five hundred others.[57]

If the Aspin Commission members and the American public needed any reminding about the importance of intelligence, they got it that morning. "I think we are going to see more of this," Admiral Studeman warned while in Milwaukee for a commission outreach event held in Aspin's old congressional district.[58] One of the many questions raised by the Oklahoma City bombing was the extent to which the FBI had succeeded in placing informants inside "patriot" groups of the kind to which McVeigh had belonged. A well-placed informant could have warned the Bureau of the planned attack; the terrorist tragedy underscored the importance of humint in the intelligence business.[59]

Within hours of the Oklahoma City bombing, security tightened dramatically around the White House and the Executive Office Buildings. The front of the NEOB was cordoned off with yellow police tape. The Secret Service was now closely inspecting each vehicle that entered the building's underground parking, and officers prohibited any trucks or vans from idling in front of the building. A long line of automobiles stretched out along 17th Street, waiting to enter the NEOB's underground garage as the Secret Service searched beneath the carriage of every vehicle with mirrors attached to poles and German shepherds sniffed the tires. A new set of police officers I had not seen in the area before paced the sidewalk, dressed in all-blue one-piece suits, pistols at their hips. Over the next week, white vans belonging to the Secret Service patrolled the streets—a *memento mori* as we walked to work each day.

On the day of the bombing, I had my commission ID badge prominently displayed around my neck as I entered the foyer of the building and passed through the security gates. Instead of lounging around in their normal casual manner, the white-uniformed Secret Service guards inside the NEOB were on high alert, matching the polished professionalism of their colleagues who guard the president. This time even my briefcase was x-rayed, an unusual procedure for badge holders.

When I arrived at my office on the third floor, I looked out the window to watch the activity on the street below, imaging what a Ryder truck parked in front of the building and filled with explosives would have done to the NEOB—as easy a target as the Murrah Building in Oklahoma City, a thought no doubt on the minds of the Secret Service officers who scurried along 17th

Street. I was no longer so happy about having a window office facing the street, and later in the day, I searched around the NEOB for a safer location on the other side of the building. In my exploration, I discovered not only a small and charming library with a friendly staff, but a gym as well. The library proved an impractical location for work, however, since I needed access to the computer at my desk . I returned to my office and looked out the window again. The state of emergency seemed to have little effect on the stately Metropolitan Club across the street. On its second floor, chandeliers glittered and elderly men sat in overstuffed chairs playing cards around a green-beige table, brandy sniffers in hand. Life goes on. I returned to my desk and got back to work.

Later that day, Aspin telephoned from the OEOB. We talked about the shock of the attack on the Murrah Building, and he said the main reason he was calling was to have me prepare a study on America's counterterrorism defenses. I told him that, coincidentally, I was scheduled that very day to visit the Agency's Counterterrorism Center (CTC), a suite of offices at Langley that looked like a CNN newsroom and was staffed mainly with personnel from the Agency's Operations Directorate. When I arrived at CTC, its external-affairs officer filled me in on what the center knew about terrorist activities that might threaten the United States, whether from inside the nation or from beyond our shores.

"Terrorism has always been with us and is here to stay," he told me, "—and will probably increase, thanks to the power that television gives to terrorists." He offered his opinion that the president should respond coolly to acts of terrorism: "Giving them undue attention just plays into the hands of the terrorists." That sounded reasonable, but how could the president ignore or downplay something as horrible as the Oklahoma City bombing? Besides, beyond being a natural human response, showing concern was good politics and leadership in the aftermath of a terrorist act or any other cataclysmic event that harmed the nation.

The CTC officer predicted that weapons used by terrorists were likely to become more lethal and sophisticated, because terrorism—like everything else—was linked to the forward march of technology. He thought that chemical-biological weapons were more likely to be used by terrorists against the United States than nuclear weapons, especially a chemical nerve gas like sarin. That substance had been used just one month earlier, fortunately with limited effectiveness, by Aum Shinrikyo, a religious group in Japan drawn to terrorist tactics against subway targets in Tokyo. Aum Shinrikyo, the commission learned, had accumulated financial assets worth billions of dollars and was planning to attack cities in Western Europe and the United States, until the

Japanese government tracked the organization down after the Tokyo subway attacks and jailed its leaders. Attacks on Japanese subways, a bombing in the American heartland, the 1993 bombing of the World Trade Center—hopes for a peaceful world after the end of the Cold War now seemed profoundly naive.

I discussed with the CTC terrorist expert how the United States might best defend itself against the threat of terrorism. "Developing better liaison relationships with foreign intelligence services is vital," he replied, "and, of course, we have to increase the quality and quantity of our humint penetrations into terrorist organizations." He also recommended improved interagency counterterrorism cooperation within the framework of the CTC, along with "tightened immigration policies." As our conversation came to an end, he informed me that the Counterterrorism Center had recently completed a paper on the subject of terrorist threats, and he would have a courier deliver the top-secret study to me tomorrow at the commission's quarters in the NEOB.

When the document arrived the next morning, I pushed everything else aside and focused on the most riveting document I had seen so far while serving on the Aspin Commission. My eyes froze at one sentence, which has since been declassified and can be presented here. "'Aerial terrorism' seems likely at some point," the document read, "—filling an airplane with explosives and dive-bombing a target."[60] America was still six years away from comprehending the full implications of this warning, and the fact that a large passenger airplane loaded with volatile aviation fuel would serve well enough as a bomb without added explosives. The document listed a number of other vulnerabilities in America's counterterrorism defenses, from local city water supplies to busy harbors and train lines. I brought the CTC study to Aspin's attention, having him read the document and my summary analysis in our secure area in the NEOB rather than risking taking it out of my office and carrying it by hand to the PFIAB suite in the OEOB. I also circulated the findings among my staff colleagues.

The CTC had sent the same information to the president and other top officials, of course, including members of SSCI and HPSCI. Only after the 9/11 attacks would I realize that both the Clinton administration and the Congress had failed to pass this information along to the Department of Transportation (DoT), airport security personnel, or the American Pilots Association—organizations and individuals with a need to know and who were in the right places to improve airport security, seal airplane cockpits, and place sky marshals on airliners. None of this happened, perhaps because the administration and Congress were paralyzed by all the other threats listed in the document and, above all, by the expense involved in trying to improve security measures against each contingency. Yet the "aerial terrorism" section of the document had leapt out at me and surely would have caused a reaction among pilots and officials at DoT. Which was more expensive—tightening airport security in 1995 or suffering the human and economic consequences of aerial terrorism in 2001? That question was easy to answer on the morning of September 11, 2001.

In a similar manner, the administration of George W. Bush would drag its feet in taking the prospect of an Al Qaeda attack against the American homeland seriously. Based on U.S. intelligence reports, the longtime government counterterrorist guru and NSC staffer Richard A. Clarke warned incoming national security advisor Dr. Condoleezza Rice in January of 2001 that Al Qaeda posed the greatest immediate threat to America's security and should be her top priority. Not until early September of 2001, however, did Rice get around to calling an NSC meeting about this danger.[61] Intelligence agencies can only do so much; at some point, policy officials have to act on the information they are provided with. Both the Clinton and the second Bush administrations failed to take intelligence warnings, such as the 1995 CTC study or Clarke's warnings, seriously enough, and 9/11 was the price to pay.

Naturally, it would have been ideal if the CIA had presented to the Bush administration the precise timing and other details of the impending Al Qaeda attacks before September 11th. This lack of "actionable" information, enormously difficult (though not impossible) to acquire when dealing with a tight-knit terrorist organization, represented an intelligence failure, to be sure; but the warnings about aerial terrorism as early as 1995, and Dick Clarke's bright red flag in 2001, were reasonably good alerts from the secret agencies—and they were ignored. The Aspin Commission, too, though momentarily shocked by the range of terrorist ploys that could grievously harm the United States, added the CTC report to the mountain of papers it was accumulating, without much attention to the specific danger of aerial terrorism. The lesson: the security of the United States depends not just on good intelligence (the more detailed, the better), but on the effective use of that intelligence by policy makers. This means taking preventive action, even if doing so costs money—perhaps lots of money. In this regard, imagine if even just a quarter of the trillions of dollars spent on the wars in Iraq and Afghanistan would have been dedicated instead to the improvement of America's intelligence capabilities and homeland defenses after the 9/11 attacks.[62]

———

During Admiral Studeman's trip to Milwaukee, he expressed his own views on what the goals of the Aspin Commission should be. Les Aspin had invited him to attend a symposium on intelligence reform at Marquette University, where the chairman had taught in the economics department before he ran for Congress. The idea was to stimulate interest in intelligence around the country, as a means of helping the commission implement its recommendations once we had written our final report. (Aspin had traveled to Harvard University for two days just prior to the Milwaukee symposium for the same purpose.) The Milwaukee event was unusual, since spy chiefs rarely give public speeches. It would have been impolitic, though, for Studeman to turn down the chairman of the commission looking into the operations of his agencies.

Speaking at the university's Alumni Memorial Union, the admiral suggested to his audience of students, faculty, and townspeople that the Aspin Commission should concentrate on the structure and costs of intelligence, since the question of collection targets had already been addressed by Presidential Decision Directive 35 (which was and remains a classified document).[63] He hoped for "evolutionary, not revolutionary" change, he said, but conceded that change was necessary. With Aspin in the audience, Studeman urged the commission to take a close look at the proper role of the director of central intelligence, especially the relationship between the DCI and the intelligence community's most demanding customer: the military. Studeman referred to "support to military operations"—SMO, in the Pentagon acronym—as the intelligence community's "defining mission." He thought the nation's intelligence budget requirements should rank at the very top of the commission's agenda, alongside the strengthening of counterintelligence. He noted, too, that the annual intelligence budget was a classified number, but that recent newspaper reports indicated the figure was around $27–28 billion. He did not dispute that estimate.

The admiral was particularly concerned about the state of imagery intelligence. He pointed out that one satellite could cost as much as $1 billion just to launch into space. The construction and management of these "birds" was less efficient than it should be, he conceded, and he expressed hope that the commission could take on this "structural problem." He raised other subjects that he thought the commissioners should probe:

- the Directorate of Operations—Should it stay within the CIA?
- covert action—Did the United States continue to need this tool?
- congressional oversight—Was it working well?
- economic intelligence—Did the CIA need to focus more on this mission?
- law enforcement—How could "the wall" between intelligence and law enforcement be lowered "to increase cooperation and reduce overlap between the two communities?"[64]

- intelligence for international organizations—Should U.S. intelligence support such entities as the United Nations and NATO?
- foreign liaison—How much should U.S. intelligence rely on foreign intelligence services and cooperate with those services against common foes?

It was useful to hear what was on the mind of the intelligence community's top acting head and to realize we were asking essentially the same questions.

———

On April 26, 1995, John Deutch appeared before the Senate Select Committee on Intelligence for his confirmation hearings. The SSCI's hearing room is a cavernous hall in the Hart Senate Office Building, which is named after the late Philip A. Hart (D-MI), a thoughtful and popular member of the Church Committee. On this morning it was filled with reporters, tourists, staff aides, and Capitol Hill police. No spooks, at Deutch's request to the CIA beforehand. The nominee was a tall man, though he walked hunched over as if he carried a heavy burden on his shoulders. He had a high forehead, wore thick, round glasses like Aspin, and displayed a brash manner that made one suspect he did not suffer fools gladly. Woe be to the MIT chemistry student who had not done his lab work, or the Pentagon general late for a meeting. According to the *Washington Post*, Deutch had acquired "a freewheeling reputation as someone willing to bend procedures, if not rules, to push cherished programs or ideas through reluctant bureaucracies."[65] The SSCI chairman, Arlen Specter (R-PA, who would switch to the Democratic Party in 2009 and go on to lose his Senate seat in 2010) said on the eve of the confirmation hearings that the Senate was looking for a "take-charge director."[66] They may have found one.

"I believe the security of the nation requires that the President, his civilian and military advisors, and the Congress have the best information," Deutch began, after the introductory formalities were over, "and the most objective assessments about the capabilities and the intentions of foreign countries and entities that may threaten the interests of this country and its allies." This was a simple statement, but it did highlight an important point: as DCI Helms once put it, "There is no greater threat to world peace than poorly informed or misinformed leaders and governments."[67] A president without good intelligence was a one-eyed Jack.

Deutch offered his own global threat matrix. First was the danger of the United States being drawn into "major regional conflicts" (MRCs, in Pentagonese) with, say, North Korea, Iraq, or Iran. Second was the danger of proliferating WMDs. Third was a collection of transnational threats: international terrorism, international crime, and international drug trafficking. I knew from earlier research that we were losing the "war" against drug trafficking, halting a mere 30 percent of the cocaine and heroin secretly shipped into the United States.[68] The last item on Deutch's threat list was Russia, despite the end of the Cold War. He had not forgotten about all the nuclear weapons that nation still possessed; even though they were not presently aimed at the United States, they could soon be if Moscow so decided.

I sat up straighter in my chair in the hearing room when the nominee began to speak of intelligence oversight, a subject seldom addressed in meetings on the third floor of the NEOB. "I state unequivocally that if confirmed as director of central intelligence, I will insist on adherence to the rules, and I will hold every person accountable for his or her actions." Bravo, I was tempted to shout from a back row. Later, when I looked at the DCI's personal transcript of his remarks (photocopied for the commission's use), I noticed that Deutch had underlined this passage in black ink.

The nominee said further that the intelligence community ought to be directing itself toward four principal goals: making sure that America's leaders had the best information available; providing "dominant battlefield awareness" for the Pentagon (the SMO argument Studeman had dwelled on in Milwaukee); taking on international terrorism, crime, and drugs (a set of issues he seemed to take with utmost seriousness, since this was the second time he had mentioned this trio of threats within five minutes); and establishing a strong counterintelligence shield to guard against any more Ames-like treacheries.

He confronted head-on the criticism about the White House's promise to place him in the cabinet. It was important to be a member of this high council, he maintained, because it highlighted the value of intelligence in the government, as well as the president's confidence in him. "I fully recognize that the director cannot allow himself to stray into offering policy advice," he reassured the senators—not very convincingly, for those who knew him well.

Deutch had a reputation for being fixated on "techint," spying using technical intelligence in the form of satellites, reconnaissance aircraft, and any other machines the government could invent to steal secrets abroad. So far, though, he had said nothing about these spy "platforms." Near the end of his formal statement, his voice grew firmer as he vowed: "I will move immediately to consolidate the management of all imagery collection, analysis, and distribution." He proposed streamlining the way in which the United States used satellites to photograph intelligence targets, as well as how the secret agencies interpreted the pictures and disseminated the information to policy makers. It was clear he intended to be an agent of change, and that techint would indeed be a major focus, as rumored.

So would the management of the intelligence community. In fact, he referred to management issues as "my first and most important challenge." Reading between the lines, this meant closer DCI attention to improved cooperation among the intelligence agencies. Deutch was going to take on the gorillas in the stovepipes. I suppressed another urge to shout "bravo!"

With the Alpirez matter in mind no doubt, he concluded his remarks by promising to have a close working relationship with SSCI and HPSCI—"my board of directors," as he put it. He assured lawmakers that he would keep them "informed about the activities for which I would be responsible—both the good news and the bad news. I understand that I am accountable to you." John Deutch was really starting to grow on me.

In responding to questions from the senators, the candidate for DCI made a courageous (some would say foolish) promise to rid the CIA of its old Cold Warriors and change the Agency "all the way down to the bare bones." He said it was "time for a generational shift."[69] These sounded like fighting words, and the sparring partner was surely the Directorate of Operations, known for its resistance to change—especially at the hands of outsiders who had never been professional intelligence officers. The halls at Langley were littered with the bones of former intelligence directors from outside the intelligence establishment who had tried to revamp the DO. The job of DO officers is to hire assets who can steal information abroad and, when necessary, to disrupt foreign governments. Those on the DO's Covert Action Staff and Special Operations Group were skilled at propaganda, political and economic manipulation, and paramilitary operations. Taking on a DCI they didn't like was a piece of cake.

The reputations of former DCIs James R. Schlesinger (1973), Adm. Stansfield Turner (1977–81), and R. James Woolsey (1993–95)—all from the outside—had been damaged by secretive retaliations by the DO, especially negative comments about the DCI leaked by operatives to friends in the American media. The sins of these particular intelligence chiefs? Schlesinger and Turner had worked together to fire many of the old guard in the Directorate of Operations, and Woolsey had the temerity to reprimand eleven DO officers for brazenly conferring medals on subordinates responsible for the lax security that had allowed Ames to operate within the directorate.

Deutch informed the senators during the confirmation hearings that, unlike Woolsey, he would have "terminated" the station chiefs and other senior DO operatives who failed to keep two consecutive DCIs apprised of the Ames case. Deutch was picking a fight with a group of professional fighters. I respected the legitimate activities of the Operations Directorate and the risks its officers took in the field (a DO officer was the first casualty in the fighting against the Al Qaeda–sponsoring Taliban regime in Afghanistan after the 9/11 attacks); nonetheless, Deutch's promise to rein in its excesses drew a third silent bravo from me. As even a former DDO would admit in testimony later in the year, the Operations Directorate had "probably got too big, too walled off, and too isolated. . . . Like the U.S. military after Vietnam, it needs an overhaul."[70]

Deutch's confirmation was considered a sure thing even before the hearings, and he was indeed quickly confirmed by the members of SSCI and approved by the full Senate as the nation's seventeenth director of central intelligence—the fourth in as many years. "He's a man for all seasons and the man of the hour," said Deputy Secretary of State Strobe Talbott after the votes.[71] Despite the new DCI's obvious talents, I had a feeling the commission might begin to miss the mild-mannered Bill Studeman.

————

As April came to an end, the buzz around the NEOB staff offices focused on the approaching commission retreat—the "offsite," as military members of the staff called it. We were taking the show to rural Virginia. "There is no need to pack a suit or dress clothes," a staff memo informed commissioners and staff. "Casual clothing, to include comfortable walking/athletic shoes, is recommended for all events." All aboard for Camp Aspin.

L ES ASPIN LOOKED FORWARD TO the retreat in the Virginia countryside, intended to help foster some degree of bonding among the diverse commissioners. The commission would escape the hectic pace of Washington for a couple of days and concentrate on the major reforms it needed to consider. The chairman worried, though, that the "A-team" in Washington—key senior security officials—might be unwilling to take time away from their busy schedules only to face an in-box piled even higher with paperwork when they returned. The staff spent the last days of April hunting down senior intelligence and policy officials who would commit to the Thursday and Friday powwow.

On Thursday, May 3, 1995, the staff and commissioners gathered at National Airport and boarded a CIA plane headed for the Farm (known more officially as Camp Peary), a "secret" 9,275-acre Agency base near Williamsburg, Virginia.[1] Flying at ten thousand feet over rolling, wooded terrain, the DASH-8 aircraft completed the bumpy trip south in an hour, touching down on an isolated landing strip at 10:15 AM. As we taxied down the runway, I peered through the window by my seat. Arrayed near a forest of pine trees stood an impressive little Air Force: a DHC-4 Caribou, a C-47, various Cessnas, an Aztec, a Volpar, a DHC-6 Twin Otter, a PC-6 Porter, and several foreign-made aircraft. Near the runway stood a decaying wood-frame building, bleached grey-white over the years by the baking sun of Virginia summers, its shutters rotted by rains that swept off the Chesapeake Bay. As we deplaned, I could hear the buzz of mud daubers in the trees.

Despite my initial impression of having landed somewhere in the Third World, we were taken to comfortable quarters a few miles away in the compound where our meetings would take place, a cluster of two-story residences, each named after a kind of tree. I checked into the "Magnolia," unpacked my suitcase, and headed for lunch. Several CIA officers awaited the commission members and staff in a rustic mess hall. The summer-camp atmosphere had the desired effect. Open collars had replaced ties and starched white shirts, and the commissioners joked casually with one another as they ate sandwiches. Almost all of those who attended the lunch ended up staying for the full two days of briefings and discussions, although five commission members—almost a third of the membership—took a pass on the entire retreat.

The Case Officers

The sessions began after lunch with a panel of case officers—the foot soldiers of the CIA's Directorate of Operations, who lived abroad and attempted to recruit indigenous agents to spy against the government of their own country (or perhaps a terrorist cell inside the country) on behalf of the United States. They spoke of how the world had changed dramatically over the past few years. "Cracking safes is irrelevant," said a bear-sized fellow with a carefully groomed beard. "Now all the secrets we're after are on computers." Another DO officer opined that the Agency didn't belong in the counternarcotics business; that mission should be reserved for the Drug Enforcement Administration. The discussion turned to the relationship between analysts in the CIA's Directorate of Intelligence (DI), where the intelligence reports for top officials are prepared, and field operatives in the DO. "Sure, we need a better partnership, but we don't need "co-location," groused a senior DO officer. "Let's don't get too carried away."

The idea of co-location, placing groups of DI analysts and DO operatives next to one another at CIA Headquarters, had not caught on with everyone at the Agency. The plan was to have these officers share office suites according to their responsibilities—all those working on the Cuban or the Cambodian portfolios, for instance, seated near one another. During the Bay of Pigs fiasco, DO planners never consulted with DI analysts on Cuba; had they done so, they would have learned that the analysts were convinced Fidel Castro was far too popular to be toppled by a paramilitary operation carried out by Cuban exiles.[2] The aim of co-location was to bring together research experts and experienced field hands, resulting in a richer understanding of circumstances abroad. The trouble was, though, that the two groups didn't like each other much. The DI intellectuals often thought the DO officers were "cowboys" with little refinement, while the DO looked upon the Agency's thinkers as clean-fingernailed, opera-loving "librarians" who lacked the imperative "ground truth" of overseas experience.

David Dewhurst and Steve Friedman were right: culture mattered, both inside the intelligence agencies and among them. The DO officer who greeted us in the lunch room and objected to co-location was willing to talk with DI specialists now and then, he explained; but to move in with them, cheek by jowl, day after day—that was asking too much. Next he would have to sit down with them for Chablis and Gouda in the afternoon. "That's a goat fuck," he said. Using more delicate language, former DCI Stansfield Turner also told the commission on another occasion that he opposed co-location. "Analysis needs to be separated from policy in order to be completely objective," he reasoned.[3]

The discussion in the lunchroom fractured into a dozen topics. "These days I contact the lawyers before I do anything," remarked another tough-looking case officer on rotation back to CIA Headquarters for a few months. By his appearance, one had to assume he was a member of the Special Operations Group (SOG) that engaged in paramilitary activities. In previous interviews, the staff had heard frequently that case officers were now risk averse; here was additional testimony to that effect. Some of the CIA personnel argued in favor of a more robust NOC (nonofficial cover, pronounced "knock") program. Most Agency case officers abroad operate out of the U.S. embassy under official cover (OC). Often they are easily identified by local intelligence services (in one country, all the CIA officers were known to drive Land Rovers); and all too frequently they tend to stick around the embassy or a few favored watering holes in the capital city, rather than integrating themselves into the local society.[4]

During the Cold War, official cover inside the embassy could be effective. The U.S. ambassador would host social events and dinners, inviting Soviet diplomats and KGB intelligence officers to attend. At these events, CIA case officers could get to know these individuals, with the hopes of recruiting some as assets who they could turn back against Moscow. (Of course, the Soviet "diplomats," many of whom were intelligence officers, hoped for the same success in reverse.) It was unlikely, though, that America's new targets for recruitment—drug dealers, international mafia figures, terrorists—were going to show up at a U.S. embassy cocktail party. One had to get out into society and the countryside to make contacts with such people, and that meant serving as a NOC, say, in the guise of an archeologist or a freelance journalist during the day, while donning a cloak as a case officer when darkness descended.

Very few CIA case officers at the time were NOCs. Nonofficial cover was expensive to administer, and it could be dangerous. If discovered engaging in espionage overseas, OCs enjoyed diplomatic immunity; but as a NOC, case officers were on their own. Still, the argument that we needed more NOCs made sense. This was the method of spying used by many other nations (witness the Russian "suburban" spy ring uncovered in the United States in 2010).

Counterintelligence came up, too, for the first time as a topic for sustained discussion before the commission. The CIA officers conceded that the "corridor file" (rumors at Agency headquarters) about Ames had been troubling long before his treachery was uncovered. He was widely known as a drunk and someone who seemed to have more money in his pockets than a bureaucrat's salary would allow. When colleagues inquired about his new Jaguar sedan and a pricey home he had purchased in Arlington, Ames brushed them off with stories of how his Columbian wife had recently inherited money from her family. Since Ames's father had been a well-regarded DO officer in the Agency, and since drunkenness was hardly page-one news at Langley, his colleagues accepted the explanation and moved on.

In most of the remarks from the CIA officers over lunch was one central message for the commission, which we had heard before in Washington: the Agency was being asked to do too many things when it came to intelligence collection. "Just say no!" seemed to be the theme—especially "no" to collection against narcotics dealers and to the notion of environmental intelligence.

We spent most of the afternoon visiting facilities around the Farm, along with sitting in on training classes that were underway for new recruits. During free time, I went for a run on the dirt roads that snaked through the pine forests. Off to the side of one road, two young Agency recruits batted a tennis ball back and forth on a well-groomed clay court. In the distance the pale blue water of a swimming pool shimmered in the sunlight, surrounded by a broad apron of manicured lawn dotted with stately oaks, towering magnolias, and lavender crepe myrtles. The Farm, Country Club for Spies.

Higher Up the Hierarchy

In the evening we had dinner with the executive director of the CIA, followed by a postprandial visit with Lt. Gen. James R. Clapper Jr., the DIA director and my friend from high school. The Agency's executive director, a high-level factotum for the DCI, was an angry man. Some of the intelligence reform proposals drifting around Washington had apparently gotten under his skin, and here was his opportunity to vent. Covert action should be hived off from the CIA and put into a separate agency; the idea of a director of national intelligence, or DNI, should be junked in favor of strengthening the existing office of the DCI; policy makers should stop tasking the intelligence agencies with an impossibly long laundry list of targets. He bristled at having to collect intelligence on the environment, on human rights, and on drug dealers. The first two were not subjects for clandestine collection, in his view; and the third was hardly a strength of the Agency—not to mention that it was flat-out dangerous.

Clapper didn't mince words either, though his style was more diplomatic. His core theme was that military intelligence was in a state of disarray and should be consolidated under the direction of a four-star flag officer—a director of military intelligence, or DMI. The more cynical members of the staff and the CIA officers in attendance privately saw this argument as Clapper's bid for another star, along with an effort to push the CIA further away from any control over military intelligence. Cynical speculation aside, it did seem as though the fragmented military agencies needed better coordination. As Wolfowitz mentioned to me during a break, "A DMI would give the DCI a focal point in the Pentagon to contact when problems arise."

The featured speaker at the retreat, Robert M. Gates, a personable former DCI, was scheduled for the 8:00–11:00 slot the next morning. Gates had earned a PhD from Indiana University in Russian studies and was the only spy chief to have come up through the intelligence ranks as an analyst. He had solid political connections around Washington, having served in the administration of George H. W. Bush as deputy national security advisor. Some critics thought he had allowed himself to become too close to the first Bush administration, even "cooking" intelligence reports to suit the administration's political needs; but I had seen no compelling evidence to support this allegation. More likely, his own professional, hard-line views on the Soviet Union simply matched up well with the thinking of the Bush administration, without Gates needing to twist any intelligence reports. One thing was certain: he was one of the most affable people in Washington and was widely liked on both sides of the aisle. Chief among his detractors were a few former analysts in SOVA, the CIA's Cold War division of Soviet experts, who stuck to their belief that Gates had become a "political director" who ignored or rejected their assessments on partisan grounds rather than because of a genuine disagreement among Sovietologists.

Either Gates didn't receive or had ignored the memo on casual dress for the retreat. He wore a button-down shirt (*de rigueur* for CIA officers at Agency headquarters), white and heavily starched, a carefully pressed suit, and a preppy stripped tie. Short and stocky with close-cropped hair and a bright smile, the former DCI knew most of the commissioners and many of the staff. He mingled with them like a fraternity brother. As he stood speaking behind the dais at the end of the table in another rustic room where we were meeting, his formal introductory remarks covered a wide range. He began by reminding the audience that the intelligence community's primary responsibility was to warn the nation of danger. The Japanese attack on Pearl Harbor in 1941 had been a primary stimulus for the creation of the CIA, he recalled. Turning briefly to the question of intelligence funding, he complained that 1986 had been the last year of budget growth in the intelligence community.

Gates grew more animated as he moved on to the issue of intelligence tasking. "The intelligence agencies are not looking for work," he emphasized. "They're overwhelmed already." Later in the year he would tell a reporter: "The CIA is probably more heavily tasked today by policymakers than at any time in the past."[5] To some extent, though, the CIA had brought this problem on itself. At the end of the Cold War, its managers had volunteered to take on almost any available task, worried that the Agency might lose status and resources in the government if it failed to make itself useful.

Gates noted, too, that—contrary to media reports—the intelligence agencies had already done much to adapt to the new world. Change was possible, even in large bureaucracies, he argued, pointing out the dramatic shift in U.S. intelligence resources away from the Soviet Union and toward new targets around the world since 1991. He also objected to Senator Moynihan's suggestion that the CIA had missed the impending collapse of the USSR in the years leading up to 1991. He insisted that the Agency had closely tracked its decline, which by my own research for Aspin confirmed, though—like everyone else in the world—it had not forecast precisely how quickly the situation in Moscow would descend into chaos. Gates then proposed a set of recommendations for reform. He was skeptical that PDD-35 was sufficient for setting collection goals. Instead, he advocated "a structure that would force policy officers to engage dynamically in providing guidance to the intelligence agencies on collection priorities." He seemed to have in mind a richer, even weekly, dialogue on targeting requirements, an ongoing conversation between the mangers of intelligence collection and high-level policy officers—even if it were merely a working group comprised of deputies to the top department secretaries in the foreign policy and security domains. The bottom line: policy makers needed to communicate their intelligence needs with greater clarity and on a more regular basis. As the former DCI had put it on another occasion: "Unless intelligence officers are down in the trenches with the policymakers, understand the issues, and know what U.S. objectives are, how the process works, and who the people are, they cannot possibly provide either relevant or timely intelligence that will contribute to better informed decisions."[6] In the same breath during his briefing at the Farm, though, Gates seemed to indicate that a robust dialogue on targeting was already underway—indeed, it was too robust, with too many requests. Raising his voice to underscore the point, Gates pleaded with the commission to help pare down the burgeoning list of intelligence-targeting priorities flowing from the various government departments—the "just say no" theme again.

On another key topic, Gates adamantly opposed the creation of a director of national intelligence. "A DNI would be like the current drug czar—weak," he said, preferring instead to beef up the DCI's authority over community-wide budgets and personnel. This was the best way, in his opinion, to overcome the powerful centrifugal forces in the intelligence community. No CIA professional, Gates included, was likely to support a DNI office located outside the Agency's headquarters; this would deprive the CIA of the central role it had enjoyed in the intelligence community since 1947, especially its analytic support to the nation's spymaster. Yet, I knew that stripping the Agency of a DCI on its seventh floor might well appeal to the many anti-CIA people around the intelligence community, who for decades had resented its status as the *central* intelligence agency. Still, I thought Gates was right. For almost fifty years, the CIA had been given by statute the job of coordinating U.S. intelligence and collating its reports; to toss this experience aside and start over with a new DNI bureaucracy located who knows where seemed foolhardy.

On Gates's checklist of intelligence reforms—and there were dozens of such lists floating around Washington—were these additional proposals:

- reducing redundancies among the eight military intelligence agencies by creating a four-star director of military intelligence. This was a reiteration of General Clapper's idea. Gates recommended, as well, a managerial consolidation of all tactical intelligence activities, to straighten out the disarray in information gathering and dissemination at the battlefield level.
- constructing better connections among the separate "stovepipes" that the thirteen intelligence agencies had become
- consolidating counterintelligence operations. Aldrich Ames remained the white elephant in the room at many of the commission's meetings; it was his treason, after all, that had helped stimulate the creation of

the Aspin panel. Gates rejected the idea of establishing a new stand-alone agency for counterintelligence, in the manner of the British MI5 organization. He wanted a new unit created for this task of a community-wide consolidation of counterintelligence, but one led by an FBI officer and located at the CIA. It would report directly to the DCI in the chain of command. He reflected on the "extraordinary hubris" of the belief inside the CIA before the unmasking of Ames that the Agency "could not be penetrated—an illusion now shattered."

- reforming the Operations Directorate—the same formidable group that John Deutch had targeted for reform. Gates expressed a preference for abolishing CIA paramilitary operations altogether ("We've never had a *secret* PM operation," he declared), turning that controversial task over to the Department of Defense.

This last recommendation made me think of a remark that former DCI and Secretary of Defense James R. Schlesinger had offered the Church Committee during a hearing on covert action in 1975. "The DoD is too big and too noisy to carry out secret paramilitary operations," he warned.

Gates remained undecided on the debate over co-location, but he recalled that "armed guards used to be placed between the two directorates, leading to an extreme isolation of the Directorate of Operations." Officers in the DO believed, he continued, that "everyone else in the headquarters building [at Langley] was irrelevant." Only DO officers possessed the "ground truth" of what was really happening overseas, while analysts—hunched over their computers thousands of miles away from the action—remained clueless. So ran feelings inside the Operations Directorate, according to this experienced former DI analyst, at least. Gates observed that most of the DCIs had chosen to ignore the obvious tensions between the CIA's two main directorates—or failed to understand the problem altogether.

One DCI in the 1960s, Vice Adm. William F. Raborn Jr. (1965–66), remained, as Gates related the story, largely in the dark about all the directorates.

"You guys are divided into divisions, right?" Raborn had asked a CIA subordinate one day.

"Yes, sir."

"Good, okay, get two of them ready to go to Vietnam," ordered the admiral, not realizing that Agency "divisions" (or, more accurately, directorates) were rather different from mobile military units.

Gates displayed some passion as he took up the subject of intelligence accountability. Back in the mid-1970s when SSCI and HPSCI were created, the committees decided to set term limits on the tenure of their members—a maximum of eight years for SSCI and six for HPSCI. In this manner, the committees hoped to reduce the risks of "co-option" (or "co-optation"); that is, having lawmakers and intelligence officers become too cozy with one another through long-standing relations. If terms were limited, perhaps the development of an "old boy" network could be curtailed. Gates thought this idea was dumb, because lawmakers were forced to rotate off the committees just as they were beginning to really understand the details of the intelligence business. Experience mattered.

He also opposed the idea of having only one oversight committee—a joint intelligence panel—to replace SSCI and HPSCI. The one-panel concept was popular among some former DCIs, as a way of reducing the amount of time directors had to spend on the Hill (one briefing, instead of two). Moreover, a single panel would supposedly diminish the risks of leaks. With astonishing candor, Gates said with a gleeful grin that with two committees, "the DCI can manipulate one against the other." If SSCI didn't like a proposed intelligence operation, perhaps HPSCI would, or vice versa; the director could use these disagreements to his own advantage. Above all, he recommended more informal meetings between the DCI and the oversight committees. I doubted that more afternoon kaffeeklatsches would have done much for the Woolsey-DeConcini relationship, but generally Gates was right. Good relationships rest on the development of rapport between individuals, and that meant getting together for informal chats—much like we hoped the retreat would increase camaraderie among the commission membership.

Gates had managed to keep everyone's attention for well over an hour—no small feat. Perhaps not wanting to push his luck too far, he wrapped up his comments, stressing "the three worst reform ideas." First was the notion of a new director of national intelligence separated from the CIA; second, the weakening or abolishment of the CIA; and, third, arbitrary cuts in the spy budget.

Now it was time for a question-and-answer session.

At the Farm, I continued a practice I had begun during the very first commission meeting in March. I wanted to record the levels of participation exhibited by each commissioner. I was interested in seeing if a chairman really did dominate the proceedings, as some of the scholarly literature on commissions suggested; and, at the same time, I sought to gain a sense of who the "movers and shakers" were on the Aspin Commission, at least as measured by personal engagement in the panel's discussions and debates and the posing of meaningful questions of witnesses. Thus, as members spoke,

1. Dicks (18)	10. Wolfowitz (2)
2. Fowler (13)	11. Dewhurst (1)
3. Aspin (10)	12. Baird (0)
4. Goss (6)	Rudman: absent
5. Friedman (6)	Allen: absent
6. Hermann (5)	Caracristi: absent
7. Pursley (4)	Coelho: absent
8. Warner (3)	Exon: absent
9. Harrington (2)	

The figures in parentheses are the number of questions and comments made by each commissioner during the two-day retreat at "The Farm" in Virginia (May 3–4, 1995), as tabulated at the time by the author.

FIGURE 5.1 Commission Participation Rates at the First Aspin-Brown Retreat, 1995

I tabulated their verbal participation rates, placing a mark by their names each time one asked a question, and another mark for follow-up comments. If the comments were extensive, I recorded a third mark.

This tabulation was not done with scientific precision, such as using a stopwatch, but it did provide a reasonably accurate approximation of who was participating and who was not. In the Q and A following Gates's remarks, for example, I came up with a "participation profile," with the name of the commissioner followed by the number of his or her questions and comments, which is illustrated in Figure 5.1.

Four former or current HPSCI overseers—Dicks, Fowler, Aspin, and Goss—dominated this particular session at the Farm. The quartet was responsible for two-thirds of the questions or comments from commissioners. If nothing else, sitting and former members of Congress knew how to talk, and, on the whole, they were shrewd questioners, having honed this skill in endless hearings on Capitol Hill.

The first question for Gates probed his views on congressional oversight (despite the proclivity of the Aspin Commission staffers and some commissioners to downplay this topic). This gave the former DCI an opening to elaborate on his earlier remarks on this subject. He complained of a tendency among SSCI and HPSCI members to "micromanage"—the word that was a favorite cudgel used by intelligence and military bureaucrats to pummel the idea of congressional involvement in the affairs of the executive branch. The argument was that lawmakers become too involved in the details of intelligence activities, even though they don't have the requisite training to understand them; as a result, delicate operations were sometimes inadvertently harmed by the clumsy meddling of congressional overseers. I had heard this critique from intelligence officers time and again since the days of the Church Committee. For some intelligence officers, it was coded language meaning: "Stay out of our business, you morons—just let us do what we think is right for the security of the United States."

At least Gates had some examples, which was rare among those who advanced this criticism. He said that lawmakers had recently forced the CIA to buy computers, while "leasing would have been smarter." If this was the best example the former DCI could come up with of "micro-management," his argument seemed weak. His second illustration, though, was more damning. "I remember Senator Malcolm Wallop [R-WY]," Gates continued, "trying to tell me exactly how many analysts to assign to each country." This was clearly over the line. The Wallop example, though, struck me as an exception to the rule; a far more frequent problem on the oversight front was congressional flaccidity—or total absence. If anything, members of Congress failed to probe enough into the details of policy, spending their time instead trying to pass bills with their names prominently displayed on them and attending fund-raisers for the next election. Among the priorities of lawmakers, scrutiny of executive branch programs—the essence of oversight—often came in last, in large measure because members of Congress received little credit from their constituents for painstakingly reviewing NRO budgets or listening to DO witnesses in closed hearings.

Gates used another question about intelligence history as an opportunity to look back on the length of service by DCIs. The intelligence community had been led by sixteen directors since 1947, compared to only four directors at the FBI—a high rate of DCI turnover, which troubled him. At another point, he mused on the "one regret" he had regarding his own tenure. "I should have made some wrenching DO personnel decisions," he said, by which he meant that he should have tossed out the deadwood that had accumulated in the Operations Directorate since the early days of the Cold War.

Previous DCIs James Schlesinger and Adm. Stansfield Turner had dismissed hundreds of DO officers and met fierce resistance to their leadership. Schlesinger had the advantage of being named secretary of defense after only a few months at the Agency and quickly escaped the heat; Turner stayed on for the full four years of the Carter administration and never really recovered from his efforts to continue Schlesinger's policy of weeding out poorly performing officers from the Operations Directorate. Turner's troubles were amplified by the fact that he personally fired the DO officers and did so, to make matters worse, by way of a coldly worded letter, while Schlesinger delegated the task to underlings. Further, the admiral dismissed many more people (820) than Schlesinger had—although Turner claims they were from the lowest 5 percent in the Agency, as measured by annual performance evaluations. At any rate, even today the names of these two former DCIs still draw groans inside the Directorate of Operations. Gates would probably have joined this DO enemies list, too, had he taken on the Agency's operatives.

Turner ended up being especially bitter about his experiences with the Operations Directorate. "I would order them to do things—and *nothing* would get done," he recalled in an interview with me.[7] One of his aides, a senior DO officer, called together the top brass in the directorate without Turner's knowledge and told them (according to a transcript of his remarks that the admiral saw later): "Now, look, Turner's not a bad guy, and in time he'll learn how we do it." This incensed Turner even more. "It wasn't a question of my having to come around and do it their way; it was a question of: I was the boss." Turner continued: "These professionals [in the DO] believe that there's just nobody who can tell them what to do. They have the attitude: 'Only we can do this.' They want a figurehead up there [on the seventh floor of CIA Headquarters], and, unfortunately, I've never been a figurehead."

Turner stressed that he had no intention of telling people in the Operations Directorate how to conduct their business. "While I'm not going to tell them where to make a dead drop [a clandestine exchange of information between an agent and a case officer], I am going to determine whether it's worth the risk of doing a dead drop," he said. "I've been enough of a manager in life to know that I didn't tell the chief engineer which valve to turn, but I told him what I needed out of him—so many knots of speed. Similarly, at the CIA I wasn't going to tell them how to spy; but I was going to say: 'What's the probability you'll get caught, and what's the product you're going to get?'"

In his further responses to questions at the Farm, Gates explained why he opposed the appointment of John Deutch to the cabinet. "This sends the wrong message about politicization," he said, referring to the worst possible sin of intelligence: coloring analytic reports to suit the political desires of policy makers. He was not saying that Deutch would necessarily commit this transgression, but that serving as a member of that distinctly political forum would be bound to raise eyebrows about the DCI's devotion to policy neutrality.

A commissioner asked whether Gates would support making public the figure for the aggregate annual intelligence budget. "No," he replied, "because then reporters will clamor to break the figure down into details, and this would jeopardize national security." It seemed an obvious red herring. The commission could simply provide the aggregate figure, reported to be about $28 billion at the time, then adamantly refuse to reveal any additional numbers—just as they had refused to reveal the total figure for forty-eight years. At least with a known aggregate figure, the public would have some sense of how much was being spent on intelligence each year to protect them. Was that asking too much in a democracy? Perhaps the real agenda for secrecy on this matter was a concern that the public might find the figure too high and press for cuts.

Another commissioner asked Gates about his views on economic intelligence. He came to the same conclusion I had through my own research, namely, that spying for U.S. companies was unneeded and unattractive to intelligence officers, though intelligence support for Washington officials on illegal trade practices of other nations, technological developments abroad, and the negotiation objectives of rivals at international trade conferences was fair game and could be quite helpful. Just as the CIA's weapons experts had supported the government with data during arms-control negotiations throughout the Cold War, so could its economic experts support America's international trade diplomacy.

Gates was asked, too, about what he had in mind with his vague remarks about the need to reform the Directorate of Operations. He explained further how the DO presented a special challenge for every DCI. "As I told Woolsey," he recalled, "the rest of the community can give you trouble; the DO can send you to jail." He painted a portrait of the directorate as a place of minimal accountability, where power and responsibility were widely dispersed—especially into the hands of its various division chiefs (organized by regions of the world or "functional" specialties, like weapons proliferation or illegal drug trade). It was, he said, a "closed circle" from the rest of the CIA. What Gates found most troubling was the directorate's "dangerous cultural problem," by which he meant "the unwillingness of lower levels to raise problems up the DO ladder." He pointed to the Ames case as an example. As we had heard from others, out of loyalty to Ames's well-liked father (himself an operations officer), the "old boys" in the DO club overlooked the weaknesses of the son—the alcoholism, the extravagant lifestyle—that by any objective accounting should have set off alarms about his vulnerability to the financial temptations of treason.

After lunch, the commissioners convened for a final business meeting before leaving to return to Washington. The corridor conversations between sessions had raised a flood of questions in their minds and now they began to flow out. How much should the nation spend on intelligence?

Was intelligence a "force multiplier" that could make our expensive weapons systems more accurate? Had the CIA fallen behind the technological curve, because of insufficient investment in research and development?

The budget process garnered the most attention. "It's fractionated," complained Senator John Warner, "and there's no accountability. Let's try and figure this out at our next meeting in Washington." Looking as stern and rigid as a cigar store wooden Indian, he went on to offer his philosophy regarding the commission's charge. "A few of us were desperately concerned that someone was going to go in and cut up the intelligence budget," he said. "This commission was meant to stop that—and it has succeeded." He warned his colleagues against "playing into the hands of politicians who will jump in to cut defense and national security. Our mission is to explain to the American people that intelligence is important."

Returning to Power City

Back in Washington, much work awaited us. The staff, and those few commissioners who wanted to join us on the front lines of our research, had scores of individual interviews lined up; we spent weeks traveling around Washington and beyond to talk with all the top intelligence and national security experts we could find. The staff already knew a lot about the core intelligence issues; that's why we were hired. No one knows everything in this arcane field, however, and the more we could learn from some of the master practitioners, the better our ability to help the commissioners decide on sensible recommendations and write a good final report. From the staff's point of view, this was a tremendous opportunity to sit down with people we might not otherwise have been able to meet—busy VIPs protected by fire-breathing gatekeepers.

For example, in May two staff members and Steve Friedman (who was rapidly becoming one of the most actively involved commissioners) went to the Washington law offices of Milbank, Tweed, Hadley & McCloy to meet with former DCI William H. Webster. "Judge" Webster, as he was known because of his earlier career as a judge on a U.S. District Court and a U.S. Court of Appeals, was widely consider "Mr. Integrity." He had a clean, wholesome look, as if he might have been an astronaut in his younger days. He also enjoyed a reputation for abiding strictly by the law and other rules of good conduct. The only person to lead both the FBI (1978–87) and the CIA (1987–91), he possessed a wealth of intelligence experience. A product of prestigious Amherst College in Massachusetts (the alma mater of Stansfield Turner and John Deutch as well), Webster had gone on to study law at Washington University. After decades of private practice in Missouri and service in his judgeships, he had become a fixture around the nation's capital— the man called in to brush up the image of an agency suffering from allegations of impropriety (most recently the CIA's involvement in the Iran-*contra* scandal).

His tenure at the CIA had been tarnished by a sense that he might have been more interested in playing tennis in the afternoons than managing spies, and by an unsatisfactory working relationship with President George H. W. Bush; nonetheless, he was still admired throughout Washington, D.C. for his devotion to ethical behavior and his knowledge of the vital relationship between the CIA and the FBI. Making the commission feel like we were listening to a broken record, Webster emphasized in his interview the absurdity of creating what he called "an unarmed DNI"—that is, a director of national intelligence set off to the side of the intelligence community with no "troops" (analysts). To be successful, a DNI would have to "have his hand on the tiller" at the helm of the CIA where most of the government's analysts resided.

Rather than create a new office of DNI, Webster argued, a smarter move would be to empower the current office of DCI by providing its incumbent with greater control over the community-wide intelligence budget. Further, the DCI should have a voice in the hiring and firing all of the "program managers"—the agency heads, or "gorillas"—and should participate in writing their "report cards" each year (their efficiency evaluations, which influence salary increases and promotions). "He who writes the report card is boss," Webster observed. He was skeptical about the idea of creating a four-star director of military intelligence, for such an office could well become a rival to the DCI. "We do not want to create islands of separateness," he said. "We want the various agencies to be responsive to the DCI, not to other managers."

The main theme running through the interview with "the Judge" was his belief that the CIA needed to regain its "centrality". It was inappropriate to turn the Agency into just a humint collection organization; it was meant, as shown by the wording of the National Security Act of 1947, to be "on top" of the intelligence community. The judge was historically correct; that is exactly what the founders of the modern American intelligence establishment had in mind when they created the CIA, but it was not a popular idea in the Pentagon or even in most of the civilian intelligence agencies.

The CIA's Historical Roots

The searing memory of one particular violent shock, and the potential for yet more violence, had led to the CIA's birth in 1947. The initial shock occurred in 1941, with the Japanese attack against Hawaii that pulled the United States into World War II. The potential for further violence was a concern very much on the minds of U.S. officials after the war ended in 1945—a fear that the Soviet Union might attempt an armed expansion into Western Europe and Asia that could jeopardize America's global interests.[8]

On December 7, 1941, Japanese warplanes swooped down on the U.S. Pacific Fleet anchored at Pearl Harbor on Oahu.[9] In two waves of strafing and bombing just after sunrise, 350 planes from six Japanese carriers managed to demolish 187 aircraft on the ground, as well as eight battleships (five sank), three cruisers, three destroyers, and four auxiliary ships in the harbor. The assault killed 2,403 American service personnel, mostly navy, and wounded another 1,178. One hundred civilians also died. In an address to Congress, President Franklin Roosevelt declared that the day of the attack would "live in infamy." The slogan "Remember Pearl Harbor!" became a rallying cry for America's entry into World War II.

Eight separate panels of inquiry examined why the United States had been taken by surprise at Pearl Harbor. None of the investigations fixed clear blame for the disaster, but one conclusion was indisputable: America's intelligence apparatus had not warned President Roosevelt that a Japanese war fleet was sailing toward Hawaii.[10] Indeed, it was the most damaging intelligence failure in the nation's history, and would remain so until the Al Qaeda terrorist attacks of September 11, 2001.

The United States had misread both the capabilities and the intentions of the Japanese. The president had no idea the Japan had developed aerial torpedoes capable of navigating the relatively shallow waters along Ford Island where the American battleships were moored. These torpedoes wreaked the greatest havoc in the attack.[11] While a U.S. intelligence program (Magic) had managed to intercept and read the Japanese military's "purple code," which indicated that Tokyo was on the verge of initiating warfare, the analysis based on this signals intelligence did not reveal when and where its military would strike. The best hunch was the Philippines. As with the months preceding the Al Qaeda strikes on American soil in 2001, plenty of "chatter" surfaced about a potential military action before the attack took place; but, amidst all the noise, insufficiently actionable signals emerged to pinpoint a specific time and place of attack.[12]

Moreover, the fragments of data available here and there in the bureaucracy about the impending outbreak of war in the Pacific were never assembled, subjected to all-source analysis, and forwarded to the White House in a timely manner—the basics of the intelligence cycle.[13] This sequestering of information resulted in part from the intention of some intelligence officers to keep the existence of "Magic" carefully compartmented and secure. The top secret that America had broken the Japanese diplomatic communications codes might be compromised, they reasoned, if information from this source were shared outside the confines of a few Navy intelligence personnel. Yet, in hiding the decoding breakthrough from the Japanese, they also succeeded in hiding it from the president of the United States.

As a U.S. senator from Missouri, Harry S. Truman was well aware of the significant loss of lives and matériel that resulted from America's poor use of intelligence in 1941. During his three-month tenure as vice president, and after becoming president following Roosevelt's death in April of 1945, Truman was further dissatisfied with the lack of coordination among America's intelligence units throughout the remaining months of World War II. As one of his top aides (and America's first intelligence director), Sidney W. Souers, once observed, during the war, "intelligence...never did reach the top level that should have had it in proper form." He noted further:

> If it was communications intelligence, it would be whispered maybe to Admiral [Harold] Stark or Secretary [Frank] Knox. They would say, "Uh-huh" and then forget it. My feeling was that messages like that should be evaluated and placed on the desks of all concerned. If intelligence had been available in that form before Pearl Harbor, it might have eliminated the disaster that occurred.[14]

This history lesson reminded me of the failure to share the CIA's Counterterrorism Center memo in 1995 on "aerial terrorism" with the Department of Transportation or the American Pilots Association in the lead-up to the 9/11 attacks.

After the Second World War, the prevention of another Pearl Harbor through the establishment of a reliable warning system became the Truman administration's foremost intelligence goal. Moreover, lawmakers on Capitol Hill evoked the memory of Pearl Harbor even more energetically than the president as they debated how to prevent future surprise attacks against the American homeland.[15]

The Truman administration soon confronted an even more compelling reason for improving U.S. intelligence: the growing sense that the United States faced a formidable and hostile adversary in the Soviet Union.[16]

War-weary GIs had just returned home from Europe and Asia when Sovietophobia began to grip the nation's capital, stirred by Winston Churchill's "Iron Curtain" speech in 1946 and waves of vitriolic anti-Western propaganda emanating from Moscow at the time. As intelligence scholar Rhodri Jeffreys-Jones has explained, "past weaknesses" like Pearl Harbor served as part of the backdrop for the debate about reforming America's intelligence capabilities in 1946–47, but more important were "present imperatives"—above all, the rise of Soviet power in the world.[17] Just as the United States could have benefitted significantly from having more effective indicators and warning (I & W) about the movements of Japanese warships in 1941, so did leaders in Washington in 1946 seek a reliable heads-up on the military capabilities and intentions of the USSR.

A CENTRAL INTELLIGENCE GROUP

In the field of intelligence, DCI Richard Helms once observed, ultimately "[warning intelligence] is everything, and underline everything."[18] Warning, in turn, rests on an ability to gather, collate, understand, and disseminate intelligence about threats rapidly to key policy officials. As one of Truman's top aides, Clark Clifford, recalled: "By early 1946, President Truman was becoming increasingly annoyed by the flood of conflicting and uncoordinated intelligence reports flowing haphazardly across his desk."[19] On January 22, 1946, he signed an executive order that created a director of central intelligence and a Central Intelligence Group (CIG) for the express purpose of achieving a "correlation and evaluation of intelligence relating to the national security." The order allowed the CIG to "centralize" research and analysis and "coordinate all foreign intelligence activities."[20]

Truman's original intent—his intelligence dream—was, in his own words, to avoid "having to look through a bunch of papers two feet high" and instead receive information that was "coordinated so that the President could arrive at the facts."[21] In today's terminology, he longed for the all-source fusion of intelligence or, in military terms, intelligence jointness. Truman supported the CIG initiative because it reflected "his dissatisfaction with what he perceived to be the haphazard nature of intelligence collection," in the words of Phyllis Provost McNeil, a member of the Aspin Commission staff who prepared a brief history of intelligence as an appendix to the panel's final report. The initiative, she continues, was in harmony with "his desire to have one authoritative source for intelligence advice, and, above all, his desire to avoid another Pearl Harbor."[22]

Yet President Truman never saw his dream fulfilled. From the beginning, the Central Intelligence Group turned out to be weak. One of its primary tasks was to put together the *Daily Summary*, the precursor to today's *President's Daily Brief*. Yet intelligence units in the various departments balked at handing over information to the CIG. Secretary of State James F. Byrnes, for example, refused to pass along cables from his overseas staff, maintaining that he would be the one to tell the president directly the most important information. In response to this intransigence, Truman weighed in on behalf of the CIG and ordered Byrnes to cooperate in the preparation of the *Daily Summary*. Nevertheless, departments remained resentful of, and often resistant to, the concept of intelligence sharing.[23] White House support for the CIG notwithstanding, putting together the *Daily Summary* quickly became "an exercise in futility."[24]

A *CENTRAL* INTELLIGENCE AGENCY

The Truman administration then turned to the idea of establishing a stronger spy organization: a Central Intelligence Agency. It soon became evident to President Truman, however, that the acquisition of a truly focused intelligence system would come at too high a price in light of an even more urgent goal the White House was pursuing: military consolidation. World War II had been rife with internal conflict among the U.S. military services, often hampering the pursuit of battlefield objectives. As a British official once commented, "U.S. Army and U.S. Navy would just as soon fight each other as the Japanese."[25] Clark Clifford remembered how the administration had to slow down intelligence reform in favor of settling the "first order of business—the war between the Army and the Navy." The "first priority," Clifford continued, "was still to get the squabbling military services together behind a unification bill."[26]

The creation of a new Department of Defense would provide an umbrella under which to bring the services closer together. The president did not wish to "complicate the fight for unification" by simultaneously carrying out a full-court press for intelligence consolidation that was bound to roil the military services, which viewed this reform as a threat to their own confederal and parochial approach to intelligence.[27] As a top CIA official recalled, "The one thing that Army, Navy, State, and the FBI agreed on was that they did not want a strong central agency controlling their collection programs."[28] So Truman and his aides entered into a compromise with the armed services, hoping this would lead to military unification. At the same time, they attempted to improve intelligence coordination to some extent, but without letting that sensitive subject get in the way of the higher goal.

The result was a series of retreats from centralized intelligence, as exhibited by the diluted intelligence language in the National Security Act of 1947. This statute provided for only a feeble DCI, and a CIA that was little different from the failed CIG. As Clifford conceded, the effort fell "far short of our original intent."[29] In this sense the CIA was, as Amy Zegart has put it, "flawed by design."[30] The landmark National Security Act would mainly address the issue of military unification, and with only moderate success at that. (More meaningful unification would have to await the Goldwater-Nichols Act of 1986.[31]) In the new law, the subject of intelligence was downplayed.

The 1947 statute did create a supposedly *Central* Intelligence Agency (at least in name), but was vague on the details of just how the new, independent agency was going to carry out its charge to "correlate," "evaluate," and "disseminate" information to policy makers in the face of the powerful grip in which the extant departments held their individual intelligence units. The portion of the law dealing with intelligence was a careful attempt to set up a CIA that, in historian Michael Warner's summary, would have to "steer between the two poles of centralization and departmental autonomy." As a result, the CIA "never quite became the integrator of U.S. intelligence that its presidential and congressional parents had envisioned."[32]

The rhetoric of "intelligence coordination" expressed in the law had a nice ring to it; however, the reality of bringing about true jointness was a different matter altogether. Genuine coordination required a strong DCI, with budget and appointment powers over all the secret agencies throughout the intelligence community. The term "intelligence community" was clearly a misnomer, coined in 1952 to describe the cluster of stovepiped espionage organizations, each with their own muscular program directors (the gorillas) and allegiance to their own department secretaries (at Defense, Justice, and State). The powers of the DCI enumerated in the National Security Act of 1947 remained at best merely suggestions, leaving America's spymaster in a position of having to cajole, persuade, plead, even beg for coordination, rather than demand unity through the threat of budget and personnel retaliation against those gorillas in the stovepipes who failed to comply with the DCI's orders. As Warner concludes: "A powerful statutory CIA never had a chance. From Day One, War and Navy leaders strenuously opposed such a scheme. With no political capital to spare, the president went along."[33]

A DCI, MINUS THE C

When Truman authorized the creation of the CIG by executive order in 1946, the group's chief counsel, Lawrence R. Houston, soon complained, "We are nothing but a stepchild of the three departments we are supposed to coordinate."[34] Matters did not improve much with the more formal statutory establishment of a CIA the next year. As the political scientists Richard C. Snyder and Edgar S. Furniss found:

> The CIA immediately ran into difficulties of the sort which seems to confront all new agencies in Washington. It inherited feuds going back to the days of the OSS [Office of Strategic Services, America's premier civilian intelligence organization during World War II, disbanded by Truman in 1946]. Over the next three years, the CIA and G-2 [the Army intelligence staff] clashed over which was to control secret agents abroad. The former finally won. A running battle raged between the State Department and the CIA over the question of whether CIA personnel attached to diplomatic establishments abroad were to be under the jurisdiction of the heads of missions. Bitterness broke out between the FBI and the CIA when the latter took charge of foreign field operations; the CIA claimed that the FBI agents did not cooperate in the change-over and the FBI claimed that CIA personnel were rank amateurs, careless about security. The Atomic Energy Commission refused for a long while to share its scientific information with CIA personnel, who were deemed unable to interpret it properly.[35]

Even twenty years after the creation of the CIA, one of its deputy directors, Adm. Rufus Taylor (1966–69), referred to the intelligence "community" as still little more than a "tribal federation."[36]

An important aspect of U.S. intelligence history since the Truman administration has been the series of efforts, running like a golden thread through the years since 1947, to overcome the flaw in the CIA's original design, namely, attempts to strengthen the DCI and the Agency in their roles as collator and disseminator of intelligence for all the secret agencies. The Dulles-Jackson-Correa Report (1948); the Eberstadt Report for the Hoover Commission (1948); amendments to the 1947 National Security Act (1949); the Clark task force of the second Hoover Commission (1954); the establishment of a United States Intelligence Board (1957); the Schlesinger Report (1971); the creation of an Intelligence Community Staff (1972); the development of communitywide oversight procedures in 1975–77; President Jimmy Carter's Executive Order 11,905 (1978); the setting up of DCI centers and task forces during the 1980s and 1990s—all pointed in one direction: the need for a more authoritative DCI to integrate the nation's fragmented intelligence organizations.[37]

Each effort lost steam after meeting resistance from the community's gorillas, especially the King Kong in the DoD—the secretary of defense, with his redoubtable allies on the congressional Armed Services and Appropriations Committees.[38] "For the duration of the Cold War, the White House kept nudging successive Directors of Central Intelligence to do more to lead the Intelligence Community," historian Warner writes. But a towering obstacle persisted: "Cabinet-level officials...saw no reason to cede power to a DCI."[39]

The DNI Solution

Judge Webster understood this history and hoped the Aspin Commission could finally pull off what so many earlier inquiries had failed to achieve: the creation of a strong DCI who could serve as a unifying leader of the intelligence community. One of the commission's next interviewees had dealt closely with the idea of creating a director of national intelligence, or DNI, instead of tinkering with the existing powers (meager as they were) of the DCI. Charles ("Charlie") Battaglia was the staff director of the Senate Select Committee on Intelligence (SSCI) in 1995, the same committee on which Britt Snider had served as counsel before becoming staff director of the Aspin Commission. Battaglia had also served as special assistant to DCI Stansfield Turner and subsequently worked for the CIA's Office of Congressional Affairs before joining the SSCI staff in 1985.

He was a sage observer of the intelligence scene and a vocal advocate on behalf of setting up a DNI to overcome, at long last, the fragmentation of the community. In 1989, he had encouraged David L. Boren (D-OK), the SSCI chairman from 1987 to 1993, and HPSCI member Dave McCurdy (also D-OK; McCurdy would chair the House Intelligence Committee from 1991 to 1993), to introduce the DNI concept in the form of legislation. The problem, he now stressed to the Aspin Commission staff, was simply stated: the DCI "didn't control anything." The titular intelligence chief was without the necessary tools to manage the sprawling espionage establishment.

The Boren-McCurdy legislation envisioned a DNI with full budgetary powers and authority to appoint the directors of the two most costly intelligence agencies: the NSA and the NRO. The DNI would not run the CIA, since the Agency's humint and covert action programs would take him or her away from community-management responsibilities; the DNI would assign a deputy to manage the Agency on a day-to-day basis. Judge Webster preferred a strengthened DCI who could lead the community from the CIA's seventh floor (to underscore the Agency's central coordinating role) *and* manage the intelligence community; Battaglia favored, in contrast, a stand-alone DNI, an intelligence spymaster located outside the Agency—precisely "the DCI without troops" that Webster viewed as impractical and unworkable.

The key to the success of a DNI or a strengthened DCI would be the preparation of reliable, insightful intelligence reports that could help the president make sound foreign policy decisions. As Judge Webster realized, this depended on a close working relationship between the intelligence chief and his or her analysts—90 percent of whom worked at the CIA's Directorate of Intelligence at Langley. If a DNI were removed from this base, "the troops" would be lost. Of course, reformers could move the Agency's Intelligence Directorate to wherever the new DNI would be housed, as Battaglia preferred; but this would amount essentially to creating a new intelligence agency, and why do that when the CIA already existed? One answer might be: because many intelligence professionals in the community didn't like the Agency and wanted to start over again. "The CIA had gotten into the habit of disdain for those things that were being done by the DIA and the military intelligence operations," former DCI James Schlesinger remembers.[40] Disdain breeds reverse disdain. The other intelligence agencies might relish the idea of cutting the Agency down to size, regardless of Truman's intent way back in 1947.

It was true that a number of people throughout the intelligence community (including prominent agency managers) viewed "the Agency" as an arrogant leader, smug in its preeminence and insensitive to the views of other intelligence professionals beyond the Langley campus. Many of the so-called interagency working groups established by the DCI during the Cold War were dominated (so the criticism went) by CIA personnel, without enough representation from the other intelligence agencies. Moreover, the CIA was often too focused on "civilian intelligence"—economic and political developments abroad—at the expense of support to military operations (SMO, the Pentagon's sacred cow). And now there was talk of environmental and global-health intelligence. The DNI proposal, from the vantage point of these critics, looked like a marvelous opportunity to pay back the CIA for a long list of grievances, real and imagined, and to refocus the community on military intelligence (as if the 85 percent of the budget already dedicated to that mission was insufficient).

Among the experts interviewed by the Aspin Commission in May, attitudes about the creation of a DNI were strongly held on both sides of the argument. It was still unclear where the commissioners would come out on this critical subject, but here was a topic we would have to address—maybe the most important, since by all accounts the broad intelligence community seemed to be poorly led—a ship without a rudder, or even a captain.

A Burgeoning Commission Agenda

Our interviews revealed several other issues prominent in the minds of intelligence specialists around Washington and across the country. The question of cabinet status for the DCI, made controversial because Deutch's insistence on this prerogative, concerned many of the individuals with whom we spoke. Judge Webster, for instance, believed that DCI membership on the cabinet would simply give critics "ammunition to allege politicization." The DCI should never make policy recommendations, in his view, and barring the DCI from cabinet meetings would reduce the pressure on the intelligence director to enter into the policy fray.

Of interest to commissioners, as well, was the matter of a fixed term for a DCI. J. Edgar Hoover had served as the director of the FBI for thirty-seven years, from the time the Bureau was founded in 1935 until he died in 1972. A lengthy tenure had the advantage of bridging presidential election cycles, providing the FBI some immunization from America's quadrennial political episodes and the resulting changes in intelligence leadership dictated by incoming administrations. Some critics felt strongly, though, that Hoover's long service had led to the ossification of the FBI. Usually unstated, but understood, was the notion, too, that Hoover had grown too powerful in Washington and had accumulated intelligence files that allowed him to blackmail government officials—even presidents—into supporting him and the Bureau. Whether or not these charges were true, no one disputed the fact that the FBI had become involved in highly questionable practices in the later years of Hoover's tenure, including COINTELPRO and the Huston Plan for domestic spying. Legislation passed after Hoover's death placed a ten-year limit on the time anyone could serve as Bureau director. Now some critics were clamoring for a similar provision applied to the office of the DCI—not that anyone so far had lasted that long in this demanding job. The record was held by Allen Dulles at eight years (1953–61).

With a fixed term, reformers hoped to ensure that a DCI would serve through national election cycles—a term length that would buffer the intelligence community against changes in its leadership according to whoever had just won the White House. Webster opposed this idea, believing that "a president must be able to pick his own intelligence director," not be stuck with someone handed down from a previous administration. The nation's chief executive and the DCI had to have a close working relationship based on personal trust and rapport.

Battaglia agreed with the Judge on this point. So did Samuel Halperin, a well regarded intelligence officer who had spoken in public on the subject and emphasized that this relationship was critical to the success of everything the intelligence agencies were trying to accomplish. In his words, "Unless the DCI is able to walk in to see the President at will, privately, except maybe for the secretary, just these persons—unless that's possible, you don't have a DCI."[41] An incoming president who inherited a DCI selected by an earlier president might not relate well to him or her; the kind of rapport Halperin found indispensable would be absent.

The Directorate of Operations was also shaping up to be one of the most important—and tangled—subjects the commission would need to address. From Webster's perspective, part of the DO challenge had to do with disciplinary matters. In the CIA, discipline was too diffuse, he believed; the DCI only dealt with the most serious infractions or the most senior managers. In contrast, the director of the FBI signed off on every disciplinary measure, even reprimands. This practice gave the Bureau director a better feel for personnel problems. In the CIA, a "culture of tolerance" had evolved, especially inside the DO. "There should be no problems the DCI doesn't know about," Webster stressed, adding that "Agency officials must learn that they will be held accountable for their transgressions."

The Judge was troubled, further, by how poorly information from the DO traveled "upstream"—that is, from the bowels of the Operations Directorate to the DCI's office on the seventh floor at the Agency. He said that he could never count on the DDO to give him "all the facts." This was a prominent theme in the memoir written by DCI Stansfield Turner as well—perhaps a feeling experienced especially by outsiders who come as strangers into the hallowed halls of Langley.[42] Turner said to me, "The chief of operations [the DDO] had difficulty getting his act together in order to answer my questions."[43]

The relationship between the CIA and the FBI was reminiscent of the borderlands between the kingdoms Scotland and England before their unification: a battleground where warring factions often clashed. Webster was well positioned to comment on yet another conflict between the FBI and the CIA: the demand of the Bureau under Louis Freeh's leadership for more FBI billets in U.S. embassies around the world. The Bureau had a compelling argument for placing its personnel overseas. As former DCI Robert Gates has said, "Organized criminal gangs—Russian, Japanese, Chinese, Nigerian—have spread to the United States from their own national borders."[44]

Countering this international criminal influence was a job for which the FBI was well suited, and Freeh had traveled throughout Eastern Europe and Russia in 1994 to meet with local law-enforcement officials about this problem. He had opened offices in Moscow, Poland, Hungary, the Czech Republic, Slovakia, several former Soviet states, Chile, Pakistan, and Beijing, with many more slated.[45] He wanted positions for his officers in several U.S. embassies.

This was a sensitive topic at CIA Headquarters. There are only so many spaces in an embassy, and the Department of State rightly demands most of them, on grounds that embassies preeminently are where the nation's diplomats carry out their assignments abroad. Over the years, though, the intelligence agencies—mostly the CIA—have been able to persuade presidents to allocate space for the case officers who need to be overseas for the purpose of recruiting local agents. Gradually, the number of "official cover" billets for the CIA expanded, but rarely without a fight between the Agency's chief of station and the DCI, on the one hand, and the U.S. ambassador and the secretary of state, on the other hand. Now another player had arrived on the embassy scene; the FBI wanted in, too. Of course, one answer would have been for the CIA and the FBI to rely on nonofficial cover; but, as I have related, NOCs are costly, dangerous, difficult to administer, and, because of the hardships involved, less appealing to young American intelligence officers. So that remedy remained less attractive to managers in both the FBI and the CIA.

Judge Webster warned that if too many Bureau agents were set loose overseas, it would invite trouble. He thought it would be useful to have a few more FBI "legal attachés" abroad, but sharply opposed the idea of allowing the Bureau to run clandestine operations. The CIA and the FBI, he told the commission staff, would simply end up "tripping over each other."

The staff also asked the Judge about some of the new intelligence requirements that had emerged since the end of the Cold War, notably economic-, environmental-, and health-intelligence tasking. I had been delving into these topics for Aspin, and I thought Webster's responses struck just the right note. On the economic side, the Judge was basically in agreement with Gates: no industrial espionage, but help the U.S. government when possible on such matters as international monetary transactions and technological transfers. He appreciated and supported an FBI economic counterintelligence role, as well, since foreign powers were persistently trying to rob the United States of its commercially viable scientific innovations and new weapons systems. As for intelligence support to guard the nation against ecological perils and pandemics, the Judge argued sensibly that intelligence agencies should be encouraged to collect and provide the government with relevant "secret pieces" of information on these subjects when they come to the attention of America's assets, case officers, and spy machines; but these missions should not be a primary focus for the intelligence community.

Each of our interviews was written up and distributed to Chairman Aspin and the other commissioners. These invaluable conversations with leading experts were shaping our understanding of the major intelligence issues then at play in Washington. They also gave us a sense of how vast our domain of inquiry was. I was beginning to understand how Admiral Noel Gayler felt as director of the NSA; we, too, had a fire hose held to our mouths.

CHAPTER 6

Weighing the Value of Estimates

TWO DAYS AFTER OUR RETREAT, Aspin had dinner with John Deutch. The newly appointed DCI was still savoring the impressive vote margin for his Senate confirmation: 17 to 0 in committee and 98 to 0 on the floor. (Senators John Warner and Daniel Patrick Moynihan were absent for the floor tally.) In contrast, Robert Gates had mustered just sixty-four votes when he became DCI in 1991. During the brief Senate debate on Deutch's candidacy, Arlen Specter, the SSCI chairman, harshly indicted the nation's intelligence agencies as a "bureaucracy that is not only incapable of meeting our security needs, but instead presents a recurring threat to our nation's credibility and legitimacy overseas, through its frequent missteps, miscalculation and mismanagement."[1]

In media accounts, Deutch was billed as an expert on intelligence technology and as someone who, while serving as number two at the Pentagon, had been responsible for overseeing the nation's military spy budgets and surveillance satellites. "Mr. Deutch's track record in science, industry and government," wrote the *New York Times*, "gives him formidable credentials as intelligence chief."[2] The media also reported that Deutch's approach to the job of DCI would be "polite, but firm" as he went about easing some top officials out the CIA's backdoor. His intention, according to *U.S. News & World Report*, was to "give a younger generation, less burdened by cold-war assumptions, a chance to lead."[3] Deutch was said to be taking aim especially at the Directorate of Operations, where "such blunders as the Aldrich Ames fiasco festered and went unpunished." While he did not anticipate a "bloodletting," Deutch told the magazine, "There will be some changes in the leadership."[4]

The new DCI planned to bring a coterie of associates with him from the Pentagon whom he would place in high Agency positions.[5] I could imagine how well that would go over at Langley. In 1977, Adm. Stansfield Turner had brought with him to "the Company," as some insiders refer to the CIA, a team of eight Navy men. They were resented by intelligence professionals inside the building and were quickly dubbed the "Navy Mafia" by old-timers who recoiled at the notion of having uniformed officers from the outside take over the seventh floor and interfering with the established way of doing things. Turner pointed out, in response to this charge, that he scattered this small group of Navy colleagues throughout the Agency rather than placing them in offices on the top floor. He concedes, however, that "it gave the wrong impression that I was trying to run the CIA with the Navy. I never saw them as a group, never once, but it was a poor public relations move."[6] To top things off, rumor had it that Turner viewed the DCI posting as merely a way station en route to the fulfillment of his true ambition: a presidential appointment as chief naval officer (CNO), the highest command post in the Navy.

One of the more benign responses from the Operations Directorate in response to the admiral's appointment was the anonymous distribution throughout the CIA Headquarters building of a bit of doggerel set to the tune of "When I Was a Lad" from the Gilbert and Sullivan musical *H.M.S. Pinafore*:

A SIMPLE TAR'S STORY

O sailors all, where'er you may be,
If you want to rise to the top of the tree;
If your soul isn't fettered to a quarterdeck stool,
Be careful to be guided by this golden rule:
    Chorus of Double-Dippers:

Keep your minds a perfect blank
And remain at sea,
And you all will be directors
Of the Company.
    Simple Tar:

For many a year I served at sea,
Living on grog and kedgeree.
I paced the deck and never went ashore,
I set the ship's course,
And pleased the commodore.
    Chorus of Double-Dippers:

He pleased the commodore
So mightily,
That now he's Director
Of the Company.

The parody went on for several stanzas, none of them flattering to Admiral Turner.

Perhaps remembering some of this history, as well as his own sharp remarks aimed at the DO at his confirmation hearings, Deutch told the media that he expected a hostile reception at Langley, at least at first. He had good reason for this expectation. As a CIA historian recalls, "His nomination struck fear . . . in the hearts of those at CIA worried that DoD's influence over national intelligence agencies had already grown too strong and would only increase under Deutch."[7] The new DCI also suggested to the media a novel interpretation of his duties in relation to the role of the Aspin Commission. He would not wait for us to come up with reforms, he said, but (as Tony Lake had warned us in his visit to the NEOB) would move ahead on his own and let us certify "the longer term changes."[8] Whatever that meant, it didn't exactly sound harmonious. As Deutch marched forward, I could see us vanishing into a crevasse of history before we had even reported.

Once convinced to take the job of spy chief, Deutch's main interest stretched beyond simply leading the CIA. "I wanted to put my focus on community matters," he recalled in 1998, "improving the relationship between the CIA and the FBI, making sure the CINCs [America's regional military commanders, known as "commanders in chief" or "combatant commanders"] were happier with the intelligence support they were getting. I wasn't going to go there and pretend that I was Richard Helms [a former DCI who had come up through the ranks of the DO] and understood human intelligence, which I didn't."[9] Deutch would have a close ally in this effort to aid the CINCs, since he had strong ties to the secretary of defense who had replaced Aspin, William J. Perry. "I had the advantage of having some of that eight-hundred-pound gorilla carry off," he recalled in my interview with him in 1998, evoking an image of the high status enjoyed by the secretary of defense and how his ties to Perry would lend some clout to Deutch's new position.

As I mentioned, Deutch was an old friend of Aspin's from their student days at MIT. As an undergraduate, Deutch studied economics and history at Amherst College, but, as he recalls, his father, an engineer, "convinced me that if I got an engineering degree, it would make me a more effective economist."[10] The plan was to complete a program in engineering at MIT, then go on to a PhD in economics. "It was a momentary foray into engineering, but then I became more interested in science," he remembers. "From engineering, I went on to chemistry." When Aspin arrived from Oxford University to pursue graduate work in economics at MIT, he met Deutch on campus.

In 1961 Deutch took a leave from the chemistry labs and went to the Pentagon to work for Secretary of Defense Robert S. McNamara, who had just put together a team of "whiz kids" to examine proposed weapons systems and other military initiatives. Impressed by Aspin's brain power, Deutch convinced him to join the McNamara team. Following this experience in the Pentagon, both men returned to MIT. Deutch finished a PhD in physical chemistry in 1965, and Aspin completed his doctorate in economics the same year. Afterward, they stayed in touch as they both rose rapidly up their respective career ladders: Deutch, as a professor of chemistry, and Aspin, as a professor of economics and soon thereafter a member of Congress. Both gravitated toward national security interests.

Aspin's attraction to security topics sprang chiefly from his work in the Pentagon under McNamara and his service in the U.S. Army; for Deutch, the roots ran deeper. Although he never served in uniform, Deutch had a lifetime exposure to the military.[11] He was born in 1938 to well-educated Jewish parents in Belgium; the family soon fled Europe to escape Hitler's Third Reich. His father had been employed at a large Belgian construction firm and his mother was a scholar of ancient civilizations. When they moved to the United States and settled in Washington, DC, Deutch's father landed a job with the War Production Board, and he continued to have an on-and-off relationship with the military side of the government throughout this life, as would his son, beginning with his days as one of the storied McNamara whiz kids.

Deutch raced up the academic ladder, first at Princeton, then back at MIT, becoming a full professor just eight years after earning his doctorate. He became head of the chemistry department while still in his thirties. The pull of Washington on his attention was strong, though, and in 1976 he was back in government, in charge of the nuclear weapons program at the Department of Energy where he became a protégé of Secretary James R. Schlesinger (who beforehand had served briefly as DCI in 1973).

Returning to MIT, Deutch sought and won the position of provost in 1985, although five years later he failed in his quest for the university's presidency. His inability to obtain that top office was one of the few setbacks in Deutch's life. Reportedly, his argumentative, impatient manner as provost had alienated too many faculty. He returned to professorial duties in the chemistry department and also kept a hand in government affairs. In 1990, the first President Bush appointed him to what was then a much smaller PFIAB, composed of only five members. When Bill Clinton won the presidency, Aspin—the new secretary of defense—assisted Deutch in his bid for the under-secretary slot at the Pentagon, confirming the old adage that it is good to know something but even better to know someone.

Deutch and Aspin even looked and acted alike to some extent. Both wore rumpled suits; both had thinning gray hair, slouching shoulders, and large brown-rimmed glasses; both had engaging wits and a high level of intellectual self-confidence. Deutch was the more aggressive of the two, however, a bear of a man, leaning forward as he walked, with an imposing bluster about him; and he was also more at ease in social settings, with a broader range of conversational interests. Aspin had a special charm, though, that came from his cheerful, ever-sanguine disposition and unassuming nature. In contrast, Deutch could be gruff and quick to dismiss anyone unable to keep up with his rapid-fire thinking.

During Deutch and Aspin's dinner together after the retreat, the DCI asked the chairman for changes in the commission's scope paper (now in its third iteration). He wanted it to concentrate more on technical improvements in intelligence gathering—the "techint" side of espionage. Deutch's knowledge of spy satellites from his time at the Pentagon had drawn him to that subject in his new capacity as DCI. There was no doubt he intended to take an active role in intelligence reform, and, given his long friendship with Aspin, Deutch was not going to be bashful about attempts to shape the commission's recommendations. In private asides during breaks in the commission's meetings over the next month, some commissioners began to question whether Aspin's relationship with Deutch was indeed too close. The commission, they whispered to one another in the small kitchen adjacent to our NEOB conference room, had to ensure a proper balance between independence and cooperation in its dealings with the aggressive director of central intelligence from MIT.

On May 9, a couple of days after the dinner with Deutch, Aspin showed up late for a staff meeting. "I's not feeling well," he mentioned to me in an aside, a worrisome comment in light of his long history of heart problems. It had only been two years since a surgeon had implanted a pacemaker in his chest. The chairman seemed to rally, though, as the meeting progressed. After staff administrative announcements (one was that Zoë Baird had organized a small task force of commissioners—Friedman, Hermann, and Coelho—to review the question of the "wall" between the intelligence agencies and law-enforcement officials), he commended us for organizing the retreat at the Farm, which he pronounced a success. Then he told the staff about the evening he had spent with Deutch. The DCI wanted to rearrange sections of the paper and make a few substantive modifications. The chairman had agreed to these changes, which meant that we would have to postpone his visit to Congress for a discussion of the scope paper until we had made the revisions—yet another rewrite of the scope paper, which was beginning to haunt us in our sleep.

Further, during the dinner Deutch had requested that the commission pay more attention to the possible creation of a more robust National Imagery Agency to replace the current Central Imagery Office. He also wanted the commission to consider a consolidation of the NRO and other space-oriented entities within the framework of the Defense Department. America's imint capabilities had reputedly been slowed by organizational inefficiencies, and that problem was clearly high on the DCI's agenda. Aspin wanted papers from the staff on these ideas by the end of the week so he could further review the possibilities with Deutch.

Despite looking bone tired and pale, the chairman listened attentively to a series of intelligence experts we had asked to drop by that afternoon. After their departure, he reminded us that we needed to strengthen the technical side of the commission's scope paper. It would then be distributed to the White House, the intelligence agencies, and key members of Congress for their comments.

———

That same day, after being sworn in at the White House, Deutch packed his personal belongings and departed from the Pentagon to take up his post as the nation's spymaster at CIA Headquarters, which was soon dubbed "Deutchland" by insiders. After a four-month pause, the intelligence community at last had a permanent director again. Deutch immediately called for a "town meeting," and on Thursday, May 11, 1995, the Agency's top brass assembled in the Agency's auditorium, known as "the Bubble," located near the front entrance of the Headquarters building. A statue of Nathan Hale, the nation's most famous spy, looked on as Agency officers filed out the front door at Langley and into the Bubble. ("I regret that I have but one life to give to my country," the young Yale University graduate reputedly told the British in 1776 as they prepared to hang him for espionage.)

The Bubble seats 478, with room for 130 more standing, and the hall was filled to capacity for the DCI's inaugural remarks. Deutch began his speech with an affirmation of the CIA's importance to the security of the United States. "We need this Agency to protect our country," he declared, adding that he had long "harbored a secret desire to be the director of central intelligence." This could have been flattering to the audience perhaps, except for the fact that everyone in the Bubble knew the president had to rope Deutch into the job, and that he had already turned down the position once. Moreover, it was widely reported that the position he truly longed for was secretary of defense. The needle on the credibility gauge was wavering. Deutch had dwelled on the topic of the Directorate of Operations during his confirmation hearings, and he now turned his attention again to that controversial component of the Agency. He promised to work with DO officers in the selection of a new person to run the directorate, most likely someone from inside the CIA.

Three years later, in 1998, I asked Deutch about his relations with the DO in retrospect. "I thought my time as DCI should be spent working on issues and serving our major customers, which were the president and the cabinet officers—not sitting around and holding hands with DO officers," he replied. "But I don't think that's the way they wanted it. They wanted the director to be a CIA guy; so there was, inevitably, a problem."[12] In a postmortem on this relationship, a journalist concluded: "The abiding theme of Deutch's tenure at C.I.A. was a kind of ongoing guerrilla war between the D.C.I.'s office on the seventh floor and the clandestine folks, marked by dis-respect on Deutch's side and increasing dislike on the D.O.'s."[13]

At the Pentagon, Deutch the scientist had been particularly interested in technical matters, and few were surprised during his town-hall remarks to hear him place an emphasis on "a new system for the management of both our military and intelligence satellite acquisition systems." His goal was to achieve "economies and efficiencies." He assured the audience this would be "an exciting event." To the non-techies in the Bubble, that was like prom-ising Wyoming cattle they would enjoy their trip to Chicago.

The speech was short, and the Director opened the floor to questions. Someone in the audience asked about the Aspin Commission and how the DCI's plans would fit in with its work. Deutch replied that Les Aspin was probably his oldest friend, who had been his classmate in college some thirty-five years ago. He noted that Aspin had been his boss when Deutch was under secretary of defense, and that they had a record of working closely together. He continued: "We had dinner together the night before last. I believe we will see a coordinated effort between his commission and our efforts to do long-range planning here and planning for change." He predicted that "there would be no seam, in my view, between our efforts and the efforts of the commission." Deutch added that he didn't see the commission or PFIAB as a problem: "I regard them as an opportunity—as a help."

In response to another question about the DI-DO partnership—the co-location experiment—Deutch ridiculed the existence of "stovepipe" barriers in the world of intelligence, in this case within the CIA. He called for greater interaction and cooperation among the Agency's directorates, as well as throughout the intelligence community. "I come from a world, a university world," he said, "where there is an enormous tendency to build stovepipes based on disciplines or based on schools.... Stovepipes are something that should be resisted."

One questioner suggested that by creating a new imagery agency, Deutch himself seemed to be setting up still another stovepipe. "I would argue," the DCI replied, "that moving to a national imagery agency is going from many stovepipes to one stovepipe." Silos, fiefdoms, stovepipes—however one referred to the divisions within the intelligence community, they seemed hard to bridge.

Given the research I was engaged in for Aspin on the quality of CIA estimating during the Cold War, I was especially interested to hear what Deutch had to say about analysis—the job of making sense of the world, widely considered the most important responsibility of the intelligence community. He observed that the Agency's Intelligence Directorate had served him well when he was deputy defense secretary, but that he had "not done a good survey of the products, nor," he added, "have I asked a broad range of consumers what they think about the products." I knew that the intelligence community's relationship with its consumers had been troubled over the years. One of the bones of contention was the usefulness of National Intelligence Estimates, or NIEs, considered by many the centerpiece of the community's analytic reports. Here was another subject the commission would have to examine.

Aspin, always a step ahead of me, telephoned after the Deutch speech and said, "Let's expand what you're doing with analytic estimates. I want you to take a broader look at the NIE process. How well does it work? Does anybody read Estimates these days? Is it just the CIA who writes them? Let me know whatever else you can find out." I turned to this project right away, putting other things on hold, given that we were about to have commission meetings with intelligence consumers whom we would be questioning closely about the quality of the reports they were receiving from the secret agencies. The NIE would no doubt be a prominent part of that discussion.

National Intelligence Estimates

A National Intelligence Estimate is an appraisal of a foreign country or international situation, authorized by the DCI and reflecting the coordinated judgment of the entire intelligence community.[14] Estimates, as NIEs are sometimes called, often serve as the building blocks of national security policy. They are the product of a thorough gathering and evaluation of intelligence drawn from all sources, with each of the "ints" (chiefly sigint, imint or geoint, humint, masint, and osint) ideally working together— what one former intelligence officer has called the "Black & Decker approach": using every tool in the box.[15] DCI Woolsey once offered an example of this synergism with respect to North Korea. "That nation is so closely guarded that humint becomes indispensable to know what is going on," he told me. "This humint then tips off sigint possibilities, which in turn may suggest where best to gather imint. These capabilities, ideally, dovetail with one another."[16]

Estimates are not limited to the task of predicting specific events; indeed, their primary function is assisting the president and other leaders by making background research available on foreign leaders, unfolding events, and the military and economic activities of other nations. An Estimate will set down on paper, and often rank, a range of possible outcomes related to developments inside another nation or faction, or will address the likely outcome of a situation developing somewhere in the world that could threaten American interests.

A CIA official has offered this definition of an NIE: "A statement of what is going to happen in any country, in any area, in any given situation, and as far as possible into the future."[17] Sherman Kent, the father of CIA analysis, observed that Estimates consist of three elements: knowledge, reasoning, and guesswork. This last dimension "may be sullied by visceral reactions," Kent warned, unless the analyst is careful not to allow personal biases to creep into his or her work.[18]

Many insiders and outsiders alike regard the NIE as the crown jewel of U.S. intelligence reporting. A respected former CIA analyst notes that an Estimate is the "most authoritative analytic product prepared by the intelligence community... the bringing together of every scrap of evidence, from the most sensitively exotic to the most openly unclassified, that the U.S. intelligence community has on the question at hand."[19] In the judgment of political scientist Harry Howe Ransom, the NIE is "the single most influential document in national security policy making, potentially at least."[20]

THE RANGE OF NIE TOPICS

The first truly interagency NIE in the United States appeared on November 8, 1950, and it addressed the subject of Chinese intervention on the Korean peninsula. The Estimate stated that there were some thirty to forty thousand

Chinese troops in North Korea, and that the Chinese intention was to maintain its presence on the peninsula. Over the years since this inaugural NIE, Estimates have sometimes been the result of formal requests from senior policy makers—the president, the national security advisor, the secretaries of state or defense, a military commander, a member (or members) of Congress—for an appraisal and prognosis of events and conditions in some part of the world. However, in a overwhelming majority of cases—75 percent in one recent year—the intelligence community itself has generated NIE proposals (pushing intelligence, rather than waiting for it to be pulled), although these initiatives are based on a perception that policy makers would like to see a more definitive study of some global topic.

As I was doing my research for Aspin, many of those knowledgeable about the production of NIEs told me that the most useful Estimates are the ones specifically requested ("pulled") by policy makers; in these cases the potential readers have indicated an interest in having more information and are thus likely to pay closer attention to the final product. They have "bought into" the process. As a former top NIE briefer to the White House told me: "Ideally, Estimates should be consumer-driven reports."[21]

The subjects for NIEs cover a wide range. Former DCI Stansfield Turner provided these examples from the Carter administration:

- the balance of strategic nuclear forces between the United States and the USSR
- the conventional military balance in Europe
- the prospects for improvement in relations between the Soviet Union and China
- the outlook for cohesiveness within the Atlantic Alliance; and
- the significance of the Third World's international debt problems[22]

On Chairman Aspin's behalf, I went through the list of Estimates prepared between 1992 and 1995. They had focused on several regions of the world, as well as non-geographic subjects.[23] Regionally, Central Asia and Russia headed the list, the subjects of forty-one NIEs during that period. A lingering post–Cold War interest in Russia made that nation—the focus of ten Estimates—outdistance all others in the Central Asian region by far in the frequency of its attractiveness as an NIE topic. Next came the Near East with twenty-four, and Africa with twenty, followed by Latin America with sixteen, and East Asia with fifteen. Substantially below these regions came Europe, along with the "functional" subjects of global weaponry and arms control (each with nine).

Bringing up the rear were a panoply of additional global issues, such as immigration and environmental degradation (seven each), health (three, including an Estimate on HIV/AIDs), drugs (two), economics (one on the effect of the General Agreement on Tariffs and Trade, or GATT), international crime (one), space (one), human rights (one), and, soon to be Public Enemy Number One, terrorism (one). During the Cold War, the list would have had roughly the same order, with Central Asia still important, but with NIEs focused even more overwhelmingly on Russia. This snapshot of post–Cold War estimating revealed the intelligence community's attempts to move slowly toward the recognition of a more complex "matrix" of threats and opportunities in a world no longer dominated by just two nations.

PREPARING ESTIMATES

Aspin wanted to know more about how Estimates were prepared, so I spoke to participants in the process about the sequence of events. First, a panel of intelligence experts, known since 1980 as the National Intelligence Council, or NIC (and earlier as the Office of National Estimates, or ONE), examines the merits of each proposed Estimate in consultation with analysts throughout the community, as well as with senior policy officials, to determine the feasibility and demand for such a study. If the decision is to move ahead, the NIC determines what segments of the community could best contribute to the Estimate and provides these selected agencies with an outline of its objectives, asking them to respond with their facts and insights by a certain deadline. This outline is known as the "terms of reference," or TOR. As a NIC document explains: "The TOR defines the key estimative questions, determines drafting responsibilities, and sets the drafting and publication schedule."[24]

In response to the TOR, data and ideas come back to the NIC from around the community and are shaped into a draft NIE by one or more of the senior analysts who comprise the NIC, in continual dialogue with experts lower on the ladder of analysts. Since 1973 the senior analysts on the NIC have been known as national intelligence officers, or NIOs. The men and women who serve as NIOs are expected, according to Sherman Kent, to have "the best in professional training, the highest intellectual integrity, and a very large amount of worldly wisdom."[25] Usually the NIO who has the most expertise on the subject at hand will lead the drafting.

The ten to sixteen or so NIOs (the number varies) are considered the *crème de la crème* of intelligence analysts. They are drawn from throughout the community, and occasionally from academe and the think tanks. The set of NIOs at the time I was looking into the estimating process for Aspin consisted of four career intelligence officers, five analysts from academe and think tanks, three from the military, and one from Capitol Hill. The NIC also maintains a list of some fifty consultants across the country with security clearances, experts from the worlds of academe and the think tanks who are consulted as the need arises.

The NIOs organize scholarly conferences with outsiders as well, in an attempt to keep themselves well informed about world affairs. Perhaps the most well known of the intelligence community's efforts to reach beyond its walls to seek academic consultation on the substance of an NIE came in 1976. Two competing groups of analysts, referred to as "Team A" and "Team B," reviewed a 1975 Estimate on Soviet military intentions and capabilities.[26] The National Security Council selected the two teams. The CIA's own Soviet experts comprised Team A, and academics (including a young Paul Wolfowitz) comprised Team B, led by Harvard University Russian historian Richard E. Pipes, known for his strongly hawkish views on the Soviet Union. Pipes and his panel were convinced that the CIA had gone soft; its liberal "civilian" outlook, reinforced by equally naive arms-control experts in the scholarly community, had led to an NIE that downplayed the Soviet plan for world conquest. In the view of Team B, the Soviets were secretly planning—and could very well implement—a first-strike, war-winning strategy. That was Moscow's goal, not peaceful coexistence with the United States. Specifically, Team B accused the CIA of miscalculating Soviet expenditures on weapons systems, thereby underestimating the formidable strength of the Red Army. Team A, in turn, charged the Pipes panel with hyping the Soviet peril.

The upshot of this attempt at "competitive analysis" using outsiders was that the CIA cut back on some of its more optimistic views about the Soviet Union in its next annual Estimate on the rival superpower, adopting Soviet military production figures slightly more in line with the Team B projections. Nevertheless, a vast gulf between the two groups remained on the subject of Soviet intentions: the relative optimism of Team A set against the pessimism of the "hard-liners" like Pipes. The "debate" probably damaged the reputation of the intelligence community; the door had been opened to doubt about the wisdom of relying only on internal judgments made by professional intelligence officers. Yet, overall, it was healthy for inside analysts to have their views tested by outside experts—although the selection of an external review board known for a particular political stance was less useful than recruiting more neutral experts free of ideological axes to grind.

During the NIE drafting process, the NIO in charge will send the first draft back to all of the intelligence agencies working on the study, and so begins the process of interagency editing, as specialists from throughout the community hammer the final document into shape. An analyst recalls the process in these painful terms: "It was like defending a Ph.D. dissertation, time after time after time."[27]

The NIC judges the appropriateness of the findings and conclusions presented in each Estimate, then sends the document along to the National Intelligence Board (NIB) for final review. In 1995, the NIB was composed of the senior representatives of the intelligence community and chaired by the DCI, who had the last say on the Estimate before it was distributed to the president and senior policy makers.[28] Sometimes, in the past, a DCI has so disliked an Estimate produced by the intelligence bureaucracy that he has written one himself on the topic instead of sending forward the NIC version. This practice is rare, however, and carries with it the danger of an Estimate becoming too personalized or even politicized.[29] Sometimes intelligence chiefs can be correct and the bureaucracy wrong, as when DCI John McCone rejected the conclusion of an NIE that predicted the Soviets would not place missiles in Cuba in the early 1960s.[30] The best bet, though, it seemed to me from my inquiries, was to rely on well-trained and experienced country or subject experts; then, if the intelligence director disagrees with the experts, he or she could forward the NIO version to policy makers along with a clearly marked dissent from the director's office.

The bulk of the NIE drafting rests in the hands of junior analysts within the intelligence community—specialists who study the daily cable traffic from the country in question or are otherwise expert in the topic under consideration (say, the efficiencies of Chinese rocket fuel, on the narrow side, or the likely path of leadership succession in China over the next two decades, on the broader side). According to an NIO, the National Intelligence Council is expected to work closely with NSC members and their staff, as well as other intelligence consumers, "scrubbing information honestly and adapting to the working style of the policy makers receiving the NIE." The NIOs are also expected to keep in touch with the various intelligence entities whose analysts contributed to the Estimate draft. The preparation of an Estimate is, according to this same insider, "an art form [that] requires a corps of floating linebackers, flexible and easily collapsible, to charge an intelligence problem."[31]

This process does not always work smoothly, I discovered, even beyond the inherent difficulty of forecasting the future.[32] Obviously, the tenor of the language in an NIE is all important, especially the confidence levels evinced in the document. NIOs must be careful not to claim more than the evidence can support, especially in the executive summary (called "key judgments," or KJs) found at the beginning of the document. This may be the only portion read by a harried (or lazy) policy official, and it needs to convey the shades of gray, and the caveats, that serve as an antidote to overly assertive and simplistic conclusions. Sometimes reporting in the NIE has been inconsistent with other intelligence reports on the same topic, in both their confidence levels and their use of assertive language, thereby sowing confusion among policy makers.[33]

Even when the language in the NIE is guarded, irresponsible policy makers can cause a "cascading" effect whereby they cherry-pick parts of the report that they like, then exaggerate their importance in subsequent speeches and conversations. Another concern is the relationship between the NIO and the decision maker. On the one hand, if the NIO becomes too cozy with those in decision-making positions, the danger of politicization rises, as the analyst is tempted to bend intelligence in support of policy objectives; on the other hand, though, if the NIO is too detached, the NIE risks being irrelevant to the information needs of the decision maker. Further, the CIA has been criticized for aggressively taking over the drafting of Estimates and, as a result, alienating participants from other agencies and undermining the important goal of all-source fusion.

An NIE can be written quickly, in two to four weeks, or even in less than a day in emergencies; in two to six months during normal times; or in as much as three years on a slow track. Historically, an Estimate has taken an average of 215 days to produce—about seven months. Estimates that are prepared on a fast-track basis during a crisis have their own name: special NIEs, or SNIEs (pronounced "snees"). During the Suez Canal crisis of 1956, the U.S. intelligence community produced a SNIE on Soviet intentions within a few hours. Analysts prefer, however, to have at least three months to produce an Estimate.[34]

THE QUESTION OF DISSENT

The question of how to represent dissenting views in an NIE has been especially tricky. To the extent that it is possible, the intelligence community attempts to resolve its disagreements before an Estimate is presented to top policy makers, although there is a danger in this of producing reports that are diluted by a search for the lowest common denominator. The various intelligence agencies sometimes have quite different perspectives on a global situation. Military intelligence organizations, for example, are notorious for their "worst case" approach to estimating. This is a result, critics contend, of pressures on analysts applied by the Department of Defense and the military-industrial complex to justify larger military budgets or new weapons systems by scaring the American people and their representatives in Congress with warnings of dire threats from abroad.[35] Conversely, military intelligence officials often consider the CIA and INR as credulous and too "civilian," unable to understand the true nature of foreign military threats.[36]

A joke about the different analytic cultures in the intelligence community draws on these differences to explain, supposedly, how the intelligence agencies perceived Soviet intentions to attack the United States during the Cold War, with the military weighing in with the most frightening forecasts:

U.S. AIR FORCE: "The Russians are here!"

DEFENSE INTELLIGENCE AGENCY: "The Russians are not here yet, but they are coming."

CIA: "The Russians are trying, but they won't make it."

BUREAU OF INTELLIGENCE AND RESEARCH (DEPARTMENT OF STATE): "The Russians? They aren't even trying."[37]

The clash of differing views among intelligence agencies—competitive intelligence—can be healthy, if driven by an objective weighing of facts rather than policy bias. Debate among analysts can provide policy makers with a wide range of views, instead of the lowest-common-denominator consensus. Sometimes NIEs are guilty of homogenization, offering up views with a tapioca consistency that deny policy officials the complexities they need to understand. The CIA has enjoyed a special advantage over the years in its capacity to ignore policy pressures. It is an independent agency, outside the framework of a policy department—the only U.S. intelligence agency that can make that claim—and, as a result, it escapes immediate, in-house policy pressures from cabinet secretaries. This is not to say there has never been politicization at the CIA; indeed, DCI William J. Casey, for example, often introduced political considerations into his handling of NIEs during the Reagan years. Nevertheless, the Agency is not embedded in a policy department and avoids some forms of political pressure that the other secret agencies must struggle against each day.

Sometimes agency dissents have been relegated to obscure footnotes, if they are included at all in an NIE. This is unfortunate, I suggested to Aspin in my report. Failing to flag uncertainties or disagreements struck me as an inexcusable error for analysts. The best NIC chairs have been careful to make sure that analytic dissents are discussed at some length in the text of the NIE itself, not hidden in a footnote—if only to avoid incurring the resentment of dissenting agencies who have had their findings and judgments shunted aside. Some dissenting agencies insist that their contrary opinions be high-lighted boldly in the text, often in a boxed format to make the dissent conspicuous. This is a useful way to encourage debate.

THE CONSUMER-LIAISON CHALLENGE

An additional responsibility of intelligence managers has been to ensure that NIOs maintain good liaison relationships with consumers and among themselves. "The difficulty lies not only in predicting the future, in a world of many variables, incomplete data, and intentional deception," writes a seasoned intelligence officer, "but in convincing policy makers that the prediction is valid."[38] Experience has shown that unless a policy maker knows and feels comfortable with an NIO or other intelligence briefer, he or she is less likely to pay much attention to the proffered product.[39] In the course of my research on Estimates, I discovered an NIO responsible for global environmental issues in the Clinton administration who had never met the NSC staff person with these same responsibilities, even though both had been in their positions for over a year.[40] This is no way to foster the rapport so necessary to the intelligence process (although such a rapport may lead to politicization unless the analyst is always on guard against the dangers of co-optation and the siren call of Washington politics).

These personal relationships are critical. A top intelligence manager has observed that when he guided the National Intelligence Council, he came to believe that NIEs "were not our real product; rather, our real product was National Intelligence Officers—not paper but people, experts, in a position to attend meetings and offer judgments."[41] Of course, the judgments presented by NIOs in meetings with decision makers are rooted in the hard research and thought that they and lower analysts have put into Estimates as they are being drafted. As for maintaining good contacts among NIOs themselves, Paul Wolfowitz once remarked to me while we were working on the commission that "the most important activity in which [NIOs] can engage is internal debate over their judgments."[42] Often, though, this debate never takes place.

NIE HITS AND MISSES

Despite all of these hazards, NIEs do get written. They try to assess current trends. Then they try to anticipate the course of history, to the extent that this is possible. Sherman Kent has said of the prime NIE goal of in-depth analysis: "The guts of the matter is the synthesizing of the pieces and setting them forth in some meaningful pattern which everyone hopes is a close approximation of the truth."[43]

Some NIEs offer a series of possible alternative scenarios about future events. Still, the end result remains something of a best guess, resulting from consultation among the top analysts in the intelligence community and others they may talk to outside the intelligence establishment. As Kent once put it, "Estimating is what you do when you do not know." In the process, he continued, one enters "into the world of speculating."[44] However shrewd the forecasts may be in an NIE, they still remain guesses—better than blind luck to be sure, but nonetheless a far cry from certainty.[45]

At times, NIEs have been as accurate as a Swiss watch in their forecasts; on other occasions they have been wide of the mark. Examples of successful predictions include the likely overall conduct of the Soviet Union in world affairs (predicting the USSR would try to expand, but avoid the risk of general war);[46] the launch of Sputnik in 1957; the Sino-Soviet split of 1962; the Chinese nuclear weapon test in 1964; the development of new Soviet weapon systems throughout the Cold War;[47] developments in the Vietnam War (1966–75); the Arab-Israeli War of 1967; the India-Pakistan War of 1971; the Turkish invasion of Cyprus in 1974; the Chinese invasion of Vietnam in 1978; the mass exodus from Cuba in 1978; the Soviet invasion of Afghanistan in 1979; the sharp deterioration of the Soviet economy just before the end of the Cold War (1984–89); the investment strategies of the Organization of Petroleum Exporting Countries (OPEC) over the years; and the rise and fall of various political leaders around the world, including the breakup of Yugoslavia in the 1990s.

As a generalization, most of the intelligence community's mistakes during the Cold War relating to the Soviet Union were about what the Kremlin intended, not about what weapons systems the Communist empire possessed.[48] The ability to track the amount and capabilities of Soviet weaponry was vital during the superpower confrontation, and it remains so today with Russia. America's arms negotiations with the Russians (and others) still depend on the ability of the intelligence agencies to detect, through a range of sources and methods, any significant violation of weapons agreements—a process known as verification. "Trust, but verify," was a statement often expressed by President Reagan in his public statements about arms accords with the Soviet Union.

Examples of analytic mistakes include: the failure to predict the outbreak of the Korean War in 1950, or the placement of Soviet offensive missiles in Cuba in 1962; the reporting—especially by U.S. Air Force Intelligence—of a (nonexistent) bomber and missile gap between the Soviet Union and the United States in the 1950s and early 1960s, in Moscow's favor; underestimating during the Vietnam War the support flowing to the Viet Cong through Cambodia; underestimating the pace of the Soviet strategic weapons program; an inability to track when and where the Pakistani physicist A. Q. Khan sent nuclear materials in the developing world; faulty forecasts about the Soviet invasions of Hungary in 1956 and Czechoslovakia in 1968, the failure to predict the Arab-Israeli war in 1973, and the fall of the Shah of Iran in 1979; and a lack of precise forecasts about the collapse of the Soviet empire in 1989–91.

I concluded in a memo to Aspin that NIEs had been uneven in their ability to provide the president and other officials with accurate predictions. Especially prone to failure were the long-range prognostications offered in some NIEs, since this ability of human beings to forecast world events accurately diminishes the farther one peers into the future. "The CIA Directorate of Science and Technology has not yet developed a crystal ball," Senator Frank Church once observed. He went on to say:

> Predicting the future must remain probabilistic. Though the CIA did give an exact warning of the date when Turkey would invade Cyprus [in 1974], such precision will be rare. Simply too many unpredictable factors enter into most situations. The intrinsic element of caprice in the affairs of men and nations is the hair shirt of the intelligence estimator.[49]

Intelligence scholar Richard K. Betts has emphasized this central point about intelligence in his writings. When it comes to predictions, he notes, "some incidence of failure [is] inevitable." Consequently, he urges a higher "tolerance for disaster."[50]

It is plain enough why policy makers need to have a realistic understanding about the limited capacities of intelligence. As a former CIA analyst has stated, "There is seldom, if ever, enough intelligence present to make absolute predictions or warnings."[51] Information is usually scarce or ambiguous, and the situation in question may be fluid and changing. Intelligence scholar Arthur S. Hulnick advises: "Policy makers may have to accept the fact that all intelligence estimators can really hope to do is to give them guidelines or scenarios to support policy discussion, and not the predictions they so badly want and expect from intelligence."[52]

This truth about intelligence limitations is unhappy news for presidents and cabinet secretaries who seek clear-cut answers, not hunches and hypotheses; but such is the reality of intelligence. Yet it bears repeating that having intelligence agencies collect information worldwide and try their best to make sense of the findings is far better than operating without information and analysis, just as it is ill advised to cross a busy street blindfolded. As CIA analyst Harold Ford has written, "There is no substitute for the depth, imaginativeness, and 'feel' that experienced, first-rate analysts and estimators can bring to the often semi-unknowable questions handed them."[53]

Moreover, I reminded Aspin, intelligence estimating might become more sophisticated in the coming years, depending on whether the United States was able to improve the capabilities of its technical and human assets to gather information overseas, as well as its ability to sift quickly through the noise and find the desired signals. It depended, too, on whether Americans were willing to expand their knowledge of foreign languages, cultures, and histories; and whether the government could attract the best young minds in the nation to prepare reliable, insightful intelligence reports for Washington decision makers. Vital, too, would be a renewed commitment among intelligence professionals to resist political pressures from policy makers to twist intelligence in a manner that suited policy preferences at the expense of the truth—the soul-destroying politicization of intelligence.

Even if NIEs are less-than-perfect instruments for predicting future events, I wrote to Aspin, they at least have the virtue of assembling in one place a dependable set of facts about a situation abroad of interest to the United States. This frees up the nation's decision makers to focus attention on sorting out the disagreements they might have over which policy options to choose. Intelligence scholar William Odom once observed, "The estimate process has the healthy effect of making analysts communicate and share evidence. If the NIEs performed no other service, they would still be entirely worth the effort."[54] Almost forty years ago, Sherman Kent noted, too, that "the intelligence estimate will have made its contribution in the way it promoted a more thorough and enlightened debate."[55]

CURRENT VERSUS RESEARCH (LONG-TERM) INTELLIGENCE

As I delved into the subject of Estimates, I discovered an important debate in the world of intelligence surrounding the question of how many resources should be sunk into the quick production of "current intelligence," which can be highly perishable, at the expense of more deeply considered products of "research intelligence" like the National Intelligence Estimate.[56] What is the proper balance between short reports on world affairs, such as the *President's Daily Brief* (PDB), and lengthier in-depth analyses, such as the NIE?

It soon became clear to me during my interviews with policy makers around Washington that almost all of them preferred to receive current intelligence reports over Estimates. Indeed, recently, consumers of intelligence (the nation's policy makers) rated NIEs eighth among products forwarded to them by the intelligence community.[57] Mark M. Lowenthal, who was HPSCI's staff director during the time of the national intelligence commission, wrote that in the past several years, the intelligence community has "put its greatest emphasis on shorter, more current products," a response to "a fairly consistent decline in policymaker interest in intelligence community products as they get longer and more removed from more current issues."[58] Former CIA analyst Harold Ford noted a similar phenomenon a generation earlier in the early 1990s, just before the Aspin Commission came along: "The great majority of policymakers have to concern themselves with fairly immediate, pressing problems. More distant and more uncertain [issues] have a lesser constituency and fewer advocates."[59] Or, as Richard Betts succinctly concludes: "Immediate problems drive out distant ones."[60]

I found that one of the items of current intelligence most desired by policy makers was foreign leadership profiles—facts and insights (sometimes salacious) about the public and private lives of the men and women who U.S. policy makers would meet at approaching conferences, summits, and other international meetings. Without these succinct profiles, presented in a format similar to baseball cards for easy reading and carrying, second-echelon political officials in other lands would remain strangers to U.S. negotiators. In one recent year, almost sixteen thousand of these profiles made their way from the CIA to government policy offices around Washington.[61]

The advent of cable news and the Internet has affected the status of NIEs. "Long-term research and in-depth analysis suffered as CIA managers and analysts became fixated on the race to get late-breaking tidbits of intelligence into the *President's Daily Brief*," writes *New York Times* reporter James Risen.[62] Adding to this *PDB* advantage, NIEs have "on occasion been wrong, or in more cases late, or in still more cases, too cloudy to be of much use."[63]

The upshot is that currently about 80 to 90 percent of the analytic resources of the intelligence community are dedicated to clarifying for policy makers what happened today and yesterday, and what is likely to happen tomorrow.[64] Estimates have receded from the agenda of priorities for the U.S. intelligence agencies even more since when I looked into this subject for Aspin in 1995. Lowenthal believes that the intelligence community has "gotten out of the knowledge-building business. Now it is: 'current, current, current.' "[65] Another leading CIA analyst ruefully agrees: "Life in the Directorate of Intelligence is no longer contemplative."[66] Happily so, critics of National Intelligence Estimates would add. They point to a series of fatal shortcomings in the Estimates process. First, NIEs are too long. "If the intelligence product is not two pages or less," an assistant secretary of defense told our commission, "it is unlikely to be read. I have only about five minutes [a day] that I can devote to reading intelligence."[67] Most policy officials devote even less time than that, if any. With tongue in cheek, but nevertheless stressing a serious point, a former intelligence officer suggests that "some policy-makers don's read, some won't read, and some can't read."[68] In a nutshell, NIEs may continue to be written, but they will likely end up sitting on a shelf somewhere, untouched by decision makers.[69]

Others, though, reject the thesis that policy makers ignore NIEs. They point, for instance, to busy political VIPs who have been avid readers of Estimates, such as secretaries of defense Les Aspin, James R. Schlesinger, and Harold Brown—all of whom devoured NIEs as if they were pulp fiction. Moreover, even if government principals never get around to reading an entire NIE (focusing, instead, on just the "key judgments" section), their aides—the deputy assistant secretaries (DASs), the work horses of Washington—usually will. The information they absorb is then recycled to their bosses in oral briefs and conversations, as well as in the memoranda and reports they prepare. And even if it were true that no policy official read NIEs, they would still serve a purpose: the drafting process educates NIOs and other analysts, who are thus better equipped to provide oral briefings to key decision makers—and these oral briefings are much in demand.[70]

One recent chairman of the National Intelligence Council with whom I spoke was Dr. Richard N. Cooper, a Harvard University economist with extensive service in the government, including as under secretary of state for economic affairs and senior staff economist at the Council of Economic Advisers. In 1994, as the NIC chair, he decided to make the rounds of policy officials to see what they thought of the NIEs they had recently received. By his account, they looked at him blankly; they had not read any of them. At the same time, though, they expressed great enthusiasm for the NIOs they knew, and they appreciated the oral briefings they provided, which were often based on newly minted Estimates.[71] Further, as Cooper states, "NIEs focus the intelligence agencies; they allow quality control for NIOs over other analysts throughout the community. They also provide valuable grist for the mill at the level of the deputy assistant secretaries and office directors."[72] Finally, as a cabinet aide put it: "No one reads an encyclopedia from A to Z, but it is still helpful to have encyclopedias."[73]

An additional criticism of NIEs is that they are too democratic: "Estimating by plebiscite," scoffs Lowenthal. "Since when is the FBI view on Darfur just as good as INR's?" he asks; yet both agencies are able to weigh in with their views in an Estimate on this subject.[74] One could pose a similar question with regard to WMDs in Iraq: Why should the DIA's view on WMDs in a foreign country be given the same weight as the judgment of intelligence officers in the Energy Department, whose primary responsibility is to monitor nuclear fuel proliferation around the world? Critics suggest, too, that NIEs are too often intellectual buffets, so broadly worded that one can find whatever one likes in them. They are, Lowenthal concludes, "intellectual and moral dead ends."[75] Former DCI Turner also worried about the "limited" value of NIEs that require "so many compromises."[76]

In the litany of concerns about NIEs that I prepared for Les Aspin, I raised the issue as well of the extent to which they sometimes became political. Some lawmakers and officials in the executive branch seemed to go after the blood of any NIO with whom they disagreed. The unfairness of this is clear, given the difficulty of predicting events. A senior intelligence officer gives this illustration of how politically dicey the art of estimating can be: "I was supposed to tell a lawmaker, who didn't know if he was going to be reelected or not, who is going to win the next Israeli elections!"[77]

Another, more famous, example comes from the Soviet invasion of Czechoslovakia in 1968. Throughout the summer of that year, the Politburo in Moscow remained divided over whether to use force to quell a rebellion in Prague. Historians now know that the Soviets went back and forth on the question of what to do, up until the eleven hour, when the decision was finally made on August 20th to launch an invasion. The CIA had reported on the fact that Soviet troops were mobilized, but the Agency was unable to say whether an invasion would actually occur. Not even the Politburo knew until the last moment. Precise predictions remain an elusive goal; nonetheless, the intelligence agencies can at least alert the White House to a developing situation, as the CIA did in the instance of the Czech invasion and during the Cuban missile crisis.

THE FREQUENCY OF NIES

As part of my examination of National Intelligence Estimates for Aspin, I researched the frequency of their production. From the first intelligence director in 1946 until John Deutch in 1995–96, the intelligence community produced 1,134 NIEs, averaging twenty-three a year over this half century.[78] I wanted to see if Estimates had, in fact, gone into decline through the years, pushed aside by the *PDB* and other forms of current intelligence. The trend line in Figure 6.1 reveals a more complex reality, with the numbers of NIEs

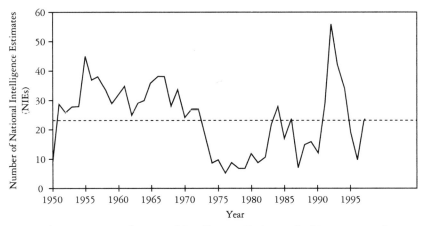

FIGURE 6.1 Frequency of National Intelligence Estimates by Year, 1950–96
My thanks to Kristin E. Swati for her assistance in the preparation of this figure.

fluctuating over the years and throughout the tenures of DCIs—although with a general decline in the number of research-intelligence products in recent decades.[79]

The frequency of NIE production in any given year is a reflection of the intelligence director's priorities at the time and the interest an administration has in receiving Estimates. Added to the mix are changing world circumstances that may require the preparation of new NIEs. In times of war, for example, policy makers are likely to be especially focused on current intelligence that reports on battlefield exigencies, with NIEs pushed to a back burner.[80]

The very first NIE was published in 1946, but it was written by just a single author inside the CIA and is not counted here because, unlike subsequent Estimates, it was not based on interagency collaboration—the hallmark of a true NIE.[81] The production of community-wide Estimates began in 1950, under the supervision of DCI Rear Adm. Roscoe H. Hillenkoetter—with nine Estimates produced that year. Gen. Walter Bedell Smith, one of the most renowned of the U.S. intelligence chiefs because of his outstanding management skills, replaced Hillenkoetter in October 1950. Under Smith, the number of NIEs leapt upward, averaging twenty-eight for 1951 and 1952. This increase reflected his determination to build up the nation's fledgling intelligence capabilities. Among Smith's first decisions as DCI was to set up the Office of National Estimates, whose sole job was to prepare Estimates. He made it clear that ONE would report directly to him, signaling that estimating would be the DCI's special province.[82]

With the advent of Allen W. Dulles's term as DCI in 1953, the production of NIEs rose further, to a new peak of forty-five in 1955—a figure that would remain unsurpassed until 1992, and which is still the second highest number. In his first two years, Dulles maintained NIE production at the same average set by Smith: twenty-eight. The frequency soon shot up, though, during the rest of his tenure (1955–61), averaging thirty-four a year.

This spike is remarkable, given Dulles's reportedly limited interest in analysis.[83] As one of his successors, Richard Helms, recalled: "Dulles tended to take the [CIA's Directorate of Intelligence] for granted. He appreciated the value and quality of the product, but rarely addressed himself to the DI or any of its problems."[84] Journalist Tim Weiner recounts how the intelligence director appeared more interested in the latest baseball scores than the latest assessments about world affairs.[85] Dulles was supposedly most devoted to the operations side of intelligence: recruiting agents, planting propaganda, secretly trying to change the course of history. He had enjoyed a life of der-ring-do in the Office of Strategic Services (OSS) during World War II, running spies against the Nazis. Nevertheless, his attention to NIE produc-tion was sufficient to continue the upward trend in their frequency; indeed, the Dulles years saw more Estimates produced—306—during his tenure than any other DCI, by far.[86]

John A. McCone followed Dulles as DCI. Like Bedell Smith, McCone was popular inside the intelligence community and similarly admired for his managerial skills. His dedication to the production of NIEs matched Smith's, at an average of twenty-eight, though it fell short of Dulles's overall average of thirty-four. It is claimed that McCone gave "new energy to the Estimates,"[87] but in fact his tenure saw an initial decline in NIE production. The figure of twenty-five Estimates for 1962 was the lowest number since the first year of interagency estimating in 1950. McCone's total of Estimates rose, however, to twenty-nine in 1963 and to thirty in 1964. Perhaps the infamous NIE of 1961, mistakenly predicting that the Soviet Union would not introduce nuclear missiles into Cuba, contributed to McCone's increased attentiveness to the Estimates process.[88] (McCone himself, recall, had personally cautioned policy makers that the NIE of 1961 on Cuba was likely wrong, and that the Soviets could in fact be expected to support their Latin American satellite state with missile emplacements.)

This upward trend continued, reaching thirty-six Estimates in 1965 under McCone's successor, Vice Adm. William F. Raborn Jr.—two more than Dulles's average.[89] The next DCI, Richard Helms, raised this level further, to thirty-eight NIEs in his first year in office (1966); but from there the number of NIEs went into their sharpest decline yet, with Helms averaging thirty-one

TABLE 6.1   Frequency of National Intelligence Estimates by DCI Administration,
1946–1996

DCI	Period of Tenure*	Number of NIEs	Average NIE Per DCI	
Souers	1946	0	0.0	very low
Vanderberg	1946–1947	0	0.0	very low
Hillenkoetter	1947–1950	50	3.0	very low
Smith	1951–1952	55	27.5	high
Dulles	1953–1961	306	34.0	very high
McCone	1962–1964	84	28.0	high
Raborn	1965	36	36.0	very high
Helms	1966–1972	216	31.0	high
Schlesinger	1973	19	19.0	low
Colby	1974–1975	19	9.5	very low
Bush	1976	5	5.0	very low
Turner	1977–1980	35	9.0	very low
Casey	1981–1986	111	18.5	low
Webster	1987–1991	78	15.5	low
Gates	1992	56	56.0	highest
Woolsey	1993–1994	76	38.0	very high
Deutch	1995–1996	29	14.5	low

* These years are not the precise full dates of service for each Director of Central
Intelligence, but rather the years in which a DCI served a preponderant number of days
in a particular year and was thus accorded the year's full total of NIEs. Dividing the
NIEs into fractions according to the number of days a DCI served each year (not shown
here) did not alter the basic analysis presented here and seemed even more arbitrary.

Estimates a year for his tenure as DCI. This decline continued to twenty-four
in 1970, and from there the frequency rose to twenty-seven in each of the
years 1971 and 1972.

In part, this downward trend reflected Helms greater interest in current
intelligence. The old newspaper man in him (his first career had been in journalism) conceded that "the pressure of meeting urgent deadlines and responding immediately to developing crises always sparked a pleasant mnemonic
echo."[90] Moreover, President Lyndon B. Johnson, who failed to mention the
subject of NIEs even once in his autobiography, *The Vantage Point*, had little
interest in lengthy intelligence reports. Chester Cooper, a CIA liaison to the
White House during the Johnson years, recalls that at the time "in-depth
analyses were far from best-sellers."[91] Johnson was, though, an avid reader of

current intelligence related to the war in Vietnam, until the rising crescendo of negative reports became too much for him to bear.

During the tenure of Helms's successors, James R. Schlesinger (who served only five months as DCI in 1973, although that was longer than any of the other DCIs that year) and then William E. Colby, the numbers continued to fall. The record shows nineteen NIEs in 1973, nine in 1974, and ten in 1975. Colby served at a time of great crisis in the intelligence community, during the "intelligence wars" of 1974–76 when the secret agencies were under investigation for domestic spying.[92] This DCI had other matters to attend to besides NIE production; the survival of the CIA itself seemed to be on the line.[93] Getting the intelligence agencies back on an even keel after the scandals preoccupied Colby's successor as well—DCI (and later President) George H. W. Bush, whose production of NIEs set a record low of five in 1976. Next came Adm. Stansfield Turner of the Carter administration (who served as DCI throughout the Carter years from 1977–81). He reversed the estimating decline but still had a relatively low production rate of nine, seven, seven, and twelve NIEs in each of his four years as DCI, for an average of nine—even less than the besieged Colby.

When the Reagan administration came to power in 1981, NIE production dipped for a year and then rebounded. Under DCI William J. Casey, the numbers jumped from nine in his first year to twenty-eight in 1984. They dipped again in the next two years, and plummeted as the administration found itself wrapped around the axle of the Iran-*contra* affair. The average during Casey's tenure of six years was 18.5 NIEs, below the overall annual average of twenty-three during the full period from 1950 to 1996. William H. Webster became DCI in 1987 when Casey died of a brain tumor, just as the Iran-*contra* scandal was heating up. While the affair was under investigation, NIEs dropped to seven in 1987 and fifteen in 1988. Clearly, DCIs find it difficult to focus on research analysis while embroiled in intelligence scandals. Webster slowly turned back to the job of more energetic estimating after the scandal cleared, recording sixteen NIEs in 1989, twelve in 1990, and ending his tenure with twenty-eight in 1991—his only year above the overall average.

When George H. W. Bush won the presidency in 1988, he soon replaced Webster with the first (and only) professional intelligence analyst ever to fill the position of DCI: Robert M. Gates, formerly a deputy director for intelligence (DDI) in the CIA. The brief Golden Age of NIEs was about to begin. In 1992, the production of Estimates under Gates hit a still-standing record of fifty-six. If you want to emphasize analysis, selecting the nation's intelligence chief from the ranks of analysts appears to be a good way to do it.[94]

Gates's successor, R. James Woolsey (the first of three DCIs for President Bill Clinton), kept the NIE production levels high, registering forty-two in 1993 (the third-highest rate ever, after Gates in 1992 and Dulles in 1955), followed by a strong thirty-four in 1994. When John M. Deutch came into the DCI office in 1995, the numbers went into decline again, to fifteen in 1995 and ten in 1996. In his town-hall meeting with CIA personnel in the Bubble on his first day as DCI in 1995, he had made some allusions to the importance of the intelligence community's products, but at the end of his tenure, the record revealed a low level of commitment to the production of National Intelligence Estimates.

As I looked over this data, it appeared to me that intelligence scandals had diverted attention away from NIE production during the middle years of this history (Colby and Bush; Casey and Webster). A decline in the frequency of NIEs had occurred as well when the CIA was run by DCIs with only a limited interest in research intelligence (Turner, Deutch), and during the CIA's early period when it was still finding its legs (Hillenkoetter). Overall, the frequency of research intelligence in the form of Estimates prospered during the 1950s and 1960s, then declined on average during the 1970s through the early 1990s—with the conspicuous exception of a year when former Agency analyst Robert Gates's reigned as DCI.

I passed these thoughts along to Aspin and suggested, too, that the argument between advocates of current intelligence and those of research intelligence was based on a false dichotomy. The nation needed both. Clearly, the conduct of warfare in Iraq and Afghanistan, for example, requires a rich flow of tactical, current intelligence to guide soldiers and their commanders, including the commander in chief. Other topics, though, cry out for more comprehensive analysis, such as the future of the Saudi royal family or the long-term appeal in the Western Hemisphere of Venezuela's anti-American president, Hugo Chavez. Policy makers and their aides are starved for information that will help them deal with problems in their in-box, but the best of these officials are usually interested in long-range forecasts as well. They will continue to want both good daily intelligence reports and long-range NIEs.

A CORNUCOPIA OF INTELLIGENCE REPORTS

The frequency of Estimates will no doubt rise and fall in the future. In between the ups and downs, though, the intelligence community steadily produces many other forms of research intelligence, whether specialized reports, memoranda, or oral briefings. According to former CIA deputy director for intelligence John L. Helgerson, "A bunch of research intelligence is done, not necessarily estimative—just everything we know about subject X; then someone says, 'It's about time we do a formal Estimate.' "[95]

The NIE, then, is just one among thousands of other reports written by the intelligence community, both current and research in nature. Among them are Intelligence Memoranda (IM), pithy analyses sent to specific policy makers; intelligence dailies, such as the *National Intelligence Daily* (NID); weekly reports; information cables; working-group reports; various research papers less detailed than NIEs (in the "middle range" of analysis, between current and research intelligence); Special Intelligence Reports and Intelligence Reports, of which there are thousands each year, focused on information requests from individuals or smaller groups of policy makers; Net Assessments, which compare foreign with U.S. military capabilities; the "baseball cards" I mentioned that feature international leadership profiles, which rose in number to account for some 60 percent of all CIA Intelligence Directorate products in a recent year;[96] e-mails and faxes over secure communications links; personal letters from the DCI or DNI to the president and other officials—a favorite of DCI George Tenet when he succeeded John Deutch;[97] and daily or on-call oral briefings. Lowenthal points to oral briefings as "probably the most important analytical service provided by the intelligence community," because of the interaction it permits between consumers and producers.[98]

When Aspin and I sat down together to discuss my findings about NIEs, we agreed that it was important for the intelligence community to continue their preparation. We also tried our hand at developing a checklist of key attributes for Estimates and other intelligence reports going to policy makers. First on the list was accuracy. In 1999, the intelligence community sent to a NATO bomber pilot the coordinates of what turned out to be the Chinese Embassy instead of an arms depot in Serbia. Afterward, Jay Leno joked that "CIA" stands for "Can't Identify Anything." (In fact, the map in question was from the NGA, not the CIA.) Three Chinese nationals were killed in this accidental bombing. Obviously, the intelligence agencies must provide accurate information. The following qualities are also vital: timeliness (history runs on nimble feet); relevance (no dissertations for the White House on local elections in Monrovia, thank you);[99] readability (no econometrics); brevity (presidents are busy); all-source fusion (tapping into the knowledge of all thirteen—today, sixteen—agencies); and, ideally, a degree of specificity—"actionable intelligence"—that can allow policy makers to take action in the nation's defense (vague "orange alerts" out; precise Al Qaeda attack plans in).

This is an exacting set of standards. Often the intelligence community will fall short, for reasons of inadequate intelligence collection; the slow translation of foreign language and coded materials, along with other data-processing problems; flawed analyses, since the brains of human beings are neither perfect nor clairvoyant; or the misuse of reports by policy makers, who may cherry pick details they like and ignore ones they don't. Despite these challenges, the secret agencies have to aim for as near flawless intelligence reporting as possible; and policy makers must constantly resist the temptation to twist these reports for political purposes.

Regarding the value of NIEs, my verdict for the chairman was unequivocal: they make a contribution. Improvements were necessary, though.[100] For example, they should be more nuanced, with dissents more boldly presented. NIE production levels needed to rise, too, and the document had to be shorter (say, thirty pages rather than a hundred), and completed in six months at the most—and faster in times of emergency. Those DCIs who allowed the number of Estimates to fall below the historical annual average of twenty-three, I suggested to Aspin, were not paying adequate attention to a core intelligence mission. To avoid the impression that the CIA was the only show in town, we agreed further that a high number of analysts and managers serving on the NIC—above all the NIOs—should come from the other intelligence agencies; it was vital for NIEs to be a truly community-wide product.

Would National Intelligence Estimates have a readership among key officials in Washington—the *sine qua non* of intelligence relevance? "If presidents read them, so will others," Aspin said to me. The most important thing is to have a president who is likely to take the nation's top intelligence findings seriously, who will read them, and who will pick cabinet officers who will read them, as if the effectiveness of their decisions depended on this practice—as it well may in some circumstances.

PART III

Leadership Transition

CHAPTER 7 | The Death of a Chairman

A S JOHN DEUTCH SETTLED INTO his duties as intelligence director, the Aspin Commission staff stepped up the pace of its interview schedule—66 to date, and 105 more pending—and began, as well, to plan a series of summer "roundtables" for the commissioners. The purpose of the roundtables, according to staff aide Kim Simpson who was organizing them, was "to invite intelligence experts and critics to a forum in which they would help commissioners and staff to hash out some very specific questions/issues."[1] The venue would be a series of continental breakfasts at the commission's NEOB conference room— coffee and rolls at 7:45. An expert would give a ten-minute presentation, say, on counterintelligence, followed by an hour of discussion. I wondered how many commissioners would attend an early-morning meeting in downtown Washington, unless the former secretary of state Henry Kissinger or some other government celebrity was the presenter. Even then, I was doubtful.

I was spending some of my time conducting interviews, but I continued to work mainly on research projects for the Chairman. In between commission meetings, talks with me about my research findings, and meetings with the staff's legal trio, Aspin attended plays at the Kennedy Center and professional basketball games at the Capital Centre, played tennis once or twice a week, spoke at forums in Washington and around the country, and was continually on the telephone discussing intelligence reform with various experts. He said nothing more about feeling ill.

The chairman had asked the staff to reduce the length of the scope paper down to three or four pages from the twenty-plus it had mushroomed to, perhaps on the theory that we would get ourselves into fewer arguments with the DCI and lawmakers if we kept things simple and general at this stage. We had now become, to paraphrase Henry James, a hippopotamus rolling a pea. Only a few of the commissioners displayed an interest in joining the staff in the nitty-gritty business of interviews and report drafting. Friedman, one of the least experienced of the commission members when it came to intelligence, had become a dynamo and joined with the staff on some of the basic grunt work—a multimillionaire with his sleeves rolled up. He was particularly interested in organizational questions and had his own one-person task force on intelligence organization; but he also joined forces with Baird (the leader), Coelho, and Hermann on the task force that was probing the relationship between cops and spies. General Allen, and Hermann again, volunteered for KP duty on issues related to spying from space. Two of the commissioners even took the time to visit some of the intelligence agencies: Dewhurst going to his old haunt, the CIA, and the indefatigable Friedman to the NSA. Of course, several of the other commissioners had been to one or another of the agencies dozens of times as congressional overseers or intelligence professionals themselves and probably didn't see the need to queue up for these local excursions; but the staff was much impressed by the "worker bees" who did participate in staff discussions, interview sessions, task forces, and agency visits.

IC21

As the staff moved forward with our scope-paper revisions and interviews, in the back of our minds was the intelligence inquiry being conducted by the House Permanent Select Committee on Intelligence.[2] On May 12, we were able to satisfy our curiosity about HPSCI's progress by talking directly with Mark Lowenthal, the Committee's staff director. A slightly built, bearded professorial figure with a keen intellect, Lowenthal had served as deputy assistant secretary for intelligence in the State Department and occasionally taught a course on the subject at Columbia University. As a younger man, he had won $154,000 on the quiz show *Jeopardy*. Lowenthal had a whimsical air and was well-known for his irreverent witticisms, although behind this jocular facade resided a serious, hard working intelligence professional with a deep knowledge of that subject and just about everything else.

He informed the commission staff members who had gone up to meet with him on the Hill that HPSCI had already spent many hours on its review of intelligence programs, titled *The Intelligence Community in the 21st Century* or simply *IC21*, but had achieved little consensus among its members on reform recommendations. He said that the committee's chairman, Larry Combest, was intrigued by General Clapper's advocacy of a director of military intelligence (DMI). Combest was interested as well in another idea, pushed by some reformers, in favor of an office that would be situated above the DMI: a new director of national intelligence—the persistent DNI proposal. Lowenthal seemed less enamored of these "structural" recommendations than his boss, but he was keeping an open mind and intended to explore the DMI proposal further with Clapper. He was sure of one thing, though: the intelligence agencies were badly disorganized. "The patchwork structure of the intelligence community made sense at the time each of the discrete pieces were added, one after another," he told the commission staffers, "but looking at the complete package today, it doesn't make any sense." The bottom line: the DCI didn't have the authority necessary to run the intelligence community.

Lowenthal worried about Deutch's plan to create a new imagery agency during a time of downsizing the government and America's intelligence capabilities, but he doubted the resolute DCI could be persuaded to drop the proposal. He expressed concern, too, about the rising number of "centers" in the intelligence community. In an attempt to overcome the organizational fragmentation that plagued the thirteen largely autonomous components of the intelligence community, DCIs had turned to the establishment of centers and interagency task forces to help them deal with specific targets or problems, such as ethnic conflict in the Balkans, the focus of one of the DCI task forces. Rumor had it that Deutch even had in mind the creation of a DCI Environmental Center to examine the possible uses of U.S. intelligence platforms to spot global ecological threats. Fourteen centers existed in 1995, along with a handful of DCI task forces. Some of them reported directly to the DCI, others to the deputy director for operations (DDO) and to the deputy director for intelligence (DDI). According to Lowenthal, they formed a "crazy quilt of staffing and reporting procedures." He thought the centers failed to include a full cross section of the intelligence community, but rather were dominated by CIA officers; as a result, there was "tremendous redundancy" between them and the rest of the community, not to mention resentment toward the Agency for trying to monopolize important career assignments.

As with the Aspin Commission staff, the HPSCI staff director had high on his investigative agenda questions about the quality of intelligence analysis. He expressed the view that National Intelligence Estimates were practically "useless," because policy officials needed "more tailored pieces" that dealt with issues they had to address immediately. The solution: analysts had to be more responsive to the information requirements of policy makers; only in this manner could analysts ensure that NIEs and other reports were relevant to urgent policy issues. Yet earlier Lowenthal had acknowledged that policy makers typically fail to express their needs with much clarity. Here was yet another dilemma we were hearing an earful about and would have to confront.

The commission staff spent an hour and a half with Lowenthal, exploring his thoughts on intelligence budgets ("the DCI needs clearer authority"); the tedious but important issue of personnel management (NSA was burdened by a top-heavy personnel profile); and DCI-presidential relations. The HPSCI staff director told us that DCI James Woolsey had never had a one-on-one meeting with President Clinton, which led him to the conclusion: "You can't legislate who the president will see and take into confidence." I was pleased to learn that the subject of oversight was on the House Committee's radar. With the comment that "it just isn't needed," Lowenthal dismissed the idea of creating a single joint oversight committee to take the place of SSCI and HPSCI. He shared with the commission staff HPSCI's plan to conduct hearings on all these subjects, and to hold an "offsite" retreat with the committee members comparable to the one we had just completed at the Farm. The House Committee also intended to introduce some type of reform legislation to improve intelligence performance. Exactly how these plans would mesh with our similar ones remained unclear.

On the same page as Senator Warner and Britt Snider, Lowenthal underscored what he believed was the most significant obligation of the Aspin Commission and HPSCI: to "revalidate the community." The American people had to be reassured that the CIA and its companion agencies were operating properly and that they were indispensable to the nation's security. I could see a place for this cheerleading, but I continued to hope we would be tough minded, too, in our examination of organizations and programs that had fallen short of reasonable expectations.

The HPSCI staff director offered the commission staff a litany of topics that his committee wanted to examine. They were essentially the same ones we had been pursuing in commission meetings and outlining in our truncated scope paper:

- Support to Military Operations: Lowenthal worried that, "left to its own devices, the Pentagon will eat up all of the intelligence community's resources." The military already took up the lion's share of the intelligence budget, and DoD's appetite had grown "astronomically" since the Persian Gulf War of 1991. He feared that John Deutch, with his Pentagon background, would further accelerate this hording of resources in the hands of military intelligence managers—the gorillas at NSA, NRO, CIO, and DIA.

- The Requirements Process: Voicing a concern we had heard many times before in our own meetings, Lowenthal expressed frustration at the inability or unwillingness of senior policy makers to define their specific intelligence-collection requirements.
- Intelligence Production: On the production side of the equation, it was hard to convince intelligence managers to explain clearly to policy makers what tradeoffs would have to occur in existing collection assignments to accommodate new tasking requirements. "The current tasking system doesn't work," he summed up glumly.
- Surge Ability: Another intelligence debate had arisen over whether, in the post–Cold War era, the United States should continue to seek an intelligence "global presence," with case officers, assets, and spy machines ringing the world; or whether, to accommodate cost cutting, the DCI should move to a posture of "global surge"—rapidly sending intelligence resources (spies, machines, money) from one hot spot to another, as needed. Former DCI Woolsey was enthusiastically in favor of surge. He often used aircraft carriers as an analogy: the United States could afford to have only so many carriers, so it moves them—surges them—from place to place, according to U.S. military requirements in the world. It seemed to me, though, that spies were fundamentally different from aircraft carriers. A good case officer knows his or her target nation well—the history, the language, the social customs. This knowledge could not be usefully transferred from one location to another; in fact, in most instances it couldn't be transferred at all, such as, say, from Afghanistan to Vietnam. One could surge selected spy machines, say, by altering the orbit of a surveillance satellite, for example—although even this could be difficult and time consuming. "Surge requires a supple management in the intelligence community," Lowenthal concluded, "which does not exist."

The Consumers

On May 16 and 17, the commission held briefing sessions with several former consumers of intelligence—senior policy makers who had been on the receiving end of the intelligence cycle. Soon the rafters of the NEOB conference room were resounding with their grievances: humint sources were often unreliable; too few CIA analysts were available to report on secondary targets (only one had been assigned to Somalia at the time of the downing of the Black Hawk in 1993); intelligence products were insufficiently tailored to the specific problems that individual policy makers faced; intelligence reports were frequently too late to be of any use—a situation intelligence professionals refer to as "OBE" (overtaken by events); and analysts cried wolf too often. On this last point, my colleague at the University of Georgia, former secretary of state Dean Rusk, had remarked to me wryly about his experience with Agency analysts during the 1960s: "The CIA predicted eight out of the last three crises."[3]

Most everyone who appeared before the commission emphasized that effective producer-consumer relationships depended on the establishment of rapport between the two groups. "A lot of this boils down to the quality of the NIO," said one veteran consumer, referring to the national intelligence officers assigned to the National Intelligence Council—the varsity squad among the community's analysts, known for their sophisticated knowledge in the area of their respective specialties and their skill in oral briefing.

One of the key issues, as I have mentioned earlier, was whether intelligence should be pushed by producers or pulled by consumers. Commissioner Wolfowitz, for one, preferred a pull system. "When it comes to satellite photography, our traditional way of doing it is to have photo interpreters at the CIA pore over it," he reminded his fellow commissioners. "They figure out what's really good, and then they forward it to troops overseas—the push side of the equation. We need to have a better capacity to distribute images to the field to help the soldier who is being shot at by someone over the next hill—an ability to let the person under fire quickly pull satellite photos of his area of the battlefield from among all those the CIO has collected in the past few hours."[4]

THE HUMINT DEBATE

Yet another area of organizational conflict came to light in these sessions, this time involving humint. The CIA's Directorate of Operations had long been involved in human intelligence—recruiting spies overseas; that was the core function of the DO. Money was not the main problem when it came to humint. Spy machines are expensive, but human assets are relatively cheap, and, for some targets, humint is superior.

One of the ironies of American intelligence is that the vast percentage of its annual budget goes into costly intelligence hardware, especially satellites, yet the value of these machines is questionable in helping the United States understand such contemporary global concerns as terrorism or China's burgeoning economic might. Cameras on satellites and reconnaissance aircraft are unable to peer inside the canvas tents, roofed mud huts, or mountain caves in Afghanistan or Pakistan where terrorists gather to plan their deadly operations, or into the deep underground caverns where North Koreans construct nuclear weapons. "Space cameras cannot see into factories where missiles are made, or into the sheds of shipyards," writes an intelligence expert. "Photographs cannot tell whether stacks of drums outside an assumed chemical-warfare plant contain nerve gas or oil, or whether they are empty."[5] As a U.S. intelligence officer aptly put it, we need "to know what's inside the building, not what the building looks like."[6]

Even within the domain of spy machines, sometimes the best results come not so much from pricey satellites as from far less expensive UAVs. On occasion, though, expensive sigint satellites do capture revealing telephone communications, such as between international drug lords or Qaeda lieutenants. Moreover, the photographic information that imint satellites yield on such matters as Russian and Chinese missile sites, North Korean troop deployments, Hamas rocket emplacements in Gaza, or the construction of nuclear reactors in Iran, is of obvious importance. In the case of terrorism, though, the most valuable intelligence coup would be to have a human agent well placed inside the Qaeda organization. For America's security, such an asset could be worth a dozen billion-dollar satellites.

Even with more routine intelligence needs, such as information to support U.S. international diplomatic negotiations, former DCI Stansfield Turner found humint a great aid. "I have seen us sit down at a negotiating table when we had the other guy's plan for negotiating in hand, thanks to a humint asset. That's pretty useful."[7] Another DCI, William E. Colby, offers this appraisal of humint: "It's one of those things you can't afford to say no to, because sometimes it can be valuable."[8] He adds: "You can go through years with nothing much happening [with regard to the CIA's assets abroad], so then you cut off the relationship. Since nothing had happened there for ten years, we were in the process of closing the [Agency's] stations in El Salvador and Portugal—just before these countries blew up!" His conclusion: "I think you'll always have some humint, and it'll pay off." Near the end of the Cold War, I asked one of the most well known of the former intelligence directors, Richard Helms, what the consequences would be if the United States eliminated humint altogether. Agitated by this thought, he responded at length:

> You would eliminate most of the information that comes into the United States government. This idea that photographic satellites, satellites that pick up electronic emissions, and all the rest of it—all those technical things...they're Jim-dandy when it comes to photographing missile installations, listening to missile firings, checking on

telemetry, looking at the number of tanks being produced in certain factories—in other words, "bean-counting" mostly. Great. But once you eliminate the issue of bean-counting, what good do those pictures do you? They're nice to have, in a situation like now in the Persian Gulf. You can count the tanks and so forth that the Iraqis are putting in there. It's a wonderful device. But it doesn't tell you what's inside [Iraqi leader Saddam] Hussein's head. It doesn't tell you what he is going to do. It doesn't give you the price of oil; it doesn't give you the price of gold; it doesn't tell you what the wheat production is going to be within a given place. Even though you photograph [something] and can make some assessments from the photographs, that isn't the final word that you want. In short, the end of the Cold War means that there's going to be more emphasis on human intelligence than there was before.[9]

Former DCI Robert Gates agrees that humint has been valuable. Acknowledging that techint was a boon to America's understanding of Soviet strategic weapons, he recalls nonetheless that "a great deal of what we learned about the technical characteristics of Soviet conventional weapons we learned through humint."[10] He adds that when it came to gauging the Kremlin's intentions, not just its capabilities, humint provided especially significant insights.

Yet humint has its limitations. Spies can be enormously difficult to recruit overseas in closed societies like Iran and North Korea, which possess effective counterintelligence defenses. So are the tightly controlled cells of Al Qaeda. Michael Goodman has commented on the difficulty of acquiring humint sources who knew anything about nuclear developments in the Soviet Union during the Cold War. The West, he notes, was "attempting to gather intelligence on a strictly compartmentalized, highly secret program within a secure police state."[11] Adding to these security barriers today is the fact that Americans focused for decades on the Communist world, largely ignoring the study of the languages, history, and culture necessary to operate spy rings in the Middle East and Southwest Asia. How many Americans speak Pashto, Arabic, and Farsi well? How many understand the nuances of slang and various dialects within these languages? And how many are willing to serve as operational officers for government pay in perilous locales, trying to recruit indigenous assets—especially as NOCs outside the comfort and safety of the U.S. embassy?

Even if they can be successfully recruited, local assets can be unreliable. These individuals are not Boy Scouts or nuns; they are often the dregs of their own societies, driven by greed and without any moral compass. Indeed, in the recruitment of such individuals, the ethics of intelligence officers "would bring a blush to Machiavelli's cheek," according to a close observer of the Great Game (as Rudyard Kipling referred to espionage activities). "Their job in life is to spot useful foreigners and then do what it takes—money, flattery, green cards and so on—to turn them into traitors."[12] The objective, after all, is to purloin useful information from one's adversaries when that information is unavailable in the public domain.

Moreover, foreign assets often fabricate reports, sell information to the highest bidder, and may become false defectors or double agents. A recent example of the risks involved in humint is the case of a German agent in Iraq during 2002, Rafid Ahmed Alwan, prophetically codenamed "Curveball." He managed to convince the German intelligence service that there were biological WMDs in Iraq; and the Germans, in turn, passed this misinformation along to a credulous CIA through their intelligence liaison relationship. Only after the war in Iraq began in 2003 did German and CIA intelligence officials begin to doubt Curveball's *bona fides*; he was, it turned out, a consummate liar.[13]

At other times, however, a humint asset can provide extraordinarily helpful information, as the Soviet military intelligence officer Oleg Penkosky did during the Cold War. Information from Colonel Penkosky helped the United States identify the presence of Soviet nuclear missiles in Cuba in 1962. With occasional successes like this in mind, the United States and most other countries persevere in their quest for reliable and productive espionage assets, even though experience shows that the benefit-cost ratio has been notoriously poor.

A humint concern of some intelligence consumers in 1995 was the fact that the Pentagon had entered into the business of asset acquisition in a big way, establishing the Defense Humint Service (DHS) within the DIA. "DHS is fairly useless," concluded one former consumer, but others felt the same way about the DO. Exactly how these two entities—DHS and the DO—were coordinating their humint efforts overseas, to avoid trying to recruit and run the same agents, remained foggy. What was perfectly clear, though, were the tensions that had arisen between the two organizations—tensions that now seemed in need of arbitration. Here was yet another item to add to the commission's growing list of responsibilities.

A Producer's Perspective

We also wanted to hear from the intelligence producers. With Deutch now safely ensconced in the DCI office, Admiral Studeman's tour of duty as acting director had came to an end; so the commission invited him back to ruminate further on his experiences, perhaps now with a greater freedom to express his own views candidly. Following our sessions with a parade of former consumers, we had the admiral join us on May 18. Thin and birdlike, with rows of ribbons on his chest and four stars on his epaulets (one more than when we'd seen him last), he looked relieved and happy. All the pressures of the intelligence directorship were behind him, and he had been lionized for his able guidance of the intelligence community through the period of transition from Woolsey to Deutch.

Peering through his thick eyeglass lenses, the admiral began his remarks with a comment on "the biggest fear at the CIA," namely, "that the military will take it over. This is the talk in the hall at 'Deutchland.' The paranoia level is rising." The rumors had some foundation. Deutch's crew of Defense Department staff aides that he had brought with him to Langley were all too reminiscent of Admiral Turner's "Navy mafia." These new employees, plus Deutch's rapid appointments of new managers at the highest levels inside the Agency, amounted to "the most sweeping such change in CIA history," according to an official in-house accounting.[14]

The commissioners were interested in the admiral's opinions on how to improve the relationship between decision makers and analysts. "The customer ought to be the driver of intelligence," Studeman said firmly—the pull theory. Even though in his earlier meeting with us he had describe the Department of Defense almost in predatory terms as an intelligence user, now he referred to the DoD as "a model customer"—at least in that it knew what kinds of intelligence it wanted and in its insistence on good analysis. "There is a large sucking sound in Washington of intelligence going into the bowels of the DoD," he joked, accurately portraying the Pentagon as a huge resource sump. The Defense Department was well organized when it came to intelligence; it knew what it wanted, and went after it—in large part because the stakes were high for the secretary of defense. The lives of troops were on the line. "Other agencies and departments are less developed," Studeman observed, adding that at the State Department "intelligence [INR] sits over on the side, like a blob, and is not well integrated into the bureaus."

The message was obvious: DoD aside, most policy customers had to be educated about the value of intelligence. They needed a more sophisticated understanding of how the three-lettered agencies could help them, and who to call. To some extent, the burden of educating rested on intelligence managers and analysts. It wasn't good enough for them merely to come up with valuable information; intelligence had to be *marketed*, just like any other product. This, in turn, required opening up dialogues with customers, reaching out from the NIC and the DI to shop intelligence around the government departments—pushing intelligence in hopes of nurturing a subsequent culture of pulling. The downside was that when analysts are sent out to brief policy makers and develop a rapport with them, it takes time away from what they do best: studying global issues. Moreover, not every intelligence officer had the right kind of outgoing personality to establish cordial working relationships with those in policy positions.

I had met with an assistant secretary in one of the policy departments for dinner a few weeks earlier, and his comments came to mind as Studeman spoke. On his second day in office during the Clinton administration, this assistant secretary received a telephone call from a senior CIA analyst. "I've been assigned to work with your department and I want to come down this afternoon to meet with you," she said, skipping preliminary niceties, such as "Congratulations on your new job" or even "How are you?" The assistant secretary explained to the analyst that he was extremely busy settling into his office and would prefer to meet later in the month. "I need to see you right away," came the icy response. She added: "You know, I have the same rank you do at the CIA. I don't want to be pushed around." The assistant secretary could hardly believe he was having this conversation. Had the analyst passed through the fire of a Senate confirmation, as he had? he thought to himself, as he felt his stomach tighten. Thoroughly irritated, he replied, "When I need you, I'll give you a call," and hung up the telephone. That ended any hope for this potentially important relationship. Fortunately, the analyst was soon replaced by someone with better "people skills," and the assistant secretary eventually enjoyed good intelligence service from the Agency. The woman on the other end of the telephone that day may have been a terrific analyst, but she failed to understand the marketing side of the intelligence business or, for that matter, basic manners. In my experience, she was an exception.

Other top analysts I had come to know, especially NIOs, were not just smart and well informed, but diplomatic and personable. But sometimes they, too, were insufficiently aware of the need—or were too busy—to cultivate ties with officials "downtown." It was not an easy assignment: senior analysts were not only expected to be experts in their field, but also to track down and "romance" overworked—and sometimes egomaniacal—policy officials. Moreover, there was a tendency for Naval officers to want intelligence from Naval analysts, Air Force officers from Air Force analysts, and so on; they trusted their own kind more than someone from the CIA, the analyst's level of knowledge and personal charm notwithstanding.

In light of all the machines and assets collecting intelligence around the globe for the U.S. government, a commissioner asked Studeman a familiar question: was the nation gathering too much information? "I'm not worried about that," he responded. "Whatever falls on the cutting room floor, we can archive, then use later when the target pops up." That was one way to look at the fire-hose problem, but how skillful were the intelligence agencies at retrieving "warehoused" information from their vast computer files when needed? I knew from interviews with NSA personnel that much of the sigint intercepted by that agency lay in dusty archives for months, even years, if not forever, without even being translated into English, let alone analyzed.

The discussion with Admiral Studeman drifted to the controversial topic of battle damage assessment (BDA in military-speak) in the Persian Gulf War; that is, estimates of how well U.S. forces had whipped the Iraqi army. He conceded that the CIA, a civilian agency, had produced a more accurate BDA in 1991, "because the military assessments [carried out by the military intelligence agencies for the DoD] were politically tilted to show 'success.'" Asked about the co-location experiment at the Agency, he said that the "partnership is magical, amazing, it really works! But for how long, I don't know." Further, Studeman warned candidly that John Deutch might steal a march on the commission, instituting reforms before we had a chance to report our findings and recommendations. For example, the new DCI was moving full steam ahead on creating a new imagery agency, along with other sweeping reforms related to the management of spy platforms in space.

Whether or not Deutch would also be able to take on "his most significant challenge"—the redesign of the DO—was a different matter, continued Studeman. That would involve "reforming a whole culture." The primary challenge presented by the Directorate of Operations was the need to modernize America's humint operations around the world. This included ironing out the conflict between the new Defense HUMINT Service and the CIA over agent recruiting, as well as settling the argument between the two over who would control how many billets (office spaces) in U.S. embassies abroad. Moreover, Studeman suggested that Deutch, and perhaps the Aspin Commission, would have to address ongoing embassy billeting disputes with the FBI and with the State Department; the development of a more robust NOC program, which was two to three times more expensive than the funding required for official-cover officers—in a time of shrinking intelligence budgets; the role of covert action in the post-Soviet world ("It's a dirty mission, hard to manage," Studeman said); the need to strengthen the Counterintelligence Staff, housed inside the DO; and the ongoing problem of "the wall" that existed between law-enforcement officers and case officers—a matter of obvious importance in fighting terrorism, since cooperation between these two groups was vital to success. He was skeptical of the "surge" concept. "Sending in 'fly aways' to another country for a short time is not good enough," he cautioned.[15]

The admiral laughed at the idea of a ten-year term limit for the position of DCI. "A guy couldn't last in the job for ten years!" he declared. Responding to a question about organizational reform, Studeman said that an Office of DNI might work, if the director had within his shop the DI, the NIC, and full budget authority over the community. In other words, create another CIA, only call it the DNI and send the existing CIA into an outer orbit of the intelligence community. Reading between the lines, this was the essence of the DNI proposal, as the admiral described it.

Despite suggesting a DNI along these lines, Studeman did not want a centralized intelligence community. "Intelligence has got to be dispersed, not centralized," he argued with some intensity. "Remember, the key consumers are 'down below,' at the tactical military level." In the same vein, the admiral opposed General Clapper's consolidation of military intelligence. The more centralized intelligence becomes, he argued, the less flexible its outer limbs and branches would be. There was clearly some logic in this viewpoint; but a fragmented intelligence community, with no real director of central intelligence, was also deficient in its capacity to share information and prepare "all source" reports for the president—the fundamental purpose of the intelligence community.

Oversight was a word that rarely came to the lips of intelligence officers when they appeared before the commission; the philosophy seemed to be to say as little as possible. Studeman broke this vow of silence, though, in a way that would have been roundly applauded in the Pentagon and much of the CIA. "The oppressive oversight needs to be thinned," he asserted. "As Acting DCI, I had six street agents overseas and 999,999 overseers at home."

I suppressed my urge to jump in and debate the admiral on this point when none of the commissioners raised objections. Wyche Fowler had once said to me that oversight is vital "to keep the bureaucrats from doing something stupid." Yet even he remained silent. In my many conversations with admirals and generals, I had the sense that if Congress were to mysteriously vanish from the face of the earth one morning, they wouldn't lose any sleep or shed any tears. Vice Adm. John M. Poindexter, the national security advisor for President Reagan, testified during the Iran-*contra* hearings that when he was planning questionable covert actions in Nicaragua, he never bothered to inform lawmakers. "I simply didn't want any outside interference," he said, as if Congress were some alien body.[16] For some of us at least, congressional "interference" lies at the heart of democracy. Here were the checks and balances spelled out in the first article of the Constitution (first for a reason) and the *Federalist* papers (especially no. 51)—the vital safeguards against a dangerous concentration of power in the executive branch. This was the core fear that animated the founders in the creation of our system of government in 1787. For many modern-day bureaucrats, though, Congress was merely an annoyance; this attitude no doubt kept the CIA from informing SSCI and HPSCI about the Alpirez murders in Guatemala.

Summing up, Studeman said that a DCI's number-one priority is to "penetrate enemy targets." After that, the director's obligation was to ensure an "all-source fusion" of intelligence, melding together information available on a target from throughout the intelligence community. Lastly, a DCI had to distribute fresh and accurate intelligence reports, as rapidly as possible, to key policy officials around the government and in command posts abroad. The admiral had ended his briefing on the most important question before the commission: how could the quality and the timeliness of information presented to decision makers in Washington be improved? It was a subject Aspin and I had been wrestling with, too, in his PFIAB offices.

The Aspin Papers: Tracking the Soviet Union during the Cold War

What I had come to think of as the "Aspin Papers"—the research studies I was writing for the chairman—had reached a point in mid-May where I was ready to give him a final draft on the subject that interested him the most: the effectiveness of the intelligence community's collection and analysis against Soviet military targets during the Cold War. He had published some findings on this subject earlier in his career and had an abiding interest in learning more.[17] My other papers on economic intelligence, environmental intelligence, and counterterrorism were nearing completion as well. I relished the opportunity to review the results with him at our "seminars" in the OEOB.

On May 18, I walked the paper on the Soviet military over to Aspin's offices and left it with his secretary. We were scheduled to discuss the findings the next week, along with a few experts joining us from around town. I had organized the study into four parts: the first examined in detail the intelligence community's successes and failures against Soviet military targets during the Cold War; the second presented a summary "report card" on this record; the third provided a visual display of the fluctuations from 1945 to 1991 in the community's under- and overestimating of Soviet military strength; and the fourth offered a set of lessons I had drawn from the analysis.

We had divided the question of the Soviet military into issues of weapons development, capabilities, adherence to arms accords, actual military events, and the Kremlin's intentions with respect to the use of military force. I won't burden the reader with a blow-by-blow account, but suffice it to say here that the CIA had recorded both successes and failures in predicting the development of new weapons in the USSR.[18] On the success side, for example, thanks to a Soviet defector (Adolf G. Tolkachev, caught and executed by the Soviets in 1986), the Agency (1) knew about Moscow's long-range bomber program as early as 1948; (2) debunked the so-called bomber- and missile-gaps (the U.S. Air Force had wrongly inflated the Soviet lead in these departments); (3) tracked its A- and H-bomb developments (although underestimating by five years how soon the Kremlin would have an atomic bomb); monitored the Soviet testing of nuclear devices; (4) forecast the advent of Soviet ICBMs; (5) knew of our adversary's submarine specifications, as well as its laser and antiballistic missile (ABM) research; (6) accumulated detailed information about the conventional capabilities of the Soviet armed forces; and, (7) throughout the Cold War, acquired the basic information on Soviet technological developments consistently in advance of major weapons production.

The list of misses was, unfortunately, also extensive. As a top Agency analyst conceded to me, "In the 'fifties, we weren't very good at all."[19] I had confirmed this point in conversations with academic specialists as well. Lacking U-2 over-flights or surveillance satellites (which were not yet invented), the CIA often joined the Air Force and other intelligence agencies in overestimating Soviet military capabilities during the 1950s. Michael Herman, a former British intelligence officer and a prominent scholar of intelligence studies in the United Kingdom, recalled that Western intelligence services had counted 175 Soviet Army divisions without understanding that in this early period of the Cold War only one-third were combat ready. "This led to a drive for nuclear weapons," he said, "to offset the inflated Soviet threat."[20] The CIA and other Western intelligence agencies also exaggerated the number of Soviet ICBMs and the Kremlin's capability to cap them with multiple warheads in the 1960s, thereby fueling an arms race between the superpowers. Subsequently, the Agency went to the other extreme of underestimating by five years the date when these warheads would be operational. Further, starting in 1974, the Soviets had advanced their ability to encrypt missile telemetry and the Agency could no longer decipher this data. The CIA was also unsure about the scope of chemical and biological weaponry in the USSR, and remained uncertain during the early 1980s about the accuracy of Soviet missilery.

Once U-2 flights and surveillance by satellites became a regular feature of American intelligence in the late 1950s and early 1960s, respectively, the

CIA, the DIA, and the NSA managed to monitor more effectively the specifications of Soviet weapons systems. The locations of Soviet troops, tanks, missiles, and aircraft were also well known. Even its submarines were reasonable well tracked, especially in the Atlantic. Further, vital intelligence on Soviet weapons plans usually continued to reach Washington officials well before the development of the weapons. Here, too, though, occasional shortcomings appeared as the CIA either overestimated or underestimated the numbers of weapons and the pace at which they would be deployed.[21] For example, the CIA overestimated the Soviet bomber force in the 1950s, the Soviet deployment of ICBMs in the same decade, missile production from 1960 to 1963, and the production of mobile missiles in the 1970s. Then the Agency underestimated ICBM production from 1965 to 1972, and the rates of deployment in the 1970s; SLBM (submarine-launched ballistic missile) production throughout out the 1970s; and missile accuracy from 1976 to 1979. Moreover, twenty-six U.S. surveillance aircraft and 108 crewmen were lost on intelligence collection missions against the USSR between 1950 and 1964 alone; and NSA warehouses were filled with sigint data that were never translated from Russian.

The mistaken estimates were a result of several shortcomings in collection and analysis. The intelligence community attributed more geo-strategic rationality to the Soviet leadership than was warranted. As in the United States, the Soviet military-industrial complex sometimes produced a larger number of weapons than Moscow's political leaders and generals really needed or wanted. Also, even the best of U.S. analysts could legitimately disagree over the meaning of data collected by our spy machines and agents. Take, for instance, the Soviet backfire bomber. The CIA classified it as a medium-ranged, tactical bomber designed for warfare in the Europe theater, which it was probably meant to be; yet it was also true that if Moscow ordered its pilots on a one-way, no-refueling kamikaze mission against the United States, the bomber could be viewed as an instrument of strategic warfare—which was how many DIA analysts saw it.

Complicating matters further, the Soviets tried to fool the West by exaggerating their military capabilities. "They wanted us to believe they were stronger than they really were," said a senior CIA analyst I interviewed as I prepared the report for Aspin. The purpose was to bolster the credibility of Soviet deterrence—just as, apparently, Saddam Hussein was attempting to do in 2002 (against Iran) by allowing the misperception that he possessed WMDs to persist. These Soviet deception measures sometimes reached absurd lengths, as when the Kremlin ordered the inflation of rubber submarines to float in Russian ports, a lame trick designed to cause an overcount by

America's surveillance satellites. The Kremlin would then offer to reduce the number of its make-believe subs in exchange for reductions in genuine U.S. weapons systems. This ploy failed, but other Soviet disinformation tricks may have been more successful.

The specifics of nuclear, biological, and chemical weapons were especially difficult to ascertain, so tightly was this information guarded by the Soviets. "That was impenetrable," conceded a senior analyst whom I interviewed, who had worked at the CIA for four decades. On the nuclear side, America's intelligence analysts were often forced to guess about the details, based on telemetry and radar emitted during Soviet missile test flights, plus assessments about nuclear technology extracted from Russian open sources and an occasional (often unreliable) Soviet defector or "walk in" agent who volunteered to serve as a spy against the Kremlin.[22]

I depicted for Aspin these oscillations between over- and underestimating Soviet military capabilities during the Cold War (see Figure 7.1). The figure displayed how America's increasing espionage prowess had reduced the wide swings in estimating that were characteristic of the first half of the superpower confrontation. The intelligence community experienced a number of technological breakthroughs leading to higher plateaus of collection capability and, subsequently, richer data banks that allowed a more accurate analysis of Soviet military developments. The most important early breakthroughs were the U-2 aircraft, which permitted high-altitude reconnaissance over Soviet territory beginning in1956, and the launching of surveillance satellites beginning in 1960. Thought less spectacular, advances in new sigint collection capabilities from satellites in the early 1970s, and again in the late 1980s, provided additional jumps forward toward more reliable coverage of Soviet military targets. This provided the United States with an ability to capture Red Army microwave communications intelligence (comint, a subset of signals intelligence), along with a sophisticated reading of telemetry (telint)—telltale emissions from Soviet rocketry and aircraft during test flights.

These technical developments led to a quantum leap in collection on the location and specifications of Soviet weaponry, a veteran intelligence analyst told me. The NIEs on the Soviet Union prepared in 1981, 1983, and 1985 are widely considered major improvements over earlier Estimates, as a result of the deeper knowledge gleaned from these more sophisticated sigint, comint, and telint capabilities.

Supplementing the breakthroughs in technical intelligence were improvements in analysis—advances of a more qualitative nature. The most important was an evolving ability to achieve an all-source fusion of intelligence. Slowly overcoming bureaucratic rivalry and distrust (to some extent), the

Key Soviet Weapons Issues During the Cold War

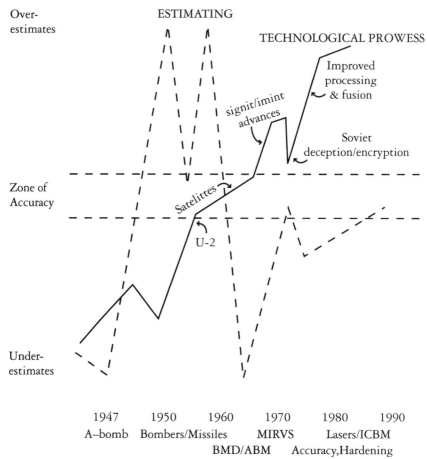

FIGURE 7.1 Approximate Error Fluctuations in Intelligence Estimates of Soviet Military Capabilities, as a Function of the Rising Prowess of U.S. Technical Intelligence and All-Source Analytic Fusion, 1947–90

ABM = antiballistic missile   ICBM = intercontinental ballistic missile
BMD = ballistic missile defense   MIRV = multiple independently targeted
reentry vehicle

secret agencies started to combine their findings into a more holistic amalgam during the 1980s, achieving a vital synergism and a more complete picture of the Soviet military. As a senior SOVA analyst recalled in one of my interviews in 1995, "It all began to come together in a critical mass to help analysts understand what was happening."

By the mid-1960s, the CIA reached the conclusion that the Soviets had no interest in a first-strike capability; instead, according to a top Agency analyst, "the Soviets were planning for a conventional war." The evidence was strong that Moscow viewed the possible use of nuclear weaponry with utmost caution; at least, that was the prevailing perspective among those at the highest level of political leadership in the Kremlin. It was true that some of the Soviet military publications occasionally engaged in worst-case analysis, including some loose talk about a first-strike against the United States, just as their counterparts in the Pentagon did; that was the blustering Soviet military literature that Professor Richard Pipes had used during the "Team B" drill in 1976 to justify his hawkish conclusions about Moscow's nefarious intentions.

During my interviews with analysts at the CIA, they remained adamant in their belief (as their leader put it) that "Team A's estimate was better." The question lingered, though: why did the Soviets build and test so many more strategic systems than the United States during the Cold War? The answer from the CIA was that, free of the kind of countervailing pressures found in American society, the Soviet defense industries ran wild. Moreover, unlike the United States, the Soviets were ineffectual at designing multipurpose weapons system and therefore produced more single-purpose weaponry. Finally, the Soviets had to test more than the United States, because they lacked the strong computer-simulation capability we used in place of extensive testing.

Looking back on the Cold War, I was beginning to see America's involvement in that superpower standoff as a story, in part, of how the U.S. intelligence community had built up an extraordinary database on the Soviet military adversary, cataloging the details of missile throw weights, bomber fuel capacity, and all the rest of the arcane specifications of weapons capabilities. From the drafting board to the final test flight, the CIA and its companion agencies knew (roughly, at least) the capabilities of Soviet weapons, how many would be deployed (though with early over- and underestimating errors), and how they were likely to operate in the field. This was no small feat, however imperfect it was in many of the details, against a tightly closed society like the Soviet Union.

Aspin was also interested in how well the United States monitored arms accords signed with the Soviet Union. Here again the picture was mixed. The intelligence community succeeded in assessing the accuracy of Soviet claims about its weapons deployments—information vital to U.S. negotiators. Similarly, it was able to verify (the "trust, but verify" mantra of America's arms negotiators during the Cold War) Soviet adherence to arms treaties and related international agreements, allowing Washington's diplomats to challenge periodic Kremlin deviations from the rules codified in these pacts. A good illustration of this capability was the DCI's disclosure in 1983 of certain Soviet violations of the ABM treaty, particularly the development of a large phased-array radar for ballistic missile early warning at a site located near the city of Krasnoyarsk in Siberia. On the "failure" side of treaty monitoring, some observers (as with those on the

Pipes-led "Team B") believed that the CIA had an "arms-control bias" that caused it to soft-pedal Soviet violations of arms accords. This criticism of the Agency, though, was advanced chiefly by hawks well known to oppose *détente* and other measures aimed at peaceful coexistence between the superpowers. The success of the U.S. intelligence agencies in monitoring compliance with various arms treaties depended on their ability to collect reliable data on Soviet weaponry. Progress, as Figure 7.1 suggests, was a tale of trial and error. At the beginning of the Cold War, this nation's inability to forecast accurately the time when the Soviet Union would obtain its first nuclear weapon, or to understand more precisely how many strategic bombers and ICBMs the USSR would build and deploy, was a result in large measure of the thin intelligence coverage the United States had over that vast territory, with its eleven time zones. This poor database meant great uncertainty, which in turn produced widespread disagreement over the Kremlin's true military capabilities and intentions.

America's intelligence services went from knowing very little about the Soviet military in the early stages of the Cold War to acquiring mountains of information. The U-2s and other reconnaissance aircraft, satellites, and listening posts on land and sea and in the air, as well as the rare well-placed agent like Oleg Penkovsky in Moscow—all provided an increasingly rich mix of intelligence data. Moreover, by the 1980s, the information gathered from these sources went into the hands of expert analysts who, in some cases, had been examining information on Soviet weaponry for over three decades. They had become much more proficient at integrating all-source intelligence and reading the tea leaves. In sum, as the Cold War unfolded, the United States benefitted from improved spy technology, smarter analysis, and an enhanced—but still immature—ethos of interagency cooperation.

When it came to tracking Soviet military movements, the intelligence community achieved near transparency in many cases, such as determining the location of the Red Army during the Six Day War of 1967, the civil unrest in Poland in 1980 and in the Baltic states in 1989–90, and the attempted coup against President Gorbachev in 1991. On the other side of the ledger, there were disquieting gaps in its knowledge, including the failure to forecast *any* of the major Soviet interventions abroad: against the Hungarian uprising in 1956, the Prague Spring in 1968, or Afghanistan in 1979. And, recall, the intelligence community had missed the initial placement of strategic and tactical nuclear missiles in Cuba in 1962; and it never realized throughout the crisis how many tactical nuclear warheads were on the island, or that Moscow had pre-delegated authority over them to local Soviet commanders.

The problem with history is that it is very hard to guess how it may unfold and, therefore, guesses about it likely direction are punctuated with analytic miscalculations. This made it difficult during the Cold War for one super-power to know exactly what the other was planning, because they themselves did not always know until the final moment. The invasion of Czechoslovakia saw the Kremlin change course several times before deciding, at the eleventh hour, to invade. Solid imagery intelligence that revealed the presence of Soviet troops along the Czechoslovak border came back to Washington from U.S. satellites, although too late to be of any use in predicting the invasion. This time lag between foreign troop movements and the determination of their whereabouts by satellite photography significantly diminished over the next two decades of technological improvements, as the United States became more adept at rapid data retrieval, processing, and dissemination. "Real-time imagery has made a *big* difference," a DDI emphasized to me.

The greatest intelligence failures involved the intelligence community's efforts to anticipate the intentions of Soviet leaders. The U.S. Air Force, for example, forecast thorough the 1950s that the Soviet Union would strike the United States with nuclear weapons; and, as the above examples indicate, the intelligence community miscalculated time and again what action the Kremlin would actually take in such places as Cuba, Hungary, and Czechoslovakia. At least, though, the CIA (and British intelligence) had correctly assessed the central importance of Moscow's likely behavior during the Cold War: the Soviets would be cautious and would refrain from a mortal confrontation with the United States.[23] Even in the case of the Cuban missile crisis, it seems clear that President Nikita Khrushchev had no idea that Washington would react so fiercely to the Soviet missile placements. When Kennedy did react strongly, the Soviets backed down.

Finally, I tried to derive some lessons from my findings. America's intelligence on the Soviet military during the Cold War was imperfect, as intelligence will always be; yet our knowledge became increasingly more accurate over the decades, a result of both growing experience among collectors and analysts in watching the Soviet target and evolving technical breakthroughs in espionage, supplemented by periodic humint achievements (though not at the highest levels of the Kremlin, just as the Soviets never succeeded in penetrating the White House). The most significant contribution made by U.S. intelligence during the Cold War was to set some parameters in the debate over Soviet military capabilities and intentions. As a former DDI said to me: "Intelligence data can be wrong, it can be misleading, it can be incomplete; but, properly understood, it does set some bounds on what is possible."

In the early days of estimating Soviet military power, Sherman Kent and other senior "wise men" at the CIA would sit back in their chairs, puff on their pipes, and ponder the likely capabilities and objectives of the USSR. In the second half of the Cold War, however, empirical data—reliable measurements from all the integrated "ints"—established a more dependable range of possibilities about the capabilities of the Soviet military. In the final decade of the Cold War, America's intelligence sources and methods had become more accurate than ever before in understanding Soviet weapons systems, capabilities, and adherence to arms accords. Nonetheless, intelligence weaknesses persisted when it came to anticipating military interventions by other countries—the confounding question of intentions.

Here are a few of the specific "lessons" I presented to Aspin:

- The overestimates of Soviet military capabilities were a result of poor databases, which led to extrapolation and worst-case forecasting.[24]
- Generally, the richer and more reliable the data on the Soviet military target, the greater was the estimating consensus and accuracy among the U.S. intelligence agencies.
- Yet, ironically, sometimes an abundance of data could lead to less agreement, as "noise" and information overload become a complicating factor.
- Large weapons systems were more easily identifiable and produced greater consensus among the intelligence agencies than did more covert weapons, such as chemical-biological ones.
- Hard data on military weapons, capabilities, and compliance with arms-control accords became steadily more reliable than softer data on potential military interventions or the question of leadership intentions.
- The intelligence agencies tended to collect too much information, which they were unable to process, let alone analyze.
- New advances in technology, among them real-time (or near-real-time) imagery and improved all-source fusion through video conferencing, brought about advances in the accuracy of analysis and forecasting.
- The most important role intelligence played against the Soviet military target was providing empirical data that set boundaries for a more realistic debate about Moscow's capabilities and intentions—a significant advance over the speculative estimating of the 1950s and 1960s.

———

Nothing fired up the chairman more than a discussion of such matters as weaponry, arms control, and intelligence verification, and I eagerly awaited the session with him and a few invited experts scheduled for the next week. In the meantime, on May 19, the commission staff met with Aspin and Vice

Chairman Rudman, along with the DCI's new liaison to the commission, Dennis C. Blair, a wiry, tightly wound, smug, and aloof rear admiral considered an up-and-coming star in the navy. He struck me as someone too used to being saluted by everyone. He had attended Oxford University as a Rhodes Scholar in the same class as President Clinton, and later commanded the *Kitty Hawk* aircraft-carrier battle group in the Pacific. Maybe he had a right to be smug.

The purpose of the meeting was to review where we stood. The interviews and the task forces were moving forward, and some commissioners planned to attend more site visits to the intelligence agencies near Washington. Eight of the commissioners were also planning a trip to discuss intelligence issues with officials in Europe, Israel, Australia, and Canada. Further, the chairman reported on his recent "town meeting" at the DIA. He said that he planned to meet with the NSA on May 22 and another American Bar Association group on May 23—all part of the commission's outreach program.

Soon after this meeting began, Blair rose from his chair to depart after his introduction by Aspin, probably not wanting to appear as a DCI "fifth column" sitting in on a commission business meeting uninvited. "No, no, stick around," Aspin said to him, and Blair returned to his seat. Rudman's faced turned red, but he said nothing. Later that day, I learned from Aspin that the vice chairman had raked him over the coals after the meeting for being too "chummy" with Blair. "What you did was totally inappropriate," Rudman told him. Aspin promised the vice chairman that he would keep the DCI's liaison officer out of our private commission business meetings in the future.

Much else was going on. That afternoon, for example, the staff held another session with RAND consultants to examine additional questions related to intelligence organization and the spy budget. At the same time, Aspin, Rudman, Dewhurst, and two of the senior staff attorneys met with former president (and former DCI) George H. W. Bush in the Jefferson House, near the White House. During the session, Bush called the *President's Daily Brief* "absolutely essential" in starting off his morning when he was president. Further, he said that he had a "traditional" view of intelligence and believed that organizationally the CIA should remain the focal point in the intelligence community. He also gave high marks to the sigint work of the NSA.

We continued to scrub the scope paper whenever we could find a spare moment. It had shrunk dramatically in size, as the chairman requested, and it would be ready for distribution to the DCI, as well as to SSCI and HPSCI, by the following week. We were making progress. The downside was that, maddeningly, our interviews had failed to produce a consensus regarding solutions to the nation's major intelligence problems—the same difficulty Mark Lowenthal was experiencing with the HPSCI inquiry.

At the CIA, John Deutch was "off to a brisk and promising start," according to my home-state newspaper, the *Atlanta Journal-Constitution*.[25] He had selected his management team, which included Nora Slatkin, a former Navy assistant secretary, as executive director (no. 3 in the Agency—the highest post ever held by a woman at the CIA). He had also impressed the *Journal-Constitution* and other newspapers with his promise to release to the public many of the Agency's historical records, the first director to do so. As well, Deutch was clearly doing his best to avoid repeating Woolsey's mistakes on Capitol Hill. A journalist noted that he "began flooding [SSCI and HPSCI] with regular reports"[26]—a smart way of signaling to lawmakers that they mattered and were constantly on his mind. Change was in the air, and, on the commission staff, so was a feeling of optimism that we could achieve good results before the year was up.

Then tragedy struck.

Death and Despair

My meeting with Aspin to discuss the Cold War record of CIA estimates on the Soviet military never occurred. The weekend before we were scheduled to sit down together, I traveled home to Georgia. On Saturday, May 19, the telephone rang in my study and on the other end was John Moseman, the commission's deputy staff director. "Aspin has suffered a massive stroke," he told me. I was stunned and spent the rest of the day in disbelief and anguish. I telephoned friends around Washington to find out more. I learned that earlier that morning Aspin had started to rise from bed, but slumped to the floor with the left side of his body paralyzed. Alone in his Georgetown townhouse, he somehow managed to telephone for help, and a few minutes later, at 9:30 AM, an ambulance rushed him to the Georgetown University Medical Center a few miles away. According to a newspaper report, Aspin was "lucid, awake and speaking" as he was carried on a stretcher into the hospital.[27] Initially there was optimism he would survive. "The next several days will be critical," said a hospital spokesman, "but his doctors are hopeful for a good recovery."[28] Later in the day, however, Aspin's brain began to swell, and he fell into a coma. Physicians used a breathing tube and administered medication to reduce the swelling, but to no avail. The next evening, at 7:55, death claimed the chairman at age fifty-six. At his bedside were his former wife, Maureen; his brother, Jim; and Aspin's close companion of many years, Sharon Sarton of Lake Geneva, Wisconsin.

"Les Aspin was unique," said the president in a statement issued by the White House. "He brought the light of his joy in living, and the heat of his intellect, to every occasion. He never met a person who didn't like him. And we will all miss him."

I felt as though the wind had been knocked out of me. I had lost a brilliant mentor and a much-valued friend. The nation had lost a talented security thinker and a loyal servant. I returned to Washington and was enveloped in the cloud of despondency that had settled over the commission's quarters. Aspin had been the primary source of energy and direction for our inquiry and, while his haphazard administrative style could be exasperating at times, he had a warmth, intellect, and knowledge about national security affairs that had won the respect and devotion of the entire staff. Each of us had a feeling of great loss.

The staff met with Vice Chairman Warren Rudman and Commissioner Tony Harrington on May 22, two days after Aspin's death. They reassured us they would stand behind the commission's mandate to complete an intelligence inquiry. Other commissioners had telephoned with similar messages. Rudman informed the staff that he would serve as interim Chairman until the White House found a replacement for Aspin. He expressed concern about whether he personally would have much time to devote to the commission's work, given his busy legal practice; therefore he had asked Harrington to help with the management responsibilities. "We will continue on the same path that Chairman Aspin laid out," Rudman said. Once again we would delay distribution of the scope paper to Congress, as Rudman advised, until John Deutch had a chance to review the most recent draft.

———

Three memorial services for Aspin were planned, one in Wisconsin on May 26 and two more in Washington in June, the first on Capitol Hill and the second in a church near the White House. The DCI had arranged for an airplane to fly mourners to the Wisconsin service, and DoD had lined up another plane as well. We were told that any of our staff wishing to attend the service could hitch a ride on one of these aircraft. At the last minute, though, no space was available—except for staff director Snider. I booked a commercial flight to Milwaukee and by chance ended up sitting next to Aspin's mentor, former Wisconsin senator William Proxmire, who served in the Senate from 1957 to 1989. He was ancient and hobbled by then, but had lost neither his radiant smile nor his nimble mind. On the trip he spoke of how Aspin had impressed him from the very start when he was a junior aide on his staff in 1960. "I don't think he ever slept," Proxmire recalled.

The service took place at the Gesu Church in Milwaukee, followed by a reception in the Monaghan Ballroom in Marquette University's Alumni Memorial Union. In May of 1994, Aspin had been appointed distinguished professor of international policy at Marquette, where he had once been a beginning assistant professor of economics. In anticipation of a VIP deluge from Washington, the church was filled with security personnel: CIA, DoD, Secret Service, city police, and campus police. Among the expected dignitaries were Vice President Al Gore; General John Shalikashvili, chairman of the Joint Chiefs of Staff; and DCI John Deutch. Across the street from the front entrance, television cameras stood waiting for the motorcade of brass to arrive. Wind ruffled the trousers and skirts of those entering the church beneath a cloudy sky. Inside, a magnificent high-vaulted ceiling inspired a sense of reverence.

As the eulogies began, it was clear that despite the somber setting this would be a joyful remembrance. "I had to set up dates for him," recalled a speaker who was a close friend of Aspin's, "because he was too distracted to arrange them himself. We'd double-date and he could be boring as..." The speaker remembered where he was. "...Er, anyway, he'd always be thinking about something else. After five minutes on the date, I'd have to entertain both of the women." Everyone laughed because they knew exactly what the speaker meant; Aspin had probably been pondering some structural flaw in a new weapons design touted by the Defense Department, which was surely more important than small talk with a date.

With good-natured humor, several of the speakers referred to Aspin's rumpled appearance, whether in hearings on the Hill or during strategy sessions at DoD. "Why didn't he ever buy a really good suit?" asked one with a grin and a shrug of his shoulders. Another recalled how skillful Aspin had become at overlooking the check at a restaurant. All agreed that he was an intensely private person whose distinction stemmed, as one friend put it, from "his concentration on the great issues of the day." Another spoke fondly of his "rumpled friend and equally rumpled dog," and how Aspin was sometimes "like a little boy who loved the pomp and circumstance of Washington." One of his friends recalled a time when his three boys were still kids. On this occasion, the boys, one of whom was nicknamed "Friebs," greeted Aspin as he came for dinner. One of them said to him: "Bet you don't know our names." Ruffling the hair of each boy, Aspin replied: "Sure I do: Friebs, Friebs, and Friebs." He ate food off their plates throughout the meal.

"He had no interest in money," reflected a former House colleague, David Obey (D-WI), "but he did want to be a player. He was a second Proxmire." Then he added, with a laugh: "He also sent more press releases to his district than there were people."

The service had its serious moments, too, as speakers recalled Aspin's enormous capacity for strategic thinking, his intelligence, his honesty, and his unmatched work ethic. They stressed, though, that he was not a drudge; he had enjoyed life. Representative Obey further observed that Aspin could conduct a seminar in economics at Yale, but also "yuk it up at the UAW." He remembered how Aspin had once told him on the House floor that a hearing he had held made the news on all three networks in the evening, plus the front page of the *Washington Post* and the *New York Times*. "Not bad, huh?" Aspin had said, poking him in the ribs. The congressman paused as he looked out at the congregation. "That's what we would say about Les. Not bad, Les! God speed."

Vice President Gore called Aspin "unique," because of his "powerful mind, strong conscience, and exuberant political skills." Then a university official ended the service with the announcement that, as of that day, Marquette University had established the Les Aspin Center for Government.[29]

The services in Washington were equally moving and well attended.[30] The president and first lady came to the ceremony held on June 13 at St. John's Church, the smallest church in the city, located directly across from the White House on Lafayette Square. "I finally found someone with four times the energy I had," said Bill Clinton, recalling Aspin's unstinting work habits. He said that he and Aspin were "policy wonks" together, and that Aspin was "a good teacher—I learned a lot from him." The president quoted a mutual friend who observed that Aspin's idea of a vacation was "thinking about defense at a different location." He joked that Aspin had once sent a postcard to his staff that asked: "Why are you wasting time reading a postcard?" Saying nothing about the Aspin Commission, Clinton concluded: "He's God's servant now. At last, he is with someone who can keep up."

Other speakers again invoked the rumpled image of Aspin in suits that rarely lay flat across his shoulders. Leslie Gelb, formerly of the *New York Times*, and president of the Council on Foreign Relations, recalled a typical dinner greeting from his close friend: "Hey, whadya say, eh? What do ya think of that MX missile, eh?" He was, Gelb noted, "the *first* policy wonk" and the "ultimate wonk." Assistant Secretary of State Richard C. Holbrooke, the president's envoy to Bosnia, referred to Aspin as "the first member of Congress...ever to understand systems analysis and the other tools of the modern military." Representative John Spratt (D-SC), a former Aspin ally on the House Armed Services Committee, added that his colleague had been "unpretentious, unaffected to the end. He took his work seriously, but not himself." General Shalikashvili summed up what all the speakers had expressed in the three memorial services: "He gave all that he had, then moved on.... His life was his work and his work was his nation."

I thought of the full life that Aspin would have had ahead of him. Later in May he was to attend his thirty-fifth reunion at Yale University; in June, he had meetings and speeches scheduled at the Council on Foreign Relations in New York City, the Army War College in Pennsylvania, and a Democratic Party conference in Wisconsin, along with the commission's trip to Europe; he had tickets to hear John Denver and Willie Nelson at Wolf Trap, an outdoor concert arena in Virginia; dinners with friends at the Kennedy Center, receptions on the Hill, lunches and dinners with various boards. July had a rare week of vacation blocked out for the celebration of his fifty-seventh birthday; August would take him to meetings of the Aspen Strategy Group in Colorado, a week of deep thinking in a stunningly beautiful valley of the Rocky Mountains. Throughout, he would have devoted himself to his main interest at the time: the work of the commission. Now none of this would happen. At least, though, as Tony Harrington eloquently said in remarks to the staff on May 22: "The commission's report can stand as a monument to Les Aspin."

| Wobbling Forward

D ESPITE THE LOSS OF OUR CHAIRMAN, the commission had to finish its work. We returned to our schedule of interviews and briefings, continuing with the search for information, and maybe even wisdom (if we were lucky), that would help us write the final report. Immediately after Les Aspin's death, Warren Rudman dropped his other obligations for a while and met with the staff leaders—the legal triumvirate—periodically to keep the work on track. On June 1, 1995, he officially assumed the title of acting chairman and called a meeting of the commission for that day.

Rudman at the Rudder

As we were gathering in the NEOB conference room, Rudman entered with an authoritative air, like a bull charging into the ring. He began the session with a moment of silence in honor of our fallen chairman. "We're going to move ahead," Rudman said, breaking the silence. "We have a tight schedule. Today we'll be hearing from more consumers of intelligence." The briefings scheduled after the business meeting would give commissioners a chance to hear from additional policy makers who had been on the receiving end of the $28 billion worth of information offered by the secret agencies. We all wanted to know more about their information needs and how well they were being served.

"How about another retreat?" Harrington began on a lighter note. "You could take us up to New Hampshire."

"Sure," said Rudman. "Lake Winnipesaukee."

"Summer camp?" asked Ann Caracristi.

"Yes," Rudman replied with a grin, then turned to the staff for an update on commission activities. The deputy staff director, Moseman, reported that we had paid RAND $881,000 so far for its assistance. Rudman noted that it was money well spent.

"We're now three to four months behind on our report to Congress," staff director Britt Snider reminded the commissioners, referring to the scope paper.

"Strike that from the record," Harrington said in mock alarm, eliciting laughter around the table.

"We commissioners have not received the scope paper yet," Bob Hermann said. "I'd like to see what the staff did with my comments."

"In case you forgot what you said?" Caracristi teased.

"I can tell you what they did," said Rudman. "They ignored them completely." More laughter.

Snider informed the commissioners that Zoë Baird was heading up a task force on law enforcement; Friedman one on "macro-organization"; Hermann on space; and Caracristi on open-source intelligence.

"What about covert action?" Wyche Fowler asked.

"Do you want a special task force?" responded Rudman.

Fowler paused. "Let's think about it…"

"You could head it, Wyche," Rudman continued.

With a sudden loss of ardor for his idea, Fowler said: "I withdraw my suggestion." More laughter. Then he added, "Let me think about it overnight."

"Why are we having task forces?" Porter Goss asked.

"This is such a big subject, we need to break it up," Rudman explained.

Goss remained unconvinced: "We need to have a review of the scope paper, and every commissioner ought to be able to join any task force."

"Yes, yes, indeed," the acting chairman agreed.

"I just wanted to clarify procedure," Goss threw in, pushing himself back in his chair.

Rudman told his colleagues that he had to leave soon and that the commission ought to get started on its briefings.

Tony Coelho raised his hand and said, "There can be no better monument to Les than to move this work forward." His colleagues nodded their heads in agreement.

On the Receiving End of Intelligence

Our first briefer was the heaviest hitter to appear before the commission to date: Secretary of Defense William J. Perry, who had served as Les Aspin's deputy at the Pentagon and replaced him when Aspin resigned as SecDef in

1994. A native of Pennsylvania, Perry held a BS and MS in mathematics from Stanford University and a PhD in mathematics from Pennsylvania State University. He had served in the Army Corps of Engineers and had held many entrepreneurial positions in civilian high-tech industries. As under secretary, Perry had been responsible for all weapon systems procurement and all Pentagon R & D, as well as serving as Aspin's principal advisor on technology, communications, intelligence, and atomic energy. He was a tall, thoughtful man with bright eyes and a reserved manner.

Perry began with a story.[1] Early one morning in October of 1994 he had greeted General John Shalikashvili, the Joint Chiefs chairman, in the SecDef's office at the Pentagon. Under his arm the general carried a portfolio of satellite photographs of Iraq. He spread the imagery across a conference table in the expansive but drab, bunker-like room. Using a pointer, Shalikashvili directed Perry's attention to a disturbing set of pictures. Improbable as it might have seemed, just three and a half years after a U.S.-led coalition had knocked Saddam Hussein's army to its knees, elements of the Republican Guard (Saddam's elite troops), supported by mechanized infantry, armor, and tank units, were moving at a rapid clip southward toward Basra, a mere thirty miles from the Kuwaiti border. The force was aimed like an arrow at the Al Jahra heights overlooking Kuwait City, in an apparent repeat of the same maneuver that led to the Iraqi conquest of Kuwait in 1990 and the First Persian Gulf War. At its current rate of speed, the Republican Guard would stream across the Kuwaiti border within a couple of days.

Perry quickly ordered a U.S. armored brigade stationed in Kuwait to the Iraqi border. With a mounting sense of uneasiness, the SecDef and the top Pentagon brass waited as young captains and lieutenants brought new batches of satellite imagery into Perry's office over the next twenty-four hours. Upwards of ten thousand Iraqi troops had amassed in an area near Basra. The number steadily rose to fifty thousand, some camped within twelve miles of the border. The American brigade had arrived, but consisted of only two thousand lightly armed marines.

While the United States also had two hundred warplanes in the area on standby alert, the Iraqi armored force dwarfed the American presence. President Clinton ordered 450 more warplanes to Kuwait, along with the 24th Mechanized Infantry Division and a Marine contingent from Camp Pendleton in California. The aircraft carrier *George Washington* steamed at high speed toward the Red Sea from the Indian Ocean. None of these forces, though, would arrive in time to block an invasion of Kuwait. Perry and Shalikashvili faced the prospect of a rout that would quickly wipe out the small American brigade assembled at the border.

The two men waited nervously for the next set of satellite photographs. When they arrived, Perry and Shalikashvili looked at them and breathed an audible sigh of relief. The Iraqi troops had suddenly stopped, and some elements were already turning back toward Baghdad.

The good news was that imagery intelligence may have prevented the outbreak of another war in the Persian Gulf. Using these timely photographs to pinpoint the location of Iraqi troops, the secretary of defense had been able to put an American brigade in place as a barrier against Iraqi incursion. "Had the intelligence arrived three or four days later, it would have been too late," Perry told the commissioners. But the episode was also cautionary. Even though vital intelligence had arrived in time to allow Secretary Perry to put up some semblance of defense at the border, the thousands of troops in the Republican Guard could have overwhelmed the single Marine brigade. The best the secretary could hope for was that the Marines might intimidate Saddam and make him think twice about another invasion. Fortunately, the bluff worked. Retrospective studies of the satellite imagery taken before the crisis suggested that Saddam had been gathering a force for weeks near Baghdad for another invasion of Kuwait. The photos displayed trickles of Iraqi troops and armor moving toward Basra that would soon turn into an invading flood. Intelligence analysts in the CIA's National Photographic Intelligence Center (NPIC) had missed these signs, as had everyone else at the Agency.

The problem had not been a lack of information; high-ranking government officials have access each day to enough imagery and other intelligence data to bury every desk in the Pentagon. Photos don't speak for themselves, however, and nobody had scrutinized them sufficiently, day-by-day, to notice the accretion of troops that suggested a gathering invasion force. "Had we analyzed the data better from techint," said Perry, looking back at the crisis, "we could have had a seven-to-ten-day-earlier alert. Better humint might have given this alert, too." The message: the United States still had much room for improvement when it came to intelligence support for military operations.

Turning to the subject of intelligence priorities, the secretary reminded the commissioners that the threat of nuclear war drove America's intelligence systems during the Cold War; now it was the proliferation of WMDs. "We're trying to prevent a nuke from going off this next decade," he said, somberly. "We're getting moderately good intelligence on this problem today, but we need to raise this to very good."

As with every briefer, Secretary Perry had a set of recommendations for the commission. Highest on his list was the need for more R & D to improve technical intelligence collection. "There has been no quantum change since the 1970s," he said, echoing John Deutch. "We're only doing incremental improvement instead of major innovations." He was especially critical about the lack of all-source fusion in the intelligence community. "We have vast information sources," he emphasized, "yet nothing exists to bring it all together—there is not enough synthesis. We need true jointness. There is enormous inertia, human and bureaucratic, in the system."

Notably lacking, he observed, was effective cooperation between the Pentagon and the CIA. As he said this, I thought of the equally poor ties between the FBI and the CIA, as well as the always-strained relations between the State Department and the Agency. Perry told the commission that he and Deutch were now getting together every Tuesday and Thursday at 8:00 AM for breakfast at the Pentagon, in an attempt to improve the DoD-CIA relationship. "It will be the closest cooperation ever between the two buildings," Perry predicted. Despite some criticism of the organizational inadequacies of the intelligence services, he had only one institutional change to recommend: the establishment of a new agency to integrate throughout the community the imagery "int"—imint (known more recently, recall, as "geoint," short for geospatial-intelligence).

This imint proposal was emerging as one of the few points of consensus among briefers before the commission, and the reform was certainly at the top of the DCI's agenda. Whether or not we supported the idea, we had the sense this reform was going to happen. The Perry-Deutch juggernaut would be hard to stop. Another point of consensus was Perry's emphasis on the necessity for humint improvements. "We focused too much on the Soviet Union during the Cold War," he said, "at the expense of places like Iraq, Iran, and North Korea." Here was another conclusion on which he and the DCI were in agreement. As Deutch recalled years later, the "human intelligence capability, especially in the CIA, suffered dramatically in the early 1990s." His explanation: "It had to do with one thing, and that was Aldrich Ames."[2] He was right with respect to the Soviet Union, but the Ames's case failed to address the question of why the United States had such poor humint in places like Iraq and Iran. As Perry went on about the nation's humint shortcomings, I thought of a retired military intelligence manager who had told us in May, "We only have twenty-six Farsi speakers in the intelligence community right now, and only three are able to understand excited Iranians talking to each other."

Next in the batting order was a Washington legend: the retired Air Force lieutenant general Brent Scowcroft, the only person to have served twice as national security advisor—once for President Gerald R. Ford and then for President George H. W. Bush. Originally from Ogden, Utah, he had earned a PhD in international relations from Columbia University in 1967; had served as vice chairman of Kissinger Associates, one of the more high-powered consulting firms in Washington; and now had his own international business advisory firm, the Scowcroft Group. He was among America's top experts on national security and he also enjoyed a reputation for honesty and good judgment. For many of us, his appearance before the commission put the gilt on the gingerbread that day.

He sat at the conference table, his large head looming over a slight body. Suspenders peeked out beneath his suit coat. "Intelligence is just as important now as it was during the Cold War," he began. "Only the emphasis has changed." The main purpose of intelligence during the Cold War had been to prevent the Soviets from surprising us in a military attack; now, in the new era, political intelligence had become most important. "What makes North Korea tick? What about the leaders of Iran?" he offered as examples. He noted further that "in a crisis, the president always acts with inadequate information; it's almost always a scramble."

As Scowcroft was talking, Porter Goss, who was sitting by me at the opposite end of the table from the general, whispered, "You know, when I was in college with Les, he never had an enemy," he said. "He used to relate well to the professors at Yale—knew them by their first names." I smiled, since as a student I had never dared to be that familiar with a professor. "He was always out of shape, slouching," Goss went on. "He tried out for a Rhodes, but failed because he was not an athlete. Really awkward with women, too." I nodded, and Goss turned back to the briefing.

"The DCI needs more control over resources," Scowcroft was saying. "He needs a bigger club." Everyone in the room knew this meant more authority over budgets and personnel. He criticized Deutch's remark in his confirmation hearings that Congress was his "board of directors." In Scowcoft's view, this was wrong: "The NSC is his board of directors."

Dennis Blair was sitting on the other side of Goss from me and whispered to him: "What we need is deep penetration of the customer." Goss grinned at this salacious pun, a play on the counterintelligence phrase "deep penetration of the adversary" (such as developing a mole in the enemy camp to see if he has already done the same against you). Maybe Blair wasn't as uptight as I had thought.

Scowcroft showed little interest in economic intelligence, arguing that "we have so much 'open source' on this." He rejected the idea, too, often advanced to the commission during briefings, that intelligence should be consumer driven—the pull argument again. "The president doesn't know what he needs until he needs it," Scowcoft went on. "It's up to the analysts to set tasking priorities, not the policy makers." This was a fundamental matter—the very starting point of the intelligence cycle—and yet renowned experts were disagreeing with one another even on this point. The former national security advisor suggested further that one had to be "squirrelly" to do intelligence in the first place.

"You're talking to a former case officer," objected Dewhurst, in mock offense.

Harrington came to the rescue: "Present company excluded. You and Porter got out."

Scowcroft was adamant that the DCI—or a DNI—should not be separated from the CIA. The director's office, he underscored, needed to have stronger budgetary authority over every intelligence agency; the SecDef could have a right of appeal to the NSC and the president.

Zoë Baird—now expecting a baby, she informed her colleagues just before the briefings began—asked about why some commissions seemed to succeed while others failed.

"It depends on the circumstances," Scowcroft replied. "President Reagan and the Congress were at loggerheads over the Commission on Strategic Forces in 1983"—the Scowcroft Commission on the MX missile. "It went nowhere. There was another commission on defense management during the Reagan years that attracted little public interest, because the subject didn't seem that urgent. Your commission suffers from that same lack of interest." Nonetheless, Scowcroft viewed our inquiry as an "unusual opportunity" to sit down with the DCI and help him focus on his problems. I wasn't sure that John Deutch thought we would be of help, especially now that his close ally, Aspin, was no longer running the commission. Besides, as Admiral Studeman had informed us on his last visit, Dennis Blair already had ten people doing studies on intelligence reform; and another of Deutch's aides, we were told by an Agency official, had ten more people looking just into management issues.

Chewing gum through most of the briefing, Bob Hermann asked Scowcroft how well the United States was likely to perform against the new post–Cold War threats to our security—Woolsey's "snakes."

"We had only modest success in penetrating the Soviet Union," Scowcroft answered, observing that the Soviets were masters of security and counterintelligence. "But it will be easier to penetrate the new targets. Still, it will take enormous patience; it might take decades in some cases. We're an impatient nation. Congress is impatient. It's very hard to achieve good penetrations, but it is doable."

The day's final briefer was Joseph S. Nye Jr., assistant secretary of defense for international security affairs. Nye was a superstar in scholarly circles: a

Rhodes Scholar with a BA from Princeton and a PhD from Harvard (both in political science), a luminary, and later dean, at the Kennedy School of Government at Harvard, and a recent chair of the CIA's National Intelligence Council (NIC). Tall, articulate, handsome, aristocratic in bearing though pleasant in manner, he had a résumé that would be the envy of anyone in the groves of academe. Given his unusual combination of high levels of academic training and practical government experience, he was an ideal candidate to speak to us about the quality of intelligence reports that came to consumers.

Nye told us that as a government official he rarely had more than forty minutes to read each day, in between meetings and telephone calls, and only about five minutes of that time was reserved for intelligence reports.[3] This was a staggering admission from one of the brightest of America's public servants. With a large annual budget, agents all around the globe, and spy satellites crisscrossing the heavens, all to provide information to policy makers, Joe Nye had only a few minutes to look at the results each day! And he was a more avid reader than most officials. It was a sobering, if not depressing, testimony.[4] He pointed to a paradox: the higher one went up the government hierarchy, the more policy makers tended to rely on oral communications; yet the intelligence community continued to pump out vast reams of paper reports. "The NIOs must *brief* policy makers on key intelligence conclusions," he emphasized, "because they're probably not going to have read the written product."

Scowcroft may have thought that intelligence collection would be easier in the new world; Nye, however, was equally convinced that analysis would be more difficult, because international affairs had become much more complex. He thought it impossible for the United States to cover the whole globe with intelligence assets, especially in a time of budget reductions; therefore, he embraced the notion of a surge capacity—Woolsey's aircraft-carrier view of intelligence motility.

Nye spoke to the commission of "mysteries" and "secrets," the dichotomy used by intelligence professionals to distinguish between things in the world that no intelligence service will ever know for sure—the mysteries ("Will President Boris Yeltsin"—in poor health at the time—"last through 1996?" was his example), compared to things the CIA could conceivably find out—the secrets (such as the warhead yield for a Soviet SS18 missile). Other examples of mysteries would include the degree of influence of the Mullahs over the people of Iran, and whether the leader of North Korea would actually start another conflict on the Korean Peninsula.[5] Further examples of secrets would include the number of tanks lined up on a field in northern China; the order of battle for North Korea's million-man army; and the location of suspected WMDs in Iraq before the U.S. invasion in 2003. One thing was certain: both during and after the Cold War, mysteries have well outnumbered secrets—and even the secrets held by some countries and factions were not easily uncovered (as tragically illustrated by the false Iraqi WMD hypothesis in 2002–3).

Nye also emphasized the importance of timing in the world of intelligence. "It must be at the right place at the right time," he said. "It can't be late, or too early." As well, he recommended a better "tailoring" of information, by which he meant that analysts needed to find out what policy makers were working on, then provide them with timely information on that topic—say, the likelihood of Iranian access to fissionable materials—instead of writing a report on, for example, a potential economic recession in South Africa that was of no interest to the policy makers at that moment. Some experts referred to the tailoring that Nye had in mind as "niche intelligence." To achieve this goal, it was vital for analysts to schedule meetings with policy makers to ascertain their information needs. Dialogue, dialogue, dialogue—here was another point of consensus on how to improve the intelligence cycle.[6]

The analyst had to be aware of boundaries, though. Becoming too chummy with policy officials would undermine the ethos of neutrality valued by intelligence professionals—the "virginity theory of intelligence," as Nye put it. This was, recall, the venerable standard advanced by Sherman Kent, the former Yale University historian and early CIA analyst who believed in the maintenance of a high wall between intelligence professionals and politicians, as a means for preventing the politicization ("spinning" or "cooking") of intelligence. The problem, though, was that walls can also lead to isolation and irrelevance for analysts. Former DCI William Colby had once said to me that he thought the relationship between the policy maker and the intelligence officer ought to be closer than Kent advocated. "Not supportive," Colby said, "but close enough to be related to what the hell is going on."[7]

Nye urged the commission to encourage outreach by the intelligence agencies. Analysts needed a "golden Rolodex" of outside experts to call on in academe, the think tanks, and the business world, he advised, adding that the culture at the CIA unfortunately encouraged the view that "we're bounded by four walls." Part of the difficulty was the security strictures—secrecy oaths, polygraph tests, background checks—that separated inside analysts from outside experts, but he thought these barriers could be overcome.

Nye complained that he got "a lot of information, but not a lot of insight" from the intelligence reports he received. This was a troubling theme that had emerged many times during the briefings in our conference room. Scowcroft, too, had stated that "the *President's Daily Brief* is frequently not very good." This raised the question of how much "value added"—a popular term at the time—came from intelligence,. Did intelligence reports, especially the *PDB* and the NIEs, really provide policy makers with information and insight beyond what they could read in newspapers? As a senior intelligence official said to me: "We're about unique information, available by no other means, that really has added value to a president's decision making. That's what we should be about."[8] But had the agencies succeeded in this objective?

The President's Daily Brief *and the Question of "Value Added"*

To measure of how good the intelligence product was for the president, Aspin had asked me to conduct an experiment at some point that would test the value added of the *President's Daily Brief*. After his death, I took up this project to keep this promise to him.

INSIDE THE *PDB*

Among the thousands of classified reports prepared each year, the *PDB* is considered the most prestigious document provided to senior policy officials by the intelligence community. George Tenet, who succeeded John Deutch as DCI, has referred to the *PDB* as "our most important product;" and Thomas H. Kean, the chair of the 9/11 Commission, dubbed it the "Holy Grail of the nation's secrets."[9]

The *Brief* is certainly the most closely guarded of the many reports written by the secret agencies. Few *PDBs* have emerged from the CIA's vaults and into the public domain.[10] The document is distributed by CIA couriers around 7:00 o'clock each morning, but only to the president and a few top cabinet officials and presidential assistants. The number of recipients has varied from administration to administration, rising to as many as fourteen in the Clinton administration and as few as five in the Reagan administration and six in the second Bush administration. Always on the distribution list are the president, the vice president, the secretaries of state and defense, and the national security advisor. The document often sets the agenda for early morning discussions among these individuals and their top aides. It serves as a "catalyst for further action," in the words of a staff aide on the NSC.[11]

In 1995, a typical day in the preparation of a *Brief* began with a meeting at the CIA of the staff responsible for assembling the document. The session started at 8:30 in the morning, about twenty-four hours before the *Brief* was due at the White House. The purpose of the meeting was to decide what subjects to include in the report, especially hot topics of the moment that were likely to be addressed in the *New York Times*, the *Washington Post*, the *Washington Times*, and the *Wall Street Journal*. As the list of items for inclusion in the document took shape, this *PDB* working group contacted analysts throughout the intelligence community who could contribute to the topics selected for the *Brief*. This calling around the intelligence community for material continued from 10:45 that morning until late into the afternoon and early evening. The various offices were asked, "What can you provide on this subject?" The responses came flowing back to the CIA, and the drafting of the document commenced.

Between 7:30 and 8:00 p.m. that same evening, the *PDB* draft was ready for review by the CIA's deputy director for intelligence (DDI) and the DCI. If they had already left their offices, the draft was sent to their homes using a secure fax machine. Any revisions they desired were returned to the *PDB* working group as soon as possible for integration into the document. The production staff took over late in the evening and labored throughout the early morning hours of the next day, printing and collating the document in a low-slung building filled with high-tech production equipment, adjacent to the CIA Headquarters building—just as printers in cities and towns around the nation were also preparing local newspapers for delivery when the sun rose. At 5:30 AM the *PDB* was ready for dissemination to those on the exclusive list of subscribers. The *Brief* was hand-carried to these principals between 6:00 and 9:00 AM, depending on when each of the policy makers wanted to receive the document. At this time, if one of the recipients wished to have a follow-up discussion, he or she could request an oral briefing from (and a Q and A with) the CIA officers chosen to travel with the document to their offices or homes.

Although the format of the *Daily Brief* has varied over the years, it has always had three core objectives: readability, logical reasoning, and faithful adherence to the intelligence community's sources. During the Ford administration it ran to over twenty pages in length on average. President Jimmy Carter reduced it to some fifteen pages. During the Clinton administration, it was nine to twelve pages long and printed with impressive four-color graphics vividly displaying, say, global economic trends in lines on a graph. Throughout the second Bush administration, the document was a "series of short, one- or two-page articles" filling a dozen pages or so, printed on heavy paper, and enclosed in a leather binder.[12]

Whatever its length or format, the *PDB*—"the book," as it is known inside the CIA—is designed to grab the attention of busy policy makers and inform them with "current intelligence" about events that have just transpired around the world. It features articles expected to be of ongoing relevance to the global concerns of the White House, perhaps the health of an aging foreign leader (such as Yeltsin in 1995) or the deployment of a new Chinese weapons system. The cadre of intelligence officers at the CIA responsible for the intense all-night production of the *PDB* takes pride in its work. The *Brief*'s glossy, spiral-bound pages are attractive and easy to read. Unlike the case with regular newspapers, policy makers don't have to turn over cumbersome pages searching for the continuation of a page A1 story on page A6; the stories in the *Brief* flow continuously. Further, the *PDB* focuses on topics known to be high on the president's agenda, rather than the daily smorgasbord offered readers by regular newspapers.

The *Brief* attempts, as well, to fully integrate information gathered clandestinely from around the world by America's intelligence agencies—an implementation of the all-source fusion concept. This integration of information provides policy makers with a comprehensive view of international affairs based on human spying, photography from surveillance satellites and reconnaissance aircraft, sigint from telephone taps, and masint from special sensors, all combined into a underlying foundation of open-source information. In this manner, the *Brief* gives busy national leaders "one-stop shopping" of up-to-date information on global events and conditions.

The *PDB* comes with another important service unavailable to subscribers of ordinary newspapers: follow-up oral briefings designed to answer the specific questions of its VIP readers—ten to sixty minutes of additional information, depending on the interest and patience of the policy maker, presented by intelligence experts on any of the articles published in the *Brief*. Here is a rare opportunity for the president and other *PDB* readers to have a conversation with their "newspaper."[13] Intelligence Director Deutch often led the oral briefing at the White House at the time I was looking into the process in 1995.

During a typical year of the Clinton administration, forty-two follow-up oral briefings took place in the offices of the fourteen *PDB* recipients; and the CIA sent an additional 426 memoranda to those recipients who requested more detailed written responses to their queries. About 75 percent of these follow-ups occurred by the next working day.[14] The *PDB* is more than a document; it is a process, allowing intelligence officers to interact with decision makers and provide useful supportive information. As an NSC staffer has noted, this interaction keeps "the CIA boys hopping, but, most importantly, it lets them know what is of interest at any given time to the President."[15]

As to whether or not the *President's Daily Brief* adds value over news available through television and newspapers, presidents and some other subscribers in the small "witting circle" of *PDB* readers have often complained about the quality of the document. George W. Bush, for instance, received the *PDB* and accompanying oral briefings during his first presidential campaign in 2000, along with other leading candidates—a service provided by the CIA since 1952 to individuals who may soon find themselves as the nation's chief executive. He found them unhelpful and remarked: "Well, I assume I will start seeing the good stuff when I become president," little knowing that the intelligence community was already giving him its best "stuff."[16] When George Tenet was the senior intelligence director on the NSC staff in the mid-1990s, however, he told me that he thought the *Brief* was "for the most part, a high-quality product. There are days when it's not earth-shattering; there are days when it's really interesting."[17]

My examination of *PDB*s while on the Aspin Commission staff showed that the intelligence agencies are often able to provide information beyond what the open media has to offer, although frequently it also falls short of this goal. Among the topics examined by the commission to test the *PDB's* "value added" were the terrorist attack of 1995 in Japan, when the group Aum Shinrikyo ("Supreme Truth" in Japanese) released lethal sarin nerve gas into the Tokyo subway system; the question of whether the Chinese were selling M-11 missile parts to Pakistan between 1989 and 1995; and intelligence reporting on unrest in Burundi in 1995.[18]

In the case of the Tokyo sarin attack, the *PDB* reader learned no more than the average newspaper subscriber about the details of the attack; but he or she found out additional facts about how the Aum Shinrikyo cult financed its operations and about the background of its leader, although not appreciably more. The subway attack took the U.S. intelligence community and Japanese authorities by surprise. The CIA and its companion agencies had virtually no information about the sect's past activities in Japan, Russia, or even the United States. Only after the attack occurred did the Agency discover that Aum Shinrikyo's leader was virulently anti-American, that he advocated chemical-biological (CB) and even nuclear war against the United States, and that he was making progress toward acquiring CB weapons of mass destruction.

As for the M-11 missile controversy, reporting in both the *PDB* and public newspapers was ambiguous.[19] In both venues, one could learn a fair amount about the alleged sale of missile parts; but the intelligence community possessed photographic and eavesdropping information that moved the case from one of pure speculation to a level of reasonably strong, if still circumstantial, evidence that the Chinese were indeed providing the Pakistanis with the weapons components.[20] The sighting of "cylindrical objects" at the Sargoha Missile Complex in Pakistan and "unidentified, suspicious cargo" being unloaded in the Karachi harbor, as reported by intelligence assets on the ground, proved nothing in themselves; however, when coupled with telephone intercepts of conversations between Pakistani and Chinese officials about M-11 contracts, plus photographs of M-11 TELs (transporter erector launchers) at Sargodha, it gave the president more evidence about what was really happening than what the *New York Times* offered.

In the Burundi case, the commission asked five public news services to provide information on the current situation in the African nation and some background on the existing unrest, all within twenty-four hours. From among the public sources of information, only Jane's Information Group provided data that was unavailable in the *PDB*.[21] Jane's, a London-based publisher that specializes in open-source intelligence, furnished the commission with two loose-leaf notebooks filled with order-of-battle statistics, detailed descriptions of weapons systems in the Burundi inventory, and a history of the local ethnic conflict. In contrast, the *PDB* had more information about the internal political polarization in Burundi, the likelihood of a humanitarian disaster that could equal the Rwandan genocide the previous year, the number and location of U.S. and European nationals in the country, and insights into ethnic patterns and arms acquisition—all based on information from human sources inside the nation. Jane's provided the most detail on Burundian weapons systems, but the American intelligence services offered what policy makers desire above all else: "actionable intelligence"—information they can act on. For instance, intelligence on a suspected arms shipment to Burundi from another nation led to quick diplomatic pressure by the United States to halt the shipment.

Satellite, U-2, and drone photography, plus wiretaps overseas and the occasional well-placed asset, are bound to give the intelligence agencies an edge in some instances over the *New York Times*, thereby giving the *President's Daily Brief* added value on some days. This was particularly evident in October of 1962 during the Cuban missile crisis, when agent reports, followed up with confirming U-2 photographic missions, proved vital for disclosing details of the Soviet threat just ninety miles from America's shoreline.

During the Cold War, the intelligence agencies added significant value over newspaper reporting when it came to knowing the number and specifications of Soviet bombers and ICBMs. Moreover, the intelligence community had the critically important capacity to discern quickly whether the Soviets were preparing for a first strike against the United States or Western Europe. A surprise attack like the one at Pearl Harbor became infinitely less likely, thanks to this capability. As a result, the hair-trigger tension on both sides of the Iron Curtain began to ease in the 1960s, as the danger of a surprise missile launch (whether accidental or intentional) declined. I found that *PDBs* were especially effective when reporting on the weapons capabilities of foreign nations and factions, on events within closed societies, and on the activities of terrorist organizations— topics that regular newspaper correspondents have a difficult time covering, because of the secretive nature of these subjects and the danger of trying to enter denied territories (like North Korea) to report on them.

Even with the advantage of its human and mechanical spying around the globe, the intelligence community's information—if better than the nation's newspapers on some occasions—still remained skimpy in significant instances, such as reporting on political machinations in Lebanon or Syria. With respect to broad political and economic issues, such as the prospects for further European integration, the latest twists in German or French politics, or the state of the economy in China, the open media often provide better insights than the intelligence community. Newspaper sometimes have correspondents who have served in some parts of the world longer than any CIA case officer.

In a fast-moving incident of short duration (like the sarin attack in Japan), the public media is apt to know as much—and sometimes more—about what has happened than the intelligence community, especially if satellite photography is irrelevant to the situation. With subjects that come to light more slowly and involve deception by nations (as with the M-11 missile story), the intelligence community has a better chance of directing its clandestine assets to acquire specific items of information, quite possibly adding value to the public reporting. Aiding the accuracy of public reporting is the fact that regular newspaper and magazine reporters often have good sources inside the intelligence community. Conversely, the secret agencies have ongoing conversations with U.S. journalists before and after they travel abroad—a controversial relationship for those concerned about keeping the media free from government influence, but one that is nevertheless widespread, persistent, and reportedly helpful to both parties.[22]

Even those in high office who have lost faith in the ability of U.S. intelligence reports to add value over newspaper reports are likely to read the *PDB* anyway, if they are fortunate enough to be on the BIGOT (distribution) list. As Secretary of State George P. Shultz of the Reagan administration wrote in his memoir, "I had no confidence in the intelligence community...[but] I continued to read *The President's Daily Brief*, in part to know what was being put before [the president]."[23]

For my review of the *PDB* in 1995, the CIA allowed me to examine only a few recent *Briefs* at its headquarters. To prepare a more meaningful evaluation of this key document, I requested access to copies going back several months or, ideally, years. In response, the door to the *Daily Briefs* suddenly slammed shut. No one on the outside had ever looked at a longer set of the *Briefs* than I had already been given, I was informed by a supercilious young liaison officer assigned to the commission (an assistant to Admiral Blair), and that policy was not going to change. So there.

I felt sure that Aspin would have weighed in on my side during this standoff; but that arch-defender was no longer available. I could not convince the commission's staff leadership to pursue the matter further. They feared that further insistence would undermine the CIA's cooperation, considered necessary to complete the rest of our work.

———

Following the enlightening sessions with Perry, Scowcroft, and Nye, the commission met the next day—June 2, 1995—with additional consumers, beginning with two senior officials well situated to address the economic side of intelligence. The first was Ronald H. Brown, the fit-looking, exuberant African American secretary of commerce; and the second, the diminutive but engaging U.S. trade representative, Michael Kantor.

"Our national and economic security are inextricably linked," Brown told the commissioners. " 'Economic diplomacy'—a term some people don't like— furthers our national interests." Singling out the NSA for its useful sigint intercepts, the secretary said he was grateful to the intelligence community for giving him "a sense of what might be put on the table" (by foreign negotiators) at international trade conferences. Intelligence helped "shape our view of the world," Brown continued. He stressed, however, that this kind of information should be gathered only for the American government, not for private businesses. The secretary wanted to see more economic intelligence collection; rather than an afterthought, he thought it should be "the center of what we're doing."

"Do you personally look at intelligence?" Ann Caracristi asked.

"Yes, I do," the secretary replied. "My intelligence people pick through the reports and provide me with a summary, plus I am usually briefed twice a week. And when I'm traveling, I normally have an intelligence officer with me.... I don't task the CIA, but my intelligence officer does."

"Is there valued added?" Friedman followed up.

"The quality is spotty. What people say on the telephone: that's what I find important."

One of the questions bandied about in conversations among commissioners and staff was whether policy agencies should be required to pay for the intelligence they received. If policy officials had to write a check for information, they might take it more seriously and give the tasking process more thought. "Intelligence should not be a free good," was the refrain some-times heard, although just as many commissioners thought this was a turkey that should stay in the oven. The pay-for-information approach posed a number of practical implementation problems the staff had been wrestling with. How would one assign a monetary value to an intelligence product, say, an analytic report, a map, or a photograph? What if the CIA had some great information, but a policy department had already depleted its budget for purchasing intelligence? Would agencies delinquent in their payments have their intelligence pipelines shut off, regardless of the national interest? Who would administer the program? Secretary Brown was asked about his views on this topic, with Tony Harrington posing the question: "Would you pay for intelligence from your budget?"

"I might not have any budget left!" Brown laughed in response. "I'd have to think through that question."

Later, Fowler approached the subject again with Brown: "What if intelli-gence were not a free good?"

"I'd be a lot more careful, more diligent, if I had to pay for it," the secre-tary replied.

Ambassador Kantor was less complimentary than Brown about the quality of intelligence. "I get better information out of the financial institutions than from the CIA," he said. "Its analysts are too young and they lack trade expe-rience.... I have two China experts on my staff who know more than all of the intelligence agencies, since they have been to China twenty-one times in the last twenty-eight months.... I had only one conversation with DCI Woolsey in over two years." The trade ambassador admitted, however, that this was partially his fault. "I'm so busy I haven't had time to lean on the CIA leader-ship," he said. "When I need the information, that's when it hits me in the gut that I don't have it."

"Do the NIOs reach out to you?" General Allen inquired.

"Contact with them has been virtually nonexistent," came Kantor's quick response. "I've had three NIO briefings in twenty-eight months in office. There is no reaching out."

Another policy maker, the chief of the international division in the Environmental Protection Agency (EPA), had also said to me in an earlier interview that "the intelligence community must become more user friendly." One of the shrewdest analysts I knew, the CIA's Jack Davis, once wrote to me in an informal memo: "As a rule, the more the clients learn about the Intelligence Directorate's capabilities, the more effectively they task it."[24] I was sure this was right, but clearly NIC analysts had failed to communicate to Kantor effec-tively, or to the EPA official, about how they could help their offices.

Friedman asked whether there was value added by intelligence and Kantor replied: "Yes, when it is specifically targeted information, such as the likely bargaining positions of foreign negotiators. This can be extremely important."

The next briefer was Robert L. Gallucci, a suave diplomat who served as ambassador at large for the Clinton administration and had been involved in negotiations with North Korea. He, too, expressed disappointment in the intelligence products he had received. He said there was virtually no sigint or humint on North Korea, noting that it was even unclear who was in charge in Pyongyang or if the nation had a nuclear weapon. The country was "a black box." In exasperation, he said: "We just have no evidence!" Further, as one would expect from the lack of good intelligence collection on this target, the CIA's analysis on North Korea was, Gallucci said, for the most part "simpleminded."

"How well is intelligence coordinated among the agencies?" Harrington asked.

"If the item is highly sexy, it is closely held," replied the ambassador. "There is little or no sharing."

Much of this testimony, and the views we had heard from several other intelligence consumers, could have left one with the impression that America's intelligence products were quite useless. Yet a number of other witnesses had pointed to their value. Just since the end of the Cold War, for instance, the secret agencies had uncovered several significant findings, including:

- instances in which radioactive materials for bomb making were being offered for sale (thanks to U.S. intervention, these materials were prevented from being sold)
- the efforts of some nations to purchase WMDs secretly (also discovered and halted)
- the location of several leading terrorists, including "Carlos the Jackal" in Sudan, the ringleader of the World Trade Center bombing in 1993, the leader of the Shining Path terrorist organization in Peru, and the Libyan perpetrators of the Pan Am 103 bombing
- information that allowed diplomatic settlements to head off military conflict between India and Pakistan
- telephone intercepts that prevented two assassination plots overseas, including one against an American ambassador and his family;
- the violation by some countries of United Nations trade sanctions against Iraq and Bosnia
- humint and sigint that led to the breakup of the Cali drug cartel

- simmering financial crises in some countries (Mexico among them) that were addressed before the effects became magnified
- the disclosure of various election irregularities abroad (in a host of new democracies)
- the discovery of human rights abuses that contributed to the criminal proceedings at the Bosnia War Crimes Tribunal in The Hague.

In addition, the intelligence agencies had played a crucial support role for U.S. combat operations in Panama, the Balkans, the Persian Gulf, Rwanda, and Haiti; and they had backed up U.S. negotiations in numerous bilateral and multilateral trade and arms-control conferences around the world.[25] In short, like every other human organization, the intelligence community had a record of pluses and minuses.

———

For each of the witnesses who appeared in our conference room, the commissioners had dozens of thoughtful questions and follow-ups. The staff was proud of their efforts to probe the details of how the intelligence community had either aided or failed to help the advancement of America's global interests. A group of eight workhorses was beginning to emerge among the commissioners: Allen, Baird, Caracristi, Dewhurst, Fowler, Friedman, Harrington, and Hermann. This amounted to half of the members (Aspin would have made it a majority) and this degree of commitment to the panel's work was heartening to the staff. We could have experienced the misfortune of more Senator Exons, who had been ignoring our requests to attend commission meetings; we hadn't seen him for months, although his visage would pop up in the media now and then, most recently in a crusade against Internet pornography.

In between the sets of briefings held on June 2, the commission had a working lunch. In the absence of Rudman, no one was really in charge and the conversation flowed freely—not to say wildly.

"Let's keep up the dialogue with Deutch," General Pursley began.

"Yes, but let's keep it formal," said Fowler with a note of caution in his voice. "We need some distance; it was too close under Les. Our value lies in a dispassionate study. This has to be *our* work, not anyone else's agenda."

"True, but we need to be relevant as well," Pursley responded.

"There was an 'appearance issue' with Les and John," Baird suggested. "We need a balance [between independence and cooperation with the DCI]."

"We've got to be tough," Fowler resumed. "The DCI and the SecDef won't criticize each other." Especially, I thought to myself, if the DCI aspires to become the SecDef.

The commission turned to its timetable, and members discussed what still had to be done. Soon they were wandering all over the map. "We should have priorities," Harrington finally declared, "not try to answer everything."

"Let me put some cards on the table," said Fowler. "We need to save some money. Where can we cut back on intelligence?"

"First you have to answer the question: what is the country's strategy in the world?" Hermann said again, as he had in an earlier commission meeting. The likelihood of us coming up with a grand strategy for U.S. foreign policy at this point in our inquiry seemed remote.

"The morning's witnesses said they didn't like what intelligence they're getting," Fowler maintained.

"Be careful, Wyche," countered Hermann, with a wry smile. "They like some of the stuff....There is some yellow journalism in your speech." No doubt Hermann was thinking of the praise we had heard for NSA's sigint prowess.

"Just a little hyperbole here and there," Fowler admitted. He enjoyed playful banter with Hermann, or with anyone else who was game. "I don't want you to be bored during my presentation."

"You two are assigned to the first task force!" Harrington declared, to laughter in the room.

"This is the last time we'll call one of these meeting," Fowler joked in return.

On a serious note, Friedman suggested, "We need another retreat in the fall for purposes of drafting the report." In response, staff director Snider recommended a commission gathering in September, followed by some final formal public hearings with witnesses.

Fowler introduced the topic of covert action again, his focus when he had served as a member of HPSCI in the late 1970s. Although he had declined to head up a task force on this subject, he maintained a lively interest in the topic anyway. "If we don't address covert action in some way, we'll be accused of being co-opted. We need to address this to give the commission legitimacy.... For example, should we support paramilitary operations?"

"Let's don't eliminate covert action," the former DO operative Dewhurst advised.

As lunch time ended and the next briefer, Adm. William A. Owens, vice chairman of the Joint Chiefs of Staff, arrived, the commissioners resolved to spend more time on another occasion looking into this controversial topic.

Admiral Owens was a highly regarded military man, described in the *New York Times* as "one of the military's most innovative officers."[26] He was a former nuclear submarine commander who now extolled the virtues, as the *Times* put it, of "new electronic surveillance systems, space-based heat-detecting systems and communications systems that would allow military commanders to have virtually perfect knowledge about enemy and friendly operations over a 40,000-square-mile area." This was music to the ears of commissioners Allen, Caracristi, and Hermann, and no doubt to DCI Deutch. From the admiral's point of view, a key challenge facing the Department of Defense was to "tie together" the new intelligence sensors, communications systems, and precision weapons that DoD had developed in recent years.[27]

Disseminating good information quickly to the soldier who pulls the trigger—that was the goal in the admiral's view. Intelligence was all about aiding the war fighter. He had a point; the protection of our fighting men and women in the field was unassailably the nation's most important intelligence objective once war had broken out. The problem was, though, this mission could be a bottomless pit when it came to spending. The goal of the military was to collect sigint and imint from satellites, process it at ground stations, and send it forward to soldiers and pilots in the "battle space"—all within seconds. As Admiral Studeman had conceded, support to military operations (SMO) presented an endless demand on America's finite intelligence resources.

In 1998, I asked Deutch about this emphasis on SMO. Was there too much of it?

"Not enough!" he replied immediately, even though he added that SMO already absorbed "about 90 percent of the intelligence budget."[28] Making sure that information went to military commanders, especially tactical intelligence, was imperative in his view. "The community's effort is really to support military operations, to be ready to tell a commander: 'We know where the Iraqi position is'...submarines...a lot of very valuable stuff.... What a huge difference that can make. In Bosnia, providing technical and human intelligence has worked great.... It prevents casualties."

I asked about whether this focus detracted from providing "national" or "civilian" intelligence to the president and other top officials—that is, insights into political, economic, and societal conditions around the world—information for officials in suits rather than uniforms that might improve U.S. diplomacy and help prevent the outbreak of warfare in the first place. For instance, with respect to Russia, "the suits" need to know not only about that nation's military capabilities, but also about the intentions of its political leadership and Moscow's use of oil as leverage in world politics. Moreover, even Russia's shockingly low birth and high death rates could be important for America's leaders to understand as they think about future relations with our former adversary. Providing better national intelligence "is an even more important function [than SMO]," Deutch responded, "but it doesn't involve more resources....Good analysis at the right time for leaders on foreign policy matters is critical, but it doesn't require you to have all that many satellites. It's a different kind of function."

That sounded logical enough, but I continued to wonder if at least a few more resources directed toward national (civilian) intelligence targets wouldn't make the United States more effective at diplomacy and less drawn toward war fighting. As a former HPSCI chair and co-chair of the 9/11 Commission, Lee H. Hamilton (D-IN), would put it a few years later, "A lot of other things are going to be neglected while you're providing military intelligence. Military intelligence is important, but it's not the whole world."[29]

The Wise Men

By mid-June of 1995, the commission brought its discovery phase to an end and entered into an analysis phase—trying to figure out what all the information we were gathering meant in terms of possible reforms. This endeavor would last throughout the summer. The tool for moving the work forward was the task force, even if it was occasionally maligned by some commissioners. The more motivated members of the commission attended task-force meetings of interest to them, and some requested the creation of additional task forces. The staff decided to prepare special "options papers" as well, so the commissioners could select from a "menu" which of several possible reform options they wished to recommend to the public in our final report. The staff and a few of the commissioners—Friedman was always ready—continued to meet with outside experts periodically; but most of our attention was now directed toward preparing draft papers on various topics for integration into our final report, along with touching base with individual commissioners to ensure their views were well reflected in our drafts.

Acting Chairman Rudman played an important role throughout June in an assignment the staff referred to as "working the Hill"—meeting with key lawmakers (notably members of SSCI and HPSCI) to keep them informed of our progress. His busy law practice barred him, though, from giving the commission the steady attention that Aspin had devoted to our work. Nor was Harrington around much. It soon became clear that we desperately needed a more fully engaged leader. Yet the White House had failed to come up with a replacement for Aspin. For over a month, from June to mid-July, the commission wobbled forward with little guidance from the top.

I was glad to see summer arrive. At last, my wife and daughter could join me in Washington. I would miss the commuting back and forth to Georgia each week like a bad case of shingles. I flew home in early June, rented a truck, and together with Nipper (a terrier), the small Johnson family made the journey back to DC. I had located a reasonably priced townhouse to rent near M Street and the Four Seasons Hotel in the heart of Georgetown, and we settled in for the summer months, enjoying the restaurants, galleries, and shopping close at hand. I was afraid that Nipper would be discombobulated by the urban setting, but he thrived in the festive atmosphere of Georgetown. Every evening he pranced down the sidewalks of M Street with us, flirting with tourists along the way as we savored the night breezes wafting off the Potomac River that eased the heat and humidity at least a little. Washington had much to offer for family outings: art galleries second in this country only to those in Chicago and New York City; the little-known Woodrow Wilson Museum off Massachusetts Avenue; the inspiring memorials along the Mall; runs and bike rides on pathways that paralleled the Potomac River; afternoon tea at the Four Seasons on Saturday and brunch on Sunday mornings; picnic trips to Annapolis and Mount Vernon. My daughter attended a summer camp at a lake in Maryland, sponsored by Sidwell Friends (John Deutch's private-school alma mater in the District); and, since the commission was part of the Office of the President, we were invited on the 4th of July for hot-dogs and Cokes on the back lawn of the White House—not a bad place to celebrate the nation's birthday. By mid-summer, we all had a heavy dose of Potomac Fever: a full-blown love affair with the capital city.

———

Still without much direction from the commission's temporary leadership (Rudman and Harrington), the staff met on June 7 to hash things out. We batted around what kind of public hearings we should hold at the end of 1995, or perhaps early in the new year. Part of the idea behind public hearings was to educate the American people about what we were finding; but we decided that we ought to use the occasion to further educate ourselves, as well, by inviting the best witnesses we could find to discuss intelligence reform. We were still uncertain about the effectiveness of our task forces. Baird was the only commissioner who seemed to have a truly deep and abiding interest in this approach. She attended several staff sessions on the task force that dealt with the relationship between law enforcement and intelligence. Two types of task forces had evolved: small staff groups that met to draft sections of the scope paper and, later, the final report; and commissioner groups that (except for Baird's) rarely met. Some staffers whimsically referred to the commissioner groups as "subsets" of the staff task forces, which they were for the most part. "I don't know how all this will work out," Snider admitted candidly at a staff meeting.

Admiral Owens's appearance had stimulated considerable debate among the members of the staff. "Surely intelligence is about more than supporting the war fighter," one staffer argued.

"I'm not so sure," replied another. "Sometimes I think the only consumers who really care about good intelligence are soldiers being shot at."

Snider observed that "the people who created this commission on the Hill were motivated by trying to downsize, economize, and make the intelligence community more efficient. We shouldn't lose sight of those objectives."

A RAND consultant who was sitting in with us during one of the staff meetings recommended that we "digest" all of the interviews we had conducted, distilling from them the most important points that would help guide the writing of the final report. In this context, "digesting" meant writing synopses that captured the essence of each interview. He advised, too, that we should "crosswalk" the work of the task forces with our preliminary table of contents for the final report, making sure our research was aligned with the key topics we wanted to present to the public.

We had certainly gathered a large amount of information from the leading experts on intelligence in the nation, along with many of the top policy officials, both currently working in government and retired. In the past few weeks, for example, we had engaged in informative meetings with professors Ernest May and Anthony Oettinger of Harvard University; Edward Levine, who had served as an SSCI staff aide since 1976; and William Hyland, a respected foreign-policy expert and former PFIAB member.

May, a well-regarded historian who sometimes wrote on intelligence topics, believed that the main business of analysts during the Cold War was to provide an accurate annual Estimate on the Soviet military. He thought the commission ought to find out how well this had been executed, unaware that Aspin and I had been working on just that topic. He suggested, too, that the commission should try to determine what issues were important enough to warrant "competitive analysis" in the future—the Team A/Team B drill that had become so celebrated in 1976. In a separate paper on NIEs read by the commission staff, May had concluded that senior policy makers rarely read these documents, but that they were valuable and ought to be written nonetheless. NIEs cost little to produce, he stressed, and provided important information and clarifications to working-level staff. This was the same conclusion I had reached before learning of Professor May's paper. Impressed by the Foreign Service entrance exam used by the State Department as a filtering screen to recruit the best young Americans possible, he further proposed a similarly rigorous method of screening would-be intelligence analysts. Finally, he suggested that the National Intelligence Council return to its old quarters on F Street near the White House, "in order to be close to the policy makers." This was the same idea that Bob Hermann was pushing inside the commission, although he wanted to rename NIC the "National Assessments Center."

Oettinger, a professor of applied mathematics, was an expert on information technology. He noted that "unfused" information is not useful for policy makers. As he emphasized, "Information must fuse all available sources." Further, he urged the commission to do what it could to renew ties between the intelligence agencies and the nation's universities, as a means for expanding the perspectives of analysts who remain overly insular inside the walls of the intelligence community. I could think of quite a few professors who would balk at that suggestion, wary of spooks and scholars working together; but I, too, thought it would be helpful if intelligence analysts could discuss their ideas with academics and think-tank experts. After all, the goal of intelligence was to make presidents and their aides wiser, and analysts did not have a monopoly on wisdom. Ties between the government and the university were not intrinsically evil, as some of my colleagues believed; however, they did need to be transparent.[30]

Philip Levine, the SSCI staff aide, had been observing the intelligence agencies from the vantage point of Capitol Hill for almost two decades. During our interview with him, he ranged agilely over a wide expanse of intelligence subjects. He was reluctant to endorse the idea that the CIA should get out of the counternarcotics business. In his opinion, the Agency's humint contacts sometimes made useful contributions in the war against illegal drugs. He supported the "co-location" experiment, because "the DI will help the DO develop a broader understanding of foreign countries." Moreover, the DI brought a longer "historical memory" to the table. He also recommended "a little more authority" for the DCI, including the ability to select the other intelligence directors—our old friends, the agency gorillas. He was concerned as well about too much "stovepiping," he said, which can lead to "jealously guarded monopolies."

Levine hoped the commission would emphasize in its report the importance of two topics that were often overlooked: intelligence accountability (oversight) and counterintelligence. As for covert action, he recalled that of all such operations he had seen reported to SSCI and HPSCI (as required by a 1974 statute known as the Hughes-Ryan Amendment[31]), about one-third made him wonder: "Why are we bothering to do this?" Finally, he came down strongly in favor of global presence over global reach or surge. "Doing El Salvador every Tuesday just doesn't work," he said, advocating at least two to three U.S. intelligence officers in every country.

I had long wanted to meet William G. Hyland, a former CIA analyst who had also directed the State Department's intelligence unit (INR). He had served as deputy national security advisor under Scowcroft during the Ford administration, and, most recently, edited the journal *Foreign Affairs*. He was something of a music aficionado, as well, and had a new book out on song-writers and American music. Well-groomed and gentlemanly, Hyland was one of the "wise men" in Washington, a small group of highly regarded experts who could be counted on to write and speak with eloquence on issues of public affairs. He was also a realist and told me during an interview, "This commission could turn out to be like most commissions: irrelevant." He explained further that "presidents have a way of picking and choosing what they like, if anything, among a commission's recommendations and discarding the rest. Besides, most of the problems with the intelligence community will not be solved by a commission report."

Hyland was skeptical about consumer-driven intelligence and observed at length that America's

> foreign policy goals change too quickly to count on. Besides, they are often vague in the minds of policy officers. When asked by intelligence officers, "What do you need [by way of information]?" their typical response will be: "Anything you can get us." One will not obtain much serious guidance on intelligence requirements from policy officials. Their answers will quite often be flippant. When they do take intelligence seriously is when it undercuts their policy objectives.

He was skeptical, moreover, that humint was worth the trouble, arguing that even Col. Oleg Penkovsky—the favorite example of a valuable U.S. asset—provided little to the United States after his early reports on the Soviet military.

Hyland had quite a different take on the Kentian notion of maintaining a wall between analysts and policy makers. "Intelligence officers are not neuters," he said. "They have policy views and often they will share them informally anyway. We might as well make it more acceptable."[32] As for reform, he believed that radical changes were unnecessary, though certainly "adjustments" were in order. His greatest concern was military intelligence. "Here is the real area for reform," he stressed. Too much money was being spent on tactical intelligence—support to the war fighter in the foxhole. Moreover, he opposed the Pentagon's efforts to enter the humint business; this was what the CIA did well already—that is, to the extent spy rings were worth much at all.

He objected, moreover, to the FBI's attempts at "building an empire overseas," because its people were "incompetent" for that kind of mission. Above all, he lamented what he saw as a decline of the CIA. "It is wounded," he observed, "and the hyenas are beginning to circle." This could lead the CIA to take on missions beyond its capacity, such as environmental intelligence, "so starved is the Agency for someone—anyone—to say, 'We need you!'" He opposed this "mission creep," but, like Levine, he thought counternarcotics was so important to the nation that the CIA needed to take this responsibility more seriously, and he thought the same of counterterrorism.

From Hyland's vantage point, Deutch's position on the cabinet was "a huge waste of time for the DCI, listening to HUD reports and the like." He dismissed the old forms of covert action, too: coups, assassination plots, bribing foreign politicians, and "worthless propaganda." Instead, the CIA's Covert Action Staff ought to be "blowing up nuclear reactors in renegade nations and otherwise disrupting WMD proliferation." He found the idea "ludicrous" that any serious person would consider separating the DCI from the CIA and calling him a DNI. "Without troops," he said, "the DCI would merely become a figurehead 'king'"—the same point that William Webster had emphasized to us. Hyland wanted to see a dramatic "cut in our intelligence overseas," relying on a surge capacity to make up for a lack of CIA stations in every country. "The president will have to understand and support this, without turning against the intelligence community when something blows up in Patagonia and we don't have an intelligence officer there," Hyland said. "Let's concentrate on the really important nations and threats." So much for any consensus on the question of surge versus global presence.

Lastly, and most painful for me as an avid proponent of congressional oversight, Hyland declared with special intensity that "Congress has no business in the area of intelligence." His primary example: all the times the poor DCI had to trek up to Capitol Hill—"more than the secretary of state!" Hyland exclaimed—to report to SSCI and HPSCI, instead of spending that valuable time running spies, managing satellites, and doing whatever he could to bring some integration to the intelligence community.

All of these interviews and briefing sessions—and so many others—with expert witnesses were extraordinarily helpful to the commission in thinking through future directions for U.S. intelligence; but, alas, the recommendations that had come forth were all over the board and often contradictory. It would not be easy for a group of commissioners from very different backgrounds and ideological inclinations to agree on which ones to adopt.

| Brown at the Helm

ONE OF THE MOMENTS IN JUNE that the commission staff looked forward to most was a session with an admiral who had become something of a legend in the intelligence community, Bobby Ray Inman. From Rhonesboro, Texas, and educated at the University of Texas, Admiral Inman had accumulated a wealth of national security experience, serving as director of naval intelligence, vice director of the DIA, director of the NSA, and deputy director of the CIA (1981–82). Since retirement to the private sector (running a high-tech business in Austin), Inman had been named by the first President Bush to join John Deutch and William Perry on PFIAB in 1990. He was among the most qualified members ever appointed to that board and he went on to serve as PFIAB's acting chair for nearly two years.

Not only had Inman been around the block a number of times, but he was exceptionally articulate and opinionated—the latter trait earning him some enemies among right-leaning members of Congress. In 1994, Congress balked at his nomination by President Clinton to serve as Les Aspin's successor at the Department of Defense. Conservative columnist William Safire accused him of tax fraud and dishonesty, and conservative lawmakers vowed to block his confirmation as SecDef. Inman finally withdrew his name from consideration, with the countercharge that Safire and his allies on Capitol Hill had engaged in "McCarthyism."[1] Our session with Inman on June 14 promised to be anything but dull.

The admiral wore a blue suit and a white shirt with a button-down collar; his year at the CIA had taught him how to dress properly as an Agency man. Tall, thin, and tanned, with delicate features, eyebrows arched in a quizzical expression, a smile on his face, and eyes bright with intelligence behind fine-rimmed silver eyeglasses, Inman had all the hallmarks of a churchman who had come to save the commission's soul. He began by addressing imagery and underscored the value of being able "to stare at a geographic area for a long period of time" with geostationary surveillance satellites. Allen, Caracristi, and Hermann, our trio of techies, nodded in appreciation. Inman noted how important access to the new technologies had become for those in the espionage business, such as being able to tap into an adversary's fax and fiber-optic communications. The primary challenge, however, remained: how to deal with the volume of information that was collected—the fire-hose problem.

Because Russia and other closed regimes had opened up since 1991, Inman saw less of a need for clandestine collection—old-fashioned spying. Open-source intelligence (osint) could now answer most of our questions. Still, he conceded, humint had a role to play even in this new era of openness. Sigint was in great shape, he said, drawing smiles from the three "NSA commissioners." Less satisfactory by far was the state of humint. As a fix, the admiral advocated more nonofficial-cover officers (NOCs) "sitting around in the coffee shops of Cairo." The current disarray in the management of human intelligence, torn as it was between the CIA and the Department of Defense, was inexcusable in his view. "We need a single manager for humint," he emphasized.

Inman's comments about sitting in coffee shops overseas brought to mind a remark former DCI James Schlesinger had made to me at the time the commission was forming. "We have to do better as a country in understanding other cultures," he said, "being better historians, and using humint—though in a different sense. I mean training people to understand societies in the way they really function, not sitting around in bars waiting for somebody to drop a nugget on you."[2] Stansfield Turner had also underscored the need to improve our knowledge of foreign societies, but he believed in mingling with locals in the streets overseas. "The DO has got to shift toward understanding *attitudes* in other countries," he told me, "and you don't get that by planting a bug, you don't get that with a microfilm. You get that by going around and talking to people, by being in the mosques and the bazaars. And only the DO can do that; it's a different style than spying."[3]

On the organizational side of intelligence, Inman favored a stronger DCI (or DNI), with full budget authority over the entire community of secret agencies—a novel position for a military man to take, since most of "the uniforms" archly defended the autonomy of those intelligence agencies within the ambit of the Department of Defense (at the time: NSA, NRO, DIA, CIO, and the intelligence units of the four military services). As for personnel authority, that should be shared—decided "concurrently," in Inman's phrase—between the intelligence chief and the department secretaries. For the office of DCI to work properly, though, it had to have the complete support of the president. "Clinton has never thought of the DCI as a member of the national security team," he said, displaying his trademark candor.

In agreement with former DCI Bob Gates, the admiral preferred moving paramilitary capabilities out of the CIA's Directorate of Operations and into the Pentagon. "The DoD is competent in the application of force," he reasoned, "whereas the CIA is good at manipulating people with covert political, economic, and propaganda operations." This sounded reasonable, until one remembered that paramilitary ops were supposed to be small and quiet—not exactly the hallmark of the Defense Department. Echoing the feelings of many intelligence officers outside the CIA (especially military officers), he chastised the Agency for its "hang-up on institutional primacy." The admiral preferred to see the secret agencies rely on "interagency teamwork," rather than subservience to the CIA—"circles instead of a hierarchy," as he put it. As he spoke, he sketched on a yellow notepad for his own amusement, drawing a triangle with "CIA" written at the top.

Without referring to any notes, Inman made some highly technical remarks about high-frequency NSA coverage, synthetic-aperture radar imagery, and space downlinks. A majority of the commission had probably never changed the oil on their car, let alone studied astrophysics; such scientific topics had the same effect on them as watching reruns of the 1968 American Bowling Association championship. Several began doodling on their notepads. Inman got their attention again, though, when he raised his voice a notch and offered a summary statement. "We must decide under what conditions the United States will use force," he said, "then make sure we have the intelligence to inform those decisions." The core question was: "Can you get relevant data in time to use force effectively?" Despite his time as DDCI at the CIA and his willingness to have a stronger national intelligence director, Inman's perspective on intelligence—as with so many of our witnesses, and certainly those in uniform—remained focused essentially on the war fighter. His own rules of thumb for the use of force were simple and sensible:

1. Don't go into civil wars—"They're like family feuds."
2. Do stop invasions that cross national boundaries.
3. Do rescue Americans in peril overseas.

A popular example among military personnel of the gaps in intelligence support to military operations was the shooting down of an American jet fighter by a Bosnian Serb antiaircraft missile in May of 1995. "The only thing worse than not having intelligence is having intelligence that does not reach the people who need it most," Admiral Studeman had observed soon after the incident.[4] The NSA director at the time, John M. "Mike" McConnell, provided some details of the mishap. As he told an audience at the U.S. Naval Institute, America's intelligence platforms detected the surface-to-air missile (SAM) twelve to thirteen minutes before the hit . That information, however, "got to everybody but the AWACS"—a radar plane that would have been able to pass the data immediately to the pilot, Capt. Scott O'Grady.[5] Miraculously, Captain Grady survived the ordeal and, thanks to the fact that our intelligence agencies had pinpointed exactly where he was after he bailed out of his crippled aircraft, the pilot was picked up quickly and evacuated by a rescue team.

Inman offered additional rules for intelligence. The secret agencies had to "get over the question of ownership." In a word, they had to share information more effectively—a common theme presented by our briefers. Moreover, the tasking for collection had to be more precise from consumers, not broad and diffuse (to which Hyland might say, "Good luck"). Finally, the commission had to be careful about the intelligence budget. In 1973, he recalled, the Congress cut back on spy funding as punishment for the CIA's failure to predict the Yom Kippur war. By 1979, the budget was running dangerously low. Only with the advent of the Reagan administration did the monies for intelligence begin to flow again. The community needed a more reliable commitment of support, he said. I knew from talking with George Tenet, then on the NSC staff, that the Clinton administration was committed to a stable intelligence budget, though one that was basically flat, with no increases envisioned for the near future.[6]

———

Two days after Inman's appearance before the panel, Rudman and Harrington met with the staff in our conference room for more planning. They told us that the long-delayed meeting with SSCI and HPSCI over the scope paper was finally set for June 22. Rudman, Harrington, and Caracristi would attend, along with HPSCI members Dicks and Goss. Rudman had already been to SSCI's hearing room the week before, to support the nomination of former SSCI staff director and NSC aide George Tenet for the number two position at the CIA under Deutch: the deputy director of central intelligence (DDCI)—a position once held by Admirals Studeman and Inman. While visiting SSCI, Rudman told its members that the commission was moving forward, "despite the unexpected and great loss of Les Aspin." He pointed out that Tenet's experience in the Senate, and more recently as the top staffer for intelligence on the NSCl, would be "most helpful" when the commission reported its findings and recommendations to the president for action. The Senate easily confirmed Tenet on June 26.

At our staff meeting, Snider reported on the latest commissioner-led task forces, such as they were (in some cases, with only one member):

Law Enforcement and Intelligence: Baird, Friedman, Coelho,
    Hermann
Macro-Organizational Issues: Friedman, Dewhurst, Pursely
International Cooperation in Space: Hermann
Open-source Intelligence: Caracristi

He noted, too, that Senator Fowler was away leading the commission's European visit and that the first part of the trip, to Great Britain, had gone well. Further, he informed Rudman and Harrington that the staff was preparing a table of contents for the final report, as a guide for the commissioners to our key subjects. "There has been no word on the appointment of a permanent chairman for the commission," Rudman said on a discouraging final note.

———

In the meantime, the restless John Deutch was anything but idle at the CIA. He held a reception for the commission on the evening of June 21 at Langley. Throughout the evening he exuded an upbeat self-confidence. Earlier that day, he had testified before the Senate Select Committee on Intelligence, six weeks into his new job.[7] He sat at the SSCI witness table with his hands forming a tepee beneath his chin and a grin that spread from ear to ear as he waited for the hearing to begin. Apparently he was enjoying his new James Bond status as the nation's spymaster.

Although he told SSCI that his experience thus far had been "quite positive," he did have one major complaint, easily anticipated by anyone who knew the slightest thing about the history of U.S. intelligence: the DCI's hands were tied.[8] "I was struck by the relative lack of executive authority that the Director of Central Intelligence has," he said in his opening statement. He was referring not so much to his control over the CIA or even his relations with agencies inside the Department of Defense, his old stomping ground; it was the "other agencies" in the community—the FBI and the additional "civilian" intelligence organizations—that seemed beyond his grasp. "He's learning fast," commented former DCI Stansfield Turner the next day.[9]

A focal point of Deutch's remarks before SSCI was the Alpirez case in Guatemala. The DCI expressed concern that the asset had been involved in human rights abuses in the Central American country and the Agency had failed to keep Congress and the Justice Department informed about worrisome developments in the case. He noted that he had already taken steps to make sure CIA personnel stationed in Latin America were more fully aware of their obligation to support democracy and human rights throughout the hemisphere. An internal investigation into the Alpirez incident was underway at the CIA and would be completed by mid-July, the DCI told the committee, and he intended to issue new guidelines to Agency field officers "that offer clear guidance on this subject beyond previous directives." It would take time to change the "culture or mind-set" at Langley, he cautioned the senators, perhaps requiring years "not weeks or months." He continued: "Strengthening the personnel system in the intelligence community, and the CIA in particular, is perhaps the single most important action that can be taken to strengthen U.S. intelligence capability in the long run."

The day before his appearance at SSCI, Deutch told *New York Times* reporters that he would soon have ready the Agency's first set of guidelines for recruiting agents overseas—a new form of quality control over the foreign nationals (assets) on its payroll. The guidelines were expected to force CIA case officers to be more discriminating in their recruitment of spies. The DCI was aware that "you are not going to be able to do the clandestine collection of intelligence with all wonderful and nice people." Nevertheless, the Agency would have to "balance here the character of the individual with respect to the intelligence you are gathering."[10]

These forthcoming "Deutch rules" on the CIA's recruitment of assets were a controversy in the making and would soon brand the DCI, at least for some critics, as hopelessly naive about the unsavory reality of gathering human intelligence. Before the regulations were released, the Agency's DDI said to the commission in one of its May meetings: "It may be necessary to recruit criminals and crooks; you can't rely on the local minister for espionage."[11] He suggested that "Joe Six-Pack"—the American public—"was much more troubled by the Ames case than by the fact that the DO had a relationship with unsavory types in Guatemala." Another senior intelligence officer stopped me in the hallway at CIA Headquarters, when I was there to interview some analysts, and spent twenty minutes ridiculing the "motherhood and apple pie intelligence" advocated by Deutch.[12]

Deutch used the occasion of his appearance before SSCI to tout his favorite projects: the organizational integration of imagery intelligence and, as part of the same package, improvements in the management of space surveillance programs—both in line with the Hermann portfolio on the commission. He informed the lawmakers that he was working closely with HPSCI's IC21 project and with the Aspin Commission on several matters concerning intelligence missions, structures, and organizations. He added:

Mr. Chairman, I would pause here to note once again my sadness at the death of Chairman Aspin and to regret that the commission can no longer benefit from his insights. I am convinced, though, that the commission's report will prove to be a fitting memorial to Mr. Aspin, and I will ensure that we continue to cooperate with its inquiries.

On Deutch's mind as well were leadership changes for the CIA's DO and DS&T, along with improvements in the relationship between intelligence officers and law-enforcement officials—Zoë Baird's pet topic. Before becoming Deutch's deputy, George Tenet told me in 1994 that he saw the relationship between law-enforcement and counterintelligence officers as "really a big deal."[13] Deutch had ordered four of his "centers" at the CIA—the Crime and Narcotics Center (CNC), the Counterterrorist Center (CTC), the Nonproliferation Center (NPC, later known as the Weapons Intelligence, Nonproliferation, and Arms Control Center or WINPAC), and the Counterintelligence Center (CIC)—to work more closely with law-enforcement personnel in the Justice Department (where the FBI resides). He also established the Law-Enforcement-Intelligence Board, which would meet bimonthly to arbitrate conflicts between cops and spooks, with the goal of better sharing of information between the two groups of professionals.

These initiatives presented by Deutch to SSCI lawmakers underscored how the commission might lose all its thunder by the time our report came out in March of 1996. At least, though, we had the satisfaction of believing that our close examination of such reform proposals had been duly reported to the DCI by his liaison officer, Admiral Blair (whom Deutch had promoted to "associate director of central intelligence for military support" and given a third star), and that reporting may have served as a catalyst to spur the DCI's push for reform.

———

On June 28, amid rumors that Wyche Fowler was lobbying the president to become the commission's chair (which Fowler denied in conversations with me), we welcomed to our conference room a visiting delegation of British parliamentarians with intelligence oversight responsibilities in the House of Commons. The leader of the delegation professed that they were "jolly keen" to visit Washington and "chat up" members of the commission. He defined the mission of British intelligence as one focused on "offsetting gaps, uncertainties, or distortions in overt information." Politicization was not the main problem in the United Kingdom, a member of this tweedy, aristocratic group of MPs averred, but rather the irrelevance of intelligence. The group inquired about the prospects of intelligence reform in the United States.

"The Department of Defense could slow down our reform proposals," our staff director ventured.

"Extraordinary," replied the delegation leader, his heavy sarcasm softened by a smile.

"I wonder if civil rights has become an inhibition in combating the evil forces the [intelligence] services confront?" inquired one of the visitors, clearly thinking it had. Another lamented that "the U.S. disease" had struck Whitehall in London as well, a reference to the growing number of intelligence-oversight staffers that had been hired by the House of Commons to keep an eye on Her Majesty's Secret Service. The visitors said that only consensus intelligence reports went from the Joint Intelligence Committee (JIC) to high-level policy makers—assessments free of the dissenting footnotes that sometimes adorned NIEs and other U.S. intelligence reports. The session ended with encomiums about the value of the "special relationship" between the British and the Americans, along with an expression of hope that intelligence "burden sharing" between the two could be further strengthened.

Harold Brown to the Rescue

During a brief burst of interest in the subject of intelligence, President Clinton finally picked a replacement for Aspin on July 13: Dr. Harold Brown, secretary of defense during the Carter administration. In a statement released by the White House, the president said:

> This appointment fills the post held by Les Aspin. Like Les, Harold Brown brings a rich combination of experience, creativity, and vision to this crucial job. I would also like to take this opportunity to thank former Senator Warren Rudman, who so ably served as Acting chairman in the interim and who will again assume the position of Vice chairman. He and Tony Harrington, as Acting Vice Chairman, have done an excellent job keeping up the momentum of the Commission's work. They and the rest of the Commission are conducting a thorough assessment of the kind of intelligence community we will need to address the security challenges of the future.

The next day Clinton made a rare presidential visit to CIA Headquarters. Under a sizzling noonday sun, he stood between John Deutch and the First Lady on a platform set up in the courtyard near the entrance to the Original Headquarters Building, an "H"-shaped, seven-story concrete edifice constructed in 1959 and nestled in the middle of the CIA's campus-like 219-acre pastoral setting. (The New Headquarters Building, constructed chiefly of green-tinted glass, was added on to the rear of this structure during the Reagan years—part of the heyday of spending on intelligence during the 1980s.)

"Mr. President, I did not know that we were going to give you such a *warm* welcome here today," said Deutch, with perspiration on his furrowed forehead as he introduced the chief executive.

Bill Clinton was in a good mood, and, after presenting Admiral Studeman with the President's National Security Medal (the highest award a member of the intelligence community can receive) for his service as acting DCI, the president offered up a humorous Arkansas tale inspired by the day's searing temperatures.

"Once in the middle of a campaign for governor," he said, "I went up to a place in northeast Arkansas to make a speech for a county judge, who was determined that I had to come to celebrate this road that he had built with funds that I gave him. He neglected to tell me that the road ended in the middle of a rice field."

The crowd of a few hundred started to chuckle as the president continued. "In the summer time in a rice field, there is nothing but heat and mosquitoes. And a swarm of mosquitoes came up in the middle of his introduction, literally hundreds of thousands of mosquitoes. It was so bad that people were slapping at their cheeks and their legs and blood was streaming down peoples' faces and cheeks. And this judge was one of the rare people that mosquitoes would never bite. I had been governor for ten years. These people knew me better than he did. He took six minutes to introduce me; it seemed like it was six years.

"And I finally was introduced and I gave the following speech: 'Folks, I have a good speech. If you want to hear it, come to the air-conditioned building down there. If we don't get out of here, we'll all die. If you reelect me, I'll kill every mosquito in the county.'" By now, most everyone in the courtyard at Langley was laughing and clapping.

"I have to tell you," said the president, concluding his story, "I never received less than two-thirds of the vote in that county." More laughter and applause. "So I'm loath to give this speech, but I will cut it down and say what I have to say to you because it's very important that I say these things, and very important that America know that you're here and what you're doing." As if written by Senator Warner, the president's remarks (probably prepared by Tony Lake and George Tenet, with help from the CIA staff) became a rallying cry to boost morale among intelligence officers, still low after the humiliation of Ames's treachery. "Today, because the Cold War is over, some say that we should and can step back from the world and that we don't need intelligence as much as we used to," Clinton said, "that we ought to cut the intelligence budget. A few have even urged us to scrap the Central Intelligence service. I think these views are profoundly wrong." He offered a further reassurance: "I believe that making deep cuts in intelligence in peacetime is comparable to canceling your health insurance when you're feeling fine."

The president offered his list of intelligence priorities, culled from the more detailed but still-classified PDD-35:

1. the intelligence needs of our military during an operation (Here was another expression, at the highest level of government, of the belief that the requirements of the war fighter—SMO—should drive intelligence.)
2. political, economic, and military intelligence about countries hostile to the United States
3. intelligence about specific transnational threats to our security, such as weapons proliferation, terrorism, drug trafficking, organized crime, illicit trade practices, and environmental issues of grave seriousness

This list closely reflected the commission's priorities, too, with the exception of environmental intelligence—tasking assets for data on Patagonian rabbits with retinal damage continued to be ridiculed by many at the CIA and by most members and staff on the commission.

Clinton noted that technical intelligence was important, but said, "We'll always need gifted, motivated case officers at the heart of the clandestine service." I was sitting close to Dewhurst; the former DO officer smiled broadly at this praise for humint. Next, the president took up the Ames scandal and reminded the crowd that this act of treason was "a terrible exception to a proud tradition of service—a tradition that is reflected in the fifty-nine stars that shine on the CIA's memorial wall in honor of those who gave their lives to serve our country." Inside the lobby of the Original Headquarters Building, stars had been carved into the marble wall over the years. Below them a "Book of Honor" displayed the names of those deceased CIA officers whose names could be revealed, along with the years of their intelligence service and dates of death. For the names that still had to remain secret, a star appeared in the book in the chronological order of the dates when they had died in the line of duty.[14]

The president made it clear while talking about Ames that he had already "ordered a comprehensive reexamination in both internal and external studies of our counterintelligence operations. As a result," he continued, "we changed the way the intelligence community does its business. Each agency now requires more attention and continuous training in counterintelligence and evaluates its employees more thoroughly and frequently." Obviously, John Deutch and the CIA had assisted in drafting this section of the speech. It made me wonder what our commission was supposed to be doing about counterintelligence, since the president and the DCI apparently already had this problem solved. I suspected there was a coded message for the commission inserted here by Deutch: "I'm already on top of these problems.—don't worry."

The president praised the DCI's efforts "to issue new rules on dealing with foreign agents suspected of human rights abuses." He went on: "We owe you [DO personnel] clear guidance on this issue; and, as a country, we have to resolve it in the right way." He looked out to where the commissioners were seated and declared: "Director Deutch and I will take with the utmost seriousness the concerns and suggestions of both the Congress and the Aspin Commission." If there was anything left to suggest, I thought to myself.

Winding down, President Clinton said: "Every morning I start my day with an intelligence report," and he added:

> The intelligence I receive informs just about every foreign policy decision we make. It's easy to take it for granted, but we couldn't do without it. Unique intelligence makes it less likely that our forces will be sent into battle, less likely that American lives will have to be put at risk. It gives us a chance to prevent crises instead of forcing us to manage them.

And, as we would be reminded in the aftermath of the 9/11 attacks and the invasion of Iraq in 2003, faulty intelligence can send forces into battle and place American lives at risk.

Oddly, the speech never mentioned Harold Brown, but everyone knew from the White House press statement the previous day that he was our new leader. In addition to his service as secretary of defense for President Jimmy Carter from 1977 to 1981 (the first scientist named to that position), Brown had been director of defense research and engineering in the Pentagon from 1961 to 1965, secretary of the Air Force from 1965 to 1969, and president of the California Institute of Technology from 1969 to 1977. After his stint as SecDef, he had served as chairman of the Johns Hopkins Foreign Policy Institute from 1984 to 1992. Like Deutch (who had recommended Brown to the White House, after pleading with him to take Aspin's place), he was a bona fide "techie" with a strong interest in intelligence platforms, from surveillance satellites to reconnaissance aircraft. Deutch and Brown had served together on the Scowcroft commission, which examined basing options for the MX missile.

Earlier that morning, the same day President and Mrs. Clinton visited the Agency (July 14), the commissioners convened to meet Dr. Brown, as well as to listen to additional expert briefings. Rudman introduced the new chairman and passed the commission's gavel to him. We were now the Aspin-Brown commission.

We soon found ourselves under quite a different style of leadership than Aspin had displayed. Chairman Brown wasted no time in establishing a commanding presence. While Aspin had been informal and casual, with his tie askew and his shoulders hunched over the table, Brown wore cufflinks and a tie pin, and sat ramrod straight in his chair. Aspin was soft-spoken and content to let others talk; Brown had a forceful, even intimidating, way of expressing himself and immediately dominated the conference room. Aspin was exceptionally smart, but Brown had a reputation for brilliance—perhaps

FIGURE 9.1 The Aspin-Brown Commission at Work, Under Chairman Brown's Gavel, 1995
At the conference table facing the camera, from left to right: former senator Wynche Fowler Jr., former representative Tony Coelho, Vice Chairman Warren B. Rudman, and Chairman Harold Brown, with the staff seated behind them and Paul D. Wolfowitz with his back to the camera.
Source: Loch K. Johnson, "The Aspin-Brown Intelligence Inquiry: Behind the Closed Doors of a Blue Ribbon Commission," *Studies in Intelligence*, 48 (2004), Center for the Study of Intelligence, Central Intelligence Agency, 12.

the brightest of all the SecDefs in the nation's history, a man with a steel-trap memory for facts and figures, and a practiced capacity for deep thinking.

Brown called the briefing session to order, as the morning's witnesses arrived and seated themselves at the conference table, now adorned with a vase of chrysanthemums. The witnesses this time included John McMahon, the sage and solidly built former DDCI whom John Deutch had recently chosen to serve on the search committee for a new deputy director to lead the Directorate of Operations—McMahon's former job during the 1980s. McMahon had earned praise in Washington's political and intelligence circles for his efforts to keep most of the DO out of the Iran-*contra* scandal, despite then-DCI William J. Casey's neck-deep personal involvement in the controversial covert actions. Accompanying McMahon was Richard Helms, one of the most popular of the former DCIs among his fellow intelligence professionals, whom a newspaper reporter had once described as "well-born, gregarious, and engaging."[15]

McMahon began his remarks with the unanticipated comment that the intelligence community was "a bit bloated." As I was recovering from the shock of that rare admission, he followed with the suggestion that intelligence oversight was important. This was my kind of witness.

Tall and patrician in manner, Helms flatly rejected the notion that a stand-alone director of national intelligence would be beneficial. A DNI had to have the analytic base of the CIA to succeed. George Tenet, a DCI in the making (he would succeed Deutch after the commission had completed its work), had expressed a similar concern to me just as our panel of inquiry was forming. "One of the problems of the concept of creating a DNI," he said, "is that you really end up with someone with a small staff, with no troops [as the DNI would be cut off from the several thousand analysts in the CIA's Directorate of Intelligence], no resources, no ability to really get anything done. So, from a bureaucratic perspective, nobody is going to follow him."[16] At the same time, though, Tenet believed—contrary to conventional wisdom—that the DCI had "enough authority" already to achieve his objectives. When he became DCI himself, he remained cautious about seeking added authority. "Every time you try to give me new authority," he said to a conference of scholars, "you get me in a fight with a building much bigger than mine [the Pentagon]."[17]

Along similar lines, another DCI, James R. Schlesinger, told me that he thought it was unnecessary "to elevate the DCI position any more than it is. . . . If the individual has high credibility, that is enough."[18] Adm. Stansfield Turner maintained, too, that he had not really required additional formal authority as DCI, because President Jimmy Carter had simply announced that—starting in 1978—the intelligence director was going to put together the whole intelligence budget. "The secretary of defense, Harold Brown, didn't like the idea, and he got me overruled in the final bout with the president and the OMB that year," Turner recalled, "but, nonetheless, I had a chance to shape the budget more than any DCI before me." The admiral remembered, too, that intelligence officers in the Pentagon gravitated toward President Carter's approach of putting the DCI in charge of the intelligence budget. "They concluded," Turner said, "that the DCI supported them better than the SecDef!"[19]

When a commissioner asked Richard Helms about congressional oversight (it was widely known he was not a fan), he conceded that at least "there had been no leaks from Congress."

"That's because you didn't tell them anything, Dick!" interjected Rudman, to the amusement of all the commissioners and staff. Helms took the jibe in fun, but the comment was closer to the truth than either Rudman or Helms would have acknowledged in public. The intelligence agencies were notorious for their reticence when it came to keeping the Congress informed.

Helms spoke of the difficulties we would encounter in trying to convince the various components of the intelligence community to work together. Intelligence and law enforcement were like "oil and water," he said. Moreover, the SecDef was "one of the biggest gorillas in town" and would not take well to being stripped of his authority over military intelligence. The relationship between the SecDef and the DCI involved a lot of pushing and shoving, Helms recalled from his days as intelligence chief, but it ought to be handled informally—not by a statute that would be doomed to fail. "In the end, the SecDef will be reasonable," Helms argued, as if gorillas were well known for reasonableness. "Tinkering with organizational remedies is something the commission should duck," he recommended.

"The failures have not been organizations," agreed Rudman. "It's been people."

Porter Goss circled back to oversight. "What's the best way to do this?" he asked Helms.

"Keep it small. Use a joint committee. Rely on trust and confidence," was the staccato response.

"Ah, the good old days," sighed Rudman, disingenuously, referring to the time before the Church Committee and the creation of SSCI and HPSCI, an era when few lawmakers looked into intelligence activities, counting on the CIA to do the right thing against the Soviet enemy and behave itself at home. While most of the time the Agency and its companion organizations did do the right thing, there had also been serious abuses of secret power—as the nation learned in the mid-1970s, and as Rudman, a leading member of the Iran-*contra* investigative committee, discovered again a decade later.

———

In January 1975, government investigators took up charges leveled by the *New York Times* that the CIA had engaged in domestic spying. The Church Committee and other panels of inquiry revealed a startling number of intelligence transgressions, in what is now remembered as the "Year of Intelligence" or—less warmly in the intelligence community—as the "Year of the Intelligence Wars." The investigations brought to light CIA assassination plots against foreign leaders; improper mail openings, wiretaps, and international cable interceptions; intelligence dossiers collected on over a million American citizens; reckless drug experiments; the unlawful stockpiling of lethal chemical and biological materials; a master spy plan to conduct surveillance against Vietnam War dissenters in the United States; intelligence infiltration of a range of associations in American society, from universities to religious and media organizations; harassment of civil-rights activists, including Dr. Martin Luther King Jr.; the incitement of violence against African American groups; and covert actions abroad aimed not just at autocracies, but democratically elected governments as well (such as the Allende regime in Chile).[20]

A counterintelligence program run by the FBI, code named COINTEL-PRO, stunned members of the Church Committee. Documents revealed that Bureau agents had conducted smear campaigns against individuals throughout the country between 1956 and 1971, simply because they had expressed opposition to the war in Vietnam or criticized the slow pace of the progress of civil rights. The attacks were aimed at people in all walks of life and of various political persuasions, reflecting an expansive hatred that included black leaders, white supremacists, feminists, and war dissenters alike. The Klan, the women's liberation movement, socialists, the New Left, antiwar and civil-rights proponents—all became enemies of the Republic that the Bureau set out to destroy.

The effects of this catalog of improprieties were profound. From 1975 on, America's support for an unrestricted intelligence capability would now be bound by another principle that had long guided the rest of the government: the safeguarding of citizens against the abuse of power by their own government, not just foreign regimes—in a word, liberty. With respect to the intelligence agencies, the nation's leaders began an unprecedented experiment in trying to balance security and liberty. The Ford administration conducted its own investigation of intelligence (the Rockefeller Commission), establishing the Intelligence Oversight Board in the White House and issuing an executive order prohibiting assassination plots. In 1976, the Senate created SSCI; and, a year later, the House followed suit with HPSCI.

The scope of intelligence oversight continued to expand. In 1978, lawmakers drew the judicial branch more directly into the realm of intelligence oversight by establishing the Foreign Intelligence Surveillance Act (FISA) court to review national security wiretap requests from the executive branch. (The second Bush administration would secretly bypass the FISA court, engaging in warrantless wiretaps in the years of anguish and fear that followed the 9/11 attacks.) In 1980, Congress enacted the Intelligence Oversight Act, a major statute that further tightened legislative supervision over the secret agencies.[21]

Each of these steps in the evolution of intelligence reform was met with debate, intense negotiations between the executive and legislative branches, and sometimes bitter quarreling. Yet lawmakers managed to establish in a bipartisan manner the precedent of a serious, ongoing review of intelligence programs and budgets within the confines of SSCI, HPSCI, and the appropriations subcommittees dealing with intelligence (and, for selected activities, the Judiciary and Armed Services committees). Congressional staff experts combed through spy budget requests, organized hearings, and, less formally, telephoned or met with intelligence officers in a continual exploration of their operations. Members of Congress asked questions at hearings (with varying degrees of earnestness), visited the secret agencies periodically, and traveled abroad to review operations in the field. As intelligence scholar and former NIC vice chairman Gregory F. Treverton has observed, the intelligence agencies had become a part of the regular government of the United States and faced the normal panoply of congressional oversight practices.[22]

John McMahon was not the only one full of surprises that morning. At one point, Helms blurted out: "The DO could easily be cut by 25 percent." Maybe the commission could take a scalpel to the intelligence budget after all, even if Senator Warner favored a hands-off policy when it came to spending for espionage.

"But surely it is not the job of this commission to draw up the intelligence community's budget," countered Brown, in his first substantive pronouncement as chairman. Helms stared at him with a bemused expression on his face, but said nothing further.

The conversation turned to the problem of the secret agencies being swamped by intelligence-gathering requests. "The way you limit that is to make the user pay for intelligence," weighed in Brown again. The room fell silent. The other commissioners had been down this road before and it seemed to lead nowhere. Fowler must have been pleased with the comment, though, since intelligence-for-pay had become one of his hobbyhorses and perhaps the only idea on which he and the new chairman agreed. Otherwise, the two men were, as the Italians say, *antipatico*.

Snider whispered something to Rudman, who then said: "Well, we better get on the bus to Langley," and everyone filed out of the conference room for the trip to hear President Clinton's speech.

When we returned from the Agency, it was time for lunch and a business meeting. Snider informed the commissioners that our second retreat was set for mid-September, although we were still trying to find a good location within easy driving distance of Washington. The staff task forces would make presentations to the commissioners during the retreat. This would help commissioners think through what recommendations they wanted to present in the final report. Snider went on to explain the staff's current labors on "options" or "focus" papers: short essays on the main intelligence issues, capped off with a set of reform choices at the end. For instance, one paper was on economic intelligence, another on the budget. The idea, Snider continued, was to guide commissioners as they worked their way through all the information we had compiled. The brief essays would spell out the core intelligence challenges and offer a range of reform ideas, each with pros and cons. The papers would be ready by August 28, in time for the commissioners to read before the retreat. The papers would also serve as first drafts for our final report.

"This should not be totally staff driven," Rudman cautioned. "The staff should be neutral and detached."

With a grin, Harrington said: "Yeah, write the papers so no member of the commission could possible criticize them."

The staff director reminded everyone that public hearings, planned for later in the year, would provide an opportunity to educate the American people about intelligence and present the case for strengthening the nation's espionage capabilities.

"Make sure we invite some people with extremist views," said Rudman, "just to let it be known that their views have been heard."

It was time for our afternoon briefings, beginning with former DCI R. James Woolsey, President Clinton's first intelligence director. He pushed hard in favor of an intelligence surge capacity. "Designing the intelligence community is like designing an aircraft carrier," he said, an analogy he had used frequently in media interviews since leaving Langley. "It needs to be flexible, for use against the unexpected. We need global reach, not global presence." He thought the biggest problem confronting the intelligence agencies was not the collection of information, however, but rather the rapid dissemination of the analyzed product—especially to the GI in the foxhole.

Bob Hermann brought the discussion back to a fundamental question before the commission: "How much intelligence do we need?" He expressed his own view that it was hard to find places to cut the intelligence budget. We had to have surveillance satellites, and, in fact, Deutch was seeking an increase in funding to finance a new generation of spy satellites for the next decade.[23] Moreover, according to several witnesses before the commission, we had already eliminated too many CIA stations overseas, especially in Africa. And, supposedly, the NSA was operating on a bare-bones budget. Plus we needed more analysts throughout the community. Woolsey nodded sympathetically as Hermann went through his litany of intelligence needs.

Addressing the matter of a creating a director of national intelligence, Woolsey became animated and exclaimed: "We already have a DNI; he's called the DCI!" He acknowledged, though, that the intelligence chief did require additional authority over budgets, personnel, and the placement of satellites in space.

Friedman asked Woolsey his opinion about "the difficult marriage between the FBI and the CIA."

"I don't know that I would call that a marriage," the former DCI responded with a laugh, but he provided no advice on how to improve this troubled relationship. It was an enduring irritant. Take counternarcotics operations, for instance. The FBI wanted to take over this mission completely and sought to have the CIA counternarcotics budget moved to its control, leading to charges at the Agency that the Bureau was "raiding" its funding (not to mention the budget of the Drug Enforcement Administration). People around Washington wondered how the CIA and the FBI would ever be able to cooperate on such matters as counterterrorism if they couldn't even cooperate on the lower-profile task of fighting international drug cartels.

As time ran out, Woolsey reflected back on his experiences as DCI. "I knew it was not a job for someone who wants to be liked," he said, "and I was right beyond my wildest dreams."

"Jim, the last four DCIs have certainly lived up to this," Rudman observed.

Wrapping up his presentation, Woolsey warned the commission about "sin number one" for intelligence: politicization, the twisting of information to suit the needs of politicians. "Intelligence will make mistakes," he said, "but they should be honest mistakes." The pressures for intelligence officers to support the world perspectives of incumbent politicians—"intelligence to please"—would remain strong. I recalled a phrase from Pushkin:

"Dearer to us the falsehood that exalts
Than hosts of baser truths."[24]

Policy makers were no exception to this rule.

Harold Brown whispered to Rudman, then slipped out of the conference room as our final guest for the day seated himself at the table. The guest was Douglas J. MacEachin, the deputy director for intelligence or DDI—the CIA's top analyst. A big, rough-hewn, extroverted individual, he wore a button-down (of course) blue work shirt (less common in the Intelligence Directorate). The most lively, if rambling, of all our briefers to date, he held the rapt attention of the commissioners and staff, even this late in the afternoon. Just what we needed: a touch of fauvism to brighten up the proceedings. I had the sense that if we had placed a drop of the DDI's blood under a microscope, it would have been all exclamation marks.

"The job of intelligence is not to give you precise answers about the future," he said, implying that this was the work of gods, not mere mortals. "Rather, our job is to provide a good understanding of what broad conditions the United States is apt to face." He asked the commission to consider the role of a football scout. "The scout is not expected to say, 'Coach, you win.' Or 'you lose,'" he said. "The scout is expected to gather data on the strength of the opposing team and, if possible, to learn about his playbook; then to use binoculars during the game and tell the coach about things he may not have noticed." The DDI emphasized that analysts were "forecasters, not fortune tellers."[25]

MacEachin considered the main Cold War target, the Soviet Union, relatively easy to cover, in contrast to the current world. During the superpower confrontation, the primary intelligence challenges were twofold: first, to monitor the missile threat posed by the Soviets; and, second, to counter their designs to take over the Third World. He thought the intelligence community had done a good job in keeping Washington officials informed about Soviet weaponry. "Most of the CIA's mistakes were about what the Soviets intended," he maintained, "not about what weapons they had." According to the DDI, the CIA's projections in the early 1960s were often way off the mark; but collection and analysis improved dramatically in the next decade. This was the trend I had found, too, in my research for Les Aspin.

Even in the 1970s, though, estimates on Soviet weapons modernization were faulty, MacEachin conceded, largely because Moscow never achieved the production levels of which the USSR was capable, and, therefore, these numbers fell below the CIA's expectations. The Agency's chief analyst was particularly proud of the intelligence community's role in marshaling weapons data for U.S. negotiators in arms-control talks with the Soviet Union, as well as its ability to monitor compliance with the negotiated accords. He complained, though, that the Reagan administration had refused to believe NIEs that concluded the Soviet economy was so poor that Moscow could not afford to build new missiles. "They didn't want to hear this," he recalled.

"Or the administration didn't want to admit it was wrong," Rudman interjected.

The DDI spoke of the intelligence producer-consumer relationship in Washington—the contacts between the intelligence agencies and the decision makers they serve. "It's our biggest problem," he said. "The relationship is close to dysfunctional." Missing were regular sit-down conversations between the two; absent this dialogue, the phenomenon of the "self-licking ice-cream cone" set in—analysts would be left to read their own reports because policy makers wouldn't know about them. Vital to the restoration of a solid working relationship between analysts and policy makers was "a good DCI relationship with the president"—missing under Woolsey and yet to be seen under Deutch.

When it came to preparing intelligence reports, MacEachin regretted not having reached out more beyond the Agency's barbed-wire fences. "We were wrong in not tapping all the best minds of the country," he reflected. "We should have acted as a Great Facilitator; we shouldn't have done all this analysis ourselves. Academe has much to offer, say, on assessing the long-range future of Egypt."

The DDI then turned to the subject of collection methods, or "tradecraft," upon which accurate analysis so heavily rests. If the information gathered by techint or humint was poor, the analysis would likely be weak as well. (Garbage in, garbage out, in the old computer maxim.) He emphasized that all of the "ints" were important. They had to work in tandem, stitching together a full tapestry on an intelligence target—though he expressed a personal preference for sigint over imint. "Pictures are great," he opined, "but we don't have the foggiest idea in the world what's in the head of many foreign leaders." For this, he said, "there is very little of more value than to hear what someone is saying over the telephone when they don't know you are listening." Assuming they weren't lying, I thought to myself, or engaging in a deception operation to fool the NSA's eavesdroppers. He acknowledged, nonetheless, that imint could be indispensable in some instances. As an example, he referred to satellite photographs of mass graves in Bosnia. These images had allowed CIA photo interpreters to confirm suspicions that Serbs had committed shocking human rights abuses. Imagery was not just for military purposes; it could also make a contribution to the prosecution of those guilty of violating international human rights.[26]

The DDI suggested further that information from humint sources could sometimes be of substantial assistance. The problem was that the CIA and the DoD simply did not have enough good assets in those places that had become global hot spots. One asset, he said, had recently helped prevent the outbreak of war between two nations, by providing the United States with enough information on the simmering confrontation to allow Washington officials an opportunity for diplomatic intervention. "If you've got *the* spy, great!" he concluded, looking over at me and adding with a grin, "You can't get this from the University of Georgia." In other words, outreach to academe was a good thing, but had its limits; better still was an agent in place with access to an adversary's top secrets.

It had been a long day, and Rudman adjourned the meeting.

———

We may have gotten a new leader in Harold Brown, but for the most part it was business as usual on the commission. Our schedule had already been worked out under Les Aspin, as had the task-force topics and the options papers. Brown needed only to preside, give authoritative backup for staff decisions, and, above all, make sure the report was pulled together by March and sold to Congress.

Yet clearly he intended to preside with a strong hand—at least when he was around. It was soon apparent that the new chairman would not come close to matching his predecessor's steady presence. Aspin had thrived on the work of the commission—here was the joy of high policy, and a chance to win back his good reputation, sullied by the disaster in Somalia and his forced resignation as SecDef. In contrast, the Washington rumor mill suggested that DCI Deutch had twisted Brown's arm to get him to take the job. (The commission had its own rumor mill, of course, like every organization, and the latest gossip was that Rudman—who possessed enough nerve to ask Mephistopheles himself for a match—had told Brown at the outset that the commission inquiry had to be completely independent, or he would resign. Brown was reportedly taken aback by Rudman's forceful warning.) So the commission had inherited a formidable but reluctant chairman, whose frenetic consulting schedule would keep him away from the nation's capital most of the time—including the entire month of November, when he would be out of the country. He flew into Washington every two weeks from his office in New York City, but otherwise planned to keep up with the commission's work by a secure telephone line and fax machine.

I had virtually no relationship with Brown, in stark contrast to my close ties to Aspin. On July 19, Snider brought the new chairman by the staff offices in the NEOB to meet each of us. The staff director introduced me as a "speechwriter for Aspin," which had constituted only a sliver of my duties for the former chairman. "If I need any speeches, I'll get ahold of you," Brown said to me. He smiled in a friendly manner, but his message was clear: don't call me, I'll call you. I failed to have the presence of mind at the time to clarify what I really did for Aspin, and what I could do for him.

I considered resigning and returning to Georgia, an idea my family liked; but I had come this far and I wanted to see things through, particularly to make sure that some of the topics of greatest interest to Aspin made their way into the final report and that I completed the history he and I had discussed (this book). In the months between the return of my family to Georgia in August and the end of the commission's work in March, I often regretted this decision—especially when frequent snow delays during the winter months stranded me overnight at the airport in Charlotte, North Carolina, on my trek homeward (which happened 20 percent of the time, I calculated). Other times, though, I was so absorbed in the commission's work and determined, with the rest of the staff, to write an outstanding final report that the unhappiness eased.

Following the chairman's visit to the NEOB offices for introductions, Snider informed the staff that Brown had spoken with him about the commission's relations with the DCI and his liaison officer, Adm. Dennis Blair. "It's fine for Blair to keep us informed of what he and the DCI are doing," Brown had advised the staff director, "but the commission should not weigh in one way or another [on Deutch's plans for reform]." As Snider relayed the chairman's remarks: "They [Deutch and the intelligence agencies] have to do what they have to do, and we have to do what we have to do. It is impossible, and undesirable, for us to attempt to take positions as a commission until issuing our final report." The new chairman's bottom line was: "We have to maintain our independence." Evidently Rudman's warning had stuck in Harold Brown's mind.

In August, we continued our quest for information about problems in the intelligence community and how they might be addressed. Our first session during those dog days of stifling heat and humidity in Washington was chaired by Rudman (Brown was scheduled to arrive soon) and started with a briefing from a technical specialist. Relying on staff notes, Rudman introduced the man with an effusive welcome, a far cry from Aspin's introduction, which often consisted of just "Go ahead." The intelligence techie went through some of the R & D challenges confronting the secret agencies, then answered a few questions. The featured briefer for the morning, though, was Anthony Lake, on a return visit to our quarters. His pale skin, thin-rimmed eyeglasses, and precise style of expressing himself bespoke of a scholarly disposition. As the president's national security advisor, he was on the front lines of America's military and intelligence activities, and this more formal reappearance before the commission was considered a noteworthy event. Brown showed up in time for Lake's opening remarks.

Earlier, in February, the national security advisor had come to the NEOB conference room to bless our efforts and to brief us on PDD-35. Now his objective was to offer commissioners his views on intelligence reform. He praised the nation's spy professionals, complimenting them for shifting so rapidly from Cold War communist targets to the "new priorities," and for their ability to answer his questions practically each day within hours or even sooner. He discerned several weaknesses, though, in their operations. To begin with, he was disappointed with National Intelligence Estimates. Too often, he said, they represented a consensus view—the lowest common denominator—without sufficient attention to dissents within the intelligence community. Further, he thought the relationship between the producers and the consumers of intelligence was woefully inadequate. "The policy makers need to ask more questions of analysts," he said, urging the commission to come up with new institutional arrangements to improve dialogue between the two groups. He noted, too, that even though he was often pleased by how quickly the intelligence agencies responded to questions he posed to them, timeliness remained a problem; he frequently had to turn to CNN for up-to-date news on global events, rather than to the CIA—the very criticism that had increasingly steered the intelligence community away from "research intelligence" like NIEs and toward "current intelligence" in an attempt to compete with CNN for the attention of policy makers.[27]

Lake reviewed the status of covert action as a hidden tool of American foreign policy, and concluded that leaks had recently made this approach "useless and dangerous." (By the time the Clinton administration came to Washington in 1993, the covert-action budget had fallen to less than 1 percent of the intelligence community's resources.[28]) Still, the national security advisor said that he wanted to "resurrect" this approach, but with better safeguards to stop the leaks. In addition, he hoped the commission could tighten the bonds between law-enforcement and intelligence officials; and that we would give attention to boosting the CIA's sagging morale, badly undermined by the disloyalty of Aldrich Ames. Other topics he thought we should address included the quality of recent intelligence recruits, as well as the skill with which the secret agencies were tracking WMDs worldwide. "Are we getting people who know about the Islamic world?" he asked. "About weapons proliferation?"

On the technical side, Lake wondered if we were purchasing the right kind of spy machines; if we—he meant the managers at NSA—were coping well with the fiber-optic revolution; and if the government was protecting the nation adequately against "information warfare." This last topic had been a focus of much attention in 1995 (and revisited with vigor by Secretary of Defense Robert M. Gates and the Obama administration in 2009). The fear was of an "electronic Pearl Harbor," in which adversaries would attack and debilitate America's computers and communications systems, shutting down Wall Street and the U.S. economy, along with the government. Finally, he expressed concern about redundancies, with the thirteen intelligence agencies spying on many of the same targets; but he cautioned, as well, against elim-inating all of the overlap, because it was healthy to have more than one opinion on many topics—what is known as "competitive analysis." Here was another one of those balancing acts that Deutch and the commission would have to consider.

Lake stayed on for Q and A. "Many of the activities of the intelligence community don't need to be changed," Harold Brown observed during this exchange, "and some are too much of a morass." This sounded like a defense of the status quo from the new chairman.

"You should focus on two or three where there is a real 'bingo,'" Lake replied, offering information warfare as an example. The cyber-warfare threat was a serious matter, of course, but many people were already working on the development of firewalls to protect computer systems in the Pentagon and elsewhere; thus, we had already decided that this particular problem did not require much added attention from the commission.

Rudman questioned the idea of revving up covert action.

"Right now there is too much supervision"—this was another way of saying "micro-management" by the Congress—"and too many leaks," Lake responded. Although the national security advisor did not go into the source of the leaks, it was well known that the Ship of State was a peculiar vessel: it leaked from the top—the executive branch.[29]

"Do you want us to 'resurrect' paramilitary operations?" Fowler asked, with a note of dismay in his voice. As a member of HPSCI, he had been a vociferous opponent of "PM ops," taking the position that all they did was embarrass the United States when they blew up in our faces—as they usually did, in his view.

The national security advisor began a partial retreat. "Well, no, but I wouldn't take it out of the picture…" His voice trailed off.

"What kind of covert action?" Fowler persisted. Lake's anemic response had failed to butter the parsnips for the former U.S. senator from Georgia.

As Lake paused, another Tony jumped in. "Counternarcotics, counterterrorism," Harrington suggested.

Lake took up this helpful thread: "…drugs, terrorism, small-scale sabotage, wiping out a murderous radio station…"

"You mean outside of the country?" Fowler asked. This seemed self-evident, but I guess it never hurt to make sure.

"We don't do this kind of thing much anymore because of leaks," replied Lake. He disregarded the question of CIA operations inside the United States, which were strictly forbidden by the National Security Act of 1947. Even in the worst days of the Agency's abuse of power (Operation CHAOS, revealed in the 1970s), the improprieties had to do with domestic spying, not with domestic covert action. The FBI's COINTELPRO activities had, in fact, amounted to domestic covert action, but that was a different story; Lake and Fowler were discussing the CIA at the moment, not the Bureau.

"We ought to be looking at paramilitary failures," Fowler went on, glancing down the conference room table toward Brown, who seemed entirely unsympathetic to the Georgian's line of questioning.

"Sometimes you want to do something without admitting it," Lake continued. "We need this gray area."

"Actions known, but not recognized," Brown added in support, ignoring Fowler. (Many years later, Fowler would run into the chairman at an airport and, as they reminisced about the inquiry, Brown said to him: "You were a pain in the ass!" Fowler had the sense that Brown was only half-joking.)[30]

Friedman changed the subject with the observation that "only the White House can resolve the fight between the CIA and the FBI."

Lake replied that he was trying to push the agencies toward working together more effectively, and he noted further that an even bigger "bureaucratic Bosnia" was the nation's approach to the counternarcotics mission. The national security advisor looked at his wristwatch and hurriedly departed for an appointment in his West Wing office.

Rudman asked Britt Snider about our schedule and the staff director reminded the commissioners that the time for our off-site retreat was rapidly approaching. "This retreat will probably be our most important meeting," Rudman said. The vice chairman also mentioned the public hearings the commission was planning for December or January. "Les wanted the public to have a chance to be heard, and I agree. Besides," he added, "this will be a self-protective exercise." That is, the commission would be able to claim a certain degree of openness to outside views, offering symbolic reassurance to the public—a common role of commissions—that the intelligence agencies were back on track after the Ames and Somalia debacles.

Later that day, after lunch, we listened to additional technical briefings. Talk of bytes, petabytes, gigabyte data rates, high-speed digital infrastructure, and hard-disk capacity soon drove all but the most ardently technical commissioners out the door, including Rudman (because he had no interest) and Brown (because he probably already knew everything they had to say).

The next afternoon the commissioners returned to the conference room for a short business meeting and a much-anticipated counterintelligence briefing on the Ames case. During the business meeting, commissioners wandered all over the intelligence map with little focus.

"Just because intelligence is redundant doesn't mean its bad," Rudman said. "I have two radios in my airplane."

"Yeah, get a second opinion if you're going to have knee surgery," Steve Friedman agreed.

"I'm worried about personnel matters," Rudman said, out of the blue, "especially at the NSA."

"Covert action is important to retain," was Brown's contribution to the meandering discussion. Fowler's face took on the appearance of a man whose new shoes were two sizes too small.

The counterintelligence witnesses arrived at the conference room. Well into the commission's existence, we at last had gotten around to addressing one of the major impetuses for the panel's creation: the Aldrich Ames affair. (The Somalia matter was being so thoroughly examined at the DoD and by the Senate Armed Services Committee that we had decided not to give it much attention in our work, even though it had spurred Aspin's initial interest in an intelligence commission.[31]) The commission had been awaiting the CIA's much-delayed "damage assessment" report on Ames's heinous activities.

The briefing began with a convoluted organizational history of counterintelligence. Once he had completed this overview, the Agency's associate deputy director for Operations/ Counterintelligence, Paul J. Redmond Jr. (who had helped crack the Ames case) told us that the traitor had essentially ruined the CIA's ability to spy against the Soviets during the final years of the Cold War. The clues to Ames's treachery had been there all along: the failed polygraph tests, the lack of a mortgage on his $540,000 home, the purchase of a new Jaguar automobile—all on a $70,000 government salary. For Ames, the motivation for treason had been chiefly financial, as well as the thrill of what for him was something of a game. The Soviets and, after the Cold War, the Russians paid him over $4 million for his handiwork. The Agency's coun-terintelligence specialist led the commissioners through the painstaking detective work ("walking back the cat," in counterintelligence terminology) that finally exposed the Soviet mole. It was an example of the CIA and the FBI working together effectively for a change.

Many of these details we had already learned about in talks with a variety of counterintelligence witnesses during our earlier interviews and conference-room briefings. New, though, was the briefer's revelation that some mid-level CIA officers were fully aware that their assets in Moscow had been compro-mised by Ames. As a result, the reports from these clandestine sources could well have been tainted with disinformation, as the Soviets attempted to deceive the United States through these channels. Even knowing this, the CIA officers never informed the White House or other policy makers about the likely double cross; they continued to pass along the clandestine reports from Russia to high councils in Washington. Apparently, the officers feared being fired if they told their superiors at Langley about the possible contam-ination; admitting that they had been taken in by the Soviets could lead to demotions or firings.[32] The end result was that an unknown number of decisions in Washington may have been contaminated by a clever Soviet deception operation.

This was a troubling disclosure, to say the least. "It's just mind boggling, the scope of what went on here," the chairman of SSCI, Senator Arlen Specter (R-PA), would conclude when DCI Deutch briefed his committee on this matter.[33] The senator said that the possibly tainted information from the Agency's compromised assets in Russia could have influenced U.S. decisions on weapons procurement—the F-22 fighter and the Seawolf attack subma-rine, for example—costing billions of dollars.[34]

The briefer finally came to the nub of the matter: what the intelligence community was going to do to prevent future counterintelligence disasters. The National Security Council, he told us, had recently dedicated an officer solely to the counterintelligence mission. (I remembered twenty years ago when the Church Committee had made a similar recommendation.[35] The wheels in Washington often turn slowly and in circles.) Further, the DCI had established a new policy board, answerable to the national security advisor, to coordinate counterintelligence activities and resolve related interagency dis-putes throughout the community. And a new "national counterintelligence center" would share and appraise information about foreign intelligence threats to the United States.

Specifically at the CIA, where Ames had carried out his treason, the DO had taken steps to involve counterintelligence experts more energetically in the evaluation of agent reporting, searching for signs of disloyalty; and the Agency now required employees to report to security officers in greater detail on their personal financial information and their foreign travel. Employees would also have to complete a new counterintelligence training course. The commissioners seemed satisfied that the intelligence agencies had taken the Ames matter seriously and adopted significant reforms to guard against further moles. Here was one topic the commission would not have to do much about, even if it had been an important *raison d'être* for starting our inquiry.

Redmond cautioned commissioners that "we're never going to stop people from 'volunteering' [spying for the enemy]. We just have to learn how to catch them earlier, and to encourage people to report on those engaged in suspicious activities."[36] Echoing Tony Lake's concern about information warfare, he concluded with the observation that computer security was currently the number one counterintelligence problem inside the intelligence community.

When I asked John Deutch in 1998 to reflect back on his achievements, he highlighted counterintelligence. "My biggest success was the change in the relationship between the FBI and the CIA," he recalled. "I worked on this; my deputy, George Tenet, worked on this. We had *one* counterintelligence effort, not two. That's very important."[37]

Rounding out the briefings in the conference room were a couple of well known authors in the field of intelligence writing: journalist David Wise and independent scholar Jeffrey T. Richelson. Wise had written extensively on the errors of U.S. intelligence, from the controversial CIA coup against the president of Guatemala in 1954 to a series of recent Agency counterintelligence failures (including Ames).[38] Wise was of leftish persuasion—a rare type to come before the commission as a witness. The litany of intelligence mishaps that he summarized for the commissioners was long, including the U-2 shoot-down over the Soviet Union in 1960, the Bay of Pigs in 1961, and the Iran-*contra* affair during the Reagan years—all, he said, "leading in part to a diminished public confidence in government." (Wise was also the coauthor of a popular introductory college text on American government.[39]) The Agency had some analytic shortcomings, he observed, but the "core problem is the DO." The Directorate of Operations was "too clubby," and it remained "encrusted with the barnacles of the Cold War." The time had come, he stressed, to spend less money on intelligence—especially on covert actions.

Wise had an even larger worry than the DO. "The animals are crashing in the forest in the Pentagon," he said with a sly grin, paraphrasing a remark that Senator Howard Baker (R-TN) had made famous during the Watergate scandal. "Watch out for military intelligence," Wise cautioned. "It has escaped the scrutiny of the press, and probably even Congress."[40]

Richelson, who had earned a PhD in political science, was an expert on the organizational evolution of the intelligence community and, especially, its achievements in science and technology.[41] He patiently scoured obscure government documents and trade magazines for details on such matters as the dates of U.S. satellite launches, their rumored payloads, and their orbiting paths. He believed that sweeping organizational changes were unnecessary in the intelligence community, although the DCI ought to be given more authority over tasking (collection assignments). He fretted about too many budget resources going into military intelligence. "The *national* intelligence function is imperiled," he declared—that is, the gathering and analysis of information about all the non-military subjects in the world that the United States needed to know about. I felt like applauding when he noted that "war prevention, not war fighting, ought to be the top intelligence priority"—a central theme in my own intelligence seminar at the University of Georgia, but rarely heard in the NEOB conference room. This meant understanding political, social, and economic trends in the world, not just military activities (as important as they were, too).

In Q and A, Rudman pressed Wise on why he was so opposed to covert action.

"The lawlessness, the lying, the violation of international norms, the secrecy—it's all contrary to what we would want done against us," Wise responded, applying the Golden Rule to intelligence.

"Aren't political campaign secrets also a violation of democracy?" asked Chairman Brown, leaning toward Wise across the conference room table, as if he had just checkmated him.

Wise dismissed that strained analogy and said: "Just because the enemy does something bad, we don't have to as well. We shouldn't adopt the methods of the KGB." He sounded like my first political mentor, Senator Frank Church, and I was pleased the commissioners could hear this point of view from such an eloquent speaker.

"The point is to justify the use of covert action in terms of its *usefulness* to the United States" retorted Brown, who had become an increasingly dominant and steely voice in the commission's briefings, "not whether the KGB does it."

Fowler avoided entering this fray, however tempting it may have been to him; but he did ask Richelson to provide the commission with a paper on how the United States could cut 20 percent out of the intelligence budget for space surveillance. At the time, Fowler attributed the reluctance of so many commissioners to embrace spending reductions to the influence of the "military-industrial-intelligence complex, as well as their fascination with spy machines."[42]

In a concluding remark, Richelson expressed his view that the consolidation of the space-based spy programs would be a mistake, "placing all of our eggs in one basket."

We had one final round of briefings with a few individuals from the private sector engaged in contract work (outsourcing) for the secret agencies, a significant component of the intelligence community often overlooked by congressional overseers and the media. In the middle of the afternoon, Rudman and Brown departed, leading to a further exodus of commissioners. Soon we were down to just a few of the panel's workhorses—Caracristi, Fowler, Friedman, and Pursely—with Coelho dropping in later in the day.

On the staff, we were beginning to reel from all the information we had accumulated. How in the world were we going to distill all of this into a set of clear-cut choices for the commissioners? If we hadn't been so busy, we might have become depressed by the daunting task before us. We soon received a memo, though, that brought cheer to everyone. On August 16, Zoë Baird gave birth to an 8-pound 6-ounce baby boy. Mother and child—Alec—were doing well.

PART IV | End Game

CHAPTER 10 | A Second Retreat

THE STAFF WAS FRANTICALLY PREPARING options papers as the date drew near for the commission's second retreat. The format of the papers was designed to make it easy for commissioners to come to the heart of the matter with a few minutes' reading on each of the core topics. An example was the paper on "The Consumer-Producer Relationship," one of the issues that seemed to sprout up at almost every commission briefing. It had become clear that the closer the relationship was between the two groups, the better the collection tasking functioned—with the caveat that the ties should not become so close as to allow the politicization of intelligence. As with so many things in life, a proper balance was necessary. In just over a page, this options paper spelled out how a balance might be achieved; then, following our adopted format, the paper presented "Options for Strengthening the Relationship." The choices were listed sequentially, with short paragraphs explaining each one.

In this example, the options we set down were:

1. *Increase the number of intelligence officers serving two- or three-year tours in policy making.* Analysts had been assigned to work within policy departments already; in fact, this practice had gone on for over two decades. Our option here would have simply raised the number of participants and tried to ensure that no consumers were overlooked.

2. *Establish "Intelligence Interlocutors."* This was an idea that had been recommended to the commission by a group of junior intelligence officers. The phrase referred to analysts or their liaison representatives who would join the staffs of policy officials during the day in the

various government departments, learning about the intelligence that the officials needed and then quickly retrieving it for them.

3. *Create more robust intelligence organizations in the policy making agencies.* This radical idea would essentially disperse the CIA's Intelligence Directorate into the government's various policy departments and agencies.

4. *Push Electronic Interaction.* This option relied less on face-to-face briefings by analysts and more on desktop computer intelligence, either "pushed" by the analyst or "pulled" by the policy maker.

For each of these options, the paper presented a succinct review of the pros and cons. For instance, for option 3, the staff noted that adopting this approach would "dilute the analytic pool [at the CIA] and carry the greatest risk of politicization." There were many other options we could have listed, of course; but we were trying to limit the choices to those we had decided were the most reasonable ones for busy commissioners to consider. We wanted to avoid complicating their decisions to the point of paralysis.

One thing was certain: commissioners needed to address this producer-consumer relationship in some manner. As former DCI Robert Gates once observed, "We have twenty-first-century methods for collecting information and getting it back to Washington, and eighteenth-century methods for getting it to policy makers."[1]

As we were preparing the option papers, we continued to hear from expert witnesses. On August 18, for instance, we invited a group of analysts to come by the NEOB. Friedman was the only commissioner to show up for the session. He sat at the conference table and took notes on a legal pad as he listened to the briefings. "We have become journalists," groused one of the analysts. "We have no time for longer-range research." It was a triumph of current intelligence over research intelligence. Another described his recent experience in the production of an NIE on Mexico. The effort brought together the NSC, the Treasury Department, the State Department, an NIO, the DIA, the DCI's Counternarcotics Center (CNC), an outside scholar, and himself (a DI analyst). "A lot of these people were hangers-on," he recalled. "We put so many nuances and caveats into the Estimate that it was practically meaningless as a forecast of future events." This problem was the opposite of NIEs that were watered down for the sake of consensus. "One thing we have discovered," observed a CIA analyst, "is that if you want the intelligence to matter, you have to be there [in the policy department] when the decision is being made"—an argument in favor of "intelligence interlocutors," or what we on the commission had begun to refer to as "liaison officers."

Each of the analysts briefing us that day lamented the lack of good communications between policy makers and analysts. "The policy maker doesn't know how to task us," said one. This reminded me of a recent conversation I'd had with a policy official. His response to my question about whether he used intelligence had been an emphatic "no," with the added admission: "Yeah, I know there are people out there, but I don't have time to find out who." The analysts longed for more opportunities to discuss intelligence requirements with the individuals they served: more videoconferencing, more faxes, more daily telephone talks (regular e-mails exchanges were still around the corner), and, best of all, more face-to-face conversations. The group felt, as well, that a better partnership between analysts and DO operatives was a good idea; but that "did not require co-location," as one of the analysts put it. They could meet frequently, but sitting next to each other all day, every day, might be pushing it—the same conclusion expressed to us at the Farm by a DO operative. As the briefings wound down, another analyst observed: "We're drowning in work, especially preparing current intelligence on the Balkans."

On my way to my office down the hallway, I bumped into Kim Simpson, Aspin's press secretary. She was handling the media for the commission, as well as organizing the public hearings we had planned for later in the year. We were the people on the staff who were closest to Aspin personally, and I felt a kinship with her. I asked how things were going. "When Aspin died, so did we," she said, referring to the commission's ties with the outside world through the media. Aspin had cultivated associations with many prominent reporters over the years, and they had apparently lost interest in the commission now that he was no longer leading us. Harold Brown seemed to have no interest in cultivating the media unless absolutely necessary.

Every few days throughout August, the staff would receive updates on the approaching retreat from the staff director or his deputy. We had found a suitable venue at last: the Xerox Document University Training and Conference Center in Leesburg, a group of modern office buildings located twelve miles from Dulles International Airport in the Virginia countryside. The dates for the conference would be September 14, 15, and 16, Thursday through Saturday. "Casual dress is suggested," advised a staff memo.

Many of the staff meetings now were dedicated to critiques of the options papers and to providing a practice forum for those on the staff who would be making oral presentations at the retreat. A flurry of memos flew between staff offices, each filled with guidance on how to strengthen one paper or another. It was a gratifying collegial experience, rather different from university research, which usually consists (at least in the social sciences) of individual faculty members working in isolation on their own projects—"stovepiping" to an extreme in the ivory towers of academe. One matter that worried us greatly on the staff was how to keep the commissioners focused on the key issues, without them wandering off on tangents. We had seen this happen too often in our business meetings and during some of the briefings.

To address this concern, we decided to convince commissioners—as diplomatically as possible—to sit down with us in the conference room for some "pre-briefings." The idea was to help orient them to the major topics they would be considering at the retreat in a few days. We invited commissioners to come by individually to the NEOB offices for personally tailored sessions on their particular intelligence interests, or we would come to their offices or homes around town, or even out of town if they were traveling. Baird was at home in Connecticut with her new baby, so we sent staff aides there to provide her with a briefing on her favorite subject: law enforcement and intelligence. Friedman and Hermann decided to request a "home delivery" briefing, too, and, since they lived relatively near Baird, they converged at her home in Hartford to consolidate the "pre-brief." The session lasted for five hours.

At a staff session in the NEOB conference room on August 28, staff director Snider told us he had made a count of how many commissioners were coming to the retreat. Nine had said yes and not a single member had said no, at least so far.

"Have we heard from Wolfowitz?" asked a staffer.

"Who?" inquired another in mock seriousness. Everyone in the room smiled; we had not laid eyes on the fabled intellect from Johns Hopkins for quite some time.

We discussed the subjects most likely to come up among the commissioners during the retreat. Commissioners are often attracted to whatever is in the morning headlines. The subject of economic intelligence had been attracting wide media coverage lately, stimulated by a currency crisis in Mexico that threatened to have a ripple effect on the U.S. economy. Others media stories warned of hostile intelligence services stealing economic information from the United States. A report issued by the White House concluded that the Russians were prime culprits in this post–Cold War espionage.[2] *Plus ça change, plus c'est la même chose.* As a result of all this media attention, commissioners were likely to bring up the issue of economic intelligence, we guessed. "And covert action," predicted one of the staffers, which drew a rhetorical plea from another: "Is there any way we can talk about covert action when Senator Fowler isn't present?"

A number of staffers found Fowler's criticism of covert action hard to take; they saw merit in this secret instrument of foreign policy, and he most assuredly did not. "It's a dirty-diaper pail," Fowler said to me in a low voice after one of our commission discussions on the topic. The former senator had a refined sense of ethics that made him recoil from the "dirty tricks" that were a specialty of the CIA's Directorate of Operations—almost always carried out at the insistence of various presidents over the years, it should be noted, not by the DO in a vacuum. Some on the staff had begun to refer to my Georgia friend as "Reverend Fowler." A few of us, though, were glad he was raising important ethical questions, which happens all too infrequently in the closed-door meetings of Washington.

I had talked with William H. Webster about covert action when he was DCI, and, like Fowler, he had strong views regarding the need for better ethical guidelines. When he periodically reviewed covert actions with his staff in the director's seventh-floor office at Langley, he posed this set of questions to officers from the Operations Directorate:

- Is it legal [with respect to U.S. statutes, not foreign or international law]?
- Is it consistent with American foreign policy, and if not, why not?
- Is it consistent with American values?
- If it becomes public, will it make sense to the American people?[3]

I hoped the commission would consider adopting a similar set of guidelines.

———

On the eve of our second retreat, our staff director met with Harold Brown and Warren Rudman. The commission's leaders told him that no votes would be taken at Leesburg; the purpose, as Britt Snider related to us in a memo (his primary way of communicating to the staff), was to discuss the issues and "see where commissioners were coming from at this juncture." The staff realized we were unlikely to reach a consensus on every issue; but the sessions with the commissioners would give us at least a sense of where each member stood, or so we hoped.

Most of the staff stayed hunched over their word processors, loaned to us by the CIA. (I sometimes wondered if the machines were sending electronic impulses back to Langley that recorded every word we wrote.) One fellow on the staff, though, seemed to find more pleasure playing solitaire on the computer, in an attempt to relieve his boredom. He was a retired CIA analyst and former *PDB* briefer, a tall, pleasant man, older than the rest of us and with a wealth of analytic experience—though he had what appeared to be only a passing interest in the work of the commission. He rallied himself at times, however, to write a couple of solid options papers related to analysis. One afternoon, I dropped by to see him about one of my own papers on this subject. I sat waiting while he finished his game of solitaire.

"How do you think the commission is doing?" I asked him after he had played the last card. I was curious to see if he even cared.

He laughed and said: "You know what this commission is all about?" Before I reply, he answered himself: "Buying time." He believed the inquiry was a charade, choreographed by the White House and Senator Warner to let the criticisms stemming from Ames and Somalia blow over. No wonder he spent his time playing solitaire.

———

During a staff meeting on September 13, Britt Snider emphasized again that Brown and Rudman wanted to avoid any votes at the retreat. "They want to listen," he said. Snider summarized the lengthy staff pre-briefing with Baird, Friedman, and Hermann in Connecticut, suggesting that some of Hermann's ideas were "crazy" and that fortunately Brown and Rudman would be at the retreat to provide a "leavening influence." Even after the five hours at Hartford, it was apparently still unclear what Baird and her allies wanted to do about improving relations between law-enforcement and intelligence officers. "Let's wait and see what they want," Snider said to us, adding: "They seem to have some revolutionary ideas." The staff director sounded skeptical about their merit.

"What do we want to do, as a staff, about covert action?" Snider asked further. He looked at me, since I was the staff member who knew Fowler best from my days on HPSCI and my residence in Georgia. "Does Wyche Fowler have any policy recommendations?" he asked. I had not had many private talks with the former senator lately, and I had no idea. Even when I saw him more frequently, his intentions were hard to read. "The heart of another is a dark forest," wrote Willa Cather in *The Professor's House*. Wyche carefully guarded his own sylvan solitude.

We spent the rest of the morning rehearsing our retreat presentations. Commissioner Bob Hermann dropped in and tried out on the staff a presentation of his own. "Titan 4 is about to take off," a young colleague whispered to me, as Hermann launched into an hour-long disquisition on how to improve space surveillance. Among his themes was his belief that it was premature to embrace the concept of a fleet of small satellites to replace the currently large and expensive systems in space—the "Battleships Galacticas" of the NRO. Could we have Chevys instead of Cadillacs? The advantages of Chevys—that is, smaller, less elaborate surveillance satellites—seemed self-evident. For example, we could fill the skies with them and, because of their lighter weight, launch them at far less cost. Yet Hermann advised, "A greater number of small satellites may not end up being cheaper. Nor do we know for sure that they could accomplish the missions of our present systems. Sure, it's great to reduce costs, but will a constellation of small satellites really meet our needs? That's not clear."[4] He offered an additional treatise on "hyperspectral imagery," and went on to suggest that "UAVs [unmanned aerial vehicles] are gathering industry momentum." Then he thanked us for listening and hastily departed.[5]

We continued to practice our own presentations, criticizing one another without restraint—a staff "murder board" (in State Department parlance) designed to help each of us make a better accounting of ourselves at the retreat. All of us had prepared too many transparencies for use in an overhead projector and we decided to pare them down to only a couple for each topic. Two more commissioners, Allen and Caracristi, showed up for part of the practice session. The NSA contingent was out in force as the endgame approached. "*Nothing* will change at NSA with the firepower it has on this commission," a staff colleague whispered to me.

———

As one would expect, the frenetic John Deutch was not playing golf or tennis as we worked away; he was resolutely advancing his own set of intelligence reforms. On the same day as our staff meeting, September 13 (the day before the retreat in Leesburg), the DCI appeared before the National Press Club in Washington. He presented this prestigious forum of journalists with a five-point program of intelligence reform.[6] Whether it was his intention or not, the DCI's efforts were overshadowing the commission's work.

Deutch's remarks to the press echoed many of the topics we were also pushing to the forefront in our options papers. First, he stressed a "customer focus." The intelligence agencies had to be more responsive to the needs of policy officials. "For example," he said, "we will not buy expensive new satellites unless there is a significant demand from our national security customers." He noted that, working hand-in-hand with Defense Secretary William J. Perry, he had moved closer toward a consolidation of the one major agency (the Central Imaging Agency) and seven minor agencies involved in imagery intelligence into a single National Imagery Agency (NIA), which would reside within the framework of the Defense Department. The purpose of the proposed agency would be to provide military commanders with "near real-time, all-source intelligence" that would give the United States a unique "dominant battlefield awareness" (DBA, in the inescapable Pentagon acronym). Deutch had come from the DoD and reportedly aspired to return to the DoD at the highest perch, so it was no surprise that he was going to take care of the Pentagon's intelligence wish list first of all.[7]

The DCI's priorities were causing major heartburn at the CIA, since the NIA plan envisioned stripping the National Photographic Interpretation

Center (NPIC) from the Agency, where it had been a fixture for decades (though housed in a building outside the Langley compound) and was considered a prized asset. Veterans at Langley worried that "imagery analysts [sent to the new NIA] would now be further away from the world of all-source analysis [at the CIA] and drawn inexorably toward supporting tactical military operations."[8] As this reorganization moved forward, several Agency imagery analysts resigned in protest rather than being forced to join Deutch's new organization.[9]

Next on Deutch's agenda was human intelligence. "Espionage is the core mission of the Central Intelligence Agency," he said, no doubt warming the cockles of DO hearts and bringing frowns inside the DI. In an attempt to shield himself from the flak, in response to his rules about vetting thuggish assets, that he was naive about the demands of espionage, he conceded that "we will continue to need to work with unsavory people." He insisted, though, that henceforth the Agency "will be different. . . . We will not do these things [recruit foreign assets] blindly, without thorough vetting and established procedures for accountability." No more Col. Alpirezes. He continued: "If questions of human rights violations or criminal involvement outweigh the value of the information to our national interest, then we will end the relationship with the asset."

Since he was on the subject of the Operations Directorate, he turned to covert action, observing that the United States "needs to maintain, and perhaps even expand, covert action as a policy tool."[10] The DCI and national security advisor Tony Lake were obviously on the same page, which would further aggravate Wyche Fowler's indigestion. This passage in Deutch's prepared statement to the media was probably a reaction to an influential article in *Foreign Affairs* that had just hit the newsstands. Written by Roger Hilsman, a former head of intelligence in the Department of State, the piece argued that "covert action has been overused as an instrument of foreign policy and the reputation of the United States has suffered"[11]—the David Wise argument. Hilsman also attacked human intelligence as a waste of time and money.

The Hilsman article inspired a thoughtful rebuttal by John I. Millis, a former CIA officer and, at the time, a HPSCI aide to Representative Porter Goss. In an unclassified photocopied essay that he distributed to the Aspin-Brown Commission staff, Millis refuted Hilsman's dismissal of humint as a useful collection method—a central theme in the *Foreign Affairs* piece. "Humint can shake the intelligence apple from the tree, where other intelligence collection techniques must wait for the apple to fall," Millis wrote.[12] The Hilsman article had caught Steve Friedman's eye as well. He wanted to know the staff's opinion on the "value added" from humint. Snider assigned me and Linda England, an affable and competent staffer with a background in the intelligence services (whom Millis would later marry), to prepare a paper on the subject for Friedman.

While speaking about the Operations Directorate to the Press Club, John Deutch touched on the subject of Aldrich Ames. (The CIA's counterintelligence staff was located within the DO.) Deutch said that he had created a position of associate deputy director of operations for counterintelligence "to assure permanent, high-level attention to counterintelligence issues."

Third on the Deutch hit parade of intelligence reforms was the question of improved relations between law-enforcement and intelligence officials—Baird's hot-button issue. He promised to seek greater cooperation between the two groups, bringing about a synergism which he vaguely stated "can produce fantastic success."

Next, the DCI vowed to carry out intelligence operations "in an efficient fashion." This was euphemistic language that meant he would insist, as DCI, on greater control over the intelligence budget of each agency in the community. His goal, Deutch claimed, was "to make a 'symphony' from the diverse instruments represented by the various agencies"—his way of advocating Harry Truman's abandoned goal in 1947 of all-source intelligence fusion coordinated by a strong DCI. Deutch was not the first intelligence chief to promote the strengthening of that office, just the most recent.

Finally, the DCI wanted to improve the quality of young Americans recruited for employment by the secret agencies. This would require better personnel management, which in turn meant closer attention to such things as ensuring a diverse workforce and incorporating greater flexibility into the intelligence organizations during a time of downsizing. He left the specifics nebulous.

Deutch came across as determined and energetic in his pursuit of intelligence reform, but behind the scenes, his hard-charging demeanor was tempered by pessimism about the prospects for success. At about the same time as the press conference, he wrote in a letter to a friend: "I am not so sure that the business of intelligence is [at] all manageable in today's climate."[13]

The Second Retreat

On September 14th, the commission convened for its fall retreat in Leesburg. It was likely to be a meeting of great importance for us on the staff, leading to a better reading of what the commissioners wanted to say in the final report—if they could decide. Further, it was probably going to be the last time the staff would have most of the commissioners together for long swaths of time, concentrating on key recommendations. As it turned out, the sessions were even more useful than the trip to the Farm, probably because the deadline for our report was approaching and commissioners felt a greater urgency about coming to grips with their final reform recommendations.

The retreat began at 1:45 on Thursday afternoon, with eleven commissioners in attendance. Absent was Exon, by now a mere memory, along with Warner, Wolfowitz, Goss, Dicks—and even Brown. (The chairman finally arrived at 4:45.) It would have been wonderful to have all the commissioners there all of the time, for each of our meetings during the retreats or in the NEOB conference room. Still, as Britt Snider pointed out, the attendance at our gatherings was better than many previous commissions; and in January and February, when we were writing the final report, all but Senator Exon took part.[14]

Rudman called the meeting to order and said: "We seek no concrete decisions, no votes. If there is a consensus, fine. Our purpose, though, is mainly to identify options." No sense riling up commissioners at this stage—that seemed to be the vice chairman's rule of thumb.

Rudman, co-chair of the budget-trimming Concord Commission in private life, signaled early in the session that he had no interest in wielding a butcher knife—or even a scalpel—when it came to intelligence spending. "Peace dividend?" he said, "That sounds good, but...China!" In other words, unanticipated potential threats had arisen that made budget cutting for intelligence risky and inadvisable. I recalled when DCI Woolsey told me in 1993 that the intelligence community was making major cutbacks at the insistence of the Congress—far too many in his view.[15] The cuts had sliced in half the number of satellites manufactured by the United States, he complained, and this had led to an even greater reduction in the number of supporting ground stations.[16]

Dewhurst agreed with Rudman's remarks on the budget. "I see more targets than ever now," he said.

Fowler objected to this line of thought: "We may need more humint, but less sigint. Let's be tough." The Georgian was of the opinion that "95 to 99 percent of sigint is just a big waste of time and money." Here was the "processing" problem in the intelligence cycle: searching for a needle in a haystack and rarely finding it. In contrast, "humint *is* intelligence," Fowler had remarked to me recently in the NEOB hallways; this is where the United States could make some headway—if the CIA would try harder. He remembered being told by DCI Woolsey that in the lead-up to the first Persian Gulf War (1990–91), the CIA had no humint assets in Iraq whatsoever.

I thought Fowler was right: the intelligence agencies continued to have plenty of money for space-based spying, but were short on humint and well-trained case officers to recruit agents in the field. At the very time the commission sat deliberating at Leesburg, the Directorate of Operations had reached a low point in its recruitment of case officers: only twenty-five new recruits were in training at the Farm in all of 1995.[17] By the end of the decade in 1999, the DO would reach its lowest level in terms of sheer numbers of officers, when the ranks fell by 20 percent from its high point during the Cold War.[18] Further, in 1995, the intelligence budget remained in decline. Since 1980, though, intelligence spending had grown at a significantly higher rate than defense spending, and had experienced far less of a downturn since the end of the Reagan years (see Figure 10.1).

"What is the purpose of this report we're writing?" Coelho asked, already agitated and we had just begun the retreat.

Fowler added: "I want specificity and credibility."

"We should say the honest thing, not pull any punches," Rudman agreed, "but let's keep in mind that we should be realistic. Don't put something up that will go *nowhere*."

"This has to be understandable to the American people," Baird advised.

"There was so much anguish over Ames and other problems," noted Rudman, drawing the commission's attention back to its origins. "Rather

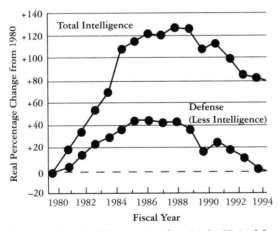

FIGURE 10.1 The Growth in Intelligence Funding in the United States, 1980–95 In constant 1996 dollars. The figure compares total intelligence (national, defense-wide, tactical) spending with non-intelligence military spending by the Department of Defense
Source: Adapted from Preparing *for the 21st Century: An Appraisal of U.S. Intelligence: Report of the Commission on the Roles and Capabilities of the United States Intelligence Community* (Washington, DC: GPO, 1996), p. 131.

than have a big fight over this on the Hill, Senator Warner wanted to move it out of the Democratic-controlled Congress. Anyway, let's hear the first presentation."

One of the staff members took her place at the podium, and the opening slide appeared on the projector screen—upside down. So much for all our days of practice. Her face turned red as she quickly corrected the error. At another point, the staff needed photocopies of a document to distribute to commissioners, but the Xerox machine at the Xerox Conference Center didn't work. Unperturbed by these minor setbacks, the commissioners sat patiently through a series of presentations, asking a few questions now and then, sympathetic to the staff's diligent preparation and willing to hear us out. At noon, we adjourned for lunch.

In the late afternoon, Harold Brown arrived and took up the gavel, with Exon, Warner, Dicks, and Goss—all of our incumbent lawmakers—still AWOL. "Let's focus on a few key topics," Chairman Brown advised, "and see if we can agree on them." He gave four examples: law enforcement and intelligence; covert action; personnel; and surveillance satellites. The temperature in the room remained normal throughout the discussion on intelligence and law enforcement, but when covert action came up, it rapidly warmed up. Opinions on this topic ran the gamut and consensus seemed unlikely.

The commission tabled (or "bracketed," in the NSC terminology adopted by the commission) the subject of covert action for the time being and took up the issue of space-based espionage. Dicks and Goss appeared in time for this discussion, just as Baird departed. Soon Fowler disappeared, too. I wondered if there was a fishing hole somewhere near the Xerox Center. Once at a Ditchley House conference near Oxford, England, I had observed him wandering up an ornate staircase at midnight, leaving behind a black-tie gala. He soon returned, still in formal attire, but with a fishing rod in one hand and a tackle box in the other. He made his way through the partygoers to the back door of the manse and vanished into the darkness. I knew from a run I had taken earlier in the day that at the end of the expansive lawn that had swallowed up Wyche and his fishing gear was a celebrated, well-stocked pond, and I knew as well that he liked nothing better than to fish—apparently even at midnight in the middle of a party.

Bob Hermann regaled his colleagues with a lengthy technical discussion of satellite spying. He went through his list of recommendations that he had tried out on the staff about developing a fleet of small satellites, then turned to an issue known as "shutter control." American firms—including Boeing, based in Representative Dicks's district—wanted to sell satellites commercially, but current policy required them to retain American control over the camera lenses on the satellites. As Hermann explained, Washington export-control officials could "curtail the use of any imaging system sold by a U.S. firm to a foreign purchaser, if U.S. government officials perceived that national security interests were being affected"—that is, if the purchaser had begun to use, or might use, the satellites and cameras against the United States or its troops overseas. This authority possessed by the U.S. government over lens control was not an attractive feature for potential buyers, and Hermann thought the policy ought to be reexamined, especially since the government in Washington could already prohibit sales to unfriendly countries through the exercise of its licensing authority.

Commissioners were wary about eliminating the shutter-control provision, however, since the idea of a "bad actor" abroad having access to sophisticated U.S.-made satellite cameras was unappealing, too. Maybe it was indeed better to have shutter-control requirements as a backstop to export-licensing safeguards. Torn on the proper way to go, the commission members leaned toward recommending a review of this complicated policy by the DCI and other officials, rather than taking a position themselves. Hermann nodded at this consensus and moved to another topic: the virtues of integrating imint and sigint collection agencies. Eyebrows soon rose at the breadth of his proposal.

"We need to think boldly about Hermann's ideas," said Wolfowitz, coming to Hermann's rescue amidst skepticism about the feasibility of the massive consolidation plan the former NSA scientist and manager had in mind. Hermann wanted nothing less than to lump together into one organization almost all of the technical collection intelligence: NSA, NRO, the CIA's DS&T, the Central Imagery Office (CIO), and a couple of other smaller organizations.

"We have no reason to be timid," agreed Rudman. "Be a little bold."

"Wait! Imint is different from sigint," objected General Allen, himself a former head of the NSA. "Let's also keep in mind that there is a boundary between boldness and common sense. Bob's plan is too bold a step." Many in the room were surprised; evidently the NSA coalition was not always in lockstep after all, as some (including me) had assumed. "The idea of a National Imagery Agency is in itself enough of a bold step," Allen concluded. The envisioned NIA, recall, would combine the CIO with a map-making intelligence agency and the National Photographic Interpretation Center (NPIC, torn from the CIA). Left out of the mix was the NSA, the NRO, and the Agency's Directorate for Science and Technology. Hermann seemed to pit himself against Allen and Caracristi, both of whom had outranked him at NSA. It was a contest he was unlikely to win.

At least, though, Hermann (a former director of the National Reconnaissance Office) had managed to convince the commissioners that the NRO should continue with its responsibilities for the research and development, acquisition, and operation of surveillance satellites—no small victory, considering the organization's disastrous public image in Washington in the aftermath of its recent cost overruns in constructing a new headquarters building. The NSA trio was skillful, too, in steering the commission away from any sweeping reforms that would touch the nation's signals-intelligence agency. "Evaluating the 'technological health' of NSA exceeded the capability of this commission," the final report stated—a preposterous claim, in light of the fact that among the commissioners was Allen, Caracristi, and Hermann, aided by senior former-NSA professionals on the staff.[19] More likely, they didn't want to evaluate its "health," as that might have opened a Pandora 's Box. Chalk up another victory for the "NSA commissioners."

However these ideas about institutional consolidation eventually played out, the idea of a consolidation of imagery intelligence would no doubt lead to strong opposition in some quarters of the intelligence community—especially at Langley and the NPIC. Before Deutch came along, DCI Woolsey had already expended much of his brief tenure in an effort to consolidate technical pieces in the intelligence community. "Security, classification, and compartmentation are such in the community that often it's difficult to get different parts working together—sort of separate baronies," Woolsey had told me once.[20] Above all, he wanted to improve the ability of the Central Imagery Office "to construct an architecture for the rapid dissemination of imagery to the battlefield." This required better integration of imint organizations in the community, he believed, but he was running into stiff bureaucratic resistance. Analysts at NPIC, for example, had dug in their heels and resisted being ripped from the Central Intelligence Agency's organizational wiring diagram, even if they were already physically apart from Langley and working in a secure building near the Potomac River in the District of Columbia.

"There was tremendous resistance from the CIA," John Deutch similarly remembers.[21] "NPIC didn't want to move. The DI felt that its analysis was significantly augmented by having NPIC institutionally allied with the Agency's Intelligence Directorate. The individual military services didn't like the idea of imagery consolidation either, because what we were doing was taking Army, Navy, and Air Force imagery analysts and putting them into a joint operation"—that is, into the proposed National Imagery Agency. Deutch continued: "But I thought the case was compelling. Shali [John M. Shalikashvili, chairman of the Joint Chiefs of Staff at the time] thought the case was compelling, and Bill [Perry, the secretary of defense] thought the case was compelling." That added up to a formidable coalition in favor of the NIA initiative.

———

As the shadows lengthened on the lawn outside the Xerox Center, the thoughts of the commissioners moved in a dozen different directions. Rudman jumped in with the topic of economic intelligence, as the staff thought he might, even though it was not on the agenda. (It was, however, one of the items on the list of nineteen topics the Congress asked the commission to examine.) The commissioners attempted to weigh whether the CIA should spy on behalf of U.S. businesses.

"Yes, let's recommend it!" said Hermann enthusiastically.

"No, let's don't!" retorted Dewhurst.

It was great to see us in such close agreement.

The discussion went on for an hour without resolution—though most leaned toward the Dewhurst side of the argument. Harrington succinctly stated the majority view: "The job of the intelligence agencies is to provide support to the government, not to companies in the private sector." Brown adjourned the meeting, with instructions to return at 9:00 o'clock the next morning.

The next day, Friday, the commission devoted itself to questions of organizational reform. Colorful autumn leaves were piled thick by the brook outside our windows, but they seemed fewer in number than the proposals offered by commissioners on the proper institutional arrangements for effective spying. Eventually, several commissioners converged on at least one main point: the authority of the Director of Central Intelligence was woefully inadequate to lead such a fractious community. General Allen, however, was having none of it. He looked at his colleagues as if they had lost their senses and asked: "Why should we give DCIs more authority, when they have been unwilling even to analyze the various agency budgets over the years?"

That evening we turned to the subject of analysis, with thirteen of our seventeen commissioners on board for the session. Exon, Warner, Baird, and Dicks were missing. It was my turn to present on the subject of National Intelligence Estimates. I began with an overhead projection that framed the central issues:

- Should the production of National Intelligence Estimates be continued?
- If so, what organization should write them, and where should it be located?

I had incorporated into my first overhead slide a clip-art image of a daffy character about to demolish his computer with a mallet, and I jokingly thanked one of my office mates, Dick Giza, for posing for the drawing of an analyst working on an NIE. This drew a few chuckles, including from the good-natured Giza, and even a slight grin from Brown.

I projected my second overhead slide that displayed a set of options on Estimates for the commissioners to consider:

- Keep the status quo, but have the NIC improve the current NIE product
- Create a new analytic organization for drafting NIEs, one that would be independent from the CIA and located in downtown DC, nearer to policy makers
- Have NIEs produced by the NSC staff or a private think tank
- Greatly reduce—or even cease to produce—Estimates

The ensuing discussion seemed to favor the first option, although a few commissioners wanted to move the National Intelligence Council (NIC, the forum for NIE production) downtown, away from the CIA and closer to the White House and the National Security Council. Bob Hermann, for example, proposed the creation of a National Assessment Center, located completely outside the intelligence community in the heart of Washington. "This would make analysts more accessible to policy makers," he reasoned. Ann Caracristi nodded her head vigorously in agreement. I remembered, too, that Joe Nye, one of our best witnesses and a former NIC chair, was drawn to the idea of making the NIC a part of the National Security Council staff, housed in the Executive Office of the President.

I offered the commissioners my recommendations, based on interviews I had conducted over the past few months with many national security officials. First, we needed NIEs, if only because they educated national intelligence officers and other analysts on key issues, making them smarter in their oral briefings to policy makers. Second, the NIC remained the most suitable place for the preparation of NIEs. And, third, it made sense to keep the NIC at the CIA, where most of the government's analysts resided and with whom the NIC could easily continue consulting on a day-to-day basis just down the hallway. Eventually, Hermann's argument for a new National Assessments Center at a downtown site would prevail in our final report, although the idea was never carried out and the NIC remained at Langley.

On Saturday, the commission conducted its wrap-up session, with Exon and Warner still absent, as were Dicks, Baird, and Pursley. The contentious topic this time was money. How much should the United States spend on intelligence? This was a fairly basic question for security planners. And a related topic: should the annual budget figure for intelligence spending be made known to the public? Our RAND consultants were on hand to make a presentation on spy funding. Spending on intelligence had been reduced each year since 1991,[22] and intelligence managers voiced mournful pleas for additional resources everywhere they went in Washington. While it was true that the spy budget had decreased, it was equally true that the Reagan administration had thrown large amounts of money at the secret agencies during the 1980s; thus, despite recent cuts, their spending base remained quite high in 1995 compared to the 1970s. From 1980 to 1990, the intelligence budget increased by a factor of some 130 percent, in contrast to about a 40 percent rise for the defense budget during this same period.[23] The community had loads of money; the problem was, it was spending it mostly on satellite hardware, then crying about not having enough funding left over for humint and counterterrorism.

Predictably, the debate over intelligence spending produced friction among the commissioners, with different factions in favor of either decreasing or increasing the budget—or keeping it the same. Ever wary, Chairman Brown grew fidgety during these clashes, his right fist doubled into a ball and quietly tapping repeatedly on the arm of his chair.

Even the discussion about making the aggregate budget figure for intelligence public turned tempestuous, just as it had in the House of Representative a year earlier when representatives voted against disclosure by a margin of 221 to 194.[24] The commission was beginning to resemble a town meeting of rival Mafiosi in a Sicilian village. Finally, Brown said: "The staff should draft two versions" for the commission to consider: one for and one against the proposal.

"Yes, both versions should say no," interjected Rudman. Fowler was seated next to Rudman, and the vice chairman slapped him playfully on the shoulder.

"No, and hell no!" Fowler added, at this prodding from the vice chairman.

"This is one of the more amusing aspects of this inquiry," Rudman added, suggesting that the fight over the disclosure of the annual aggregative figure was a tempest in a teapot. Brown concurred.

Despite nods by the chairman in the direction of change every now and then, Tony Coelho had grown increasingly frustrated by the embrace of rosewater reforms by his colleagues. "We are in danger of becoming a status quo commission," he finally burst out. The room fell silent for thirty seconds, but it felt like enough time to recruit a whole ring of agents in the Federally Administered Tribal Areas (by which I refer not to the U.S. intelligence community, but to the mountainous region between Afghanistan and Pakistan).

"We will have some changes," Brown said at last, with an edge to his voice, as if Coelho and Fowler were a couple of badly behaved students and he the headmaster.

"According to whom?" asked Coelho, pushing the envelope. "The DCI? The SecDef?" He may as well have been emptying his pipe on an open powder keg. Some people are born brave—or foolhardy.

The chairman's jaw hardened. Who had let this arrant knave into the meeting? His tone harsh and his brow contracting into furrows, Brown glowered at Coelho and said, "Let's put this discussion off to later."[25]

———

As the end of the retreat approached, the chairman offered a summary of the three-day sessions. He observed that the commission was unlikely to make "very much change" when it came to economic intelligence. On law enforcement and intelligence, Brown said that we could "at least bring these matters to the attention of senior officials, and if the officials don't get along, we'll buck them up to a decision authority." As for covert action, he doubted "that we are going to say anything terribly new and startling, but we should say something, and there may be a footnote"—in other words, perhaps a dissent from Wyche Fowler or Tony Coelho.

"If we don't at least address the subject," said Fowler, "then you will open up a credibility gap." His desperate hopes for a close look at paramilitary operations fading, he added: "I just hope you won't close your mind. I go back to the vice chairman's statement about some areas of boldness; this is something that is crying out to be addressed, and it should be."

Unfazed by Fowler's eloquence, Brown ignored him and went on to the matter of organizational reform. Here the commission was going to "suggest some changes at the margin," the chairman suggested, "and perhaps even significant changes. They are not bold changes." Brown expressed his belief that the DCI and the secretary of defense were determined to create a National Imagery Agency—regardless of what the commission might think. On the matter of a director of military intelligence, Brown was leery of trying to pass a new law to create such an office; let the eight-hundred-pound gorilla in the Pentagon, the SecDef, decide such matters. "It is really telling the secretary of defense how to run his shop," the chairman said, "so, as a member of the club, I'm of two minds about that." He added: "I would not want to write this into legislation, but urge the secretary of defense to make some changes." As for personnel matters, he insisted that "What we are talking about [downsizing] is *big stuff*." And on the subject of space espionage, Brown again thought that what Hermann had in mind was "big change." The chairman wanted more information about Hermann's plans before making any final decisions.

With respect to the aggregate budget figure, "there has been discussion," the chairman noted, "but I don't think there has been unanimity."

"The intelligence community is overwhelmingly against [releasing the annual figure]," Rudman reminded his colleagues.

The room fell silent again, so the chairman turned to the idea of intelligence as a free good. He and Fowler had floated the idea of charging policy makers a fee for intelligence, as a way to make them take the information more seriously. "I'm not sure we got anywhere with that," Brown concluded, and Fowler remained quiet, perhaps battered enough for one day.

Porter Goss entered the fray on the side of more attention to oversight. "It is important," he pleaded.

"Does that mean recommending to Congress what it ought to do?" asked Brown, warily.

"Yes, I think that's a very important thing to do."

Brown stared at Goss skeptically, but said: "Having active members [of Congress] on the commission gives us something of a license to do that, and I think we should."

Wolfowitz asked for the floor and told his colleagues that his two biggest concerns were counterintelligence and the poor state of human intelligence. "These were the most spectacular failures going into this inquiry," he observed.

Rudman nodded and looked at his watch. It was time to stop. "I think we've made a very important start," he concluded, smiling around the room, "but there is a lot more to be done."

As with our meetings in the NEOB and at the Farm, I kept a record during our second retreat of the participation rates for the individual commissioners, jotting down a mark in my notebook each time they spoke and giving extra marks for follow-up commentary. A sense of the involvement of each commissioner at the Leesburg retreat comes from the number of questions and comments they made—though, of course, some individual comments (usually from the chairman) had greater influence and significance than others, regardless of how brief they may have been (see Figure 10.2 below).

Chairman Brown dominated the Leesburg meetings, in terms of questions to the staff and his colleagues, as well as remarks of his own. Vice Chairman Rudman was not far behind. Hermann scored high, too, because of his prominence during the discussion on "techie" topics: space and satellites,

1. Brown (367)	7. Fowler (69)	13. Pursley (36)
2. Hermann (260)	8. Harrington (59)	14. Goss (18)
3. Rudman (224)	9. Dicks (52)	15. Caracristi (16)
4. Coelho (87)	10. Dewhurst (51)	16. Warner (0)
5. Allen (81)	11. Wolfowitz (46)	17. Exon (0)
6. Friedman (73)	12. Baird (42)	

The figures in parentheses are the number of questions and comments posed by each commissioner during the three-day retreat in Leesburg, Virginia (September 14–16, 1995), as tabulated at the time by the author.

FIGURE 10.2 Commission Participation Rates at the Second Aspin-Brown Retreat, 1995.

NSA listening capabilities, and CIO imagery. He was joined in this scientific domain by General Allen, fifth on the list. Coelho and Friedman were steady contributors, too, and Fowler weighed in regularly on a number of subjects, from budgets to covert action. Senator John Warner, so enthusiastic about the commission at the beginning, was a nonentity in these key proceedings, along with the phantom senator from Nebraska, James Exon. Of the top seven participants, five were presidential appointees, while only two—Coelho and Fowler—had been chosen by Congress.

The participation rates varied according to the topics before the commissioners. Figure 10.3 examines the degree of involvement of the top four participants in commission deliberations at the second retreat, arranged by subject matter. Except in the instance when Brown arrived very late (intelligence collection was the subject at hand), the chairman and the vice chairman both tallied high on these tabulations for each issue. Further, as one would anticipate in light of the interests they expressed in earlier commission meetings, Baird excelled when it came to law enforcement; Fowler on covert action; Hermann on organization, personnel, and space; Friedman on analysis; and Allen, on the budget and on spying from space (Brown had asked him to head up commission task forces on these subjects). In addition, Coelho, Harrington, and Dicks, when he was around (which was infrequently), exhibited substantial levels of involvement in two or more issue areas. As a general rule, the leadership steadily dominated the proceedings, yielding the floor to a few other commissioners who felt strongly about selected topics before the panel and had special expertise they could bring to bear.

Subjects (with Number of Questions and Comments in Parentheses)	Rankings	
A. Opening Comments; Collection	1. Rudman (51) 2. Coehlo (19)	3. Fowler (16) 4. Harrington (13)
B. Law Enforcement	1. Rudman (26) 2. Brown (23)	3. Baird (20) 4. Harrington/Coehlo (tied at 13)
C. Covert Action	1. Brown (32) 2. Rudman (25)	3. Harrington (13) 4. Fowler/Coehlo (tied at 12)
D. Intelligence Organization	1. Hermann (49) 2. Brown (43)	3. Dicks (21) 4. Rudman (16)
E. Personnel	1. Brown (55) 2. Hermann (33)	3. Rudman (23) 4. Dicks (16)
F. Space	1. Hermann (80) 2. Brown (59)	3. Rudman (25) 4. Allen/Dicks (tied at 15)
G. Analysis	1. Brown (51) 2. Rudman (24)	3. Hermann/Friedman (tied at 22) 4. Coehlo (13)
H. Spending	1. Brown (98) 2. Hermann (57)	3. Rudman (34) 4. Allen (27)

FIGURE 10.3 Commission Participation Rates at the Second Aspin-Brown Retreat in 1995, by Subject Matter

A Closer Look at Intelligence Oversight

At a work session in the NEOB conference room in the late fall after the Leesburg retreat, an uncommon liberal-conservative alliance sprang into being. The occasion was a Goss recommendation, which Fowler seconded, that "we need strong language on oversight." Naturally, I was pleased to see this union in support of what I believed, contrary to most of the staff and commissioners, should be a central topic in our proceedings.[26]

During the early days of modern congressional oversight, beginning in 1975, HPSCI junior members Les Aspin and Roman Mazzoli (D-KY) became that committee's most vocal critics of questionable spy operations. Although supportive of the worthwhile intelligence operations that came before them for review, Aspin and Mazzoli were also indefatigable in their cross-examination of intelligence officials who appeared before the House committee in executive-session hearings. Some members would ask one or two questions of witnesses; Aspin and Mazzoli posed a larger number of questions that probed the details of operations. Vigilant but fair, they achieved a balance between criticism of and support for the secret agencies.[27]

All too often, though, lawmakers on SSCI and HPSCI have lacked such vigilance; as a result, oversight has become far less rigorous than what reformers in 1975–76 had hoped for and anticipated.[28] Indeed, these committees held few hearings on terrorism in the years preceding the 9/11 attacks, nor did they bother to probe the "aerial terrorism" warnings from the CIA's Counterterrorism Center from 1995 forward.[29] No wonder a frustrated observer recommended in 2004: "Bring members of Congress's oversight bodies before a public hearing and ask what they could have done to prevent Sept. 11."[30]

APPROACHES TO INTELLIGENCE OVERSIGHT

Lawmakers have displayed four general approaches to their supervisory responsibilities while serving on the House and Senate Intelligence Committees.[31] The first type of intelligence overseer is the "ostrich": a lawmaker who embraces a philosophy of benign neglect toward the intelligence agencies (see Figure 10.4). This view characterized almost all members of Congress before the domestic spy scandal of 1974–75. A classic illustration of the ostrich was Senator Barry Goldwater (R-AZ), who rose to the chairmanship of SSCI in 1981. (For a list of SSCI and HPSCI chairs over the years, see Appendix C.) He had previously served as a member of the Church Committee that investigated the spy scandals in 1975–76. Ironically, Goldwater at that time had voted against the creation of SSCI—the very committee he would come to lead. He also opposed most of the other reforms recommended by the Church

		Responsibility for Intelligence Support	
		Low	High
Responsibility		1	2
for	Low	The Ostrich	The Cheerleader
Intelligence		3	4
Evaluation	High	The Lemon-Sucker	The Guardian

FIGURE 10.4 A Typology of Roles Assumed by Intelligence Overseers in Congress

Committee, including closer judicial scrutiny of wiretapping operations inside the United States (via the FISA court established in 1978) and more extensive congressional hearings on CIA covert actions.

The senator from Arizona was content with the system of oversight that existed before 1975: an occasional review of secret activities by a few subcommittees on intelligence housed within the Armed Services and Appropriations Committees.[32] These panels were passive for the most part. They did nothing to halt the rampant domestic spying revealed in 1974, the plots carried out by the CIA to assassinate selected foreign heads of state, the FBI's COINTELPRO operations, or many other controversial spy activities uncovered by the Church Committee. Indeed, according to a recent study, when he was in Congress (R-MI), President Gerald R. Ford served on the House Intelligence Oversight Subcommittee in the days prior to HPSCI and never heard a word about the CIA's domestic spying or assassination plots.[33]

The second type of intelligence overseer is the "cheerleader." In this case, the member of Congress has removed his or her head from the sand, but only for the purpose of cheering for the intelligence agencies.[34] The cheerleader is interested in the advocacy of spies and their activities, the support of intelligence budgets (along with the virtually automatic granting of supplements when requested), and the advancement of clandestine operations at home (by the FBI) and abroad against suspected U.S. enemies.

During hearings, the cheerleader specializes in "softball" pitches—easy questions for witnesses from the CIA and the other intelligence agencies, such as: "Do you need additional funding for counterterrorism?"[35] In press conferences, the cheerleader acts as a defense attorney for America's spies, hinting at their behind-the-scenes, "if you only knew" successes; lauding the heroism of intelligence officers and agents; castigating journalists for printing leaked secrets that supposedly imperil the nation; and warning of threats at home and abroad that could lead to a disaster if the intelligence agencies are hamstrung in any way. Although such statements by cheerleaders are often true (such as those concerning the heroism of many intelligence officers who have been under fire over the years in Vietnam, Iraq, and Afghanistan), they are generally one-sided and uncritical.

An example of a cheerleader is Rep. Edward P. Boland (D-MA) when he became the first chair of HPSCI in 1977. Boland witnessed firsthand how a 1975 House investigative committee, led by Rep. Otis Pike (D-NY), had prepared a shrill final report, widely discredited for its ideological anti-CIA bias. Appalled by the Pike Committee episode, a majority of House members refused to create an intelligence oversight committee of their own when the Senate established SSCI in 1976; it took another year of debate before representatives finally voted to establish HPSCI. To demonstrate to House members that the new intelligence oversight committee could behave more maturely than the Pike panel, Boland made a concerted effort from 1977 to 1980 to cooperate with intelligence officials. He often suppressed personal skepticism about some covert operations and expressed his support for the government's secret bureaucracy, determined to prove that HSPCI could be a leak-free and responsible partner in the world of espionage. The Pike Committee had ended its inquiry in a state of disarray, with its top-secret report leaked in 1976 to a New York City newspaper, the *Village Voice*.[36] Boland was determined to prove that HPSCI was not going to be another version of the Pike Committee.

A third role is the "lemon sucker"—a label I borrow from a Bill Clinton phrase for those economists who express a sour point of view toward almost any policy initiative.[37] This approach is similarly one-sided, only in the opposite direction of the cheerleader. For the lemon sucker, no activities undertaken by the intelligence agencies are likely to be considered worthwhile. The secret agencies are inherently immoral, engaged in such repugnant acts as reading other people's mail, eavesdropping on telephone conversations, stealing documents, and perhaps even killing people. The lemon sucker also points a finger at the intelligence agencies for incompetence, noting the CIA's inability to eliminate any of the foreign leaders on its assassination hit list (despite many attempts), the failure to anticipate the fall of the Soviet Union or the 9/11 terrorist attacks, and the errors in prediction regarding unconventional Iraqi weaponry in 2002.[38]

For the most extreme skeptic among the lemon suckers, there is but one solution: shut down the CIA and the other secret agencies, à la Senator Moynihan's recommendation in 1994. Rep. Robert Torricelli became such a zealous skeptic of the CIA in 1995 that he resorted to a highly unprofessional tactic: as a member of HPSCI, he disclosed in a press conference classified information regarding the Agency's employment of Colonel Alpirez, the army office in Guatemala charged with complicity in the murder of an American citizen.[39] Few thoughtful observers of intelligence embrace the role of the lemon sucker—and none have emulated Torricelli's extreme behavior. Most overseers believe that the intelligence agencies, whatever their flaws, are necessary for providing information and insight on world affairs to decision makers.

The fourth type of intelligence overseer is the "guardian." This role conforms best with the aspiration of reformers in 1975. Senator Frank Church favored a Congress that would carry out a serious, ongoing review of the nation's secret operations. Rather than simply respond to crises, his hope was to prevent spy scandals and intelligence failures from occurring before they happened. Rep. Lee H. Hamilton, HPSCI chair from 1985 to 1987, has argued that the ideal intelligence overseers are both "partners and critics" of the secret agencies.[40] Norm Dicks of the Aspin-Brown Commission similarly argues that "overseeing the intelligence community is like being a good parent: you have to encourage and discipline."[41]

As members of the intelligence community themselves (the legislative wing), lawmakers on SSCI and HPSCI must educate the American people on the virtues of having an effective espionage capability—the goal championed by John Warner on the Aspin-Brown Commission. Moreover, when the secret agencies legitimately need a friend in court, these lawmakers have the credibility to defend them against unreasonable charges, such as a "failure" to anticipate surprise calamities that no mere mortal could have foreseen. Without defenders on Capitol Hill, the secret agencies are at a major disadvantage in gaining public support for their often valuable secret activities and their sizeable budgets, since they cannot advertise their own achievements in public. Members of Congress can provide citizens with some assurance that the secrecy and the funding for intelligence are being used properly to bolster the security of the United States.

But to be truly effective as overseers, lawmakers must also be critics, searching for and correcting program flaws—the Wyche Fowler approach. When mistakes of collection-and-analysis are made and when scandals occur, citizens expect their representatives to take steps that will prevent the errors from happening again—or, better yet, reduce the number of mistakes and scandals in advance by way of thorough hearings, field investigations, and budget reviews. This side of the equation requires a capacity, above all, to leave the pom-poms in the locker room and speak out against questionable activities (in closed hearings whenever intelligence operations are too sensitive for public review). Lee Hamilton has come as close to the ideal of an intelligence guardian as any member of SSCI or HPSCI. As head of HPSCI, he regularly convened committee meetings, paid close attention to memos and reports from his staff and the intelligence agencies, followed up on media allegations of mistakes or wrongdoing, and spent time carefully going over budgets and discussing proposed operations with intelligence professionals. "The key requirement [for effective oversight] is for individual members to be skeptical," he emphasized, while at the same time providing support for appropriate intelligence activities.[42]

Even Hamilton faltered, however, during the Iran-*contra* scandal in the mid-1980s. When staffers on the National Security Council assured him they were not involved in illegal intelligence operations, Hamilton (along with other SSCI and HPSCI leaders) took their word at face value—always a mistake for overseers of serious intent. When *Al Shiraa* (a Lebanese weekly) subsequently revealed the scandal, it was clear that national security advisor Robert C. McFarlane and his deputy, Lt. Col. Oliver L. North, had misled Hamilton about their involvement in the affair.[43] "They lied to me," Hamilton said to me recently. "So did Elliott Abrams"—another Iran-*contra* figure on the NSC staff during the Reagan years.[44]

Lying is the most extreme approach used by some intelligence officers to fend off congressional overseers, but it is not the only method. Simply refusing to inform lawmakers has been the choice of some officials in the executive branch who don't understand, or refuse to honor, the concept of checks and balances in America's government. In 2009, for example, a report surfaced indicating that Vice President Dick Cheney had ordered the CIA not to inform Congress of a sensitive intelligence program. Rather than remind the vice president (who was presumably acting with the president's knowledge) that the law requires reporting to SSCI and HPSCI, the CIA evidently saluted Cheney and kept the program under wraps.[45] Were the program simply at a stage of early planning and discussion, there would be no legal requirement to report to Congress (although it is always smart politics to keep the lawmakers who fund your agency well informed); but once a program approaches the operational stage, HPSCI and SSCI expect to be briefed. Cheney's order, though, appeared to be a blanket command to keep Congress in the dark. In a related revelation in 2009, the new director of the Central Intelligence Agency (D/CIA), Leon E. Panetta, acknowledged publicly that the CIA had "concealed significant actions" from the Congress since the 2001 terrorist attacks. Panetta vowed to halt the evasiveness.[46]

On other occasions, an intelligence agency may claim the right to brief only a few members of Congress, rather than the full memberships of SSCI and HPSCI. In times of emergency, oversight laws do allow reporting to just the Gang of Eight—the top leaders in the House and the Senate who deal with intelligence. (The Speaker, the ranking minority leader, and the senior Democrat and Republican on HPSCI in the House; and the majority leader, ranking minority leader, and the senior Democrat and Republican on SSCI in the Senate.) Yet, after the emergency subsides, there is the clear expectation expressed in the law that HPSCI and SSCI's full membership will be briefed— all within a few days.[47]

Some in the intelligence agencies and in Congress would like to tighten this circle even further, preferring a Gang of Four and cutting out HPSCI and SSCI altogether. Yet it is often members of the two intelligence committees, and frequently the most junior members, who have the temerity to ask the tough questions that need to be raised.[48] Cutting out members of SSCI and

HPSCI defeats the constitutional purpose of genuine checks and balances, extolled so brilliantly in James Madison's fifty-first *Federalist* paper. Still others in the intelligence community, while perhaps longing for a Gang of None, would settle for a Gang of One, whispering in the ear of a HPSCI or SSCI chair and swearing him or her to secrecy. I witnessed the CIA try this tactic a number of times against HPSCI in its early days; the chairman, Edward P. Boland, had the good sense and firmness of backbone to reject this approach. He demanded—and received—full committee briefings.[49]

All of these efforts to report to some number of "Gang" members or another—the smaller the better, from the viewpoint of many intelligence officers—is a form of game playing that rests on the unspoken but underlying assumption that HSPCI and SSCI can't be trusted to keep secrets. The Torricelli case aside, the evidence is strongly to the contrary; national-security leaks come chiefly from within the executive branch. Those who play such hide-and-seek games, as if they were employees in Charles Dickens's notorious Circumlocution Office, fail to appreciate two fundamental tenets of America's government. First, it works best when all the cylinders are firing, not just the executive cylinder. The members of SSCI and HPSCI have much to contribute to the evaluation of U.S. intelligence activities; all wisdom does not lie in the executive branch. Indeed, the major abuses of power by intelligence agencies have occurred when Congress was kept in the dark. Second, the most successful foreign policy and security initiatives of the United States have been those based on the support of the American people as expressed through their surrogates in Congress. When lawmakers are excluded, so are the citizens they represent. If an intelligence operation can't stand up under the scrutiny of the SSCI and HPSCI memberships, it should not be pursued.

Perhaps fearful of being tagged as weak on national security—the favorite label for Republicans to stick on the Democrats—President Barack Obama threatened in 2009 and again in 2010 to veto the Intelligence Authorization Act if it included language to require full SSCI and HPSCI committee briefings on covert action.[50] Yet the proposed language in the act would be more in the fashion of a reminder than a new initiative; earlier oversight statutes already require full briefings. For example, even in the days when Chairman Boland of HPSCI was trying to develop comity with the CIA and restore the credibility of the House after the Pike Committee debacle, his committee consistently met as a whole for all covert action briefings.

Former DCIA Gen. Michael Hayden has complained that legislative overseers "pressure the intelligence community to push to the legal limit, and then cast accusations when aggressiveness goes out of style, thereby encouraging risk aversion." This is simply inaccurate. Yes, lawmakers encourage spies to push to the legal limit—but not over that limit; only when intelligence officers cross this bright line do overseers criticize their actions and require a return to the rule of law. As an intelligence officer in the field, one can—indeed, one must—be aggressive and risk taking; but one can, and one must, also obey the laws of the United States.[51] Members of SSCI and HPSCI have no intention of undermining the effectiveness of America's intelligence agencies; but they have an obligation to serve as a check on the misuse of secret power.

The United States must have enough confidence in its form of government to believe that as a nation we can be both strong and lawful. These are not mutually contradictory objectives; they are entirely compatible. A former DCI has stated as well as anyone the importance of full intelligence reporting to lawmakers. According to Robert M. Gates, "Some awfully crazy schemes might well have been approved had everyone present not known and expected hard questions, debate, and criticism from the Hill. And when, on a few occasions, Congress was kept in the dark, and such schemes did proceed, it was nearly always to the lasting regret of the Presidents involved."[52]

THE DYNAMIC NATURE OF INTELLIGENCE ACCOUNTABILITY

During their tenures, individual members of SSCI and HPSCI have sometimes embraced more than one approach to the job of intelligence supervision. Moreover, even those lawmakers who may fall into just one of the four categories depicted in Figure 10.4 (ostrich, cheerleader, lemon sucker, and guardian) can often be some distance apart from one another within that center. For example, some cheerleaders and lemon suckers may be mild in their advocacy or criticism, respectively, while others may be zealous. In the case of the ostriches, some may poke their heads out of the sand at least once in a while, if only to cheer for the CIA. As for guardians, some may be better than others at keeping an even keel between offering praise and finding fault.

Illustrations of the migratory habits of lawmakers when it comes to oversight roles are presented in Figure 10.5. Representative Boland may have felt compelled to be a strong partner of the intelligence agencies in 1977–80 to offset the bad impression left by the Pike Committee's strident attacks against the CIA. As the 1980s progressed, however, he began to drift away from the posture of cheerleading to assume a more balanced stance as guardian. By 1982, the HPSCI chairman had become a full-fledged lemon sucker, increasingly skeptical of then-DCI William J. Casey and his use of covert action to advance the fortunes of the *contras* against the Sandinista Marxist regime in Nicaragua.

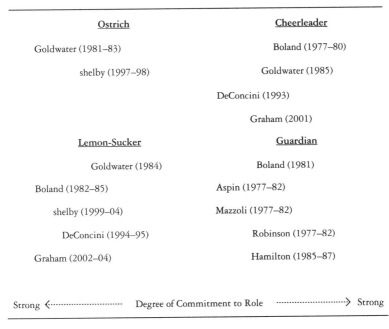

Ostrich	Cheerleader
Goldwater (1981–83)	Boland (1977–80)
shelby (1997–98)	Goldwater (1985)
	DeConcini (1993)
	Graham (2001)
Lemon-Sucker	**Guardian**
Goldwater (1984)	Boland (1981)
Boland (1982–85)	Aspin (1977–82)
shelby (1999–04)	Mazzoli (1977–82)
DeConcini (1994–95)	Robinson (1977–82)
Graham (2002–04)	Hamilton (1985–87)

Strong ⟵····················· Degree of Commitment to Role ·····················⟶ Strong

FIGURE 10.5 Role Migration and Stability among Intelligence Overseers

The Democrats ran the House at the time and a majority agreed with Boland that the mining of Nicaraguan harbors and the blowing up of power lines (along with other extreme paramilitary operations) were excessive responses to the minimal threat posed by the Sandinista regime. Between 1982 and 1985, Boland introduced and guided to passage seven successive amendments bearing his name (drafted with guidance from Wyche Fowler). Each amendment more tightly restrained the use of covert action in Nicaragua. Finally, both the House and the Senate prohibited the CIA from conducting covert action against the Sandinistas altogether.

By the time his tenure had come to an end in 1985, Boland's relations with Casey had profoundly deteriorated, as the HPSCI chairman metamorphosed from cheerleader to guardian to lemon sucker. In Boland's case, the stimuli for these changes were twofold: first, what he perceived as the Reagan administration's overheated response to events in Central America; and second, a new, aggressive and arrogant DCI (Casey) who did nothing to hide his disdain for the notion of congressional intelligence oversight. Policy (paramilitary operations in Nicaragua) and personality (Casey's irascibility) dramatically transformed Chairman Boland's approach to intelligence accountability.

Senator Goldwater went on a similar, though more extensive, odyssey at the helm of the Senate Select Committee on Intelligence. With his head in the sand during the first few years of his SSCI chairmanship (1981–83), Goldwater initially played the role of ostrich, deferring to DCI Casey and the secret agencies. He believed that the spy bureaucrats should be trusted to do a good job under the trying circumstances of the Cold War. During the debate on the War Powers Resolution and efforts by Congress to restore its war powers in 1973, Goldwater opposed the resolution, arguing that the president knew best when it came to matters of war making.[53] When Boland began introducing his restrictive amendments against covert action in Nicaragua, Goldwater (his Senate counterpart) declared that the laws proposed by the HPSCI chair were "unconstitutional."[54] He added: "It's another example of Congress trying to take away the constitutional power of the President to be Commander in Chief and to formulate foreign policy."[55] Like Vice President Dick Cheney in the second Bush administration, Goldwater was a leading proponent of the so-called unitary theory of presidential supremacy.[56]

Then, in 1984, William Casey managed to achieve the seemingly impossible; President Reagan's DCI single-handedly turned the intelligence community's most reliable ostrich into one of its most vocal skeptics: Goldwater became a lemon sucker. The catalyst in this dramatic transformation was Casey's misleading testimony during an appearance before SSCI. When asked by a committee member whether the CIA was mining harbors in Nicaragua, the intelligence director responded with an unequivocal "no." Only later did it become evident that Casey, in an artful dodge, had relied on a technical point: the CIA was not mining harbors, it was mining *piers* within harbors.[57] This attempt to toy with SSCI angered its chairman, Goldwater. Institutional pride trumped (temporarily at least) his feelings of blind deference toward the intelligence community. The chairman fired off a letter to one of the best forums for venting in the nation's capital: the *Washington Post*. Castigating Casey for his attempts at legerdemain before SSCI overseers, the letter said in part: "It gets down to one, little, simple phrase: I am pissed off!"[58]

As Goldwater's ire over Casey cooled down, the chairman drifted into a comfortable cheerleading role for the remainder of his tenure through 1985. This approach to oversight better suited his long-standing deference to the executive branch in the conduct of foreign and security policy. Yet never again while on SSCI did the Arizonian find it prudent to keep his head in the sand. As least as a cheerleader, he kept up with current intelligence initiatives, leaving open the possibility that once again he just might discover some activities worthy of serious questioning. Herein lies the slim advantage of having a cheerleader as overseer rather than an ostrich.

In another example, recall how former intelligence chief R. James Woolsey, whose personality could shift rapidly from charming to churlish, managed a similar feat of alienating another SSCI chairman, Dennis DeConcini, to the detriment of the intelligence agencies. Again, a DCI's style, coupled with basic policy disagreements over operations (Woolsey for techint and DeConcini for humint), led to an estrangement between an intelligence chief and an oversight committee chairman, turning the SSCI leader from advocate to staunch critic.

The government of the United States is built on a foundation of shared powers among the three branches of government. In addition to making laws, a primary duty of the legislative branch is to keep watch over the sprawling bureaucracy that lies beneath the president. An especially difficult assignment is to maintain vigilance over the hidden side of this bureaucracy—the nation's secret agencies. Before 1975, lawmakers largely overlooked this assignment, because the job was viewed as too time consuming, as well as daunting in the level of expertise required. Moreover, intelligence oversight provides little opportunity for credit claiming back home; most intelligence operations are too sensitive to discuss in public.

Even since the advent of the post-1975 era of more serious intelligence oversight, members of Congress have continued to feel these tugs that pull their attention away from supervising the nation's espionage activities. The time and study required to become an effective agent of accountability in this hidden domain, plus the lack of pats on the back in the home district for engaging in intelligence oversight activities, adds up to an unattractive result for lawmakers concerned about reelection (as most always are). Members of Congress usually conclude that their time is better spent raising campaign funds and pursuing legislative objectives that are more visible in their constituencies and better covered by the media. As a former SSCI chair put it, "There are no turkeys to be handed out that you can talk about."[59]

Yet what about when intelligence failures lead to devastating attacks against the United States or ill-fated military interventions by our nation abroad? What if lawmakers could have prevented outcomes like these through a more energetic review of such matters as the quality of intelligence collection and analysis, and the effectiveness of information sharing among the secret agencies? When a terrorist bomb goes off in an American city, what member of Congress will want to explain to constituents why he or she was too busy fundraising or drafting earmarks to ensure—by means of serious hearings and budget reviews—the readiness of America's intelligence agencies? Here is why Goss and Fowler's interest in intelligence oversight was so vital in 1995, and remains so today.

| The Final Stretch

Throughout our inquiry, the work of the commission was buffeted by global, national, and local events.[1] Globally, the collapse of the Mexican peso in 1994, as the commission was organizing, sent the Clinton administration into a whirlwind of economic activity. During his presidential campaign two years earlier, Clinton had focused his attention on domestic economic problems facing the United States. Now, on the international front, he confronted more headaches related to the health of the world economy than he had counted on. After advancing the North American Free Trade Agreement (NAFTA) to passage on Capitol Hill, the president had a political investment in making sure commerce in North America prospered.

The initial responses of the Clinton administration to the crisis in Mexico were clumsy, in part because the Treasury Department and the Federal Reserve had weak ties to America's intelligence agencies and had little access to information about the events unfolding south of the Rio Grande.[2] Fortunately, the talents of Treasury Secretary Robert Rubin offset this unsatisfactory information flow; he managed to help bail out the Mexicans anyway with an ingeniously crafted $20 billion aid package. The crisis underscored the significance of economic intelligence, as well as the need for the trade-oriented departments and agencies in Washington (Treasury, Commerce, State, Agriculture, and the Office of U.S. Trade Representative) to improve their ties with the intelligence community—and vice versa.

Further, in early 1995, a CIA operative was caught attempting to recruit a high-level economic official in Paris, straining relations between the United States and France for a time and raising questions about the value of risky economic espionage activities.[3] Little wonder, with these Mexican and French experiences fresh in mind, that many of the commissioners displayed an abiding interest in the subject of economic intelligence.

More vexing still were conditions in the Balkans during this period. The mass rapes carried out by Serbs against Bosnian Muslims, a shocking tool of warfare; the incidents of ethnic cleansing throughout the region; and the widespread atrocities committed by Bosnians, Serbs, and Croats—all part of a four-year war in the former Yugoslavia—were impossible to dismiss as someone else's business. The initial reaction of the Clinton administration was to enlist NATO members in the bombing of the primary aggressors, the Bosnian Serbs. This failed to halt the fighting and the raping, however, so the administration escalated its diplomatic initiatives, dispatching Assistant Secretary of State Richard Holbrooke to negotiate a peace settlement (in Dayton, Ohio) among the warring factions. The resulting pact, known as the Dayton Accords, was a success; but the war had cost some 250,000 lives in the Balkans and displaced three million people. In the intelligence community, the Balkan conflict siphoned off considerable resources as the CIA assigned hundreds of case officers and analysts to the region. For example, the Agency's Directorate of Operations mobilized scores of paramilitary officers to train the Croatian Army covertly for the defense of its people against the Serbian army. It was an illustration of how "intelligence surge" could work, to some extent, while at the same time allowing the intelligence community to keep up a semblance of "global presence."

Other foreign crises diverted the energy and attention of the White House and the intelligence agencies, including persistent unrest in Haiti; concern about rumors of a nuclear weapons program in North Korea; international trade tensions between the United States and Japan; a soaring U.S. trade deficit, especially with China; Iran's construction of suspicious nuclear reactors; endless fretting about the state of Israel and its Arab enemies; and the declining health of Russian president Boris Yeltsin, a friend of the United States. Terror, too, had taken on an increasingly high profile in the world. In January 1995, right at the beginning of the commission's inquiry, a bomb-making laboratory exploded in Manila. While investigating the incident, the Philippine national police discovered evidence of a terrorist plot led by Ramzi Yousef to bomb the U.S. embassy in Manila, dynamite a dozen American airplanes in Asia, and crash a jet airliner into the CIA's headquarters—an example of the increasing chances for the "aerial terrorism" the Agency had warned about in its 1995 memo to the commission and others. In March of 1995, the Japanese religious cult Aum Shinrikyo attacked the Tokyo subway system, killing a dozen people and injuring 5,500 more; the next month, it attacked again in Japan, this time using cyanide aimed at a crowded commuter train at the Shinjuku Station, leading to the hospitalization of over three hundred victims. In Paris during the summer, a bomb exploded on a commuter train, killing four people and harming eighty more—the first case of terrorism in France since a series of bombings in the mid-1980s. In November, terrorists struck facilities in Saudi Arabia.

Happily, there was also some good news on the terrorist front during the commission's investigations. Working with local authorities and the CIA, the FBI captured Ramzi Yousef, who was planning not only the attacks referred to above but was the suspected mastermind of the 1993 bombing of the World Trade Center in New York City. The agencies tracked him down in Islamabad, Pakistan, in February of 1995, and extradited him to New York. Further, a federal jury convicted Sheikh Omar Abdel-Rahman, an Egyptian, and nine codefendants, on charges of conspiracy to wage "a war of urban terrorism" in the United States. Most of the evidence against Abdel-Rahman came from a humint asset who had infiltrated his terrorist cell.

Nationally, the Clinton administration had to cope with the rising specter of violence perpetrated by homegrown terrorists, displayed most vividly in the destruction of the Alfred P. Murrah Federal Building in Oklahoma City. It was not known how many similar events were being planned by disaffected "patriot groups" in the Midwest and the West. The capture of former football star O. J. Simpson and his trial for murder further preoccupied the nation's attention in 1995, drawing the media and the public away from issues of intelligence reform.

Locally, in Washington itself, the administration had its hands full politically with a GOP-controlled Congress led by the combative Speaker of the House, Newt Gingrich of Georgia. Periodically throughout November and December of 1995, the Speaker threatened to shut down the government for spending too much money. While shoveling piles of money at the secret agencies away from the media's view, the Republicans openly advocated $1 trillion in domestic spending cuts (chiefly in entitlement programs) and $245 billion in tax cuts. The primary bones of contention between the two parties were Medicare and Medicaid, both of which the GOP sought to reduce dramatically. (Ironically, it would be the Clinton administration that balanced the federal budget—indeed, leaving behind a substantial surplus in the federal treasury—and the GOP under George W. Bush that would drive he nation deeply into debt.)

The president finally called the Speaker's bluff and closed down federal agencies and departments (including the commission staff), blaming Gingrich. The move idled over a million federal employees and contract workers, paralyzed a range of government operations, and irritated the usual throng of tourists visiting Washington. President Clinton eventually won the public-relations battle with the Speaker by reminding Americans about the value of government services. The president remained embattled, though, in the Whitewater real-estate scandal back in Arkansas, which Gingrich and other Republican officials tried to pin on the Clintons—unsuccessfully but with zeal.

At the very local level, inside the Oval Office, the president (we subsequently learned) was not exactly riveted to the subject of intelligence reform. As winter laid a thick mantle of snow over DC in the last days of 1995, Bill Clinton was becoming increasingly caught up in a relationship with a White House intern, Monica Lewinsky, which would lead to his impeachment by the House on charges of perjury and obstruction of justice. In 1998, the Senate acquitted Clinton after a three-week trial, when the vote fell short (by seventeen ballots) of the Constitutional requirement of a two-thirds majority to convict and remove the president from office.

Lewinsky, a twenty-two-year-old from California, began her infamous White House internship in July of 1995. Later that November, after a staff party in the midst of the government shutdown, she and the president had the first of ten sexual encounters that took place between the months of November 1995 and March 1997. According to the report of the independent counsel assigned to investigate the affair, in February 1996—at the time we were about to report our findings to the White House—President Clinton confided to Lewinsky that he felt "uncomfortable" about their relationship, and he ended it, though only temporarily as it turned out.[4] His personal troubles were about to deepen further as a former acquaintance from Arkansas, Paula Jones, filed a lawsuit against him for sexual misconduct and as Lewinsky began to demand more attention from the president.

That winter even the weather was nasty. Washington experienced one of its highest levels of snowfall, which produced the fifth worst winter in the history of the nation's capital. The severe weather caused some commissioners to miss our meetings, and delayed or cancelled the flights of commission witnesses scheduled to travel to Washington.

In short, like every other investigative panel to come along, the Aspin-Brown Commission moved forward haltingly and without the luxury of operating in a vacuum. At the staff level, we may have been obsessed with the subject of intelligence reform; but, throughout 1994–96, our activities were just one of many events in the daily lives of White House officials, bureaucrats, lawmakers, pressure groups, and our own commissioners.

Even before the commission came to life in 1994, the intelligence community had taken impressive steps to face the new challenges that emerged in the aftermath of the superpower confrontation. Robert M. Gates was the first DCI to serve following the disintegration of the Soviet empire. "There was a massive reallocation of resources inside the CIA," he remembers. While some 60 to 80 percent of America's intelligence personnel and funding had been focused on the USSR in any given year during the Cold War, by fiscal year 1993 , according to Gates, "only 13 percent of the CIA's resources were directed against the former Soviet Union. Huge reassignments of people took place."[5]

All these events aside, our race with John Deutch toward the goalpost of intelligence reform was enough to remind us each day that we were not alone, even in the small world of intelligence experts. "[Deutch] has a wonderful opportunity to get out in front of these reform groups," observed David Whipple, a former CIA station chief who was the executive director for the Association of Former Intelligence Officers at the time.[6]

Indeed, several other groups were preparing their own proposals to remedy the ills of the secret services, including scholars at Georgetown University—a favorite hangout for retired spooks who signed up as adjunct or visiting professors—and by the Twentieth Century Fund. (My experience with the Fund suggested that, when it came to intelligence, its staff didn't know wood from canvas, in the old British Navy expression.) One of the most prestigious of the intelligence study groups, which Aspin had met with a couple of times earlier in the year, was the Council on Foreign Relations in New York City. The Council beat our publication date by a month when its director of national security programs, Richard N. Haass, wrote an op-ed piece in the *Washington Post* in February 1996 filled with proposals for intelligence reform.[7]

While we were trying to turn the clock forward, Haass appeared intent on turning back two decades of bipartisan intelligence reform. He recommended the resumption of assassination plots (banned by an executive order signed by President Ford in 1976[8]); the use of the Peace Corps as a cover for CIA officers abroad (never used before and also formally banned in the 1970s as an intelligence cover); authority for intelligence officers to pretend they were American journalists, academics, or clergy traveling overseas (thereby endangering the real ones); and more aggressive participation in *coups d'état* against regimes deemed unfriendly to the United States—the kind of extreme covert actions that had given the nation a black eye during the Cold War. The Church, Pike, and Rockefeller panels of inquiry had strongly rejected all of these initiatives in the mid-1970s, and I hoped the Aspin-Brown Commission would, too.

Bringing Things Together

In the middle of these events and the growing partisan wars between the Clinton-led Democrats and the Gingrich-led Republicans, the commission staff continued to polish drafts of the final report and listened to a final round of witnesses. The triumvirate of staff attorneys had taken charge of writing the final report, with the rest of us in the role of drafting sections for their review. They were talented, at least, and their outline of a table of contents for the final report looked sound, but it might have been even better with a broader involvement of the staff in this planning. Maybe even the former CIA analyst addicted to computer solitaire would have gotten more involved in our work. Although we were all confined in a suite of offices just steps away from one another, the mode of communication between the staff brass at one end of the hall and the rest of us at the other end was usually the inter-office e-mailed memo. (While e-mails were still rare in most of the government, the CIA had set up this method of internal communication for use by the commission staff.) "This will constitute the week's staff meeting," was an increasingly common introduction to these communications. "The staff director doesn't like face-to-face interaction," confided one of the ruling attorneys during a rare *tête-à-tête* with me in late September.

———

Whenever the commission could find a former high-ranking member of the National Security Council to visit with us, we jumped at the chance. On September 19, 1995, right after the retreat, on the schedule for the NEOB conference room was former secretary of defense Melvin Laird. He had been a kingpin on the Armed Services Committee in the House of Representatives for years. As we waited for Secretary Laird to arrive, the staff talked informally about the retreat in Leesburg.

"Brown's memory is amazing," Snider observed.

"Incredible," agreed one of our staff experts on military intelligence, Dick Giza. "He probably remembers the first movie he went to, the row he sat in, and the candies he ate."

One of the things I had noticed about Brown was his wide-ranging knowledge. Aspin was brilliant on many topics, especially related to arms control, weapons systems, and strategic doctrine; but Brown could discuss, impressively, most *everything* that came before the commission.

Laird entered the room as this conversation was going on, and he observed that "Brown is the most brilliant of the SecDefs." Bald except for a fringe of hair at the back of his head, and with pouches beneath his eyes and a furrowed brow, Laird smiled cheerfully at the staff and the few commissioners in attendance. Pursley was close to the former SecDef and made the formal introduction. Removing his suit coat to reveal glittering cuff links and a blue dress shirt, Laird began his remarks by reflecting back on his days in the House of Representatives during the 1970s. The Defense Department appropriations bill was tightly held at that time, he recalled, with only five lawmakers meeting in the Speaker's office to hammer out the annual spending for the Pentagon and the intelligence services. These House members had four counterparts in the Senate. No one in either chamber knew who made up these elite groups; they were kept completely insulated from the rest of the Congress.

When he turned to the subject of intelligence, Laird immediately expressed opposition to the idea of a director for military intelligence—Gen. James Clapper's prized concept. "The secretary ought to handle these coordination responsibilities himself," he declared. He also dismissed the notion that the United States needed a large fleet of surveillance satellites. "We should rely on allies for much of this," he said, "—even the Russians." This position would surely have drawn scowls from Allen, Caracristi, and Hermann, but they were absent, as was Dewhurst, who would have balked at the idea of cozying up to Moscow. Laird praised NSA's sigint contributions during the time he was SecDef and took the opportunity to slam former DCI Richard Helms for being condescending to President Nixon—or so, evidently, the president had often complained to Laird.

———

Near the end of September, the commission had its first—and only—problem with internal leaks. Somebody had revealed to a DIA officer details of our discussions at the Leesburg retreat. This became distorted and grew into a rumor that we had in mind drastically cutting the budget of the DIA, or maybe even abolishing the Agency altogether (a favorite proposal advanced by a number of previous intelligence commissions and committees). This was not true for the Aspin-Brown panel as a whole, however much it may have been an appealing idea to a few individual commissioners and staff members who found the work of the DIA redundant to a fault, given the intelligence units in each of the four military services. Generals in the Pentagon contacted the commission about the rumor, and Chairman Brown knew we had a leak.

Moreover, a few newspaper stories surfaced after the Leesburg retreat that directly quoted a commissioner's views on the subject of economic intelligence. All of this created a flurry of additional rumors within our own NEOB office suite: Chairman Brown was going to order FBI interrogations and CIA polygraph tests for all staff, with the objective of finding out who the leaker was. Heads would roll.

In fact, Brown was much more sensible than that. In a dispassionate memo that displayed experience and wisdom, he wrote to the staff and the commissioners:

> It has come to my attention over the last few days that information discussed at the retreat has been shared both with the press and with people in the Intelligence Community....
>
> Needless to say, this does not help our process. We now have a commissioner being harassed by the press. DIA appears to be more defensive towards us than heretofore. It is only a matter of time before efforts begin to lobby individual commissioners and staff, and we see news stories appear in the local press.
>
> Apart from distracting us and skewing our process, there is also a price to be paid in terms of our subsequent deliberations and our communications with each other. If we cannot rely on everyone involved to protect the confidentiality of the Commission's process, communications between us are unavoidably going to suffer.
>
> I know that each and every one of you wants this effort to succeed. I know that none of you wants to complicate our lives.
>
> I suspect that whoever leaked this information did so without realizing the repercussions for our process.
>
> I do not plan to do anything more about this. I simply reiterate the need for everyone involved to keep the Commission's deliberations to themselves.

We never found out who on the commission had spoken to someone in the DIA; but a staffer did admit to a telephone conversation with a reporter about economic intelligence, in which he had inappropriately mentioned a few comments made by a commissioner at the retreat. The staffer was embarrassed and contrite; it was clear he had learned a lesson. The commission moved on, with no more leaks. The staffer was also lucky; on some commissions he would have been summarily dismissed.

———

The reports of financial irregularities at the National Reconnaissance Office grew into a media spectacle in late September of 1995. The NRO had secretly accumulated over $1.5 billion in public monies without keeping Congress informed about these unspent funds. The agency then asked the legislature to appropriate more satellite monies, again without admitting that it already had enough stowed away from past appropriations to cover the costs of new satellites. John Deutch said publicly that the NRO had "ignored a directive from Congress" issued several years ago to reduce the amounts it was carrying over from year to year.[9] On top of these charges, news surfaced in January of 1996 that the agency had managed to misplace more than $2 billion in classified funds the previous year, a result of its chaotic accounting system and poor management.[10] The lost appropriations were found when Deutch ordered an outside audit.

Defenders of the NRO pointed out that, given the unpredictability of when a U.S. satellite in orbit might wear out and fall from the skies, the agency had to have money in reserve—what it called "forward funding" or a "carry-forward account"—so it could quickly launch a new replacement satellite. Otherwise, the United States might become blind with respect to certain important parts of the globe. While it was true that the life span of a satellite was somewhat unpredictable, this did not relieve NRO managers of a responsibility to explain carefully their special funding needs to lawmakers and to keep them well informed of the agency's current reserves. That was a key aspect of meaningful oversight: keeping lawmakers informed.

This was not the first time the NRO had gotten itself into trouble. In 1994, members of Congress were astonished to learn that the agency had constructed a new upscale headquarters building near Dulles International Airport in northern Virginia. The $347 million spent on the facility had been hidden in other budget lines.[11] The agency admitted what it referred to blandly as "its accounting negligence."[12] Further, the NRO had a signed a multibillion dollar contract for ocean surveillance satellites, despite explicit instructions not to do so from the House Appropriations Committee.[13] An unhappy HPSCI chairman, Larry Combest, said, "[The National Reconnaissance Office] has a credibility problem here." He added: "One of the real complaints I have [is that] they have had a history of evading questions. They do not answer a question fully."[14] A Pentagon official offered this judgment about the NRO: "They've been living the good life."[15] And some people on the Aspin-Brown Commission considered intelligence oversight a matter of secondary importance! In response to complaints from SSCI and HPSCI about the NRO's budget legerdemain, Deutch ordered a management shake-up at the spy satellite organization and dismissed its top leadership.[16]

Throughout the autumn of 1995, DCI Deutch conducted his own form of intelligence oversight at the CIA, in his usual brash manner. As September came to an end, he dropped a bureaucratic bombshell at Langley and he would never fully recover from the resulting shockwaves. The cause was the Alpirez case—the failure of officials in the Latin American division of the Operations

Directorate to inform lawmakers about the misdeeds of its military asset in Guatemala, Col. Julio Roberto Alpirez. The colonel, recall, was accused of complicity in the murder of an American citizen and the husband of another American citizen. The question was whether or not Agency officers complied with the Intelligence Oversight Act of 1980, which required the intelligence agencies to keep SSCI and HSPCI "fully and currently informed...of any significant intelligence activity and any significant intelligence failure."

The results of the CIA's inquiry into this matter were in, and the DCI was ready to issue his disciplinary sentencing on September 27, 1995. The former chief of station in Guatemala at the time, as well as another DO officer, were fired outright; a third officer was demoted; and twenty-three additional Agency officers received from Deutch either formal letters of reprimand or, if they had already retired from the CIA, less formal letters chastising their behavior in the Alpirez case.[17] One of the letter receivers was a recently retired DO officer on the staff of the Aspin-Brown Commission staff, a twenty-seven-year Agency veteran.

Tony Harrington had been investigating this case, too, as chairman of the Intelligence Oversight Board.[18] Gen. Lew Allen and Ann Caracristi were on the IOB with him, along with Harold W. Pote, an investment banker named to PFIAB by President Clinton. In a public statement, the IOB announced in concurrence with the DCI's findings that "as a result of management inattention, congressional notification [regarding the Alpirez human rights abuses] was delayed for over three years with regard to one key report [about the events in Guatemala]."[19]

The punishments meted out by Deutch were, according to a newspaper report, "the most severe discipline imposed at the CIA in recent years."[20] Agency insiders were quoted as saying that the incumbent DCI "was not going to make the same mistake as Woolsey."[21] Deutch's predecessor had been criticized for being too lenient on the eleven CIA officers who had been accused of maintaining insufficient security in the DO during Aldrich Ames's ten years of treason. Not a single DO officer had been demoted or fired by Woolsey—which SSCI had blasted as "seriously inadequate."[22]

At 8:00 o'clock on Friday morning, September 29, Deutch entered "the Bubble" at the CIA to address a large crowd of employees about his actions. Contrary to long-standing Agency tradition, the audience remained seated when the DCI entered the auditorium. Deutch's greetings were met with an icy silence. Early in his remarks, he said: "I want people to know that when they take risks required to perform their job within understood rules, I will back them fully." At these words, anger erupted from the crowd, which consisted chiefly of officers from the Directorate of Operations. Several laughed derisively at the DCI's claim that he would support them; others in the audience responded with shouts of dismay at his punishments in the Alpirez case. At the end of the short meeting, CIA officers booed the intelligence chief—a spectacle never witnessed before, back to the days in 1959 when Agency officers first began to assemble in the Bubble, or since.[23]

Deutch's detractors that morning resented what they saw as an unfair application of new standards to old and formerly acceptable modes of behavior, namely, recruiting useful agents abroad no matter what kind of personal lives they might lead. The highest ranking officer reprimanded by the DCI, Richard J. Kerr, the former deputy director of the CIA from 1989 to 1991, who was on duty when the misdeeds took place, objected publicly to the "Star Chamber" proceedings and the "revisionist history" employed by Deutch and his aides.[24] Kerr claimed to have been unsure at the time whether the Alpirez case rose to the threshold of requiring a report to lawmakers—as if the telephone with lines to Capitol Hill had been severed to prevent him from checking on that point, or that the CIA lacked a team of legislative liaison officers who could have found out the answer readily enough.[25]

Another officer brushed aside the Deutch punishments as political, a fresh attempt by the DCI and Democrats in Congress—whose resentment over the Iran-*contra* scandal continued to smolder, according to this argument—to do away with the Operations Directorate. One Agency official said on the day of the announced disciplinary action that "those who have been punished are scapegoats....Deutch must make amends with Congress, because he has another job in mind"[26]—a thinly veiled reference to the rumors of the DCI's ambitions to become secretary of defense. Another top DO official and former head of the CIA's Counterterrorism Center, Duane "Dewey" Clarridge, would later write: "Deutch instead of sorting out the Clandestine Services [the DO] and then supporting it, simply drove a knife into its back."[27] The individuals Deutch had fired or reprimanded were now victims and martyrs, at least in the eyes of fellow DO officers. The Operations Directorate rallied beneath the banners of mutual protection and professional loyalty.

As a reporter on the intelligence beat noted at the time, "Like a host rejecting an invading virus, [the DO] has foiled repeated reform attempts by a long string of directors."[28] To use a different simile, previous intelligence directors had learned that criticizing the DO was like poking a finger into a hornet's nest. Now it was Deutch's turn.

———

On my way to a staff meeting on September 26, I bumped into Admiral Blair, the DCI's liaison contact with the commission, as he was coming out of our suite of offices. He exuded a warmth I had not seen before. "Personnel issues will be the toughest for the commissioners to deal with," he said, "and where the commission can help the most." He headed for the elevators on the way out of the NEOB, and I continued on to the conference room. The staff was assembling, and an informal discussion was already under way about how to organize our public hearings. We were about to raise sails and turn toward the open sea.

Les Aspin had been critical of Hillary Clinton's pursuit of healthcare reform behind closed doors, with the debate hidden from the public; he had favored at least some sort of open presentation by the commission. In that spirit, we intended to sponsor an open forum on intelligence reform. The questions went round the NEOB conference room as the staff discussed the approaching hearings: How many sessions would we have? What would be their purpose? Would they be carefully choreographed to make a few central points, or should they be freewheeling? Should commissioners disclose their own views, or should they just listen to more witnesses? It was decided that November would be the best time to hold the hearings, if Chairman Brown could make it back from his foreign travels sometime during that month. At the end of the meeting, the staff reviewed the NRO's plight and speculated as well about the rumor of a government shutdown spurred by the Clinton-Gingrich confrontation that might affect our own progress.

The next morning an e-mail about the hearings showed up on the screens of the staff member's computers, sent by the staff director. Brown would be unable to return to Washington any time during November, the message read, and Rudman had scheduling conflicts during that month. The commission leaders wanted the hearings rescheduled for January. Moreover, the hearings would be just one day, rather than two or three.

As he reviewed our original statutory mandate, the staff director remembered that of the nineteen issues formally assigned to us for investigation, the very last one dealt with the United Nations. "My perception is, this is not a big problem area," Snider said in a follow up e-mail to a few staffers, "although it has been a touchy one politically, which is why it is on the list of 19." The topic was sensitive for a couple of reasons. First, some lawmakers—including the chairman of the Senate Foreign Relations Committee, the arch-conservative Jesse Helms (R-NC), seemed to despise the UN. He wanted to stop paying America's dues to the organization, as a precursor to complete withdrawal. Second, since Communists nations and other adversaries of the United States were members of the UN, the idea of sharing intelligence with that international organization to make it more knowledgeable about world events made no sense whatsoever to some lawmakers, particularly Helms. They wanted the commission to make sure the Clinton administration wasn't giving away important secrets to the UN's secretary general.

Snider asked staffer Linda England to have a look at this subject, if only to be able to say we had not overlooked one of our formal assignments. Since my good friend and occasional co-author Ambassador Karl F. Inderfurth was part of our UN delegation in New York, she in turn recruited me to help out. Even though I was no longer writing papers for Les Aspin, my plate was full with this and many other projects for the commission. On her behalf, I flew to New York City and interviewed various people at the UN, including our top ambassador (and later secretary of state) Madeleine K. Albright. Based on these talks, my impression was that the intelligence community had been very careful in sharing information with the UN, and that the relationship had been mutually beneficial. A flap over lost U.S. intelligence documents in Somalia in 1993 had led to a tightening of UN procedures for handling classified materials on loan from member nations. I was disturbed to find out later, however, that U.S. intelligence officers had been embedded into the framework of the United Nations soon after America's first invasion of Iraq in 1990. The purpose of this intelligence operation was to help UN officials determine if the Saddam Hussein regime had WMDs. While this objective appeared reasonable enough to some, the use of the UN as cover for U.S. intelligence operations was controversial to others. What did this do to the integrity of the United Nations?[29] When Saddam discovered this U.S. intelligence operation, he forced the entire UN inspection team out of Iraq, leaving the West blind about his WMD activities.

I was sure of one thing: the commissioners were not going to enter this political minefield. They would follow Warner's advice and steer clear of details about U.S. intelligence support for the United Nations.

———

On September 28, Brown, Rudman, and a few staff aides visited the Congress to bring lawmakers up to date on the commission's progress, and to solicit their opinions about subjects for our final report. The first destination was the House Permanent Select Committee on Intelligence for a chat with its chairman, Larry Combest. Goss and Dicks, HPSCI members as well as members of the commission, volunteered to attend, too.

The commission delegation arrived at 11:00 and spent forty minutes in a cordial discussion with the HPSCI chairman about our work and his own IC21 project. Combest repeated an idea that he had shared with Brown, Rudman, and Harrington back in June: there was a possible benefit in proposing "radical" intelligence reform for the shock effect, then pulling back to a more reasonable position. Brown said it was possible he was right; but, happiest with anchor to windward, the commission chairman indicated that he would leave the radical overtures to HPSCI. Combest said that he personally wouldn't mind taking some bold positions in favor of reform, if that would achieve some meaningful intelligence improvements.

Brown informed the HPSCI chairman that the commission would make significant recommendations in four or five main areas, including the DCI's authority, law enforcement, satellite architecture, personnel, and military intelligence. In addition, the commission would "comment" on a few other matters, such as economic intelligence and covert action. Brown was beginning to form our final report in his head, and our staff leaders took careful notes about his expressed interests.

Brown mentioned to Combest, with a nod to Goss, that matters of intelligence oversight had been raised at the commission's retreat in Leesburg. In the hallways at the Xerox Center, Goss had expressed an interest to Brown in establishing a joint oversight committee to replace SSCI and HPSCI, but Goss didn't restate this preference now. Brown, however, brought it up anyway. "That's a bad idea," Combest responded immediately. "Hell, we can't even get those senators to a conference committee meeting!" Goss remained quiet; junior members of congressional committees normally do their best to avoid arguments with their chairman.

Combest did believe, however, that the commission should look at some oversight issues, such as whether the eight- and six-year ceilings (respectively) on SSCI and HSPCI membership should be removed, since it prevented the accumulation of experience and expertise among committee members. As a former HPSCI Chair has recalled, "I was on the intelligence committee at least two years, and maybe three, before I understood the terminology."[30] Most observers had become critics of the fixed terms of tenure on the two oversight panels, even though in the 1970s the ceilings had made sense. At the time, lawmakers feared that future overseers might become too close to the intelligence agencies they were supposed to be supervising if they stayed on the intelligence committees too long. Lost, though, was the kind of accumulated experience that lawmakers need to perform well as overseers, and thus the pressure to remove the ceilings had mounted. "About the time the members become effective on the committees—they've learned enough to become effective—they're gone," former DCI Robert Gates had noted. "The result is that you're always starting over with people who don't know anything about the business, and you waste a lot of time bringing them up to speed."[31]

Worth examining, too, Combest said, were jurisdictional controversies on the Hill. As things stood in 1995 (and even today), the Judiciary Committees, the Armed Services Committees, and the Appropriations Committees shared intelligence jurisdiction with SSCI and HPSCI, which created a confusing state of oversight responsibilities. Cautiously, Brown mentioned that the commission might look at these issues "but leave the solutions to Congress." Combest, Dicks, and Goss nodded their heads in approval.

Representative Dicks brought up the subject of personnel reductions in the intelligence community. He said that "smaller might be better"—especially in the Directorate of Operations. Combest kept his cards close to his vest about his committee's likely recommendations, but it was clear that he was interested in breaking down (as he put it) "the tyranny of the stovepipes"—especially by integrating the major collection agencies (NSA, CIO, NRO) into one vast Technical Collection Agency, or TCA, similar to Bob Hermann's proposal at our Leesburg retreat. According to an HPSCI staff aide, this was the "most striking area of disagreement" between Combest and the Aspin-Brown Commission, since we—aside from Hermann and perhaps Wolfowitz—were not prepared to embrace such a dramatic amalgamation of sigint and imint.[32]

Combest's staff director, Mark M. Lowenthal, had mentioned when Brown and Rudman first arrived at the HPSCI offices that the Combest Committee would not release its IC21 findings until April 1996—a month after we planned to publish our report. That was welcome news; we were already being overshadowed by Deutch's fast-moving reforms and by various outside study groups like the Council on Foreign Relations.

Brown and Rudman returned to Capitol Hill later that afternoon at 5:00 for another meeting, this time with SSCI chairman Arlen Specter. Brown reiterated for Specter's benefit the list of topics on which our panel would make "significant recommendations"—the same lineup he had presented to Combest. The commission chairman paused, then said, half-joking: "By significant, I refer to the number of persons who will be upset." Brown added: "The more outcry, the more significant the recommendation." He might well have used a phrase popular in the Pentagon at the time: some rice bowls were going to be broken.

On the walk to Specter's office in the Hart Senate Office Building, Rudman said to Brown that the idea of a joint oversight committee was a "non-starter." Most lawmakers liked the oversight setup as it was, with a separate SSCI and HPSCI. So Brown did not mention that proposal as he and Rudman visited with Specter, but the commission chairman did say that his panel would have a look at some oversight issues. "I would welcome the commission's views on the subject," was Specter's noncommittal response. The SSCI leader observed that his committee was already loaded up with things to do—the Alpirez case and the NRO scandal being two examples. He implied that he wasn't looking for additional work and would rely on the commission to blaze any new reform trails.

Specter expressed his disappointment with Deutch's tenure as DCI so far. "He has not taken hold of the Agency," lamented the SSCI chairman. He spoke vaguely for a while about how his committee was looking into ways to enhance the DCI's authority over the intelligence community. Following this soliloquy, Brown and Rudman shook hands cordially with Specter and went to the office of Senator Daniel Patrick Moynihan, who was heading up a special commission of his own on government secrecy.[33]

Enjoying a chance to rib his old colleague, Rudman began the twenty-minute visit with Moynihan by telling him that the Aspin-Brown Commission would "recommend moving the State Department to the CIA." Moynihan, who had made just the opposite recommendation the previous year, was as feisty as ever and replied: "I don't care, just as long as you get rid of one or the other!" He had backed away from abolishing the CIA, but the New York senator did have in mind a spate of intelligence reform proposals. Above all, he criticized CIA analysts for their inability to "think beyond traditional ideas." Claiming that he had predicted the crumbling of the Soviet empire long ago, he said the CIA lacked the imagination to envision that possibility. Rudman asked him what major issues the commission should be looking into. In response, Moynihan lambasted the Agency for "too much bureaucratic layering" in its preparation of intelligence reports. He recommended that the commission try to reduce the time and the distance that it took draft reports to travel from the front line junior analysts up to the CIA's senior managers.

———

On October 12, the staff and five commissioners—Hermann, Allen, Caracristi (the NSA trio), Pursley, and the ubiquitous Steve Friedman—gathered in the conference room for a briefing on military intelligence. Although Friedman didn't fall into that categories, the presence of the others indicated that the techies were out in force. Brown was expected to attend but had to cancel at the last minute, and he asked the voluble Hermann to chair the session. Across the table from the commissioners sat three generals and an admiral, the day's witnesses.

During the military briefing, Rear Adm. Michael W. Cramer, the director of naval intelligence, stressed that "technology has saved us [in the armed services]. We can do more with fewer people. Moreover, we are working better as a team, thanks to the Goldwater-Nichols reforms that forced us down this line and heightened our awareness of jointness." It was great to hear some good news for a change. The conference room soon filled with Pentagon jargon: "According to the algorithm..." "By orders of magnitude..." "The tooth-to-tail ratio..." plus a deluge of acronyms, as if the conference room had become a giant bowl of alphabet soup: JROC, TIARA, C4I, PDD, SOCOM, RMA, JMIP, JSTARS. Which was worse—RAND or the DoD—when it came to the use of esoteric phrases and abbreviations was hard to say. As the session came to an end, one of the generals shook his head in dismay and groused: "This DCI has injected himself into military matters never gone into before by an intelligence director."

As Friedman had requested at the Leesburg retreat, we reconvened that afternoon for a discussion among commissioners on the subject of humint—the intelligence community's human spies ("informants," as the FBI preferred to call them). The former case officer David Dewhurst showed up for this part of the meeting, joining the group of commissioners who had been there that morning. Brown and Harrington arrived a half hour later. The consensus among the commissioners was that the United States needed a much more robust humint capability around the world. Here was one reform on which everyone seemed to agree. Certainly the development of global spy rings was a relatively inexpensive proposition—"the cost of one whistle on a satellite," a commission staffer liked to say. It took time to build agent networks, however, especially in regions of the world ignored by the United States during the Cold War years—five to ten years, in the view of most experts.

Chairman Brown said that he opposed the idea of folding the DIA's Humint Service into the CIA's Operations Directorate. "That would make the DIA's assets too civilian from the CINC point of view," he explained, using the Pentagon acronym for "commanders in chief"—the top U.S. military commanders in various parts of the globe. Yet in the *Washington Post*, a senior congressional aide had rightfully asked just a few weeks after our retreat: "Do we need two clandestine human intelligence services?"[34]

———

On Friday, the 13th of October, we gathered again in the NEOB so the commissioners could further review a range of reform proposals. Brown called the morning segment of the meeting to order at 9:00 o'clock sharp. The panel's attendance had increased to eight members. The seven AWOL commissioners included Exon and Warner, of course, plus Baird (her physician did not want her spending so much time away from her new baby), Dicks, Goss, Hermann (in a rare absence), and Wolfowitz.

First, the chairman reported on his recent trip with Rudman to Capitol Hill. "The Senate committee [SSCI] is not as far along as HPSCI," Brown

324 | THREAT ON THE HORIZON

said, his cufflinks sparkling under the room's neon lights, "and it would like us to lead, whereas it is unclear what the House wants." I knew an aide on the HPSCI staff who had confided to me the previous day that no serious discussion about intelligence reform was taking place among the House committee members at all, even if Combest and Lowenthal were striding vigorously down the pathway of reform. He added that there was virtually no collegiality on the panel. He thought HPSCI lawmakers were more interested in political posturing than hard thinking about the future of U.S. intelligence. They couldn't have been much more disengaged than our senators, Exon and Warner, I thought to myself at the time. At least HPSCI had Mark Lowenthal as staff director; I had no doubt he would try hard to draw the committee's members into the reform debate.

The staff reviewed the topics that had come to the forefront at the Leesburg retreat. With commissioners leaving the conference room for telephone calls periodically, a staffer presented an overview of the intelligence budget options, noting at one point that funding for espionage activities "has gone up 80 percent since 1980."

"How much to spend depends on how much you want to know," Rudman observed. "How much insurance do you want?"

Brown nodded vigorously. He and the vice chairman had developed a close working relationship over the past few months, and jocularity between them was a regular feature of commission meetings. Both seemed to be enjoying themselves, and indeed Rudman revealed in an op-ed in December of 1995 looking back on his career in the Senate: "I left in 1992. I am 65 years old. I felt 75 in the Senate. I feel 35 now."[35]

Covert action, counterintelligence, and open-source intelligence could be "held harmless" in any budget reductions the commission might propose, the staffer suggested, as he listed some of the spending options. Regardless of how one felt about the intelligence budget, it was becoming increasingly clear that the tide was turning against the idea of reaping a peace dividend from the intelligence purse. In an interview for a CIA employee newsletter, Chairman Combest noted that the House had voted to *increase* the intelligence budget.[36] Indeed, the vote was in favor of a 5 percent rise in the spy budget for fiscal year 1996, pushing the total funding for the community close to $30 billion for the coming year.[37] Moreover, Speaker Gingrich was reportedly attempting to provide the CIA with an amount of anywhere from $18 million to $36 million (newspaper accounts differed) for a single covert action against Iran that he supported.[38] The operation had been conceived by the Speaker himself, probably a first in U.S. history.[39] Those commissioners who wanted to cut funding for intelligence—most notably Fowler and Coelho, whom Brown seemed to view more and more as Jacobins who had somehow infiltrated the commission—would be swimming against the tide.

In his CIA newsletter interview, Combest observed further that "while there are many bright people on the Brown Commission, they don't have intelligence backgrounds." So much for Allen, Caracristi, and Hermann, not to mention the former and incumbent lawmakers who had served for years on SSCI or HPSCI, or Brown, Pursley, and Wolfowitz's long exposure to intelligence as consumers, or the service of Dewhurst and Goss in the CIA early in their careers.

At the end of the presentation on budget options, Brown asked General Allen to take another close look into the details of the spending issue. For several months, Allen had already been in charge of an informal commission task force that was reviewing the spy budget; now the chairman was formalizing this review with the creation of a special budget subcommittee, headed by Allen and composed also of Friedman, Hermann, and Coelho. Fowler, who had complained the most at the retreat about the need for spending cuts, was left off the roster; Brown understood the powers of a chairmanship.

Porter Goss arrived in time for the next briefing, on organizational reform; so the total was now up to eleven members present. Key options included creating an NSC Committee on Foreign Intelligence to give greater prominence to intelligence at the highest levels of government, and elevating the stature of PFIAB as a presidential advisory body. The staff also laid out the argument for creating several new positions in the intelligence community, each designed to help the DCI achieve better coordination among the dispersed agencies. Ideas for institutional consolidation soon filled the room. One staff model envisioned gathering the fragmented "ints" together into discrete agencies, according to function—the idea Aspin and I had tossed around the previous winter: one agency for imint (the Central Imaging Office expanded into a larger National Imagery Agency), another for sigint (an augmented NSA), and yet another for the humint elements in the community (the DO and the Defense Humint Service combined). Aspin and I had concluded that this seemed like merely rearranging the stovepipes.

The proposals for moving boxes around on the community's organizational chart were becoming highly convoluted, and the commission meeting soon began to sound like a graduate seminar on organization theory. We had been hanging out with RAND consultants too long. "This is confusing," Hermann finally said. "I want to be able to explain imint reform in a two-floor elevator ride." Brown told the staff to work some more on the proposals.

On the law enforcement and intelligence front, Steve Friedman presented Baird's proposal in her absence. "I'm sorry I'm not able to attend the meeting this month," she had written to her colleagues in early October. "My doctor hasn't shared my enthusiasm for jumping right back in after Alec's birth." In the memo, she said further that "law enforcement, intelligence and our other assets would each be more effective if coordinated at a high level under the National Security Council."[40] She had in mind the creation of an NSC Executive Committee to coordinate the CIA and the FBI when it came to national security threats, as well as serving as a venue where their disputes over defector bona fides could be arbitrated. In Baird's scheme, the committee would be headed by the vice president, or perhaps by co-chairs comprised of departmental deputies (State, DoD, Treasury), assisted at the staff level by a "transnational issues coordinator."

Baird expressed some reservations about the ambiguity of the term "transnational" in her proposal. Later in the month, rumors would drift back to the commission staff that Senator Warner didn't like the term "transnational" either; it sounded too much like "Trilateral," as in the Trilateral Commission— a New York City–based study group that some viewed as a liberal conspiracy to control the United States, if not the world. These two commissioners may have been unhappy with the term; but, for better or for worse, it was already firmly entrenched in the vocabularies of national security officials and academic scholars of international affairs.

Brown questioned the notion of a transnational issues coordinator at a deeper level, saying that we would just be creating another job for "some defeated senatorial candidate, and we have enough of them already." It seemed a jibe at Wyche Fowler's expense. The former senator smiled, but his face turned slightly red, and I knew him well enough to know the remark stung.

The chairman did have a point, however, about establishing new entities for intelligence within the framework of the NSC. That high forum already had a group dealing with intelligence issues, recently led by the former SSCI staff director George J. Tenet, who had become number two at the CIA under Deutch.[41] The NSC intelligence staff group consisted of three individuals, including a senior director for intelligence. Its purpose was, and remains, to ensure that the policy priorities of an administration were reflected in the operations of the intelligence community—essentially a liaison function, coupled with management and oversight duties. It also carried out the president's annual review of the nation's ongoing covert actions.

The senior director for intelligence on the NSC works for the national security advisor, making sure that intelligence operations are properly vetted, and that the risks and policy considerations are fully considered. As Tenet told me in 1994, the office provides a two-way street: "The DCI may come in with a list of operational or collection issues, and the national security advisor may raise his own agenda items. It's a very, very important forum for constant contact [between the intelligence community and the policy making principals in the government]." Moreover, the intelligence community, Tenet emphasized, "is a full participant in all of the interagency working groups on the National Security Council."[42] So it was not as though the NSC was not in contact with the intelligence community, or vice versa. I thought this existing group, perhaps with an added staffer or two, could have handled the issues that Baird had in mind; but the temptation to create new boxes on the organizational charts is always strong.

In the afternoon, the commission took up personnel matters. Some members of the staff had traveled to Canada and they returned impressed by how its intelligence service had handled a problem similar to the one faced by the NSA and some of the other American intelligence agencies: a workforce that had grown too large The Canadian Parliament had given that nation's intelligence chief in Ottawa a one-time opportunity to reduce the size of the secret service significantly by offering reasonable incentives for retirement. Our staff was taken by the idea; and, more importantly, so was Harold Brown, which meant it had a good chance of being incorporated into our recommendations. Specifically, the proposal involved giving, as the staff director summed it up in a memo, "the DCI and the Secretary of Defense a one-time, one-year special authority to terminate and reallocate positions in the interests of operational efficiency and the well-being of the Community." The Canadian approach contained a clever "exchange" provision. An employee whose position was marked for termination could stay on, if he or she exchanged places with another individual in a position not scheduled for termination who wanted to retire. The whole subject was about as exciting as cream of wheat for breakfast on a hot summer morning; but it was important, nonetheless, in light of the excessive size of some U.S. intelligence agencies—especially the NSA.

Next on the agenda was the question of whether to release the annual aggregate budget figure, a topic that had temporarily paralyzed the commission during the Leesburg retreat. Brown at last took a semi-bold stance, arguing for a one-time release of the figure (for the year 1996), as well as the percentage of the budget that went to the CIA (about 8–10 percent of the total, or $3 billion[43]). That CIA percentage was so small—most of the aggregate budget went to military intelligence agencies, especially NRO, CIO, and NSA—that it would signal to the American public that the Agency was not the giant monster often portrayed in the newspapers. Some thought this whole matter was one big yawn. As Goss put it, "My heart does not beat very fast on this issue."

"This horse has already left the barn," Rudman said, noting that the media and others believed the figure was going to be released as a minimal indication that the commission had at least done something. "The commission's credibility is at stake on this one," he continued. "Besides, it would teach the public that the CIA is not a huge organization."

By prior agreement between Goss and Brown, oversight was on the agenda, too. Goss's concerns about this subject, expressed at the Xerox Center retreat, had taken on added weight because of the budget scandal at the National Reconnaissance Office. The NRO's shell games with its congressional appropriations were being reported in newspapers throughout early October, just as we were winnowing down our long list of topics for inclusion into the final report. Once again, Goss brought up the possibility of a single joint committee for intelligence oversight, in place of one in the Senate (SSCI) and another in the House (HSPCI). This would make it easier for a DCI and other officials to report to Congress, he maintained, and one committee would be more secure from leaks than two.

"That's not even worth talking about," Rudman replied, pointing out that most lawmakers did not want to have only one committee on intelligence. The Senate and the House liked to have their own separate review panels. As usual, a Brown or Rudman criticism of a proposal was equivalent to sticking a pin into a balloon. Goss retreated to a follow-up recommendation that would allow SSCI and HPSCI members a ten-year term on those committees (rather than eight or six, respectively), and that would give committee chairs a six-year run at the helm (rather than four). This became known as Goss's "ten and six" proposal. It was only a modest step toward ensuring greater experience on the congressional intelligence panels, and it drew no opposition. Fowler and Goss further proposed strong language in the report that would emphasize the importance of vigilant intelligence oversight in Congress. The expression on Brown's face suggested that whatever he had for lunch did not agree with him. He gave Fowler a withering glance.

Evening was approaching and commissioners were beginning to drift out of the conference room. "We haven't focused enough on counterintelligence," Friedman said in frustration as the number of attendees dwindled.

"Yeah, and we need more work on personnel and on budgeting," Rudman added. We no longer had a quorum, however, and the chairman postponed further discussion until our next meeting. Given that Brown would be overseas in November, that might not be until December. As the chairman was leaving the room, he remarked to Rudman: "Personnel and budget will be the two most important areas for review by the commission."

Outside the NEOB, a storm had darkened the streets, and a cold, wet wind blew off the Potomac. Cars heading home formed rivers of red, their rain-jeweled taillights flowing through the concrete, steel, and glass canyons of the city. I turned up my coat collar against the wind, opened an umbrella, and made my way down Pennsylvania Avenue toward Georgetown in search of solace and a Scotch at the Bistro Français.

Preparing for a "Markup"

The rest of October, as well as November and December, passed by in a blur of heavy snowfalls outside the NEOB and a flurry of white paper inside, with drafts of final report language circulating endlessly from office to office. Review and revise, review and revise—this was our routine, interrupted only briefly by Thanksgiving and December holiday celebrations, along with a mandated government furlough that lasted one week in November as the president and Speaker Gingrich fought over the budget.

The staff director notified us by memo in mid-October that he did not want to share any of the drafts of the final report with commissioners "until we have a version we are satisfied with at the staff level." The plan was to let Brown and Rudman read our work first for a "sanity check," as the staff director put it; then the drafts would pass on to those commissioners most interested in a particular subject, such as Hermann and Caracristi on space surveillance or Baird on law enforcement and intelligence. Finally, after incorporating their suggestions, the draft of the final report would move on to the rest of the commissioners.

Not until early in the new year would Brown and Rudman receive a draft of the full report that the staff considered in solid shape. With a green light from them, we would distribute the document (incorporating their changes and amendments) to the rest of the commissioners in time for them to read it prior to a decisive January 18th commission meeting.

At that meeting, we would begin hammering out precisely what final language and recommendations the members desired. Here was where things were really going to take form. The procedure would be similar to what was known on Capitol Hill as a markup, in which the specifics of legislation are determined by a few people with strong ideas of their own sitting around a table, along with instructions from their staff, lobbyists, constituents, and fellow lawmakers. Now we would get down to the nitty gritty, selecting the few topics that would actually make it into our report to the public. I wondered if oversight would survive the commission's markup sessions, and what budget figures the commissioners would recommend.

In addition to drafting the final report, the staff was preparing for the commission's public hearing, now scheduled for January 19th. The witnesses had to be selected and invited; the hearing room on Capitol Hill scheduled and the appropriate security measures taken (hearings on the CIA often attracted nutcases in Washington), and Brown and Rudman would need opening statements and a script for introducing the witnesses. Further, we would be expected to have briefing materials available for the commissioners, as well as suggested questions they could pose during the session along with those they came up with themselves. We had decided to call back Bobby Ray Inman and Joe Nye, along with some new witnesses: Frank Carlucci, a former SecDef and, at one time, the second in command at the CIA; James R. Lilley, a former ambassador to China (a consumer of intelligence); William P. Barr, general counsel of the GTE Corporation (to address economic intelligence); and Dr. Richard N. Haass, the director of national security programs at the Council on Foreign Relations.

I was busy, too, providing Wyche Fowler, my Georgia compatriot, a little extra assistance in preparation for the commission's markup of the final report. Given his interest in covert action, in early December I sketched out for him some language he might try to include in the report. I recommended that the wording should make it clear that this secret approach to foreign policy ought to be used only as a last resort, and with some clear moral constraints. These thoughts were among the suggestions I sent to him:

> We should recommend that the United States resort to covert action only in the most discriminating manner, because this approach in the past has often discredited the nation's good name. Whenever feasible, the United States should rely on a diplomatic resolution to international disputes, rather than cover action.... Covert action, moreover, should never involve operations that, if exposed, would unduly embarrass the United States, and they should not be directed against fellow democracies.... In almost all cases, the United States should reject secret wars, *coups d'état*, and other extreme uses of covert action.[44]

I hoped that Wyche Fowler could encourage the commission to adopt a code of ethics for covert action in its report, along the lines DCI Webster had discussed with me. It was important for the United States—the good guys—to define clearly what the nation stood for in the conduct of its foreign policy, whether the initiatives were open or secret. The failure of Congress or the president to articulate clearly what covert action operations were permissible had been unfair to operatives in the CIA's Operations Directorate and, when overzealous schemes were allowed to go forward, they had stained the nation's reputation abroad.

———

Even though Chairman Brown was out of town in November, the commission gathered in our conference room on the 9th for a business meeting led by Warren Rudman. "I've never seen a more opportune time for a commission to have an impact," observed Senator John Warner, in a rare appearance, as the session began. "The mood in Congress is that something has to be done. This is an important moment. Our report will be read. It is a convergence of the right minds at the right time." He went on: "We need a press hook or two, though. It can't be dry legal language."

"What are we going to say about counterintelligence?" Ann Caracristi asked.

"We'll have something on that," Rudman assured her, without elaboration.

"We need dramatic cultural change in the community," Friedman said, sounding a valid theme he had latched onto months earlier. He expressed special concern about FBI counterintelligence and its tendency to isolate itself from the rest of the intelligence community.

We turned to that morning's scheduled staff briefings on military intelligence and on budget matters. When they were completed, we called Vice Adm. Dennis Blair (Deutch's aide) into the room to discuss counterintelligence improvements at the CIA, especially what steps the intelligence community was taking to understand and thwart the uses of deception against the United States by hostile secret services. The upshot of Blair's review was that henceforth intelligence officers would receive more training on the importance of counterintelligence and deception. Following Admiral Blair came a string of analysts in a continuation of the commission's investigation into how the community's analytic products, from the *PDB* to the NIE, might be improved. Among them was the CIA's Jack Davis, who argued that "an increase in annual DI funding of, say, 25 percent would—at modest expense—give the Directorate the personnel and other resources it needs to help the nation cover nearly all its bets as it moves into an uncertain future." Yet another request for additional resources—a popular refrain for the chorus of briefers who visited Suite 3201 in the NEOB.

The vice chairman for estimates on the National Intelligence Council, John E. McLaughlin (also an accomplished amateur magician), emphasized that analysts were being encouraged to be candid in those cases when they had no good answer for questions raised by policy makers. He advised them to respond: "I don't have enough ground truth [empirical evidence] to answer that question, but I'll see what I can find out." It was a simple point, but one fraught with significance. If only intelligence analysts in 2002 had been more forthright with the president and other senior officials in highlighting the ambiguities and gaps in the data on the subject of WMDs in Iraq.

The Commission Hones Its Recommendations

On December 1, 1995, the commission gathered in the NEOB for further consideration of the final report, with everyone (except Exon, of course) making an appearance—though Senator Warner, as was his wont, stayed only a short while. Fowler limped into the conference room dressed casually and on crutches. "Knee operation," he explained.

"We have to *sell* our report," Warner emphasized when the session began. This drew nods around the table.

"Let's be cautious about supporting co-location," said Goss as the commission launched into more substantive matters. "We don't want a breakdown of compartmentation." The word "compartmentation" referred to separating information on a "need to know" basis, keeping it in small compartments and thus more secure. Opening doors between Agency units (in this instance, the DI and the DO) might undermine this principle, Goss reasoned. The problem was, though, that compartmentation ran counter to another important goal: sharing information among units to enhance all-source fusion—knocking down the stovepipes. Rudman suggested that the commission simply present the pros and cons of co-location and leave it at that.

The thorny issue of budget cuts came up again as General Allen reported on the work of the commission's budget subcommittee. His thesis was that there was fat in the intelligence community and it needed to be cut; but the cutbacks would have to be pursued with great care, so as not to harm important intelligence operations. "We could achieve a 15 percent reduction [in the total intelligence budget] over ten years," he suggested.

"That's a non-starter," responded Dicks instantly. "That proposal wouldn't get a hundred votes in the House. We ought to be stabilizing the intelligence budget, just like defense. I would have to dissent strongly against that recommendation."[45]

"Gee, what a surprise," said Hermann with a smile, no doubt thinking of future Boeing intelligence contracts in Dicks's constituency.

"I agree with Dicks," Goss added.[46] The HPSCI contingent on the commission was unifying.

"I think we can squeeze some money out of the budget," Rudman said.

"I predicted this moment months ago," said Fowler. Taking a page from the writings of the philosopher Immanuel Kant, he urged the commission to do what is right, no matter what the consequences. "The public expects savings," he argued. "We should recommend the *best* solution, not what is politically palatable. The appetite [for funding] in the intelligence community is insatiable."[47]

"We can't cut the budget at that rate," complained Dicks as he stared down the table toward General Allen.

"Whether we're credible is the key point," said Coelho, "—not counting votes on the Hill."

"Liposuction works better than a machete for reducing the budget," Hermann noted vaguely.

"What is driving this is the quixotic goal of war-fighting without any casualties," Fowler weighed in again. His attempts to piece together the shards of an argument for cutting the intelligence budget ran into a strong blitz from Norm Dicks, the former linebacker. The representative from Washington enumerated instances in which military operations desperately required *more* intelligence resources, not less, noting that information was a vital "force multiplier." His face turning red, he practically shouted in the conference room: "*We've already cut $100 billion from the DoD!*"

After nearly an hour of the commissioners haggling over the budget proposal, Rudman, Harrington, and Friedman (the three Concord Coalition members on the panel) eventually sided with Dicks and Goss, abandoning the anti-deficit philosophy of their outside interest group. The swirl of debate around the table soon made it clear that if it came to a formal division of the house, the Dicks faction had the votes on the commission to defeat the budget cuts proposed by the Allen task force—including the most important ballot of all, Chairman Brown's.

A realist, General Allen threw in the towel. "If I can't convince you to save money," he said, "then, okay, I'll go along." The concept of a 15 percent reduction proved to be a weigh stone too heavy for even a man of Allen's considerable stature.

Fowler, though, was not quite ready to give up. "How are you going to answer the question 'How much money have you saved us?'"

"Our job is not to come up with a specific budget," Rudman replied.

"I don't disagree with that, but the public expects savings," said an exasperated Fowler. At this point, though, he was just running on fumes.

The work session made it clear that on a good many issues the staff would have a hard time getting the commissioners to find common ground for the language in the final report. Further, even when the report was completed, the work of the commission would not be over; we still had to build a consensus outside our panel in favor of the recommendations—particularly on Capitol Hill. "Senator Warner is right," Rudman stressed. "We will have to sell this report to the public and the media."

"And to the DCI," Dicks added.

———

Fowler telephoned me on December 27 and said, "I'm going to Mexico to try to catch a big fish. We ought to hang firm on covert action. Your stuff is right on target, and I'll help you fight when I get back." I shared my draft language on covert action with my office mates, a military intelligence expert and a former DO operative. They balked at its "liberal" tenor and advised against trying to incorporate it into the report. I also sent the former Georgia senator unclassified information on environmental intelligence (another interest of his), along with some unclassified materials on economic intelligence. I had found a new Les Aspin to write for, only this one had gone fishing.

During January staff meetings, we reviewed the comments of commissioners on drafts of the final report. This never took long to assimilate, because few members had given us any guidance whatsoever; in fact, only Friedman, Baird, and Caracristi had responded to our request for specific comments. We had a flare-up at an early session when one of the younger researchers suggested that the staff should vote on each of the recommendations before sending a list of them to the commissioners. Snider exploded with a rare outburst of profanity, caught himself, then said: "Just tell me if you disagree with something. Let's work this out together. Tell me—or you're going to be ignored."

"Could we at least talk about the report?" ventured a more senior staffer.

"It's better for me to get things in writing," Snider snapped. Then, after further cooling down, he added: "But we can talk."

"We need more detail in the report," the senior staffer continued. "And we have too much emphasis on the CIA."

"Yeah," chimed in another. "Also, there is an unevenness in the importance of all the recommendations."

"Who's our audience?" asked a staffer.

"The public," Snider replied, exhibiting more patience than he had earlier, "but Congress is a key audience, too. We need to write this report in simple language, very simple. At the same time, though, we have to offer guidance to the intelligence community. This will be a difficult balancing act. Remember, this is not set in stone yet. We have time to make changes. We haven't even heard from most of the members yet. This is a starting place."

At a subsequent staff meeting later in January, we had received a little more commentary from the commissioners, including the chairman. Most of their comments, though, were too broad to be of much help in revising. (Fowler dismissed the draft of the first chapter outright as an apologia.) One of the staff attorneys applauded Chairman Brown for giving us "comments we can actually do something with." The chairman's stock rose dramatically in my eyes, too, when it became clear that he also was something of a grammarian, among all his other talents. For example, he had crossed out "hopefully" in one segment of the draft and penciled in: "we hope that." (Not every grammarian agreed with this rule but I liked it, and I was pleased to see that the chairman did, too.) I knew Fowler was a stickler for proper English, as well, and that would help us polish the prose. Brown was basically pleased with the draft and focused on a few passages that needed clarification. "Did the commission discuss this?" he asked about one recommendation that advocated a continuing CIA role in counternarcotics. I didn't think the commissioners ever advocated this point as a specific conclusion for our report, although some witnesses had briefly mentioned the value of the CIA's antinarcotics work during our briefings. At this stage this proposal was a staff suggestion.

To my surprise, the chairman was sticking with his recommendation that we disclose the CIA budget figure, along with the aggregate amount for the entire community. I doubted that this idea would get by Senator Warner, or some of the other commissioners wedded chiefly to the status quo.

———

On January 18, 1996, our panel convened in the NEOB to walk through the report again—in what would prove to be their penultimate review of the document. The weather was cooperating for a change, unlike the week before when "the Blizzard of '96"—as newspapers labeled it—had shut down Washington's airports. I was left stranded in Georgia, an inconvenience I didn't mind at all, since I was becoming more reluctant each week to board the plane to Washington and leave my family behind.

For this important session, attendance was almost complete, with Exon the only exception. "Let's do this by going around the table and hearing each commissioner's view," suggested the chairman.

"No, let's do it chapter by chapter," Rudman countered, and Brown relented—a rarity.

Senator Warner noted early in the meeting that he opposed cutting personnel at the CIA, because the Agency's "morale is very low." He argued that downsizing was a "budget issue" and therefore not within the commission's purview. He also advised the commission to drop most of the language about enhancing the intelligence role of the United Nations, a "hot button" topic that, in his opinion, would discredit the report on the Hill. He was prepared, albeit reluctantly, to allow disclosure of the aggregate intelligence spending figure, but without further budget details on spending by the CIA or any of the other individual agencies. "I'm from the old school," he said, "and I normally oppose disclosure; but I know the reality. Still, I draw the line at one aggregate figure—no more."

Several of the commissioners thought the staff language in the report was too critical of the intelligence services. "Remember the underlying reason for the commission," Warner weighed in again: "to restore confidence in intelligence."

Goss agreed. "The language is lurid," he said. "We shouldn't paint such a black picture. I'm not trying to whitewash, but let's tone this down. This will hurt morale at the agencies." Goss and Dewhurst, our former DO alum, had become champions of protecting the CIA's public image, although several others also felt that the tenor of the report was sometimes too harsh.[48]

"I think that's right," said Rudman. "Some of the language is too inflammatory."

The commissioners often got sidetracked. At one point, they spent twenty minutes debating how to define intelligence—narrowly to mean collection and analysis, or more broadly to encompass counterintelligence and covert action? As in some academic circles, most commissioners seemed to prefer the narrow definition. I thought that was like describing a duck as a bird that swims, ignoring the fact that it also flies and waddles across the ground. Regardless, the final stages of our inquiry hardly seemed the time for basic definitional debates.

As the commissioners moved forward under Brown's sometimes heavy hand, they compromised on their differing views. A senior staffer whispered to me: "This will be like drafting a National Intelligence Estimate: we'll get the lowest common denominator." The wide range of opinions among commissioners, coupled with a hope for consensus, had the effect of blurring some important issues—a common criticism leveled at commissions over the years.[49]

"This will be viewed as an extraordinary apologia for the intelligence community," Fowler warned midway through the markup, drawing grimaces from Brown, Warner, and Goss. "We don't say enough about counterintelligence," the Georgian pointed out. "What about Ames? What about Colonel Alpirez in Guatemala? What about covert action? The stuff on economic intelligence strains credulity. And what about environmental intelligence?"

"The tree huggers are a pain in the ass," was Dewhurst's contribution to the discussion.

"We need to do something about sexual discrimination at the CIA," Baird declared, having entered the room late.

"Oh, you missed that," grinned Harrington. "Porter suggested we write a whole chapter in the report on that subject."

Brown looked at his wristwatch and said, "We've got to move along."

"I plead for self-restraint," Rudman seconded. "We'd all write this differently."

"Yes, but we need to be comfortable with this report if our names are going to be on it," argued Coelho, as he weighed in on Fowler's side for more extensive reform.

Nerves were beginning to fray, so the commissioners took a break, heading for restrooms and telephones. When they returned, Friedman raised the subject of consumer-producer relationships. "There seems to be a high correlation between consumer satisfaction [with intelligence products] and a close personal relationship between intelligence officers and policy makers," he said, voicing one of the key lessons we had learned from our interviews and briefings. If consumers knew where to drop the hook to catch the information they needed, they would be satisfied. The implication was that the commission needed to suggest ways to have the two groups interact more frequently.

Other commissioners advanced their favorite proposals, most of which Brown dismissed brusquely—such as Fowler's preference for tighter restrictions over CIA paramilitary action and other features in the "code of ethics" for covert action that he and I had discussed briefly before the meeting. Intelligence funding received the most attention. Brown observed that "the intelligence budget didn't go down much after the Cold War because of the need to provide support for military operations"—our old friend SMO. Rudman returned to the question of a budget reduction. "We better try to cut 5 percent if we are going to have any credibility—except with the defense contractors," he said. The vice chairman had apparently remembered, at least to some extent, his reputed passion for debt reduction.

"I say to the president of the Concord Coalition," Fowler agreed, happy to suddenly have such a powerful budget-cutting ally in Rudman, "this is our chance to save money."

Goss remained unconvinced. "It's more difficult to track a bunch of snakes [emerging world threats] than one dragon [the Soviet Union during the Cold War]," he said, paraphrasing the metaphor made popular by Jim Woolsey.

"Therefore, we need more money for intelligence, not less." Once again, forces pulled in opposite directions and seemed to leave the commission stuck in the middle with the status quo—another common outcome for blue-ribbon panels over the years.

One of the few budget matters that most commissioners could agree on was the release of the aggregate budget figure for 1996. "Nothing will give us more credibility than releasing the top figure," said Rudman.

"We'll look silly if we don't," Brown agreed—although, after listening to Senator Warner, he backed away from his initial willingness to disclose the CIA budget as well.

By the time the commissioners had worked their way through the full draft, they looked exhausted. Fatigue had begun to take hold of even the most patient commissioners and the chairman brought the session to an end. "My head is exploding," Fowler said to me in an aside, as we walked out of the conference room. "These people [the commissioners] don't understand that the press and the public are going to be interested mainly in account-ability, covert action, and counterintelligence, not dry, sterile treatises on bureaucratic changes—moving boxes from here to there." His face was a por-trait of dismay.

————

The next day was show time: the commission's only public session. On the morning of Friday, January 19, at 9:00, we gathered for the event in Room 106 of the Dirksen Senate Office Building. A small audience had assembled in the hearing room—eighteen spectators (intelligence officers, most likely) and seventeen reporters, by my count. Even Senator Exon magically appeared for a cameo appearance, although not until 3:42 in the afternoon. David Dewhurst had brought an elaborate camera with him and was busy snapping photographs of his commission colleagues as they sat behind a U-shaped bench, waiting for Chairman Brown to gavel the hearings to order.

Assistant Secretary of Defense Joseph S. Nye Jr. repeated his insightful tales of life as a harried intelligence consumer, underscoring again the limited amount of time he had to read intelligence reports; Bobby Inman called boldly for a separation of the Operations Directorate from the CIA, establish-ing the clandestine service as an agency on its own (a position favored by former DCI Stansfield Turner, too, though strongly opposed by DCI Deutch); and Richard N. Haass, with the Council on Foreign Relations, reviewed the findings of his study group on intelligence, which highlighted the possible value of allowing the CIA's case officers overseas to pretend they were U.S. journalists or even members of the clergy. Haass recommended, as well, that the United States adopt a more robust use of covert action.[50]

"The use of American journalists to spy and American spies to pose as journalists is an appalling idea," responded the *New York Times* to Haass's suggestion in our hearing about new modes of intelligence cover.[51] This territory had been covered rather thoroughly in the 1970s by Les Aspin's HPSCI Subcommittee on Intelligence Oversight, when I served as its staff director. At that time, the CIA had promulgated formal internal regulations that prohibited it from using accredited journalistic cover or recruiting any U.S. journalists (except freelance writers) for purposes of espionage.[52] The reigning philosophy at that time was that recruiting American journalists to work on the side as U.S. intelligence agents, or employing the profession as a cover for espionage, put the personal safety of America's accredited journalists at risk, not to mention striking a heavy blow at the concept of a free press clearly separated from the government. I thought the Aspin Subcommittee had it right in 1978 and Haass was badly wrong.[53]

The renewed debate on this topic stirred by our public hearing brought to light an admission from John Deutch that although the CIA had honored the established journalist prohibitions since the 1970s, the DCI had the right to waive these strictures in times of a life-or-death emergency—say, using a journalist to gain access to a terrorist who intended to detonate a nuclear device in the United States. Former DCI Stansfield Turner then conceded to the media that he had invoked this right three times during the Carter administration.[54] This apparent loophole in the written prohibitions worried some outsiders; if a DCI had this kind of discretion to ignore a formal set of regulations, would he or some successor misuse the privilege?[55] And why hadn't Turner reported this waiver to the congressional oversight committees? Deutch attempted to quell the criticism by stating that he was unlikely ever to use the waiver option; moreover, if he did, he would report any exceptions immediately to SSCI and HPSCI, thereby providing appropriate accountability.

The president of the Council on Foreign Relations, the former journalist Leslie Gelb (a longtime friend of Les Aspin who had spoken at his memorial service in Milwaukee), quickly tried to distance himself from the recommendations offered by Haass and the Council on Foreign Relations study group.[56] The Council's task force had only suggested that "a fresh look be taken" at the problem of providing CIA officers with credible cover abroad, Gelb wrote. Moreover, the task force was "independent"—that is, not within Gelb's control. Further, the Council itself was not taking a position on the controversy. Finally, Gelb added, not even all of the task force members agreed with Dr. Haass. As for Gelb himself, he said that he personally opposed the use of journalistic cover, as well as the lifting of restrictions that prohibited the CIA's secret employment of accredited American journalists.

———

The commission's last meeting to hear testimony took place on February 2, another day of heavy snowfall in Washington. We had called only a single witness: John Deutch. The DCI was being given a final opportunity to lay out—and lobby for—his own reform plans, many of which paralleled those of the commission. In earlier remarks presented on December 19 during a HPSCI public hearing on that committee's IC21 study, Deutch had spoken of an increase in terrorist danger in the world—"tremendous growth," he said.[57] Newspapers everywhere featured this warning. Further, Deutch would soon be praised by the *New York Times* as a "reform-minded Director" who had dealt "candidly" with the Ames betrayal and released many historical documents that had been archived in the basement vaults of the intelligence agencies. The newspaper said that he was a "reformer ready to try new ideas and throw out old practices."[58] The DCI was on a roll.

Deutch brought many of the same messages to our conference room in February that he had presented to HPSCI in December. In both testimonies, his remedy for the rising terrorist threat was clear: the United States needed more spies abroad. "One has to rely, to an extraordinary degree, on human intelligence," he said, "as opposed to the technical intelligence capabilities." We knew, however, that as DCI he had concentrated mainly on techint; but we welcomed this attention to humint as well, which was widely embraced by the commissioners and most of our witnesses. The Clinton administration was now taking terrorism seriously, especially the radical Palestinian faction known as Hamas; the Egyptian group, Gama'a al-Islamiyya; and a pro-Iranian fundamentalist group in Lebanon, Hezbollah. Within a few years, in 1998, Al Qaeda would become the largest blip on the terrorism radar screens at the White House and the CIA.

In the context of discussing terrorism, Deutch reiterated his support for covert action or, at any rate, some forms of it. "The use of covert action to get rid of governments, as we did in the fifties and sixties, is counterproductive," he said. "However, if directed against proliferation or terrorism, it is highly useful." In a subsequent interview with me in 1998, he used this example: "If you find out that Osama bin Laden has a chemical plant, you may want to go there and destroy that plant. If you use the U.S. Marine Corps, you've got a military battle on your hands, but if you do it covertly...so I think it is important, but not for the classical reasons" [that is, to overthrow regimes].[59]

I had listened to his predecessor, R. James Woolsey, speak similarly on this subject. "There are some cases in which there is nothing else that can be done except covert action," he told me a year before the Aspin Commission formed. "You're not going to persuade terrorists not to do something by démarcheing them. The same for weapons proliferators. You've got to figure out some way to stop them." He continued: "But in terms of the big covert actions of the past—Afghanistan, Nicaragua—this was more of a Cold War phenomenon. It's an important, but relatively small, share of what the Agency will do. In volume, *way, way* down from what it would have been four or five years ago."[60]

In our session with Deutch, Q and A began with the former president of Cal Tech, our chairman, showing off a little. "We need to keep in mind," he said, "that if you have a list of ten priorities, the most important ten percent of the eighth priority is probably more important than the 99th percent of the first priority." Deutch smiled. Here was the music of Cal Tech and MIT.

Friedman returned the discussion to plain English, asking the DCI how well the CIA and the FBI were working together against terrorist targets. Deutch's forehead crumpled into furrows as he expressed concern that they were still far less united than they needed to be. "Good cops don't make good spies," he said, "and good spies don't make good cops"—echoing an observation he had made as well during the HSPCI hearings. In the old adage, the FBI still thought mainly about stringing up suspects, while the CIA wanted to string them along.[61] The DCI stressed, however, that he was working hard to improve cooperation between the agencies.

Deutch had another major theme to offer the commissioners: the need for intelligence reorganization. He sought the commission's assistance in his quest for legal authority to formulate nearly all of the annual intelligence budget, including spending for each of the military intelligence agencies. Here was Harry Truman's original idea come back to life. As things stood right now, Deutch reminded us (though we hardly needed any tutoring on this subject), the budget was negotiated between the DCI and the secretary of defense. "It's an ad hoc process," he said. Although Deutch's relationship with Secretary of Defense William Perry was good, there were no guarantees that the two offices might not be at loggerheads in the future. If Deutch had owned a crystal ball, he could have seen ahead to the administration of George W. Bush and observed Secretary of Defense Donald Rumsfeld blocking efforts by DCI George Tenet to exercise leadership over the military intelligence agencies in the name of all-source fusion.

When HPSCI members had asked about this proposal in December, Deutch acknowledged that the managers of the various intelligence agencies—the gorillas in the stovepipes—would "go out of their minds." He continued: "I mean, it's unheard of...especially for [agencies] other than the Department of Defense" to give such authority to the CIA director.[62] And, he could have added, rare for DoD as well. Deutch told us that he would not mind foregoing control over the relatively small budgets of INR in the State Department, the intelligence unit in the Energy Department, or the FBI—a mere sliver of the community's overall budget—just as long as the DCI had authority over the big-ticket agencies: NSA, NRO, CIO, and the DIA.

After the intelligence chief's departure, the commissioners resumed their ongoing discussion of the final report—a last chance for them to lobby for any specific proposals that were dear to their hearts. Brown the Technocrat sarcastically deflated the idea of increased funding for environmental intelligence, an initiative promoted by Fowler the Humanist. "While there are hard targets [dangerous states and terrorist groups], we should spend time on the environment?" the chairman jeered. For him, global-disease and environmental intelligence ("bugs and bunnies") should never be a principal focus of the intelligence agencies. To get Harold Brown to budge on this proposal, Fowler would have required the lever of Archimedes.

Brown's response to Fowler's interest in environmental intelligence put my fellow Georgian in a sour mood. Rudman left the room for a moment and returned with some cookies from the staff kitchen. "This commission needs to sweeten up," he said, with a mischievous grin. "Here, Wyche, have about eight of these." Fowler managed a smile for Rudman, despite Brown's *auto-da-fé*.

While the commission chairman clearly had no interest in the greening of intelligence by assigning satellites to examine vanishing rain forests and other environmental concerns, Fowler did have one consolation: he was not entirely alone in his belief that U.S. intelligence could help us understand global ecology. The vice president, Al Gore, had also asked the CIA and the NRO to engage more in environmental activities.[63] Gore spoke publicly, to the amusement of Harold Brown and a few other commissioners, about using spy satellites to track the migration of whales at sea, the extent of worldwide earthquake damages, and the effects of global warming on Arctic glaciers and ice floes.

John Deutch, too, had taken up the subject of environmental intelligence, with some pushing from the vice president. He established a DCI Environmental Center, which worked with U.S. scientists in the private business and university sectors to explore how the rich imagery archives of the intelligence community might be used for ecological research. Deutch remained enthusiastic about environmental intelligence after he left the DCI position. "I think it's very important," he told me in 1998. "Environmental matters are influencing economics and political relationships. It's a natural for intelligence collection. The EPA collects nothing—zippo—on international matters. What is happening to water around the world? Food? Collection on such matters requires only a minor investment of intelligence resources. When you have satellite time available, why wouldn't we do this?"[64]

Fowler was hardly the only target of the chairman's periodic scorn. When Bob Hermann brought up again his interest in a National Assessment Center, placed in a building somewhere near the White House, Brown snorted in ridicule: *"This* is going to be the solution to our analytic problems?"

"The chairman has a certain yellow-journalism approach," replied the good-natured former NSA and NRO manager, using one of his favorite expressions and absorbing Brown's blunt judgment with less pain than Fowler had felt. As it would turn out, the wily Hermann managed to have his National Assessment Center proposal entered into the final report despite Brown's skepticism.

Moving through each chapter of the draft of the final report, the commissioners commented as they saw fit. If their suggestions sparked interest in other members, discussion might lead to changes in wording—unless Brown or Rudman expressed opposition, the kiss of death. Time crawled by on arthritic knees as we went through the document almost line by line. At last, well into the afternoon, Brown called for a formal vote on the commission's final report. Not a dissenting voice was heard, and the staff's smiling faces lit up the conference room.

| The Commission Reports

A FTER WEEKS OF FINE-TUNING THE PROSE, with multiple drafts sent out to the commissioners for comments, the Aspin-Brown Commission report was ready for printing in mid-February of 1996. Though some of the commissioners—Coelho and Fowler especially—were unhappy with the compromises that had been made, each signed the document, and early on the morning of March 1, they gathered in the Oval Office to brief the president. Even Senator J. James Exon miraculously surfaced for the occasion.[1] In an amusing denouement to the commission's many months of labor, the president turned to Exon first and asked about the report and how it was likely to play on Capitol Hill. "Senator Warner and I were unable to attend all the commission meetings," he said, fidgeting, no doubt to the amusement of commissioners in the room (all but Dicks, Hermann, and Warner were in attendance). They knew the Nebraskan had skipped almost every meeting we had held. This didn't keep Exon, though, from offering his appraisal that the report would be well received. The president was on Clinton Time: having arrived forty-five minutes late, he asked a couple of broad questions, schmoozed for a few minutes, and departed, leaving Vice President Gore to hear the details about our findings and recommendations.

Chairman Brown was in good spirits, perhaps happy to be sitting in the Oval Office rather than in the NEOB conference room listening to more briefings. He told a Pentagon joke, skillfully gave the president a little taste of our recommendations (Brown focused on our disclosure of the aggregate intelligence budget figure), then, after Clinton left, offered the vice president a more complete account of our findings.

The timing of the report's release became something of a headache for the commission staff. John Deutch, who *Time* magazine referred to that week as "becoming the most powerful spymaster Washington has ever seen,"[2] wanted multiple advanced copies so he could review the report in a video conference with his staff at the CIA and prepare himself for public comment. The same was true for most of the other intelligence agency heads. We were reluctant to send copies all over town, though, because of the high leak potential; Brown and Rudman wanted the report to be today's news, not yesterday's. Admiral Blair came to the NEOB offices and got into a tiff with the staff director about our unwillingness to allow widespread distribution of the report within the intelligence community. It took a few days for Brown and Deutch to reach a *modus vivendi*, arriving at a plan for limited dissemination to top intelligence managers.

Later on the morning of March 1, the two-hundred-page document—dedicated to Les Aspin, as well as to intelligence officers who had given their lives in service to the country—was ready for public release. After twelve months, eighty-four formal witness testimonies, and over two hundred interviews from the time we began in early 1995, *Preparing for the 21st Century: An Appraisal of U.S. Intelligence, The Report of the Commission on the Roles and Capabilities of the United States Intelligence Community* was printed, bound, and on the streets, replete with thirty-nine proposals for reform.[3] The birds would now fly where they may.

I circled March 7 on my calendar. I was going home to Georgia to stay; no more weekly commuting. Henceforth, instead of discussing billion-dollar budgets for intelligence, I'd be on the University Council's Education Affairs Committee, pondering how many days in a semester should be allocated for drop-add, and I would be enjoying every moment.

As Brown and Rudman wrote in the preface to the report, the commission had three overarching goals: closer working ties between policy makers and intelligence officers, an integrated community that more effectively shared information, and improved management of the secret agencies. More specifically, here were our major recommendations:

- Economic intelligence: We rejected "industrial espionage" (CIA spying on foreign companies); but we did advocate some forms of economic intelligence, such as reporting on unfair trade practices being used against U.S. firms competing for contracts with foreign governments (chapter 2 of the report).
- Counternarcotics: Over the objection of many DO officers, we concluded that the CIA should stay in the war against drug dealers, coordinating

its work closely with the Drug Enforcement Administration and the FBI (chapter 2).

- Environmental and health intelligence: In brief commentaries, we favored some attention to these topics, though (I thought) far less than they warranted[4] (chapter 2).
- Elevating intelligence: We proposed the creation of an NSC "Committee on Foreign Intelligence" (the Baird initiative) to give intelligence a higher profile in the White House, and we recommended, as well, a subordinate NSC "Consumers Committee" to improve responsiveness to the information needs of policy makers (chapter 3).
- Law enforcement: We advocated another NSC committee (also Baird's idea), the Committee on Global Crime, to work on improving relations between law enforcement and intelligence, especially in the struggle against international criminal cartels (chapter 4).
- Jointness: With an eye toward the goal of all-source fusion, we proposed that the DCI be provided with two new deputies; one would focus on community management and the other on the day-to-day operations of the CIA (freeing the DCI to coordinate the wider community).[5] In this same vein, the DCI would have the right to "concur" on the appointment of military intelligence agency heads (here at least was an implicit veto power for the intelligence director), and would be "consulted" on other senior appointments in the community. In short, the commission backed away from a truly strong DCI (or DNI) with full appointment and budgetary powers. Instead, the report concluded that "the DCI's existing legal authorities with respect to the Intelligence Community are, on the whole, sufficient" (p. 54). Where long strides were needed, we had taken some baby steps toward bringing greater cohesion to the secret agencies. It would take the 9/11 attacks to change the political climate in favor of a DNI with true management authority—although (as I show in the next chapters) even then the powers of the office remained weak (chapter 5).
- DO: The commission report urged that officers in the Directorate of Operations rotate into other intelligence units (both within the CIA and throughout the intelligence community) on occasion to reduce the insularity of the DO—a slight nod toward the spirit, if not the full implementation of, "co-location." Several commissioners remained wary that DI/DO co-location might become too cozy and undermine the independence of DI analysts—thus, the report's lack of effusive praise for this experiment in intra- and interagency cultural bonding (chapter 6).[6]

- Global presence: the commission came out firmly in favor of global presence over the competing concept of surge. "The offices [overseas] need not be large," the report noted (p. 68).
- Liaison: We stressed the importance of improving communications between policy makers and analysts by placing either a few CIA liaison contacts directly within the policy departments or at least by having the Agency provide daily intelligence briefings to the departments. This was one of my favorite recommendations, which some on the staff had begun to refer to as "forward liaison."[7] Moreover, we advised the intelligence agencies to strengthen their outreach to experts in academe and think tanks, to use open-sources more effectively, and to increase computer compatibility among the agencies within the intelligence community (chapter 8).
- Analysis: The commissioners adopted, though narrowly, Dr. Hermann's concept of a National Assessment Center to replace the NIC, located somewhere outside the CIA—ideally, near the White House. The NAC was never established (chapter 8).
- Personnel: Influenced by the staff trip to Canada, commissioners recommended that the CIA and the military agencies "right-size" their workforce through at least a 10 percent staff reduction, accompanied by fair compensation for early retirements—a proposal that held little appeal to Warner, who was not interested in any CIA personnel cuts.[8] We suggested, too, the creation of a "senior executive service" for the community, as a means for encouraging management centralization under the DCI—a proposal soon adopted by the intelligence community. In the text of the report, we noted that rising personnel costs continued to prevent investments in new technologies and operational initiatives, especially at the NSA where the problem was "acute" (p. 96). The commission's NSA trio let this criticism make it into the report, because personnel reductions might free up funding for the new spy technology so dear to them (chapter 9).
- Efficiencies: Chairman Brown inserted a pet recommendation of his own into the report at the eleventh hour, namely, that the SecDef should conduct a review of military intelligence production as a means of eliminating waste and duplication. This was mild stuff, and the chairman made sure the commission report embraced the status quo when it came to DoD control over most of the intelligence budget. "As a general proposition, the Commission believes it would be a serious mistake to weaken the relationship between intelligence and defense," the report stated (p. 53). In other words, the SecDef

would remain an eight-hundred-pound gorilla and the DCI the organ grinder's monkey with tin cup in hand, begging for contributions to civilian intelligence. We rejected Gen. James R. Clapper Jr.'s idea of a director of military intelligence inside the Pentagon, but this proposal would eventually come to fruition anyway after the 9/11 attacks (chapter 10).[9]

- Consolidations: We proposed that all humint be placed within the CIA's Operations Directorate, stripping DIA of its Defense Humint Service; and, in support of the most sweeping organizational reform that would take place in 1996, we backed the DCI/DoD proposal for a new National Imagery and Mapping Agency, or NIMA—the name preferred by the DoD over "National Imagery Agency," which we had tossed around in commission meetings. The NIMA would soon come into being.[10] The all-CIA humint proposal languished, however, until after 9/11 when the government created (in 2005) the National Clandestine Service (NCS) to replace the DO. The NCS would serve as an overarching framework for both CIA/DO and DoD humint activities, with the old DO (now the NCS) remaining at Langley and the Defense Humint Service surviving and staying within the military at the DIA's building on the grounds of Bolling Air Force Base across the Potomac from National Airport. A Marine Corps major general became director of this bifurcated organization, with an office at the Agency and the title "CIA deputy director for community HUMINT" (chapters 10 and 11).[11]

- Space surveillance: Dr. Hermann got much of what he wanted. The commission supported his plans for improved satellite management. Further, we proposed the adoption of new rules for selling U.S. surveillance hardware abroad, calling for a serious review of the current policy that required American firms to permit U.S.-government "shutter control" over imint systems sold overseas—a liability for firms competing with other nations for foreign commercial satellite sales. The commission advised, further, that the United States proceed forward on two fronts: working with allies to develop "low-end tier" surveillance satellites and sharing the costs, while maintaining exclusive U.S. control over a second "high-end tier" fleet of highly sophisticated spy satellites (chapter 11).

- Spending: On the question of espionage spending levels, we passed the buck to the president and Congress, although the commission did come out in favor of disclosing the aggregate annual budget figure (chapter 12).[12]

- Burden sharing: We noted how the United States could benefit from intelligence sharing with other nations and with international organizations, although the language in the report remained vague for fear that Senator Warner was right that key lawmakers might recoil at the idea of sharing information with the United Nations (chapter 12).
- Oversight: We weighed in on the question of oversight, though modestly, suggesting that the current maximum term limits for SSCI and HPSCI members be raised a couple of years to enhance the experience quotient on the two panels. The report concluded: "By most accounts, [SSCI and HPSCI] provide rigorous and intensive oversight" (p. 143)—a stretch, to say the least, although no doubt politic, as we were about to ask these very committees to advance our recommendations on the Hill (chapter 14).

In the report, covert action was essentially ignored, and counterintelligence—the concern that contributed so much to the creation of the commission in the first place—was discussed in less than a page (the message in the report was that the government had to take counterintelligence more seriously). Still, we had advanced some useful reform ideas, even if many of them—personnel cuts, rules for satellite sales abroad, and institutional consolidations—were hardly sexy, headline-making departures from the status quo. "Major surgery was not the solution," staff director Snider later opined.[13]

———

On March 1st, the commission held a press conference at 9:30 AM in the main lounge of the National Press Club to comment on our final report. Eleven commissioners attended the gathering, but the exchange with reporters was dominated by Harold Brown. The chairman began by reviewing the main proposals for the media throng. "Since I assume you have read the report," he said, like a headmaster addressing a classroom of suspect jackanapes, "I'll remind rather than inform you about it." The panel had examined the merits of several radical reforms, Brown observed, such as taking the Operations Directorate out of the CIA, engaging in industrial espionage, elevating the DCI to a position of intelligence czar, and lumping all of the intelligence agencies into the Defense Department (I could recall no serious discussion or support for that "reform"). But, he concluded, "we decided that whatever their virtues, the deficiencies of the proposals were greater."

Brown highlighted the commission's efforts to make the intelligence agencies more responsive to consumers, notably by creating better liaison ties between policy makers and analysts. He pointed, as well, to the creation of a

Committee on Foreign Intelligence within the framework of the NSC, arguing that it would help clarify targeting priorities for the president, as well as provide a forum for reviewing the recruitment rationales for the hiring of especially unsavory foreign agents (a reference to the Alpirez case and the "Deutch rules"). The chairman stressed the importance of having this special NSC committee to arbitrate disputes between the DCI and law enforcement officials. These were all efforts to untangle the often snarled lines of bureaucratic relations between the intelligence agencies, especially the CIA and the FBI.

When it came to the powers of the DCI, Brown had successfully blocked any effort to turn the DCI into a countervailing eight-hundred-pound gorilla, able to stand up to the secretary of defense. Instead, the commission had settled on the establishment of special deputies who would assist the intelligence chief coordinate the thirteen secret agencies—our limited attempt to offset the centrifugal forces that pushed against the goal of more centralized all-source fusion. At least, though, this small movement toward better integration of the intelligence "community" offered some symbolic reassurance to reformers that *something* was being done to help the DCI cope with its institutional fragmentation.

In this same spirit, the commission advocated a little more say for the director of central intelligence over who would be appointed to head each of the intelligence agencies beyond the CIA (already led by the DCI). The director, however, would only be allowed to provide "concurrence" with respect to appointments to the military intelligence agencies. According to this prescription, the DCI would be given veto power over the appointment of an agency head by the SecDef, but would not have the sole say over the selection. For the civilian agencies, the DCI's authority would be weaker still; the intelligence chief would merely be "consulted" on appointments. Nor would the DCI have the final say over the budgets for each of the intelligence agencies. Some director of *central* intelligence!

With particular pride, Brown underscored the personnel changes the commission had proposed. The secretary of defense and the DCI would be given a year to reduce the staff of the intelligence agencies using the incentive of generous retirement benefits. Rudman told the reporters that, "particularly for the NSA, unless this is done, and done soon, we will wake up about five years from now with an NSA that does not have the ability to supply the president and the other parts of the executive branch . . . the kind of information it needs." As Chairman Brown would tell the American Bar Association later in the month, this personnel initiative could be "the toughest one of all to get through [Congress], because people don't like their rice bowls cracked."[14] During the session at the National Press Club, Brown lauded as well some of the Allen-Caracristi-Hermann technical reforms, including a recommendation that the United States sell spy satellites mounted with sophisticated cameras to friendly nations, but only if they agreed to share their photography with Washington.

After suggesting that Congress and the executive branch think of ways to trim redundancy and waste in the budget (as if that responsibility had not been part of the commission's charge in the first place), the commission's leaders gave a brief rhetorical nod to the need for better oversight. Then came what Brown and Rudman expected would be the climax to the press conference: the recommendation that the DCI disclose the aggregate annual intelligence budget figure. After all, Brown explained, as he glanced around the assembled press corps with a wry grin, "You've got to throw meat to the lions every once in a while—otherwise, they'll eat people."[15]

———

At 3:00 o'clock that afternoon, Brown and Rudman went through a review of the commission report again, this time before the leadership of the intelligence community—a rare gathering of all the agency gorillas and their top staff in the Bubble. There were neither hoorays nor boos. A few days later, the duo would brief SSCI and HPSCI on our report in separate hearings. It was a time of salesmanship—though, as we would soon discover, not everyone liked the product.

The following Monday, HSPCI released its IC21 report.[16] It proposed the establishment of a new covert entity, the U.S. Clandestine Service, where all humint and covert action personnel would be housed (either within the CIA or outside)—Admiral Inman's recommendation. The House Intelligence Committee saw merit, as well, in stripping the Directorate of Science and Technology from the Agency and dispersing its parts into other intelligence agencies. What would remain, as a *New York Times* reporter put it, would be a CIA that had devolved into "a small box on a big flow chart."[17]—essentially, analysts in the Directorate of Intelligence, a security contingent, and janitors to sweep the hallways at Langley.

The HPSCI report boldly advocated a stronger DCI who could "break down the stovepipes." Under its scheme, the nation's spy chief would have much greater control over military intelligence, with clear veto power over appointments to the military intelligence agencies and—the most dramatic initiative—authority to transfer funds between military and civilian spy agencies. Exactly where the new DCI would be housed, whether at the weakened CIA or somewhere else, was left unstated. Wishing to avoid what it saw as yet another stovepipe, the House committee opposed the creation of a National Imagery and Mapping Agency. This position went against not just our recommendation in favor of NIMA but, more importantly, against the inexorable tide of the DoD and the DCI. NIMA would happen.

On March 6, Brown and Rudman traveled to the SSCI hearing room in the Hart Senate Office Building to present the commission report. Rudman told the senators that the personnel adjustments proposed for the community, and especially for the NSA, were "the single most important" part of the report. Brown reviewed the other proposals and ended his remarks by stating that he had brought with him draft legislation and copies of proposed executive orders designed to implement the report's prescriptions—both the good handiwork of our staff legal troika. In Q and A, Chairman Arlen Specter noted that, in his opinion, the core question was: "Why not put *all* intelligence under the DCI?" It was a point well taken. What kind of intelligence chief was it who had little control over the entire spy budget or agency appointment powers?

Next, the commission leaders made their way through the underground passages that connect the Senate offices and the Capitol Rotunda to repeat their briefing to House members. Just off the rotunda was HPSCI's cozier suite of offices, guarded by police officers. Only four HPSCI members bothered to show up for the session: Chairman Combest, Goss, Dicks, and, the future Speaker of the House, Nancy Pelosi (D-CA). Two other members arrived halfway through the briefing, leafed through their copies of the report for a few minutes, then departed. Here was the "rigorous and intensive" legislative oversight we had touted in our report! Rudman spoke at length about the commission's important personnel recommendations. When he had completed his remarks, Pelosi sagely inquired about the ongoing struggle between the DCI and the SecDef over who was really the nation's intelligence director. As Brown temporized, voting bells went off and the meeting came to an end.

That same day, Senators Specter and Bob Kerrey introduced legislation (S 1593) in the Senate to carry forth the commission's objectives.[18] Combest had already brought before the HPSCI membership a draft bill designed to achieve the sweeping intelligence reforms he had embraced—especially the establishment of a muscular DCI. According to *Congressional Quarterly*, the Combest proposal went "well beyond" the Aspin-Brown Commission recommendations.[19]

Reflecting on the value of commissions, Jonathan Yardley once observed that most of them have provided "brief amusement for newspaper columnists and other deep thinkers but none [have] led to action of any genuine consequence."[20] We would now see if the Aspin-Brown Commission report would end up in this graveyard.

Public Reaction

The editors of the *New York Times* quickly dismissed the "anodyne" report of the Aspin-Brown Commission for its lack of "imagination and courage." The commissioners had exhibited the "the spine of a rag doll," according to the newspaper, by leaving "a flawed system essentially intact."[21] The *Times* was especially unhappy that we had not spent more time criticizing the CIA, nor had we called for the abolition of the scandal-ridden NRO. Further, the newspaper wanted to see deep budget cuts. I could imagine Tony Coelho and Wyche Fowler nodding their heads in agreement as they read the damning critique.

Intelligence officers interviewed by the *Times* expressed similar disapproval. Evidently they saw no need for the reforms we had proposed, from strengthening the DCI to addressing the bloat at NSA. The report was "underwhelming," observed one of them.[22] A former CIA analyst concluded that the commission's recommendations "do not serve the White House, the State Department or the American people."[23] Lt. Gen. James R. Clapper Jr., the former DIA director (soon to be the director of the new NIMA), singled out for criticism the idea of dismantling the Defense Humint Service and combining it with the DO into a "National Clandestine Service." In his words, "Intelligence gathering through technological means will not make up for human intelligence in the military."[24] This comment missed the mark. The question was not whether technical intelligence would dwarf humint— that had already happened—but rather whether it was more efficient and sensible to combine DoD and CIA human-agent activities overseas. Also, Clapper vigorously opposed giving the DCI any form of budget and personnel authority over military intelligence, using the scare tactic that America could end up with a Soviet-like intelligence czar. "Do you want something like the KGB and GRU in this country?" he asked in vintage, over-the-top DoD rhetoric on the subject of a strong DCI with "civilian" proclivities.[25] Fifteen years later in 2010 when he was named DNI, I wondered if Clapper would soon grow frustrated by the lack of authority that comes with this high office title.

Reflecting back on the commission report, former DCI John Deutch remembered that "there were three people who liked the Aspin-Brown Commission report: the president, Tony Lake [the national security advisor], and myself. I thought it was a step forward. Everybody else hated it. The secretary of defense hated it; the secretary of state hated it; the attorney general hated it." I asked him why this was the case. "Because when the smoke cleared," he replied, "the commission gave the director of intelligence more authority."

He paused, then added: "But then this authority vanished virtually without a trace. It never went anywhere. Tony [Lake] said to me, 'John, you ought to push this.' But I did not want to have a fight with Chris [Warren Christopher, the secretary of state] and Bill [Perry, the secretary of defense]."[26]

Joining the editors of the *Times*, some intelligence scholars were likewise unimpressed with our work. In their view, the commission report offered only limited insights and reform. One critic berated the commissioners, fairly, I thought, for arguing "that we need everything and since everything is expensive, we need to spend just as much as before."[27]

Journalist David Wise, one of the witnesses who had been most critical of the CIA during our briefings, observed that "a Commission made up of members of the establishment is not likely to clobber the establishment, or step on many toes—and it didn't."[28] He properly slammed us for ducking the key question of "how much money the United States should be spending on intelligence now that the Cold War is over"—exactly the kind of public criticism Coelho and Fowler had worried about. Further, Wise regretted that we had said "little" about reforming the Directorate of Operations, "the inbred, arrogant, secret club where Ames worked—for the wrong side." Moreover, he found it disconcerting that "in the wake of the worst spy scandal ever to hit the CIA [Ames], the Commission has proposed a beauty treatment for the spy agencies that leaves their formidable problems—and blemishes—intact." His conclusion: "There may be audible sighs of relief in Langley, but there is scant reassurance for the public."

The *Washington Post* was kinder, noting that the commission report was "the most comprehensive, high-level government review of U.S. intelligence gathering to be conducted in nearly 20 years." The newspaper quoted Senator John Warner's praise of the panel for its success in fending off "the 'slash and burn' measures" advocated by some of his fellow lawmakers.[29]

A commission staffer knew someone at the *New York Times* and contacted him about the nasty editorial on the commission's report. According to this well-placed individual on the newspaper's staff, the *Times* writer who had penned the unsigned, negative opinion had covered the CIA during the years when William J. Casey served as DCI and "had come away with a sour taste that affected his whole view of the subject." The contact, who also covered the national security beat for the newspaper, noted that he had not been consulted on the piece and personally found it too harsh.

The *Times* editorial outraged Harold Brown. He joined Rudman (who tempered the chairman's language) in writing a letter of rebuttal to the newspaper. Among Brown's overheated comments removed by Rudman: "You appear to think the nation should satisfy its intelligence needs through news columns and CNN, and satisfy its requirements for a military capability with rolled-up copies of your newspaper." When the toned-down Brown-Rudman rebuttal arrived at the *Times* building in New York City, its editors objected to the length of the letter and sent back to the commission a pare-down version that removed Brown's remaining snide remarks, as well as a reference to a factual error that Brown and Rudman had pointed out to the newspaper. (We had proposed a six-year term for a deputy director to the DCI who would manage the CIA, not for the DCI office itself, as the *Times* mistakenly printed.)

By the time the *Times* edited version of the Brown-Rudman letter made it back to the commission, the chairman was in an airplane headed for a speaking engagement. On behalf of Brown and himself, Rudman decided to accept the newspaper's redactions, although he insisted that the *Times* restore the reference to the newspaper's factual error. Contacted in midflight by our staff director, Brown grudgingly agreed to Rudman's compromise. The final printed letter noted: "We were established to review roles and capabilities, not to rehash allegations of wrongdoing or mismanagement."[30] The CIA was but one of a baker's dozen agencies we examined, Brown and Rudman further pointed out, and "accounts for less than one-eighth of the intelligence budget." Therefore, it did not warrant a full-scale critique in its own right in our report; we had too much other ground to cover.

As for the NRO, the commission leaders referred in their letter to our recommendations for tightening up the management of that errant agency. On the budget, Brown and Rudman weakly noted how we had suggested places to effect savings, but it was up to the administration and Congress to make specific cuts. Appropriately, they took a shot back at the *Times* for arguing the intelligence agencies were in need of major overhaul, without ever pinpointing "what overhaul should take place or how it would improve the existing system."

————

We fared somewhat better on the Hill than we had with the *Times*. The SSCI chairman, Arlen Specter, for example, offered at least a modicum of unwonted praise, calling our study a "good report." Even he made it clear, though, that our recommendations were just a "starting point."[31] He thought we had failed to go far enough in addressing the "biggest problem," namely, the intelligence "old boy network" that eschewed accountability—a reference to the CIA's Operations Directorate. His examples included ignoring Aldrich Ames's foibles for far too long; giving "tainted information" to the president and other officials (a reference to the information forwarded to the CIA from Moscow assets known to have been fingered by Ames, then passed along by

Agency analysts to policy makers); and failing to inform lawmakers about the Alpirez case. The SSCI chief said that he wished the commission had granted the DCI far more authority than the report recommended—my major criticism as well. "He should have control of all intelligence budgets, and not just be consulted," Specter concluded.[32]

Our reform proposals, limited as they were, did not travel well on their journey through the congressional labyrinth, despite Rudman's hopeful handwritten inscription—"Get it done!"—on the personal copy of the report sent to HSPCI chairman Larry Combest. On April 15, 1996, Combest referred to his own proposed reform package (HR 3227) as an opportunity to achieve a "truly corporate" intelligence community that was well integrated and shared information more effectively.[33] He envisioned a DCI office that had command over all intelligence appointment and budget decisions. In addition to a stand-alone Clandestine Humint Service (separate from the CIA) that would meld DO and DIA humint assets, the HSPCI chairman continued to advocate the creation of a new Technical Collection Agency to consolidate the NSA, NRO, and CIO—sigint and imint in one package, as Bob Hermann had radically proposed at our Leesburg retreat. This TCA organization would report directly to the DCI. "I don't want all the imagery controlled by Defense," Combest declared, explaining his preference for a TCA over a National Imagery and Mapping Agency.

These bold ideas for reform eventually proved too much to take for Combest's HPSCI colleagues, and, inside the confines of the committee's quarters, they strongly objected to the direction their chairman was leading them. The Aspin-Brown Commission's own Norm Dicks, who was also the ranking Democrat on HPSCI, led the counteroffensive against Combest's comprehensive reform package. "We're changing here very fundamental relationships between the Department of Defense and the director of Central Intelligence," he said, "which is going to cause problems."[34]

Combest retreated in the face of this opposition and softened the bill, which finally (on May 9) garnered a favorable 6-to-3 vote from HPSCI members.[35] Yet even this watered-down version so upset the Pentagon that it mobilized its considerable lobbying resources to rally members of the House against the measure. On July 17, the House National Security Committee (the old Armed Services Committee, with a temporary name change)—firmly in the clutches of Defense Department lobbyists—proposed an even more diluted intelligence reform bill that removed all vestiges of a strengthened DCI. "We're going to hold the line on an erosion of the Secretary of Defense's authority," the committee's chairman, Floyd D. Spence (R-SC), declared.[36]

The DoD attack was so potent that Combest no longer saw any reason even to take the HPSCI proposal to the House floor.

The Pentagon managed as well to undermine the pro-reform legislation in the Senate, introduced by Arlen Specter. When the DoD lobbying effort struck the Senate, the SSCI chairman was left staring at an anemic intelligence authorization bill. Aiding the defeat in both chambers was the lukewarm championing of the reform measures by John Deutch and the president. It was reported that, even though the DCI had testified in favor of the Aspin-Brown and Combest bills during congressional hearings, "he was torn by his own close ties to the Pentagon."[37] Deutch, now eyeing the coveted SecDef position for himself from his perch at Langley, backed away from the idea of giving too many powers to the intelligence director, which he might want to have in his own hands as the Pentagon's top man. As for Bill Clinton, intelligence remained distant from his main interests—a detachment that effectively nullified what could have been the most powerful force in Washington in favor of intelligence reform: the White House.

Although Combest's more radical legislation never even made it to the House floor, SSCI chairman Arlen Specter, an iron-willed individual, had not given up completely on his support for the commission's recommendations, even if debate over intelligence reform was beginning to unfold, according to the *Congressional Quarterly*, "in a more contentious fashion in the Senate."[38] Specter started out by including our recommendations largely intact into the Intelligence Authorization Act for Fiscal Year 1997 (S 1718).[39] This Senate-sponsored bill, approved by SSCI members on April 24, granted the DCI four new deputies to improve community coordination—two more than we had suggested in our report. The proposed legislation also provided the DCI's Community Management Staff with more personnel and funding. Moreover, the legislation gave the DCI a stronger role in the selection of all the intelligence agency heads, and it increased the intelligence chief's leverage over budget allocations and transfers within the intelligence community—although, even under this proposal, the SecDef would retain ultimate control over both appointments and budgets for the military intelligence agencies.

The most striking reform embraced by the Senate bill was the creation (within the framework of the Defense Department) of a National Imagery and Mapping Agency, designed to consolidate the community's high-tech imagery and mapping capabilities—including the Central Imaging Office and the Agency's cherished NPIC. This was a relatively easy sell, since both Deutch and Perry were already on record in favor of NIMA. Chalk up another bureaucratic victory for the SecDef at the expense of the CIA and contrary to the institutional reforms favored by HPSCI's Combest.

Strom Thurmond (R-SC) and Sam Nunn (D-GA) of the Senate Armed Services Committee, two of the Pentagon's most dependable cheerleaders, led the Senate effort to block any attempt at increasing the DCI's authority—however slightly—over intelligence appointments and budgets. Members of SSCI and the Armed Services Committees attempted for a month to seek a compromise between their respective positions for and against a strong DCI, but to no avail. The clinching argument that crippled Specter's legislation (and Combest's in the House) was simple. If passed, it would supposedly create a "monolithic intelligence community." So predicted Thurmond, the chairman of the Senate Armed Services Committee, aged ninety-two and a veteran of the Normandy landing.[40] Further, it would jeopardize America's war fighters—as if any DCI (or DNI, if that was to be the new label for America's spymaster) would ever make a decision that would knowingly endanger our men and women in uniform. The Armed Services Committee abandoned further discussions with SSCI and approved its own anti-reform bill, which was supported by the Governmental Affairs Committee as well.[41]

On September 17, the Specter bill went to the Senate floor, but ran immediately into a substitute measure: the Armed Services Committee's paler version of intelligence reform. This substitute quickly passed in lieu of Specter's proposal. The House-Senate conference committee accepted this weakened version, which even rejected the modest proposal to disclose the annual budget figure for the intelligence agencies. "The American public doesn't want to know that number," declared HSPCI member Jon Kyl (R-AZ). "It is being requested by those who are opponents of our intelligence community."[42] Perhaps he had in mind such disloyal American radicals as Harold Brown, Warren Rudman, John Warner, and John Deutch. Both chambers adopted the conference committee report by voice vote on September 25, and President Clinton signed the emaciated Intelligence Authorization Act (Public Law 104–293) on October 11.

Once again, the powerful coalition of the Pentagon and its congressional allies had ganged up to halt more serious measures to provide the DCI with real authority over America's scattered intelligence services. One casualty was the proposal to transfer the DoD's humint assets to the CIA. On this point, General Clapper had won. (Within a few years, however, the proposal for a CIA National Clandestine Service, backed by both the commission and Combest in 1996, would finally be adopted—though, as I have noted earlier, it continued to keep DoD humint in the Pentagon's organizational framework, not the CIA's.) The Aspin-Brown Commission did manage to gain approval for the two DCI assistant positions it had recommended (one for community management and one to help run the CIA), plus two more positions added on by the Congress, but their roles remained limited.[43]

The DoD's efforts to sabotage the intelligence reform legislation sought by the commission and leaders of SSCI and HPSCI received helpful assistance from Rep. Dicks during the congressional debates on the commission's recommendations, as he spoke on the floor against several initiatives. For example, some House members tried to cut the budget of the NRO as punishment for its sloppy spending practices. "Great Britain is dealing with mad cow disease," observed Rep. Patricia Schroeder (D-CO). "Here today on this floor we are dealing with sacred cow disease"—namely, the intelligence budget. Dicks successfully argued, however, that DCI Deutch had already taken action against the NRO by firing its top officials. He warned that a reduction in the agency's budget would have serious repercussions for the launching of new spy satellites. The NRO builds "incredible satellites," he said, and he might have added: "in my home district." He did grant the point, though, that the agency had "lousy accountants."[44]

In the approved bill, the DCI was stripped of any unilateral authority over appointments and budgets—even the right to reveal the aggregate spy budget. In 1997, spending on intelligence was expected to climb by 4.9 percent over the previous fiscal year, reaching a level of some $30 billion.[45] This increase represented a 3.9 percent rise over the president's request, which in itself was a far cry from Warren Rudman's muted advocacy during the commission's discussions of a 5 percent cut in spending for spies—let alone the initial recommendation of the Allen task force in favor of a 15 percent reduction.

The authoritative chronicle of Capital Hill politics, the *Congressional Quarterly*, concluded that the "ambitious, two-year effort to reshape the U.S. intelligence community ended with modest results."[46] Former DCI Robert Gates had speculated almost a year before the creation of the Aspin-Brown Commission: "I don't think you'll ever get legislation to create, in effect, a DCI who is the line manager for the intelligence community. It can't happen when five-sixths of the budget is in the Defense Department, and when the director of NSA, the head of NRO, [and] the director of DIA have dual responsibilities that only partly fit into the *national* intelligence community."[47]

As our recommendations were wending their way through the corridors of Capitol Hill like a Calistoga wagon in Apache territory, the DCI initially made a strong case on their behalf to the president—even though both men ultimately retreated from a full-court-press lobbying effort in Congress. In a memorandum dated April 5, 1996, Deutch wrote to Clinton: "I propose that you take initiatives, based on the Aspin-Brown report, to strengthen U.S.

intelligence during the next decade."[48] He offered two reasons why the moment was propitious for reform: first, the Aspin-Brown recommendations were sound, needing only some tweaking here and there; and, second, quick action would stop the progress of the more radical HPSCI proposals being pushed by Larry Combest. The rest of the memo explained our key reforms, often drawn verbatim from the commission's report.

The White House had nothing to say about the reform proposals, however, until April 23. On that day, the president publicly endorsed one of our least significant recommendations: the release of the aggregate intelligence budget figure for the year.

PART V | Reform Unraveled

CHAPTER 13

In The Commission's Wake

IN THE AUTUMN OF 1996, charges appeared in the *San Jose Mercury News* that CIA officers had been involved in drug sales in the United States, peddling cocaine from Nicaragua in the back streets of Los Angeles. The implication of the report was that the drug dealing had been sanctioned by the Agency to finance its secret operations beyond congressional appropriations—another Iran-*contra*-like scandal in the making. No one had any hard evidence to prove this allegation, and it seemed far-fetched; but politically the story created a sensation. Bravely, DCI Deutch flew out to Watts, California, the site of riots in the 1960s, to defend the Agency before a hostile crowd. He may not have convinced them the allegation was false, but many in the audience admired his pluck. It was a chaotic encounter, covered on national television. After answering questions at length—some shouted at him—the DCI limped off the stage of the local high school auditorium, using a cane to support an old leg injury that had flared up.[1]

Deutch returned to Langley for a few months; but, frustrated and dispirited, he hung up his DCI hat in December of 1996. He had served for nineteen months as Director, just as his immediate predecessors (Woolsey and Gates) had also served for less than two years. He said that the DCI position had been so frustrating that he should have followed his initial instinct not to be "pushed into" the task.[2] "It's a tough job," he concluded.[3] Many at Langley were happy to see him depart, especially inside the DO. A journalist who covered intelligence during this 1990s summed up Deutch's tenure as a period of "relentless self-criticism of the Agency, to its great detriment."[4] Nonetheless, he received high marks from the *New York Times* for his reform efforts, even though the newspaper ultimately considered him something of a disappointment for having been unable to "break" the rebellious Operations Directorate, and for his premature departure from Langley.[5]

Deutch fell short in his bid to become secretary of defense, having alienated the White House in a disagreement about the likely results of President Clinton's policies toward Iraq. In a Senate hearing, Deutch had observed that Saddam Hussein was stronger in 1996 than he had been after the first Persian Gulf War in 1990–91—not what the president wanted the public to hear, however true.[6] The DCI later explained that he meant stronger *politically*, not militarily, but this qualification was too little, too late from the vantage point of the White House.[7] After his retirement from the DCI position, Deutch reflected back on his tenure and declared that four years had been enough time in the government for him; he had grown tired of the political jockeying in Washington. "I never dreamed I would be in the government for so long, giving up my position at MIT," he told me.[8]

The Commission's Residual Effects

The intelligence community was unaffected in any large way by the Aspin-Brown inquiry—or HPSCI's IC21 reform efforts.[9] The intelligence community's budget remained intact and began to move upward; the effort to disclose the aggregate budget figure was squelched; counterintelligence and counterterrorism received far less attention than warranted; the ethical limits of covert action were never defined, nor its role in the future; the strained relations between the CIA and the FBI continued; the weaknesses in accountability went largely unaddressed; and the DCI's powers remained stunted. It would take the tragic events of September 11, 2001, to bring about stronger demands for intelligence reform.

This is not to say that the commission was without purpose. Presidential commissions have a multiplicity of functions. Traditionally, they offer symbolic reassurance, provide information to shape policy, educate experts and the general public, and allow delay (a "cooling off" period) while a problem undergoes further study.[10] The Somali disaster had led to Aspin's interest in an intelligence inquiry. Most members of the commission, though, were initially concerned about the Ames treason case and—in light of Moynihan's widely reported attack against the CIA for failing to predict the fall of the Soviet Union—with providing legitimacy to the nation's intelligence mission and protecting its budget. The Somalian intelligence and the Ames counterintelligence failures were investigated chiefly by the DoD and a CIA/FBI team, respectively, with relatively little attention given to these subjects by our commissioners—ironically, in light of the panel's origins. We did review the DoD and CIA/FBI findings on these topics, though, and found them sufficiently thorough to stand on their own without us duplicating this work. Our final report reassured the public that valuable preventive lessons had been learned from both the Somalian and the Ames disasters. In the pages of the report, Warner achieved his original goal: we had provided a treatise on the merits of good intelligence that would help lift the CIA's sagging reputation and morale in the aftermath of Somalia, Ames's treason, and Moynihan's perorations.

The commission retreated from an endorsement of a powerful director of national intelligence; this would have been far too bold a move for Harold Brown, a former secretary of defense and a bona fide member of the eight-hundred-pound gorilla club. We did give some legitimacy, though, to the idea of strengthening the DCI's authority, at least a little; and this notion of trying to make the intelligence director more effective began to gain currency in reform circles, despite ongoing objections from the Pentagon. In 2001, following the September terrorist attacks against the United States, a special PFIAB task force on intelligence, led by the board's able chairman at the time, General Brent Scowcroft, adopted this view in a written report that has never been published. President George W. Bush quickly buried the Scowcroft study when Secretary of Defense Donald Rumsfeld and his powerful ally, Vice President Dick Cheney, complained about Scowcroft's attempts to move the NSA, NRO, and NGA (the National Geospatial-Intelligence Agency, which by then had replaced NIMA) out of the Pentagon's control and firmly into the hands of the DCI. Henceforth, Scowcroft became *persona non grata* in the administration, even though he had been President George H. W. Bush's top foreign policy and security adviser. The general soon resigned from the president's intelligence board.

While many of the commission's reform proposals foundered, some did become policy. As I have mentioned, George J. Tenet (Deutch's replacement as DCI) finally released the aggregate intelligence budget figure for fiscal year 1996, despite the unwillingness of Congress to mandate its disclosure.[11] Moreover, as advocated by the commission, the intelligence agencies made long-overdue personnel cuts to downsize their burgeoning staffs; and intelligence managers consolidated imagery intelligence into NIMA (soon renamed NGA). Some of these changes may have occurred anyway (especially the creation of NIMA), but the commission's support gave them added legitimacy and moved the proposals along. Even when formal policy change was not the end result, the commission's efforts to define and highlight key issues helped intelligence managers understand the weaknesses in their organizations and where they needed to concentrate their day-to-day efforts toward improvements.

Certainly the commission aided the education of experts and the public alike on questions of intelligence, even if the *New York Times* and some other critics were unimpressed by our findings. The serious debates over intelligence problems inside the commission's NEOB conference room allowed members and staff to learn more about the intricacies of espionage. In this sense, the panel served as an advanced leadership seminar for these individuals, several of whom would rise to important government positions. When Wyche Fowler became U.S. ambassador to Saudi Arabia soon after the inquiry, his up-to-date knowledge of intelligence operations proved useful. This was true, as well, for Norman Dicks and Porter Goss in their oversight duties on HPSCI. Goss would soon chair the House Committee from 1997 to 2004, where he continued to be a strong critic of the CIA's humint inadequacies.[12] He then assumed the duties of DCI in 2004 for a "turbulent" eighteen months of service as the nation's spy chief.[13]

Further, Warren Rudman soon became PFIAB chairman, and from 1999 to 2001 he also co-chaired (with former senator Gary Hart, D-CO) the U.S. Commission on National Security/21st Century.[14] Friedman went on to be chief economic adviser to President George W. Bush, starting in 2002 and lasting through 2004. He continued to served on PFIAB (which had a name change to PIAB, President's Intelligence Advisory Board, during the second Bush years), where he followed Rudman as its chairman, and he also served as the IOB chairman—both leadership positions beginning in 2005. President Clinton appointed Anthony Harrington as ambassador to Brazil in 2000; Paul Wolfowitz served on the Rumsfeld Commission in 1998 (it concluded that long-range missile attacks from countries like Iran, Iraq, and North Korea were a genuine threat to the United States), was named deputy secretary of defense in 2001, and, following a bumpy career at DoD, left to become president of the World Bank (where he had another rough ride); David Dewhurst, the cowboy commissioner, headed the Texas Office of Homeland Security in 2002 and was subsequently elected lieutenant governor of Texas.

At the staff level, in addition to L. Britt Snider becoming the CIA's inspector general, DCI Tenet named our deputy staff director John Moseman as the CIA's director of the Office of Congressional Affairs and then chief of staff to Acting CIA Director John McLaughlin; and, the third member of the commission's legal troika, John Bellinger, took a position on the NSC staff and, subsequently, served as an aide to Secretary of State Condoleezza Rice and the highest-ranking lawyer in the Department of State. Bellinger found himself in the brave and lonely role of an inside critic of the Bush administration's adoption of torture and other extreme intelligence methods.[15] All of these individuals were better at their jobs, and in some cases helped into those jobs, because of their experience on the commission. John Deutch's military assistant, Dennis Blair, would serve in a number of command roles in the Navy, retiring as a four-star admiral. He would come out of retirement in 2009 to lead the intelligence community as the nation's third director of national intelligence—the new title (since 2004) for the U.S. spymaster.

In addition, largely through newspaper stories about the commission and its findings, the public acquired a better understanding of intelligence budgets and organizations. Moreover, scholars in the field of intelligence studies found in the commission's report a useful archive for research on a subject where information is difficult to acquire.

Clearly, delay was a consideration in the commission's proceedings, as the computer-solitaire player on the staff maintained from the beginning. While the Clinton administration searched for a new DCI, pondered how to prevent another Ames from undermining America's security, and tried to head off Moynihan's calls for shutting down the CIA, the establishment of an intelligence commission gave the public a sense that something was being done about these troubling matters. "The irresponsible cries for cuts in intelligence have faded," Senator Warner observed triumphantly at a commission meeting just before release of our final report. As he rose to leave for another appointment, he turned to Brown, smiled, and said: "The commission has fulfilled the original objective. I commend you."

———

Studies on commissions have suggested that their chairmen tend to dominate the proceedings.[16] My experience with the Aspin-Brown Commission confirmed this generalization. The commission chairmen, Les Aspin and then Harold Brown, definitely shaped the direction of the inquiry, over and above the influence of any other member. Vice Chairman Rudman, though, was an active player, too, and individual commissioners shined within certain policy domains, such as Robert Hermann when it came to matters of space surveillance and Zoë Baird on relations between law-enforcement officers and intelligence officials. The overall participation rates of members in commission meetings for the entire thirteen months of the inquiry are displayed in Figure 13.1.

A second generalization in the research on commissions is that they often have a major effect on policy. The Aspin-Brown Commission did have some influence on policy, but certainly nothing major. Well-positioned defenders of the intelligence status quo, notably the Pentagon and its allies on key congressional committees, stood as sentinels on guard against sweeping

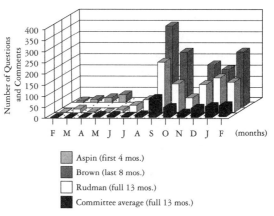

FIGURE 13.1 Overall Levels of Member Participation on the Aspin-Brown Commission, 1995–96

Number of questions and comments per month (for February 1995 to February 1996). Based on the author's tabulations at the Commission's fourteen meetings (one per month, plus an additional public hearing in January of 1996). Chairman Aspin's rates reflect the first four months of participation; Chairman Brown's, the last eight months; and Vice Chairman Rudman's, the entire thirteen months. The September 1995 meeting took place over four days and provided an opportunity for the highest levels of participation; other meetings normally lasted one day, but occasionally two. The "Commission Average" is based on the participation rates of all seventeen members, except in June when the commission had a membership of sixteen. According to their total number of questions and comments, the commissioners displayed the following hierarchy of participation rates (the presidential appointees are in italics):

1. *Brown* (1,278)
2. *Rudman* (957)
3. *Hermann* (573)
4. *Friedman* (457)
5. Fowler (373)
6. Coelho (366)
7. *Harrington* (339)
8. *Allen* (263)
9. Pursley (231)
10. Dewhurst (213)
11. Goss (197)
12. Dicks (192)
13. *Wolfowitz* (151)
14. *Baird* (146)
15. *Caracristi* (125)
16. Aspin (73)
17. Warner (64)
18. Exon (11)

intelligence reform—particularly the creation of a director of national intelligence with full budget and appointment powers over all the civilian and military intelligence agencies. Even inside the commission, a majority of members (and especially Chairman Brown) had no interest in building up a muscular DCI or DNI against the wishes of the incumbent secretary of defense and the Pentagon's allies on Capitol Hill. My guess is that Les Aspin, another former SecDef with an increasingly pro–status quo orientation, would have come out in a similar place, although he might well have pushed harder for some trimming of the budget, and he certainly would have weighed in more persistently on the Hill than Brown did in lobbying for the commission's recommendations.

It should be emphasized that before, as well as during and after the days of the Aspin-Brown Commission, the DCI and the intelligence agencies were anything but passive observers. The first individual to serve as the nation's intelligence chief after the end of the Cold War, Robert M. Gates, had made dramatic changes in the orientation of the CIA as early as 1991, by shifting most of its resources away from Russia as a target and toward new threats—especially the growing problem of global weapons proliferation. Similarly, the NSA director moved to prepare his agency for changes in technology affecting electronic surveillance, notably the trend toward fiber-optic transmissions; burned by the Ames treachery, the CIA's Counterintelligence Staff tightened its security reviews, adopting closer auditing procedures over personal spending by intelligence officers. Moreover, DCI Deutch energetically pursued his interest in the consolidation of space photographic surveillance; and both he and his successor, George Tenet, took important steps to improve humint, through an aggressive recruitment of new CIA case officers and the establishment of rigorous language-training programs for Agency personnel. Deficiencies in "America's first line of defense" remained, however. The number of NOCs, for example, stayed flat until 2000, when there was a slight increase.[17] And, as late as 2006, not a single person at the FBI could speak Arabic in the section of the Bureau responsible for investigations into international terrorism.[18]

America's spy chiefs in the post–Cold War era found change difficult to achieve in some areas, especially overcoming the separateness of the intelligence organizations—replacing the agency fiefdoms (stovepipes) with a sense of corporate teamwork. The Aspin-Brown Commission could have been more aggressive in this quest for greater jointness. Clearly we fell short of achieving the kind of all-source fusion (integration) of intelligence that many reformers hoped to see. As intelligence scholar Amy Zegart has written, America's spy agencies were "nowhere close" to being as good as they should have been on the eve of the 9/11 attacks in 2001.[19] They might have been, though, had Congress fully embraced even the limited reforms we sought—and had Deutch, Brown, Rudman, and, especially, President Clinton (and, after him, President George W. Bush) lobbied harder for improvements in America's intelligence capabilities.

It is unnecessary to review in detail the many intelligence errors that pre-ceded the 9/11 tragedy, followed by the mistakes in ascertaining the presence of unconventional weaponry in Iraq; these subjects have been the focus of several good government reports, as well as books and articles by journalists and scholars.[20] A summary of the major shortcomings, though, will illus-trate how a great many of the issues examined by the Aspin-Brown Commission continued to plague the United States in the years following its inquiry.

Even though the intelligence community was weaker than one would have liked in the run-up to 9/11, its agencies deserve more credit for warning policy makers about a terrorist attack against the United States than is usu-ally accorded them. Recall that as early as 1995, the CIA's Counterterrorism Center reported to the White House, the Aspin Commission, and other top levels of government that terrorism was likely to head in a startling new direction ("Aerial terrorism seems likely at some point—filling an airplane with explosives and dive-bombing a target"). The CTC erred only in not understanding that a commercial airliner does not need additional explo-sives; filled with highly volatile jet fuel, it already has the capacity to be a powerful guided missile. In early 2001, another panel, the Hart-Rudman Commission, sponsored by the Department of Defense and led by former senators Hart and Rudman, drew on intelligence reports to warn officials once again about the likely imminence of a terrorist attack against the American homeland.[21]

THE 9/11 INTELLIGENCE FAILURE

In their 1995 document, the CTC's analysts had good reason to be concerned about aerial terrorism. After all, there had been public reports in 1994 and 1995 about terrorist schemes to fly an airplane into the Eiffel Tower or into the CIA Headquarters building. The Agency's multiple and strong warnings on this topic surfaced in high policy circles, including the NSC, SSCI, and HPSCI, with regularity between 1995 and 2001. This is why George Tenet, the DCI at the time, asserted after the 9/11 attacks that this tragic event had not been an intelligence failure: the CIA had fulfilled its obligation to warn policy officials.

Tenet's argument is badly flawed, of course, because the intelligence community never provided officials with precise information about the tim-ing and location of the anticipated airplane hijackings and the kamikaze assaults against New York City and the Pentagon. Missing from the intelligence reports was "actionable" information that would have allowed law enforcement and security personnel to arrest the terrorists before they boarded the ill-fated flights.

Moreover, during the period from 1995 to 2001, the intelligence agencies flooded officials with many other dire—but also unspecified—predictions about additional perils, from trucks or vans filled with dynamite that might explode in urban commuter tunnels to attacks against the nation's ports, railroad system, livestock, crops, and water supplies. These reports lacked guidance about which threats were most likely, and most of the time they did not offer enough detail to give decision-makers an opportunity to set up pinpointed defenses. Since the protection of the American people costs money, and lots of it—say, to inspect all of the large cargo containers coming to these shores aboard ocean freighters, or to reinforce cockpit doors on every commercial aircraft—policy makers become paralyzed at the thought of preparing for every conceivable attack scenario. Rather than spend billions, and in the process run up the national debt and risk public criticism for excessive taxation and spending, they are inclined just to hope nothing bad will happen.

One can see in the actions of the government preceding the 9/11 attacks a parallel with the wishful thinking that took place before Hurricane Katrina devastated New Orleans in 2005. Officials in Louisiana had received many warnings from professional engineers and other experts that a category 5 hurricane could demolish the levees that protected the city from floods. Improvements to bolster the levees, however, would have been extraordinarily expensive. Moreover, category 5 hurricanes are extremely rare. Thus, the temptation was strong to spend the money on other pressing policy needs (education, healthcare, streets, sewers, crime prevention) and hope that such a powerful storm would never come—or, if it did, that the levees would somehow hold. When the storm did come and the levees failed, as predicted, the costs of response and rehabilitation went far beyond what it would have cost to strengthen the levees before the storm.

One might think the 9/11 attacks would have taught the United States something about the importance of spending money on homeland security. To some extent it did; for example, the second Bush administration created (albeit begrudgingly) a Department of Homeland Security. Yet the spending priorities of the administration belied a genuine willingness to address vulnerabilities at home. Much of the new department's counterterrorism funding ended up as pork-barrel benefits for states that were unlikely candidates for a terrorist attack (rescue equipment for North Pole, Alaska, for instance, and chemical suits for Outagamie, Wisconsin), in contrast to such major potential targets as America's metropolitan areas, transportation centers, nuclear reactors, and ports of entry. Moreover, as national security expert Stephen Flynn notes, during every three days of warfare in Iraq the second Bush administration routinely spent the equivalent of its entire $600 million budget request of 2006 for "safeguarding all of the nation's seaports, mass transit systems, railways, bridges, tunnels, and energy facilities."[22] It is one thing to insist on actionable intelligence, and to demand a sense of probabilities about impending dangers—this is vital; but it is important, too, for policy makers to take intelligence warnings more seriously, and to fund adequately projects that will truly help defend the nation against lethal threats highlighted by the intelligence agencies.

The 9/11 surprise, then, was indeed a policy failure, as illustrated by the minimal efforts of both the Clinton and the second Bush administrations to tighten airport security, warn pilots, seal off cockpits, field air marshals, or even alert top officials in the Department of Transportation—despite the CIA's persistent warnings from 1995 to 2001 about anticipated aerial terrorist operations. The events of 9/11, though, amounted to a major intelligence failure as well, even if DCI Tenet preferred not to call it that. Government inquiries since 9/11 have discovered that the nation's secret agencies proved unable to coordinate and act on many important pieces of specific information in their possession about Qaeda operatives and their planned attacks against the United States.[23] For example, the FBI failed to locate two of the nineteen hijackers, Nawaf al-Hazmi and Khalid al-Mihdhar, despite an alert from the CIA about their arrival in San Diego—although in an unfortunate bureaucratic lapse the Agency's warning wasn't passed along to the Bureau until late in August 2001, after the terrorists had been in Southern California for several months. Hazmi's name was even listed in the local San Diego phone book, but still the Bureau was never able to track him down.[24] Here again one could see the lingering problem of a poor CIA-FBI working relationship. For all of our efforts on the Aspin-Brown Commission, reinforced by the prodding of DCI John Deutch, to push the two agencies toward a better union, for all intents and purposes they remained stovepipes.

The Bureau also displayed a lack of responsiveness to warnings from its own agents in Phoenix and Minneapolis about suspicious flight training for foreigners taking place in those cities. For good reason, the FBI agent in Minneapolis had requested a warrant from Bureau headquarters to enter the apartment in Minneapolis where a suspect (Zacarias Moussaoui) lived. This would have allowed his computer to be examined for evidence that he might be enrolled in flight training for nefarious purposes. Despite the fact that this man had known ties to foreign terrorists, FBI Headquarters rejected the warrant request, apparently out of concern that the justification to the Foreign Intelligence Surveillance Act (FISA) court would not be strong enough—a poor judgment call by Bureau officials in Washington, DC. Access to Moussaoui's laptop computer might well have unraveled the 9/11 plot, since he did indeed prove to have a Qaeda connection and is sometimes referred to as the "twentieth highjacker."[25]

At a deeper level, 9/11 was an intelligence failure because the CIA had no assets within Al Qaeda; because the NSA fell far behind on translating relevant sigint intercepts involving suspected terrorists, including telephone conversations between Qaeda lieutenants on the eve of the attacks; and because the intelligence community lacked language skills and a deep understanding of nations and factions in the Middle East and Southwest Asia, or even about the objectives and likely motivations of the Qaeda leader Osama bin Laden.

IRAQI WMDS

In the case of weapons of mass destruction in Iraq—the second major intelligence failure to follow on the heels of the Aspin-Brown inquiry—the mistakes of the secret agencies were in some ways even more troubling. A National Intelligence Estimate of October 2002 concluded, as did most intelligence agencies and outside analysts, that WMDs were probably present in Iraq. This assessment appears to have been based on three primary sources of inaccurate information.[26]

First, because the CIA and DoD had so few well-placed human assets inside Iraq during the interwar years (1992–2002), analysts in the intelligence community had to extrapolate from what they knew about Iraq when Americans last had boots on the ground in that rogue nation, as part of the war effort in 1991. At that time, the CIA learned that its estimates regarding the progress of the Iraqi WMD program prior to the first Persian Gulf War had been inaccurate; Saddam's development of unconventional weapons had advanced some five years beyond what the Agency and other intelligence organizations had projected. Absent reliable ground-based sources once U.S. troops departed from Iraq in 1991, soon followed by UN weapons inspectors (who were thrown out of the nation by Saddam because CIA officers were embedded in the inspection team), intelligence analysts were no doubt tempted to overcompensate for their earlier underestimates by overestimating the likelihood of WMDs in 2002.

Second, the reports of two seemingly important humint interrogations proved false. Testimony from a German asset (Rafid Ahmed Alwan) from

Iraq, a Baghdad scientist known—prophetically, as it turned out—by the intelligence codename "Curveball," factored into the CIA's assessments. German intelligence officials vowed that Alwan was a valuable and reliable source, and rebuffed the requests of Agency counterintelligence officers to interview him themselves. Only two years after the second war against Iraq started in 2003 did the Germans acknowledge that Curveball had, in fact, turned out to be a fabricator—indeed a pathological liar and a convicted sex offender. Moreover, the confessions of an Al Qaeda member named Ibn al-Shaykh al-Libi, captured by the U.S. military in Afghanistan after the 9/11 attacks and initially interrogated by the DIA, did not hold up either. He admitted after the United States had invaded Iraq that he made up stories about Saddam's WMD advances just to stop the torture inflicted on him by Egyptian intelligence interrogators, to whom American intelligence had rendered him for further questioning.[27]

Third, the exiled Iraqi National Congress, led by Ahmed Chalabi, claimed to know what was going on in Iraq. Chalabi, a charming, well-educated, middle-aged physician from Baghdad, encouraged the U.S. intelligence agencies and the second Bush administration to believe that Saddam was determined to acquire a nuclear weapons capability. Chalabi's reliability was called into question, though, after the U.S. invasion of Iraq in 2003. Belatedly, it was determined that his hidden agenda had been to push for an American attack so that he might advance his personal political agenda: the toppling of Saddam Hussein, followed by his own rise to power in Baghdad.

On top of this "evidence," U.S. intelligence analysts were also aware that the British secret service, along with the espionage agencies of several other countries, were worried about the possibility of Iraqi WMDs. Yet an official British government inquiry into this issue (the Butler Report) in 2004 revealed that the worries of British intelligence (MI6) analysts had more to do with the possible use of *tactical* chemical-biological weapons by Saddam on the battlefields of Iraq if he faced a foreign invasion force, not *strategic* WMDs that could strike the United Kingdom, the United States, or even their support forces in the Middle East at a distance from the fighting.[28] The speeches of Saddam himself buttressed the WMD hypothesis, since he often boasted of his capabilities in the realm of unconventional weapons—perhaps in a misguided rhetorical attempt to deter a feared Iranian invasion of his country.

It is often claimed that the second Bush administration pressured CIA analysts to write an NIE (finally requested by the Congress in 2002) that pointed to the presence of WMDs in Iraq, thereby providing useful intelligence support to legitimize a military intervention against the Iraqi regime—

what some argue was the goal of the administration in the first place, the question of WMDs aside. Vice President Dick Cheney visited analysts at Agency Headquarters an unprecedented eight times leading up to the publication of the 2002 NIE. He sharply questioned the estimates of analysts whenever they seemed not to share his conviction that unconventional weaponry must surely exist in Iraq, and that Al Qaeda and Saddam had a secret alliance. The CIA analysts with whom Cheney visited, though, say they were not intimidated by the vice president ("despite his perpetually curled lip," as one put it to me). On the contrary, they were pleased to have such rare high-level attention paid to their work, and they didn't change a single word in their analyses because of the vice president's interrogations.[29]

In addition, Secretary of State Colin Powell visited with CIA officials several times to probe the strength of their evidence on Iraqi WMDs, especially on the eve of his appearance before the United Nations on February 3, 2003, to make the case before the world for armed intervention into Iraq. During his visits to Langley, the secretary discovered some disagreements among intelligence analysts. Even within his own intelligence shop, the Bureau of Intelligence and Research (INR) in the Department of State, dissent was in the air, as it was inside the U.S. Air Force intelligence service and the Department of Energy intelligence unit (an organization notably expert when it comes to global nuclear issues, which it tracks daily). These relatively small agencies offered assessments that disagreed in some important ways from the intelligence community's majority viewpoint in support of the WMD hypothesis.

The dissents from the three small but well-regarded agencies should have triggered some skepticism in the administration regarding the hypothesis that Saddam had a robust WMD program. Yet a trio of behemoths in the intelligence community—the CIA, NSA, and DIA—continued to argue that Saddam most likely did have highly dangerous unconventional weapons, whether nuclear, biological, or chemical. Moreover, DCI Tenet, who had frequent access to the White House, backed the intelligence community's majority opinion. One point of dispute centered on the sixty thousand high-strength aluminum tubes purchased by Iraq that might have been meant for an uranium centrifuge in a nuclear weapons program. Important, too, especially for Powell's UN presentation, was the testimony of Curveball and some imint products that seemed to indicate the presence of mobile chemical-weapons labs in Iraq. Yet INR analysts in Powell's own department and other analysts in the Department of Energy's intelligence unit maintained that the aluminum tubes were most likely combustion chambers for conventional rockets, not components of a uranium centrifuge. Moreover, the mobile labs could just as well have been (and indeed turned out to be) fire trucks, not the chemical-decontamination vehicles that accompany chemical weapons.[30] Further, analysts in Air Force intelligence questioned the majority opinion that Iraq's UAVs had a long-range weapons-carrying capability.

Nonetheless, Powell deferred to the powerful majority coalition. Further, these debates were internal ones among professional intelligence analysts for the most part, outside the purview of the American public. The three small agencies were swamped by the judgments of their mighty companion organizations—and the DCI himself.[31] In the end, Powell went to the UN to make his argument on behalf of the administration for the Iraqi invasion. He now states that "the sourcing was inaccurate and wrong and, in some cases, deliberately misleading, and for that I am disappointed and I regret it."[32]

To his credit, President George W. Bush questioned DCI Tenet directly about his confidence in the hastily prepared 2002 NIE conclusion that supported the WMD hypothesis. Was he absolutely sure there were unconventional weapons in Iraq? Tenet's response, reported by Bob Woodward of the *Washington Post*, is now well known: "It's a slam dunk, Mr. President."[33] Those who have read the 2002 NIE indicate, however, that the analysts who wrote it were by no means claiming any such sweeping conclusion.[34] While they did state that, on balance, the odds were in favor of finding WMDs in Iraq, the Estimate contained a number of caveats about the assessment's empirical softness. This uncertainty is precisely what DCI Tenet should have underscored for the president: that the NIE was hardly a definitive report and that more on-the-ground fact finding was badly needed to fill in the gaps; and that the CIA was uneasy about the humint from Curveball and Al-Libi, as well as the motives of Chalabi. A briefing along these lines from the DCI to the president would have highlighted the need for a delay in the invasion plans until new UN weapons inspectors were able to reenter Iraq and clear up the intelligence ambiguities. Certainly this is what two of our major allies at the UN, France and Germany, strongly advocated at the time. Instead, the White House seems to have been all too ready to accept the majority findings of the intelligence community, which conveniently happened to run parallel to their own policy aspirations for an Iraqi invasion.

George Tenet evidently fell into an enticing trap that awaits any spy-master: the politics of the White House. Caught up in the administration's enthusiasm for war against Saddam, which would have (the administration believed) eliminated a primary threat to Israel, enhanced the prospects for democracy in the Middle East, avenged Saddam's assassination plot against former President George H. W. Bush (who had humiliated Iraq in the first Persian Gulf War with a quick victory), and ensured access to Iraqi oil, Tenet provided the clinching reassurance for a White House in need of public support. In reality, however, the only real slam dunk was the guarantee that war would now come on winged heels.

Even before his "slum dunk" remark, the DCI had failed to correct the record at another significant moment in the WMD debate. Inserted into the president's State of the Union address in 2003 was an assertion that Saddam had sought to purchase yellow-cake uranium from Niger, suggesting that the Iraqi dictator was indeed pursuing a nuclear weapons program. The CIA had looked into this allegation, dispatching a former U.S. ambassador to make direct inquiries on the ground in the African nation. The ambassador found no evidence to support the allegations and reported this finding to the CIA, which in turn passed on the information to deputy national security adviser Stephen Hadley—all well in advance of the State of the Union address. Yet, the speech included the yellow-cake claim anyway, even though Tenet himself had personally telephoned Hadley and advised removal of the passage.[35] The notion that Saddam had tried to buy yellow-cake uranium was now cloaked in the legitimacy of the President's own words in the important nationally televised event. Tenet claimed that he had never seen an advance copy of the final State of the Union remarks (odd for a leading government official) and therefore was unable to correct the record before the address to Congress. He also failed to correct the public record after the speech.

A number of conclusions may be derived from the 9/11 and Iraqi WMD cases, only one of which was clearly addressed by the Aspin-Brown Commission. First, intelligence officers—and most notably the nation's intelligence chief—must be brutally candid about the limits of their analyses, cautioning presidents and others whenever their findings and estimates are on shaky ground. What is firmly rooted in empirical findings, and what is largely speculation; which agent reports are fully vetted and which are from second- or third-hand sources—these matters must be carefully delineated. The Aspin-Brown Commission did not emphasize this point sufficiently in its report, although it is basic to the preparation of good intelligence products and we should have underscored it.

Second, intelligence collectors and analysts must be more forceful in vetting their sources, another point we never addressed in our report. When the Germans balked at allowing the CIA to conduct its own interviews with the asset known as Curveball, the Agency should have downgraded the dependability of this source—or stop relying on him at all.

Most importantly, intelligence officials must maintain a wall between themselves and the policy desires of an administration. Here is a fundamental principle of analysis—the Kentian imperative—that the Aspin-Brown

Commission did highlight. The siren song of White House politics must be as anathema to intelligence managers and analysts as the beckoning witch with a poisonous apple should have been to Snow White. Speaking truth to power is a notoriously difficult task. Those in power usually do not want to hear facts that run counter to their established policies. In the days of antiquity, the messenger with bad news was not warmly greeted.

Further, policy makers frequently convince themselves that they are too busy to read intelligence reports, or even to listen to oral briefings. Perhaps the greatest paradox regarding American intelligence is that so much effort and funding go into the gathering and analysis of intelligence for policy makers, only to have those in high office pay no (or little) attention to the results.

Then comes the even more vexing problem of "politicization"—the cardinal sin of intelligence, as Jim Woolsey reminded the Aspin-Brown Commission. The politicization of intelligence can take two forms. Intelligence officers can "cook" information to suit the needs of policy makers, currying the favor of political superiors to advance their own careers: what is known as "intelligence to please." Fortunately, this occurs fairly infrequently since, like academicians and journalists, most analysts are imbued with a sense of professional ethics that forbids this practice.

More common is the second form, whereby policy officials distort intelligence reports provided to them when the analytic conclusions fail to support their policy objectives. As a character in John Steinbeck's *The Winter of Our Discontent* sagaciously remarks: "No one wants advice—only corroboration."[36] One instance of this is "cherry picking," that is, selecting from intelligence reports only those items of information and analysis that uphold one's policy or political preferences, ignoring countervailing facts. Sometimes, even more blatantly, policy officials simply ignore entire reports, as President Lyndon B. Johnson was inclined to do with CIA analyses that presented a dismal prognosis about the likelihood of military success in Vietnam,[37] or as the second Bush administration did with CIA reports on the lack of an Al Qaeda–Iraq connection.[38] In such instances, the unenviable but vital responsibility of intelligence officers is to call policy officials to account for their distortions—publicly if necessary, even though it may place their jobs in jeopardy.

The CIA and its British counterpart, MI6, both of whom understood that policy makers were exhibiting an unwarranted alarmist stance toward Iraq in 2002, stood by mutely for the most part. An exception was when CIA analysts complained publicly (through anonymous media leaks) that Vice President Cheney was wrong to insist there was a significant tie between Al Qaeda and Saddam Hussein. Intelligence reporting had come to just the opposite conclusion, although CIA analysts cautioned that a bond might in fact be forged between global terrorists and the Iraqi dictatorship (or its insurgent remnants) if the West invaded Iraq. Despite the CIA's unambiguous findings to the contrary, the vice president continued to argue on television and radio talk shows prior to the U.S. invasion of Iraq that Al Qaeda and Saddam's secular regime were secretly allied.

In Search of Further Intelligence Reform

The American public must come to understand that intelligence agencies, like every other human enterprise, will always have their share of failures. Such is the existential dilemma of trying to forecast world events. Nevertheless, much can be done to lessen the odds of failure. The various phases of the intelligence cycle provide a roadmap for improvements that can be made in America's intelligence capabilities.

PLANNING AND DIRECTION

First, as the Aspin-Brown Commission emphasized in 1996, policy officials must still make a better effort to define precisely what their intelligence needs are. Decision makers need to communicate exactly what they want to know, so the intelligence agencies can focus their attention on these requirements. The tasking of the intelligence agencies continues to be vaguely explained, if at all, and only irregularly updated; the result has been an overly diffuse, and sometimes irrelevant, intelligence effort—one of the key complaints registered by Robert Gates to the commission at the Farm in 1995.

COLLECTION

As every government study of 9/11 and of the allegations about WMDs in Iraq has concluded, the balance between techint and humint remains out of kilter in favor of spy machines, to the detriment of establishing effective spy rings around the world—a problem underlined by the Aspin-Brown Commission. Yet, even nine years after 9/11, the United States has a long way to go in developing the language skills and knowledge of foreign cultures necessary for intelligence officers if they are to succeed in the recruitment of well-placed assets overseas. Just in sheer numbers of case officers, the CIA is woefully understaffed. The FBI has more agents in New York City alone than the CIA has operations officers around the world.

Further, when it comes to electronic surveillance, the government of the United States must examine anew the relationship between the FBI, the FISA court, and the Patriot Act of 2001. With the appropriate safeguards to civil liberties, steps must be taken to ensure that wiretap warrants can be acquired with dispatch in properly documented cases of national security threats, as failed to happen in the Minneapolis case during events leading up to the 9/11 attacks. At the same time, however, the original purpose of the FISA court—requiring warrants for the surveillance of Americans suspected of endangering national security—must be fully restored since its secret abandonment by the second Bush administration in 2001; and the telecommunications companies involved in these violations of the FISA statute must be reminded (apparently periodically, because there were similar wiretap violations uncovered by the Church Committee in 1975) that they have no right to break the law, even if a misguided President asks them to do so.[39]

PROCESSING

The intelligence agencies are behind the learning curve on data sifting. The federal government must pay higher salaries to attract state-of-the-art computer specialists, and should call upon Silicon Valley to assist the intelligence agencies in overcoming their information-technology deficiencies. The challenge is twofold. First, intelligence managers must connect more effectively all the computers of the intelligence agencies (horizontal integration), then down to state and local counterterrorism officials (vertical integration), so that information can be rapidly shared—with all the necessary counterintelligence firewalls—with security and law enforcement officials on America's front line defenses. The goal should be to ensure the smooth electronic communication of intelligence warnings throughout the nation's security establishment in Washington, throughout the nation, and to American troops and diplomats overseas. Second, as information is gathered, intelligence managers must develop improved methods of filtering out the high percentage of "noise" from the small but important strand of "signals" that stream into the secret agencies from platforms and assets around the globe. These are profound IT challenges that deserve as much attention as was recently garnered by the danger of cyber warfare.

ANALYSIS

In the realm of analysis, better language skills and understanding of foreign cultures is once again vital for intelligence success. Further, analysts will need to be more careful about highlighting important nuances in their reporting and making it clear how good (or bad) their sources are. Useful, too, would be a better sense of what the analysts believe the probabilities are that their predictions are likely to happen: low, moderate, or high. This approach is sometimes used by analysts, but inconsistently. When an analyst presents a list of threats without any sense of which are most likely to occur, the end result is to paralyze the will of the policy maker to confront any of the threats. Especially important are efforts to ensure that policy makers better understand the reasons for dissent by some agencies or analysts. Intelligence reports should red-flag these dissents, so that America's leaders have a full understanding of all the key arguments involved, not just the majority opinions. During the Iraqi WMD debate, the contrary views of the Energy Department, INR, and Air Force intelligence were inadequately underscored, especially by the DCI in his conversations with the president. Though rarely used, Team A/Team B exercises in competitive analysis are useful, too, as a means for flushing out dissent—if Team B is staffed by objective experts.

DISSEMINATION

Analysts and intelligence managers must be trained to resist pressures from policy makers to "cook" intelligence; and they must be determined to set the record straight for the public if intelligence reports are twisted for political purposes by those in high office. Other than telling the truth as best they can discern it, no responsibility is greater for intelligence officers. On the policy side, the American people must chose leaders who are fact-seekers, individuals who are open minded and able to change course in light of new evidence—who, in other words, take the intelligence reports they receive seriously even when they run counter to their hopes.

Important, too, is the development of better ties between the producers and consumers of intelligence, a dominant theme in the Aspin-Brown Commission report. The best approach is the one recommended by the commission, that is, for the intelligence agencies to place (openly, and with permission, of course) liaison officers inside the policy departments—individuals who can attend staff meetings, periodically discuss with decision makers their information needs, and otherwise learn by hanging out at the water cooler what is on the minds and in the in-boxes of decision makers. In this manner, the intelligence agencies can improve their ability to help with relevant factual information and objective analysis. This is the most surefire way to ensure that intelligence is related to the pressing decision agendas of government officials. If the work of intelligence officers lacks relevance to the workaday demands of decision making, they may as well close their offices, return the entire spy budget to the federal treasury, and go fishing with Wyche Fowler.

These objectives will not be easy to meet; but the United States should set high goals for its intelligence services, if we expect to ward off another 9/11 attack (or worse). The starting point is effective leadership. The *sine qua non* for the success of intelligence reform is a president who understands the importance of strengthening America's security shield, and who is willing to carry on the effort to bring greater cohesion to the nation's fragmented intelligence community by finally establishing a genuine director of national intelligence.

| Intelligence Reform Redux

THE CREATION OF A STRONGER INTELLIGENCE chief with full budget and appointment powers over all of the agencies in the intelligence community—someone with the authority to bring about an all-source sharing of information—has been the main recommendation of every intelligence-reform panel since 1949, most recently the Aspin-Brown Commission in 1996 and the Kean (9/11) Commission in 2004.[1] Yet this idea has yet to be adopted in a manner that would truly integrate the civilian and military intelligence agencies in the United States. The Department of Defense has jealously guarded its military intelligence prerogatives and persistently refused to allow the creation of a true director of central intelligence (DCI) or, using a different name, a director of national intelligence (DNI), to guide the nation's intelligence mission.

Finally, though, with the Intelligence Reform and Terrorism Prevention Act of 2004, the Kean Commission appeared to have convinced policy makers of the previously impossible: that a true national intelligence director should be established.[2] Yet, digging beneath the surface of the Reform Act, it becomes clear that once again the Defense Department and its allies in Congress were able to dilute and obfuscate the authority of the newly created intelligence chief. As intelligence scholar Amy Zegart has accurately concluded, the 2004 legislation "left the secretary of defense with greater power, the director of national intelligence with little, and the Intelligence Community even more disjointed."[3]

The New Intelligence Debates

During 2002–04, in the aftermath of the 9/11 attacks and the faulty intelligence analysis regarding WMDs in Iraq, a fresh spate of inquiries into the performance of the intelligence community pointed again to the need for a strengthened intelligence director—whether called a DCI or DNI—a leader with broad authority who could improve information sharing among the secret agencies and integrate their other activities as well.[4] This time the well-treaded reform proposal gained traction, a consequence of the 9/11 attacks that left the Twin Towers in ruins, the Pentagon in flames, nearly three thousand Americans dead, and the United States in a state of shock and anger. Telling, too, was the growing realization that an intelligence estimate written in 2002 predicting the likely presence WMDs in Iraq—the trigger for the second Persian Gulf War—had been flat-out wrong. The expectations of the intelligence community that the transition from the tyranny of Saddam Hussein to democracy in Iraq would be relatively smooth were also in error; the reality instead was stiff resistance from insurgents, leading to mounting U.S. casualties and a prolonged, unpopular war—one that has lasted longer than the Second World War.

Just as the memory of Pearl Harbor and the specter of a threatening Red Army had concentrated Washington's attention on intelligence reform in 1947, so, too, did the stunning destruction and carnage on American soil on the morning of the 9/11 attacks. More than ever since the passage of the flawed National Security Act in 1947, Washington officials seemed ready to increase the stunted powers of the DCI.[5]

In July 2004, the 9/11 (Kean) Commission advocated, along with a series of other reform proposals, the creation of a national intelligence director with full budget and appointment powers over the key entities in the intelligence community—an idea sharply opposed by the CIA.[6] Briefly tagged with the acronym "NID," the proposed national intelligence director was soon more commonly referred to in intelligence circles and the media as the director of national intelligence, or DNI, an analogue of the more familiar abbreviation of DCI for the nation's existing spymaster. As the Kean Commission made clear, the new intelligence chief would need to have power over the budget of each intelligence agency, as well as the right to hire and fire their managers (the "gorillas")—or else remain a mere figurehead.

Under the initial DNI proposal, lower-level "tactical" military intelligence programs would stay within the purview of the SecDef—contrary to scare-mongering claims by some DoD officials who sought to sway opinion against the proposal (as the Defense Department had succeeded in doing when the Aspin-Brown Commission attempted to enhance the powers of the

DCI in 1996). Further, the DNI would be located in the Executive Office of the President and would no longer run the CIA; the Agency would have its own leader, a director of the central intelligence agency (DCIA or D/CIA), who would report to the DNI.[7] The Kean Commission also advocated the creation of a National Counterterrorism Center (NCTC), an organization for joint operational planning and the sharing of intelligence regarding terrorists, with staffing from throughout the community—similar to a DCI center, only with more equitable representation by officers from across the intelligence community, not overwhelmingly from the CIA. The NCTC was to be part of the DNI office, but would also report directly to the president (a split allegiance that seemed bound to cause confusion). Presented forcefully, with gripping evidence and readable prose, and presaged by widely seen televised hearings, the commission's report became a national bestseller and a topic of discussion during the 2004 presidential election.[8]

In fits and starts, the White House acceded to the commission's DNI plan (itself a variation of a proposal advanced unsuccessfully by Oklahoma lawmakers Senator David L. Boren and Rep. Dave McCurdy in the 1990s). At an August 2004 press conference announcing the intelligence changes, President George W. Bush said: "I think that the new national intelligence director ought to be able to coordinate budgets...[and] work with the respective agencies to set priorities."[9]

President Bush had reservations, though, about how deeply the DNI should be allowed to reach into the purse of DoD's military intelligence organizations, and to what extent the DNI should be allowed to appoint the intelligence-agency managers—the same issues that had hounded the Aspin-Brown Commission's deliberations about strengthening the DCI office.[10] The *New York Times* worried that the president was turning a potentially useful new leadership position into "a neutralized bureaucratic cipher by depriving the office of any real authority."[11] The ambiguity surrounding the new DNI's powers led the ranking minority member on HPSCI, Jane Harmon (D-CA), to remind her congressional colleagues: "If the national intelligence director has no real budgetary authority, he or she will have no real power."[12]

Later in August of 2004, the president issued executive orders that gave his DCI designate, Porter Goss, authority to "determine" the budget for the National Foreign Intelligence Program (NFIP), which is the label given to all foreign intelligence activities above the level of purely tactical military operations (later known as the National Intelligence Program or NIP). Among the NFIP's major agencies are the CIA, NSA, NGA, NRO, INR, intelligence units in the Departments of Treasury and Energy, and the FBI's intelligence division. They account for approximately three-fourths of the annual intelligence budget that, by 2004, had reached some $40 billion.[13] Exactly what the word "determine" meant remained unclear, since on another occasion the president said that the DNI would "coordinate" the intelligence budget.[14] Moreover, also in August, Secretary of Defense Donald H. Rumsfeld expressed his opposition to DNI control over defense intelligence spending.[15]

Vacillating between trying to please the pro–Kean Commission lobbyists (most notably, the families of the 9/11 victims, who were determined to bring about intelligence reform), on the one hand, and the powerful insider Rumsfeld faction, on the other hand, the president in early September leaned toward the Kean Commission's recommendation and declared that the new DNI would have "full budgetary authority."[16] Later, in September, the president switched again, sending forward to Congress a detailed twenty-three-page proposal that limited the DNI's authority over military intelligence.[17] The Rumsfeld camp was a force to be reckoned with inside the private sanctums of the White House, with an influential ally in Vice President Dick Cheney. Where the president would stand in October, as intelligence reform accelerated toward a vote in Congress, was anybody's guess.

In the months leading up to this jockeying over intelligence changes, many experts and government officials put in their oars, as another national debate over intelligence reform ensued. The Aspin-Brown Commission had planted some of the seeds for this debate; the 9/11 attacks added the water and the fertilizer. The Democratic presidential challenger, Senator John Kerry (D-MA) endorsed the Kean Commission's reforms *in toto*, free of any of the conditions designed to protect the DoD's dominance over such agencies as the NSA, NGA, and NRO—just as the Scowcroft Report from PFIAB, rejected earlier by the president, had stood up to the Pentagon's efforts to shelter the military intelligence agencies from control by a civilian Intelligence Director. Several prominent lawmakers also backed the drive for a muscular DNI, although a few cautioned that the drafting of major intelligence reforms in the midst of a presidential election was problematic. They recommended waiting until the new year, when the electoral dust had settled. The vast majority on Capitol Hill, however, wanted immediate action—Republicans and Democrats alike—if only so that they could display for voters back home a pre-election determination to make the United States a safer place.

Congress Turns to Intelligence Reform—Again

During August and September of 2004, members of Congress entered into a flurry of committee work on the proposed DNI legislation. A spokesman for the House Speaker, J. Dennis Hastert (R-IL), noted that considerable uncertainty surrounded how much budgetary and other authority the new intelligence director should have. "That's the big issue," he said, "and it's a matter of negotiation not only with our committees but also with the White House."[18] Finally, in October, both chambers of Congress passed intelligence reform bills, indeed mammoth and complicated proposals.

The Senate bill came in at over five hundred pages and received eighty-one amendments during floor debate. The House bill was even longer, at over six hundred pages, with multiple amendments of its own. The two bills differed in content—sharply so on some issues. Many observers looked upon the House bill as an effort to counter the more pro-DNI Senate bill. "The Senate bill is fiercely resisted by miffed Defense officials and turf-jealous committee lions," concluded the *New York Times*.[19] Provisions introduced by House Republicans limited the DNI's budget powers over the military intelligence agencies, including the largest ones (NSA, NGA, and NRO).[20] The GOP initiatives raised the distinct possibility, according to an experienced Hill staffer, that the Defense Department might be able—as it had in 1996 (and many times earlier)—to block reform efforts meant to provide the nation's intelligence chief with broad budget authority.[21] It seemed as though the DoD could do exactly that under the provisions of the House bill, the language of which gave the DNI authority merely to "develop" the intelligence budget. Here was wording similar to the weak proposal that had prevailed in the Congress during its deliberations over the Aspin-Brown recommendations. In contrast, the Senate bill would have endowed the DNI with much bolder authority to "determine" the intelligence spending levels—more in the spirit of Senator Arlen Specter's bill in 1996 and the second President Bush's initial granting of budget authority to DCI Goss.

The House Republican bill also provided the Justice Department with wider surveillance and deportation authority on law-enforcement and immigration cases related to counterterrorism. One of these amendments, which would have permitted the Department of Homeland Security to detain illegal immigrants indefinitely and deny their right of *habeas corpus* review by a judge, even drove a wedge between the White House—reluctant to go that far—and the House GOP leadership. In the midst of all this elbowing over compromise language in late October, national security advisor Condoleezza Rice and budget director Joshua B. Bolten wrote a letter to lawmakers on behalf of the White House in favor of the Senate's more expansive powers for the DNI. At the same time, though, the White House continued to support House Republican efforts to strengthen counterterrorist surveillance techniques for law-enforcement officers.[22] Unbeknownst to most members of Congress and the public alike, the president had already authorized the NSA to ignore the FISA court and—without judicial warrants, required since 1978—carry out wiretaps and other forms of surveillance that might involve American citizens.[23]

The House bill gave the DNI substantial control over a new position called director of the CIA (DCIA or D/CIA), as well, while the Senate bill allowed the CIA chief greater autonomy. Moreover, the two chambers differed on the issue of whether the aggregate intelligence budget figure should be revealed each year—the Senate for its disclosure, and the House (and the White House) against—as well-worn a debate as one could find in intelligence circles. The Senate wanted, too, an independent civil-liberties board to provide added accountability over intelligence and law-enforcement activities; the House and the White House stood against this measure. The Senate sought to move the Office of the DNI to downtown Washington, away from any specific intelligence agency—a blow to the CIA, where the DCI had resided for decades. (This was one of the main reasons the Agency opposed replacing the DCI with a DNI.) The White House and the House wanted this provision dropped, leaving open the possibility that the new DNI could be housed in the old DCI offices at the Agency in Langley. Hundreds of additional differences separated the two bills; a conference committee faced the tough job of seeking a compromise intelligence-reform package palatable to both the Senate and the House, as well as to the Bush White House.

Of greatest significance would be the eventual position taken by lawmakers regarding the DNI's authority over budgets and personnel. A widely discussed possible compromise would give the DNI budget authority over the CIA, NSA, NGA, and NRO (all in the space-based surveillance business, except for the Agency). With respect to the other intelligence organizations (INR, along with the intelligence units in the Energy and Treasury Departments, the FBI, and the DIA and the armed forces intelligence units in DoD), the DNI would have to consult with—and probably defer to—each of the department secretaries in which an intelligence agency was embedded. The same would be true for the newest members of the intelligence community: the intelligence unit in the Department of Homeland Security (DHS), created in 2003; Coast Guard Intelligence, created in 2001, then shifted within the framework of DHS in 2003; and the Drug Enforcement Administration, a well-established agency in the Justice Department assigned to the community in 2006. (See Appendix B for a depiction of the contemporary U.S. intelligence community.) Regarding the power to hire and fire each of the program managers (the agency gorillas, now sixteen in number), the DNI might have to seek concurrence with the SecDef and the other department secretaries.

Senior intelligence officials worried about the outcome of the struggle over the DNI's eventual authority. As one put it, "I am not very sanguine that much will come of this either—other than something that is worse than what we have now."[24] The "either" was a reference to the earlier Aspin-Brown Commission attempts to bolster the DCI's ability to manage all the intelligence agencies.

Whether or not the nation would have a new intelligence law to restructure the community by the end of 2004—or ever in the near future—remained unclear as the presidential campaign came to an end in November, with George W. Bush winning a second term. The 9/11 Commission leaders, Chairman Thomas H. Kean (a Republican and former governor of New Jersey) and Vice Chairman Lee H. Hamilton (a Democrat and former House member from Indiana), warned that the nation stood "at a crossroads. . . . There is very little time left in this Congress to act."[25] The four most senior conferees held out hope, though, that they could pass an acceptable bill in a lame-duck session.[26]

At first, Congress failed to pass an intelligence-reform bill in any form. Speaker Hastert pulled the House bill from consideration when the chairmen of the Armed Forces and Judiciary Committees objected to provisions related, respectively, to the DNI's authority over tactical military intelligence budgets and to immigration matters—a fate similar to Rep. Combest's bill in 1996. Proponents continued to lobby for the legislation, nevertheless, and persuaded Congress to take up the bill again in a rare lame-duck session held during December of 2004. Thanks in no small part to the perseverance of a few relatives of the 9/11 victims who felt fervently about the need for intelligence reform,[27] the conferees finally crafted a compromise that went to the floors of the House and the Senate.

Vital to the outcome was acceptance of the word "abrogate" in the language of the proposal. The compromise language stated that the powers of a new DNI would not abrogate the military chain of command, which had the effect of mollifying the pro-DoD faction.[28] Indeed, as a leading military intelligence official observed, this wording "effectively neutered the legislation."[29] Following this and a few other last-minute adjustments, and aided by increased pressure from the White House on the House GOP leadership (again in response to lobbying by the victims' families), the bill was passed in the House of Representatives by a vote of 336 to 75 on December 7. The next day the Senate followed suit, voting 89 to 2 in favor.

On December 17, the president signed the Intelligence Reform and Terrorist Prevention Act (IRTPA) into law.[30] At the signing, Bush referred to the new statute as "the most dramatic reform of our nation's intelligence capabilities since President Harry S. Truman signed the National Security Act of 1947." He added that "under this new law, our vast intelligence enterprise will become more unified, coordinated, and effective."[31] The rhetoric was as wide of the mark as ever had come out of the White House from any administration.

The end result of the much-amended 600-page law was an Office of DNI that was still nowhere near dominant enough to draw the intelligence agencies together into one cooperative enterprise. Despite the urging of the Aspin-Brown Commission, the horrors of the 9/11 attacks, the far-reaching mistakes related to the war in Iraq, the impressive work of a Congressional Joint Committee that investigated the 9/11 intelligence errors,[32] and all the publicity associated with the findings of the Kean Commission, the most Congress seemed able to achieve were half-measures that failed to knit together the long-standing rents in the vast tent of the intelligence community. The DNI would have to go on sharing authority with the SecDef over military intelligence—the same situation faced by the DCI before the bill was passed. This meant that the eight-hundred-pound gorilla in the Pentagon, the SecDef, would continue to dominate U.S. intelligence, maximizing support to military operations (SMO) while minimizing resources for global political, economic, and cultural matters that might help prevent the outbreak of wars in the first place. Vaguely stated in the law, the new intelligence chief would be allowed to "monitor the implementation and execution" of intelligence operations. Tribal warfare in the intelligence "community" would continue; institutional diffusion had trumped consolidation.

The new law also established the National Counterterrorism Center (NCTC)—a useful organizational reform; increased the number of border guards and immigration agents; set minimum standards for issuing driver's licenses (in an effort to prevent would-be terrorists from traveling easily in the United States); required visa applicants to have in-person interviews; granted surveillance and wiretap authority to pursue "lone wolf" terror suspects who have no connection to foreign countries or organizations (a troubling feature for civil libertarians); and, in a long overdue improvement, buttressed aviation security. The director of the NCTC would report straight to the president but with ambiguous ties as well to the DNI, adding further fragmentation and confusion over the chain of command in the intelligence community. Yet another stovepipe. In addition, the bill created an oversight board on civil liberties, but, farcically, one whose members would serve at the whim of the president and without subpoena powers.

After examining the new law, an intelligence official concluded: "It's a black hole we're looking into."[33] The Congress had retreated from even the innocuous idea that we had recommended in 1996 of disclosing the annual aggregate budget for intelligence. In 2008, the Bush administration attempted, through a revision of Executive Order 12333 (originally signed at the beginning of the Reagan administration), to bolster the authority of the DNI somewhat by encouraging intelligence managers in each of the agencies to follow the leadership of the director; but the new language reinforced the point that the DNI could not "abrogate" departmental authorities. Secretary of Defense Robert M. Gates, national security advisor Stephen Hadley, and DNI Vice Adm. Mike McConnell guided this revision effort in 2008 and selected the permissive verb "shall" in the wording for the executive order that urged the elements of the intelligence community to implement the director's orders—a subtle invitation to continue politics as usual. On one point practically every observer of these antics agreed: the 2004 statute and the 2008 executive-order were riddled with ambiguities and contradictions that would have to be hammered out over the coming years and improved through legislative amendments—if a new president were interested and tough enough to take on the challenge.

———

A Nesting Place for the DNI

Of less sweeping import, but still significant and controversial, was the issue of where the DNI would sit. Some proposed the seventh floor at Langley, thereby reinforcing President Truman's concept of the CIA as a *central* intelligence agency with a strong director at the helm who could guide all of the secret agencies toward the production of all-source intelligence reporting. The DNI would rely on a deputy—a DCIA—to run the day-to-day affairs of the Agency, while the national intelligence chief concentrated on problems of community coordination, intelligence fusion, and the speedy dissemination of information to decision-makers. According to this perspective, a DNI would work best when he or she had the National Intelligence Council (NIC), the National Intelligence Officers (NIOs), the Directorate of Intelligence (DI), the Directorate of Science and Technology (DS&T), and other major CIA staff support close at hand. After all, 90 percent of the nation's intelligence-analysis capacity was located just down the corridors from the old DCI's seventh floor aerie at the CIA Original Headquarters Building in Langley. As with the DCI, the new DNI's power (such as it was) would depend on his or her access to deep and timely knowledge of world affairs, and that knowledge would come mainly from the NIC, the DI, and related CIA entities, complemented by data and analysis coming into Langley from the other agencies in the community. This was the Truman model of an intelligence hierarchy led by a genuine director of central intelligence—or, in the new terminology, director of national intelligence.

If the Office of the DNI were removed away from these CIA sources of information and located downtown near the White House or somewhere else apart from Langley, the new intelligence chief would be stripped of a power base that depended on superior knowledge and, therefore, emasculated—much like the nation's drug czar, who has operated without being directly in charge of a major anti-drug agency or department. As two savvy reporters noted during the 2004 debates over intelligence reform, a DNI distant from Langley "would not have the intimate knowledge of the human intelligence operations and the daily analyses [produced by the CIA]."[34]

Former DCI Robert Gates predicted that were a DNI left "without troops [NIC and DI analysts]...the intelligence czar would, in fact, be an intelligence eunuch."[35] A more recent DCI, George Tenet, agreed: "If you separate the DCI"—Tenet saw no need for the new title of "DNI"—"from troops, from [CIA] operators and analysts, I have a concern about his or her effectiveness, his or her connection."[36] Further, running covert actions would be more difficult for a DCI or a DNI who was not in proximity to the CIA's Directorate of Operations (DO, with its new name today of National Clandestine Service or NCS). Intelligence scholar and journalist James Bamford joined the chorus of those who advocated the placement of the intelligence community's new boss on the seventh floor at Langley: "The head of CIA should once again be made the director of central intelligence and given overall responsibility for America's spy operations."[37]

A second school of thought—the anti-CIA contingent—strenuously opposed locating the DNI at Langley. "It would mean that *nothing* has changed," emphasized the NGA director, former Air Force Lt. Gen. James R. Clapper, Jr.[38] Similarly, many others in the intelligence community (not counting Agency officers) looked upon the placement of the DNI at Langley as a slide backward toward the old CIA that had left them out in the cold and would probably continue to do so when it came to assignments on important centers, task forces, and other interagency groups. It would be a case of "CIA capture," a phrase that floated around the national security establishment in the autumn of 2004. These critics preferred a more "neutral" location for the DNI, somewhere in downtown Washington; or perhaps at Bolling Air Force Base in southeast Washington, where space was available in the new DIA Headquarters Building ("DIA capture" perhaps). To keep the DNI from becoming an "intelligence eunuch," proponents of this school were willing to allow the NIC and elements of the DI to move with the DNI into the new location away from Langley—essentially the creation of another "CIA" that wasn't the CIA.

On practical grounds, the sheer difficulty of finding an appropriate building near the White House to house the DNI and related staff proved too expensive. One possibility was to provide space for the spy chief and staff in the Old Executive Office Building. The DCI, recall, already had a suite of offices there, and, given the colossal size of the structure, additional rooms for the DNI could surely be found to accommodate a larger staff. But nobody who was already housed in the building wanted to give up space in this prestigious location, a stone's throw from the West Wing of the White House.

Another idea was to place all the program managers on the seventh floor at Langley, a convocation of gorillas meant to overcome the perception of "CIA capture" by having each of the agency heads clustered together on the same floor as the DNI. From a management point of view, placing all the program managers and the DNI in the same location might lead to improved interagency dialogue and coordination. Maybe even close friendships would develop that would smooth relations among the agencies. As Under Secretary of State George Ball once noted, "Nothing propinques like propinquity."[39] This plan, though, was widely unpopular with the program managers. As one declared to me, insisting on anonymity: "No! I won't go. I need to be here [in my own agency] with my troops."[40] This defiance reflected a different, but also compelling, management argument: agencies separated from their program manager on site could well flounder.

If he were still around, which option would Harry Truman have endorsed? Given his "liking for centralization and clear lines of responsibility,"[41] he would probably have leaned toward a DNI at Langley. He would have been attracted to the idea of pulling together intelligence from around the world and depositing it within the Agency, which already enjoyed an extensive information base (NIC, DI, DS&T); and then for the CIA to reach out aggressively to the rest of the community in search of all-source fusion, through the use of interagency centers and task forces with equitable community-wide representation. This design seems most in harmony with the original motivation behind Truman's attraction to the creation of a Central Intelligence Agency in the first place.

In December of 2004, though, lawmakers rejected the Truman approach. Under pressure from the Pentagon, they decided to ban the DNI from a permanent office at Langley—over the objections of the White House.[42] (During George Tenet's reign at Langley, the CIA Headquarters Building had been renamed the George H. W. Bush Intelligence Center, in honor of the only DCI to become president of the United States; George W. Bush, the son of the eponymous honoree, may have been reluctant to undermine the central role of the Agency.) It was payback time for the CIA from supporters of the other intelligence services, for all its slights and perceived arrogance over the years.

————

The first DNI appointee, Ambassador John D. Negroponte, initially found space for his office in cramped quarters near the White House, then a year later moved into the Defense Intelligence Agency Center (DIAC), the glassy new DIA Headquarters Building at Bolling Air Force Base, located across the Potomac River from National Airport. The ambassador brought with him a few analytic components from the CIA and other agencies around the community. The NIC, the DI, and the DS&T remained twelve miles away at Agency headquarters in Langley. Nesting at Bolling only temporarily (the DIA wanted all of its space returned), Negroponte and the White House set in motion plans to construct a facility for the Office of the DNI at Liberty Crossing near Tysons Corner in northern Virginia, a large and up-scale facility ready for use in 2008. This would bring the nation's intelligence director to within six miles of Langley and the analytic resources he or she needed, if the spymaster wished to be anything more than a shadow. Why not just move the DNI back into CIA Headquarters? That would require an amendment to the 2004 intelligence reform law, one likely to be blocked by the anti-Agency faction in the community and its allies in the Congress. "That horse is out of the barn," concluded an experienced intelligence officer, waving aside any thoughts about revisiting this battle.[43]

Though weak in authority, the DNI Office has not been idle since its creation in the waning days of 2004. For instance, in 2006, Ambassador Negroponte addressed the tasking dilemma that we had confronted on the Aspin-Brown Commission, that is, the difficulty of acquiring clear intelligence requests from policy makers. His solution: the creation of a National Intelligence Priorities Framework (NIPF), designed to gather together the collection needs of senior policy makers on a semi-annual basis. This was a worthy effort to gauge shifts in intelligence priorities in government offices around Washington—one of our objectives and the reason we proposed the concept of a "forward liaison".[44] The ambassador also established "mission managers" to identify and coordinate the expertise of the intelligence community to address key national security issues, such as Iran, North Korea, and Venezuela—a variant of the DCI's use of centers.[45] Progress was made, as well, toward strengthening the NCTC, also located at Liberty Crossing near Tysons Corner, along with setting up a new National Counterproliferation

Center (NCPC) in the same Virginia neighborhood—an area that was rapidly becoming Spy Central U.S.A.

Negroponte soon fled back to the Department of State, however, after serving for less than two years as DNI. His successor, Vice Admiral Mike McConnell, one of our witnesses in 1995 when he was NSA director, moved into the Bolling office for the time being and continued to build up a staff. McConnell didn't last long in the DNI job either, though, stepping down in 2009. His replacement: none other than Admiral Dennis Blair, John Deutch's liaison to the Aspin-Brown Commission and to the Pentagon in 1995–96. He vowed to make sure the intelligence agencies obeyed the law (a reaction to criticism over the NSA warrantless wiretaps controversy still boiling in 2009).[46] He also got into a spat with the new DCIA, former representative Leon E. Panetta (D-CA), over the question of who would name the chiefs of station in U.S. embassies around the world—the head of the CIA (as had traditionally been the case since 1947) or the DNI. The argument was a continuation of an earlier round of jousting over this question between the staffs in the Office of the DCIA and the Office of the DNI.[47]

Negroponte, McConnell, and Blair are all talented, bright individuals, but they found the DNI job frustrating. The United States, in a search for greater cohesion in the intelligence community, had ended up instead with an intelligence chief even weaker than the old DCI—a "spymaster" with ambiguous authority, a small staff, and detached from most of the government's reservoir of intelligence analysts at Langley. Just what the nation needed: an isolated intelligence director leading the Office of the DNI in what was, essentially, a hollowed-out seventeenth spy agency.

During the confirmation hearing for Admiral McConnell's appointment as DNI, the SSCI chairman, Jay Rockefeller (D-WV), raised thoughtful questions about the weaknesses of the office. The senator observed:

> We did not pull the technical collection agencies out of the Defense Department [the Scowcroft proposal] and we did not give the DNI direct authority over the main collection or analytic components of the community. We gave the DNI the authority to build the national intelligence budget, but we left the execution of the budget with the agencies. We gave the DNI tremendous responsibilities. The question is: did we give the position enough authority?[48]

For most observers—outside of the DoD at least—the answer was an unequivocal "no." Even McConnell, after serving two months as DNI, could only offer a euphemistic description of a job that he had clearly found unwieldy. The office was, in his gentle expression, a "challenging management condition."[49]

In particular, he complained about his inability to dismiss incompetent people. "You cannot hire or fire," he told a reporter.[50] The admiral soon announced a "hundred-day plan," in which he proposed a searching review of the DNI's authority and an ongoing effort to integrate the components of the intelligence "community." He vowed: "We're going to examine it; we're going to argue about it; we're going to make some proposals."[51] Appearing before the Senate in February of 2008, he further testified: "Our current model...does not have operational control over the elements that conduct intelligence activities. The DNI also does not have direct authority over the personnel in the sixteen agencies in the community."[52] This is what the Aspin-Brown Commission and the Kean Commission had been talking about over the past decade.

At least the retired SecDef, Donald H. Rumsfeld, who opposed the idea of a strong intelligence chief to begin with, was no longer in Washington to stymie the development of a more effective DNI Office. In his place came Robert M. Gates, a former DI analyst and DCI, who understood intelligence probably better than any SecDef in the nation's history. Moreover, he had long been an advocate of a better working relationship between military and civilian intelligence agencies, as he had expressed to the Aspin Commission at our first retreat in 1995. Whether this happy alignment of the stars could overcome the DNI's inherent statutory weaknesses, though, was unlikely—especially with McConnell becoming more and more preoccupied with (and defensive about) the debate over controversial CIA torture methods and the secret NSA warrantless wiretap program that had come to light. His support for the administration's warrantless wiretaps was tepid at best, since this program appeared to violate the Foreign Intelligence Surveillance Act of 1978.[53]

———

A Dream Still on Hold

As in the past, the dream of better intelligence coordination in 2004 had run head first into the community's stovepipe tradition and the dominance over intelligence exercised by the secretary of defense. To a significant degree, agency parochialism continues to block all-source fusion, even though close observers and practitioners like the former NSA director and recent DCIA Lt. Gen. Michael V. Hayden concede that the old form of "plumbing" (a term of art referring to the organizational structure of the intelligence community) does not work properly when it comes to the goal of sharing information among the secret agencies.[54] The major impediment to fulfilling Truman's aspirations for intelligence integration during the reign of Donald Rumsfeld in the Pentagon continued to be the Office of the Secretary of Defense and the chairman of the Joint Chiefs of Staff (JCS), along with their allies on the Armed Services Committees in Congress.[55]

A closer look at the dynamics of the political forces that diluted the 2004 Intelligence Reform legislative reveals the obstacles that proponents of a strong DNI face. In September 2004, while Congress was debating the reform bill, an eyewitness account by lawmaker Christopher Shays (R-CT) revealed that Secretary Rumsfeld "trashed everything about the national intelligence director" at a closed briefing in the Senate.[56] The SecDef's major concern was the placing of authority over intelligence spending into the hands of a DNI. "There may be ways we can strengthen intelligence," he reportedly argued to the president, "but centralization is not one."[57] Rumsfeld evidently believed that a powerful DNI might fail to provide sufficient support to military operations—the SMO imperative that came up time and again during the Aspin-Brown Commission inquiry. The co-chair of the 9/11 Commission, Thomas Kean, had a rather different view. "If you're not going to create an intelligence director who has the powers of budget and appointment," he said, "don't do it."[58]

During the October 2004 debate over the various legislative proposals to restructure the nation's intelligence community, the chairman of the Joint Chiefs of Staff, Gen. Richard B. Myers, wrote a letter to a key House conferee, Armed Services chairman Duncan Hunter (R-CA), urging him and his colleagues to preserve the Pentagon's control over intelligence spending for agencies with a military mission, including all the big spenders: NSA, NRO, and NGA. Hunter heartily agreed, sending up the smokescreen that he opposed the Kean Commission reforms because they would remove the Pentagon's control over tactical (battlefield) intelligence, which was not true.[59] This put both men, Myers and Hunter, at odds with the commander in chief in the White House—especially unusual for a sitting JCS chief— since the president claimed to be in support of the Senate bill, which allocated broad spending powers to the proposed DNI.

In a late October surprise, Hunter also produced an e-mail from the former executive director of the Kean Commission, Philip Zelikow, that suggested his willingness to endorse the House's more limited grant of DNI spending authority. The commission's former members quickly distanced themselves from the message of their former staff leader, while a spokesperson for the 9/11 victims' families, Mary Fetchet, told the media, "Obstructionists, in particular the Department of Defense . . . are jeopardizing" the reform bill.[60]

In November, as part of his effort to block the creation of a strong DNI, Rep. Hunter told the American people: "If we don't have a chain of command—and that means have a direct responsiveness to the Department of Defense and to those war fighters on the ground—a chain of command between them and the people that run those satellites, we are not going to have the responsiveness that we have right now." He continued: "We're going to have more power for the National Intelligence Director and, unfortunately, pull away the tight working relationship [that the military intelligence agencies have] with DoD."[61] Not acknowledged in Hunter's argument was the fact that the proposed legislation kept all of the tactical military intelligence units under the command of the SecDef.

Moreover, no DNI would ever ignore the needs of the fighting man and woman in uniform. The top priority, whether for a strong or a weak DNI, would remain SMO—or else the president would properly fire the spy chief. A strong DNI, though, would be in a better position to draw together the whole range of intelligence coming into the United States—military, political, economic—and, therefore, provide the president and other policy officers with a broader, integrated view of world affairs: the elusive goal of all-source fusion. Senator John Warner—the champion of the status quo on the Aspin-Brown Commission–took Hunter's side, using his chairmanship of the Senate Armed Services Committee to fight any initiative that might erode DoD authority over the military intelligence agencies.[62]

Taking an unexpected position during these debates, the strongly pro-Pentagon SSCI chairman, Pat Roberts (R-KS), dismissed Hunter's premise that reform would interrupt the flow of intelligence to the battlefield as a "canard."[63] Undeterred by Robert's criticism, however, Hunter went on to warn his congressional colleagues that the reform bill would "sever the lifeline" of intelligence for U.S. troops overseas; it would cause confusion in the chain of command and, therefore, cost the lives of America's young men and women in uniform.[64] It sounded like a replay of the jeremiads delivered by Senator Strom Thurmond and General Clapper in 1996.

The president, as well as JCS chairman Myers (now back in line with the White House after some scolding from his commander in chief), countered with assurances that the bill, as the president put it, "preserves the existing chain of command."[65] It was this standoff between Hunter and the pro-reformists that finally led to a reluctant willingness by the latter to insert the word "abrogate" into the statutory language, which had the effect of making the DNI's authority over budgets and personnel ambiguous at best.

It is entirely reasonable—indeed, necessary—for Defense Department officials and members of the Armed Services Committees to seek reassurance that intelligence support for America's fighting men and women would not be degraded by the creation of a strong DNI. Yet, contrary to the fears that SMO would deteriorate, it should be understood that one of the DNI's top assistants would be a military person with three stars, assigned to work with the Office of the DNI day by day to ensure that tactical and strategic military intelligence concerns have top priority in the intelligence community, especially in times of war. (This was the primary job Dennis Blair had in 1995, working for DCI Deutch.) Should the DNI fail to provide adequate support to military operations, the remedy would be clear: the SecDef would complain to the White House, and the commander in chief would no doubt dismiss the spy chief and select as a replacement someone who understood the importance of timely military intelligence, especially to combatants in the field.

Conversely, the ax would fall as well on any DNI who became a mere pawn of the Pentagon, ignoring his or her responsibilities to evaluate worldwide political, economic, and cultural topics—collectively known as "civilian" or "diplomatic" intelligence. Among the advantages of having a real director of national intelligence is the greater likelihood that the person in this office could effectively combine military and civilian intelligence into an integrated product for policy makers—the president and his assistants, who must gauge the chances for a diplomatic settlement to an international dispute before sending in the military. James R. Clapper Jr., the newest DNI, vowed in his confirmation hearings before SSCI (July 20, 2010) to achieve a proper balance between civilian and military intelligence needs. He said that he would expand the DNI's authority when possible to ensure this objective.

Would a strong DNI with full authority over the spy agencies and a mandate to bring about information fusion solve America's intelligence woes and ward off future 9/11s and WMD errors? In itself, of course not. Improvements in intelligence must continue across a broad front. Necessary reforms include the ongoing development of better human intelligence, especially in the Middle East and Southwest Asia; improved foreign-language skills and knowledge of foreign countries among case officers and other collectors, as well as analysts and policy makers; an enhanced capacity for "lingering" aerial surveillance;[66] better data sifting in search of signals in the flood of information noise that rushes into Washington from collection points around the globe; intelligence dissemination that is more sensitive to the informational (though certainly not the political) needs of policy makers; and fully integrated and secure information-sharing technology, both horizontally throughout the federal government and vertically from Washington down to state and local counterterrorism officials.

Even in Washington, DC, the physical barriers that block communications among the sixteen intelligence agencies remain considerable. "I am unable to send email, and even make secure phone calls, to a good portion of the intelligence community from my desktop," a senior aide to the DNI complained in 2007, in an echo of grievances I heard frequently on the Aspin-Brown Commission over a decade earlier.[67]

Information radiating out from Washington to state and local security officials has been even more problematic. To aid this vertical intelligence integration, the intelligence community has established over forty "fusion centers" around the nation, called Joint Terrorism Task Forces (JTTFs), to provide a conduit through which information (especially on counterterrorism) can flow downward in the federal government from DC to the nation's cities and local law enforcement officers.[68] According to the guidelines set up by the Department of Justice and the Department of Homeland Security, an intelligence fusion center is "a collaborative effort of two or more agencies [in DC] that provide resources, expertise, and/or information to the [local] center with the goal of maximizing the ability to detect, prevent, apprehend, and respond to criminal and terrorist activity."[69] The number of JTTFs rose steeply from thirty-five soon after the 9/11 attacks to 106 in 2010.

The fusion centers are a useful approach to intelligence sharing, yet a survey from the National Governors Association indicated in 2006 that "sixty percent of responding state homeland security directors are dissatisfied or somewhat dissatisfied with the specificity of the intelligence they receive from the federal government."[70] Further, a congressional report concludes, "numerous fusion center officials claim that although their center receives a substantial amount of information from federal agencies, they never seem to get the 'right information' or receive it in an efficient manner."[71]

Improvements in the integration of intelligence IT, both horizontally and vertically, will have to go hand in hand with the erection of sophisticated counterintelligence firewalls to protect U.S. intelligence against hostile penetrations—the potential calamity of a future Aldrich Ames with access up, down, and around the integrated intelligence community computer network. In addition, to guard against bioterrorism, the Centers for Disease Control and Prevention, along with the Department of Health and Human Services, must be more closely integrated into the network of intelligence-sharing with federal, state, and local security offices.[72]

In the mix, too, must be the preservation of competitive analysis, so that the desired intelligence centralization under a stronger DNI does not stifle freedom of expression within the various agencies. Encouraging dissenting footnotes in intelligence reports—or, even better, conspicuously "boxed" dissents in the executive summary (known as the "Key Judgments" in an NIE) as well as in the body of a report—would preserve the ability of agencies to explain the logic of their analyses to policy officials even when in the minority.

Further, the oversight morass on Capitol Hill cries out for reform, with consolidation of the many intelligence review committees an imperative. If the DNI is provided the powers the office needs to manage the sprawling intelligence community, the director must be subject to continuous and meaningful legislative review—but by SSCI and HPSCI, not the confusing array of multiple committees on Capitol Hill that currently takes up too much of the time of the intelligence director.

As with the reform recommendations offered by the Aspin-Brown Commission, the proposal for a sweeping intelligence-reform bill in 2004 represented another step toward the goal of a real (not cosmetic) director of national intelligence. Here was a chance to establish a leader with full authority over America's secret agencies, a spy chief who could overcome the twin causes of ineffective intelligence: interagency rivalry and parochialism. A last minute watering down of the reform legislation, though, left the DNI enfeebled and cut off from his vital corps of analytic "troops" at the CIA. The next step is to restore that part of the Intelligence Reform and Terrorism Prevention Act that was omitted in 2004: full budget and appointment powers for the DNI over all the secret agencies. Success in this objective will require a determined effort by President Barack Obama, working together with the new DNI, James Clapper, as well as SSCI and HPSCI. Clapper, opposed to a strong DNI at the time of the Aspin-Brown Commission and during the 2004 Great Debate on intelligence, is likely to have a different view as he now experiences the frustrations of the office firsthand. Moving quickly, by November 2010 he had reached an agreement with Secretary of Defense Robert M. Gates for the DNI to have unprecedented authority over budgets and personnel for the National Intelligence Program (NIP—the large, strategic intelligence agencies and programs), with DoD handling the Military Intelligence Program (MIP—the smaller, tactical intelligence agencies and programs). Whether these arrangements would last after Gates and Clapper left office was another matter, since they lacked the permanency of law. If the Obama national security team can address these weaknesses in the office, the phrase "intelligence community" will finally mean something, and the safety of the United States will be significantly strengthened by virtue of an integrated intelligence system.

The List of Subjects Mandated for Commission Study

October 14, 1994

Public Law 103–359; 108 *Stat.* 3458

(1) to review the efficacy and appropriateness of the activities of the United States intelligence community in the post-cold war global environment; and

(2) to prepare and transmit the reports described in section 904.

(b) IMPLEMENTATION.—In carrying out subsection (a), the Commission shall specifically consider the following:

(1) What should be the roles and missions of the intelligence community in terms of providing support to the defense and foreign policy establishments and how should these relate to tactical intelligence activities.

(2) Whether the roles and mission of the intelligence community should extend beyond the traditional areas of providing support to the defense and foreign policy establishments, and, if so, what areas should be considered legitimate for intelligence collection and analysis, and whether such areas should include, for example, economic issues, environmental issues, and health issues.

(3) What functions, if any, should continue to be assigned to the organizations of the intelligence community, including the Central Intelligence Agency, and what capabilities should these organizations retain for the future.

(4) Whether the existing organization and management framework of the organizations of the intelligence community, including the Central Intelligence Agency, provide the optimal structure for the accomplishment of their missions.

(5) Whether existing principles and strategies governing the acquisition and maintenance of intelligence collection capabilities should be retained and

what collection capabilities should the Government retain to meet future contingencies.

(6) Whether intelligence analysis, as it is currently structured and executed, adds sufficient value to information otherwise available to the Government to justify its continuation, and, if so, at what level of resources.

(7) Whether the existing decentralized system of intelligence analysis results in significant waste or duplication, and, if so, what can be done to correct these deficiencies.

(8) Whether the existing arrangements for allocating available resources to accomplish the roles and missions assigned to intelligence agencies are adequate.

(9) Whether the existing framework for coordinating among intelligence agencies with respect to intelligence collection and analysis and other activities, including training and operational activities, provides an optimal structure for such coordination.

(10) Whether current personnel policies and practices of intelligence agencies provide an optimal work force to satisfy the needs of intelligence consumers.

(11) Whether resources for intelligence activities should continue to be allocated as part of the defense budget or be treated by the President and Congress as a separate budgetary program.

(12) Whether the existing levels of resources allocated for intelligence collection or intelligence analysis, or to provide a capability to conduct covert actions, are seriously at variance with United States needs.

(13) Whether there are areas of redundant or overlapping activity or areas where there is evidence of serious waste, duplication, or mismanagement.

(14) To what extent, if any, should the budget for United States intelligence activities be publicly disclosed.

(15) To what extent, if any, should the United States intelligence community collect information bearing upon private commercial activity and the manner in which such information should be controlled and disseminated.

(16) Whether counterintelligence policies and practices are adequate to ensure that employees of intelligence agencies are sensitive to security problems, and whether intelligence agencies themselves have adequate authority and capability to address perceived security problems.

(17) The manner in which the size, missions, capabilities, and resources of the United States intelligence community compare to those of other countries.

(18) Whether existing collaborative arrangements between the United States and other countries in the area of intelligence cooperation should be maintained and whether such arrangements should be expanded to provide for increased burdensharing.

(19) Whether existing arrangements for sharing intelligence with multinational organizations in support of mutually shared objectives are adequate.

The U.S. Intelligence Community (IC), 2010*

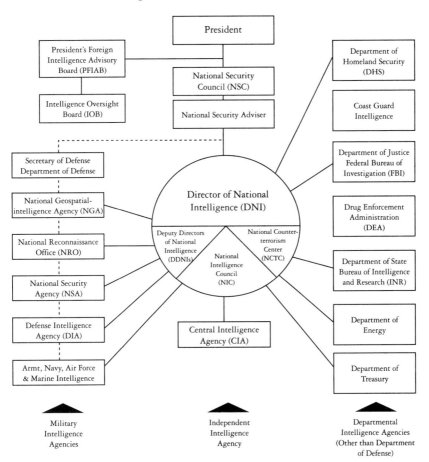

*From 1947 to 2004, a Director of Central Intelligence (DCI) led the intelligence community. In 2005 a Director of National Intelligence (DNI) replaced the DCI office. The Coast Guard became a part of the community in 2001, and was subsequently placed under the Department of Homeland Security when DHS became a member of the community in 2003. The most recent member of the intelligence community is the Drug Enforcement Administration, a long-time fixture in the Justice Department, admitted in 2006.

U.S. Intelligence Leadership, 1947–2010

Director, National Intelligence

2005–2007	John D. Necroponte
2007–2009	J.M. "Mike" McConnell
2009–2010	Dennis C. Blair
2010–	James R. Clapper, Jr.

Directors, Central Intelligence

1947–1950	Rear Adm. Roscoe H. Hillenkoetter
1950–1953	Gen. Walter Bedell Smith
1953–1961	Allen W. Dulles
1961–1965	John A. McCone
1965–1966	Vice Adm. William F. Raborn, Jr.
1966–1973	Richard Helms
1973	James R. Schlesinger
1973–1976	William E. Colby
1976–1977	George H. W. Bush
1977–1981	Adm. Stansfield Turner
1981–1987	William J. Casey
1987–1991	William H. Webster
1991–1993	Robert M. Gates
1993–1995	R. James Woolsey
1995–1997	John M. Deutch
1997–2004	George J. Tenet
2004–2005	Porter J. Goss

Chairs, Senate Select Committee on Intelligence

1976–1977	Daniel K. Inouye, Democrat, Hawaii
1977–1981	Birch Bayh, Democrat, Indiana
1981–1985	Barry Goldwater, Republican, Arizona
1985–1987	David Durenberger, Republican, Minnesota
1987–1993	David L. Boren, Democrat, Oklahoma
1993–1995	Dennis DeConcini, Democrat, Arizona
1995–1997	Arlen Specter, Republican, Pennsylvania
1997–2001	Richard C. Shelby, Republican, Alabama
2001–2003	Bob Graham, Democrat, Florida
2003–2006	Pat Roberts, Republican, Kansas
2007–2008	John D. Rockefeller, IV, Democrat, West Virginia
2009–	Dianne Feinstein, Democrat, California

Chairs, House Permanent Select Committee on Intelligence

1977–1985	Edward P. Boland, Democrat, Massachusetts
1985–1987	Lee H. Hamilton, Democrat, Indiana
1987–1989	Louis Stokes, Democrat, Ohio
1989–1991	Anthony C. Beilenson, Democrat, California
1991–1993	Dave McCurdy, Democrat, Oklahoma
1993–1995	Dan Glickman, Democrat, Kansas
1995–1997	Larry Combest, Republican, Texas
1997–2004	Porter J. Goss, Republican, Florida
2004–2006	Peter Hoekstra, Republican, Michigan
2006–	Silvestre Reyes, Democrat, Texas

NOTES

Preface

1. For accounts, see Loch K. Johnson, *A Season of Inquiry: The Senate Intelligence Investigation* (Lexington: University Press of Kentucky, 1985); Loch K. Johnson, "Congressional Supervision of America's Secret Agencies: The Experience and Legacy of the Church Committee," *Public Administration Review* 64 (2004): 3–14; Frederick A. O. Schwarz Jr., "Intelligence Oversight: The Church Committee," in *Strategic Intelligence*, ed. Loch K. Johnson (Westport, CT: Praeger, 2007), 5:19–46; Frederick A. O. Schwarz Jr. and Aziz Z. Huq, *Unchecked and Unbalanced: Presidential Power in a Time of Terror* (New York: New Press, 2007); and Frank J. Smist Jr., *Congress Oversees the United States Intelligence Community, 1947–1994*, 2nd ed. (Knoxville: University of Tennessee Press, 1994).

2. Quoted in a letter to the author from Frank S. White, Ministry of Defense, London, September 1, 1967.

3. Richard J. Aldrich, *The Hidden Hand: Britain, America and Cold War Secret Intelligence, 1945–1964* (London: John Murray, 2001), 5.

4. Vice Admiral J.M. "Mike" McConnell, Director of National Intelligence, remarks (author's notes, conference on "Intelligence Strategies: New Challenges and Opportunities," National Defense Intelligence College, Washington, DC, September 26, 2007). See also Amy B. Zegart, "An Empirical Analysis of Failed Intelligence Reforms Before September 11," *Political Science Quarterly* 121 (Spring 2006): 33–60; Zegart, "Blue Ribbons, Black Boxes: Toward a Better Understanding of Presidential Commissions," *Presidential Studies Quarterly* 35 (June 2004): 366–93; and Zegart, *Spying Blind: The CIA, the FBI, and the Origins of 9/11* (Princeton, NJ: Princeton University Press, 2007).

5. These committees are informally referred to under the names of their respective chairs. On the first Hoover Commission (led by former President Herbert Hoover), see Commission on the Organization of the Executive Branch of Government, *The Hoover Commission Report on the Organization of the Executive Branch* of Government (New York: McGraw-Hill, 1949); on the Dulles Commission, see William M. Leary, ed., *The Central Intelligence Agency: History and Documents* (Tuscaloosa: University of Alabama Press, 1984); and on the second Hoover Commission, see Commission on the Organization of the Executive Branch of Government, *Intelligence Activities: A Report to the Congress* (Washington, DC: GPO, 1955). The Schlesinger Report (*A Review of the Intelligence Community*) can be found at the National Security Archive, George Washington University, Washington, DC, and is available online: http:// www.gwu.edu/~nsarchiv/NSAEBB/NSAEBB144/document%204.pdf; and for the Murphy Commission report, see Commission on the Organization of the Government for the Conduct of Foreign Policy: *Report* (Washington, DC: GPO, 1975). For the other reports, see: Commission on CIA Activities within the United States, *Report to the President* (Washington, DC: GPO, June 1975) (the Rockefeller Commission); Select Committee to Study Governmental Operations with Respect to Intelligence Activities, *Final Report*, 6 vols, (Washington, DC: GPO, 1976) (the Church Committee); the Select Committee on Intelligence(Pike Committee), whose final, still-classified report was leaked to a New York newspaper: *Village Voice*, "The CIA Report the President Doesn't Want You to Read: The Pike Papers," (February 16 and 23, 1976); Senate Select Committee on Secret Military Assistance to Iran and the Nicaraguan Opposition and House Select Committee to Investigate Covert Arms Transactions with Iran, *Hearings and Final Report* (Washington, DC: GPO, 1987) (the Inouye-Hamilton Committee); the Gore Commission (led by Vice President Al Gore): National Performance Review, *The Intelligence Community: Accompanying Report of the National Performance Review* Office of the Vice President (Washington, DC: GPO, 1993); National Commission on Terrorist Attacks upon the United States, *The 9/11 Commission Report: Final Report of the National Commission on Terrorist Attacks Upon the United States* (New York: Norton, 2004) (The Kean Commission or 9/11 Commission); and Commission on the Intelligence Capabilities of the United States Regarding Weapons of Mass Destruction, *Report to the President of the United States* (Washington, DC: GPO, 2005). According to the 9/11 Commission staff, since 1965 there have been 640 blue-ribbon commissions on various subjects. Cited in Philip Shenon, *The Commission: The Uncensored History of the 9/11 Investigation* (New York: Twelve, 2008), 386. Though little studied or understood, commissions have become a significant component of governance in the United States.

6. A former Director of Central Intelligence has referred to the Aspin-Brown Commission as "the largest and most inclusive review of the Intelligence

Community since 1975." Stansfield Turner, *Burn Before Reading: Presidents, CIA Directors, and Secret Intelligence* (New York: Hyperion, 2005), 231. For a preliminary study of the commission that served as a springboard to this book, see Loch K. Johnson, "The Aspin-Brown Intelligence Inquiry: Behind the Closed Doors of a Blue Ribbon Commission," *Studies in Intelligence* 48 (2004): 1–20. Despite the importance of the Aspin-Brown Commission in the evolution of U.S. intelligence, one recent book on the CIA that purports to cover the period since the end of the Cold War only devotes one sentence to the panel in its 536 pages—in a footnote, no less. John Diamond,*The CIA and the Culture of Failure: U.S. Intelligence from the End of the Cold War to the Invasion of Iraq* (Stanford, CA: Stanford University Press, 2008), 473n139.

7. See, for example, Morton H. Halperin, "The Gaither Committee and the Policy Process,"*World Politics* 13 (1961): 360–84; Kenneth Kitts, *Presidential Commissions & National Security: The Politics of Damage Control* (Boulder, CO: Rienner, 2006); Ernest R. May, "When Government Writes History: A Memoir of the 9/11 Commission," *New Republic*, May 23, 2005, 30–35; and Shenon, *The Commission*, also about the Kean Commission.

8. On this approach to the study of government activities, see Richard F. Fenno Jr.,*Watching Politicians: Essays on Participant Observation* (Berkeley: Institute of Governmental Studies, University of California at Berkeley, 1990).

9. For examples of the genre, see Richard F. Fenno Jr., *Home Style: House Members in Their Districts* (Boston: Little, Brown, 1978); May, "When Government Writes History"; Richard E. Neustadt, *Report to JFK: The Skybolt Crisis in Perspective* (Ithaca, NY: Cornell University Press, 1999); and Eric Redman, *The Dance of Legislation* (New York: Simon and Schuster, 1973).

10. Winston S. Churchill,*The Second World War*, vol. 1, *The Gathering Storm* (Boston: Houghton Mifflin, 1948), iii.

11. John Updike, "The Blessed Man of Boston," in *Pigeon Feathers, and Other Stories* (New York: Knopf, 1962), 157.

12. Johnson, *Season of Inquiry, 2*.

Chapter 1

1. See Kenneth Allard, *Somalia Operations: Lessons Learned* (Washington, DC: National Defense University Press, 1995); Walter Clarke and Jeffrey Herbst, eds., *Learning from Somalia: The Lessons of Armed Humanitarian Intervention* (Boulder, CO: Westview, 1997); John L. Hirsch and Robert B. Oakley, *Somalia and Operation Restore Hope: Reflections on Peacemaking and Peacekeeping* (Washington, DC: U.S. Institute for Peace Press, 1995); Robert Patman, *Strategic Shortfall: The Somalia Syndrome and the March to 9/11* (Santa Barbara, CA: Praeger Security International, 2010); and Karin Von Hippel, *Democracy by Force: U.S. Military Intervention in the Post–Cold War World* (New York: Cambridge University Press, 2000).

2. John McCain, press release, Washington, DC (August 2, 1993).

3. Senate Armed Services Committee, *Review of the Circumstances Surrounding the Ranger Raid on October 3–4, 1993, in Mogadishu, Somalia*, 104th Cong., 1st sess., 1995, 8.

4. Ken Adelman, "Living and Departing with Grace," *Washington Times*, May 23, 1995, A18.

5. See James Bamford, *Body of Secrets: Anatomy of the Ultra-Secret National Security Agency; From the Cold War through the Dawn of a New Century* (New York: Doubleday, 2001); Bamford, *The Puzzle Palace: A Report on America's Most Secret Agency* (New York: Penguin, 1983); Patrick Radden Keefe, *Chatter: Dispatches from the Secret World of Global Eavesdropping* (New York: Random House, 2005); Keefe, "The Challenge of Global Intelligence Listening," in *Strategic Intelligence*, ed. Loch K. Johnson (Westport, CT: Praeger, 2007), 2:23–39; Matthew M. Aid, "A Post-9/11 Report Card on the National Security Agency," in ibid., 2:41–59; Aid, *The Secret Sentry: The Untold History of the National Security Agency* (New York: Bloomsbury, 2009).

6. Patrick J. Sloyan, "How the Warlord Outwitted Clinton's Spooks," *Washington Post*, April 3, 1994, A6. While the NSA is the nation's preeminent code-breaking and sigint agency engaged in telephone eavesdropping and e-mail snooping, on some occasions the CIA is involved in these activities as well, often backed by NSA technicians.

7. For an account, see Mark Bowden, *Black Hawk Down: A Story of Modern War* (New York: Atlantic Monthly, 1999). Aideed died from gunshot wounds in a firefight with a rival Somalian clan in 1996.

8. Michael Ross, "Aspin Rejects Calls for Resignation," *Los Angeles Times*, October 8, 1993, A1. The appropriations bill was 107 Stat. 1475–77, sec. 8151 (1993); see Louis Fisher, *The Politics of Shared Power: Congress and the Executive*, 4th ed. (College Station: Texas A&M University Press, 1998), 204.

9. Quoted by Bruce Van Voorst, "Man in a Minefield," *Time*, April 5, 1993, 30.

10. R. W. Apple Jr., "The Lives They Lived: Les Aspin; Vietnam's Student," *New York Times Magazine*, December 31, 1995, 8; see also R. Jeffrey Smith and Charles R. Babcock, "Transformed Aspin Prepares to Take Over Former Target," *Washington Post*, January 7, 1993, A12.

11. See Richard A. Serrano, "Aspin Clears Combat Policy for Women," *Los Angeles Times*, January 12, 1994, A4.

12. Lawrence Freedman and Efraim Karsh, *The Gulf Conflict, 1990–1991: Diplomacy and War in the New World Order* (Princeton, NJ: Princeton University Press, 1993).

13. Steven L. Burg and Paul S. Shoup, *The War in Bosnia-Herzegovina: Ethnic Conflict and International Intervention* (Armonk, NY: Sharpe, 1999).

14. John R. Ballard, *Upholding Democracy: The United States Military Campaign in Haiti, 1994–1997* (Westport, CT: Praeger, 1998).

15. Gérard Prunier, *The Rwanda Crisis: History of a Genocide* (New York: Columbia University Press, 1995); Philip Gourevitch, *We Wish to Inform You That*

Tomorrow We Will Be Killed with Our Families: Stories from Rwanda (New York: Farrar, Straus, and Giroux, 1998).

16. Daniel S. Papp, Loch K. Johnson, and John Endicott, *American Foreign Policy: History, Politics, and Policy* (New York: Pearson Longman, 2005), 200.

17. Adam B. Ellick, "64 Journalists Killed Worldwide in 2007, the Most Since '94," *New York Times*, December 18, 2007, A6.

18. Daniel P. Bolger, *Savage Peace: Americans at War in the 1990s* (Novato, CA: Presidio, 1995).

19. Walter Pincus, "Discontent at CIA Unveils New Charges of Questionable Conduct," *Washington Post*, July 15, 1994, A9.

20. Walter Pincus, "White House Labors to Redefine Role of Intelligence Community," *Washington Post*, July 13, 1994, A2. Another source offers this same figure, but suggests further that the costs per year might have surpassed $35 billion (John J. Fialka, "Congress Is Set to Approve Big Review of Costly U.S. Intelligence Community," *Wall Street Journal*, September 26, 1994, A6).

21. Quoted in Pincus, "White House Labors."

22. Quoted in John M. Broder, "Russian Premier Warns U.S. Against Role as Policeman," *New York Times*, July 28, 1999, A8.

23. Quoted in James Risen, "CIA Still Reeling from Ames Ties to Soviet Agents," *Los Angeles Times*, November 27, 1995, A1.

24. *Ibid.*, A10. For a more complete appraisal of the damage caused by Ames, see John Deutch, *Statement on the Clandestine Services and the Damaged Caused by Aldrich Ames*, Office of the Director of Central Intelligence (December 7, 1995); and Senate Select Committee on Intelligence, *An Assessment of the Aldrich H. Ames Espionage Case and Its Implications for U.S. Intelligence*, 103rd Cong., 2nd sess., November 1, 1994.

25. Daniel Patrick Moynihan, "Do We Still Need the C.I.A.? The State Dept. Can Do the Job," *New York Times*, May 19, 1991, E17. For an assertion that other members of Congress also questioned the value of keeping the CIA, see Steven Komarow, "In Turnabout, the CIA Finds Itself under a Microscope" *USA Today*, July 15, 1994, A5.

26. George Tenet, (senior director for intelligence, National Security Council, and, later, DCI), interview with author, Old Executive Office Building, Washington, DC, June 11, 1994.

27. Paul F. Horvitz, "Aspin to Step Down as Defense Secretary," *New York Times*, December 16, 1993, A1.

28. AP report in the *New York Times*, "Aspin's Pacemaker Operation Called Successful," March 19, 1993, A19.

29. David E. Rosenbaum, "Les Aspin, 56, Dies; Member of Congress and Defense Chief," *New York Times*, May 22, 1995, B10.

30. Pat M. Holt, *Secret Intelligence and Public Policy: A Dilemma of Democracy* (Washington, DC: CQ, 1995), 203–5; Kenneth Michael Absher, Michael C. Desch, and Roman Popadiuk, "The President's Foreign Intelligence Advisory

Board," in ed. Loch K Johnson, *The Oxford Handbook of National Security Intelligence* (New York: Oxford University Press, 2010), 172-188. Initially, PFIAB was known as the President's Board of Consultants on Foreign Intelligence Activities (PBCFIA); then, in 2008, by Executive Order no. 13,462, President George W. Bush renamed the panel the President's Intelligence Advisory Board (PIAB). For four years under President Jimmy Carter, the board was disbanded. Members of the board serve without financial compensation, other than transportation costs and a per diem to attend its periodic meetings. During the Clinton administration, the board as a whole met infrequently: only about every six weeks—and never with the president (according to an interview conducted by Absher, Desch, and Popadiuk). Under Clinton, the board expanded from eight to a dozen members, with terms limited to two years; the president named a total of twenty-one individuals to the panel during his two terms in office (1993–2001).

31. James Bennet, "Thinking About the Day After Tomorrow," *New York Times*, December 24, 2000, A14; Donna Cassata, "Congress Jumps to CIA's Aid in Its Quest for Identity," *CQ Weekly Report*, January 7, 1995, 41. In a memoir, a leading senator at the time and chair of the Senate Select Committee on Intelligence, Dennis DeConcini, also portrays the president as uninterested in intelligence. Dennis DeConcini and Jack L. August Jr., *Senator Dennis DeConcini: From the Center of the Aisle* (Tucson: University of Arizona Press, 2006), 198–99. This seeming indifference to questions of intelligence and national security only added to Clinton's unpopularity at the CIA; its employees were already disenchanted with the president for failing to attend the ceremony that honored two employees murdered by an anti-American Pakistani extremist, Mir Aimal Kasi, in early 1993 (the First Lady went in his place). Kasi gunned down the intelligence officers with an AK-47 assault rifle as they sat in their cars on the way to work, waiting for the traffic light to change before entering the Agency's compound. Kasi fled to Pakistan, where the FBI and the CIA finally tracked him down over four years later and brought him back for trial in the United States. Convicted of the killings in 1997, he was put to death by lethal injection at the Greensville Correctional Center in Virginia in 2002.

32. Walter Pincus, "White House Labors," A2.

33. Professor Harry Howe Ransom of Vanderbilt University, one of the most important and prolific of the early intelligence-studies scholars in the United States, eschews the phrase "intelligence community" in order not to overstate the organizational cohesion among the intelligence agencies. He prefers the phrase "intelligence system" (e-mail to the author, December 17, 2007). Because the "community" designation is so widely adopted among intelligence professionals, however, I continue to use it here, even though I understand and appreciate Professor Ransom's reasoning.

34. Interview by the author with a DO manager, Washington, DC, February 11, 1986.

35. For a vivid, if one-sided (anti-CIA), history of covert action and its negative consequences, see Tim Weiner, *Legacy of Ashes: The History of the CIA* (New York: Doubleday, 2007).

36. See Loch K. Johnson, *America's Secret Power: The CIA in a Democratic Society* (New York: Oxford University Press, 1989); John Prados, *Presidents' Secret Wars: CIA and Pentagon Covert Operations since World War II* (New York: Morrow, 1986); Prados, *Safe for Democracy: The Secret Wars of the CIA* (Chicago: Dee, 2006); Gregory F. Treverton, *Covert Action: The Limits of Intervention in the Postwar World* (New York: Basic Books, 1987).

37. William J. Daugherty, *Executive Secrets: Covert Action and the Presidency* (Lexington: University Press of Kentucky, 2004); Steve Coll, *Ghost Wars: The Secret History of the CIA, Afghanistan, and Bin Laden, from the Soviet Invasion to September 10, 2001* (New York: Penguin, 2004).

38. R. James Woolsey Jr., DCI, interview with author, CIA Headquarters, Langley, VA, September 19, 1993. For a graph depicting the CIA's use of covert action over time, see Loch K. Johnson, *Secret Agencies: U.S. Intelligence in a Hostile World* (New Haven, CT: Yale University Press, 1996), 33.

39. See Loch K. Johnson, "Ostriches, Cheerleaders, Skeptics, and Guardians: Role Selection by Congressional Intelligence Overseers," *SAIS Review of International Affairs* 28 (Winter-Spring 2008): 93–108; Fred F. Manget, "Intelligence and the Rise of Judicial Intervention," in *Handbook of Intelligence Studies*, ed. Loch K. Johnson (New York: Routledge, 2007), 329–42.

40. Hans Born, Loch K. Johnson, and Ian Leigh, eds., *Who's Watching the Spies? Establishing Intelligence Service Accountability* (Washington, DC: Potomac Books, 2005); Loch K. Johnson, "Accountability and America's Secret Foreign Policy: Keeping a Legislative Eye on the Central Intelligence Agency," *Foreign Policy Analysis* 1 (Spring 2005): 99–120.

41. For an example of the *Times* reporting on intelligence abuses, see Seymour M. Hersh, "Underground for the C.I.A. in New York: An Ex-Agent Tells of Spying on Students," *New York Times*, December 29, 1974, A1. Representative Otis Pike (D-NY) led the Pike Committee, the House counterpart to the Church Committee.

42. Art Pine, "Ex-Defense Secretary Aspin Dies After Suffering Stroke," *Los Angeles Times*, May 22, 1995, A15.

43. Bob Woodward, "The Secretary of Analysis," *Washington Post*, February 21, 1993, W8.

44. Ward Just, "A 'Whiz Kid' Among the Ruff-Puffs," *Newsweek*, June 5, 1995, 31.

45. Apple, "Vietnam's Student," 9. See also R. W. Apple Jr., "Change in the Pentagon," *New York Times*, December 16, 1993, A1; Barton Gellman and Jeffrey R. Smith, "Hesitant by Design," *Washington Post*, November 14, 1993, A1; Norman Kempster and Robin Wright, "For Aspin, This was the Year from Hell," *Los Angeles Times*, December 16, 1993, A33; John Lancaster, "A Man Who Seemed Miscast," *Washington Post*, December 16, 1993, A1.

46. Richard Pearson, "Former Defense Secretary Les Aspin Dies at 56," *Washington Post*, May 22, 1995, B4.

47. L. Britt Snider, "A Different Angle on the Aspin-Brown Commission,"*Studies in Intelligence* 49 (2005): 85.

48. Tim Weiner, "Congress Decides to Conduct Study of Need for C.I.A.," *New York Times*, September 28, 1994, A1.

49. See Snider, "A Different Angle," 85–86.

50. Senate Armed Services Committee, *Review of the Circumstances*, 4, 6, 8. See also Bill Gertz, "Aspin's Decision on Tanks Was Political," *Washington Times*, October 3, 1995, A3; and Allard, *Somalia Operations*.

51. Les Aspin, telephone conversation with author, December 12, 1994.

52. Tim Weiner, "Looking for the Enemy; For C.I.A., History Is the Big Traitor," *New York Times*, January 1, 1995, Wk3. Severely undermining the CIA's reputation, in Weiner's view, was the fact that a "slacker like Mr. Ames could flourish in the clandestine service."

53. Kenneth Kitts, *Presidential Commissions and National Security: The Politics of Damage Control* (Boulder, CO: Rienner, 2006), 173.

54. In fact, the CIA had done a reasonably good job of closely tracking the decline of the Soviet economy in the 1980s and the likelihood of the ensuing political disintegration of the Soviet Union; it just had not predicted the exact day and hour—nor had anyone else in the world. See Johnson, *Secret Agencies*, 187–91; Bruce D. Berkowitz and Jeffrey T. Richelson, "The CIA Vindicated: The Soviet Collapse Was Predicted," *National Interest* 41 (Fall 1995): 36–47; Bruce D. Berkowitz, "U.S. Intelligence Estimates of the Soviet Collapse: Reality and Perception," *International Journal of Intelligence and Counterintelligence* 21 (Summer 2008): 237–50.

55. Kitts, *Presidential Commissions*, 168–69.

56. Komarow, "In Turnabout."

57. See Ernest R. May, "The Twenty-first Century Challenge for U.S. Intelligence," in *Transforming U.S. Intelligence*, ed. Jennifer E. Sims and Burton Gerber (Washington, DC: Georgetown University Press, 2005), 6–7.

58. See John Diamond, *The CIA and the Culture of Failure: U.S. Intelligence from the End of the Cold War to the Invasion of Iraq* (Stanford, CA: Stanford University Press, 2008), 224–25.

59. Douglas Waller, "Master of the Game: John Deutch," *Time*, May 6, 1996, 42; Diamond, *The CIA and the Culture of Failure*, 225.

60. Waller, "Master of the Game."

61. Les Aspin, telephone conversation with author, November 3, 1994.

62. See Thomas Powers, "Computer Security: The Whiz Kid vs. the Old Boys," *New York Times Magazine*, December 3, 2000, p. 16.

63. Snider, "A Different Angle," 86.

64. *Congressional Quarterly Weekly Report*, "Intelligence Authorization," September 10, 1994, 69.

65. Douglas F. Garthoff, *Directors of Central Intelligence as Leaders of the U.S. Intelligence Community, 1945–2005* (Center for the Study of Intelligence, Central Intelligence Agency, Washington, DC, 2005), 232.

66. Snider, "A Different Angle," 86.

67. Fialka, "Congress Is Set to Approve Big Review."

68. Walter Pincus, "Politics Marks Intelligence Study Panel; Last-Minute Language Limits Democrats' Role," *Washington Post*, November 1, 1994.

69. Quoted in ibid.

70. Senator Warner's concerns were not unfounded. A *National Journal* poll of the American people in 1994 found that an overwhelming majority—72 percent—had only "some" or "very little" confidence in the CIA. *National Journal*, "Opinion Outlook: Views on National Security," April 4, 1994, 802.

71. 103d Cong., 2nd sess., *Congressional Record* 140 (August 12, 1994), S11379–89.

72. See the commission's final report, *Preparing for the 21st Century: An Appraisal of U.S. Intelligence* (Washington, DC: GPO, 1996), appendices E, E-2, and E-3. The commission treated this list as a general guide and departed from it, as deemed appropriate, to deal with matters the original statute had failed to anticipate. As Snider has noted, not all the items on the original list that he prepared rose "to the same level of significance," and they "missed a few key issues and do not frame others in the right way." L. Britt Snider, unclassified memo to the author (undated, but received on July 27, 1995).

73. 103d Cong., 2nd sess., *Congressional Record* 140 (August 12, 1994), S 11379–89; *Congressional Quarterly Weekly Report*, "Intelligence Authorization," September 10, 1994, 69. The House had passed a similar measure in support of the commission by a vote of 410 to 16 on July 20, 1994. On a procedural second vote in the Senate, the leadership brought up the House bill (HR 4299) as a substitute for the Senate bill (S 2082), just passed unanimously. On this go-round, which provided a final bill with the same language for both chambers (and therefore, ready to move on to the conference committee), the vote continued to be overwhelmingly in favor: 97 to 2. 103rd Cong., 2nd sess., *Congressional Quarterly Almanac* 50 (1994).

74. Robert Pear, "A Shake-Up at Spy Agency as Secret Fund is Disclosed," *New York Times*, September 25, 1995, A12.

75. Additional views of Senator John Warner, in *Preparing for the 21st Century*, 149.

76. H.R. Rep. No. 103–753, 103rd Cong. 2nd. sess., 65, reprinted in 1994 U.S.C. 2751, 2773. Both chambers accepted the conference report by voice vote on September 30th. 103rd Cong., 2nd sess., *Congressional Quarterly Almanac* 50 (1994).

77. Snider memo to the author.

78. *Intelligence Authorization Act For Fiscal Year 1995*, tit. IX, 50 U.S.C., 401 note (Su1995), Public Law 103–359.

79. Tim Weiner, "Commission Has Begun Task of Redefining Role of C.I.A.," *New York Times*, March 18, 1995, A1.

80. Elizabeth A. Palmer, "Congress Creates Commission to Study CIA's Performance,"*Congressional Quarterly Weekly Report*, October 1, 1994, 2824.

81. Pincus, "Politics Marks Intelligence Study Panel," A5.

82. Kitts, *Presidential Commissions*, 5.

Chapter 2

1. Unsigned editorial, *New York Times*, "Mr. Aspin: Pick Up the Pace," January 16, 1995, A16.

2. Larry Combest, letter to the editor, *New York Times*, January 23, 1995, A12.

3. Kenneth Kitts, *Presidential Commissions and National Security: The Politics of Damage Control* (Boulder, CO: Rienner, 2006), 170.

4. Donna Cassata, "Intelligence Panel Belatedly Filled," *Congressional Quarterly Weekly Report*, February 4, 1995, 374.

5. See, for example, Tim Weiner, "Clinton Chooses Retired General to be C.I.A. Head," *New York Times*, February 8, 1995; and Joe Klein, "Closework," *New Yorker*, October 1, 2001, 44–49, which refers to the president's interest in national security issues as "cursory" (p. 49).

6. Several incumbent PFIAB members found themselves left out of the action, including Thomas S. Foley, the former Democratic speaker of the House, who had helped picked the congressional appointees on the commission before he was defeated for reelection; Thomas F. Eagleton, the former senator from Missouri; Dr. Sidney D. Drell, a noted physicist; Maurice Sonnenberg, a trade and security expert; and Lois D. Rice, an education activist. A list of all PFIAB members and their dates of service can be found in Kenneth Michael Absher, Michael C. Desch, and Roman Popadiuk, "The President's Foreign Intelligence Advisory Board," working paper (March 2008), appendix. Aspin attempted to mollify the rejected PFIBA members by inviting them to attend Commission meetings on an informal basis as observers. Only Sonnenberg and Rice took him up on the offer; and once it was clear how marginal their roles would be, they stopped attending most meetings.

7. See Kitts, *Presidential Commissions*, 12.

8. For his memoir, see Warren B. Rudman, *Combat: Twelve Years in the U.S. Senate* (New York: Random House, 1996).

9. William S. Cohen and George J. Mitchell, *Men of Zeal: A Candid Inside Story of the Iran-Contra Hearings* (New York: Penguin, 1988), 19.

10. Press conference, Washington, DC, May 7, 1989, quoted in ibid., 76.

11. Jill Smolowe, Margaret Carlson, and Elaine Shannon, "The Zoe Baird Debacle: How It Happened," *Time*, February 1, 1993, 4.

12. Ibid., 6.

13. Patrick McGeehan, "Economic Adviser from Other Side of the Deficit—Stephen Friedman," *New York Times*, December 13, 2002, A28.

14. See Loch K. Johnson, *A Season of Inquiry: The Senate Intelligence Investigation* (Lexington: University Press of Kentucky, 1985).

15. Elaine Sciolino, "In a Humble World, Defense Deputy Stands Firm," *New York Times*, April 2, 2001, A10.

16. Peter J. Boyer, "The Believer," *New Yorker*, November 1, 2004, 46–57.

17. John Cassidy, "The Next Crusade," *New Yorker*, April 9, 2007, 36–51.

18. See James Bamford, *The Puzzle Palace: A Report on America's Most Secret Agency* (Boston: Houghton Mifflin, 1982), 111–12; Douglas Martin, "Gen. Lew Allen, 84, Dies: Directed Security Agency," New York Times, January 9, 2010, A15.

19. Based on the author's ongoing research, as yet unpublished, into congressional roll-call votes on Senate opposition to intelligence reform. The preliminary data indicate that on roll-call votes in the Senate on several intelligence reform proposals from the 1950s through recent times most Republicans were strongly opposed to intelligence reform and most Democrats were strongly in favor (chiefly because of the latter's concern about questions of privacy and civil liberties). See also Loch K. Johnson, "Playing Ball with the CIA: Congress Supervises Strategic Intelligence," in *The President, the Congress, and the Making of Foreign Policy*, ed. Paul E. Peterson (Norman: University of Oklahoma, 1994), 49–73, for similar findings, but based on the degree of difficulty in questions posed by Democrats and Republicans to CIA witnesses during congressional public hearings on intelligence.

20. Brigid Schulte, "Warner's Career marked by Courage to Buck Conventional Wisdom," *Washington Post*, September 2, 2007. A1.

21. Laura Blumenfeld, "Goss Hailed As Old Pro, Assailed as Partisan," *Washington Post*, September 13, 2004, A1.

22. Quoted in Philip D. Duncan and Christine C. Lawrence, eds., *Politics in America 1998: The 105th Congress* (Washington, DC: CQ, 1997), 344.

23. William O. Studeman, remarks, "Teaching Intelligence," Intelligence Conference, Center for the Study of Intelligence, Central Intelligence Agency, Tysons Corner, VA, author's notes, October 1, 1993. See also Tim Shorrock, *Spies for Hire: The Secret World of Intelligence Outsourcing* (New York: Simon & Schuster, 2008); and Dana Priest and William M. Arkin, "Top Secret America: A Washington Post Investigation; Day 2: National Security Inc.," Washington Post (July 21, 2010), at http://www.postandcourier.com/news/2010/jul/21day-2-national -security-inc

24. Duane Hutchinson, *Exon: Biography of a Governor* (Lincoln, Nebraska: Foundation Books, 1973).

25. Associated Press report, *New York Times*, "Former Senator J. James Exon, 83, Dies," June 13, 2005, A10.

26. J. James Exon, remarks, quoted in Senate Committee on Armed Services, *MX Missile Basing System and Related Issues: Hearings before the Committee on Armed Services*, 98th Cong., 1st sess., 1983, 17.

27. See Loch K. Johnson, "Wyche Fowler," *The New Georgia Encyclopedia* at http://www.georgiaencyclopedia.org/nge/Article.jsp?id=h-1093&hl=y, 21.

28. For an account, see Richard F. Fenno Jr., *Senators on the Campaign Trail: The Politics of Representation* (Norman: University of Oklahoma Press, 1996), 160–238.

29. Frederick A. O. Schwarz Jr., remark to the author, Dirksen Senate Office Building, Washington, DC, June 26, 1975.

30. See, for example, Johnson, *Season of Inquiry*, 34.

31. "Aspin Outlines Role of Intelligence Commission," *National Security Law Report* 17 (February-March 1995), 1, 4–6.

Chapter 3

1. Laura Blumenfeld, "Goss Hailed As Old Pro, Assailed as Partisan," *Washington Post*, September 13, 2004, A1.

2. Janet Hook, "Republicans Step Up to Power in Historic 40-Year Shift," *Congressional Quarterly Weekly Report*, January 7, 1995, 7.

3. John M. Deutch, interview with author, MIT, Cambridge, MA, October 29, 1998.

4. "Washington Whispers," *U.S. News & World Report*, February 20, 1995, 23.

5. On Goldwater-Nichols, see James R. Locher III, *Victory on the Potomac: The Goldwater-Nichols Act Unifies the Pentagon* (College Station: Texas A&M University Press, 2002).

6. Robert M. Gates, interview with author, Washington, DC, March 28, 1994.

7. William O. Studeman, e-mail to the author, October 10, 2001.

8. Les Aspin, remark to the author, Washington, DC, July 14, 1994.

9. The figure of 85 percent is from the Aspin-Brown Commission final report, *Preparing for the 21st Century: Appraisal of U.S. Intelligence* (Washington, DC: Government Printing Office, March 1, 1996, 49. For the unofficial (but widely reported) total budget figure of $28 billion, see *Congressional Quarterly Weekly Report*, "Intelligence Authorization," September 10, 1994, 69; and Tim Weiner, "Let's Play Spy! (And the Money Is Real!)," *New York Times*, August 14, 1994, Wk15. In 2007, the *Washington Post* reported that the total U.S. intelligence budget for that year was just over $50 billion ("2007 Spying Said To Cost $50 Billion," October 30, 2007). This figure refers to the National Intelligence Program (NIP): primarily the budgets of the NSA, NGA, NRO, CIA, and some of the smaller civilian agencies, leaving aside the Military Intelligence Program (MIP), which is dedicated to tactical military intelligence requirements, When the two programs are combined, my interviews with intelligence officials in 2010 indicated that the budget is as much as $80 billion or over two-and-a-half times the size of the intelligence budget on September 11, 2001. In September 2009, the Director of National Intelligence (an office created in 2004 to replace

the DCI) said publicly that the overall intelligence budget figure is around $75 billion. For purposes of comparison, the annual projected intelligence budget for France in 2008 was reportedly about $1 billion; and for the United Kingdom, about $5 billion (cited in Steve Aftergood, "Deliberating the Intelligence Budget in France," *Secrecy News*, Federation of American Scientists Project on Government Secrecy, December 14, 2007, http://www.fas.org/blog/secrecy/2007/12/deliberating_the_intelligence_.html).

10. After the 9/11 attacks, the civilian side of the intelligence community was augmented by three additional agencies: an intelligence unit in the new Department of Homeland Security (DHS), Coast Guard Intelligence (soon placed organizationally within the framework of the DHS), and the Drug Enforcement Administration (DEA), long part of the Justice Department and now accorded new status as a major intelligence entity in the community (see Appendix B). These additions bring the total to seven intelligence agencies embedded in civilian policy departments today, eight in the Department of Defense, and, adding the independent CIA, sixteen agencies in the overall "community." For an excellent account of how the Coast Guard became a member of the intelligence community, see Kevin E. Wirth, *The Coast Guard Intelligence Program Enters the Intelligence Community: A Case Study of Congressional Influence on Intelligence Community Evolution* (Washington, DC: National Defense Intelligence College, 2007). The main figure in this case study is central to this book as well: Rep. Porter Goss (R-FL), an avid sailor with an appreciation for the work of the Coast Guard and a willingness to use his pivotal position as chairman of HPSCI to assist in its aspirations to join the community.

11. On the evolution of the American intelligence establishment, see William R. Corson, *The Armies of Ignorance: The Rise of the American Intelligence Empire* (New York: Dial, 1977); Rhodri Jeffreys-Jones, *The CIA and American Democracy* (New Haven, CT: Yale University Press, 1989), as well as his "The Rise and Fall of the CIA," in ed. Loch K. Johnson, *The Oxford Handbook of National Security Intelligence* (New York: Oxford University Press, 2010), 122–137; Mark M. Lowenthal, *U.S. Intelligence: Evolution and Anatomy*, 2d ed. (Westport, CT: Praeger, 1992); John Ranelagh, *The Agency: The Rise and Decline of the CIA* (New York: Simon and Schuster, 1986); Harry Howe Ransom, *The Intelligence Establishment* (Cambridge, MA: Harvard University Press, 1970); Jeffrey Richelson, *The US Intelligence Community*, 5th ed. (Boulder, CO: Westview, 2008); Douglas T. Stuart, *Creating the National Security State: A History of the Law That Transformed America* (Princeton, NJ: Princeton University Press, 2008); and Michael Warner, "The Rise of the U.S. Intelligence System: 1917–1977," in ed. Johnson, *The Oxford Handbook of National Security Intelligence*, 107–121.

12. R. James Woolsey, interview with author, CIA Headquarters, Langley, VA, September 29, 1993.

13. Stansfield Turner, interview with author, at Turner's residence, McLean, VA, May 1, 1991. For a vivid description of his difficulties in trying to manage the

CIA—let alone the larger intelligence community—see his memoir, *Secrecy and Democracy: The CIA in Transition* (Boston: Houghton Mifflin, 1985). Today, two of the CIA's directorates have different names: the Directorate of Support (instead of the Directorate of Administration) and the National Clandestine Service (instead of the Directorate of Operations).

14. On the various spending units in the intelligence community, see Mark M. Lowenthal, *Intelligence: From Secrets to Policy*, 4th ed. (Washington, DC: CQ, 2009).

15. R. James Woolsey, testimony, *Hearings*, U.S. Senate Select Committee on Intelligence, 103d Cong., 2nd. sess., March 6, 1993.

16. David Gries, interview with author, Center for the Study of Intelligence, CIA, Rosslyn, VA, July 9, 1993.

17. For a critique of the intelligence cycle's failure, in its simplicity, to capture the complex reality of real-world intelligence, see Arthur S. Hulnick, "What's Wrong with the Intelligence Cycle?" in *Strategic Intelligence*, ed. Loch K. Johnson (Westport, CT: Praeger, 2007), 2:1–22.

18. James R. Clapper Jr., cited in *Intelligencer* (AFIO newsletter), October 1995, 3.

19. R. V. Jones, "Intelligence in a Democracy" (lecture, author's notes, U.S. Department of State, Washington, DC, December 4, 1975).

20. This "river" metaphor comes from former DCI Robert M. Gates (1991–93) and is used often by intelligence officials (and later in this book by an acting director of central intelligence).

21. See *The 9/11 Commission Report: Final Report of the National Commission on Terrorist Attacks upon the United States* (New York: Norton, 2004). For a critique of the commission report, see Loch K. Johnson, "An Elephant Rolling a Pea," *Diplomatic History* 30 (April 2006): 327–33.

22. Not everyone thinks this is a problem. David Gries, a former intelligence officer at the CIA, states: "Do we know what the policy makers want? Most of what is written on this subject is rubbish. We see these people almost every day of the week; they read our reports. You can be sure, they tell us very frankly what's on their minds and whether we are meeting their needs." "Teaching Intelligence" (lecture, author's notes, Center for the Study of Intelligence, CIA, Tysons Corner, VA, October 1, 1993).

23. For an example from that era, see Richard Pipes, "What To Do About the CIA," *Commentary*, March 1995, 42.

24. John Hollister Hedley, "Checklist for the Future of Intelligence," occasional paper, Institute for the Study of Diplomacy, Georgetown University, Washington, DC, 1995, 3–4. For an account of the Georgetown University intelligence-reform group, see Walter Pincus, "Military Espionage Cuts Eyed," *Washington Post*, March 17, 1995, A1.

25. Preston Niblack, Arnold Kanter, and John Schrader, "Developing an Analytic Framework for the Commission: Workshop Notes," project memorandum, PM-390-CRCIC, March 1995, 2, italics in original.

26. Ibid., 9.

27. For this early history, see Loch K. Johnson, "A Centralized Intelligence System: Truman's Dream Deferred," *American Intelligence Journal* 23 (Autumn/Winter 2005): 6–15.

28. *9/11 Commission Final Report*, 417.

29. James R. Clapper, telephone conversation with author, January 9, 1995.

30. In 1980, Les Aspin had written: "I believe there is a case to be made that Congress needs to revise the way it oversees covert action. But the problem is not that congressional oversight is too strict already; the problem is that it is not strict enough yet." "Covert Acts Need Even More Oversight," *Washington Post*, February 24, 1980, B7.

31. *9/11 Commission Final Report*, 420.

32. As I was thinking to myself about these matters at one of the staff meetings, an old saw came to mind (supposedly uttered during a heated debate in the British House of Commons years ago). In response to cries for "Reform! Reform!" a member of Parliament replied: "Reform, sir? Don't talk to me of reform. Things are bad enough as they are."

33. For accounts, see Loch K. Johnson, *Secret Agencies: U.S. Intelligence in a Hostile World* (New Haven, CT: Yale University Press, 1996), 187–91; Bruce D. Berkowitz and Jeffrey T. Richelson, "The CIA Vindicated: The Soviet Collapse Was Predicted," *National Interest* 41 (Fall 1995): 36–46; Bruce D. Berkowitz, "U.S. Intelligence Estimates of the Soviet Collapse: Reality and Perception," *International Journal of Intelligence and Counterintelligence* 21 (2008): 237–50; Kirsten Lundberg, "CIA and the Fall of the Soviet Empire: The Politics of 'Getting It Right'," Kennedy School of Government, Harvard University, Case Study C16-94-1251.0, Cambridge, MA, 1994; David M. Kennedy, "Sunshine and Shadow: The CIA and the Soviet Economy," Kennedy School of Government, Harvard University, Case Study C16-91-1096.0, Cambridge, MA, 1991; Douglas J. MacEachin, *CIA Assessments of the Soviet Union: The Record Versus the Charges* (Washington, DC: Center for the Study of Intelligence, CIA, 1996); and James Risen, "Files Show CIA Warned of Soviet Decline," *Los Angeles Times*, September 26, 1995, A6.

34. For a more elaborate listing of successes and failures, see Johnson, *Secret Agencies*, ch. 7; and, with a focus on the failures, Tim Weiner, *Legacy of Ashes: The History of the CIA* (New York: Doubleday, 2007).

35. Cited in Mark M. Lowenthal, "Intelligence Collection in Transition," *World Politics Review*, February 2, 2009, 16.

36. See James G. Blight and David A. Welch, eds., *Intelligence and the Cuban Missile Crisis* (London: Cass, 1998).

37. Robert S. McNamara, the former secretary of defense in the Kennedy years, who was among those given access to these Soviet documents, quoted in James G. Blight, Bruce J. Allyn, and David A. Welch, *Cuba on the Brink: Castro, the*

Missile Crisis, and the Soviet Collapse (New York: Pantheon Books, 1993), 379, italics in original.

38. Lawrence Wright, "The Spymaster," *New Yorker*, January 21, 2008, 57.

39. Memorandum from Kim M. Simpson to Les Aspin, "Commission Outreach Action Plan," March 9, 1995.

40. Recounted in David E. Rosenbaum, *New York Times*, "Les Aspin, 56, Dies; Member of Congress And Defense Chief," May 22, 1995, A1.

41. See Les Aspin, "The MX Bargain," *Bulletin of the Atomic Scientists* 39 (November 1983): 53–57; Elizabeth Drew, "A Political Journal," *New Yorker*, June 20, 1983, 55; and Steven V. Roberts, "The Congressmen Say MX Still Faces a Tough Battle," *New York Times*, April 12, 1983, A20.

42. Three months after Mark Lowenthal of HPSCI had sent out a solicitation letter asking experts for advice on intelligence reform, Les Aspin mailed out a similar (although far less detailed) plea—in part sincere and in part a public relations gesture. For instance, his letter to AFIO said: "I am writing to ask for your help. . . . Your input is very much appreciated and we urge you to write or phone the Commission staff." Les Aspin, letter to AFIO members, received on May 4, 1995, and reprinted in *Intelligencer* 6, June 1995, 3.

43. See Hedley, "Checklist for the Future of Intelligence." This report was specifically prepared as a checklist for consideration by the Aspin Commission and was carefully read by its commissioners and staff. For a summary of its section on military intelligence duplication, see Pincus, "Military Espionage Cuts Eyed."

44. In 2008, the Department of Homeland Security established the National Applications Office (NAO). One of its duties was to promote the use of intelligence capabilities, such as surveillance satellites, for domestic homeland security. In response, the chairman of the House Homeland Security Committee warned: "Turning America's spy satellites on the homeland for domestic law enforcement purposes is no trivial matter." He and other members of the committee vowed to terminate the program unless NAO's plans complied with a "detailed legal framework" and were vetted by "the privacy and civil liberties community." See Siobhan Gorman, "Privacy Fears Threaten Satellite Program," *Wall Street Journal*, April 8, 2008, A3. In the 1970s, the CIA properly refused a request from the Alcohol and Tobacco Tax and Trade Bureau of the Treasury Department to provided imint assistance in the form of infrared photography during a search for moonshine stills in the mountains of North Carolina. See Commission on CIA Activities Within the United States, *Report to the President by the Commission on CIA Activities Within the United States* (Washington, DC: Government Printing Office, 1975), 231, note 5.

45. "Exon Says This Congress Will Be His Last," *Congressional Quarterly Weekly Report*, March 18, 1995, 786.

46. Walter Pincus, "Panel Rejects Intelligence Shift," *Washington Post*, July 18, 1996, A25.

47. Among several sources claiming that military intelligence agencies within the institutional framework of the Pentagon control some 85 percent of the annual intelligence budget percentage (a figure often cited in interviews conducted by the author with intelligence officials over the years), see Mark T. Kehoe, "Spy Agencies to See Minor Change," in *Congressional Quarterly Almanac 1996* (Washington, DC: CQ, 1997), 9–17; see also note 9 in this chapter.

48. Joint Committee on Events Surrounding the Terrorist Attacks of September 11, 2001, *Hearings*, U.S. Congress, 107th Cong., 2nd sess., October 3, 2002, 7.

49. Robert M. Gates, comment to the author, referring to his relationship with Secretary of Defense Dick Cheney, Washington, DC, March 27, 1994.

50. In 1959, President Dwight David Eisenhower approved a PFIAB reform recommendation that "action be taken to effect strong, centralized direction (both through the NSC and the DCI) of the Intelligence Community and its resources, in order to strengthen our national intelligence effort and to contain its costs." James S. Lay, NSC Executive Secretary, to the DCI, Washington, DC, January 29, 1957, cited in Kenneth Michael Absher, Michael C. Desch, and Roman Popadiuk, "The President's Foreign Intelligence Advisory Board," working paper (March 2008), 38, note 126. Little was done, however, toward achieving this objective.

51. *9/11 Commission Final Report*, 267–72.

52. On these and other CIA-FBI counterintelligence disputes, see Tom Mangold, *Cold Warrior: James Jesus Angleton; The CIA's Master Spy Hunter* (New York: Simon & Schuster, 1991).

53. Tim Weiner, "Looking for the Enemy; For C.I.A., History is the Big Traitor," *New York Times*, January 1, 1995, Wk3.

54. Tim Weiner, "New C.I.A. Chief Wants to Revamp U.S. Spying Overseas," *New York Times*, July 3, 1995, A1.

55. This phrase is widely attributed to Jesse Unruh, the former California state legislative leader in the 1960s.

Chapter 4

1. Quoted in Donna Cassata, "Choice of Deutch to Head CIA Wins Qualified Praise," *Congressional Quarterly Weekly Report* 53, March 18, 1995, 826.

2. Robert Pear, "A Shake-Up at Spy Agency as Secret Fund Is Disclosed," *New York Times*, September 25, 1995, A12.

3. Elaine Sciolino, "C.I.A. Chief Charts His Own Course," *New York Times*, September 29, 1996, A1.

4. Cassata, "Choice of Deutch," 825.

5. George Tenet succeeded Deutch as DCI and also enjoyed cabinet status, although he rarely attended cabinet meetings; and when George W. Bush became president in 2001, he removed Tenet's cabinet rank. Thus, three DCIs have been members of the cabinet—William Casey, Deutch, and

Tenet—although Casey is the only one to have vigorously exercised this pre-rogative through participation in policy debates.

6. Cassata, "Choice of Deutch," 826.

7. John M. Deutch, interview with author, MIT, Cambridge, MA, October 29, 1998.

8. Sherman Kent's classic book on intelligence is *Strategic Intelligence for American World Policy* (Princeton, NJ: Princeton University Press, 1949).

9. Stansfield Turner, interview with author at Turner's residence, McLean, VA, May 1, 1991.

10. Randall M. Fort, remarks, "Intelligence and Policy Review Project," John F. Kennedy School of Government, Harvard University, Cambridge, MA, April 12, 1990.

11. Richard Helms, interview with author, Washington, DC, December 12, 1990.

12. Fritz Ermarth, remarks, "Intelligence and Policy Review Project," John F. Kennedy School of Government, Harvard University, Cambridge, MA, April 12, 1990.

13. See Paul R. Pillar, "Intelligence, Policy, and the War in Iraq," *Foreign Affairs* 85 (March/April 2006): 27; and David D. Gries, "New Links Between Intelligence and Policy," *Studies in Intelligence* 34 (Summer 1990): 1–6, reprinted in *Inside CIA's Private World: Declassified Articles from the Agency's Internal Journal, 1955–1992*, ed. H. Bradford Westerfield (New Haven, CT: Yale University Press, 1995), 357–65.

14. Stansfield Turner, "Intelligence for a New World Order," *Foreign Affairs,* Fall 1991, 151–52.

15. Robert M. Gates, remarks, Economic Club of Detroit, April 13, 1992.

16. R. James Woolsey, testimony, Select Committee on Intelligence, U.S. Senate, February 2, 1993; Woolsey, "The Future of Intelligence on the Global Frontier" (lecture at the Executive Club of Chicago, November 19, 1993).

17. William E. Colby, interview with author, Washington, DC, January 22, 1991.

18. R. James Woolsey, response during a question-and-answer period following his address, entitled "The Future Direction of Intelligence," Center for Strategic and International Studies, Washington, DC, July 18, 1994.

19. See Loch K. Johnson, *Secret Agencies: U.S. Intelligence in a Hostile World* (New Haven: Yale University Press, 1996), chap. 7; and Johnson, *Bombs, Bugs, Drugs, and Thugs: Intelligence and America's Quest for Security* (New York: New York University Press, 2000), chap. 2.

20. Mostafa K. Tolba and Iwona Rummel-Bulska, *Global Environmental Diplomacy: Negotiating Environmental Agreements for the World, 1973–1992* (Cambridge, MA: MIT Press, 1998), 13–14; Lydia Polgreen and Sabrina Tavernise, "Water Dispute Raises Tension Between India and Pakistanis," *New York Times* (July 21, 2010), A1.

21. For more on environmental intelligence, see Johnson, *Bombs, Bugs, Drugs, and Thugs*, chap. 2.

22. According to a newspaper report, the DO is comprised of some five thousand people, of whom about one thousand are case officers stationed abroad. See Walter Pincus and Dana Priest, "Goss Reportedly Rebuffed Senior Officials at CIA," *Washington Post*, November 14, 2004, A6.

23. Quoted in David Wise, "Is U.N. the Latest Cover for CIA Spies?" *Los Angeles Times*, January 17, 1999, M2.

24. See William J. Daugherty, *Executive Secrets: Covert Action and the Presidency* (Lexington: University Press of Kentucky, 2004); Loch K. Johnson, *America's Secret Power: The CIA in a Democratic Society* (New York: Oxford University Press, 1989); Johnson, *Secret Agencies: U.S. Intelligence in a Hostile World* (New Haven, CT: Yale University Press, 1996); John Prados, *Safe for Democracy: The Secret Wars of the CIA* (Chicago: Dee, 2006); Gregory F. Treverton, *Covert Action: The Limits of Intervention in the Postwar World* (New York: Basic Books, 1987); Tim Weiner, *Legacy of Ashes: The History of the CIA* (New York: Doubleday, 2007); Leslie Gelb, "Should We Play Dirty Tricks in the World?" *New York Times Magazine*, December 21, 1975, 10–20; Senate Select Committee to Study Government Operations with Respect to Intelligence Activities, *Alleged Assassination Plots Involving Foreign Leaders: An Interim Report* (New York: Norton, 1976); and Hugh Wilford, *The Mighty Wurlitzer: How the CIA Played America* (Cambridge, MA: Harvard University Press, 2008).

25. See Johnson, *Secret Agencies*, 33.

26. See, respectively, the memoir written by the CIA's lead operative in the coup, Kermit Roosevelt, *Countercoup: The Struggle for the Control of Iran* (New York: McGraw-Hill, 1979); and Richard H. Immerman, *The CIA in Guatemala: The Foreign Policy of Intervention* (Austin: University of Texas Press, 1982); see also David Wise and Thomas B. Ross, *The Invisible Government* (New York: Random House, 1964); Peter Chapman, *Bananas: How the United Fruit Company Shaped the World* (Edinburgh: Canongate, 2007). These coups, though, were by no means blood free. For example, in Guatemala at least forty-three of the CIA's local "rebels" were killed in the covert action. See Tim Weiner, "C.I.A. Destroyed Files on 1953 Iran Coup," *New York Times*, May 29, 1977, A11.

27. See Peter Wyden, *Bay of Pigs: The Untold Story* (New York: Simon & Schuster, 1979); and John Prados, "The Bay of Pigs: Failure at Playa Girón," in *Safe for Democracy: The Secret Wars of the CIA* (Chicago: Dee, 2006), 236–72. For a broader critique of CIA covert actions, see Loch K. Johnson, *Seven Sins of American Foreign Policy* (New York: Pearson Longman, 2007).

28. Senate Select Committee on Secret Military Assistance to Iran and the Nicaraguan Opposition and House Select Committee to Investigate Covert Arms Transactions with Iran, *Report of the Congressional Committees Investigating the Iran-Contra Affair*, 100th Cong., 1st sess., November 1987.

29. On the Nicaragua covert actions, see William S. Cohen and George J. Mitchell, *Men of Zeal: A Candid Inside Story of the Iran-Contra Hearings* (New York: Viking, 1988); on the CIA in Afghanistan during the 1980s, see Steve Coll, *Ghost Wars: The Secret History of the CIA, Afghanistan, and Bin Laden, from the Soviet Invasion to September 10, 2001* (New York: Penguin, 2004); and George Crill, *Charlie Wilson's War: The Extraordinary Story of the Largest Covert Operation in History* (New York: Grove, 2003).

30. Anthony Lewis, "Costs of the C.I.A.," *New York Times*, April 25, 1997, A19.

31. McGeorge Bundy, remark to the author, Athens, GA, October 6, 1987.

32. On the details of why these plots failed, see Committee to Study Government Operations, *Alleged Assassination Plots*.

33. See Frank Church, "Covert Action: Swampland of American Foreign Policy," *Bulletin of the Atomic Scientists*, February 1976, 7–11.

34. William E Colby, interview by Larry King, *Larry King Live*, CNN, February 2, 1987.

35. Stansfield Turner, interview with author, Turner's residence, McLean, VA, May 1, 1991. On the CIA's use of propaganda during the Cold War, see Wilford, *Mighty Wurlitzer*.

36. Elaine Sciolino, "C.I.A. Asks Congress for Money to Rein in Iraq and Iran," *New York Times*, April 11, 1995, A1; Sciolino, "C.I.A. Asks Congress for $19 Million to Undermine Iraq's Rulers and Rein In Iran," *New York Times*, April 12, 1995, A4. For an extensive account of a classic covert action that failed against Saddam Hussein in Iraq after the Cold War, see Jim Hoagland, "How CIA's Secret War on Saddam Collapsed; A Retired Intelligence Operative Surfaces With Details and Critique of U.S. Campaign," *Washington Post*, June 26, 1997, A21.

37. On the difficulties in bridging the DO and DI cultures, see Charles G. Cogan, "The In-Culture of the DO," *Intelligence and National Security* 8 (January 1993): 78–86.

38. William E. Colby, interview with author, Washington, DC, January 22, 1991. For the complete published interview, see Loch K. Johnson, "A Conversation with DCI William E. Colby: Spymaster during the 'Year of the Intelligence Wars,'" *Intelligence and National Security* 22 (April 2007): 250–69.

39. Twelve years later, President George W. Bush would name McConnell as director of national intelligence (DNI).

40. Siobhan Gorman, "Bush's Choice of McConnell Said to Revive 'Career' Model," *Baltimore Sun*, January 6, 2007, A1.

41. This attribution may be apocryphal, but it is widely cited and was never denied by Secretary Stimson, who closed down a code-breaking unit in his department in 1929; see John Ranelagh, *The Agency: The Rise and Decline of the CIA* (New York: Simon and Schuster, 1988), 27.

42. Quoted in Loch K. Johnson, *A Season of Inquiry: The Senate Intelligence Investigation* (Lexington: University Press of Kentucky, 1985), 83. DCIA Gen.

Michael Hayden has stated that the NSA, where he served as director, intercepted 200 billion minutes in telephone conversations in 2003 (comment, C-SPAN interview, January 23, 2006). In 2010, Priest and Arkin reported that the NSA intercepts 1.7 billion e-mails, phone calls and other types of communications every day (Dana Priest and William M. Arkin, "Top Secret America: A *Washington Post* Investigation; Part 1: A Hidden World, Growing Beyond Control," *Washington Post*, July 20, 2010, at http://www.postandcourier.com/news/2010/jul/20/part-1-hidden -world). Also in 2010, the Office of the Director of National Intelligence noted that the amount of foreign intelligence that comes to the intelligence community each day from around the world "vastly" exceeds the entire text holdings of the Library of Congress (which is estimated at 10 terabytes). Every day, too, the National Counterterrorism Center (NTCT) receives 8,000-10,000 pieces of counterterrorist information, including some 10,000 names of terrorist suspects and over forty specific warnings of terrorist attacks and plots ("ODNI Provides Detailed Facts about the IC Post-9/11," e-mail to the author, July 19, 2010).

43. James Risen and Ronald J. Ostrow, "East Germany's Spy Files at Center of FBI-CIA Clash," *Los Angeles Times*, October 25, 1995, A16; Michael Wines and Ronald J. Ostrow, "Cuban Defector Claims Double Agents Duped U.S.," *Washington Post*, August 12, 1987, A8; Bud Shuster, "Hi-Tech versus Human Spying," *Washington Times*, February 11, 1992, F3; Robert M. Gates, *From the Shadows: The Ultimate Insider's Story of Five Presidents and How They Won the Cold War* (New York: Simon & Schuster, 1996), 560; Ernest Volkman, *Espionage: The Greatest Spy Operations of the Twentieth Century* (New York: Wiley, 1995), 16, 22–25.

44. George Tenet (senior director for intelligence), interview with author, National Security Council, Old Executive Office Building, Washington, DC, June 11, 1994.

45. In 1990, on the eve of the U.S. invasion of Iraq in the First Persian Gulf War, the Defense Intelligence Agency had forty-two people assigned to review reports on POWs and MIAs from Vietnam and just two assigned to Iraq. House Armed Services Committee, *Report*, 103 Cong., 1st sess., 1993, cited in Rick Maze, "Probe Finds Gaps in Spy Effort," *Defense News*, August 23–29, 1993, 7.

46. Title V of the *National Security Act of 1947*, 50 U.S Code , 413 (Accountability for Intelligence Activities) 15.

47. Carroll J. Doherty, "On Hill, Latest CIA Uproar Revives Issue of Trust," *Congressional Quarterly Weekly Report*, April 15, 1995, 1073.

48. *New York Times*, "Robert Torricelli for the Senate," October 28, 1996.

49. These quotes from Cohen, Shelby, and Studeman are from the transcript, "Guatemala and the Reported Murders of Michael Devine and Efrain Bamaca," Senate Select Committee on Intelligence, *Hearings*, 104 Cong., 1st sess., April 4, 1995, 42, 50–53.

50. Senate Select Committee on Intelligence, *Hearings on the Huston Plan*, 94th Cong., 1st sess., September 23, 1975; Johnson, *Season of Inquiry*. Often witnesses known for their brilliance and steel-trap minds will suddenly develop amnesia when questioned about past intelligence excesses—a condition known in the Pentagon as CRS—"Can't Remember Shit"—a most convenient affliction. See Seymour M. Hersh, "The General's Report," *New Yorker*, June 25, 2007, 60.

51. William E. Colby, testimony, House Permanent Select Committee on Intelligence, *Hearings on Congressional Oversight of Covert Activities*, 98th Cong., 2nd sess., 1983, 29.

52. Senate Select Committee on Secret Military Assistance to Iran and the Nicaraguan Opposition and the House Select Committee to Investigate Covert Arms Transactions with Iran, *Report*, 100th Cong., 1st sess., November 1987, 142.

53. In 2008 newspapers filled with stories about how the CIA's Operations Directorate failed to inform HPSCI lawmakers about its destruction of videotapes on torture, which key members of the committee had asked the directorate to preserve. See, for example, Mark Mazzetti and Scott Shane, "Account of C.I.A. Tapes Is Challenged," *New York Times*, January 17, 2008, A8. While most of the blame for poor reporting to Congress falls on the intelligence agency managers, especially the DCI (now known as the DNI), lawmakers are not without blame; often they don't even bother to demand access to information they need to know as intelligence overseers. There is always a tug-of-war between the legislative and executive branches over information, and, as former HPSCI staff director Mark M. Lowenthal has pointed out, neither executive branch officials nor members of Congress have adequately provided "firm rules about what you can provide [to lawmakers] when" (interview, *NewsHour with Jim Lehrer*, PBS, December 7, 2007). In 2010, President Obama vowed to veto a bill that called for full reporting to HPSCI and SSCI on intelligence activities—a unfortunate lack of understanding on behalf of the White House (carried over from the second Bush administration) about the right of lawmakers on these committees to be kept informed.

54. Office of the White House Press Secretary, memorandum for Anthony S. Harrington, released to the public on April 10, 1995.

55. See Beverly Gage, *The Day Wall Street Exploded: A Story of America in Its First Age of Terror* (New York: Oxford University Press, 2009). This crime was never solved.

56. Jo Thomas, "In a Letter, McVeigh Told Of Shifting To 'Animal'," *New York Times*, May 9, 1997, A1.

57. For an account, see Stuart A. Wright, *Patriots, Politics, and the Oklahoma City Bombing* (New York: Cambridge University Press, 2007).

58. Quoted in Craig Gilbert, "Expect More Terrorism," *Milwaukee Journal Sentinel*, April 21, 1995, A12.

59. In 2007 researcher Stuart A. Wright, drawing on a 2003 Associated Press investigation, charged that the federal Bureau of Alcohol, Tobacco, and Firearms (ATF) had an informant inside the McVeigh camp who provided advanced warning about the Oklahoma City attack, but was discounted (*Patriots, Politics*, 183). If true, this would be another illustration of good intelligence being trumped by a poor policy decision—a phenomenon that would arise again in the September 11, 2001, Al Qaeda attacks against the United States, when (as I soon relate) officials in Washington from 1995 to 2001 once more paid insufficient attention to intelligence warnings, in this case, about the possibility of "aerial terrorism."

60. A CIA internal review of events leading up to 9/11 found no intelligence reporting on the possible use of aircraft in a U.S. terrorist attack, but the reviewers somehow overlooked this and other subsequent reports from its own Counterterrorism Center. For the CIA review, see John L. Helgerson, *Report on CIA Accountability with Respect to the 9/11 Attacks* June 2005, summarized in a declassified (originally top-secret) nineteen-page executive summary released in June 2005, xvii, cited (and accepted as correct) by John Diamond in *The CIA and the Culture of Failure: U.S. Intelligence from the End of the Cold War to the Invasion of Iraq* (Stanford, CA: Stanford University Press, 2008), 500 n91.

61. Richard A. Clarke, *Against All Enemies: Inside America's War on Terror* (New York: Free Press, 2004), 229–331.

62. See Stephen Flynn, *America the Vulnerable: How Our Government Is Failing to Protect Us from Terrorism* (New York: HarperCollins, 2004).

63. William Studeman, remarks, Marquette University, Milwaukee, WI, April 20, 1995.

64. This wall had been put into place, for a good reason, in the 1970s. Intelligence officials face a much lower standard of suspicion when obtaining judicial warrants for wiretaps and other eavesdropping. If information gathered by intelligence officers were shared with law-enforcement authorities across "the wall," the evidence (under rules in 1995) would be considered tainted and, therefore, inadmissible in criminal cases. Yet law-enforcement authorities often seek access to intelligence evidence that might prevent a criminal act from taking place. Finding the right balance between an appropriate sharing of information between intelligence and law enforcement to protect the American people, on the one hand, and ensuring that civil liberties are honored, on the other hand, is a dilemma that the commission would spend a fair amount of time considering. On this "wall," see James E. Baker, *In the Common Defense: National Security Law for Perilous Times* (New York: Cambridge University Press, 2007), 85. Still unresolved in 2004, the 9/11 Commission would grapple with this dilemma, too. Philip Shenon, *The Commission: The Uncensored History of the 9/11 Investigation* (New York: Twelve, 2008), 329. The debate continues about the proper relationship between law enforcement and intelligence agencies.

65. R. Jeffrey Smith, "If Confirmed, Deutch Intends to Reform CIA, Officials Say," *Washington Post*, April 26, 1995, A2.

66. Ibid.

67. Richard Helms, *A Look over My Shoulder: A Life in the Central Intelligence Agency* (New York: Random House, 2003), 164.

68. Johnson, *Bombs, Bugs, Drugs, and Thugs, 44.*

69. Quoted in Tim Weiner, "Nominee for C.I.A. Vows to Clear Out Cold War Culture," *New York Times*, April 28, 1995, A1.

70. Richard J. Kerr, testimony, House Permanent Select Committee on Intelligence, *Hearings*, U.S. of Representatives, 104th Cong., 1st sess., November 16. 1995.

71. Quoted in Robert Parry, "The Spymaster," *Boston Magazine*, July 1995, 33.

Chapter 5

1. As described in Tim Weiner, "Careers Are Among the Casualties of C.I.A.'s Latest Security Breach," *New York Times*, November 20, 1996, A1, among several other public sources.

2. See Peter Wyden, *Bay of Pigs: The Untold Story* (New York: Simon & Schuster, 1979).

3. Stansfield Turner, remarks to the commission, April 26, 1995.

4. The gifted journalist David Ignatius once observed that what the CIA does instead of using NOCs is post case officers "mostly in embassies and consulates around the world, often with quite flimsy diplomatic cover. They're marching in formation, like the British Redcoats, against an enemy that is hiding behind trees." David Ignatius, "Reinvent the CIA," *Washington Monthly*, April 1994, 40.

5. James Risen, "Do We Still Need the CIA," *Los Angeles Times Magazine* (October 8, 1995), 14.

6. Quoted in Roy Godson, ed., *Intelligence Requirements for the 1990s: Collection, Analysis, Counterintelligence, Covert Action* (Lexington, MA: Lexington Books, 1989), 111.

7. Stansfield Turner, interview with author, Turner's residence in McLean, VA, May 1, 1991.

8. Bradley F. Smith, "The American Road to Central Intelligence," in *Eternal Vigilance? 50 Years of the CIA*, ed. Rhodri Jeffreys-Jones and Christopher Andrew (London: Cass, 1997), 1–20; and, more generally, John Lewis Gaddis, *The United States and the Origins of the Cold War, 1941–1947* (New York: Columbia University Press, 1972).

9. James C. Bradford, "Attack on Pearl Harbor," in *The Oxford Companion to United States History*, ed. Paul S. Boyer (New York: Oxford University Press, 2001), 585; Edwin T. Layton, *"And I Was There": Pearl Harbor and Midway— Breaking the Secrets* (New York: Morrow, 1985); Gordon W. Prange, *At Dawn We Slept: The Untold Story of Pearl Harbor* (New York: McGraw-Hill, 1981); John Costello, *Days of Infamy: MacArthur, Roosevelt, Churchill, the Shocking Truth*

Revealed: How Their Secret Deals and Strategic Blunders Caused Disasters at Pearl Harbor and the Philippines (New York: Pocket Books, 1994).

10. For the views of a chief counsel for the Joint Congressional Investigating Committee on Pearl Harbor, see Seth W. Richardson, "Why Were We Caught Napping at Pearl Harbor?" *Saturday Evening Post*, May 24, 1947, 79–80. See also Kenneth Kitts, *Presidential Commissions and National Security: The Politics of Damage Control* (Boulder, CO: Rienner, 2006), chap. 2.

11. John Deane Potter, *Yamamoto: The Man Who Menaced America* (New York: Viking, 1965).

12. Roberta Wohlstetter, *Pearl Harbor: Warning and Decision* (Stanford, CA: Stanford University Press, 1962.

13. Alvin D. Coox, "Pearl Harbor," in *Decisive Battles of the Twentieth Century: Land, Sea, Air*, ed. Noble Frankland and Christopher Dowling (New York: McKay, 1976), 148.

14. Sidney W. Souers, interview with William Hillman and M. Noyes, Kansas City, MO, December 15, 1954 (CIA, box 23, B file, Harry S. Truman Library, Independence, MO), reprinted in *Spymasters: Ten CIA Officers in Their Own Words*, ed. Ralph E. Weber (Wilmington, DE: SR Books, 1999), 5.

15. Rhodri Jeffreys-Jones, "Why Was the CIA Established in 1947?" in *Eternal Vigilance?* 21–40.

16. See the documents in Michael Warner, ed., *CIA Cold War Records: The CIA under Harry Truman* (Washington, DC: History Staff, Center for the Study of Intelligence, Central Intelligence Agency, 1994).

17. Jeffreys-Jones, "Why Was the CIA Established," 23.

18. Richard Helms, quoted in Bob Woodward, *Veil: The Secret Wars of the CIA, 1981–1987* (New York: Simon & Schuster, 1987), 49.

19. Clark Clifford, *Counsel to the President: A Memoir* (New York: Random House, 1991), 166.

20. Michael Warner, "Central Intelligence: Origin and Evolution," in *Central Intelligence: Origin and Evolution*, ed. Michael Warner (Washington, DC: History Staff, Center for the Study of Intelligence, Central Intelligence Agency, 2001), reprinted in *Intelligence and the National Security Strategist: Enduring Issues and Challenges*, ed. Roger Z. George and Robert D. Kline (Washington, DC: National Defense University Press, 2004), 43.

21. Quoted in Merle Miller, *Plain Speaking: An Oral Biography of Harry S. Truman* (New York: Berkeley, 1973), 420n.

22. Phyllis Provost McNeil, "The Evolution of the U.S. Intelligence Community— An Historical Overview," in *Preparing for the 21st Century: An Appraisal of U.S. Intelligence*, Report of the Commission on the Roles and Capabilities of the United States Intelligence Community (Washington, DC: GPO, 1996), A-1 to A-25, reprinted in *Intelligence and National Security: The Secret World of Spies; An Anthology*, ed. Loch K. Johnson and James J. Wirtz, 2nd ed. (New York: Oxford University Press, 2008), 5–20, quotation from p. 9.

23. Christopher Andrew, *For the President's Eyes Only: Secret Intelligence and the American Presidency from Washington to Bush* (New York: HarperCollins, 1995), 165–66.

24. Anne Karalekas, "History of the Central Intelligence Agency," Supplementary Detailed Staff Reports on Foreign and Military Intelligence, *Final Report*, Senate Select Committee to Study Governmental Operations with Respect to Intelligence Activities, April 23, 1976, 4:12.

25. Quoted in Smith, "The American Road," 16.

26. Clifford, *Counsel to the President*, 168, 169.

27. Ibid., 168–69.

28. Ray S. Cline, *The CIA Under Reagan, Bush, and Casey: The Evolution of the Agency from Roosevelt to Reagan* (Washington, DC: Acropolis Books, 1981), 112.

29. Clifford, *Counsel to the President*, 169.

30. Amy B. Zegart, *Flawed by Design: The Evolution of the CIA, JCS, and NSC* (Stanford, CA: Stanford University Press, 1999).

31. James R. Locher III, *Victory on the Potomac: The Goldwater-Nichols Act Unifies the Pentagon* (College Station: Texas A & M University Press, 2002).

32. Warner, *Central Intelligence*, 45, 47.

33. *Ibid.*, 38.

34. Clifford, *Counsel to the President*, 168.

35. Richard C. Synder and Edgar S. Furniss Jr., *American Foreign Policy: Formulation, Principles, and Programs* (New York: Rinehart, 1954), 230.

36. Quoted in Victor Marchetti and John D. Marks, *The CIA and the Cult of Intelligence* (New York: Knopf, 1974), 70.

37. McNeil, "Evolution of the U.S. Intelligence Community"; Warner, *Central Intelligence*; Larry C. Kindsvater, "The Need to Reorganize the Intelligence Community: A Senior Officer's Perspective," *Studies in Intelligence* 47 (2003): 33–37.

38. Loch K. Johnson, *Bombs, Bugs, Drugs, and Thugs: Intelligence and America's Quest for Security* (New York: New York University Press, 2000).

39. Warner, *Central Intelligence*, 49.

40. James R. Schlesinger, interview with author, Washington, DC, June 16, 1994.

41. Quoted in Ralph E. Weber, ed., *Spymasters: Ten CIA Officers in Their Own Words* (Wilmington, DE: SR Books, 1999), 129.

42. Stansfield Turner, *Secrecy and Democracy: The CIA in Transition* (Boston: Houghton Mifflin, 1985).

43. Stansfield Turner, interview with author, Turner's residence, McLean, VA, May 1, 1991.

44. Robert M. Gates, "Security Challenges in the Post-Cold War World," (lecture, the Richard B. Russell Symposium, University of Georgia, Athens, October 16, 1995).

45. Author's interviews with CIA and FBI intelligence officials in 1995; see, also, R. Jeffrey Smith and Thomas W. Lippman, "FBI Plans To Expand Overseas;

23 New Offices Slated, Raising Some Criticism At State Dept. and CIA," *Washington Post*, August 20, 1996, A1.

Chapter 6

1. Quoted in Tim Weiner, "Emphatically, Senate Votes to Confirm C.I.A. Chief," *New York Times*, May 10, 1995, A21. A dozen years later, this would be Weiner's own thesis in his history of the CIA, entitled *Legacy of Ashes: The History of the CIA* (New York: Doubleday, 2007).

2. Unsigned editorial, *New York Times*, "Another New Man at the C.I.A.," March 14, 1995, A16.

3. "Spring Housecleaning at the CIA," *U.S. News & World Report*, May 8, 1995, 14.

4. Ibid.

5. R. Jeffrey Smith, "Deutch Is Confirmed Without Senate Dissent; New CIA Chief to Move on Shake-Up," *Washington Post*, May 10, 1995, A6.

6. Stansfield Turner, interview with author, Turner's residence, McLean, VA, May 1, 1991.

7. Douglas F. Garthoff, *Directors of Central Intelligence as Leaders of the U.S. Intelligence Community, 1946–2005* (Washington, DC: Center for the Study of Intelligence, Central Intelligence Agency, 2005), 236.

8. Stansfield Turner, interview with author, Turner's residence, McLean, VA, May 1, 1991.

9. John M. Deutch, interview with author, Massachusetts Institute of Technology, Cambridge, MA, October 29, 1998.

10. Ibid.

11. See Robert Parry, "The Spymaster," *Boston Magazine*, July 1995, 32–36.

12. Ibid.

13. Thomas Powers, "Computer Security; The Whiz Kid vs. the Old Boys," *New York Times Magazine,* December 3, 2000, p.16.

14. See Loch K. Johnson, "Glimpses into the Gems of American Intelligence: the *President's Daily Brief* and the National Intelligence Estimate," *Intelligence and National Security* 23 (2008): 333–70, from which this chapter draws.

15. Quoted in Stewart Bell, "How CSIS 'Tool Box' Broke Up Terror Cell," *National Post* (Toronto), April 26, 2005, A1.

16. James Woolsey, interview with author, CIA Headquarters, Langley, VA, September 29, 1993.

17. Lyman B. Kirkpatrick, "United States Intelligence," *Military Review* 41 (May 1961): 18–22, quote at 20, based on a speech presented in Detroit, Michigan, in November 1960, cited in Harry Howe Ransom, *The Intelligence Establishment* (Cambridge, MA: Harvard University Press, 1970), 147. For samples of NIEs that have been declassified, see Johnson, *Strategic Intelligence*, 2:241–95; Benjamin B. Fischer, ed., *At Cold War's End: US Intelligence on the Soviet Union and Eastern Europe, 1989–1991* (Langley, VA: Center for the Study of Intelligence, Central Intelligence Agency, 1999).

18. Sherman Kent to Allen Dulles, May 3, 1963, Sterling Library Collection, Series 1, Box 18, Folder 390, Yale University Library.

19. Harold P. Ford, *Estimative Intelligence*, Intelligence Profession Series 10 (McLean, VA: Association of Former Intelligence Officers, 1993); see also his *Estimative Intelligence: The Purposes and Problems of National Intelligence Estimating* (Lanham, MD: University Press of America, 1993). Declassified portions of an NIE on Iran released in 2007 refer to NIEs as "the Intelligence Community's (IC) most authoritative written judgements [*sic*] on national security issues and designed to help US civilian and military leaders develop policies to protect U.S. national security interests." National Intelligence Council, National Intelligence Estimate, *Iran: Nuclear Intentions and Capabilities* (November 2007); *CNN News*, CNN, December 3, 2007.

20. Ransom, *Intelligence Establishment*, 147. For an example of the occasionally strong influence an NIE can have on policy, see former DCI Stansfield Turner's discussion of how an Estimate in 1954, which concluded that the U.S. use of a nuclear weapon against Vietnam that year would ignite World War Three, contributed to President Eisenhower's decision against the bombing. Stansfield Turner, *Burn Before Reading: Presidents, CIA Directors, and Secret Intelligence*(New York: Hyperion, 2005), 79. Another illustration comes from Robert M. Gates, the former DCI and the secretary of defense during the second Bush and the Obama administrations. He recalls an NIE written in 1978 that warned of a growing effort by the Soviet Union to expand its military assistance programs abroad as a means of influencing the developing world—a warning that, according to Gates, President Carter took seriously, increasing U.S. attention to the developing world (no doubt also at the urging of his hawkish national security advisor, Zbigniew Brzezinski); Robert M. Gates, *From the Shadows: The Ultimate Insider's Story of Five Presidents and How They Won the Cold War* (New York: Simon & Schuster, 1996), 74–75. Michael Herman is correct, though, in his observation that it is as unrealistic to think that NIEs will lead to immediate policy actions as it is to think that "daily newspapers expect to change the world with every issue." Michael Herman, *Intelligence Power in Peace and War* (Cambridge, UK: Cambridge University Press, 1999), 143.

21. Former CIA official Charles Peter, interview with author, Washington, DC, June 26, 1995.

22. Stansfield Turner, *Secrecy and Democracy: The CIA in Transition* (Boston: Houghton Mifflin, 1985), 243.

23. An example of a non-geographic subject is the spread of WMDs around the world.

24. National Intelligence Council, *Iran: Nuclear Intentions*, 5.

25. Sherman Kent, *Strategic Intelligence for American World Policy* (Princeton, NJ: Princeton University Press, 1949), 64–65.

26. See Anne Hessing Cahn, *Killing Detente: The Right Attacks the CIA* (University Park: Pennsylvania State University Press, 1998); Rhodri Jeffreys-Jones, *The*

CIA and American Democracy (New Haven, CT: Yale University Press, 1989), 212–13; Richard Pipes, "Team B: The Reality Behind the Myth,"*Commentary*, October 1986, 24–40; John Ranelagh, *The Agency: The Rise and Decline of the CIA*, rev. ed. (New York: Simon & Schuster, 1987), 622–24; and Weiner, *Legacy of Ashes*, 351–52.

27. Chester Cooper (retired CIA analyst), interviewed by Ron Nessen, "Intelligence Failure: From Pearl Harbor to 9/11 and Iraq" (radio transcript), *America Abroad Media*, July 2004, 11.

28. For an account of this process, see Senate Select Committee on Intelligence, *Report on the U.S. Intelligence Community's Prewar Intelligence Assessments on Iraq*, 108th Cong., 2nd sess., July 7, 2004, excerpted in Johnson, *Strategic Intelligence*, 2:318–20.

29. For examples of DCI-penned NIEs, see the discussion of DCI Stansfield Turner in Douglas F. Garthoff, *Directors of Central Intelligence as Leaders of the U.S. Intelligence Community, 1946–2005*, Center for the Study of Intelligence (Dulles, VA: Potomac Books, 2005), 153n; Gerald K. Haines and Robert E. Leggett, eds., *Watching the Bear: Essays on CIA's Analysis of the Soviet Union* (Langley, VA: Center for the Study of Intelligence, Central Intelligence Agency, 2003), 169–70; and Ranelagh, *The Agency*, 662. Stansfield Turner has said that, from time to time, he elected to "inject [his] views into [NIEs] in order to give them some real substance," rather than settling for the watered-down comprise documents he thought they sometimes were. Turner, *Burn Before Reading*, 96. Turner was careful, however, to make sure that, as he recalled, "the President clearly knew that the opinion expressed in the NIE was that of his intelligence advisor, and me alone" (184). He adds, "It was probably the most unusual NIE on record, where the DCI was the dissenter from everybody." Stansfield Turner, interview with author, Turner's residence, McLean, VA, May 1, 1991. Both Garthoff and Turner note that DCI William J. Casey of the Reagan Administration often appended his own personal notes to NIEs, registering his dissent (Turner, *Burn Before Reading*, 153n and 199, respectively). According to one authoritative account, the senior Latin America analyst at the CIA (John R. Horton) resigned in 1984 after Casey insisted that he revise an intelligence assessment on Mexico so it would support the Reagan administration's alarmist views about Communist activity south of the U.S. border. Philip Taubman, "Analyst Said to Have Quit C.I.A. in Dispute," *New York Times*, September 28, 1984, A1.

30. For an account by Sherman Kent, see his "A Crucial Estimate Relived," *Studies in Intelligence* 8 (1964): 1–18, reprinted in *Studies in Intelligence* 36 (1992): 111–19. A history of the CIA refers to this Estimate as "a high-water mark of misjudgment for forty years, until the CIA assayed the state of Iraq's arsenal [in 2002]." Weiner, *Legacy of Ashes*, 195. See also Michael Douglas Smith, "The Perils of Analysis: Revisiting Sherman Kent's Defense of SNIE 85-3-62," *Studies in Intelligence* 51 (September 2007): 29–32.

31. Senior DO officer George Carver, interview with author, Bonn, West Germany, November 19, 1984, quoted in Johnson, *America's Secret Power*, 93.

32. See, for instance, Stephen J. Flanagan, "The Coordination of National Intelligence," in *Public Policy and Political Institutions: United States Defense and Foreign Policy—Coordination and Integration*, ed. Duncan L. Clarke (Greenwich, CT: JAI, 1985), 157–96.

33. See George Tenet, *At the Center of the Storm: My Years at the CIA* (New York: HarperCollins, 2007), 370.

34. See Senate Select Committee on Intelligence, *Report on the U.S. Intelligence Community's Prewar Intelligence Assessments on Iraq*, 108thg Cong., 2nd sess., July 7, 2004, reprinted in Johnson, *Strategic Intelligence*, appendix H, NIE reference at 2:320.

35. See, for example, Select Committee to Study Governmental Operations with Respect to Intelligence Activities (the Church Committee), U.S. Senate, *Final Report*, 94th Cong., 2d. Sess., Sen. Rept. No. 94–755, Washington, DC: Government Printing Office, 1976, vol. 1; Richard Helms, *A Look Over My Shoulder: A Life in the Central Intelligence Agency* (New York: Random House, 2003), 235; and Turner, *Burn Before Reading*, 245.

36. See, for instance, the debate over Soviet military intentions during the Reagan years, described in the Church Committee, *Final Report*, vol. 1.; Robert M. Gates, *From the Shadows: The Ultimate Insider's Story of Five Presidents and How They Won the Cold War* (New York: Simon & Schuster, 1996), 264–66; and Daniel O. Graham, "Estimating the Threat: A Soldier's Job," *Army Magazine*, April 1973, 14–18.

37. Richard K. Betts has commented on the repercussion of worst-case analysis: "The norm of assuming the worst poses high financial costs and potential risks increasing political friction that could make crises escalate unnecessarily." *Enemies of Intelligence: Knowledge and Power in American National Security* (New York: Columbia University Press, 2007), 36.

38. Arthur Hulnick, review of *Estimative Intelligence: The Purposes and Problems of National Intelligence Estimating*, by Harold P. Ford, *Conflict Quarterly* 14 (Winter 1994): 73.

39. See, for instance, Ford, *Estimative Intelligence*, 41–42, 48–49; Chester L. Cooper, "The CIA and Decision-Making," *Foreign Affairs* 50 (January 1972): 223–36.

40. Author's interviews with officials who requested anonymity, August 28, 1997, Washington, DC.

41. Gregory F. Treverton (RAND Corporation analyst and former vice chair of the National Intelligence Council), "Intelligence for an Era of Terror," memorandum sent to the author, March 23, 2007.

42. Remarks to the author, Washington, DC, November 9, 1995.

43. Sherman Kent to Frank Wisner, November 18, 1963, Sterling Library Collection, Series I, Box 18, Folder 390, Yale University Library.

44. Sherman Kent, "Estimates and Influence," *Foreign Service Journal* (April 1969): 17. Former secretary of state Dean Rusk once said to me that all intelligence reports ought to begin with the caveat: "We really don't know what is going to happen, but here is our best guess." Remark to the author, Athens, GA, July 4, 1988.

45. President George W. Bush said in a press conference on September 21, 2004, that the CIA was "just guessing" when it came to analyzing foreign affairs. The president had in mind specifically the pessimistic predictions coming from the Agency about the U.S. occupation of Iraq, but he seemed to imply that intelligence in general was merely guesswork. This was an overstatement by the president, which did not help morale in the intelligence community; nevertheless, strategic intelligence does involve an element of guessing, although normally by people who have closely studied the subject in question and are better informed than most policy makers.

46. British intelligence came to the same conclusion. One of its leaders has written that correctly "identifying Soviet strategic caution [was] perhaps the most important single judgment of the [Cold War] period." Percy Cradock, *Know Your Enemy: How the Joint Intelligence Committee Saw the World* (London: Murray, 2002), 292.

47. Senator Frank Church (D-ID), known as a harsh critic of the CIA, noted in 1975 that "in the last twenty-five years, no important new Soviet weapons system, from the H-bomb to the most recent missiles has appeared which had not been heralded in advance by NIEs." *Congressional Record*, November 11, 1975, S35787. An example is the Soviet Polaris-type "Y" missile and the submarines on which it was carried, both well anticipated before the first boats were launched. See also Lawrence Freedman, *US Intelligence and the Soviet Strategic Threat*, 2nd ed. (Princeton, NJ: Princeton University Press, 1986); and John Prados, *The Soviet Estimate: U.S. Intelligence Analysis and Russian Military Strength* (New York: Dial, 1982).

48. See also United States General Accounting Office, *Foreign Missile Threats: Analytic Soundness of Certain National Intelligence Estimates*, Report to the Chairman, Committee on National Security, House of Representatives, August 1996.

49. Church, *Congressional Record*, S35786.

50. Richard K. Betts, "Analysis, War and Decision: Why Intelligence Failures Are Inevitable," *World Politics* 31 (October 1978): 78. See also Betts, *Enemies of Intelligence*.

51. Ford, *Estimative Intelligence*, 7. An experienced intelligence officer has acknowledged that "you have to come up with a timely answer, yet it is apt to be based on incomplete information whose validity you're often not positive about. The best an analyst ever has is enough evidence to indict: probable cause. That's the best. We rarely get evidence that would convict before a jury. And often we don't even achieve the probable cause standard." William O. Studeman,

"Teaching Intelligence" (lecture, author's notes, Center for the Study of Intelligence, CIA, Tysons Corner, VA, October 1, 1993).

52. Hulnick, review of *Estimative Intelligence*, 74.

53. Ford, *Estimative Intelligence*, 49.

54. William E. Odom, *Fixing Intelligence: For a More Secure America*, 2nd ed. (New Haven, CT: Yale University Press, 2004), 81.

55. Kent, "Estimates and Influence,"45.

56. See, for example, Richard L. Russell, *Sharpening Strategic Intelligence: Why the CIA Gets it Wrong, and What Needs to be Done to Get it Right* (New York: Cambridge University Press, 2007), 122.

57. Mark M. Lowenthal (remark, author's notes, Canadian Association for Security and Intelligence Studies [CASIS] Conference, Ottawa, October 27–28, 2006).

58. Mark M. Lowenthal, "Intelligence Analysis: Management and Transformation Issues," in *Transforming U.S. Intelligence*, ed. Jennifer E. Sims and Burton Gerber (Washington, DC: Georgetown University Press, 2005), 220–38, quote at 227.

59. Ford, *Estimative Intelligence*, 38.

60. Betts, *Enemies of Intelligence*, 70.

61. Author's interview with a senior DI official who requested anonymity, Washington, DC, August 28, 1997.

62. James Risen, *State of War: The Secret History of the CIA and the Bush Administration* (New York: Free Press, 2006), 6.

63. Ford, *Estimative Intelligence*, 38.

64. The figures of 80 to 90 percent come from the author's interview with a senior CIA manager in the Agency's Intelligence Directorate, Washington, DC, August 28, 1997; Risen, *State of War*, quotes former CIA analyst Carl Ford as saying, "Today, about 90 percent of analysts do nothing but current reporting" (7). Amy B. Zegart underscores how performance evaluations in the CIA have been based on the number of reports produced by analysts—an intelligence analogue to the "publish or perish" requirements for professors in research universities. "For career-minded analysts, the message was clear," she writes, "stay away from strategic assignments." *Spying Blind: The CIA, the FBI, and the Origins of 9/11* (Princeton, NJ: Princeton University Press, 2007), 92.

65. Lowenthal, remarks at CASIS Conference.

66. Author's interview with a former Vice Chairman for Estimates who requested anonymity, Washington, DC, August 28, 1997.

67. Joseph F. Nye Jr., testimony before the Aspin-Brown Commission, open hearing, Washington, DC, January 19, 1995.

68. Allan E. Goodman, remark, "Teaching Intelligence," conference, Center for the Study of Intelligence, CIA, Tysons Corner, VA, October 1, 1993.

69. An NIO confided to me in a 1990 interview that "the number of reports one produces determines one's promotion in the intelligence community. This leads to far more intelligence reports than policy makers have time to read."

70. Betts states, "Most intelligence products, even NIEs, are never read by high-level policymakers. At best, they are used by second-level staffers as background material for briefing their seniors" (*Enemies of Intelligence*, 40).

71. Richard Cooper, interview with author, Washington, DC, November 9, 1995.

72. Ibid.

73. Interview with author under conditions of anonymity, Washington, DC, August 22, 1997.

74. Lowenthal, remarks at CASIS Conference.

75. Ibid. Elsewhere, Lowenthal has referred to NIEs as "pie-in-the-sky papers," given the difficulty of peering into the future. Mark M. Lowenthal, "The Intelligence Time Event Horizon," in *International Journal of Intelligence and CounterIntelligence* 22 (2009): 369–81, quote at 381.

76. Turner, *Burn Before Reading*, 243.

77. William Nolte, remarks at CASIS Conference.

78. The author is grateful to the CIA for providing these statistics, which come independently from two different sources within the Agency. Of course, a much more important question than the annual production rates (the frequency) of NIEs is their quality. Unfortunately, this question cannot be systematically addressed here, since most NIEs remain classified. In 2007, Director of National Intelligence Vice Admiral J.M. "Mike" McConnell vowed to keep them classified, arguing that "the integrity of the NIE process could be harmed by expectations that all or portions of the NIE are likely to be declassified." "Guidance on Declassification of National Intelligence Estimates Key Judgments," memo, DNI to the Intelligence Community Workforce (October 24, 2007). For examples of some Estimates that have been made available to the public, see Johnson, *Strategic Intelligence*, appendix F, 2: 241–95. For attempts at an evaluation of some NIEs that have become a part of the public record, see the remarks of Senator Frank Church on the Senate floor (*Congressional Record* [November 11, 1975], S35787), quoted in Loch K. Johnson, *A Season of Inquiry: The Senate Intelligence Investigation* (Lexington: University Press of Kentucky, 1985), 119–20; Freedman, *US Intelligence*; Ford, *Estimative Intelligence*; Johnson, *Secret Agencies*, 197–201; Prados, *Soviet Estimate*; and Weiner, *Legacy of Ashes*. For an insightful and eloquent appraisal by a leading British intelligence official, see Cradock, *Know Your Enemy*, especially 271–80. As these and other studies indicate, NIEs are certainly fallible; there have been many miscalculations over the years, such as the misreading of the imminence of the Arab-Israeli war in 1973. For a testy exchange between DCI Tenet and the Kean 9/11 Commission about the failure of an NIE on Somalia in 1993 to warn the White House of early Al Qaeda involvement in operations against U.S. soldiers abroad, see the Commission's public hearing on April 14, 2004, cited in Amy B. Zegart, "'CNN with Secrets:' 9/11, the CIA, and the Organizational Roots of Failure," *International Journal of Intelligence and*

Counterintelligence 20 (2007): 18–49, at note 107. Yet, at the same time, Estimates have often proved to be accurate and valuable, as with the CIA's reliable monitoring of military weapons systems in the Soviet Union and its tracking of petrodollars worldwide during the Cold War. As Michael Herman has put it, with classic British understatement, "When the full history of the Cold War is written, the record of CIA's Directorate of Intelligence in assessing the USSR may well emerge with some credit" (*Intelligence Power*, 369). See also Les Aspin, "Debate Over U.S. Strategic Forecasts: A Mixed Record," *Strategic Review* 8 (1980): 29–43, 57–59; and Aspin, "Misreading Intelligence," *Foreign Policy* 43 (Summer 1981): 166–72.

79. The data came to the author organized by year, not by DCI tenure; the decision here was to associate all of the Estimates in a given year with the intelligence director who served the most time in that particular year. The figures presented here, then, should be considered accurate yearly portrayals of NIE production, but the distribution of NIEs by DCI is approximate. The author also looked at the data by dividing NIEs proportionally according to how much time a DCI served in a given year; this approach did nothing to alter the conclusions offered in the text. For the precise dates of service for each of the DCIs, see David S. Robarge, "Directors of Central Intelligence, 1946–2005: A Long Look Back," *Studies in Intelligence* 49 (2005): 2.

80. This point is stressed by Lowenthal, "Intelligence Analysis," 227.

81. See Garthoff, *Directors of Central Intelligence*, 19.

82. See Ranelagh, *The Agency*, 192.

83. See Richard Kovar, "An Interview with Richard Lehman: Mr. Current Intelligence," *Studies in Intelligence* 9 (2000): 27; Ranelagh, *The Agency*, 242; and Turner, *Burn Before Reading*, 78, 88.

84. Helms, *Look Over My Shoulder*, 236.

85. Weiner, *Legacy of Ashes*, 122.

86. This is in part a function of the fact that Dulles was in the DCI office longer than any other director; but his average per year was still the third highest, outpaced only during the brief tenures of DCI Robert M. Gates in 1991–1993 and R. James Woolsey in 1993–94 (see Table 6.1).

87. Ranelagh, *The Agency*, 414.

88. Kent, "A Crucial Estimate."

89. In this examination of NIE production, it should be understood that any particular DCI may not deserve the credit apportioned here; in the case of Raborn, for instance, some historians of the CIA have concluded that Richard Helms, the deputy to Adm. Raborn, actually ran the Agency during the Admiral's tenure (Weiner, *op.cit.*, 252). Nevertheless, just as with presidents, DCIs reap the praise and the blame for what happens while they are in the wheelhouse.

90. Helms, *Look Over My Shoulder*, 237.

91. Chester Cooper, "CIA and Decision-Making," 227.

92. For an account, see Johnson, *Season of Inquiry*.

93. See William E. Colby and Peter Forbath, *Honorable Men: My Life in the CIA* (New York: Simon & Schuster, 1978.

94. Ironically, though, Gates told the commission at the Farm that he believed NIEs had only had a marginal influence on policy during his career.

95. Remarks to the author, "Accountability of Intelligence and Security Agencies and Human Rights," International Symposium, sponsored by the Dutch Review Committee on the Intelligence and Security Services & the Faculty of Law, Radboud University, Nijmegen, The Hague, Holland (June 8, 2007). Journalists Dana Priest and William M. Arkin reported in 2010 that America's secret agencies produce 50,000 intelligence reports each year—in their words, "a volume so large that many are routinely ignored" ("Top Secret America: A *Washington Post* Investigation; Part 1: A Hidden World, Growing Beyond Control," *Washington Post*, July 20, 2010, at http://.postandcourier.com/news2010/jul20/part-I-hidden-world).

96. Author's telephone interview with a senior CIA analyst who requested anonymity, February 20, 2006.

97. See Tenet, *At the Center of the Storm*, 122.

98. Lowenthal, "Intelligence Analysis," 227.

99. According to a former number 2 at the CIA (the deputy director of central intelligence), "If you leave it to its own devices, the intelligence community will write scholarly tomes that can fill your walls." Bobby Ray Inman, interview in *U.S. News & World Report*, December 20, 1982, 32.

100. For additional thoughts on this subject, see Johnson, *Strategic Intelligence, vol. 2*; Lowenthal, "Intelligence Analysis"; and Russell, *Sharpening Strategic Intelligence*.

Chapter 7

1. Kim M. Simpson "Preliminary Roundtable Strategy" (memo to Aspin Commission, May 17, 1995), 1.

2. Early in the year, HPSCI sent out letters to experts around Washington and beyond soliciting advice on useful intelligence reforms "to help us create a baseline for our own review." Mark M. Lowenthal to the author, February 7, 1995.

3. Dean Rusk, comment to the author, Athens, GA, October 5, 1979.

4. For similar testimony by Wolfowitz, this time arguing that we now had such a capability, see Joint Committee on Events Surrounding the Terrorist Attacks of September 11, 2001, *Hearings*, 107th Cong., 2nd sess., September 19, 2002, 18.

5. Solly Zuckerman, *Nuclear Illusion and Reality* (New York: Viking, 1982), 130.

6. Quoted in Steven Emerson, *Secret Warriors: Inside the Covert Military Operations of the Reagan Era* (New York: Putnam, 1988), 35.

7. Stansfield Turner, interview with author, Turner's residence, McLean, VA, May 1, 1991.

8. William E. Colby, interview with author, Washington, DC, January 22, 1991). For the complete published interview, see Loch K. Johnson, "William E. Colby: Spymaster during the 'Year of the Intelligence Wars,'" *Intelligence and National Security* 22 (April 2007): 250–69, reprinted in *Exploring Intelligence Archives: Enquiries into the Secret State*, ed. R. Gerald Hughes, Peter Jackson, and Len Scott (London: Routledge, 2008), 255–69.

9. Author's interview with Richard Helms, Washington, D.C. (December 12, 1990). For the complete published interview, see Loch K. Johnson, "Spymaster Richard Helms," *Intelligence and National Security* 18 (Autumn 2003), 24–44.

10. Author's interview with Robert M. Gates, Washington, D.C. (March 28, 1994).

11. See Michael S. Goodman, *Spying on the Nuclear Bear: Anglo-American Intelligence and the Soviet Bomb* (Stanford, California: Stanford University Press, 2007), 206.

12. Jonathan Clarke, "The CIA Drifts Between Fear and Loathing,"*Los Angeles Times*, September 3, 1995. M5. Clarke served as a British diplomat.

13. "Faulty Intel Source 'Curve Ball' Revealed," *60 Minutes*, CBS, November 4, 2007. The CIA did attempt to gain access to Curveball while he was in the hands of German intelligence officers, but was rebuffed by the Germans. Since the CIA doesn't allow German intelligence to vet Agency assets, reasoned the Germans, why should they allow the CIA to vet German assets?

14. Douglas F. Garthoff, *Directors of Central Intelligence as Leaders of the U.S. Intelligence Community, 1946–2005* (Washington, DC: Center for the Study of Intelligence, Central Intelligence Agency, 2005), 238.

15. Arguing against relying on a surge capability, another senior intelligence officer said to me a few days later: "You never know when you might need something from an agent in 'Falklandia.' You better have him available, just in case."

16. Senate Select Committee on Secret Military Assistance to Iran and the Nicaraguan Opposition and House Select Committee to Investigate Covert Arms Transactions with Iran, *Hearings*, 100th Cong., 1st Sess., Washington, DC, 1987, 159.

17. See, for example: Les Aspin, "Debate Over U.S. Strategic Forecasts: A Mixed Record," *Strategic Review* 8 (1980): 29–43, 57–59; and Aspin, "Misreading Intelligence," *Foreign Policy* 43 (Summer 1981): 166–72.

18. See Loch K. Johnson, *Secret Agencies: U.S. Intelligence in a Hostile World* (New Haven, CT: Yale University Press, 1996).

19. As I was exploring these questions for Aspin, I spent considerable time with high-level CIA and DIA analysts, some of whom had been working the Soviet military target for decades. Especially helpful was a meeting with several senior analysts on May 9, 1995, at Agency Headquarters, and I would like to

express my appreciation once again to these experts for patiently answering my questions at length.

20. Michael Herman, "Intelligence during the Cold War" (lecture, University of Georgia, Athens, GA, April 6, 1962).

21. See William J. Broad, "Russian Says Soviet Atom Arsenal Was Larger Than West Estimated," *New York Times*, September 26, 1993, A1.

22. See Goodman, *Spying on the Nuclear Bear*.

23. Percy Cradock, *Know Your Enemy: How the Joint Intelligence Committee Saw the World* (London: Murray, 2002).

24. This was the same problem the United States would face in 2002 when it assessed the likelihood of WMDs in Iraq.

25. *Atlanta Journal-Constitution* "Fresh Air at CIA," May 20, 1995, A4.

26. Nick Kotz, "Mission Impossible," *Washingtonian*, December 1995, 63.

27. David E. Rosenbaum, "David E. Rosenbaum, "Les Aspin, 56, Dies; Member of Congress and Defense Chief," *New York Times*, May 22, 1995, A1.

28. *Atlanta Journal-Constitution*, "Ex-Defense Chief Aspin Listed as Critical After Stroke," May 21, 1995. A11.

29. Within a year, $700,000 had been raised for the center, assisted by John Deutch as the master of ceremonies at a major fund-raising event. Frank A. Aukofer, "Friends of Aspin Raise $700,000 for MU Center," *Milwaukee Journal Sentinel*, June 12, 1996, A3.

30. See unsigned editorial, *Washington Post*, "Aspin, The Wonk's Wonk," June 14, 1995, C4.

Chapter 8

1. For a public account, see William J. Perry, *Report of the Secretary of Defense to the President and the Congress* (Washington, DC: GPO, 1996). This military confrontation is described in Loch K. Johnson, "The CIA's Weakest Link," *Washington Monthly* 33 (July/August 2001): 9–14, from which this narrative is drawn.

2. John Deutch, testimony, National Commission on Terrorist Attacks upon the United States, *Hearings*, October 14, 2003.

3. British journalist Peter Hennessy maintains that members of the British Cabinet also spend about five minutes on any given topic (remarks, author's notes, St. Antony's College, Oxford University, June 11, 2003).

4. In 1993 I had heard another seasoned analysis from INR in the Department of State say that "intelligence reports of any length work their way from the in-box to the burn bag unread, because consumers don't have time to read them. The demands today are for the quick report and the quick answer" (remarks, author's notes, Intelligence Conference, CIA Headquarters, Langley, VA, September 30, 1993).

5. See Tim Weiner, "Iraq's Top Secret; Intent Is the Ultimate Mystery," *New York Times*, November 16, 1997, WK 1.

6. Perhaps the lowest point in intelligence producer-consumer relations in the modern era came during the Reagan years. Secretary of State Shultz writes: "I had no confidence in the intelligence community.... I had been misled, lied to, cut out." George P. Shultz, *Turmoil and Triumph: My Years as Secretary of State* (New York: Scribners, 1993), 864.

7. William E. Colby, interview with author, Washington, DC, January 22, 1991.

8. George Tenet (senior director for Intelligence, National Security Council), interview with author, Old Executive Office Building, Washington, DC, June 11, 1994.

9. George Tenet, *At the Center of the Storm: My Years at the CIA* (New York: HarperCollins, 2007), 30; the Kean quote is from Linton Weeks, "An Indelible Day," *Washington Post*, June 16, 2004, C1. In a court deposition, the CIA argued recently that the *PDB* "is the quintessential pre-decisional, deliberative document." Quoted in Steven Aftergood, "An Intimate Look at the President's Daily Brief (1970)," *Secrecy News*, November 30, 2007, http://www.fas.org/blog/secrecy/2007/11/an_intimate_look_at_the_presid.html. The *PDB* has a new companion: in 2009 the CIA began sending top policy officials every morning the *Daily Economic Brief* or *DEB*, a reaction to the economic turmoil that had struck the globalized economy in 2008–9 and heightened attention to world trade issues.

10. For examples from the Johnson administration, as well as the *Brief* on Bin Laden acquired by the Kean Commission, see Loch K. Johnson, ed., *Strategic Intelligence* (Westport, CN: Praeger, 2007), 2:296–307.

11. Interview with author under conditions of anonymity, Washington, DC, November 19, 1984, quoted in Loch K. Johnson, *America's Secret Power: The CIA in a Democratic Society* (New York: Oxford University Press, 1989), 90. For a look at the *PDB* process as it operated in 1970, see Andrew W. Marshall to Henry A. Kissinger, March 18, 1970, Nixon Presidential Library, cited in Aftergood, "An Intimate Look."

12. These figures come from the author's interviews with CIA personnel involved with the *PDB* production in each of these administrations; the description of the Bush *PDB* draws on an e-mail message to the author from a *PDB* briefer, August, 7, 2008, and also Tenet, *At the Center of the Storm*, 31.

13. A DDI study during six months in 1994–95 indicated that policy makers had asked 1,300 follow-up questions after reading a *PDB*. In 57 percent of the cases, the questions were answered at the time of the briefing, and in 43 percent of the cases, the CIA was queried later and provided answers within a day or two.

14. Author's interviews with Clinton administration officials, Washington, DC, throughout 1992–97.

15. Quoted in Johnson, *America's Secret Power*, 90.

16. Quoted in Richard L. Russell, "Low-Pressure System," *The American Interest* 2, no. 6 (Summer 2007): 123. On the practice of providing the *PDB* and oral

briefings to presidential candidates, see John L. Helgerson, *Getting to Know the President: CIA Briefings of Presidential Candidates, 1952–1992* (Washington, DC: Center for the Study of Intelligence, Central Intelligence Agency, n.d., ca. 1996); see also Richard J. Kerr and Peter Dixon Davis, "Ronald Reagan and the *President's Daily Brief,*" *Studies in Intelligence* (Winter 1998–99), 51–56.

17. George Tenet, interview with author, Old Executive Office Building, Washington, DC, June 17, 1994.

18. These observations are based on the author's interviews with intelligence officers, Washington, DC, 1998.

19. See Tim Weiner, "C.I.A. Chief Defends Secrecy, in Spending and Spying, to Senate," *New York Time,* February 23, 1996, A5.

20. In 2008, imint would again provide compelling evidence that the North Koreans had helped the Syrians build a nuclear reactor capable of generating plutonium. See David E. Sanger, "Bush Administration Releases Images to Bolster Its Claims About Syrian Reactor," *New York Times,* April 25, 2006, A5.

21. The other sources consulted by the Aspin-Brown Commission were the Institute for Scientific Information Research Services Group, Oxford Analytica, East View Publications, and LexisNexis. This is not to say that these groups would have failed to perform well on other occasions; but at least in this instance they did not stack up well against the *PDB* (and the Institute missed our deadline by four days).

22. See Johnson, *America's Secret Power,* chap. 9.

23. Shultz, *Turmoil and Triumph,* 864.

24. Jack Davis, memo to the author, "CIA's Directorate of Intelligence: Challenges and Choices," October 30, 1995.

25. For a more extensive list of recent intelligence successes, see the commission's final report: Commission on the Roles and Capabilities of the United States Intelligence Community, *Preparing for the 21st Century: An Appraisal of U.S. Intelligence* (Washington, DC: GPO, 1996), 11–13.

26. Eric Schmitt, "No. 2 Officer at Pentagon Plans to Quit," *New York Times,* September 15, 1995, A12. Among the admiral's many publications is William A. Owens, *High Seas: The Naval Passage to an Uncharted World* (Annapolis, MD: Naval Institute Press, 1995).

27. See Howard Banks, "Fewer Ships, More Microchips," *Forbes,* June 19, 1995, 124.

28. John M. Deutch, interview with author, Massachusetts Institute of Technology, Cambridge, MA, October 29, 1998.

29. Lee H. Hamilton, testimony, Joint Committee to Investigate Events Surrounding the September 11, 2001, Attacks, *Hearings,* U.S. Congress, 107th Cong., 2nd. sess., October 3, 2002, 4.

30. For more on this delicate relationship, see Johnson, *America's Secret Power,* chap. 8.

31. Co-sponsored by Senator Harold E. Hughes (D-IA) and Representative Leo J. Ryan (D-CA), the amendment to section 662 of the Foreign Assistance Act of 1961 (U.S Code 22, 2422) became law on December 30, 1974.

32. In 2003, British Prime Minister Tony Blair asked the JIC (Joint Intelligence Committee, roughly comparable to the American NIC) "to provide not only estimates but also for the first time recommendations on policy," according to Michael S. Goodman, *Spying on the Nuclear Bear: Anglo-American Intelligence and the Soviet Bomb* (Stanford, CA: Stanford University Press, 2007), 208. So much for a "Kentian wall" separating policy and intelligence in the United Kingdom.

Chapter 9

1. William Safire, "Cold Comfort Level," *New York Times*, December 23, 1994, A18; Judy Keen and Steve Komarow, "Inman Out; Claims Plot by Critics," *USA Today*, January 14, 1994, A1.

2. James R. Schlesinger, interview with author, Washington, DC, June 16, 1994. An experienced DO officer scoffed at the strategy of hanging out at bars and cafes, hoping a recruit will fall into one's lap. As he recalls, with astonishment: "'Just sit in the cafés and bars nearest to the foreign and defense ministries and try to meet people' was the *serious* advice given by a performance-award-winning senior operative to a hapless, quintessentially American junior case officer tasked to recruit European officials." Reuel Marc Gerecht, "A New Clandestine Service: The Case for Creative Destruction," in *The Future of American Intelligence*, ed. Peter Berkowitz (Stanford, CA: Hoover Institution, 2005), 118, emphasis in original.

3. Stansfield Turner, interview with author, Turner's residence, McLean, VA, May 1, 1991.

4. Quoted by Dana Priest, "System Failed Downed Pilot, CIA Official Says," *Washington Post*, June 28, 1995, A15.

5. Ibid.

6. George Tenet (senior director for intelligence, National Security Council), interview with author, Old Executive Office Building, Washington, DC, June 11, 1994.

7. R. Jeffrey Smith, "Deutch Cites Concerns on CIA Failings," *Washington Post*, June 22, 1995.

8. John Deutch, Statement, Select Committee on Intelligence, *Hearings*, U.S. Senate, 104th Cong., 1st sess., June 21, 1995.

9. Quoted in Sam Vincent Meddis, "CIA Chief Says He May Require Broader Powers," *USA Today*, June 22, 1995, A16.

10. James Risen, "CIA to Issue Guidelines on Hiring Foreign Operatives," *New York Times*, June 30, 1995, A4.

11. The CIA's general counsel, a former aide to Senator Sam Nunn of Georgia and counsel to the Senate Armed Services Committee—in short, no shrinking

violet—has said: "In my experience the guidelines did not prove an unnecessary burden in recruiting human assets. . . . We must know who we're dealing with and case officers must have the knowledge that they will be backed up by headquarters in their dealings with these people. That can only be assured by a system in which headquarters knows what is going on and approves. That is what these guidelines provide, and I believe they will prove in the long run to be a great benefit to CIA and its officers." Quoted in Paul Schott Stevens, "An Interview with Former CIA General Counsel Jeffrey H. Smith," *National Security Law Report* 18, no. 6 (October 1996): 6]. Over and over again, Deutch assured the DO and the public that his new rules would in no way prohibit case officers from aggressively recruiting terrorists or those close to terrorist organizations; in these cases, the rules would be lifted. Similarly, from the vantage point of the case officer, a savvy and seasoned DO operative states that "there is simply no such thing as a case officer who didn't try to recruit a Middle Eastern terrorist because of concerns about the possible legal blow back from associating with someone who may have engaged in criminal behavior"(Gerecht, "A New Clandestine Service," 107). Nevertheless, Smith later concluded that the Deutch rules were a mistake, in part because "many in the field resented the guidelines, and some may have used them as an excuse when they were not able to recruit sources in terrorist groups. . . . It became a kind of mantra that the guidelines were a tremendous hindrance to recruiting." Quoted in Douglas Jehl, "An Abundance of Caution And Years of Budget Cuts Are Seen to Limit C.I.A.," *New York Times*, May 11, 2004, A18. DCI George Tenet rescinded the rules in 2002; the thought, however wrong minded, that they were interfering with intelligence operations against terrorists had become politically unpalatable. Among those in favor of scrapping the Deutch rules was commissioner Porter Goss. After the commission had completed its work, he observed in a speech that some think "we should only deal with clean assets, that we should only work with reputable and morally responsible individuals. Well, you don't get the penetrations and you don't get the asset you need [with that approach]." "Representative Porter Goss Responds to CIA Critics," *National Security Law Report* 18, no. 8 (December 1996), 11.

12. His comment was reminiscent of Secretary of State Henry Kissinger's *realpolitik* perspective on the work of the State *Department* in 1973. Complaining in a meeting with officials from the Department's Latin American division that the briefing papers it was producing were too oriented toward questions of human rights, he declared: "The State Department is made up of people who have a vocation for the ministry. Because there were not enough churches for them, they went into the Department of State." Quoted in Larry Rohter, "Word for Word/Kissinger on Pinochet; The Human Rights Crowd Gives Realpolitik the Jitters," *New York Times*, December 28, 2003, Wk 7, based on documents acquired by the National Security Archive at George Washington University in Washington, DC.

13. George Tenet, interview with author, Old Executive Office Building, Washington, DC, June 11, 1994.

14. For a moving account of some of the people whose names are in the "Book of Honor," see Ted Gup, *The Book of Honor: Covert Lives and Classified Deaths* at the CIA (New York: Doubleday, 2000).

15. Richard Harris, "Reflections: Secrets," New Yorker, April 10, 1978, 44.

16. George Tenet, interview with author, Old Executive Office Building, Washington, DC, June 11, 1994.

17. George Tenet (comment, National Intelligence and Technology Symposium, CIA, Langley, VA, November 6, 1998).

18. James Schlesinger, interview with author, Washington, DC, June 16, 1994.

19. Stansfield Turner, interview with author, Turner's residence, McLean, VA, May 1, 1991.

20. See Loch K. Johnson, *A Season of Inquiry: The Senate Intelligence Investigation* (Lexington: University Press of Kentucky, 1986); Johnson, "Congressional Supervision of America's Secret Agencies: The Experience and Legacy of the Church Committee," *Public Administration Review* 64 (2004), 3–14; Frederick A. O., Schwarz Jr., "Intelligence Oversight: The Church Committee," in *Strategic Intelligence*, ed. Loch K. Johnson (Westport, CT: Praeger, 2007), 5:19–46; Frederick A. O. Schwarz Jr. and Aziz Z. Huq, *Unchecked and Unbalanced: Presidential Power in a Time of Terror* (New York: New Press, 2007); and Frank J. Smist Jr., *Congress Oversees the United States Intelligence Community*, 2nd ed. (Knoxville: University of Tennessee Press, 1994).

21. Loch K. Johnson, "Legislative Reform of Intelligence Policy." *Polity* 17 (1985), 549–73.

22. Gregory F. Treverton, "Intelligence: Welcome to the American Government," in *A Question of Balance: The President, Congress, and Foreign Policy*, ed. Thomas E. Mann (Washington, DC: Brookings Institution, 1990), 70–108.

23. Tim Weiner, "New C.I.A. Chief Wants to Revamp U.S. Spying Overseas," *New York Times*, July 3, 1995, A2.

24. Quoted in "Gooseberries," a story by Anton Chekhov, *The Wife and Other Stories*, translated by Constance Garnett.

25. An NIO had observed to me the week before: "We are a non-Prophet institution."

26. See Steve Tsang, ed., *Intelligence and Human Rights in the Era of Global Terrorism* (Westport, CT: Praeger, 2007).

27. The former president and DCI, George H. W. Bush, once wrote to me that the intelligence "product was better than CNN and the WSJ [Wall Street Journal] on almost every count. Sometimes, CNN's on the spot coverage was very helpful. Sometimes, I felt CNN was being used by Saddam Hussein." George H. W. Bush to author, January 23, 1994.

28. R. James Woolsey, interview with author, CIA Headquarters, Langley, VA, September 29, 1993.

29. In 1971, for example, an internal CIA investigation concluded that only 5 percent of serious leaks seemed to have come from Capitol Hill. George Lardner Jr., "Moynihan Unleashes the C.I.A.," *Nation*, February 16, 1980, 177.

30. Wyche Fowler, interview with author, Athens, GA, February 28, 2008. While he and Brown agreed on very little that year, Fowler remembers admiring in retrospect the discipline that Brown brought to the commission after Aspin's loose style of management, as well as Brown's insistence on keeping the media at arm's length.

31. Senators John Warner (R-VA) and Carl Levin (D-MI), the two leaders of the Armed Services Committee, had spearheaded the panel's inquiry into the Somali debacle. Their committee interviewed hundreds of people, including U.S. soldiers who had been stationed in Somalia in 1993, UN personnel, CIA officers and managers, State Department diplomats, and even Aideed and other warlords involved in the conflict. I have summarized the committee's harsh indictment of Aspin's political and military decisions earlier in this book (Chapter 1). On the intelligence front, the committee's findings were mixed. The U.S. military-intelligence units received high marks, although the number of rocket-propelled grenades (RPGs) in the hands of the Somali fighters had been badly underestimated. The committee's primary criticism, though, centered on the CIA's poor humint in the region, calling it "limited." Plainly put, that meant not enough assets, and the few who were available proved unreliable. Especially vexing was the inability of local assets to tell the U.S. forces where Aideed was hiding. See John Warner and Carl Levin, *Review of the Circumstances Surrounding the Ranger Raid on October 3–4, 1993, in Mogadishu, Somalia*, Senate Armed Services Committee, 104th Cong., 1st sess., 1995, 42. C. Kenneth Allard also discusses some of the security problems in the dissemination of U.S. intelligence in Somalia during 1991–93, when American forces were working hand-in-hand with other allied nations. See his *Somalia Operations: Lessons Learned* (Washington, DC: National Defense University Press, 1995). In my own research on the commission, I had found that on some occasions UN officials carelessly handled U.S. intelligence documents shared with them, even leaving some classified papers behind during their withdrawal from Somalia in 1994; see also Bill Gertz, "Clinton Wants Hill Off His Back," Washington Times, November 1, 1995, A1.

32. See the series by James Risen: "CIA Heavily Infiltrated in Russia, Report Finds," *Los Angeles Times*, October 31, 1995, A1; "3 Ex-CIA Directors Blamed for Agency Role in Misdeeds," *Los Angeles Times*, November 1, 1995, A1; and "Gates Says Aides Failed to Tell Him About Ames," *Los Angeles Times*, November 2, 1995, A1; see also Tim Weiner, "C.I.A. Tells Panels it Failed to Sift Tainted Spy Data," *New York Times*, November 1, 1995, A1; and Maureen Dowd, " Liberties; Lies And Kisses," *New York Times*, November 2, 1995, A27.

33. Quoted in John Diamond, *The CIA and the Culture of Failure: U.S. Intelligence from the End of the Cold War to the Invasion of Iraq* (Stanford, CA: Stanford University Press, 2008), 232.

34. Subsequent internal investigations concluded that decisions in Washington had not been appreciably affected by the questionable intelligence reporting from Moscow (e-mail communication from the CIA reported in ibid.? 239).

35. See John T. Elliff and Loch K. Johnson, "Counterintelligence," in *Final Report*, Book 1, Foreign and Military Intelligence, Senate Select Committee to Study Governmental Operations with Respect to Intelligence Activities, 94th Cong., 2nd sess., April 26, 1976, 163–78.

36. At the very time of this briefing on counterintelligence, a CIA veteran officer by the name of Harold J. Nicolson—the highest ranking Agency officer ever to be charged with treason—was busy spying for the Russians; he was caught in November of 1996; see David Johnston and Tim Weiner, "On the Trail of a C.I.A. Man, Trips and Big Cash Transfers," *New York Times*, November 21, 1996, A1. The new procedures that required intelligence officers to disclose their personal finances helped catch Nicolson; see Walter Pincus and Roberto Suro, "Rooting Out the 'Sour Apples' Inside the CIA," *Washington Post*,, National Weekly Edition, December 1, 1996, 30. 19. Soon after, two more "volunteers" would be caught: Earl Pitts, an FBI agent spying for the Russians, and Robert C. Kim, spying for South Korea. Tim Weiner, "Ex-Analyst Pleads Guilty in Spy Case," *New York Times*, May 8, 1997, A16. Redmond was right: there were no complete cures for treason. For more on his views about counterintelligence, see Paul J. Redmond, "The Challenges of Counterintelligence," in ed. Loch K. Johnson, *The Oxford Handbook of National Security Intelligence* (New York: Oxford University Press, 2010), 537–554.

37. John M. Deutch, interview with author, Massachusetts Institute of Technology, Cambridge, MA, October 29, 1998. He considered his other major successes the improvement of consumer satisfaction with intelligence, along with better support to military operations—a goal that he had clearly signaled to everyone in 1995 when he elevated his aide, Admiral Blair, to the position of associate director of central intelligence for military support. As for failures, "there were so many," he said. "They're hard to describe."

38. See, for example, David Wise and Thomas B. Ross, *The Invisible Government* (New York: Random House, 1964), on the Guatemala coup; and David Wise, *The Spy Who Got Away: The Inside Story of Edward Lee Howard, the CIA Agent who Betrayed His country's Secrets and Escaped to Moscow* (New York: Random House, 1988); Wise, *Nightmover: How Aldrich Ames Sold the CIA to the KGB for $4.6 Million* (New York: HarperCollins, 1995); and Wise, *Spy: The Inside Story of How the FBI's Robert Hanssen Betrayed America* (New York: Random House, 2002).

39. Milton C. Cummings Jr. and David Wise, *Democracy Under Pressure: An Introduction to the American Political System*, 10th ed. (Belmont, CA: Thomson, 2005).

40. Efforts by Congress to monitor military intelligence operations would prove challenging to lawmakers in the coming years. In 2009, for example, HPSCI would report on "the blurred distinction between the intelligence-gathering activities carried out by the Central Intelligence Agency (CIA) and the clandestine operations of the Department of Defense (DOD)." The Agency routinely reported to SSCI and HPSCI on its activities; the Pentagon, taking advantage of this "blur," did not—even thought the Intelligence Oversight Act of 1980 required activity reports from all intelligence entities. See "Oversight of Intelligence Activities," Intelligence Authorization Act for Fiscal Year 2010, *Report No. 111–86*, House Permanent Select Committee on Intelligence, 111th Cong., 1st sess., July 2009; and Jennifer D. Kibbe, "Covert Action and the Pentagon," in Loch K. Johnson, ed., *Strategic Intelligence*, (Westport, CT:Praeger, 2007), 3:131–44.

41. See, for example, Jeffrey T. Richelson, *A Century of Spies: Intelligence in the Twentieth Century* (New York: Oxford University Press, 1995); and Richelson, *The Wizards of Langley: Inside the CIA's Directorate of Science and Technology* (Boulder, CO: Westview, 2001).

42. Wyche Fowler, interview with author, Athens, GA, February 28, 2008.

Chapter 10

1. Robert M. Gates, interview with author, Washington, DC, March 28, 1994.

2. The report came from the National Security Council, *Annual Report to Congress on Foreign Economic Collection and Industrial Espionage*, July 1995, discussed in Bill Gertz, "Economic Spying in U.S. Is Done by Allies, Report Says," *Washington Times*, August 9, 1995, A3.

3. Similarly, former national security advisor McGeorge Bundy once said to me that "if you can't defend a covert action if it goes public, you'd better not do it at all—because it will go public usually within a fairly short time span." Interview with author, Athens, GA, October 6, 1987. Former DCI Stansfield Turner has also written: "There is one overall test of the ethics of human intelligence activities. That is, whether those approving them feel they could defend their decisions before the public if their actions became public." *Secrecy and Democracy: The CIA in Transition* (Boston: Houghton Mifflin, 1985), 178.

4. In 1996, after the commission had completed its work, Hermann chaired a DCI panel on space surveillance that recommended building a fleet of small, light, and relatively cheap satellites.

5. Hermann was prescient about UAVs; they have now become the hottest platform for intelligence collection in Iraq, Afghanistan, and Pakistan, and—when armed with Hellfire missiles—are the most lethal new form of paramilitary covert action. In November 2002, a CIA Predator flying at thirty

thousand feet over Yemen launched a Hellfire missile that struck a vehicle and incinerated its six passengers (including an American citizen) who were suspected of terrorism; see Walter Pincus, "U.S. Strike Kills Six in Al Qaeda," *Washington Post*, November 5, 2002, A1. Needless to say, this event (and others more recently involving missiles fired from drones) raise serious questions about due process, as well as who has the right to approve such an operation—questions yet to be answered satisfactorily.

6. John Deutch, "The Future of U.S. Intelligence—Charting a Course for Change" (speech, National Press Club, Washington, DC, September 12, 1995).

7. See Walter Pincus, "Pentagon Gaining Turf From the CIA," *Washington Post*, November 16, 1995, A14.

8. Douglas F. Garthoff, *Directors of Central Intelligence as Leaders of the U.S. Intelligence Community, 1946–2005* (Dulles, VA: Potomac Books, 2005), 245.

9. David A. Fulghum and Robert Wall, "Operation Allied Force: Intel Mistakes Trigger Chinese Embassy Bombing," *Aviation Week & Space Technology*, May 17, 1999, 55.

10. This part of the speech made the news, as anything about covert action has a way of doing; see R. Jeffrey Smith, "Expansion of Covert Action Eyed," *Washington Post*, September 13, 1995.

11. Roger Hilsman, "Does the CIA Still Have a Role?" *Foreign Affairs* 74, no. 5 (September/October 1995): 112.

12. John I. Millis, "Why Spy?" (unclassified draft essay, no date, but circulated to the Aspin-Brown Commission staff in September 1995).

13. Quoted in Garthoff, *Directors of Central Intelligence*, 253.

14. L. Britt Snider, quoted in "The Brown Commission and the Future of Intelligence: A Roundtable Discussion," *Studies in Intelligence* 39 (1996), 9.

15. R. James Woolsey, interview with author, CIA Headquarters, Langley, VA, September 29, 1993.

16. Ibid.

17. According to DDO James L. Pavitt, (remarks, *Dateline NBC*, October 17, 2004); see also *The 9/11 Commission Report: Final Report of the National Commission on Terrorist Attacks upon the United States* (New York: Norton, 2004), 90.

18. Douglas Jehl, "Abundance of Caution and Years of Budget Cuts Are Seen to Limit C.I.A.," *New York Times*, May 11, 2004, A18, quoting DDO James L. Pavitt. So much for the Aspin-Brown Commission's emphasis in 1996 on building up the government's humint capabilities. Views on the meaning of these numbers varied, however. In 1997, for example, even a former head of the Directorate of Operations, retired DCI Richard Helms, would tell a reporter that there were "too many people" and too much "bloat" in the clandestine service. Tim Weiner, "Aging Shop of Horrors: The C.I.A. Limps to 50," *New York Times*, July 20, 1997, Wk6. Despite the humint declines in the 1990s, by 2004 the Agency was able to graduate from the Farm its largest

class of DO operatives ever. David E. Kaplan, "Mission Impossible," *U.S. News & World Report*, August 2, 2004, 42. By 2009, the CIA was recording its largest number of job applications: 180,000 in the first half of the year, and of high quality as measured by SAT scores. Reported on "Morning Edition," National Public Radio, July 6, 2009.

19. Commission on the Roles and Capabilities of the United States Intelligence Community, *Preparing for the 21st Century: An Appraisal of U.S. Intelligence*, (Washington, DC: GPO, 1996), 125.

20. R. James Woolsey, interview with author, CIA Headquarters, Langley, VA, September 29, 1993.

21. John M. Deutch, interview with author, Massachusetts Institute of Technology, Cambridge, MA, October 29, 1998.

22. *9/11 Commission Report*, 93.

23. See Commission on the Roles and Capabilities, *Preparing for the 21st Century*, 131.

24. *Congressional Record*, 103d Cong., 2d sess., July 19, 1994, H21321.

25. As historian Ernest R. May has noted with respect to the Kean Commission, the leaders of panels of inquiry in Washington do their best to avoid dissolving "into a partisan wrangle." "When Government Writes History: A Memoir of the 9/11 Commission," *New Republic*, May 23, 2005, 31.

26. For a brief overview on the importance of intelligence oversight, see Loch K. Johnson, "Congress's Experiment in Overseeing Spies," *New York Times*, June 9, 2002, Wk 5. See also David M. Barrett, *The CIA and Congress: The Untold Story from Truman to Kennedy* (Lawrence: University Press of Kansas, 2005); Loch K. Johnson, "Accountability and America's Secret Foreign Policy: Keeping a Legislative Eye on the Central Intelligence Agency," *Foreign Policy Analysis* 1 (Spring 2005): 99–120; and L. Britt Snider, *The Agency and the Hill: CIA's Relationship with Congress, 1946–2004* (Washington, DC: Center for the Study of Intelligence, Central Intelligence Agency, 2008).

27. For a detailed examination of their approaches to oversight, see Loch K. Johnson, *Secret Agencies: U.S. Intelligence in a Hostile World* (New Haven, CT: Yale University Press, 1996), 89–94.

28. See Loch K. Johnson, "Supervising America's Secret Foreign Policy: A Shock Theory of Congressional Oversight for Intelligence," in *American Foreign Policy in a Globalized World*, ed. David P. Forsythe, Patrice C. McMahon, and Andrew Wedeman (New York: Routledge, 2006), 173–92.

29. From January of 1998 until the Qaeda attacks on 9/11, SSCI held eight hearings on terrorism, and HPSCI held two. Greg Miller, "Panel Headed by CIA Nominee Was Singled Out in 9/11 Report," *Los Angeles Times*, August 12, 2004, A1.

30. Victoria Toensing, "Oversee? More Like Overlook," *Washington Post*, June 13, 2004, B7.

31. See Loch K. Johnson, "Ostriches, Cheerleaders, Skeptics, and Guardians: Role Selection by Congressional Intelligence Overseers," *SAIS Review of International Affairs* 28 (2008): 93–108.

32. See David M. Barrett, "Congressional Oversight of the CIA in the Early Cold War, 1947–1963," in *Strategic Intelligence*, ed. Loch K. Johnson (Westport, CT: Praeger, 2007), 5:1–18; Loch K. Johnson, *America's Secret Power: The CIA in a Democratic Society* (New York: Oxford University Press, 1987), Johnson, *A Season of Inquiry* (Lexington: University Press of Kentucky, 1985); and Harry Howe Ransom, *The Intelligence Establishment* (Cambridge, MA: Harvard University Press, 1970).

33. Tim Weiner, *Legacy of Ashes: The History of the CIA* (New York: Doubleday, 2007), 337.

34. Acting in this role, Porter Goss once observed that "the Hill has filled the vacuum [left by the executive branch under President Clinton] on championing the cause of intelligence," quoted in Gregory McCarthy, "GOP Oversight of Intelligence in the Clinton Era," *International Journal of Intelligence and Counterintelligence* 15 (2002): 41.

35. On the frequency and seriousness with which intelligence officers have been questioned by lawmakers in public hearings, see Loch K. Johnson, "Playing Ball with the CIA: Congress Supervises Strategic Intelligence," in *The President, the Congress, and the Making of Foreign Policy*, ed. Paul E. Peterson (Norman: University of Oklahoma Press, 1994), 49–73.

36. *Village Voice*, "The CIA Report the President Doesn't Want You to Read: The Pike Papers," February 16 and 23, 1976.

37. Cited in Steve Roberts, "The 1973 Oil Crisis," *America Abroad Media*, Audio Case Studies, Disc 2 (2007).

38. For chronicles of these failures, see Weiner, *Legacy of Ashes*; and Amy B. Zegart, *Spying Blind: The CIA, the FBI, and the Origins of 9/11* (Princeton, NJ: Princeton University Press, 2007). On the assassination plots, see Senate Select Committee to Study Governmental Operations with Respect to Intelligence Activities, *Alleged Assassination Plots Involving Foreign Leaders: An Interim Report* (New York: Norton, 1976). And on the faulty WMD forecast, Robert Jervis, *Why Intelligence Fails: Lessons from the Iranian Revolution and the Iraqi War* (Ithaca, NY: Cornell University Press, 2010).

39. For an account of the Torricelli case, see Mark M. Lowenthal, *Intelligence: From Secrets to Policy*, 4th ed. (Washington, DC: CQ, 2009), 294–95; and R. H. Melton, "Ethics Panel Will Take No Action on Torricelli," *Washington Post*, July 13, 1995, A1.

40. Quoted in F. Davies, "GOP-Controlled Senate Expected to Give Less Scrutiny to War on Terror," *Miami Herald*, November 7, 2002, A1.

41. Norman Dicks, interview with Cynthia Nolan, Washington, DC, October 15, 2003, "More Perfect Oversight: Intelligence Oversight and Reform," in Johnson, *Strategic Intelligence*, 5:115–40, quote at 126–27.

42. Lee H. Hamilton, testimony, *Hearings*, Joint Committee to Investigate Events Surrounding the September 11, 2001, Attacks, 107th Cong., 2nd sess., October 3, 2002, afternoon session, 2.

43. See Senate Select Committee on Secret Military Assistance to Iran and the Nicaraguan Opposition and House Select Committee to Investigate Covert Arms Transactions with Iran, *Report of the Congressional Committees Investigating the Iran-Contra Affair*, S. Rept. No. 100–216 and H. Rept. No. 100–433, 100th Cong., 1st sess., November 1987.

44. Lee H. Hamilton, remark to author, Athens, GA, April 9, 2008.

45. See Scott Shane, "Cheney is Linked to Concealment of C.I.A. Project," *New York Times*, July 12, 2009, A1. In this piece, a former HPSCI chair (and ongoing member of the committee), Rep. Peter Hoekstra (R-MI) stated: "We have to pull the information out of them [the intelligence agencies] to get what we need."

46. Siobhan Gorman, "Democrats Say Panetta Admits CIA Misled Them," *Wall Street Journal*, July 10, 2009, p. A1.

47. See the 1980 *Intelligence Oversight Act* (Title V of the *National Security Act of 1947*, U.S. Code 50, 413) and the 1991 *Intelligence Authorization Act* (U.S. Code 50, 413b).

48. Recall the examples of the junior lawmakers Aspin and Mazzoli on HPSCI serving as model intelligence overseers; see Johnson, *Secret Agencies*.

49. For an example of an SSCI chair (David Boren, D-OK) succumbing to this approach, see John Diamond, *The CIA and the Culture of Failure: U.S. Intelligence from the End of the Cold War to the Invasion of Iraq* (Stanford, CA: Stanford University Press, 2008), 202.

50. Gorman, "Democrats Say Panetta Admits." The fact that the president failed to name a single member to PIAB until after six months into his tenure raised questions about his interest in the subject of intelligence.

51. Michael Hayden and Michael B. Mukasey, "The President Ties His Own Hands on Terror," *Wall Street Journal*, April 17, 2009, A13. General Hayden was D/CIA from 2006 to 2009 and, before that, director of the NSA at the time it entered into an inappropriate warrantless wiretapping agreement with the White House, in violation of the Foreign Intelligence Surveillance Act of 1978; Michael B. Mukasey was attorney general of the United States from 2007 to 2009.

52. Robert M. Gates, *From the Shadows: The Ultimate Insider's Story of Five Presidents and How They Won the Cold War* (New York: Simon & Schuster, 1996), 559.

53. See *Congressional Record* 119 (1973): 24532; and Pat M. Holt, *The War Powers Resolution: The Role of Congress in U.S. Armed Intervention* (Washington, DC: American Enterprise Institute for Public Policy Research, 1978).

54. Quoted in *U.S. News & World Report*, "U.S. Aid to Nicaraguan Rebels— Lawmakers Speak Out," May 2, 1983, 29.

55. Ibid., 29.

56. The unitary theory of the presidency embraces the idea that the president should be all-powerful in foreign and security policy, especially when the nation faces a security crisis like global terrorism. For a proponent of this view, popular with

Vice President Dick Cheney in the second Bush administration, see John Yoo, *War by Other Means: An Insider's Account of the War on Terror* (New York: Atlantic Monthly Press, 2006). In contrast, see David Cole and James X. Dempsey, *Terrorism and the Constitution: Sacrificing Civil Liberties in the Name of National Security*, 3rd ed. (New York: New Press, 2006); Louis Fisher, *The Constitution and 9/11: Recurring Threats to America's Freedom* (Lawrence, KS: University Press of Kansas, 2009); Jack Goldsmith, *The Terror Presidency: Law and Judgment inside the Bush Administration* (New York: Norton, 2007); Loch K. Johnson, *Seven Sins of American Foreign Policy* (New York: Pearson Longman, 2007); and Frederick A.O. Schwarz Jr. and Aziz Z. Huq, *Unchecked and Unbalanced: Presidential Power in a Time of Terror* (New York: The New Press, 2007).

57. DCI Casey devoted all of twenty-seven words to this important mining operation in over an hour's briefing to SSCI members. John McMahon (senior DO officer), interview with author, Washington, DC, June 12, 1984.

58. Barry Goldwater, letter to the editor, *Washington Post*, April 11, 1984, p. A17.

59. Bob Graham (D-FL), interviewed on August 8, 2009, by intelligence scholar Jennifer Kibbe and cited in "Congressional Oversight of Intelligence: Is the Solution Part of the Problem?" conference paper presentation, annual meeting, American Political Science Association, Toronto, September 5, 2009, 31.

Chapter 11

1. For a recent history of this period, see Derek Chollet and James Goldgeier, *America Between the Wars: From 11/9 to 9/11: The Misunderstood Years Between the Fall of the Berlin Wall and the Start of the War on Terror* (New York: BBS Public Affairs, 2008).

2. See Ernest R. May, "Intelligence: Backing into the Future," *Foreign Affairs* 71, no. 3 (Summer 1994): 65.

3. William Drozdiak, "France Accuses Americans of Spying, Seeks Recall," *Washington Post*, February 23, 1995, A1.

4. For a time line of the scandal and the "uncomfortable" characterization, see *Washington Post*, September 13, 1998, A1.

5. Robert M. Gates, interview with author, Washington, DC, March 28, 1994.

6. Quoted in James Risen, "Do We Still Need the CIA?" *Los Angeles Times Magazine*, October 6, 1995, 34.

7. Richard N. Haass, "Don't Hobble Intelligence Gathering," *Washington Post*, February 15, 1996, A27.

8. As documented in Executive Order no. 12333: "No person employed by or acting on behalf of the United States Government shall engage in, or conspire to engage in assassination." The language has been interpreted to exclude legitimate military targets in times of authorized warfare. See James E. Baker, *In the Common Defense: National Security Law for Perilous Times* (New York: Cambridge University Press, 2007), 155.

9. Quoted in Robert Pear, "A Shake-Up at Spy Agency as Secret Fund is Disclosed," *New York Times*, September 25, 1995, A12.
10. Tim Weiner, "A Secret Agency's Secret Budgets Yield Lost Billions, Officials Say," *New York Times*, January 30, 1996, A1.
11. Tim Weiner, "Let's Play Spy! (And The Money Is Real!)," *New York Times*, August 14, 1994, Wk 16.
12. Pear, "Shake-Up at Spy Agency." Congress reacted with legislation to require from the intelligence community specific notification of any new construction costing $500,000 or more. *Intelligence Authorization Act for FY 1995*, U.S Code 50, 403-2b (supp. 1995), 602.
13. Pear, "Shake-Up at Spy Agency."
14. Tony Capaccio, "CIA Ends Reagan-Era Pact That Kept Pentagon From NRO Books," *Defense Week*, October 2, 1995, 1. An intelligence official who came into the NRO after the scandal recalls that the agency had a largely negative view toward SSCI and HPSCI in its early days. "'We're not going to tell you anything, and you can't make us,' was the attitude," he said (remarks, author's notes, "National Intelligence and Technology Symposium," CIA Conference, Langley, VA, November 6, 1998).
15. Capaccio, "CIA Ends Reagan-Era Pact."
16. Tim Weiner, "Spy Satellite Agency Heads are Ousted for Lost Money," *New York Times*, February 27, 1996. A9.
17. See R. Jeffrey Smith and Walter Pincus, "CIA Chief to Punish Employees," *Washington Post*, September 27, 1995, A23; Tim Weiner, "C.I.A. May Dismiss Chief Officer Involved in Guatemala," *New York Times*, September 27, 1995, A1; R. Jeffrey Smith and Walter Pincus, "Punishment in Guatemala Affair Sparks Angry Backlash at CIA," *Washington Post*, October 3, 1995, A14; and Walter Pincus, "CIA Chief Castigates 7 Agency Officials," *Washington Post*, November 1, 1995, A1. News reports underestimated the actual numbers of letters sent out by the DCI ("Update on Guatemala Punishments," unclassified memo, Aspin-Brown Commission, September 27, 1995).
18. Under President Clinton, the IOB became a PFIAB standing committee, rather than a separate entity in the Executive Office of the President, as it had been when created by President Ford in 1976. Clinton also specified that the IOB chair would be selected by the PFIAB chair, and Aspin had selected Harrington.
19. Smith and Pincus, "CIA Chief to Punish Employees." For the IOB findings, see Anthony S. Harrington, *Report on the Guatemala Review*, presented to Anthony Lake, national security advisor, on April 7, 1995, which concluded, too, that the CIA had on its payroll a number of military officers suspected of torture, kidnapping, and assassinations.
20. Weiner, "Breaking With Past."
21. Cited in "Update on Guatemala Punishments," unclassified memo, Aspin-Brown Commission, September 27, 1995.

22. Senate Select Committee on Intelligence, *An Assessment of the Aldrich H. Ames Espionage Case and Its Implications for U.S. Intelligence*, 103d Cong., 2nd sess., November 1, 1994, 78.

23. Author's interviews with CIA officers who had been present at the meeting (October 1995); also: Smith and Pincus, "Punishment in Guatemala Affair."

24. Smith and Pincus, "Punishment in Guatemala Affair."

25. Years after the Aspin-Brown Commission inquiry, its staff director would dismiss the brouhaha over the Alpirez case, the Deutch rules, and the DO firings as "oversight gone berserk," causing morale to plummet at the CIA. L. Britt Snider, interviewed by John Diamond, quoted in *The CIA and the Culture of Failure: U.S. Intelligence from the End of the Cold War to the Invasion of Iraq* Stanford, CA: Stanford University Press, 2008, 278.

26. Smith and Pincus, "Punishment in Guatemala Affair."

27. Duane R. Clarridge, *A Spy for All Seasons: My Life in the CIA* (New York: Scribner, 1997), 411.

28. James Risen, "Do We Still Need the CIA?" *Los Angeles Times Magazine*, October 6, 1995, 14. The same theme would appear in the newspapers over a decade later. In response to a request in 2005 that the CIA's inspector general conduct an investigation into questions of improper destruction of Agency videotapes on torture, the incumbent deputy director of operations, Jose A. Rodriguez Jr., told the DCI at the time—none other than the Aspin-Brown Commission's own Porter Goss—not to worry about doing that; the DO would investigate itself. Years earlier, DCI Stansfield Turner had said that he agreed with a former CIA deputy director (Frank C. Carlucci) who told him that "running the CIA from the director's office was like operating a power plant from a control room with a wall containing many impressive levers that, on the other side of the wall, had been disconnected." Stansfield Turner, *Secrecy and Democracy: The CIA in Transition* (Boston: Houghton Mifflin, 1985), 185. In 2005 Goss told an associate (subsequently quoted in the media) that when DO officers ignored his requests it gave him the sense that "when he pulled a lever to make something happen in the DO, it wasn't just that nothing happened. It was that the lever came off in his hands." Mark Mazzetti and Scott Shane, "Tape Inquiry: Ex-Spymaster In the Middle," *New York Times*, February 20, 2008, A1.

29. For more on this subject, see David Wise, "Is U.N. the Latest Cover for CIA Spies?" *Los Angeles Times*, January 17, 1999, M2; Loch K. Johnson, *Bombs, Bugs, Drugs, and Thugs: Intelligence and America's Quest for Security* (New York: New York University Press, 2000); and Steven Greenhouse, "Conflict in the Balkans: In Washington; U.N. Bosnia Force to Get U.S. Spy Planes," *New York Times*, June 5, 1995, A1.

30. Lee H. Hamilton, testimony, *Hearings*, Joint Committee to Investigate Events Surrounding the September 11, 2001, Attacks, 107th Cong., 2nd sess., October 2, 2002, 21.

31. Robert M. Gates, interview with author, Washington, DC, March 28, 1994.

32. Susan M. Ouellette, "The Intelligence Community in the 21st Century—IC21" (conference paper, International Studies Association Annual Meeting, San Diego, CA, April 18, 1996).

33. For his reflections on this commission, see Daniel Patrick Moynihan, *Secrecy: The American Experience* (New Haven, CT: Yale University Press, 1998).

34. Quoted in Walter Pincus, "Pentagon to Spy More Overseas," *Washington Post*, October 30, 1995, A17.

35. Warren B. Rudman, "A Senator's Day," *Washington Post*, December 21, 1995, D7.

36. "HPSCI Chairman Combest Outlines Vision for the Future of Intelligence," *What's News at CIA*, November 13, 1995, 4.

37. Thomas W. Lippman, "Defense and Diplomacy," *Washington Post*, September 14, 1995, A17.

38. Donna Cassata, "Iran Covert Fund Proposal Delays Authorization," *Congressional Quarterly Weekly Report*, October 28, 1995, 332, for the $36 million figure; Tim Weiner, "U.S. Plan to Change Iran Leaders Is an Open Secret Before it Begins," *New York Times*, January 26, 1996, A1, for the $18 million figure.

39. In 1998, the Speaker telephoned DCI George Tenet on a secure line and said breathlessly: "Can you get me a list of things to spend $1 billion on in four hours?" As Tenet remembers, sardonically, "I resisted mightily," adding with a smile: "The Speaker is a great man." Behind the scenes, Porter Goss (who had become head of HPSCI) had urged the Speaker to offer the "plus-up." George J. Tenet and Porter Goss (remarks, author's notes, "National Intelligence and Technology Symposium," CIA Conference, Langley, VA, November 6, 1998).

40. Zoë Baird, "Staff Paper on Law Enforcement and Intelligence," memorandum to commissioners, October 12, 1995, 2. During the commission's examination of the topic, she wrote an op-ed piece laying out her views on the cops-and-spooks relationship: "When Crime and Foreign Policy Meet," *Wall Street Journal*, October 24, 1995, A22. See also Stewart Baker, "Panel Discusses Problems of Law Enforcement and Intelligence," *National Security Law Report* 17, no. 10 (October 1995): 1, 4. The Baird piece caused a brief dustup on the commission. During our proceedings, no one—commissioner or staff—was supposed to be talking to the media or writing about topics that were before the commission. Baird told Brown and Rudman about the forthcoming op-ed article, but only after the presses were running—presenting the commission leaders with a *fait accompli*. They were not pleased, but it was too late to do anything about it.

41. George Tenet became John Deutch's deputy—DDCI—in July of 1995, acting DCI in December of 1996 (when Deutch left the job) and, after national security advisor Tony Lake lost a bruising nomination fight on the Hill in 1997 to replace Deutch, the new DCI. See Tim Weiner, "Clinton Proposes Acting C.I.A. Chief As Agency Leader," *New York Times*, March 20, 1997, A1.

42. George Tenet, interview with author, Old Executive Office Building, Washington, DC, June 17, 1994.

43. Author's interview with CIA officer in the Office of Legislative Liaison who asked for anonymity, CIA, Langley, VA, April 15, 1993; see, also, Walter Pincus, "Curtain Is Falling on Another Intelligence Drama: Reform," *Washington Post*, July 8, 1996, A13.

44. Back in the 1970s, Les Aspin had said that "covert actions should be as consistent as possible with the moral character of the American public, so that if some action becomes public, it would not be terribly embarrassing to the government of the United States because it is not something most Americans would consider immoral." "Foreign Intelligence: Legal and Democratic Controls" (remarks, AEI Forums, American Enterprise Institute, Washington, DC, December 11, 1979), 5.

45. Perhaps Dicks could sense the kind of GOP attacks that would occur later if the commission cut the intelligence budget. In 2004, for example, the Bush administration policy director for the presidential campaign that year claimed on national television: "[The Clinton administration] gutted our intelligence." Tim Adams, remark, *The NewsHour with Jim Lehrer*, PBS, September 24, 2004. That allegation came even though the Aspin-Brown Commission had, if anything, built up the U.S. intelligence capability and certainly never reduced espionage funding. Imagine the charges if there had been a 15 percent cut, as the Allen subcommittee recommended. On spending for spies, a DCI has claimed that "when you get away from L.A. and New York, the rest of the country loves us; they want us to catch the bad guys—and they don't care about budgets." George Tenet (remarks, author's notes, "National Intelligence and Technology Symposium," CIA Conference, Langley, VA, November 6, 1998).

46. In two years, HSPCI chair Goss would remark at an intelligence conference: "We have hollowed out our intelligence capability dangerously; this is what motivates me every day" (remarks, author's notes, "National Intelligence and Technology Symposium," CIA Conference, Langley, VA, November 6, 1998).

47. Lieutenant General James R. Clapper, Jr. once offered this vision of future intelligence: "The ultimate ideal here is to have a constant God's-eye view of the battlefield. Anywhere, anytime, all the time." Quoted in Steve Komarow "'Lesser Conflicts': Big Defense Challenge," *USA Today*, November 1, 1994, 8. Similarly, another senior military intelligence officer told me that the United States should fill the skies with surveillance satellites and reconnaissance drones looking down on every country. He referred to this network as "a series of automated systems behaving like border collies." A common theme from John Deutch was his aspiration for "dominant battlefield awareness," delivering to American commanders detailed data on enemy forces in all types of weather and on a continuous basis. See, for example, R. Jeffrey Smith, "CIA to Alter Its Priorities In Information Gathering," *Washington Post*, September 13,

1995, A1. I could hardly imagine how much these objectives would cost. Further, in 2004, a DDO would proclaim, "I need hundreds and hundreds, thousands [of additional personnel]"—quoted in Douglas Jehl, "An Abundance of Caution and Years of Budget Cuts Are Seen to Limit C.I.A.," *New York Times*, May 11, 2004, A18. Another experienced former DO officer observes, however, that the Agency, "like any other bureaucracy, will always plead for more cash, even when operatives in the field have more money than they know what to do with." Reuel Marc Gerecht, "A New Clandestine Service: The Case for Creative Destruction," in *The Future of American Intelligence*, ed. Peter Berkowitz (Stanford, CA: Hoover Institution Press, 2005), 107. When he succeeded John Deutch in 1997, DCI George Tenet became a master of repeating before Congress the sorrowful refrain "If I'd only had more money to fight terrorism." In his memoir, he maintained that "by the mid-to late 1990s, American intelligence was in Chapter 11" (George Tenet, with Bill Harlow, *At the Center of the Storm: My Years at the CIA* (New York: HarperCollins, 2007, 108)—even though the intelligence budget remained at levels 80 percent higher than it had been in 1980. Moreover, the government's counterterrorism budget from 1995 to 2000 doubled, including a 350 percent increase in the FBI's counterterrorism funding and a (still classified) substantial increase in the CIA's counterterrorism resources. See the testimony of national security advisor Samuel "Sandy" Berger of the Clinton administration, *Hearings*, Joint Committee to Investigate Events Surrounding the September 11, 2001, Attacks, 107th Cong., 2nd sess., September 19, 2002, 4. After 9/11, the intelligence budget really took off; for example, NSA's funding doubled from 2001–06 [Siobhan Gorman, "NSA Has Higher Profile, New Problems," *Baltimore Sun* (September 8, 2006), A1]. The DIA staffed spiraled upward from 7,500 employees in 2002 to 16,500 in 2010 (Dana Priest and William M. Arkin, "Top Secret America: A *Washington Post* Investigation; Part 1: A Hidden World, Growing Beyond Control," *Washington Post*, July 20, 2010, at http://www.postandcourier.com/news/2010/jul/20/part-1-hidden-world). And, as I have mentioned before, by 2010 the combined National Intelligence Program and the Military Intelligence Program had grown to some $80 billion, according to my interviews with intelligence officials that year. (DNI Blair referred publicly to a figure of around $75 billion in September of 2009.) On top of this growth came new records in the hiring of outside contractors to work on intelligence matters—a veritable explosion of ties between the three-letter secret agencies in Washington and the private sector, raising serious questions of accountability, redundancy, and waste (see Dana Priest and William M. Arkin, "Top Secret America: A *Washington Post* Investigation; Day 2: National Security Inc.," *Washington Post*, July 21, 2010, at http://www.post-andcourier.com/news/2010/jul/21/day-2-national-security-inc).

48. In 2004, an unsigned editorial in the *Los Angeles Times* would conclude: "Goss has been a patsy for the Agency he's now supposed to rebuild [as the newly

appointed DCI]....Goss loves the CIA not wisely but too well." *Los Angeles Times*, "Goss Will Keep Status Quo at CIA," reprinted in the *Athens Banner-Herald* (Georgia) on August 15, 2004, A6.

49. See, for example, Joseph A. Pika, John Anthony Maltese, and Norman C. Thomas, *The Politics of the Presidency*, 5th ed. (Washington, DC: CQ, 2002).

50. His reform proposals were published in *Making Intelligence Smarter: The Future of U.S. Intelligence: Report of an Independent Task Force*, Sponsored by the Council on Foreign Relations, Richard N. Haass, Project Director (New York: Council on Foreign Relations, 1996); see, also, Walter Pincus, "Relaxed CIA Covert Action Rules Urged," *Washington Post*, January 30, 1996, A13.

51. *Unsigned editorial, New York Times* , "Again, the CIA and the Press," February 21, 1996, A18; see, also: Jim Hoagland, "The CIA: No Cover for Failure," *Washington Post*, February 22, 1996, A25.

52. See Loch K. Johnson, "The CIA and the Media," *Intelligence and National Security* 1 (May 1986): 143–69.

53. See "The CIA and the Media," *Hearings*, House Permanent Select Committee on Intelligence, Subcommittee on Oversight, 95the Cong., 1st sess., April 20, 1978.

54. Walter Pincus, "Turner: CIA Nearly Used a Journalist in Tehran," *Washington Post*, March 1, 1996, A15.

55. See Tim Weiner, "Chief Defends Secrecy, in Spending and Spying, to Senate," *New York Times*, February 23, 1996, A1; and Walter Pincus and R. Jeffrey Smith, "CIA Defends Rule on Use of Reporters," *Washington Post*, February 23, 1996, A1. The renowned constitutional authority Louis Fisher has noted: "If you don't put it [any guidance that you seriously want the executive branch to honor] in a statute, it becomes a plaything for the president" (remarks, author's notes, panel on intelligence studies, International Studies Association, annual meeting, Washington, DC, March 28, 1994).

56. Leslie H. Gelb and Henry Grunwald, letter to the editor, *New York Times*, February 20, 1996, A10.

57. John M. Deutch, testimony, "The Role of the Intelligence Community in the 21st Century," *Hearings*, House Permanent Select Committee on Intelligence, 111th Cong., 2nd sess., December 19, 2008. See, also, James Risen, "CIA Director Predicts Terrorism Rise; Seeks to Boost Spy Network," *Los Angeles Times*, December 20, 1995, A39; and Bill Gertz, "CIA Chief Sees More Terrorism," *Washington Times*, December 12, 1995, A7.

58. Unsigned editorial, *New York Times*, "The Struggle Against Secrecy," January 3, 1996, A14; unsigned editorial, *New York Times*, "Spy Pablum," March 3, 1996, Wk14.

59. John M. Deutch, interview with author, Massachusetts Institute of Technology, Cambridge, MA, October 29, 1998.

60. R. James Woolsey, interview with author, CIA Headquarters, Langley, VA, September 29, 1993

61. Malcolm Gladwell uses this phrase in his "Connecting the Dots: The Paradoxes of Intelligence Reform," *New Yorker*, March 10, 2003, 88.

62. R. Jeffrey Smith, "Deutch Outlines Plan to Centralize Control of Intelligence Community," *Washington Post*, December 20, 1995, A18.

63. Johnson, *Bombs, Bugs, Drugs, and Thugs*, 61.

64. John M. Deutch, interview with author, Massachusetts Institute of Technology, Cambridge, MA, October 29, 1998.

Chapter 12

1. Perhaps Senator Exon warranted a special category of intelligence overseer all to himself: not so much an ostrich (see chapter 10) as a prairie dog, hiding underground most of the time, but popping up for inaugural meetings, public hearings, and visits to the Oval Office.

2. Douglas Waller, "Master of the Game: John Deutch," *Time*, May 6, 1996, 41.

3. Commission on the Roles and Capabilities of the United States Intelligence Community, *Preparing for the 21st Century: An Appraisal of U.S. Intelligence* (Washington, DC: GPO, 1996).

4. For my own research findings on these topics, see Loch K. Johnson, *Bombs, Bugs, Drugs, and Thugs: Intelligence and America's Quest for Security* (New York: New York University Press, 2000).

5. These proposed DCI assistants were designated deputy director for the intelligence community (DDIC, superseding the existing deputy director of central intelligence, or DDCI) and the deputy director for the Central Intelligence Agency (DDCIA).

6. One former CIA analyst concluded in 2004 that, "in the end, nothing was done to change old ways of doing business [between the DI and the DO]"; see Flynt Leverett, "Force Spies to Work Together,"*New York Times*, July 9, 2004, A19. Nevertheless, when he became DCI in 2005, Porter Goss continued to emphasize the importance of co-location. "I expect a closer symbiosis between the DI and the DO," he said in remarks to CIA employees in the Bubble on September 22, 2005, according to an intelligence officer who attended the meeting (interview with author, Washington, DC, October 28, 2005). President Obama's DCIA, Leon Panetta (a former member of Congress, D-CA), said in 2010 that there would be "more co-location of analysts and operators at home and abroad" over the next five years, and that the fusion of the two "has been key to victories in counterterrorism and counterproliferation" (quoted in Greg Miller, "CIA to Station More Analysts Overseas as Part of Its Strategy," *Washington Post*, April 30, 2010, A1).

7. For an elaboration, see Loch K. Johnson, "Analysis for a New Age," *Intelligence and National Security* 11 (1996): 657–71.

8. One intelligence official estimated that more than five thousand people would be let go if this recommendation became law; see Tim Weiner, "Commission Recommends Streamlined Spy Agencies," *New York Times*, March 1, 1996, A17.

It did not become law. Defeating Senator Warner in the commission's conference room did not mean defeating him on Capitol Hill, where it really mattered.

9. In 2006, Clapper would be named to the new post of under secretary of defense for intelligence; and, in 2010, he became the nation's fourth DNI in five years. On this first appointment, see Walter Pincus, "Gates Picks Intelligence Undersecretary," *Washington Post*, January 4, 2007, A1; on the second, see the unsigned editorial, "Misdirection of National Intelligence," *New York Times*, July 22, 2010, A11; and Loch K. Johnson, "Intelligence Agency at the Crossroads," *Atlanta Journal-Constitution*, July 22, 2010, A14.

10. In 2003, at the request of its director at the time, Gen. Clapper, NIMA would adopt the tongue-twisting name National Geospatial-Intelligence Agency (NGA). By 2009, imint had come to be referred to in the intelligence community as geoint.

11. See Walter Pincus, "CIA Spies Get a New Home Base," *Washington Post*, October 14, 2005, A1; and Defense Intelligence Analysis Center, *Intelligence Strategy: New Challenges and Opportunities*, Office of the Director of National Intelligence and the National Defense Intelligence College, Bolling Air Force Base, Washington, DC, September 26, 2007, 13.

12. After recommending that the secret agencies "reduce the costs of their operations" (xxv), the report went on to say: "Where such reductions should be made and at what level are judgments which the Commission is not in a position to make" (137). After a year's study, why the commissioners could not at least make some concrete suggestions in this regard was more a matter of the politics on the panel than anything else. In a slipup, the report included a chart on the intelligence budget (132) that inadvertently suggested fairly specific intelligence funding and staff levels for fiscal year 1996. Steve Aftergood, of the Federation of American Scientists, noted that one could extrapolate from the chart the specific annual budget and staff figures for the NSA, CIA, DIA and NRO, by comparing them with the publicly known budgets for the Community Management Staff (CMS) and the Defense Mapping Agency (DMA), which were part of the chart; see R. Jeffrey Smith, "Making Connections with Dots to Decipher U.S. Spy Spending," *Washington Post*, March 12, 1996, A11. Two years earlier, the House Defense Appropriations Subcommittee had accidently revealed the CIA, NFIP, and TIARA intelligence budgets. "Congress Mistakenly Publishes Intel Budget," *Secrecy & Government Bulletin* 41 (November 1994), published by the Federation of American Scientists.

13. L. Britt Snider, quoted in "The Brown Commission and the Future of Intelligence: A Roundtable Discussion," *Studies in Intelligence* 39 (1996): 9. Elsewhere Snider recalls: "The name of the game was not beefing up the [intelligence] function, as it is today, but rather preserving it in the face of mounting attacks." L. Britt Snider, "A Different Angle on the Aspin-Brown Commission," *Studies in Intelligence* 49 (2005): 86.

14. "Harold Brown Reports on Work of Intelligence Commission," *National Security Law Report* 18, no. 3 (April 1996): 8.

15. A Freedom of Information Act lawsuit filed by the Federation of American Scientists forced official disclosure in 1997, requiring DCI George Tenet to reveal the aggregate figure for fiscal year 1998 (a sum of $26.6 billion). Subsequently, in 1998, Tenet voluntarily announced the figure for the following year ($26.7 billion). The Office of the DNI, which replaced the DCI position in 2005, announced in June of 2008 that the aggregate annual figure had risen to $43.5 billion in 2007—a result of a legislative requirement that the DNI declassify and reveal the aggregate budget figure for the National Intelligence Program (NIP) at the end of each fiscal year. A centerpiece of the Aspin-Brown Commission recommendations had finally become a matter of routine policy, although in 2010 some lawmakers threatened to nullify this requirement by allowing a White House waiver of the rule each year. In October of 2008 the DNI said the budget for the NIP had moved up to $47.5 billion (this did not include the Military Intelligence Program or MIP, estimated at another $25 billion at least). In 2010, the Office of the DNI stated that the NIP budget was "approximately $48 billion" (Office of the Director of National Intelligence, e-mail entitled "ODNI Provides Detailed Facts about the IC Post-9/11," July 19, 2010). As I have noted earlier, the NIP and the MIP combined now stand at some $75-80 billion. On some of this history, see Steven Aftergood, "Intel Budget Disclosure and the Myths of Secrecy," *Secrecy News* 104 (October 28, 2008), 1, http://www.fas.org/blog/secrecy/2008/10/budget_disclosure.html; and ODNI News Release no. 17–08 (October 28, 2008); and, on the intelligence budget generally, see Loch K. Johnson and Kevin J. Scheid, "Spending for Spies: Intelligence Budgeting in the Aftermath of the Cold War," *Public Budgeting & Finance* 17 (Winter 1997), 7–27.

16. House Permanent Select Committee on Intelligence, *The Intelligence Community in the 21st Century: Hearings*, 104th Cong., 2d sess., March 4, 1996; see also Walter Pincus, "Untangling the Spy Network's Webs," *Washington Post*, March 5, 1996, A12.

17. Tim Weiner, "Proposal Would Reorganize U.S. Intelligence Agencies," *New York Times*, March 5, 1996.

18. "Section Notes," *Congressional Quarterly Weekly Report*, March 9, 1996, 635.

19. Ibid.

20. Jonathan Yardley, "When Words Won't Do the Trick," *Washington Post*, October 16, 1995.

21. Unsigned editorial, *New York Times*, "Spy Pablum," March 2, 1996, Wk14.

22. Quoted in Tim Weiner, "Commission Recommends Streamlined Spy Agencies," *New York Times*, March 1, 1996, A17.

23. Melvin A. Goodman, "The C.I.A.'s Reason for Living," *New York Times*, March 15, 1996, A15.

24. Pat Cooper, "Reshuffling May Limit Pentagon's Spy Role," *Defense News*, March 4–10, 1996, 3.

25. Quoted in Walter Pincus, "Curtain is Falling on Another Intelligence Drama: Reform," *Washington Post*, July 8, 1996, A1.

26. John M. Deutch, interview with author, Massachusetts Institute of Technology, Cambridge, MA, October 29, 1998.

27. John Prados, "No Reform Here: A Blue-Ribbon Panel Proved Once Again That 'Intelligence Reform' Is Something of an Oxymoron." *Bulletin of the Atomic Scientists* 52, no. 5 (September/October 1996): 56.

28. David Wise, "A Report That Blesses Espionage-as-Usual," *Los Angeles Times*, March 17, 1996.

29. In bold print in the first chapter, the commission report offered up for public consumption the theme that Senator Warner had advanced over the past year: "Intelligence is an important element of national strength. The country should not lose sight of this amid the spy scandals and management failures of recent years" (13).

30. Harold Brown and Warren B. Rudman, letter to the editor, *New York Times*, March 7, 1996, A24.

31. Arlen Specter, remarks, press conference, Senate Select Committee on Intelligence, March 1, 1996.

32. Quoted by Michael Kilian, "Panel Sees Spy Units as Crime Fighters," *Chicago Tribune*, March 2, 1996, A3.

33. "Spy Agencies to See Minor Changes," in *Congressional Quarterly Almanac 1996* (Washington, DC: CQ, 1997), 9–17.

34. Ibid., 9–18.

35. HR 104–620, part 1, House Permanent Select Committee on Intelligence 104th Cong., 2nd sess., 1996.

36. "Spy Agencies to See Minor Changes," 9–18.

37. "Spy Agencies to See Minor Changes," 9–16.

38. Ibid., 9–18.

39. S. Rep. 104–258, Senate Select Committee on Intelligence, 104th Cong., 2nd sess., 1996.

40. *Congress and the Nation*, vol. 9 (Washington, DC: CQ, 1997), 246; Walter Pincus, "Panels Continue Impasse on Intelligence," *Washington Post*, June 7, 1996, A21.

41. Senate Committee on Armed Services, 104th Cong., 2nd sess., 1996, S. Rep. 104–277; and, Senate Committee on Governmental Affairs, 104th Cong., 2nd sess., 1996, S. Rep. 104–337

42. Quoted in "Section Notes," *Congressional Quarterly Weekly Report*, April 17, 1996, 1181.

43. See Richard A. Best Jr., *Proposals for Intelligence Reorganization, 1949–2004*, Congressional Research Service Report 325000 (September 24, 2004), 37. Soon after Deutch left the DCI office (in December of 1996), the two additional deputy positions provided by the Intelligence Authorization bill at the time—one for collection (assistant director of central intelligence/collection,

ADCI/C) and one for analysis (assistant director of central intelligence/analysis and production, ADCI/AP—were filled, at the insistence of SSCI and HPSCI lawmakers. George Tenet, the DCI, hired HPSCI's Mark Lowenthal for the analysis slot and he became a close confident to the director. See Philip Shenon, *The Commission: The Uncensored History of the 9/11 Investigation* (New York: Twelve, 2008), 77–79.

44. For this exchange, see "Spy Agencies to See Minor Changes," 9–20; and Mark T. Kehoe, "House Passes Bill to Protect Spy Agencies from Cuts," *Congressional Quarterly Weekly Report*, May 25, 1996, 1477.

45. Kehoe, "House Passes Bill."

46. "Spy Agencies to See Minor Changes," 9–19.

47. Robert M. Gates, interview with author, Washington, DC, March 28, 1994. He said he had been able to achieve a high degree of control over the community without formal legislation, but rather by persuading and cajoling the gorillas in the stovepipes to rally behind his leadership—or face more dire congressional efforts to integrate the intelligence agencies.

48. *Intelligence Community Response to the Aspin-Brown Commission and Recommendations for an Administration Initiative,* unclassified Memorandum to the president from John Deutch, April 5, 1996, with copies to the vice president, secretaries of state and defense, attorney general, director of OMB, chief of staff to the president, national security advisor and chairman of the Joint Chiefs of Staff.

Chapter 13

1. For accounts, see Maureen Dowd, "From D.C., With Love," *New York Times*, November 17, 1996, Wk13; John M. Deutch, "A Time to Open Up the C.I.A.," *New York Times*, May 18, 1997, Wk17.

2. R. Jeffrey Smith, "Having Lifted the CIA's Veil, Deutch Sums Up: I Told You So," *Washington Post*, December 26, 1996, A11.

3. Quoted in Charles E. Lathrop, ed., *The Literary Spy: The Ultimate Source for Quotations on Espionage and Intelligence* (New Haven, CT: Yale University Press, 2004), 118.

4. John Diamond *The CIA and the Culture of Failure: U.S. Intelligence from the End of the Cold War to the Invasion of Iraq* (Stanford, CA: Stanford University Press, 2008), 422.

5. Unsigned editorial, *New York Times*, "The Incorrigible C.I.A.," December 8, 1996, A14.

6. John Deutch, testimony, Senate Select Committee on Intelligence, 104th Cong., 2nd sess., September 19, 1996; see Elaine Sciolino, "C.I.A. Chief Charts His Own Course," *New York Times*, September 29, 1996, A33; and Tim Weiner, "Nominations Have Made C.I.A. Chief Odd Man Out," *New York Times*, December 6, 1996, B7.

7. Sciolino, "C.I.A. Chief Charts."

8. John M. Deutch, interview with author, Massachusetts Institute of Technology, Cambridge, MA, October 29, 1998. Deutch returned to his position as a chemistry professor at MIT. Soon after his departure, Agency security officials accused him of having taken unauthorized materials home while still serving as DCI. By all accounts, he had violated rules against removing classified papers from CIA Headquarters, but for the simple reason that he was conscientiously trying to catch up with his heavy workload, with no intention (and no allegations made against him) of misusing secret documents for some illicit purpose. While a member of PFIAB, former secretary of state Henry Kissinger often used intelligence documents outside the board's meeting rooms—equally against the rules—but there was less of an uproar. (See Jeff Gerth and Sarah Bartlett, "Kissinger and Friends and Revolving Doors,"*New York Times*, April 30, 1989, A1.) I doubt that Deutch was the first and only DCI to take home a classified document to study in the evening. While he was unwise to handle documents in this manner because of the security risks involved, Deutch was hardly a careless person or a security risk. Nonetheless, responding to the recommendations of the CIA inspector general (L. Britt Snider, our staff director who had been named to this important Agency position after the commission completed its work), DCI Tenet stripped his predecessor of his security clearance and opened the door to the possibility that Deutch might face federal prosecution for mishandling classified documents. Before it came to that, Deutch was pardoned by President Clinton in the last days of his administration. The charges against Deutch seemed overheated for someone who had served the nation well and in many sensitive government positions. Some suspected this public embarrassment was the result of skillful DO operatives settling a score for the former DCI's rough handling of their Directorate. Under Warren Rudman's chairmanship, PFIAB took the stance that Deutch's offense should have been investigated even more vigorously than had been the case with Tenet's probe. See Vernon Loeb, "Panel Criticizes CIA's Investigation of Deutch,"*Washington Post*, May 6, 2000, A9; Diamond, *CIA and the Culture of Failure*, 246–47.

9. On HPSCI's inquiry, see Abraham H. Miller and Brian Alexander, "Structural Quiescence in the Failure of *IC21* and Intelligence Reform," *International Journal of Intelligence and Counterintelligence* 14 (Summer 2001): 234–61.

10. See, for example, David Flitner, *The Politics of Presidential Commissions* (Dobbs Ferry, NY: Transnational, 1986).

11. Tim Weiner, "For First Time, U.S. Discloses Spying Budget," *New York Times*, October 16, 1997, A17.

12. See, for example, House Permanent Select Committee on Intelligence, Report on Intelligence Authorization, 109th Cong., 1st sess., June 21, 2005.

13. Dafna Linzer and Walter Pincus, "Goss Forced Out as DIA Director," Washington Post, May 6, 2006, A1.

14. For his reflections on his PFIAB service, see Warren Rudman, "Perspectives on National Security in the Twenty-First Century" (lecture, Seminar on

Intelligence, Command, and Control, Harvard University, April 22, 2002), http://pirp.harvard.edu/pubs_pdf/rudman/rudman-io2-1.pdf.

15. See Jane Mayer, The *Dark Side: The Inside Story of How the War on Terror Turned into a War on American Ideals* (New York: Doubleday, 2008).

16. See, for instance, Kenneth Kitts, *Presidential Commissions and National Security: The Politics of Damage Control* (Boulder, CO: Rienner, 2006).

17. According to an interview with an intelligence official quoted in Amy B. Zegart, *Spying Blind: The CIA, the FBI, and the Origins of 9/11* (Princeton, NJ: Princeton University Press, 2007), 94.

18. Dan Eggen, "FBI Agents Still Lacking Arabic Skills," *Washington Post*, October 11, 2006, A1.

19. Amy B. Zegart, "September 11 and the Adaptation Failure of U.S. Intelligence Agencies," *International Security* 29 (Spring 2005): 78–111, quote at 111; and Zegart, Spying Blind.

20. Among them: National Commission on Terrorist Attacks upon the United States, *The 9/11 Commission Report: Final Report of the National Commission on Terrorist Attacks Upon the United States* (New York: Norton, 2004) (The Kean Commission or 9/11 Commission);; Senate Select Committee on Intelligence and House Permanent Select Committee on Intelligence, *Report: Joint Inquiry Into Intelligence Community Activities Before and After the Terrorist Attacks of September 11, 2001*, 107th Cong., 2nd sess., December 2002; Senate Select Committee on Intelligence, *Report on the U.S. Intelligence Community's Prewar Intelligence Assessments on Iraq*, 108th Cong., 2nd sess., July 2004; Richard K. Betts, *Enemies of Intelligence: Knowledge & Power in American National Security* (New York: Columbia University Press, 2007); Richard A. Clarke, *Against All Enemies: Inside America's War on Terror* (New York: Free Press, 2004); Diamond, *CIA and the Culture of Failure*; Senator Bob Graham, with Jeff Nussbaum, *Intelligence Matters* (Lawrence, KS: University Press of Kansas, 2008); Melvin A. Goodman, "9/11: The Failure of Strategic Intelligence," *Intelligence and National Security* 18, no. 4 (December 2003): 59–71, and Goodman, *Failure of Intelligence: The Decline and Fall of the CIA* (Lanham, MD: Rowan & Littlefield, 2008); Robert Jervis, "Reports, Politics, and Intelligence Failures: The Case of Iraq," *Journal of Strategic Studies* 29 (2006): 3–52, and Jervis, *Why Intelligence Fails* (Ithaca, NY: Cornell University Press, 2010); Mayer, *Dark Side*; James P. Pfiffner and Mark Phythian, eds., *Intelligence and National Security Policymaking on Iraq: British and American Perspectives* (Manchester, UK: Manchester University Press, 2008); Paul R. Pillar, "Intelligence, Policy, and the War in Iraq," *Foreign Affairs* 85, no. 2 (March/April 2006): 15–28; Richard L. Russell, *Sharpening Strategic Intelligence:Why the CIA Gets It Wrong, and What Needs to Be Done to Get It Right* (New York: Cambridge University Press, 2007); Tim Weiner, *Legacy of Ashes: The History of the CIA* (New York: Doubleday, 2007); Bob Woodward, *Bush at War* (New

York: Simon & Schuster, 2002); Woodward, *Plan of Attack* (New York: Simon & Schuster, 2004); and Zegart, *Spying Blind*.

21. United States Commission on National Security/21st Century, *Road Map for National Security: Imperative for Change* (Wilkes-Barre, PA: Kallisti, 2002).

22. Stephen Flynn, *America the Vulnerable: How Our Government Is Failing to Protect Us from Terrorism* (New York: Harper Perennial, 2005), 175. Flynn cites the mid-1990s when the consensus among counterterrorism experts was that "it would take a catastrophic terrorist attack on U.S. soil to get the federal government to embrace real change" (178). He ends his valuable study on a somber note, observing that even after 9/11 members of Congress remained disengaged from reforms to strengthen the nation's defenses against terrorism. A similar sense of disappointment, even despair, runs through Zegart, *Spying Blind*. On the misuse of counterterrorism funding for pork-barrel projects, see Eben Kaplan, "Q or A: Risk-Based Homeland Security Spending," *New York Times*, February 11, 2006, A6.

23. *The 9/11 Commission Report*. See also Loch K. Johnson, "A Framework for Strengthening U.S. Intelligence," *Yale Journal of International Affairs* 1 (Winter/Spring 2006): 116–31, from which some of this chapter is drawn.

24. *9/11 Commission Report*, 223.

25. Ibid., 273.

26. See Commission on the Intelligence Capabilities of the United States Regarding Weapons of Mass Destruction, *Final Report* (Washington, DC: GPO, 2005); David Barstow, William J. Broad, and Jeff Gerth, "How the White House Embraced Disputed Arms Intelligence," *New York Times*, October 3, 2004, A1; Jervis, *Why Intelligence Fail*; and Johnson, "A Framework."

27. See "Faulty Intel Source 'Curve Ball' Revealed," *60 Minutes*, CBS News, November 4, 2007; Bob Drogin, *Curveball* (New York: Random House, 2007); and Douglas Jehl, "Report Warned Bush Team about Intelligence Doubts," *New York Times*, November 6, 2005, A14. The report in the title refers to a DIA analysis prepared and circulated to government officials in February 2002.

28. "Review of Intelligence on Weapons of Mass Destruction," *Report of a Committee of Privy Counsellors*, HC 898, July 14, 2004.

29. Author's interviews with CIA analysts, CIA Original Headquarters Building, Langley, VA, June 15, 2005.

30. See Diamond's summary in *CIA and the Culture of Failure*, chap. 9.

31. Barstow et al., "Disputed Arms Intelligence."

32. Karen DeYoung, *Soldier: The Life of Colin Powell* (New York: Knopf, 2006), 508.

33. Woodward, *Plan of Attack*, 249. Tenet maintains that he used the phrase "slam dunk" merely to underscore for the president his belief that CIA could come up with a stronger case for the public that Iraq probably had WMDs.

George Tenet, *At the Center of the Storm: My Years at the CIA* (New York: HarperCollins, 2007), 362. One way or the other, though, the DCI seems to have left the president with the impression that Saddam clearly possessed unconventional weaponry—not that the second Bush administration needed much convincing.

34. See, for example, the memoir of former SSCI chairman Bob Graham, *Intelligence Matters: The CIA, the FBI, Saudi Arabia, and the Failure of America's War on Terror* (New York: Random House, 2004).

35. Tenet, *Center of the Storm*, 449.

36. During the commission's inquiry, an NIO half joked to me: "In the fairy tale about the emperor who wore no clothes, the little boy was rewarded; in real life, he was taken behind the wall and beaten by the secret police."

37. See, for example, Thomas L. Hughes, "The Power to Speak and the Power to Listen: Reflections in Bureaucratic Politics and a Recommendation on Information Flows," in *Secrecy and Foreign Policy*, ed. Thomas M. Franck and Edward Weisband (New York: Oxford University Press, 1974): 13–50.

38. Clarke, *Against All Enemies*; Mayer, *Dark Side*.

39. For an official account of the events surrounding the slide of the second Bush administration into warrantless wiretapping, see the Offices of the Inspector Generals of the Department of Defense, Department of Justice, Central Intelligence Agency, National Security Agency, and Office of the Director of National Intelligence, *Unclassified Report on the President's Surveillance Program*, Report No. 2009-0013-AS, Washington, DC, July 10, 2009. Much to its credit, Qwest Communications stands alone among America's major telephone companies in refusing to participate when NSA requested (both before and after the 9/11 attacks) that it engage in warrantless surveillance programs, which the agency's own lawyers viewed as illegal. See Scott Shane, "Former Phone Chief Says Spy Agency Sought Surveillance Help Before 9/11," *New York Times*, October 14, 2007, A27.

Chapter 14

1. *The 9/11 Commission Report: Final Report of the National Commission on Terrorist Attacks upon the United States* (New York: Norton, 2004).

2. See James E. Baker, *In the Common Defense: National Security Law for Perilous Times* (New York: Cambridge University Press, 2007); James Bamford, "Forum: Intelligence," *Harper's*, June 2007, 55–56; Richard K. Betts, "The New Politics of Intelligence: Will Reforms Work This Time?" *Foreign Affairs* 83, no. 3 (May/June 2004): 2–8; Helen Fessenden, "The Limits of Intelligence Reform," Foreign Affairs 84, no. 6 (November/December 2005), 106–20; David E. Kaplan and Kevin Whitelaw, "Intelligence Reform—At Last," *U.S. News & World Report*, December 20, 2004, 31–32; Stan A. Taylor and David Gaush, "Intelligence Reform: Will More Agencies, Money, and Personnel Help?" *Intelligence and National Security* 19 (2004): 416–35.

3. Amy B. Zegart, *Spying Blind: The CIA, the FBI, and the Origins of 9/11* (Princeton, NJ: Princeton University Press, 2007), 183. An intelligence professional, retired army Lt. General William E. Odom, Director of the NSA from 1985 to 1988, declared that Americans have "less security than we had before" the 9/11 attacks, because the Defense Department and the intelligence agencies had managed to fend off key reforms advocated by the Kean Commission, HPSCI, and SSCI. Quoted in Jim McGee, "Spies: More Than Two Years After 9/11, the Dots Remain Farther Apart Than Ever," *Congressional Quarterly*, December 16, 2003, http://homeland.cq.com/hs/display. do?dockey=/cqonline/prod/data/docs/html/hsnews/108-000000946531. html@allnewsarchive&metapub=HSNEWS&seqNum=1&searchIndex=1.

4. In addition to the *9/11 Commission Report*, see the final report of the Graham-Goss Committees, Senate Select Committee on Intelligence and House Permanent Select Committee on Intelligence, *Joint Inquiry Into Intelligence Community Activities Before and After the Terrorist Attacks of September 11, 2001*, 107th Cong., 2nd sess., Washington, DC, December 2002; and Report on the U.S. Intelligence Community's Prewar Intelligence Assessments on Iraq, Select Committee on Intelligence, U.S. Senate, 108th Cong., 2nd sess., Washington, D.C. (2004); and the final report of the Silberman-Robb Commission, Commission on the Intelligence Capabilities of the United States Regarding Weapons of Mass Destruction, *Report to the President of the United States*, Washington, DC: GPO, 2005).

5. See Arthur S. Hulnick, "Does the U.S. Intelligence Community Need a DNI?" *International Journal of Intelligence and Counterintelligence* 17 (2004): 710–30.

6. Philip Shenon, "9/11 Panel Is Said to Urge New Post for Intelligence," *New York Times*, July 17, 2004, A1; Shenon, "9/11 Report Calls for a Sweeping Overhaul of Intelligence," *New York Times*, July 23, 2004, A1. See also Shenon, *The Commission: The Uncensored History of the 9/11 Investigation* (New York: Twelve, 2008). On CIA opposition, see Elisabeth Bumiller, "Intelligence Chief Without Power?" *New York Times*, August 3, 2004, A15.

7. *9/11 Commission Report*, 407–19; as far back as 1955, the Second Hoover Commission had urged that the management of the CIA be separated from the management of the intelligence community. See Alfred Cummings, "The Position of Director of National Intelligence: Issues for Congress," *Report*, Congressional Research Service, August 13, 2004, 18.

8. *9/11 Commission Report*. For a critique of the report, see Loch K. Johnson, "An Elephant Rolling A Pea," *Diplomatic History* 30 (April 2006): 327–33.

9. *New York Times*, "Excerpts From Bush News Conference Calling for a National Intelligence Director," August 3, 2004, A15.

10. Richard W. Stevenson and Philip Shenon, "Bush Endorses Naming a Chief on Intelligence," *New York Times*, August 3, 2004, A1; Bumiller, "Intelligence Chief Without Power?"

11. Unsigned editorial, *New York Times*, "Sidestepping Reform at the C.I.A.," August 11, 2004, A22.

12. Quoted in Bumiller, "Intelligence Chief Without Power?"

13. Walter Pincus, "CIA Chief's Power a Hurdle in Intelligence Reform," *Washington Post*, October 17, 2004, A13.

14. Elisabeth Bumiller and Philip Shenon, "Bush Now Backs Budget Powers in New Spy Post," *New York Times*, September 9, 2004, A1.

15. "We wouldn't want to place new barriers or filters between the military Combatant Commanders and those agencies when they perform as combat support agencies," the secretary opined. Statement by Donald Rumsfeld before the Senate Armed Services Committee, 105th Cong., 2nd sess., August 17, 2004; see, also, Stevenson and Shenon, "Bush Endorses Naming a Chief."

16. Bumiller and Shenon, "Bush Now Backs Budget Powers."

17. Philip Shenon, "Bush Shows Congress Plan for Spy Czar," *New York Times*, September 17, 2004, A10.

18. John Feehery, spokesman for the Speaker, quoted in Philip Shenon, "Intelligence Proposals Gain in Congress," *New York Times*, September 16, 2004, A15.

19. Unsigned editorial, *New York Times*, "Avoiding Distractions," September 27, 2004, A30.

20. Philip Shenon, "Delays on 9/11 Bill Are Laid to Pentagon," *New York Times*, October 26, 2004, A17.

21. Cited in Walter Pincus, "Senators Offer Intelligence Plan," *Washington Post*, October 25, 2004, A3.

22. Philip Shenon, "White House Urges Quick Passage of 9/11 Bill," *New York Times*, October 20, 2004, A23.

23. See James Risen and Eric Lichtblau, "Bush Lets U.S. Spy on Callers Without Courts," *New York Times*, December 16, 2005, A1; James Risen, *State of War: The Secret History of the CIA and the Bush Administration* (New York: Free Press, 2006); Eric Lichtblau, *Bush's Law: The Remaking of American Justice* (New York: Pantheon Books, 2008); and the Offices of Inspectors General of the Department of Defense, Department of Justice, Central Intelligence Agency, National Security Agency, and Office of the Director of National Intelligence, *Unclassified Report on the President's Surveillance Program*, Report No. 2009-0013-AS, Washington, DC, July 10, 2009.

24. Author's interviews, Washington, DC, October 1–8, 2004.

25. Charles Babington, "9/11 Panel Leaders Give Warning," *Washington Post*, October 26, 2004, A15.

26. Walter Pincus, "Collins Eyes the Powers Bush Gave to CIA Chief; Intelligence Negotiations Still Deadlocked," *Washington Post*, October 30, 2004, A4.

27. Dana Milbank, "Two Mothers Helped Move Mountain on Post-9/11 Bill," *Washington Post*, December 9, 2004, A1.

28. Martin Kady II, "Cleared Intelligence Rewrite Is Big Finish for the 108th," *Congressional Quarterly Weekly Report*, December 11, 2004, 2937. The

language read: "The president shall issue guidelines to ensure the effective implementation and execution within the executive branch of the authorities granted to the Director of National Intelligence...in a manner that respects and does not abrogate the statutory responsibilities of the heads of departments" (section 1018).

29. James R. Clapper Jr., "The Role of Defense in Shaping U.S. Intelligence Reform," in *The Oxford Handbook of National Security Intelligence*, ed. Loch K. Johnson, (New York: Oxford University Press, 2010), 1068.

30. Public Law 108-458, U.S. Statutes at Large 118 (2004): 3638. See Kady, "Cleared Intelligence Rewrite"; and "Intelligence Overhaul Enacted," 2004 *Congressional Quarterly Almanac* (Washington, DC: CQ, 2005), 11–3 to 11–13.

31. Quoted in Thomas H. Kean and Lee H. Hamilton, *Without Precedent: The Inside Story of the 9/11 Commission* (New York: Knopf, 2006), 316.

32. See Senate Select Committee on Intelligence and House Permanent Select Committee on Intelligence, *Joint Inquiry Into Intelligence Community Activities Before and After the Terrorist Attacks of September 11, 2001*, 107th Cong., 2nd sess., Washington, DC, December 2002.

33. Quoted in Dana Priest and Walter Pincus, "Director's Control Is a Concern," *Washington Post*, December 8, 2004, A4.

34. Walter Pincus and Charles Babington, "Intelligence Bills Lack Details," *Washington Post*, October 6, 2004, A25.

35. Robert M. Gates, "Racing to Ruin the C.I.A.," *New York Times*, June 8, 2004, A18.

36. Quoted in Walter Pincus, "Intelligence Reform Will Not Be Quick," *Washington Post*, May 4, 2004, A1. Mark M. Lowenthal, the former HPSCI staff director, had become a top official at the CIA under DCI George Tenet, an old Capitol Hill friend of his, and feared all along that the objective of the 9/11 staff director, Philip D. Zelikow, was to make the Agency a scapegoat for the failure of the entire intelligence community to warn of the terrorist attacks in 2001 (according to interviews with Lowenthal quoted in Shenon, *The Commission*, 78–79).

37. Bamford, "Forum: Intelligence," 56.

38. James R. Clapper Jr., interview with author, NGA Headquarters, Bethesda, MD, October 7, 2004. Clapper is now the Director of National Intelligence (DNI).

39. Quoted by Elizabeth Drew, "A Reporter at Large: Brzezinski," *New Yorker* (July 1, 1978), 95.

40. Author's interview, Washington, DC, October 7, 2004.

41. Alonzo L. Hamby, *Man of the People: A Life of Harry S. Truman* (New York: Oxford University Press), 310.

42. Charles Babington and Walter Pincus, "White House Assails Parts of Bills," *Washington Post*, October 20, 2004, A10.

43. William M. Nolte (former NSA official, remark, panel on intelligence analysis, International Studies Association, annual meeting, San Francisco, CA, March 27, 2008). Intelligence scholar Jeffrey T. Richelson has noted that "the creation of the DNI creates a fragmented national analytic activity—divided between the CIA and DNI centers" [review of Robert Jervis's *Why Intelligence Fails* (Ithaca: Cornell University Press, 2010) in *Diplomatic History*, H-Diplo Roundtable Review XI, 2010, 17, http://www.h-net.org/~diplo/roundtables/PDF/Roundtable-XI-32.pdf].

44. Director of National Intelligence, *The 2006 Annual Report of the United States Intelligence Community* (February 2007), 7.

45. Kevin Whitelaw, "At DNI, a Mission Manager to Track North Korea," *U.S. News & World Report*, November 3, 2006, http://www.usnews.com/usnews/news/articles/061103/3dni.web2.htm.

46. Eric Lichtblau and James Risen, "U.S. Wiretapping of Limited Value, Officials Report," *New York Times*, July 10, 2009, A1.

47. Mark Mazzetti, "Fight for Control over U.S. Spies," *International Herald Tribune* (June 6–7, 2009), 7; Pamela Hess, "CIA, Intel Director Locked in Spy Turf Battle," WFED Radio, May 27, 2009. Some intelligence observers wondered at the time if this was a further attempt to militarize U.S. intelligence. A majority of the gorillas in the stovepipes were already flag-rank military officers, and Blair was a retired member of the club. Was the goal now to put military people in charge of the intelligence units in most of the U.S. embassies around the world? This standoff was to be arbitrated by the national security advisor in the Obama administration, James L. Jones—yet another retired flag officer (a former commandant of the U.S. Marine Corps). When the dust settled in 2010, DNI Blair had lost this battle, as the president sided with his old Democratic political ally Panetta. Since humint is run primarily out of the U.S. embassies abroad and is a CIA function, it makes sense to select most COSs from the Agency's senior ranks; however, in some countries, the most important U.S. intelligence activities have to do with sigint and having a NSA officer in charge would be logical. Elsewhere, geoint may be preeminent and would benefit from a NGA officer as COS.

48. John D. Rockefeller, "Opening Statement," *Confirmation Hearings of John M. McConnell to be DNI*, Senate Select Committee on Intelligence, 110th Cong., 1st sess., February 1, 2007.

49. Quoted in Mark Mazzetti, "Intelligence Chief Finds that Challenges Abound," *New York Times*, April 7, 2007, A10.

50. Bloomberg News, "Director Wants More Authority in Intelligence," *New York Times*, April 5, 2007, A13.

51. Quoted in Mark Mazzetti, "Intelligence Chief Announces Renewed Plan for Overhaul," *New York Times*, April 12, 2007, A13. See also Richard A. Best Jr. and Alfred Cumming, "Director of National Intelligence Statutory Authorities: Status and Proposals," *Report for Congress*, Congressional Research Service, November 2, 2007.

52. Mike McConnell, testimony, "DNI Authorities," *Hearings*, Senate Select Committee on Intelligence, 110th Cong., 2nd sess., February 14, 2008.

53. See, for example, David Johnston and Scott Shane, "Debate Erupts on Techniques Used by C.I.A.," *New York Times*, October 5, 2007, A1; and Stephen Labaton, "House Panels Vote for More Scrutiny Over Foreign Eavesdropping," *New York Times*, October 11, 2007, A21. The *Unclassified Report on the President's Surveillance Program* documents the questionable legal foundations of the warrantless wiretaps. For a range of views on the warrantless wiretap program, see the Yale University School of Law Symposium on the subject, "Opening Arguments: Warrantless Wiretaps," reprinted in *Intelligence and National Security: The Secret World of Spies: An Anthology*, 2nd ed. Loch K. Johnson and James J. Wirtz (New York: Oxford University Press, 2008), 404–12. In the midst of these controversies, Admiral McConnell released a "five-hundred-day plan" with additional ideas on how to "create a culture of collaboration"—but with no new authorities for the DNI. 500 Day Plan: Integration and Collaboration, United States Intelligence Community, Washington, DC, October 10, 2007.

54. Eric Lipton, "Spy Chiefs Say Cooperation Should Begin at the Bottom," *New York Times*, October 14, 2004, A16.

55. See Lisa Getter, "CIA Tumult Causes Worry in Congress," *Los Angeles Times*, November 15, 2004, A1.

56. Quoted in Shenon, "Delays on 9/11 Bill." See also Martin Kady II, "Pentagon Wields an Iron Hand in National Director Debate," *Congressional Quarterly Weekly Report*, October 2, 2004, 2308, 2310, which reports that Rumfeld's message to lawmakers was "if it ain't broke, don't fix it"—in short, back off. Kady notes, too, that "Pentagon leaders have been working quietly for months—in open hearings, classified briefings and one-on-one lobbying—to reduce the role that an NID [that is, the DNI] would be able to play in controlling the military agencies, "including NGA, NSA, and NRO (2310).

57. Quoted by Scott J. Paltrow and David S. Cloud, "Reports on 9/11 Say Clinton, Bush Missed Chances in Terrorism," *Wall Street Journal*, March 24, 2004, A1.

58. Kady, "Pentagon Wields an Iron Hand," 2312.

59. Philip Shenon, "Joint Chiefs Chairman Urges Curbs on Intelligence Post," *New York Times*, October 23, 2004, A15; Walter Pincus and Charles Babington, "Intelligence Bill Unlikely to Be Ready by Nov. 2, Negotiators Say," *Washington Post*, October 23, 2004, A2; Charles Babington and Walter Pincus, "Intelligence Overhaul Bill Blocked," *Washington Post*, November 21, 2004, A1; Martin Kady II, "Uproar Over Intelligence Bill Puts Hunter in the Bull's Eye," *Congressional Quarterly Weekly Report*, November 27, 2004, 2770.

60. Martin Kady II, "Chances for Intelligence Rewrite Grow Slim as Pentagon Digs In," *Congressional Quarterly Weekly Report*, November 13, 2004, 2701.

61. Interview, NewsHour with Jim Lehrer, PBS, November 2, 2004.

62. Helen Fessenden and Martin Kady II, "Hill Finds Intelligence Shake-Up Daunting Task From Step One," *Congressional Quarterly Weekly Report*, September 4, 2004, 2061; and Kady, "Pentagon Wields an Iron Hand," 2308. See also Philip Shenon, "Rumsfeld Wary about Shuffling Spy Duties," *New York Times*, August 18, 2004, A6.

63. Elisabeth Bumiller and Philip Shenon, "Bush Urged to Get Pentagon in Step on Intelligence Bill," *New York Times*, November 23, 2004, A1.

64. John M. Donnelly, "Troop Safety at Heart of Debate Over Stalled Intelligence Bill," *Congressional Quarterly Weekly Report*, November 27, 2004, 2774.

65. Martin Kady II and Jonathan Allen, "Bush Banks on His Influence to Move Intelligence Rewrite," *Congressional Quarterly Weekly Report*, December 4, 2004, 2879.

66. While director of NGA, General Clapper suggested to me that the government should use relatively inexpensive camera-equipped pilotless blimps flying at eighty thousand feet as a promising way to improve battlefield transparency. James R. Clapper Jr., remarks to author, NGA Headquarters, Bethesda, MD, October 7, 2004.

67. Quoted by Demetri Sevastopulo, "U.S. Intelligence Launches 'MySpace' for Analysts,'" *Financial Times*, August 21, 2007, A1.

68. John Rollins, *Fusion Centers: Issues and Options for Congress*, Congressional Research Service, Library of Congress, Washington, DC, January 18, 2008.

69. *Fusion Center Guidelines: Developing and Sharing Information and Intelligence in a New World*, Department of Justice and Department of Homeland Security, July 2005, 4.

70. Reported in Steven Aftergood, "Intelligence Fusion Centers Emerge Across the U.S.," *Secrecy News*, April 25, 2006, http://www.fas.org/blog/secrecy/2006/04/intelligence_fusion_centers_em.html.

71. "Fusion Centers: Issues and Options for Congress," *Report*, Congressional Research Service, Library of Congress, July 6, 2007, 5; see, also, Milton W. Nenneman, "An Examination of State and Local Fusion Centers and Data Collection Methods" (paper, Naval Postgraduate School, March 2008).

72. Deep Jayendrakumar Shah, "Unsuspecting Targets: Preparing America's College Towns for a Bio-Katrina," (honors thesis, University of Georgia, 2008), 28.

Allen, Lew Jr., (*continued*)
  suggests cuts in intelligence
    spending, 333
Allende, Salvador, 258
Alpirez, Julio Roberto, 118–20, 128,
    202, 300, 322
  commission's views on, 351
  Deutch's views on, 248–49
  rattles CIA, 316–18
Alwan, Rafid, Ahmed
    ("Curveball"), 197, 375–76
American Bar Association, 66, 86,
    211, 351
American Pilots Association, 123, 146
American Political Science Association, v
Americans with Disability Act, 49
Ames, Aldrich Hazen, 9, 15, 21, 75,
    133, 157, 355–56
  CIA morale and, 266
  capture of, 269–70
  Deutch comments on, 221, 285
  guarding against repeat, 402
  repercussions at CIA, 317,
    366–67
  use of tainted intelligence and, 270
Amherst College, 144, 159
Analysis, 205–10, 347, 379, 382–83
Analysts, testimony from, 332–333,
    377
Antiballistic missile, 203, 206–07
Appropriations Committees,
    151, 321
Arab-Israel War of 1967, 173;
    Arab-Israel War of 1973, 174
Aral Sea, 104
Argonne National Laboratory, 75
Aristide, Jean-Bertrand, 7
Armed Services Committees, 151, 321,
    391, 399–400
Arms control, 166, 173, 207
Army, U.S., 148; Army Intelligence
    Service, 70, 151
Army War College, 216

Asia, 15, 166–67
Aspen Strategy Group, 216
Aspin, Les, 23, 37, 114
  approaches to organizing the
    commission, 28, 58
  approaches to conducting the
    commission's work, 65, 67–68,
    72, 76, 88, 369
  as chair of House Armed Services
    Committee, 18–19
  as critic of the Pentagon, 16
  as member of HPSCI, xii, 12
  as PFIAB chairman, 11, 19, 58
  as political centerist, 19
  at Oxford University, 20
  at MIT, 20
  at Yale University, 20
  background of, 160
  brother of, 212
  Brown, Harold, and, 255, 264, 371
  Clinton, Hilary, critical of, 319
  comments on power of secretary of
    defense, 91
  covert action and, 464 n. 44
  death of, 212
  Deutch, John, friendship with, 157,
    160–61
  election to Congress of, 18, 20
  former wife of, 212
  health of, 9–10, 86, 161
  intelligence targets and, 79
  investigates CIA-media
    relations, 340
  leisure activities of, 189
  media relations of, 85, 279
  meets with President George H.W.
    Bush, 211
  memorial services for, 212–15
  named chair of commission, xii
  named secretary of defense, 3, 161,
    177
  NIEs and, 185
  oversight roles, 305

criticizes commission
proposals, 354, 359, 400
opposes moving DNI to CIA, 394
Clarridge, Duane "Dewey," 318
Clifford, Clar, 147–49
Clinton, Bill, xii, 6, 8, 10–11, 22, 308,
330
addresses CIA and
commissioners, 251–54
appoints commission members, 35
appoints Brown as commission
chair, 251
death of Les Aspin and, 213, 215
impeachment proceedings, 311
Lewinsky, Monica, and, 311
meets with commission, 345
naming of new DCI, 65
pardons Deutch for alleged misuse of
classified documents, 472 n. 8
reacts to potential re-invasion of
Kuwait by Iraq, 219
supports commission's findings, 354
supports release of aggregate annual
budget figure, 360
tepid lobbying for commission
reforms, 358, 360
terrorism and, 341
thanks Harrington and Rudman for
filling in between Aspin and
Brown, 251
Clinton administration, 4, 123, 172,
226–27, 310–11
CNN, 356
Coast Guard Intelligence, 390,
423 n. 10
Coelho, Tony, 37, 62, 65
background of, 49–50
comments on death of Les
Aspin, 218
intelligence spending and, 91, 326,
334
member of task force on
budgets, 326

member of task force on CIA-FBI
relations, 161, 190, 248
participation rates on
commission, 139, 296–97, 370
purpose of commission and, 89
urges stronger reforms, 88, 287,
293–94, 338, 345
Cohen, William S., 118–20
COINTELPRO, Operation (FBI), 75,
84, 153, 258, 299
Colby, William E.,
consumer-producer relations and, 225
covert action and, 112
economic intelligence and, 103
humint and, 195
intelligence collection and, 114
NIEs and, 181–83
Cold War, xiv, xvi, 70, 81, 342
Co-location, 131, 163, 241, 347,
467 n. 6
Combest, Larry, 33, 316, 353, 409
advocates radical reform as a
strategy, 320–21, 353, 357, 361
attracted to DMI concept, 190
criticizes commission, 326
embraces DNI concept, 191
intelligence spending and, 325
introduces reform bill, 353, 357
major disagreement with
commission, 322
retreats from his own reform
package, 358
visits with Brown and
Rudman, 320–22
Comint, 205
Commerce, Department of, 308
Commission on National Security/21st
Century, 368
Commissions, functions of, 366,
369–70, 457 n. 25
Committee to Protect Journalists, 7
Community Management Staff, 70, 92,
358

Dewhurst, David H. III, 37, 61, 87,
    132, 223
  advocated reform, 89
  appointed head of Texas Office of
    Homeland Security, 468
  as photographer, 339
  background of, 50
  covert action and, 236
  elected lieutenant governor of
    Texas, 368
  expresses concern about Russian
    spying against U.S., 116
  favors less critical language in the
    report, 337
  joins task force on
    macro-organizational issues, 248
  meets with President George H.W.
    Bush, 211
  opposes increase in economic
    intelligence activities, 291
  participation rates on
    commission, 139, 296–97, 370
  scoffs at environmental
    intelligence, 338
  spending and, 286
  visits CIA, 190
Dickens, Charles, 303
Dicks, Norman D., 37, 368
  background of, 47–48
  district intelligence ties, 288
  downsizing the intelligence
    community and, 64, 322
  opposes budget cuts, 333
  opposes HPSCI reform
    package, 357, 360
  oversight and, 301, 322
  participation rates on
    commission, 139, 296–97, 370
  selling report to DCI, 335
Diplomacy, 232, 237–38
Director, Central Intelligence Agency
    (DCIA or D/CIA), 393, 397,
    470 n. 43

Director of Central Intelligence
    (DCI), 13, 63, 70
  cabinet status of, 153
  centers and task forces, 150, 152,
    191
  commission's views on, 347
  controversy over cabinet status, 99
  early history of, 149
  fixed term of office (proposed), 153,
    201
  given more authority by
    commission, 354
  job of, 101
  turnover and, 140
  weakness of, 151, 191, 245–46,
    351, 353, 354, 360, 366,
    427 n. 50
Director of Military Intelligence
    (proposed), 134–35, 144, 191,
    314
Director of National Intelligence
    (DNI), 72, 134
  calls for, 385
  established, 391–92
  home for, 393–96
  opposed by Department of
    Defense, 385–93
  weaknesses of, 394, 397–98, 403
Directorate of Administration (CIA), 71
Directorate of Intelligence (CIA), 71,
    152, 393
  Deutch's views on, 164
  focused on current intelligence, 176
Directorate of Operations (CIA), 8, 71,
    108–09, 127, 129. See also
    National Clandestine Service.
  as a club, 271
  commission's views on, 347
  complaints of an officer, 131
  covert action and, 332
  DIA and, 297
  dislike for DCIs Schlesinger and
    Turner, 141, 158–59

Surface-to-air missile (SAM), 247
SVR, 9
Swati, Kristin E., 179

Tactical Intelligence and Related
    Activities (TIARA), 72
Talbott, Strobe, 129
Taliban, 15
Tasking, 93, 135;
    functional targets, 166;
    transnational targets, 327
Taylor, Elizabeth, 46
Taylor, Adm. Rufus, 150
Technical Collection Agency
    (proposed), 322, 357
Technical intelligence (techint), 127,
    205, 220, 341
Telemetry, 203, 205
Tenet, George, 184, 342, 408
    as DCI, 371, 463 n. 29
    as DDCI, 463 n. 41
    as senior intelligence officer on the
        NSC, 65, 327–28
    CIA-FBI relationship and, 250
    emphasizes need for U.S. grand
        strategy, 117
    failures to fully brief president on
        Iraqi WMD debate, 377–78,
        474–75 n. 33
    intelligence spending and, 247
    investigates Deutch for misuse of
        classified documents, 472 n. 8
    9/11 attacks and, 372–74
    nominated for DDCI position, 247–48
    PDB and, 226, 229
    opposes DNI concept, 256, 394
Terms of reference (TOR), 167
Terrorism, 14–15, 122–24, 298,
    309–10, 341, 457 n. 29. See also
    Counterterrorism
Third Option, 110. See also Covert
    Action
Third World, 166

Threats to the United States, "matrix
    of," 90, 167
Thurmond, Strom, 46, 359, 400
Thomas, Clarence, 53
Time, 346
Tolkachev, Adolf G., 203
Torricelli, Robert G., 118–19, 300
Tower Commission, 36
Tradecraft, 263
Transportation, Department of, 123,
    146, 374
Treason, 271
Treasury, Department of, 69, 278, 308
Treverton, Gregory F., 29, 259
Trilateral Commission, 327
Truman administration, 146–49
Truman, Harry S., 77, 147–48, 392–93;
    intelligence goal of, 394–95, 398
Turkey, 15, 173–74
Turner, Adm. Stansfield, 71, 100, 128,
    151, 248, 339, 408
    admits secretly waiving CIA-media
        prohibitions, 340
    covert action and, 112
    critical of DO, 154, 462 n. 28
    critical of NIEs, 178
    criticized by DO officers, 158
    economic intelligence and, 102
    ethics and, 455 n. 3
    favors separate analysis from
        operations, 132
    fires members of DO, 140–41
    humint and, 195, 245
    Navy "Mafia" and, 158, 198
    NIEs, examples of, 166; frequency
        of 181–83
    opposes DNI concept, 256–57
    releases intelligence budget figure, 367
Twentieth Century Fund, 312

U-2 surveillance aircraft, 16, 82–83,
    203–05
United Auto Workers, 215